D0786875

DATE

The United Nations
Blue Books Series, Volume I

# The United Nations and
# Apartheid
## *1948-1994*

With an introduction by
Boutros Boutros-Ghali,
Secretary-General of the United Nations

Department of Public Information
United Nations, New York

Published by the United Nations
Department of Public Information
New York, NY 10017

Editor's note:

Each of the United Nations documents and other materials reproduced in this book ("Texts of documents", pages 221-544) has been assigned a number (e.g. Document 1, Document 2, etc.). This number is used throughout the Introduction and other parts of this book to guide readers to the document text. For other documents mentioned in the book but not reproduced, the United Nations document symbol (e.g. S/1994/717, A/48/691) is provided. With this symbol, such documents can be consulted at the Dag Hammarskjöld Library at United Nations Headquarters in New York, at other libraries in the United Nations system or at libraries around the world which have been designated as depository libraries for United Nations documents.

The United Nations and Apartheid, 1948-1994
The United Nations Blue Books Series
Volume 1
ISBN: 92-1-100546-9

United Nations Publication
Sales No.: E.95.I.7 (Soft)

Printed by the United Nations Reproduction Section
New York, NY

# Contents

## Section One:
## Introduction by Boutros Boutros-Ghali, Secretary-General of the United Nations

## Section Two:
## Chronology and Documents

# Section One
# Introduction

# I  Overview

1    The inauguration on 10 May 1994 of Mr. Nelson Mandela as President of the Republic of South Africa, chosen unanimously by a National Assembly elected by all the people of that country, signalled a historic transformation of that nation. On that day, a country bedevilled by the inhumanity of apartheid became a non-racial democratic State deeply committed to the principles of the Charter of the United Nations and the Universal Declaration of Human Rights. South Africa had regained its rightful place in Africa, in the United Nations and in the family of nations.

2    The inauguration marked not merely the liberation of a country from racist tyranny, but the triumph of the aspiration of Africa for the total emancipation of the continent and the successful resolution of one of the gravest problems that had faced the United Nations from its very inception.

3    Attending that ceremony on my first visit to South Africa to welcome the newborn nation on behalf of the world community, I was moved—as an African and as the Secretary-General of an organization which had so resolutely supported the struggle against apartheid—by the spirit of reconciliation that the new leaders had so successfully promoted, and by their determination to ensure that the country made its rightful contribution to Africa and to the world. I assured South Africa of the United Nations' continued support as the nation embarked on building a truly non-racial society and fulfilling the rightful aspirations of the great majority of the population.

4    When the new South African delegation, led by its Foreign Minister, was seated in the General Assembly on 23 June 1994, I noted that the fight against apartheid had been one of the major struggles of our century and that the destruction of apartheid was both a tribute to the people of South Africa and a testament to what could be achieved when the international community acted in concert in the pursuit of justice.[1]

1/Document 217
See page 537

5    When, on 3 October 1994, President Mandela addressed the United Nations General Assembly, he observed that it was the first time in its 49 years that it had been addressed by a South African head of state drawn from among the African majority. Welcoming the vanquishing of apartheid, President Mandela said: "That historic change has come about not least because of the great efforts in which the United Nations engaged to ensure the suppression of the apartheid crime against humanity."[2] Apartheid, he added, represented the very opposite

2/Document 221
See page 541

of all the noble purposes for which the United Nations was established, and in fact "constituted a brazen challenge to the very existence" of the Organization.

6       The struggle against apartheid extended far beyond South Africa's borders, and was one that helped to define the role that the United Nations could play in resolving seemingly intractable issues. It also helped to shape the conscience of the international community as a whole. South Africa's success, therefore, was also a success for the United Nations. I am proud that the United Nations played such a central, determining role in the international efforts to promote the establishment of a democratic and non-racial South Africa. Indeed, there are few causes for which the United Nations strove as hard as it did to eliminate apartheid in South Africa. It is not far-fetched to assert that, had the United Nations not demonstrated its solidarity with the South African people's anti-racist struggle, that struggle could have been a much more cataclysmic one.

7       However important the role that the United Nations played in bringing South Africa to freedom from racial domination, nothing can take away from the fact that it was the determination of the South African people themselves to resist and overthrow racist domination that resulted in victory for democracy and equality. Each stage in the growth of international resolve to apply pressure can be directly traced to the level of the intensity of internal resistance, and indeed no amount of outside support could of itself have brought about the elimination of apartheid. But the South African people recognized that they needed international assistance in their struggle, and they openly appealed for it. The United Nations played an indispensable role in mobilizing such moral, political and material assistance by the world community.

8       It was, of course, not easy for the United Nations to under-take this task. While abhorrence of apartheid became universal, it took many years of patient and persistent efforts by the United Nations to build a consensus among Member States on the desirability of going beyond mere condemnation to action, and to secure agreement on measures and to assist the oppressed people in their legitimate struggle to force the South African Government to desist from its disastrous course.

9       Finally, when a solution through negotiations became feasible, the United Nations was able to play a central role in facilitating consultations in South Africa and assisting in the transition to a non-racial democratic State. This facilitating diplomatic role is not widely known, as it was naturally conducted discreetly.

10       In the early phase, the United Nations condemnations of apartheid were a great source of encouragement for South Africans fighting racist tyranny. When Nelson Mandela was charged in court on

7 November 1962 for leading a nationwide strike, he was able to refer in his statement to the previous day's General Assembly resolution calling for sanctions against South Africa. He said: "I hate the practice of race discrimination, and in my hatred, I am sustained by the fact that the overwhelming majority of mankind hate it equally."

11    In subsequent years, the United Nations provided a forum for the liberation movements and undertook an international campaign against apartheid. The United Nations excluded representatives of the South African Government from its meetings and recognized the liberation movements as the authentic representatives of the South African people. It devoted considerable time and resources to developing international pressure on the South African authorities and assisting the growing worldwide movement against apartheid, by involving not only Governments but peoples all over the world in the campaign against apartheid.

12    There were three main phases in the work of the United Nations in dealing with apartheid after the South African Government first formalized the policies that denied the basic rights of the majority of South Africans and enshrined domination by a racial minority.

13    In the first period, from 1948 to 1966, the United Nations repeatedly appealed to South Africa to reassess its policies in order to ensure full equality for all South Africans. When South Africa refused to countenance such appeals, and particularly after the 1960 Sharpeville massacre, the principal organs of the United Nations considered measures, including economic sanctions, which might be taken to persuade the South African Government to seek a peaceful solution. While the Security Council adopted an arms embargo in 1963, its five permanent members disagreed over the need for the wider economic sanctions that were repeatedly urged by the General Assembly. Through the establishment of the Special Committee against Apartheid, however, the General Assembly prepared the way for mobilizing concerted international action.

14    In the second period, from 1967 to 1989, in response to the continuing intransigence and aggression of the South African authorities, the United Nations launched its international campaign, which eventually extended across the globe and increasingly isolated South Africa in most of its international relations. Despite differences among Member States on whether or not sanctions and other measures should be mandatory, the United Nations promoted the arms, oil and other economic embargoes, as well as sports and cultural boycotts and other forms of public action. By ensuring publicity for the question of apartheid and making active efforts to reach public opinion all over the world, the campaign was able to attract support in all countries, includ-

ing those which were South Africa's main trading partners and whose Governments were reluctant to impose sanctions against South Africa.

15    In the third and most recent phase, from 1990 to 1994, the United Nations sought to encourage the South African authorities as they finally legalized the liberation movements and moved towards a negotiated solution. The Declaration on Apartheid and its Destructive Consequences in Southern Africa, adopted by the General Assembly in December 1989, initiated the process which led to the historic election of April 1994. The United Nations played a crucial role in promoting negotiations and in helping to ensure free and fair elections, at the request not only of all the major parties but of the minority South African Government itself. Vital assistance was provided when wide-ranging violence threatened to derail the process of negotiations, and in 1994 the United Nations coordinated the international observation of democratic elections under universal suffrage.

16    This book traces the actions by the United Nations in support of the legitimate aspirations of the South African people until apartheid was eliminated as a State policy and the South African people were able, in a remarkable spirit of reconciliation, to bury the past and establish a non- racial democratic State. The shared vision of South Africa's leaders ultimately overcame the inheritance of fear and bitterness that apartheid had engendered.

17    The long campaign to support the liberation of South Africa from racism posed many challenges to the Organization, but it was a campaign from which it learned valuable lessons. It learned, for example, the meaning and implication of the commitments Member States had made when they adopted the Charter of the United Nations and the Declaration of Human Rights. As President Mandela observed in his 3 October 1994 address to the General Assembly, it was "of great importance to the universal efficacy of, and respect for, the Declaration of Human Rights and the Charter of the United Nations that the United Nations should have spurned the pleas of the apartheid regime that the gross violation of human rights in South Africa was a domestic matter

3/Document 221
See page 541

of no legal or legitimate concern to the world body".[3]

18    In its exercise of moral suasion in the campaign against apartheid, the United Nations learned also the value of parallel efforts by regional and subregional organizations, both inter- and non-governmental. Throughout this period, the United Nations was the medium through which an effective global campaign against apartheid could be maintained and which, in the end, was uniquely well-placed to provide critical support and encouragement in the final phase of reconciliation, negotiation and elections.

19    More than four decades of debate, evolution and dynamic action—with hundreds of resolutions, thousands of meetings and docu-

ments, scores of conferences and seminars, as well as a great variety of actions by United Nations organs and agencies in promoting the international campaign against apartheid—can only be covered selectively in this volume. But it is hoped that it will indicate the contribution of the United Nations to the historic transformation in South Africa and provide a deeper understanding of the capacity of the Organization for dealing with the major issues of concern to humanity.

20      This Introduction, which comprises Section One, traces the evolution of the United Nations position regarding apartheid, the international actions it engendered, and finally the role the Organization played in the crucial period of transition to a non-racial democratic State. Section Two provides an extensive chronology and bibliography of United Nations documentation on the subject. It also contains texts from many of the most important documents relating to the decisions, resolutions and activities recounted in the Introduction.

# II    United Nations consideration of apartheid, 1948-1966

21    From its inception, the United Nations has been acutely conscious of its obligation to promote the elimination of all forms of racial discrimination. In the very first session of the General Assembly in 1946—at which decisions were taken that led to the adoption of the Universal Declaration of Human Rights—a complaint was lodged by India against South Africa's increasing discrimination against people of Indian origin. India also made the first formal reference at the United Nations to the policy of apartheid soon after it was adopted by South Africa's newly elected National Party in 1948. The first General Assembly resolution specifically aimed at apartheid was adopted in 1952.

22    The focus of the following pages is on the years between 1948 and 1966, when the General Assembly regularly appealed to the South African Government to reconsider its apartheid policies. Faced with the South African Government's persistent rejection of General Assembly resolutions, the principal organs of the United Nations began to consider measures, including economic sanctions, which might be taken to persuade South Africa to renounce its policies. As early as 1955, such pressure led the Government of South Africa to withdraw from membership in the United Nations Educational and Scientific Organization (UNESCO), and subsequently, in 1963 and 1964, also to withdraw from the Food and Agriculture Organization of the United Nations (FAO) and the International Labour Organisation (ILO) respectively.

23    The period after 1960 was marked by an increasingly more determined approach by the General Assembly—as its ranks swelled with newly independent States in Africa and elsewhere—as well as by the beginning of the involvement of the Security Council. The international revulsion which followed the killing of 68 peaceful protesters in Sharpeville in March 1960 prompted the Security Council to adopt its first resolution deploring the policies and actions of the Pretoria Government.[4] In November 1962, the General Assembly for the first time recommended specific diplomatic and economic measures to press the South African Government to abandon apartheid, and also established the Special Committee against Apartheid. In August 1963, the Security Council called on all States to cease the sale of arms to South Africa—a recommendation that was complied with by several major arms-supplying countries.

24    As South Africa, defying the United Nations and world opinion, began to resort to increasing repression against all opponents of

4/Document 15
See page 244

apartheid, there was virtual unanimity in the United Nations that the Organization should take measures to exert pressure on that Government to abandon its racial policies and to promote humanitarian assistance to the victims of apartheid. But there were serious differences of opinion on the appropriate means, especially on the imposition of comprehensive sanctions against South Africa, a course favoured by a majority of Member States.

## Building a consensus against apartheid

25    The United Nations was founded on the principle of equality for all human beings. At its very first session, in 1946, the General Assembly unanimously adopted a resolution proposed by Egypt—resolution 103 (I) of 19 November 1946—in which the Assembly declared that it was "in the higher interests of humanity to put an immediate end to religious and so-called racial persecution and discrimination" and called on the Governments and responsible authorities to conform both to the letter and to the spirit of the Charter of the United Nations. The Assembly later set up a Commission, chaired by Mrs. Eleanor Roosevelt, to prepare a bill of rights; the draft submitted by the Commission was then adopted by the Assembly, on 10 December 1948, as the Universal Declaration of Human Rights (resolution 217 (III)), which affirmed: "All human beings are born free and equal in dignity and rights . . . Everyone is entitled to all the rights and freedoms set forth in this Declaration, without distinction of any kind, such as race, colour, sex, language, religion, political or other opinion, national or social origin, property, birth or other status."

26    The question of racial discrimination in South Africa itself also came before the General Assembly at its first session in 1946 when the Government of India lodged a complaint asserting that people of Indian origin in South Africa were being subjected to discrimination and deprived of their elementary rights, in contravention of agreements concluded between the Governments of India and the Union of South Africa in 1927 and 1932. The actions of the South African Government, it said, had impaired friendly relations between the two Member States and deserved consideration by the United Nations.

27    The dispute had been provoked by the South African Government's enactment, in 1946, of the Asiatic Land Tenure and Indian Representation Act, which prohibited people of Indian origin from acquiring land. In June of that year, the Indian organizations in South Africa launched a passive resistance campaign resulting in the imprisonment of almost 2,000 people. After attempts at negotiation failed, the

Indian Government recalled its High Commissioner in South Africa and prohibited trade with the country.

28    The General Assembly took up India's complaint, rejecting South Africa's contention that the United Nations could not consider the matter as it was within that country's domestic jurisdiction. After lengthy discussions, the Assembly adopted a resolution expressing the opinion that "the treatment of Indians in the Union should be in conformity with the international obligations under the agreements concluded between the two Governments and the relevant provisions of the Charter".[5]

5/Document 1
See page 221

29    There was no progress towards a resolution of this problem. Despite repeated appeals by the General Assembly and the appointment of a Good Offices Commission to promote negotiations, the South African Government continued to maintain that the matter was within its domestic jurisdiction.

30    Instead, racial tensions escalated when the National Party came to power in South Africa in 1948, espousing the policy of apartheid. Under that policy, the new Government began implementing a series of discriminatory measures designed to segregate the population on racial lines and denying basic rights to the non-White majority. In its continuing complaint about the treatment of people of Indian origin, India in 1948 made the first formal reference to apartheid at the United Nations in a letter requesting consideration of the matter.[6]

6/Document 2
See page 221

31    While the earliest concern voiced in the United Nations was specifically related to the question of discrimination against people of Indian origin, consideration of this matter by the General Assembly helped bring the wider racial situation in South Africa to international attention. The attempts of the South African Government to justify its policy of apartheid, and to claim that it was not based on racial discrimination, failed. The General Assembly declared for the first time on 2 December 1950[7] that "a policy of 'racial segregation' (apartheid) is necessarily based on doctrines of racial discrimination".

7/Document 3
See page 223

## Consideration of apartheid by the General Assembly

32    On 26 June 1952, the African National Congress of South Africa (ANC) and the South African Indian Congress, together with organizations representing the Coloured people as well as White opponents of apartheid, launched a non-violent "Campaign of Defiance Against Unjust Laws" in which over 8,000 people contravened selected discriminatory legislation and regulations and risked imprisonment. This campaign of passive resistance helped focus world public opinion on the serious situation in South Africa and the legitimate aspirations of the great majority of the country's people. At the request of the Govern-

ments of 13 Asian and African States—Afghanistan, Burma, Egypt, India, Indonesia, Iran, Iraq, Lebanon, Pakistan, the Philippines, Saudi Arabia, Syria and Yemen—an item entitled "The question of race conflict in South Africa resulting from the policies of apartheid of the Government of the Union of South Africa" was included in the agenda of the seventh session of the General Assembly in September 1952.

33    In an explanatory memorandum, the 13 Governments stated that the founding of the United Nations and the acceptance by Member States of the obligations embodied in the Charter of the United Nations, had given the peoples in parts of the African continent new hope and encouragement in their efforts to acquire basic human rights.[8] But in direct opposition to the trend of world public opinion, the policy of the South African Government was "designed to establish and to perpetuate every form of racial discrimination which must inevitably result in intense and bitter racial conflict".

8/Document 4
See page 223;
Document 5
See page 225

34    The non-White people of South Africa, according to the memorandum, had felt compelled to launch a completely non-violent resistance movement against the Government's unjust and inhuman racial policies. In its efforts to suppress the movement, the Government had arrested thousands of people and had used physical violence such as flogging. The race conflict in South Africa resulting from the Government's apartheid policies was creating a "dangerous and explosive" situation; it constituted both a threat to international peace and a flagrant violation of the basic principles of human rights and fundamental freedoms enshrined in the Charter of the United Nations. It was therefore imperative that the General Assembly give this question its urgent consideration "in order to prevent an already dangerous situation from deteriorating further and to bring about a settlement in accordance with the purposes and principles of the Charter of the United Nations".

35    The General Assembly rejected the South African contention that it was not competent to consider the matter, and on 5 December 1952 adopted a resolution establishing a three-member United Nations Commission on the Racial Situation in the Union of South Africa (UNCORS) to study the problem in the light of both the purposes and principles of the Charter and the United Nations resolutions on racial persecution and discrimination. In a separate resolution the Assembly also declared that "in a multiracial society, harmony and respect for human rights and freedoms and the peaceful development of a unified community are best assured when patterns of legislation and practice are directed towards ensuring equality before the law of all persons regardless of race, creed or colour". Government policies which were in contravention of these goals and designed to perpetuate or increase discrimination were inconsistent with Article 56 of the Charter, by which

Members pledged to respect human rights and fundamental freedoms for all.[9]

9/Document 6
*See page 226;*
Document 7
*See page 227;*
Document 8
*See page 228*

## Commission on the Racial Situation in South Africa

36    The members of UNCORS were Mr. H. Santa Cruz, former Permanent Representative of Chile to the United Nations, who acted as Chairman; Mr. Dantès Bellegarde, former Permanent Representative of Haiti to the United Nations; and Mr. Henri Laugier of France, a former Assistant Secretary-General of the United Nations. The Commission submitted annual reports to the General Assembly in 1953, 1954 and 1955. In the first of these, it affirmed the competence of the United Nations to consider the matter, and gave a detailed account of the racial situation in South Africa and its effects.[10] Concluding that the racial policies of the South African Government were contrary to the Charter of the United Nations and the Universal Declaration of Human Rights, it declared that "the doctrine of racial differentiation and superiority on which the apartheid policy is based is scientifically false [and] extremely dangerous to internal peace and international relations". Warning of the risk of escalating violence making settlement by conciliation more difficult, it held that the United Nations had a duty to give moral support to the oppressed people and, in a spirit of international solidarity, to assist South Africa in solving the problem.

10/Document 9
*See page 228*

37    In its second report, in 1954, the Commission, at the request of the General Assembly, offered suggestions which, it believed, could alleviate the situation and promote a peaceful settlement.[11] It suggested ways of raising the standard of living of the non-White people, as well as the progressive abolition of the migrant labour system and "pass laws" (which required African men to carry a pass in order to be in urban areas), elimination of the "colour bar" in employment, equal pay for equal work, trade union rights and a plan for universal education. It stressed, however, that while equal economic opportunities for all were necessary, steps to achieve political equality among ethnic groups were of primary importance and "cannot be continually deferred without serious danger". It suggested that the United Nations family of agencies offer assistance to South Africa in implementing such a programme.

11/Document 10
*See page 231*

38    In its third report, the Commission made special reference to the Bantu Education Act, which imposed a segregated system of education throughout the country. It warned that "apartheid in education, symbolized by the words 'Bantu education' . . . , is liable to accentuate even more and to spread among the entire native population a Bantu nationalism with a strong anti-White orientation. The Commission

believes that the Nationalist Government, in carrying its policy of school segregation to extremes, may receive some sad surprises . . . ."[12]

39    The South African Government objected strongly to the inclusion of the issue of apartheid on the agenda of the General Assembly. The Government refused to cooperate with UNCORS and ignored the invitation of the General Assembly (in its resolution 820 (IX) of 14 December 1954) to consider the suggestions of the Commission for a peaceful settlement of the racial problem. In 1955, it withdrew its delegation from the tenth session of the General Assembly in protest against the inclusion of the item on apartheid in the agenda. South Africa withdrew again from the General Assembly's session in 1956 when the question was included, and announced that it would maintain only a token representation at meetings of the Assembly and at United Nations Headquarters. South Africa had already withdrawn from UNESCO in 1955 in protest against the Organization's activities against racial discrimination and was to similarly withdraw from the FAO in 1963 and from the ILO in 1964. Nevertheless, the General Assembly annually adopted resolutions appealing to the South African Government to revise its racial policies.

40    Meanwhile, the situation in South Africa continued to deteriorate. In 1953, the South African Government enacted stringent laws providing for the proclamation of a state of emergency and imposing heavy penalties, including whipping, for contravention of laws in a protest campaign. In 1956, it arrested 156 leaders of the freedom movement and charged them with high treason, an offence carrying the death penalty. In the same year, it extended the pass laws to African women. For its part, the national movement continued to organize opposition to apartheid with boycotts, strikes and demonstrations, despite severe restrictions and increasing repression. Of particular significance were the adoption of the Freedom Charter by a multiracial conference in 1955[13] and a demonstration of women against the pass laws on 9 August 1956.

### The Sharpeville massacre

41    The Sharpeville massacre of 21 March 1960, when the police fired at a peaceful demonstration against the pass laws, killing 68 Africans and wounding more than 200 was a turning point in the international community's consideration of apartheid. The incident provoked widespread condemnation around the world.

42    At the urgent request of 29 African and Asian Member States,[14] the Security Council considered the matter and on 1 April adopted resolution 134 (1960)—by 9 votes in favour and none against, with 2 abstentions, by France and the United Kingdom—in which it

12/Document 11
See page 233

13/Document 12
See page 241

14/Document 14
See page 244

recognized that the situation in South Africa had led to international friction and, if continued, might endanger international peace and security.[15] The Council deplored the policies and actions of the South African Government and called upon it to initiate measures aimed at bringing about racial harmony based on equality in order to ensure that the situation did not continue or recur, and to abandon its policies of apartheid and racial discrimination. It also requested the Secretary-General, in consultation with the South African Government, to make such arrangements as would adequately help uphold the purposes and principles of the Charter of the United Nations. The South African representative participated in the discussion in the Security Council but maintained that consideration of the matter violated Article 2, paragraph 7, of the Charter, which restricts United Nations authority on issues within the domestic jurisdiction of Member States.

15/Document 15
See page 244

43     United Nations Secretary-General Dag Hammarskjöld informed the Security Council on 19 April 1960 that he had agreed to a suggestion by the South African Government that he hold preliminary consultations with it in London at the conclusion of the Commonwealth Prime Ministers' Conference in May and that he visit South Africa after a Judicial Commission appointed to investigate the Sharpeville incident had completed its inquiry. He met the South African Minister of External Affairs in London in May and, at the invitation of the South African Government, visited South Africa between 6 and 12 January 1961. He reported to the Security Council that no mutually acceptable agreement had been reached in the course of his discussions with the South African Prime Minister.[16]

16/Document 18
See page 246

44     Meanwhile, resistance had spread in South Africa after the Sharpeville massacre. The South African Government declared a state of emergency on 30 March 1960, mobilized the Citizens' Force to supplement the police, army and air force and detained thousands of people. In an effort to suppress strikes, it issued emergency regulations making refusal to work punishable by five years in prison, a heavy fine or both. On 8 April, it banned the ANC and the Pan Africanist Congress of Azania (PAC) and detained their leaders. Several PAC leaders were tried for organizing protests against the pass laws and given heavy sentences. Mr. Robert Mangaliso Sobukwe, President of the PAC, was sentenced to three years' imprisonment.

45     The Government conducted a referendum restricted to White voters on 5 October 1960 on its proposal to declare a Republic and proceeded with arrangements to proclaim a Republic, in May 1961. By contrast, an All-In African Conference—with 1,400 delegates from 145 religious, cultural, peasant, intellectual and political bodies— met in Pietermaritzburg on 25 and 26 March 1961 and denounced the proposed Republic which, it said, "rests on force to perpetuate the

tyranny of a minority". It called for a national convention of elected representatives of all the people to decide on a new constitution, and planned mass demonstrations on the eve of the establishment of the Republic unless this demand was accepted.[17] Nelson Mandela was chosen to lead the protests as secretary of the action committee.

17/Document 19
See page 247

46    In May 1961, the Government resorted to a massive show of force to suppress the planned demonstrations and industrial action. All police leave was cancelled and defence legislation was amended to enable the use of the armed forces for the suppression of internal disorder. One amendment provided for the detention of persons for 12 days and for trial without jury in certain cases, with the proof of innocence resting on the accused. The Government's security measures ensured that a planned nationwide strike turned out to be only partially successful.

47    Meanwhile, in June 1960, the Second Conference of Independent African States, meeting in Addis Ababa, had called for sanctions against South Africa.[18] Several Governments broke relations with South Africa and instituted economic and other sanctions against it. Opposition in the Commonwealth forced the South African Government to leave that organization when the country became a Republic. ANC President Chief Albert J. Luthuli's call in 1959 for a consumer boycott of South African goods was taken up by people in a number of Western countries. From these intial groups, wider anti-apartheid movements, which were to play such an important role in raising international consciousness, arose to support the struggle of the South African people against apartheid.[19]

18/Document 16
See page 245

19/Document 13
See page 243

48    A number of African States attained independence in 1960. The African Group of States at the United Nations, now with a larger and growing membership, began to press for stronger United Nations action against apartheid. At the fifteenth and sixteenth sessions of the General Assembly, in 1960 and 1961, African and other States proposed diplomatic, economic and other measures against South Africa, but their proposals did not obtain the required two-thirds majority. Instead, the Assembly adopted, by overwhelming majorities, alternative drafts by several Asian States, which contained a more general provision requesting all States to consider taking such separate and collective action as was open to them, in conformity with the Charter of the United Nations, to bring about the abandonment by the South African Government of its racial policies.

49    In these resolutions, the General Assembly deplored the South African Government's continued and total disregard of the repeated requests and demands of the United Nations and world public opinion. It also deplored the Government's aggravation of racial issues by the passage and enforcement of ever more discriminatory laws. It affirmed

that the racial policies being pursued by the South African Government were "a flagrant violation of the Charter of the United Nations and the Universal Declaration of Human Rights and are inconsistent with the obligations of a Member State". The votes were 95 to 1 on resolution 1598 (XV) of 13 April 1961,[20] and 97 to 2, with 1 abstention, on resolution 1663 (XVI) of 28 November 1961. Compared with earlier resolutions, in which the General Assembly merely appealed to South Africa to reassess its racial policies, these votes showed not only growing international concern but also great progress towards a consensus in the United Nations on the issue of apartheid, and a growing conviction that the international community should take action to exert pressure on the South African Government to abandon its policies. For example, the attitude of the United Kingdom, South Africa's main trading partner, which had hitherto denied the competence of the United Nations, underwent an appreciable change after Sharpeville, and its representative declared in 1961 that his Government regarded apartheid as being so exceptional as to be *sui generis* and now felt able to consider proposals on the subject.[21]

20/Document 21
See page 249

21/Document 20
See page 248

22/Document 22
See page 250

## Action against apartheid begins

50   Despite almost universal condemnation of apartheid by the international community, the South African Government continued to reject the requests and demands of the principal organs of the United Nations. Its response to the march of freedom in Africa was to build up its military establishment and the apparatus for internal repression, and establish an arms industry. The brutal repression which ensued left the freedom movement with no legal means of continuing the struggle. The ANC and the PAC, having been banned, went underground, abandoned their adherence to non-violence and set up military wings for armed struggle.

51   On 16 December 1961, *Umkhonto we Sizwe* (Spear of the Nation), the military wing of the ANC, set off a series of explosions, damaging a post office, several offices of the Department of Bantu Administration and Development and an electric power station.[22] Over 300 acts of sabotage were reported between December 1961 and the end of 1963. Explaining why *Umkhonto* chose to resort to sabotage, Mr. Mandela said in 1964: "Sabotage did not involve loss of life, and it offered the best hope for future race relations. We believed that South Africa depended to a large extent on foreign capital and foreign trade. We felt that planned destruction of power plants and interference with rail and telephone communications would tend to scare away capital from the country, make it more difficult for goods from the industrial

areas to reach the seaports on schedule and would in the long run be a heavy drain on the economic life of the country, thus compelling the voters of the country to reconsider their position."

52    On 26 June 1962, the South African Government promulgated the General Law Amendment Act (the "Sabotage Act") which prescribed the death penalty for a wide range of offences and enabled the Government to place persons under virtual house arrest. The authorities served "banning orders"—involving severe restrictions of freedom—on many opponents of apartheid and imposed house arrest on a number of leaders. Mr. Mandela, who had gone underground in May 1961, was arrested on 5 August 1962 and charged with incitement and leaving South Africa without a passport. The Minister of Justice banned all meetings held to protest against the arrest, trial or conviction of any person.

53    At the seventeenth session of the General Assembly, in 1962, the two items on "race conflict" in South Africa and the treatment of people of Indian and Indo-Pakistan origin in that country were merged into a single item: "The policies of apartheid of the Government of the Republic of South Africa". On 6 November 1962, the General Assembly adopted resolution 1761 (XVII) in which it recommended specific measures which had failed to receive the necessary two-thirds majority at earlier sessions.[23] It deplored the failure of the South African Government to comply with the repeated requests and demands of the General Assembly and the Security Council and its flouting of world public opinion by refusing to abandon its racial policies, and also reaffirmed that the continuance of South Africa's policies seriously endangered international peace and security.

23/Document 23
*See page 251*

54    The General Assembly also requested Member States to take specific diplomatic and economic measures, separately or collectively, in conformity with the Charter of the United Nations, to bring about the abandonment of those policies. The steps proposed were: to break off diplomatic relations with the Government of South Africa, or refrain from establishing such relations; to close their ports to all vessels flying the South African flag; to enact legislation prohibiting their ships from entering South African ports; to boycott all South African goods and refrain from exporting goods, including all arms and ammunition, to South Africa; and to refuse landing and passage facilities to all aircraft belonging to the Government and to companies registered under the laws of the Republic of South Africa.

55    The General Assembly further requested the Security Council to take appropriate measures, including sanctions, to secure South Africa's compliance with the resolutions of the Assembly and the Council and, if necessary, to consider action under Article 6 of the Charter

(concerning the expulsion from the United Nations of a Member State which has persistently violated the principles of the Charter).

56    This was also the occasion when the Special Committee against Apartheid came into being. Established by the General Assembly, it was initially known as the Special Committee on the Policies of Apartheid of the Government of the Republic of South Africa. Subsequently, in 1971, the General Assembly shortened its name to "Special Committee on Apartheid" and in 1974 renamed it the "Special Committee against Apartheid" (the title used in all references to the Committee in this publication). The creation of this Committee, which held its first meeting on 2 April 1963, ensured that apartheid would remain under continuous consideration in the United Nations.

57    Many Member States broke diplomatic, economic and other relations with South Africa prior to, or in response to, resolution 1761 (XVII), or refrained from establishing such relations. South African Airways aircraft were obliged to follow circuitous routes, as African States prohibited flights over their territories. The traditional and major trading partners of South Africa, however, did not support or implement the resolution. As a result, the economic consequences for South Africa were rather limited.

58    On 7 November 1962, the day after this important resolution was adopted, Nelson Mandela was sentenced to six years in prison. In a statement to the court, Mr. Mandela declared that the resolution was proof of the world's hatred of racial discrimination.

59    Less than three weeks later, on 26 November 1962, disturbances broke out in Paarl when, according to press reports, about 100 Africans surrounded the police station in an effort to release seven African prisoners. The police opened fire and five Africans died. Two Whites were killed and three others were critically injured. Approximately 400 Africans were arrested, and the Government appointed the Snyman Commission to inquire into the disturbances. The Commission warned in an interim report that terrorism by *Poqo*, an underground organization associated with the PAC, would increase to alarming proportions in 1963 unless drastic action was taken immediately. The Government then proceeded to detain thousands of persons—not only alleged or suspected members of *Poqo* but also members of the ANC and the PAC.

60    In May 1963, the Government enacted a law for the detention of suspects without trial for 90 days at a time. The Special Branch of the Police resorted to the assault and torture of detainees, held *incommunicado*, in an effort to extract confessions and to obtain information about underground activities. Many persons were tried under various repressive laws, and were sentenced to long terms of imprisonment. A special law was enacted to enable the Government to keep in detention PAC

President Robert Sobukwe, who had completed a three-year prison sentence in connection with the campaign against the pass laws in 1960.

61    In view of these grave developments, the newly established Special Committee against Apartheid submitted an interim report to the General Assembly and the Security Council on 6 May 1963, in which it recommended that the Security Council consider the situation in South Africa as a threat to international peace under Chapter VII of the Charter, which provides for mandatory action by all States. The Summit Conference of Independent African States, held in Addis Ababa in May, endorsed the report of the Special Committee and designated four Foreign Ministers (from Liberia, Madagascar, Sierra Leone and Tunisia) to speak for all African States in the Security Council.[24] The same year, South Africa was excluded from the work of the United Nations Economic Commission for Africa (ECA).

24/Document 26
See page 253

62    In July, the Special Committee submitted a second interim report drawing attention to the expansion of military and police forces in South Africa since 1960 and recommending an arms embargo against South Africa "as the first and most urgent step to deal with the situation in the Republic of South Africa". The Committee said that the expansion of all branches of the armed forces, the setting up of air commando units, the establishment of police reserves and home guards, the training of civilians in the use of arms, the development of the radio network to link all of the nearly 1,000 police stations in the Republic, the importing of large quantities of modern arms and the great increase in the defence and police budgets were indicative of the increasing tension in the country. It pointed out that the defence budget had grown from 43.6 million rand in 1960/61 to 157 million rand in 1963/64 and that the budget provision for the manufacture of munitions had risen from 368,000 rand to 23.6 million rand in the same period. The military build-up, it stressed, not only was meant to suppress resistance to apartheid, but also posed a threat to the security of other States which abhorred the apartheid policies.

63    The Special Committee also worked closely with the emerging anti-apartheid movements outside South Africa, particularly in the United Kingdom and the United States, to help raise international consciousness about developments in South Africa and the need for action. In 1963, it granted a hearing to the American Committee on Africa and was in contact with the Reverend Dr. Martin Luther King, Jr., who had co-sponsored an appeal for action against apartheid with ANC President Chief Albert J. Luthuli.[25] The Committee promoted contributions by Governments to the Defence and Aid Fund for Southern Africa, initially set up in the 1950s in the United Kingdom to assist the victims of apartheid, to enable the Fund, after the mass arrests, to cope with the greatly increased need for international assistance to the fami-

25/Document 24
See page 252

lies of political prisoners. It recommended that ways should be found for international agencies to provide relief and assistance for opponents of apartheid and their families.[26] In 1964, the Special Committee sent a delegation to the International Conference for Sanctions against South Africa, organized in London by the British Anti-Apartheid Movement.

26/Document 29
*See page 257;*
Document 43
*See page 284*

64    The consumer movement also now spread in order to isolate South Africa in other areas, particularly sports. The exclusion of South Africa from the 1964 Olympic Games reflected the effectiveness of this campaign.

## The Security Council's arms embargo

65    By mid-1963, there was sufficient consensus over the alarming developments in South Africa for the Security Council to take stronger action. At the request of 32 African States, the Council considered the "explosive situation" in South Africa from 31 July to 7 August. On 7 August, it adopted—by 9 votes in favour and none against, with 2 abstentions—resolution 181 (1963), the first call ever for an arms embargo against a Member State.[27] Noting with concern the arms build-up by the South African Government, "some of which arms are being used in furtherance of that Government's racial policies", it solemnly called upon all States "to cease forthwith the sale and shipment of arms, ammunition of all types and military vehicles to South Africa". The resolution was not adopted under Chapter VII of the Charter and was therefore not "mandatory". A separate vote on a paragraph calling for a boycott of South African goods and prohibiting the export to South Africa of strategic materials of direct military value received only 5 votes and was not adopted.

27/Document 28
*See page 257*

66    An international campaign for an arms embargo had been launched in the United Kingdom in May 1963, when ANC President Chief Albert J. Luthuli pointed out that arms imported from the United Kingdom, such as Saracen armoured cars, had been used against peaceful demonstrators. The United States had announced an arms embargo in August 1963, prior to the adoption of resolution 181 (1963).[28] The United Kingdom, which had abstained on that resolution, decided on an embargo after a change of government in November 1964. France, which had also abstained, maintained for several years that it embargoed arms destined for internal repression but not those for defence.

28/Document 27
*See page 254*

67    Because of widespread repression and the charging of Mr. Mandela and other leaders under the Sabotage Act, the General Assembly took up the question of political prisoners early in its 1963 session. Several prominent members of the ANC and associated organizations had been arrested at Rivonia in July and had been charged, along with Mr. Mandela, who was already in prison, for leading *Umkhonto we*

*Sizwe*. On 11 October 1963, the General Assembly adopted a resolution in which it requested the Government of South Africa "to abandon the arbitrary trial now in progress and forthwith to grant unconditional release to all political prisoners and to all persons imprisoned, interned or subjected to other restrictions for having opposed the policy of apartheid".[29] The vote was 106 to 1, with only South Africa voting against. In a further resolution adopted on 16 December 1963, the General Assembly took note of the serious hardship faced by the families of persons persecuted by the South African Government for their opposition to apartheid, requested the Secretary-General to seek ways and means of providing relief and assistance through appropriate international agencies to the families of such persons, and invited Member States and organizations to contribute generously to their relief and assistance.[30]

29/Document 32
*See page 267*

30/Document 35
*See page 270*

68    In a resolution adopted unanimously on 4 December 1963—resolution 182 (1963)—the Security Council condemned the South African Government's non-compliance with the General Assembly and Security Council appeals. It appealed to all States to comply with resolution 181 (1963), in which the Council had called for an arms embargo, and requested the Secretary-General "to establish under his direction and reporting to him a small group of recognized experts to examine methods of resolving the present situation in South Africa through full, peaceful and orderly application of human rights and fundamental freedoms to all inhabitants of the territory as a whole, regardless of race, colour or creed, and to consider what part the United Nations might play in the achievement of that end". It invited the South African Government to avail itself of the assistance of this group in order to bring about such a peaceful and orderly transformation.[31]

31/Document 34
*See page 269*

69    This decision arose from an initiative put forward earlier by the Foreign Minister of Denmark, Mr. Per Haekkerup, in a statement in the General Assembly on 25 September 1963.[32] Mr. Haekkerup had said that while the Danish Government supported the use of pressure to induce the South African Government to change its policy, pressure and sanctions alone were not sufficient to bring about a peaceful resolution of the South African question. The United Nations had to show an alternative to apartheid—a truly democratic society with equal rights for all individuals, irrespective of race. The transformation might prove to be a task which could not be accomplished by the people of South Africa alone. In that process, the United Nations would have to play a major role in assisting the South African people in the transitional period and in laying the foundations of a new society. He suggested that careful studies be initiated without delay.

32/Document 30
*See page 265*

## Expert Group on South Africa

70    The Secretary-General appointed the following members to the Expert Group: Mrs. Alva Myrdal (Sweden), Chairman; Sir Edward Asafu-Adjaye (Ghana); Mr. Josip Djerdja (Yugoslavia); Sir Hugh Foot (United Kingdom), Rapporteur; and Mr. Dey Ould Sidi Baba (Morocco). (Mr. Djerdja resigned from the Group in March 1964.) In response to a request by the Secretary-General, the South African Government replied on 5 February 1964 that it refused to grant facilities to the Group or to cooperate with it in any form whatsoever.

71    Nevertheless, the Expert Group held extensive consultations and submitted a report on 20 April 1964. On the same day, Nelson Mandela, during the Rivonia trial, made his statement that was to echo around the world: "I have cherished the ideal of a democratic and free society in which all persons live together in harmony and with equal opportunities. It is an ideal which I hope to live for and to achieve. But if needs be, it is an ideal for which I am prepared to die."[33]

33/Document 39
*See page 280*

72    In its report, the Group gave expression to the same vision as that of Mr. Mandela, affirming that "the future of South Africa should be settled by the people of South Africa—all the people of South Africa—in free discussion . . . all the people of South Africa should be brought into consultation and should thus be enabled to decide the future of their country at the national level."[34] In order to give effect to this essential principle, the Group considered that all efforts should be directed towards the establishment of a national convention fully representative of the whole population. Once a convention had been convened "it might decide" to create a constituent assembly charged with the task of drawing up a detailed constitution and thus opening the way to the election of a representative parliament. For a constituent assembly, elections might well be required, perhaps undertaken with United Nations assistance and supervision, it added, stressing the importance of an amnesty to enable the national convention to be fully representative.

34/Document 36
*See page 271;*
Document 37
*See page 272*

73    The Group indicated that the United Nations could provide its good offices to facilitate consultations on the formation and the agenda of the national convention. At the convention itself, if so requested, it could offer expert advice on constitutional, economic and social problems. At a later stage, it could help in administrative reorganization, and in particular, could help to meet any request for the organization and supervision of elections. If the necessity arose, the United Nations could contribute to the maintenance of law and order and the protection of life and civil rights, and thus both allay fears and secure confidence.

74    The Group's report suggested that the United Nations and the specialized agencies could assist in the vital field of education and

training, because of the acute need for very large numbers of non-Whites to be qualified for the professions, the civil service and teaching. The Group therefore recommended that a United Nations South African Education and Training Programme be created.

75     The Group proposed that the South African Government be invited to send its representatives to take part in discussions under the auspices of the United Nations on the formation of the national convention. If no satisfactory reply was received by a stipulated date, the Security Council would be left with no effective peaceful means of assisting in resolving the situation, other than applying economic sanctions. The Expert Group, therefore, recommended an urgent examination of the logistics of sanctions.

76     It concluded: "The struggle in South Africa is not a struggle between two races for domination; it is a struggle between the protagonists of racial domination and the advocates of racial equality . . . We have no doubt that the cause of emancipation will prevail in South Africa . . . A political, economic and social system built on the domination of one race by another by force cannot survive. What is now at issue is not the final outcome but the question whether, on the way, the people of South Africa are to go through a long ordeal of blood and hate."

77     In June 1964, when the Security Council, at the request of 58 Member States, again considered the South African question, it had before it the report of the Group of Experts as well as two reports by the Special Committee against Apartheid. In a report of 25 March, the Special Committee had drawn the Security Council's attention to new developments in South Africa, particularly the death sentences imposed on several persons and the threat of death sentences for others, including the accused in the Rivonia trial (see paragraph 67). Convinced that effective mandatory measures ought to be taken urgently to meet the grave situation and to prevent irrevocable consequences, the Committee recommended that the Council, as a first step, call on South Africa to refrain from executing those sentenced to death for opposing its racial policies; abandon current trials under arbitrary laws; desist from adopting further discriminatory measures; and refrain from all other action likely to aggravate the situation.

78     In another report, of 25 May, the Special Committee had reviewed further developments and recommended that the Council: declare that the situation in South Africa was a grave threat to the maintenance of international peace and security; take effective measures to save the lives of the South African leaders condemned for acts arising from their opposition to apartheid; request that all States which maintained relations with South Africa—especially the United States, the United Kingdom and France—take effective measures to meet the pre-

sent grave situation; and decide to apply economic sanctions, in accordance with Chapter VII of the Charter.

79    The Security Council considered the matter from 8 to 18 June. In resolution 190 (1964) of 9 June 1964, with particular regard to the death sentences and the Rivonia trial, which was coming to an end, the Security Council urged the South African Government: to renounce the execution of the persons sentenced to death for acts resulting from their opposition to apartheid; to end the Rivonia trial forthwith; and to grant an amnesty to all persons already imprisoned, interned or subjected to other restrictions for their opposition to apartheid, particularly the defendants in the Rivonia trial.

80    The resolution was adopted by 7 votes to none, with 4 abstentions by some members who felt that the Security Council should refrain from action which might be construed as interference in the due process of law of a Member State.

35/Document 41
See page 283

81    Further discussion of the situation led to the adoption of Security Council resolution 191 (1964) of 18 June 1964.[35] By that time Mr. Mandela and his colleagues had been sentenced to life imprisonment.[36] The Council urgently appealed to the South African Government: to renounce the execution of any persons sentenced to death for their opposition to apartheid; to grant immediate amnesty to all persons detained or on trial, as well as clemency to all persons sentenced, for their opposition to the Government's racial policies; and to abolish the practice of imprisonment without charges, without access to counsel or without the right of prompt trial.

36/Document 39
See page 280;
Document 40
See page 282

82    Noting the recommendations and the conclusions in the report of the Group of Experts, the Council endorsed and subscribed in particular to the main conclusion of the Group that "all the people of South Africa should be brought into consultation and should thus be enabled to decide the future of their country at the national level". It requested the Secretary-General to consider what assistance the United Nations might offer to facilitate such consultations among representatives of all elements of the South African population. It invited the South African Government to accept the main conclusion of the Group of Experts, to cooperate with the Secretary-General and to submit its views to him with respect to such consultations by 30 November 1964.

83    By the same resolution, the Security Council established an expert committee, composed of representatives of all members of the Security Council, to undertake a technical and practical study and report to the Council as to the feasibility, effectiveness and implications of measures which could be taken by the Council under the Charter of the United Nations. It also invited the Secretary-General, in consultation with appropriate United Nations specialized agencies, to establish a

programme for the purpose of arranging for education and training abroad for South Africans.

*84* In a letter to the Secretary-General on 13 July, South Africa stated that it regarded Security Council resolution 190 (1964) as intervention by the United Nations in the judicial process of a Member State and therefore beyond the authority of the Charter. In another letter, on 16 November, it rejected the invitation to accept the main conclusion of the Group of Experts, on the grounds that what was being sought was that a Member State should abdicate its sovereignty in favour of the United Nations.

## Expert Committee of the Security Council

*85* The Expert Committee submitted its report to the Security Council on 2 March 1965.[37] It revealed disagreement among its 11 members. A set of conclusions was adopted by a majority of 6 to 4 (France did not participate in the Expert Committee). The Committee also transmitted other drafts which did not obtain a majority, as well as a dissenting note by the delegations of Czechoslovakia and the Union of Soviet Socialist Republics (USSR).

37/Document 44
*See page 285*

*86* In the conclusions adopted by a majority vote of 6 to 4, the Committee stated that although South Africa would not be readily susceptible to economic measures, it would not be immune to damage from them. There were several areas of vulnerability in the South African economy. Emphasis was placed on the importance of a total trade embargo, an embargo on the sale of petroleum and petroleum products and on arms. Also considered were a cessation of emigration of technicians and skilled manpower to South Africa, interdiction of communications with South Africa and political and diplomatic measures referred to in the resolutions already adopted by the Security Council and the General Assembly.

*87* The conclusions recognized the need for adequate international machinery under the aegis of the United Nations to prevent the circumvention of the various measures by States and individuals. They stated that an international effort should be made to mitigate the hardships which such measures might bring upon the economies of some Member States. Certain Committee members stressed the importance of a total blockade to make the measures effective, as well as the costliness of such an operation. Consequently, they said that in the event of a total blockade, a proportionate sharing of costs should be considered.

*88* In their dissenting note, the representatives of Czechoslovakia and the USSR stated that the Committee had every ground for concluding that economic and political sanctions against South Africa were feasible and would have the effect of inducing the South African authorities to abolish apartheid and comply with the decisions of various United Nations organs.

89    The report of the Expert Committee contained no proposals with sufficient support for adoption by the Security Council, and was therefore not considered by the Council.

## Building a consensus for action

90    By 1966, there was virtual unanimity in the United Nations on its objectives with respect to the situation in South Africa. The United Nations categorically condemned apartheid as a flagrant violation of the Charter of the United Nations and the Universal Declaration of Human Rights. It sought to promote equality before the law for all persons regardless of race, creed or colour, as well as the economic, social, cultural and political participation of all the people on a basis of racial equality. All the people of South Africa should be brought into consultation and enabled to decide the future of their country at the national level. The Organization demanded that the South African Government end repression and grant amnesty to all persons sentenced, detained, restricted or forced into exile for their opposition to apartheid.

91    To achieve these objectives there was agreement on three main lines of action: (1) pressure on the South African Government to persuade it to end repression, abandon apartheid and seek a peaceful solution through consultation with the genuine representatives of all the people of South Africa; (2) appropriate assistance to the victims of apartheid and those struggling for a society in which all people would enjoy equal rights and opportunities; (3) dissemination of information to focus world public opinion on the inhumanity of apartheid and to encourage such opinion to exert its influence in support of United Nations efforts for a peaceful and just solution.

92    By 1966, the United Nations had also called for an arms embargo against South Africa—the first such step taken against any Member State.[38] Even the countries which did not support a total arms embargo said they were restricting their sales of arms to South Africa. The Organization had also established funds for humanitarian and educational assistance to the victims and opponents of apartheid. The provision of legal and other assistance to those persecuted under repressive laws—including those involved in activities of banned organizations and acts of sabotage—was without precedent in the history of the world Organization. The General Assembly had already requested that the Secretary-General, in consultation with the Special Committee against Apartheid, take appropriate measures for the widest possible dissemination of information on apartheid and United Nations efforts to deal with

38/Document 28
See page 257

it, and had invited all Member States, specialized agencies and non-governmental organizations to cooperate in that regard.

93    But there were sharp differences of opinion between Member States as to what further action was needed—differences which inevitably limited the ability of the United Nations to exert effective pressure on the South African Government to secure an amelioration of the situation inside the country. A majority of Member States believed that the total isolation of the South African Government and its supporters through diplomatic, economic and other sanctions, which would be mandatory under Chapter VII of the Charter, was essential to secure a peaceful solution in accordance with the purposes and principles of the Charter. The USSR and other socialist countries were early and strong advocates of more vigorous action to bring about the end of apartheid. A large number of States, many of them newly independent and developing countries, ended their relations with South Africa, often at considerable economic sacrifice, or refrained from establishing them.

94    However, some States, especially the major trading partners of South Africa, opposed sanctions. They argued that the isolation of South Africa, and its exclusion from the United Nations and other international bodies, would be counter-productive. These States included three permanent members of the Security Council—France, the United Kingdom, and the United States—whose support was essential for a mandatory decision by the Security Council. As a result, the foreign trade of South Africa, and foreign investments in South Africa, continued to grow despite the resolutions of the General Assembly. African and other countries advocating sanctions began to accuse South Africa's main trading partners of collaborating with apartheid, nullifying the sacrifices of other States and thereby encouraging the South African regime to persist in its behaviour.

95    In a 1966 resolution, the General Assembly deplored the attitude of the main trading partners of South Africa, including three permanent members of the Security Council, which "by their failure to cooperate in implementing resolutions of the General Assembly . . . and by their increasing collaboration with the Government of South Africa, have encouraged the latter to persist in its racial policies". Such collaboration, the Assembly stated, "has aggravated the danger of a violent conflict", and it requested them to take urgent steps to disengage from South Africa.[39] The disagreement among Member States on measures to exert effective pressure on the South African Government was a factor in enabling the regime to defy the United Nations and proceed with its plans to consolidate and entrench White domination. In doing so, it resorted to ever-increasing repression.

39/Document 49
See page 293

96    Despite the disagreements, the General Assembly, in its 1966 resolution, acting on the recommendation of the Special Committee

against Apartheid, endorsed "an international campaign against apartheid" as a means to overcome the impasse through a comprehensive programme of action involving the United Nations, Governments, intergovernmental and non-governmental organizations and individuals. This campaign was to involve not only intensified efforts to secure agreement on sanctions, but partial measures on which a wide measure of agreement could be obtained—such as public boycotts of South Africa—and greater efforts to promote political and material support to the opponents of apartheid.

# III International campaign against apartheid, 1967-1989

*97* The period from 1967 to 1989 was characterized, on the one hand, by escalating tension and conflict in southern Africa resulting from the policies and actions of the South African Government and, on the other, by determined efforts by the United Nations to develop the international campaign against apartheid to secure both an end to that system of racial discrimination and the establishment of a non-racial society through consultations among the genuine representatives of all the people of South Africa.

*98* The political and human rights situation inside South Africa deteriorated further after 1967 as the authorities continued to impose apartheid policies, resorting to increasing repression in response to mounting opposition from movements representing the majority of the people. As neighbouring countries attained independence, the South African Government also undertook overt and covert aggression against several of them, so as to limit their ability to support liberation in South Africa and to increase those countries' economic dependence on South Africa. By the late 1980s, this destabilization policy had caused enormous loss of life and had severely undermined their economies.

*99* The military might of the South African State could not, however, suppress the demand for freedom of the majority of South Africans, which was expressed forcefully in protests in the 1970s and 1980s. Nor could the South African Government effectively counter the growing international campaign against apartheid, which consistently received the backing of the entire United Nations system and included support for the liberation movements, political prisoners and victims of apartheid. The campaign also promoted the arms, oil and other economic embargoes as well as sports and cultural boycotts—the first such actions that the United Nations had ever called for against any country. By ensuring wide publicity for the question of apartheid, the campaign was able to attract public support in all countries, including South Africa's main trading partners whose Governments were reluctant to impose sanctions.

*100* From 1967 onward, the United Nations encouraged Governments and peoples to take a wide range of measures to isolate the South African regime and demonstrate solidarity with those who were oppressed. In 1973, the General Assembly declared that "the South African regime has no right to represent the people of South Africa" and that

40/Document 71
*See page 328*

"the liberation movements recognized by the Organization of African Unity are the authentic representatives of the overwhelming majority of the South African people".[40] South Africa was excluded from participation in the General Assembly, as well as from most specialized agencies of the United Nations. It was expelled from many governmental and non-governmental organizations and conferences. The sports and cultural boycotts of South Africa also made great advances, showing clearly to the supporters of the regime how greatly apartheid was despised around the world. From as early as 1964, South Africa could no longer participate in the Olympic Games. Its sports teams were no longer welcome around the world. Prominent entertainers refused to perform to segregated audiences in South Africa, and consumer boycotts spread through many countries. An increasing number of States began to favour the use of economic sanctions. By 1975, the South African Government was effectively excluded from all the organs of the United Nations as a direct consequence of its violation of the Charter of the United Nations and the Universal Declaration of Human Rights.

101    The following pages trace the increasing isolation of apartheid South Africa in its international relations. When in 1977, under resolution 418 (1977), the Security Council imposed a mandatory arms embargo against South Africa,[41] Secretary-General Kurt Waldheim pointed out that it was the first time in the history of the United Nations that action had been taken under Chapter VII of the Charter against a Member State, and that thereby the United Nations had entered "a new and significantly different phase of the long-standing efforts of the international community to obtain redress of these grievous wrongs".[42]

41/Document 89
*See page 348*

42/Document 90
*See page 348*

102    In 1985, when the South African Government proclaimed a state of emergency and escalated repression, the international community again reacted strongly, and the Security Council, for the first time, called on Governments to take significant economic measures against South Africa.[43] There was a widespread response—from the United States Congress, the European Community, the Commonwealth and Member States which had maintained economic relations with South Africa. International banks stopped making new loans to South Africa and hundreds of transnational corporations began to divest themselves of their holdings in the country. Such measures eventually harmed the long-term prospects of the South African economy and brought home to the apartheid regime and its supporters that they had to move towards an accommodation with the majority of South Africans and their representatives. By 1989, the end of the cold war made it easier for the international community to take concerted action. The United Nations endorsed the assessment of the ANC and African States that a conjuncture of circumstances had finally arisen for the settlement of the South African problem through negotiations.

43/Document 116
*See page 392*

# Escalating crisis in South Africa

*103* One of the major aims of apartheid was the denationalizing of Africans, who constituted over four fifths of the population, by making them citizens of several ethnic "homelands". From 1951 onward, these territories were carved out of scattered and impoverished reserves, and by the 1980s they still covered less than 13 per cent of the land area of the country. According to the ideology of apartheid, Africans who were needed to work in factories, mines and homes were to be regarded as temporary sojourners in White South Africa and those whose labour was not required—including the old and the infirm, who were referred to as "superfluous appendages"—were to be deported to the "homelands".

*104* The regime hoped to deceive world public opinion with the fiction that it was promoting African "self-determination" by staging fraudulent elections in the homelands in collaboration with pliant chiefs and declaring a number of them "independent". Four of them—Transkei, Ciskei, Bophuthatswana and Venda—were declared "independent" in the 1970s, thereby denationalizing millions of Africans, while the others retained their homeland status. In other parts of South Africa, apartheid also implied the segregation of the Coloured people and people of Indian origin; these groups were given councils with little power. With the use of such far-reaching apartheid measures, White domination was intended to become entrenched. However, the implementation of these plans required brutal repression, and entailed the removal of nearly 5 million people from their homes.

*105* In many resolutions, the United Nations stressed the territorial integrity of South Africa and refused to give credence to the apartheid regime's creation of the entities that became widely known as "Bantustans" when the regime moved to declare them "independent".[44] Both the General Assembly and the Security Council specifically denounced the proclamations of the so-called "independence" of the four Bantustans as invalid and called on Governments to deny any form of recognition to them. No Member State recognized those entities.[45]

44/Document 60
See page 313

45/Document 77
See page 335;
Document 84
See page 342;
Document 85
See page 343;
Document 104
See page 367

*106* Ultimately, apartheid's ambitious plans for comprehensive racial separation were destined to fail in the face of resistance from the South African people, who received strong backing from African and other countries and vital encouragement from the international campaign against apartheid. The campaign was launched by the United Nations when the liberation movements in South Africa were struggling to recover from a number of reverses and when the apartheid regime, confident of its military might, had become more ruthless and aggressive. By 1965, the South African authorities had been able to suppress temporarily the resistance which had been led by the underground

## South Africa's homelands under apartheid, 1986

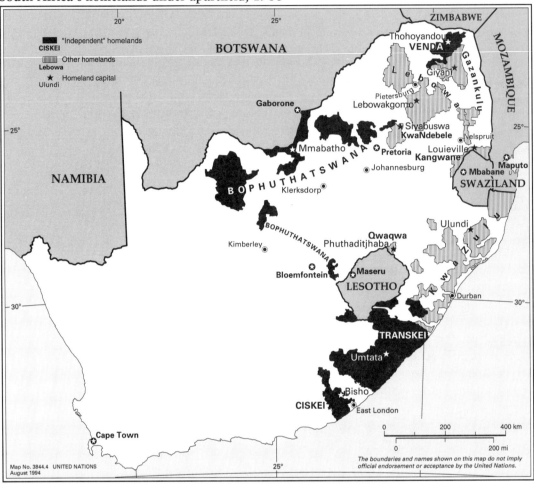

The ten homelands created by the apartheid system were highly fragmented and usually located across infertile rural areas, giving them little chance of economic viability.

structures of the ANC and the PAC and the armed wings they had set up to conduct sabotage and other actions. Thousands of their leaders and activists had been jailed or restricted, scores executed or tortured to death and many others forced into exile. Military and police establishments had been greatly expanded and an armoury of repressive laws had been added to the statute-books. An appearance of peace had been imposed by terror.

*107* In 1966, the General Assembly, by an overwhelming vote, terminated South Africa's mandate over the Territory of South West Africa (Namibia), but the South African regime defied the United Nations and continued its occupation of Namibia. The same year, the Security Council imposed mandatory sanctions against the illegal racist minority regime in Southern Rhodesia, which had declared independence in November 1965, but South Africa again defied the United Nations and sustained that regime. In 1967, when freedom fighters of the Zimbabwe African People's Union and the ANC of South Africa crossed into Southern Rhodesia, the South African regime sent its security forces there in defiance of the United Nations and the Administering Authority, the United Kingdom.

108    Despite the South African Government's aggression in defending the apartheid system, the spirit of freedom was irrepressible. New and more intense waves of resistance against apartheid emerged in South Africa after every reverse. Moreover, the international campaign was building up pressure on the apartheid regime and its supporters, increasing assistance to the liberation struggle and reinforcing the morale of the opponents of apartheid. By the late 1960s, a Black Consciousness Movement had emerged in South Africa and gained a wide following among students and workers. It supported solidarity among the oppressed—Africans, Coloured people and Indians—and denounced the chiefs and others who collaborated with the regime and betrayed popular aspirations. In the early 1970s, there was a wave of strikes by African workers, despite laws prohibiting such actions. The underground structures of the national liberation movement had begun to revive. The oppressed people in South Africa were further encouraged when Portuguese colonial rule ended in Mozambique and Angola in 1974 and 1975, respectively.

109    Inside South Africa, resistance continued to grow. On 16 June 1976, students protested in Soweto against the system of Bantu education and the imposition of Afrikaans as a compulsory medium of instruction. Police shot and killed many schoolchildren, and the student uprising spread nationwide. Hundreds of thousands of workers then went on strike in solidarity with the students, thousands of whom fled the country and joined the liberation forces.[46]

46/Document 82
*See page 339;*
Document 83
*See page 340*

110    Once again, the regime resorted to repressive tactics. Steve Biko, a founder and leader of the Black Consciousness Movement, was tortured to death in police custody on 12 September 1977. A month later, Black Consciousness organizations, as well as other groups and two newspapers with Black readerships, were banned.

111    The Soweto massacre, the murder of Mr. Biko and the banning of organizations engaged in peaceful opposition to apartheid heightened demands for effective international action and prompted the Security Council to decide unanimously on the imposition of a mandatory arms embargo against South Africa in 1977.[47]

47/Document 89
*See page 348*

112    At this point, not only was there a large increase in international assistance to South African refugees and exiles, but some Western Governments, following the example set by Sweden, began to make direct contributions to South African liberation movements. Smaller

Western countries, led by the Nordic group, began to take national measures to restrict their economic and other relations with South Africa. Previously they had withheld taking national economic measures, considering them ineffective without a decision by the Security Council. Now they felt it was more important to take a lead that other countries might follow.

*113*    After 1980, as student resistance again spread across the nation and as armed struggle expanded, the South African regime continued with further repression. It adopted a so-called "total strategy" to deal with its opponents. The military establishment began to exercise enormous influence in government; it conducted raids against refugees in neighbouring countries and employed death squads to assassinate leaders of the national liberation movements at home and abroad.

*114*    With the international campaign against apartheid beginning to have an effect, the regime, in order to counteract it, greatly expanded its propaganda network, reinforced with secret operations, to try to persuade the world that real reforms and adjustments were under way in South Africa. For example, it permitted the holding of some multiracial sports competitions in an effort to gain readmission to international sporting events. Similarly, to avert international trade union action, the regime amended its legislation to allow registration of African and multiracial trade unions, but with severe restrictions to control their independence.

*115*    In 1983, the Government announced plans for a new constitution providing representation in segregated chambers of Parliament for the Coloured people and Indians, but not for Africans. It was approved by an exclusively White referendum held on 2 November 1983. This failure to address the fundamental political demands of the majority of South Africans led to the formation of the United Democratic Front (UDF), an alliance of anti-apartheid organizations representing millions of people, which opposed the manoeuvre and was supported in its views by the international community.

*116*    Throughout the 1970s and 1980s, the South African regime sought to become the dominant regional Power in southern Africa. With the march of freedom in Africa and the liberation of Mozambique (1974), Angola (1975) and Zimbabwe (1980), it embarked on threats and acts of aggression and destabilization against independent African States. This was intended to intimidate those countries into denying refuge or facilities to South African freedom fighters and to keep them economically dependent. In particular, it instigated and supported proxy forces to destroy the economic and social infrastructure of the newly independent countries, especially Angola and Mozambique, and it also intervened directly with its own forces. A colonial war was conducted in Namibia for more than two decades, causing great loss of human life.

117    The South African Government's efforts to entrench White domination and extend its hegemony in the region resulted in enormous human suffering. At home, in addition to the millions who were forcibly removed, thousands more were killed, wounded, tortured or imprisoned.

118    The cost to neighbouring States of South African aggression and destabilization was enormous. Hundreds of thousands of people were killed and millions were displaced. A study published by the ECA in 1989 estimated that the economic cost to the nine member States of the Southern African Development Coordination Conference (SADCC) was over $60 billion during the period 1980-1988 and $10 billion in 1988 alone. The SADCC subregion's output would have been over 40 per cent higher in the absence of a hostile South Africa, according to the report (*South African Destabilization; The Economic Cost of Frontline Resistance to Apartheid*, Addis Ababa, 1989).

119    At various times the apartheid regime tried, with the encouragement of some Western Powers which espoused a policy of "constructive engagement" with South Africa as an alternative to sanctions, to project itself as being interested in peace in the region. It was able to persuade Mozambique, devastated by South African–supported depredations, to sign an "Agreement on Non-Aggression and Good Neighbourliness", known as the Nkomati Accord, in March 1984. It hoped that, with its claims of seeking peace in the region and reform at home, it could break out of its isolation.

120    During this period, which was one of heightened international tension, the relations between the major Powers adversely affected United Nations action against apartheid. Such was the situation in the early 1980s when the United States, and in some cases the United Kingdom, opposed or abstained on proposals for action concerning South African acts of aggression against the Front-line States—Angola, Botswana, Mozambique, Tanzania, Zambia and Zimbabwe—and violence against the African people in South Africa, as well as resolutions on concerted action against apartheid co-sponsored by several Western Powers. This happened at a time when France, led by President François Mitterrand, was moving towards meaningful action against apartheid and a growing number of Western States were committing themselves to sanctions. But even resolutions with overwhelming majorities proved ineffective in deterring the South African Government, which had by then come under the influence of its military establishment, so long as one or more of the Great Powers were opposed to those resolutions.

121    However, when the South African Prime Minister P. W. Botha visited Western European capitals in 1984, he encountered mass demonstrations organized by anti-apartheid forces. He failed to win the

support for his Government's limited and racially-exclusive reforms that he sought from European Governments.

122    Soon after Mr. Botha's return to South Africa, domestic mass resistance against the constitution proposed in 1983, as well as other apartheid measures, grew so strong that the regime placed parts of the country under a state of emergency. In 1985, after becoming President, Mr. Botha declared a state of emergency which was extended throughout the entire country in 1986 and which was then renewed annually until 1990. During this period, tens of thousands of people were detained without trial, including thousands of children, some as young as eight years old.

123    Resistance became so widespread after 1984 that it could not be suppressed by a show of force, by the stationing of troops in African townships or by brutal violence against demonstrators. Trade unions were able to organize general strikes of millions of workers despite the emergency regulations, and many townships became fortresses of resistance. The regime began to look for ways out of its self-imposed crisis. In response to the campaign for the release of Nelson Mandela and other leaders, the regime offered Mr. Mandela a conditional release in January 1985, which he refused. In a message to the people sent through his family the following month, he said: "I cannot and will not give any undertaking at a time when I and you, the people, are not free."

124    The continuing resistance of South Africa's people, including schoolchildren, and the regime's brutal attempts at repression caught the attention of the world media. People worldwide—but especially those in Western countries—demanded that their Governments take action. The United Nations actively encouraged this growing anti-apartheid sentiment. The different forms of action taken between 1967 and 1989 are briefly reviewed below.


## Concerted action by the United Nations

125    The United Nations responded to South Africa's defiant actions not only by condemnations, but by taking action and by continually affirming its commitment to eliminating apartheid. After South Africa repeatedly refused to accommodate international public opinion, there was a growing belief that the international community should support the struggle for majority rule.

126    Because the effects of apartheid pervaded every aspect of life in South Africa, the issue also came before numerous organs and specialized agencies of the United Nations. There was a consistency of approach by all organs and agencies. Although some duplication was unavoidable, despite efforts at coordination, this concerted action by many agencies and on many aspects of the issue helped to make the world

aware of the effects of apartheid in various spheres, and encouraged the involvement of diverse segments of world public opinion to take appropriate action against apartheid.

127 In all activities against apartheid, close cooperation was established by the United Nations system with the Organization of African Unity (OAU), as well as with the South African liberation movements recognized by the OAU, namely, the ANC and the PAC. Such wide interaction on an issue of considerable controversy is unique in the annals of the United Nations.[48]

48/Document 98
See page 353;
Document 99
See page 354

128 The General Assembly and the Security Council were the principal organs concerned with action against apartheid. During the 1960s and early 1970s, while the General Assembly pressed for sanctions against South Africa and requested the Security Council to take action, the latter did not impose sanctions because of the opposition of three permanent members, so that the approaches of the principal organs seemed at variance. There was, however, growing convergence by the 1980s which, after 1989, greatly facilitated parallel action to secure the transition to a non-racial democratic Government in South Africa.

129 The increasing level of commitment to end apartheid and assist the liberation of the South African people can be seen over successive resolutions. In 1972, the General Assembly expressed its strong conviction "that the United Nations has a vital interest in securing the speedy elimination of apartheid". In 1975, the Assembly proclaimed that the United Nations and the international community had "a special responsibility towards the oppressed people of South Africa and their liberation movements, and towards those imprisoned, restricted or exiled for their struggle against apartheid". It reiterated its determination to devote increasing attention and resources, in close cooperation with the OAU, for "the speedy eradication of apartheid in South Africa and the liberation of the South African people".[49] In 1983, the General Assembly affirmed that "the elimination of apartheid constitutes a major objective of the United Nations".

49/Document 79
See page 336

130 Both the General Assembly and the Security Council increasingly emphasized that apartheid could not be reformed or adjusted. In 1984, the Security Council declared that "only the total eradication of apartheid and the establishment of a non-racial democratic society based on majority rule, through the full and free exercise of universal adult suffrage by all the people in a united and non-fragmented South Africa, can lead to a just and lasting solution of the explosive situation in South Africa".[50]

50/Document 113
See page 390

131 While apartheid was unanimously denounced as a crime, there was disagreement over defining it as a crime against humanity. From 1966 onward, the General Assembly condemned apartheid as a "crime against humanity". In 1973, it adopted and opened for signature

the International Convention on the Suppression and Punishment of the Crime of Apartheid, which declared in its Article 1: "The States Parties to the present Convention declare that apartheid is a crime against humanity". Although the resolutions and the Convention were adopted by large majorities, a substantial number of delegations continued to oppose the reference to "crime against humanity".[51]

51/Document 70
*See page 325*

## Role of the General Assembly

*132*  From the 1960s onward, the General Assembly expressed its conviction, by large majorities, that the situation in South Africa constituted a threat to international peace and security and that mandatory economic and other sanctions under Chapter VII of the Charter were essential to solve the problem. It repeatedly requested that the Security Council impose sanctions and deplored the opposition of South Africa's major trading partners, including three permanent members of the Security Council, to such action. It condemned the actions of States and transnational corporations which continued and even expanded their relations with South Africa. There was a deliberate attempt to secure wider support for action against apartheid both through consultations with all groups of States, and by the adoption of resolutions expressing serious regret at, or condemnation of, actions of Governments which opposed the isolation of the South African regime and which continued relations with it. By substantial majorities, the Assembly deplored collaboration with South Africa by certain countries, and called on them to take measures to terminate such collaboration. In such resolutions, Israel, the United States of America, the United Kingdom, France and the Federal Republic of Germany were the countries most frequently mentioned; Japan, Italy, Portugal, Belgium, Chile and Switzerland were also cited in one or more resolutions. The Assembly also made numerous appeals to the Member States, intergovernmental and non-governmental organizations, and individuals to help eliminate apartheid by isolating the South African Government internationally.

*133*  The General Assembly dealt with all aspects of apartheid and was responsible for the consistency of approach in the United Nations campaign against apartheid. Under its authority and with its endorsement, the Special Committee against Apartheid, which had been established in 1962, promoted the international campaign against apartheid (see paragraphs 157-169 for the role of the Special Committee).

*134*  After 1970, the Group of African States at the United Nations and the Movement of Non-Aligned Countries began proposing a series of resolutions on various aspects of the campaign against apartheid, rather than a single resolution, not only to focus attention on particular facets of the problem, but also to secure the widest possible support for each course of action. This ensured the adoption by virtual unanimity, of resolutions concerning such issues as assistance to victims of apartheid, demands for the release of political prisoners and cessation of executions of opponents of apartheid.[52]

135 On matters such as economic sanctions, arms and oil embargoes and other measures to isolate South Africa, the size and composition of the majorities varied and partly depended on the language of the resolutions. There was, however, a steady increase in the majorities for these resolutions, and more and more Member States proceeded to new levels of action.[53] The discussions in the General Assembly, the consultations by the Special Committee against Apartheid and the efforts of the OAU and other bodies, as well as the strength of world public opinion, promoted this trend.

136 From 1984 to 1988, the progress towards a consensus was manifest in a series of resolutions entitled "Concerted international action for the elimination of apartheid", co-sponsored by several Western States together with African and non-Aligned States. The resolutions were adopted with only two votes cast against—by the United Kingdom and the United States. Resolution 43/50 K of 5 December 1988 provides a good example of the level of agreement at that time on a wide range of appeals for, among other things: the cessation of further investment in, and financial loans to, South Africa; an end to all promotion of and support for trade with South Africa; the cessation of military, police or intelligence cooperation with South African authorities; a halt to the export and sale of oil to South Africa; and the cessation of academic, cultural, scientific and sports relations that would support the apartheid regime.

### Role of the Security Council

137 The Security Council first considered the situation in South Africa in 1960 and thereafter adopted several significant resolutions, especially in 1963 and 1964. Although the Council did not recognize the situation as a threat to international peace and security under Chapter VII of the Charter, as the General Assembly had asked it to do, and did not impose mandatory economic sanctions, it issued ever stronger condemnations of the apartheid regime and its acts of aggression against neighbouring States. It demanded an end to repression, recognized the legitimacy of the struggle against apartheid, demanded a series of measures by the South African Government, and called for various actions by Member States.[54] And it imposed a mandatory arms embargo against South Africa in 1977—the first time such action was ever taken against a Member State.[55]

138 A hardening of the Security Council position against apartheid also occurred in 1977, when in resolution 417 (1977) it for the first time referred to the South African regime as "racist" and affirmed the right to self-determination of the people of South Africa.[56]

52/Document 91
See page 349

53/Document 80
See page 336;
Document 86
See page 344;
Document 92
See page 349;
Document 93
See page 350;
Document 96
See page 351;
Document 122
See page 407;
Document 123
See page 408

54/Document 64
See page 316;
Document 82
See page 339

55/Document 89
See page 348

56/Document 88
See page 347

*139*　In the same resolution the Security Council strongly condemned the regime for its resort to massive violence and repression against the Black people, as well as all other opponents of apartheid. (The term "Black people" has often been used in United Nations resolutions to denote all the oppressed people of South Africa—Africans, Coloured people and Indians). Among other things, it demanded that the South African regime: release all persons imprisoned under arbitrary security laws; cease its indiscriminate violence against peaceful demonstrators, murders in detention and torture of political prisoners; and abolish the policy of Bantustanization, abandon the policy of apartheid and ensure majority rule based on justice and equality. Again in 1980, following more repression by the South African regime, especially against workers, students and church workers, the Security Council issued a strong condemnation in resolution 473 (1980).[57]

57/Document 97
*See page 352*

*140*　After 1984, the Security Council recommended even stronger action, when the regime's imposition of a new constitution and other measures led to widespread resistance. In resolution 554 (1994), passed on the eve of elections for racially segregated chambers under the new constitution, it expressed its conviction that the new constitution would continue the process of denationalization of the indigenous African majority, depriving it of all fundamental rights, and further entrench apartheid. It noted that the inclusion in the new constitution of the Coloured people and people of Asian origin was aimed at dividing the oppressed people of South Africa and fomenting internal conflict. It rejected and declared as null and void the constitution and the elections to be organized under it.[58]

58/Document 113
*See page 390*

*141*　With the worsening of the situation in South Africa and the declaration of a state of emergency in 36 districts in 1985, the Security Council responded with resolution 569 (1985) in which, for the first time, it called for specific economic measures against South Africa, including a suspension of all new investment, suspension of guaranteed export loans, restrictions in the field of sports and cultural relations, and prohibition of all new contracts in the nuclear field.[59] Although not mandatory, this call by the Security Council amounted both to a significant tightening of the pressure on the apartheid regime and to an acceptance of the validity of sanctions in helping to eliminate apartheid. While the Governments of several major Powers, including some permanent members of the Security Council, were still opposed to the use of mandatory economic sanctions against South Africa, the Security Council resolution reflected recognition by some of the major industrialized nations that the policy of "constructive engagement" with Pretoria was not effective in persuading the South African regime to abandon apartheid.

59/Document 116
*See page 392*

### Other organs of the United Nations

*142* Over the years, many other United Nations organs also acted against apartheid.

*143* The Economic and Social Council considered the reports of the commissions on Human Rights, the Status of Women and Transnational Corporations (see below) and, at the request of the ILO, also acted on complaints of infringements of trade union rights in South Africa.

*144* The Commission on Human Rights devoted great attention to apartheid at its twenty-third session in February/March 1967, partly because of a request by the Special Committee against Apartheid that it urgently consider the torture and ill-treatment of political prisoners and detainees in South Africa. It established an Ad Hoc Working Group of Experts to investigate the matter, and also appointed a Special Rapporteur on apartheid.[60]

60/Document 52
*See page 298*

*145* As a result of the Commission's attention to the treatment of political prisoners, and the Working Group's investigation, the South African Government invited the International Committee of the Red Cross to visit the prisons and also made some improvements in the conditions of political prisoners. (However, it continued to deny access to detainees.)

*146* Thereafter, apartheid became a major item on the Commission's agenda. The annual reports of the Ad Hoc Working Group documented and publicized human rights violations in South Africa. The Commission also prepared the draft of the International Convention on the Suppression and Punishment of the Crime of Apartheid, adopted by the General Assembly in 1973, and monitored its implementation. In addition, a series of reports prepared by a Special Rapporteur of the Commission on the effects of collaboration with South Africa, especially by transnational corporations, led to a number of resolutions by the Commission, the Economic and Social Council and the General Assembly.

*147* The Commission on the Status of Women concentrated on the situation of women and children under apartheid and recommended special assistance to projects for refugee women and children.

*148* The Commission on Transnational Corporations requested the Secretary-General to prepare reports on the activities of transnational corporations in South Africa and their linkages with the apartheid system in the military and other fields. On its recommendation, the Centre for Transnational Corporations arranged two public hearings by panels of eminent persons, in 1985 and 1989, on the activities of transnational corporations in South Africa and Namibia.

*149* The Disarmament Commission dealt with reports on the efforts of the South African Government to obtain a nuclear-weapon capability.

*150* The United Nations Council for Namibia and the Special Committee on the Declaration on Granting Independence to Colonial Countries and Peoples examined the policies and actions of South Africa in Namibia and other colonial territories.

*151* Successive Secretaries-General were deeply involved in all efforts to eliminate apartheid and promote a peaceful solution, as were Secretariat units such as the Department of Public Information and the Centre against Apartheid.

## Specialized agencies and other institutions

*152* South Africa withdrew from the United Nations Educational, Scientific and Cultural Organization (UNESCO) in 1955, the Food and Agriculture Organization of the United Nations (FAO) in 1963 and the International Labour Organisation (ILO) in 1964 because of those organizations' condemnation of apartheid. Most of the other United Nations agencies took action to expel or suspend South Africa from membership or to restrict its participation in their activities and meetings. South Africa was excluded from the work of the Economic Commission for Africa from 1963, but it remained a member of the World Bank and the International Monetary Fund (IMF). The World Bank, however, following consultations with the United Nations, refrained from approving any loans to South Africa from 1966 onward. In 1974, South Africa lost its seat on the Board of Executive Directors of both the World Bank and the IMF. Its last use of IMF resources was in 1982, until a loan was made during the country's transition to majority rule in 1993.

*153* As the South African Government became increasingly isolated, several United Nations agencies invited the representatives of South African liberation movements to their meetings and conferences.

*154* The United Nations Development Programme (UNDP) provided assistance to South African liberation movements from 1974 onward, as did FAO, ILO, UNESCO, the United Nations Children's Fund (UNICEF), the World Health Organization (WHO) and the World Intellectual Property Organization (WIPO). FAO, ILO, UNESCO, UNICEF, and WHO published studies on apartheid and contributed to the dissemination of information about South Africa. ILO and UNESCO, in particular, developed extensive programmes of action against apartheid.

*155* In 1964, the ILO General Conference unanimously adopted a Declaration concerning Action against Apartheid and approved a Programme for the Elimination of Apartheid in Labour Matters. Thereafter, successive Directors-General submitted annual reports on the Declaration's application. In subsequent years, the ILO decided on stronger measures and expanded its activities against apartheid. It provided considerable assistance to the South African liberation movements and to Black workers and trade unions in South Africa. The Workers' Group of the ILO Governing Body, in cooperation with the United Nations Special Committee against Apartheid, organized three international trade union conferences against apartheid in 1973, 1977 and 1983.

156    UNESCO published a number of studies as well as educational materials on various aspects of apartheid, organized or hosted a number of conferences and seminars to promote action against apartheid and provided fellowships and training to members of South African liberation movements. It broke off relations with all international non-governmental organizations cooperating with apartheid.

## The Special Committee against Apartheid

157    Established by a decision of the General Assembly in 1962 to keep developments concerning South Africa's racial policies under constant review and to report to the General Assembly and/or the Security Council, the Special Committee against Apartheid received a steady broadening of its mandate in subsequent years, and became the United Nations' central arm for following the situation and for making recommendations for action by the Organization's major organs. Its specific major function soon became the promotion of the international campaign against apartheid under the auspices of the United Nations.[61] The Committee itself had proposed the need for a comprehensive programme of action in 1966 as a way to break out of the impasse resulting from the Member States' disagreement on sanctions and to sustain a momentum of action against apartheid.[62] The programme was conceived as relying not only upon continued efforts to secure sanctions, but also upon a multi-pronged effort to promote action at various levels on all aspects of the problem and to facilitate the broadest possible participation in the struggle against apartheid.

158    From the Special Committee's first meeting in 1963, its initiatives led to new levels of action by the General Assembly and the Security Council.[63] After extensive consultations by the Special Committee with Governments and organizations, in particular the OAU, the South African liberation movements and anti-apartheid movements, the programme for the international campaign began to crystallize. It was reflected in annual resolutions of the General Assembly and later set out in programmes of action adopted by the General Assembly[64] and by many conferences and seminars organized by the United Nations.

159    In December 1966, the General Assembly endorsed the Special Committee's proposal for an international campaign against apartheid and authorized the Committee to consult specialized agencies, regional organizations, States and non-governmental organizations on ways to promote the campaign. The campaign had a dual purpose.

61/Document 53
*See page 300;*
Document 58
*See page 311*

62/Document 46
*See page 291*

63/Document 25
*See page 253*

64/Document 111
*See page 379*

It sought to press South Africa's major trading partners to facilitate the adoption of effective mandatory sanctions by the Security Council while promoting all possible actions which could be taken by the General Assembly and other United Nations organs and agencies, pending the imposition of sanctions. It also sought to encourage Governments, organizations and individuals to isolate South Africa and to support those struggling for a non-racial democratic society.

160    The Special Committee against Apartheid gave primary importance to economic sanctions and related measures designed to secure the speedy eradication of apartheid. It also suggested the arms and oil embargoes and various other partial steps to secure certain minimum but vital objectives. In addition, the Special Committee was concerned with action to prevent the serious aggravation of the situation and the growth of racial bitterness and hatred, and to help alleviate distress among the victims of apartheid. It sought to enable wide segments of the international community to demonstrate, by action, their concern for a peaceful solution of the problem in South Africa.[65]

65/Document 46
See page 291

161    The Group of Western European and Other States at the United Nations declined membership in the Special Committee. While this lack of participation prevented dialogue within the Committee between supporters and opponents of sanctions and other measures and could be seen to weaken the authority of its recommendations, the Committee nevertheless proceeded to initiate a wide range of actions against apartheid. The Committee's composition, in fact, enabled it to act expeditiously and with unanimity. The Committee gave special attention to frequent consultations with Western Governments, sent missions to their capitals and gained wide respect. The Committee was able to take advantage of the fact that the long struggle for freedom in South Africa had already earned the sympathy and support not only of Asian and African countries, but also of organizations and people in Western countries which had maintained extensive and long-standing political, economic and military relations with South Africa. It was assisted in its work by the regular endorsements of the General Assembly, which repeatedly appealed to all agencies within the United Nations system, as well as other organizations, to take action against apartheid within their mandates.

162    The Special Committee against Apartheid placed great emphasis on the role of world public opinion and action by the public as a means of isolating the South African regime and its supporters, demonstrating solidarity with the struggle for liberation and persuading Governments, including the major Powers, to join in concerted action against apartheid. It gave United Nations support to developing, extending and coordinating the movement for solidarity with the South African people.

163    In June 1968, the Special Committee held special sessions in Stockholm, London and Geneva, and invited many organizations, politicians and leaders of opinion to participate in its meetings for extensive discussions on the situation in South Africa and the campaign against apartheid. The same year, the General Assembly decided that the international campaign against apartheid must be intensified, and requested the Special Committee to promote the campaign.[66]

66/Document 56
*See page 308*

164    In later years, the Special Committee went on to establish closer relations with anti-apartheid organizations, and lent active support to boycotts and other campaigns which would come to involve millions of people, especially in Western countries. It invited anti-apartheid movements to its meetings, conferences and seminars, so that they might join with Governments, United Nations agencies, the OAU and international non-governmental organizations in discussing the situation and formulating proposals for action. It thereby helped the national anti-apartheid movements to receive broad international support and attention. It took account of their suggestions and requests in formulating its own recommendations to the General Assembly and the Security Council.[67]

67/Document 67
*See page 318;*
Document 81
*See page 337;*
Document 107
*See page 369*

165    The support of the United Nations helped anti-apartheid groups to counter vested interests and lobbies in their countries which opposed action against apartheid. In turn, consultation with anti-apartheid movements helped the Special Committee against Apartheid in all its efforts to promote international action. Such close cooperation between the United Nations and non-governmental organizations was unprecedented.[68] The United Nations was thereby engaged in promoting action within the territories of Member States, often at variance with the policies of national Governments, with little active opposition by Governments; that was a reflection of the public sentiment against apartheid which had developed under the democratic traditions in Western countries.

68/Document 114
*See page 391*

166    While promoting action against apartheid as an imperative international duty, the Special Committee always emphasized that the role of the United Nations and the international community was supportive. The Chairman of the Special Committee, Mr. Achkar Marof (Guinea), said in 1967: "The main role in the liberation of southern Africa should rightfully go to the oppressed people themselves. The international community can assist them and help create conditions in which they can secure the liberation with the least possible violence and delay, but it cannot aspire to deliver liberation to them. The efforts of the international community should only complement the efforts of the oppressed people."

167    The Special Committee always looked forward to racial harmony and eventual reconciliation in South Africa. The statements of two

**69/Document 33**

*See page 267;*

**Document 72**

*See page 329*

chairmen of the Committee, Diallo Telli (Guinea) and Edwin Ogebe Ogbu (Nigeria), are illustrative.[69] In 1963 Mr. Telli said: "The present Government of the Republic of South Africa offers for all time no other future to its non-White population than perpetual subordination. Though it describes itself as engaged in a struggle for the survival of the White population, it deliberately imperils their own safety and offers them no other destiny than a hopeless struggle for domination . . . South Africa has been described as a microcosm of the world. Its racial groups are derived from or have close kinship with the peoples of many Member States. South Africa could be an example to the world if all groups within the country were permitted to live together in amity, on the basis of equality."

168    In 1974, Mr. Ogbu noted: "When the White minority in South Africa abandons its dream of perpetual domination over the Africans, and when it is ready to seek, hopefully by concerted international action, to negotiate with the genuine representatives of the overwhelming majority of the people the destiny of the nation as a whole, I have no doubt that the African people of South Africa will show their traditional tolerance and magnanimity."

169    While the Special Committee fully supported the struggle against apartheid and opposed the South African regime, it always kept in view the ultimate goal of a negotiated peaceful settlement in the interests of all the people of South Africa. When such a settlement became possible, it played a key role in securing consensus on the Declaration on Apartheid and its Destructive Consequences in Southern Africa, adopted by the General Assembly in 1989.[70] Thereafter, it worked in close cooperation with the Secretary-General in promoting the transition to a non-racial democratic Government in South Africa.

**70/Document 135**

*See page 419*

## The liberation movements

170    After 1966, the legitimacy of the South African Government was increasingly denied, while the liberation movements came to be accepted as the authentic representatives of the South African people in the forums of the United Nations. In November 1962, the General Assembly had requested the Security Council to consider, if necessary, action under Article 6 of the Charter, which reads: "A Member of the United Nations which has persistently violated the Principles contained in the present Charter may be expelled from the Organization by the General Assembly upon the recommendation of the Security Council."[71] Such action was not, however, pressed in the Security Council for over a decade.

**71/Document 23**

*See page 251*

*171*    From 1965 onward, a number of Member States began to declare at sessions of the General Assembly that they did not accept the credentials of the South African delegation. Thereafter, on the proposal of African States the Assembly resolved to take no decision on the credentials submitted on behalf of the representatives of South Africa. This, however, did not lead to the unseating of the South African delegation. In 1970, during the observance of the twenty-fifth anniversary of the United Nations, the Assembly decided, on the proposal of African States, to ask the Credentials Committee to consider as a matter of urgency the credentials of the South African representatives. After the Committee had submitted its report, ten African delegations moved an amendment—which was adopted—to the effect that the report be approved "except with regard to the credentials of the representatives of South Africa". The President of the General Assembly, Mr. Edvard Hambro of Norway, stated before the vote that adoption of the amendment would be a very strong condemnation of the South African Government's policies and would constitute a very solemn warning to that Government. As he understood it, the South African delegation could continue to sit in the Assembly, and its rights and privileges of membership would not be affected.[72] The statement was not challenged.

72/Document 59
*See page 313*

*172*    In September 1974, the General Assembly not only rejected the credentials of the South African delegation but also requested the Security Council to review relations between South Africa and the United Nations.[73] In the Security Council, the African members proposed a draft resolution to reaffirm that the policies of apartheid were contrary to the principles and purposes of the Charter and inconsistent with the provisions of the Universal Declaration of Human Rights, and to recommend to the General Assembly to expel South Africa from the United Nations for persistent violations of the Charter. The resolution received 10 votes, but was not adopted because of the negative votes of three permanent members.

73/Document 73
*See page 332;*
Document 74
*See page 332*

*173*    Subsequently, in the General Assembly, the President, Mr. Abdelaziz Bouteflika of Algeria, was requested to give his interpretation of the earlier decision of 30 September rejecting the credentials of the South African representatives. He ruled that the consistency with which the Assembly had refused to accept the credentials of the South African delegation was tantamount to saying that the General Assembly refused to allow that delegation to participate in its work. The status of South Africa as a member of the United Nations was, however, left open as a matter requiring a recommendation from the Security Council. The President's ruling was upheld by 91 votes to 22, with 19 abstentions.[74]

74/Document 75
*See page 333*

*174*    Meanwhile, in 1973, after considering the report of the International Conference of Experts for the Support of Victims of Colonialism and Apartheid in Southern Africa,[75] the General Assembly had

75/Document 68
*See page 319*

declared that the South African regime had no right to represent the people of South Africa and that the liberation movements recognized by the OAU were "the authentic representatives of the overwhelming majority of the South African people." It authorized the Special Committee against Apartheid, in consultation with the OAU, to associate the liberation movements closely with its work. It also requested that all specialized agencies and other intergovernmental organizations deny membership or privileges of membership to the South African regime and invite, in consultation with the OAU, representatives of the South African liberation movements recognized by that organization to participate in their meetings.[76]

76/Document 71
*See page 328*

*175*   In March 1974, the Special Committee against Apartheid decided to invite the liberation movements recognized by the OAU—the ANC and the PAC—to attend its meetings as observers. And on the Special Committee's recommendation, in the same year the Special Political Committee of the General Assembly also invited the liberation movements to attend its meetings as observers during its discussions of apartheid. In 1976, when the General Assembly decided to examine apartheid directly in plenary meetings, it invited the ANC and the PAC to participate as observers at those meetings where apartheid was being considered. Representatives of the liberation movements were always permitted, without objection, to make statements.

*176*   The General Assembly kept up its pressure on the South African regime. In resolution 3324 E (XXIX) of 16 December 1974, it recommended that the regime should be "totally excluded from participation in all international organizations and conferences under the auspices of the United Nations so long as it continues to practice apartheid". In a 1975 resolution, it declared that "the racist regime of South Africa is illegitimate".[77] Many resolutions of the United Nations organs from 1973 onward refer to the "regime", "racist regime" or "apartheid regime" of South Africa rather than the South African "Government".

77/Document 80
*See page 336*

*177*   By 1975, South Africa was effectively excluded from all organs of the United Nations. The denial of legitimacy to the regime and the recognition of the liberation movements signalled a new stage in international action against apartheid.

## Arms embargo

*178*   The first resolutions of the Security Council calling for an arms embargo, adopted in 1963, were not mandatory.[78] They had not been unanimously adopted, nor had they been fully implemented by all States. Embargoes had been imposed by South Africa's two traditional

78/Document 28
*See page 257;*
Document 34
*See page 269*

arms suppliers, the United States and the United Kingdom, in 1963 and 1964 respectively. Some countries had prohibited only arms for "repression", allowing sophisticated weapons for "external defence"; or else they had continued to sell "dual purpose" equipment which could be used for both military or civilian purposes; or they had failed to abrogate earlier contracts for the supply of military *matériel* or licences for the manufacture of arms.

*179* The General Assembly repeatedly called on all States to implement the Security Council resolutions fully and scrupulously. Member States also pressed the Security Council to widen the embargo, close any loopholes, prevent restrictive interpretation, and decide on a mandatory embargo, under Chapter VII of the Charter of the United Nations. The Special Committee against Apartheid reported all available evidence of circumventions and violations of the embargo as well as South Africa's continued military build-up. It encouraged campaigns by anti-apartheid groups to press their national Governments for a total arms embargo against South Africa and the cessation of all military cooperation with that country. It also supported campaigns by anti-apartheid movements for the arms embargo.

*180* The call for an arms embargo had become a political issue in the United Kingdom in 1963, when Labour Party leader Harold Wilson addressed an anti-apartheid rally in Trafalgar Square, London, pledging the support of his party for the embargo. The United Kingdom imposed the embargo when the Labour Party came to power the next year. The campaign nevertheless continued. It pressed for a total cessation of all military cooperation with South Africa and opposed all moves to reverse the arms ban.

*181* In 1970, when a new Government in the United Kingdom considered relaxing the embargo, there was strong public opposition in the country and in the Commonwealth. On 23 July 1970, in resolution 282 (1970), the Security Council reaffirmed its previous resolutions, condemned violations of the arms embargo and called upon all States to strengthen the embargo by implementing it unconditionally and without reservations; by withholding the supply of all vehicles and equipment for use of the armed forces and paramilitary organizations; by revoking licences and patents granted to the South African Government or companies for the manufacture of arms and ammunition, aircraft and naval craft or other military vehicles; and by ceasing provision of military training for members of the South African armed forces and all other forms of military cooperation with South Africa. The resolution, however, was not mandatory, and three permanent members (France, the United Kingdom and the United States) abstained from the voting.

*182* After further deterioration of the situation in South Africa and in southern Africa as a whole, repeated requests by the General

Assembly and Member States and increasing public demands, the Security Council finally imposed, under Chapter VII of the Charter, a mandatory arms embargo against South Africa in resolution 418 (1977), adopted unanimously on 4 November 1977.[79] In that resolution, the Council strongly condemned the South African Government for its acts of repression, its defiant continuance of apartheid and its attacks against neighbouring independent States; expressed grave concern that South Africa was at the threshold of producing nuclear weapons; and recognized "that the existing arms embargo must be strengthened and universally applied, without any reservations or qualifications whatsoever, in order to prevent a further aggravation of the grave situation in South Africa". The Council determined that "the acquisition by South Africa of arms and related *matériel* constitutes a threat to the maintenance of international peace and security". It decided that all States "shall cease forthwith any provision to South Africa of arms and related *matériel* of all types". The Council further decided that all States should refrain from any cooperation with South Africa in the manufacture and development of nuclear weapons.

79/Document 89
See page 348

183    Stressing the significance of the resolution, United Nations Secretary-General Kurt Waldheim said that it marked "the first time in the 32-year history of the Organization that action has been taken under Chapter VII of the Charter against a Member State".[80] He added that it was abundantly clear that the policy of apartheid, as well as the measures taken by the South African Government to implement that policy, were "such a gross violation of human rights and so fraught with danger to international peace and security that a response commensurate with the gravity of the situation was required." It was also significant, he added, that this momentous step was based on the unanimous agreement of the Council members. By this action, the Secretary-General declared that the United Nations had entered a "new and significantly different phase" of the effort to redress the wrongs of the South African situation.

80/Document 90
See page 348

184    In December of the same year, the Security Council established a Committee, consisting of all its members, to examine the progress of the implementation of resolution 418 (1977), study ways in which the embargo could be made more effective and make recommendations to the Council. The work of the Committee was, however, hindered by the fact that it failed to receive information from Governments on violations of the embargo.

185    The Special Committee against Apartheid, which had been promoting effective campaigns for the arms embargo, addressed an appeal to trade unions and other organizations as well as to individuals to inform the Committee of any breaches or planned breaches of the embargo by governmental agencies, corporations and institutions. It

encouraged the establishment by the British Anti-Apartheid Movement of the World Campaign against Military and Nuclear Collaboration with South Africa in 1978.

186    The World Campaign had as its founding patrons the Heads of State of Angola, Botswana, Nigeria, Tanzania and Zambia. Its sponsors were Mr. Olof Palme of Sweden, Mrs. Coretta Scott King of the United States and Mr. David Steel and Mrs. Joan Lestor of the United Kingdom. The objectives included campaigning for an end to all forms of military, nuclear and security collaboration with the South African regime; working for the effective implementation and reinforcement of the United Nations arms embargo; making representations to Governments violating the embargo; and cooperating with the United Nations and the OAU on the implementation of effective measures to combat military, nuclear and security collaboration with South Africa.

187    Working in close collaboration with the British and other anti-apartheid movements, the World Campaign became the main source of information to the Security Council Committee and the Special Committee against Apartheid on violations of the arms embargo and on the means to strengthen the embargo. Mr. Abdul S. Minty, director of the World Campaign, appeared on several occasions before the two committees and the Security Council. The Special Committee, in cooperation with the World Campaign, held hearings on the arms embargo and organized several conferences and seminars to discuss the reinforcement of the embargo. The initiatives of the Special Committee and the World Campaign helped the Security Council Committee to contact Governments about alleged violations and to report, with recommendations, to the Security Council, on the tightening of the embargo.

188    Meanwhile, the General Assembly continued to press for the strengthening and full implementation of the arms embargo. In 1979, it also appealed to the youth of South Africa "to refrain from enlisting in the South African armed forces, which are designed to defend the inhuman system of apartheid, to repress the legitimate struggle of the oppressed people and to threaten, and commit acts of aggression, against neighbouring States".[81] It invited all Governments and organizations to assist persons compelled to leave South Africa because of a conscientious objection to assisting in enforcing apartheid through service in military or police forces.

81/Document 94
*See page 350*

189    On 13 June 1980, the Security Council, concerned by widespread violence in South Africa, as well as the country's military aggression against independent African States, adopted resolution 473 (1980),[82] calling on all States strictly and scrupulously to implement resolution 418 (1977), which imposed a mandatory arms embargo. It requested its own Committee to recommend "measures to

82/Document 97
*See page 352*

close all loopholes in the arms embargo, reinforce and make it more comprehensive".

190    In response to the worsening situation inside South Africa, the Security Council made further extensions to the embargo during the 1980s, although these were not mandatory. On 13 December 1984, in resolution 558 (1984), the Security Council requested all States "to refrain from importing arms, ammunition of all types and military vehicles produced in South Africa". In resolution 569 (1985) of 26 July 1985, it urged Member States to adopt further measures such as the prohibition of new contracts in the nuclear field and of sales of computer equipment that might be used by the South African army and police.[83]

83/Document 116
See page 392

191    In resolution 591 (1986) of 28 November 1986, the Security Council made a series of requests to all States in order to strengthen the embargo. The Council urged States to take steps to ensure that components of embargoed items did not reach the South African military establishment and police through third countries, and to prohibit the export to South Africa of items which they had reason to believe were destined for the military and/or police forces of South Africa, had a military capability and were intended for military purposes, namely, aircraft, aircraft engines, aircraft parts, electronic and telecommunications equipment, computers and four-wheel-drive vehicles. It also requested all States to refrain from any cooperation in the nuclear field with South Africa which would contribute to the manufacture and development by South Africa of nuclear weapons or explosive devices, and renewed its request to all States to refrain from importing arms, ammunition of all types and military vehicles produced in South Africa.

192    Despite the mandatory embargo, the South African Government was able to amass military equipment and *matériel*. Because the embargo was voluntary for several years, Governments failed to revoke earlier contracts and licences, and some Governments allowed the export of dual purpose equipment. South Africa was also able to build a substantial domestic arms manufacturing industry with the collaboration of the arms industries of certain countries, despite the embargo. The General Assembly, in emphasizing the importance of the arms embargo, in several resolutions called on Western and other States — particularly France, the Federal Republic of Germany, Israel, the United Kingdom and the United States of America — to cease all cooperation with South Africa in the military and nuclear fields. As late as 1989, it found it necessary to deplore the actions of Israel, Chile and two corporations in the Federal Republic of Germany.[84] Yet the embargo did have a significant effect, both in retarding the military build-up in South Africa and in greatly increasing its cost in obtaining military *matériel* by illicit means. It also prevented South Africa from obtaining many items of military equipment.

84/Document 106
See page 369;
Document 131
See page 415;
Document 141
See page 430;
Document 149
See page 439

## Oil embargo

*193*　As a country with a substantial industrial base, South Africa has long depended heavily on imports of oil. The United Nations, therefore, recognized that an embargo on oil and petroleum products would be an effective means to exert pressure and could complement the arms embargo. Beginning in 1963, the General Assembly adopted several resolutions calling on States to refrain from supplying petroleum and petroleum products to South Africa. In November 1973, the Summit Conference of Arab States in Algiers decided to impose a complete oil embargo on South Africa. The Special Committee against Apartheid, building on this important advance which could make an effective oil embargo feasible, commissioned studies on oil sanctions against South Africa and appealed to other Governments and organizations to take action.

*194*　On 21 September 1978, the Special Committee submitted a special report to the General Assembly and the Security Council on "Oil sanctions against South Africa". It recommended that the Security Council consider the matter urgently and take a mandatory decision, under Chapter VII of the Charter, for an embargo on the supply of petroleum and petroleum products to South Africa. It also recommended that all States be urged to enact legislation to prohibit: the sale or supply of petroleum or petroleum products to South Africa, directly or through third parties; the shipment in vessels or aircraft of their registration, or under charter to their nationals, of any petroleum or petroleum products to South Africa; and the supply of any services (technical advice, spare parts, capital, etc.) to the oil companies in South Africa. The Security Council could not consider the matter because of the opposition to oil sanctions by three permanent members of the Council.

*195*　The General Assembly endorsed those recommendations at its next session—in a separate resolution on "Oil embargo against South Africa"—resolution 33/183 E of 24 January 1979—by 105 votes to 6, with 16 abstentions. Although there was now the prospect of a cessation of oil exports from the major oil-producing countries to South Africa, there remained the problem of tanker companies and other interests finding ways to thwart the actions of those countries. There was a continuation of secretly negotiated supplies, despite the insistence by the Governments of a number of oil-producing countries—notably Nigeria—that the embargo on sales to South Africa must be respected by companies operating on their territory. During the 1970s, Iran was an important source of oil for South Africa, until the new Government announced in 1979 that sales would be discontinued.

*196*　In its next report to the General Assembly and the Security Council in 1979, the Special Committee against Apartheid suggested that those bodies call on all States to take effective action against oil supplies to South Africa. It also urged the General Assembly to encourage the creation of appropriate machinery by the petroleum-exporting countries to monitor shipments of petroleum and petroleum products to South Africa and to penalize all companies involved in such illegal shipments.

*197*   The General Assembly, in its resolution 34/93 F of 12 December 1979, requested the Security Council to consider urgently a mandatory oil embargo under Chapter VII of the Charter of the United Nations. It called upon all States to enact appropriate legislation. It specifically requested them to prohibit: the shipment in vessels or aircraft of their registration, or under charter to their nationals, of any petroleum or petroleum products to South Africa; the provision of facilities in their ports or airports to vessels or aircraft carrying petroleum or petroleum products to South Africa; and any investments in, or provision of technical or other assistance to, the petroleum industry in South Africa.

*198*   The General Assembly also requested States to include in all contracts for the sale of petroleum or petroleum products provisions prohibiting direct or indirect resale to South Africa, and to take effective legislative and other appropriate measures to prevent petroleum companies and shipping companies, as well as banks and other financial institutions, from giving any assistance to the South African regime in circumventing the oil embargo, including the seizure of vessels which violated the embargo and their cargoes.

*199*   Since the Security Council was unable to take any action in this respect, in view of continuing opposition from some of its permanent members, the Special Committee held extensive consultations with Governments and promoted public campaigns for an oil embargo. The General Assembly endorsed its recommendations in a number of subsequent resolutions. The Special Committee also co-sponsored with two non-governmental organizations of the Netherlands—the Holland Committee on Southern Africa and Working Group Kairos (Christians against Apartheid)—an International Seminar on an Oil Embargo against South Africa, held in Amsterdam in March 1980, and publicized the Declaration of the Seminar. In addition, it promoted the observance of an International Day for an Oil Embargo against South Africa on 20 May 1980.

*200*   The following month, the Netherlands Parliament voted in favour of an oil embargo against South Africa. The Special Committee then consulted with members of the Parliament and organized, in cooperation with them, a Conference of West European Parliamentarians on an Oil Embargo against South Africa, held in Brussels on 30 and 31 January 1981. In 1980, the Special Committee also had encouraged and assisted the Holland Committee on Southern Africa and Working Group Kairos in establishing a Shipping Research Bureau in Amsterdam to investigate violations of the oil embargo by tanker companies and other interests. The reports of the Bureau assisted the Special Committee (and later the Intergovernmental Group to Monitor the Supply and Shipping of Oil and Petroleum Products to South Africa) in making representations to Governments about the need to take firm action.

201    The General Assembly, in 1982, authorized the Special Committee to appoint a Group of Experts to make a thorough study of the oil embargo and requested the Secretary-General to organize meetings of oil-producing and oil-exporting countries committed to the oil embargo so that they could consult on national and international arrangements to ensure the effective implementation of the embargo.

202    While consulting with the Governments of those countries, the Special Committee, with the assistance of the Shipping Research Bureau, drew the attention of Governments concerned to suspected violations by tanker companies and others of the embargoes instituted by the oil-exporting countries. It promoted public campaigns for the embargo, including an international campaign against the Shell oil company. It organized an International Conference of Maritime Trade Unions on the Implementation of the United Nations Oil Embargo against South Africa, held in London in October 1985, and a United Nations Seminar on the Oil Embargo against South Africa, held in Oslo in June 1986.

203    In 1986, the General Assembly established an Intergovernmental Group to Monitor the Supply and Shipping of Oil and Petroleum Products to South Africa. The Group made contact with Governments, as well as with many non-governmental organizations. It obtained information from all available sources on the South African port calls of ships capable of carrying oil and petroleum products and communicated with Governments concerned. In 1989, in cooperation with the Special Committee against Apartheid, it organized hearings on the oil embargo.

204    The Group's investigations and reports led to several General Assembly resolutions calling on the Security Council to impose a mandatory embargo "on the supply and shipping of oil and petroleum products to South Africa as well as on the supply of equipment and technology to financing of and investment in its oil industry and coal liquefaction projects", and requesting States concerned, pending a decision by the Security Council, to adopt effective measures and/or legislation "to broaden the scope of the oil embargo in order to ensure the complete cessation of the supply and shipping of oil and petroleum products to South Africa".[85]

85/Document 130
See page 413;
Document 143
See page 432 ;
Document 150
See page 440;
Document 175
See page 460

*205*    Although South Africa was able to obtain oil and petroleum products despite the United Nations efforts at an effective embargo, it was obliged to pay a high price to secure illicit shipments. The Intergovernmental Group noted in its 1991 report that the oil embargo, despite its deficiencies, had imposed costs on South Africa estimated at between $25 billion and $30 billion over the previous 12 years. The General Assembly—in resolution 47/116 D of 18 December 1992—also recognized that the embargo made a major contribution to the pressure exerted on South Africa towards the eradication of apartheid.

## Other economic measures

*206*    While the arms and oil embargoes were particularly important in increasing South Africa's costs in continuing repression at home and aggression against independent African States, a large majority of Member States felt that comprehensive economic sanctions were essential to secure the elimination of apartheid. They argued that the South African White minority Government utilized the country's rich resources to provide a high standard of living for Whites and to suppress resistance by the majority of the population. The South African economy, however, required loans and investment, as well as imported technology, to sustain growth. It was able to attract investments from transnational corporations and financial interests because the apartheid system offered cheap labour and high profits. If effective economic sanctions were imposed on South Africa, and all benefits of international cooperation were denied to it, the Government would have no alternative but to negotiate political transformation with the representatives of the oppressed majority.

*207*    At the request of African and other States, from 1962 onward the General Assembly called for mandatory economic sanctions as essential to solving the problem of apartheid. The Assembly deplored the action of States which increased their economic relations with South Africa, and condemned the activities of transnational corporations and financial interests involved in the country. While reaffirming that position, the Assembly began in 1969 to call for specific measures in order to focus on feasible and significant action, to encourage Governments which were not prepared to end all economic relations with South Africa to implement partial measures and to facilitate public campaigns, especially in countries which maintained economic relations with South Africa.

*208*    A number of countries continued to maintain economic relations with South Africa throughout the years of the international campaign against apartheid. Several Western countries had substantial trade with South Africa, and invested in its mining, industrial and agricultural enterprises. South Africa was the main source of several strategic minerals. There was therefore a reluctance among many Member States, including some major Powers, to censure or antagonize the South African Government. Because the conduct of trade was less visible than the sports and cultural exchanges that attracted media attention and international opprobrium, these economic ties often passed unnoticed, although the United Nations and anti-apartheid movements did their best to publicize them.

209    In the "Programme of Action against Apartheid", adopted on 9 November 1976, the General Assembly called upon all Governments to terminate all economic collaboration with South Africa and, in particular, to refrain from supplying petroleum, petroleum products or other strategic materials to South Africa; to refrain from extending loans, investments and technical assistance to the South African regime and companies registered in South Africa; to prohibit loans by banks or other financial institutions in their countries to the South African regime or South African companies; to prohibit economic and financial interests under their national jurisdiction from cooperating with the South African regime and companies registered in South Africa; to deny tariff and other preferences to South African exports and inducements or guarantees for investment in South Africa; to take appropriate action in international agencies and organizations—such as the European Economic Community, the General Agreement on Tariffs and Trade, the IMF and the World Bank—for denial by them of all assistance and commercial or other facilities to the South African regime; to refuse landing and passage facilities to all South African aircraft; to close ports to all vessels flying the South African flag; and to prohibit airlines and shipping lines registered in their countries from providing services to and from South Africa; to prohibit or discourage the flow of immigrants, particularly skilled and technical personnel, to South Africa.

210    In subsequent resolutions, the General Assembly also asked Governments to: terminate all Government promotion of trade with or investment in South Africa; end exchanges of trade missions with South Africa; ban the import of gold, uranium, coal and other minerals from South Africa; prohibit the sale of krugerrands and all other coins minted in South Africa; deny any contracts or facilities to transnational corporations collaborating with South Africa; take action against corporations and tanker companies involved in the illicit supply of oil to South Africa; expose the influence of transnational corporations operating in South Africa on news media in their countries; and encourage non-governmental organizations engaged in campaigns against collaboration by transnational corporations in South Africa.[86] At the same time, the General Assembly requested the Special Committee against Apartheid to

86/Document 111
*See page 379*

promote campaigns on these issues. Although the response from Western and other Governments was limited or slow, public sentiment in support of such measures grew.

211    The appeals to Governments found little support until 1976 when, after the Soweto massacre, Norway and Sweden took steps to stop new investments in South Africa. Thereafter, a growing number of States proposed resolutions annually in the General Assembly urging the Security Council to consider steps to achieve the cessation of further foreign investments in, and financial loans to, South Africa. The resolutions received increasing majorities of votes: 124 to none, with 16 abstentions, in 1976; as against 140 to 1, with 7 abstentions, in 1983.

212    In 1984, with the encouragement of the Special Committee, the Nordic countries and other Western States co-sponsored a resolution on "Concerted international action for the elimination of apartheid". The resolution contained an appeal to all States, pending mandatory sanctions by the Security Council, to consider national measures such as cessation of further investments in, and financial loans to, South Africa, and an end to the promotion of trade with South Africa. The resolution received 146 votes in favour and 2 against, with 6 abstentions. In subsequent years, similar resolutions called for additional national measures.

213    The process of building wider support for specific national measures, pending Security Council action, finally led to the adoption by the Security Council, on 26 July 1985, of resolution 569 (1985).[87] In it the Council urged all Member States to adopt such measures as suspension of new investment in South Africa; prohibition of the sale of krugerrands and all other coins minted there; suspension of guaranteed export loans; prohibition of all new contracts in the nuclear field; and prohibition of all sales of computer equipment that might be used by the South African army and police. The Council also commended those States which had already adopted voluntary measures against the South African Government, urged them to enact new provisions and invited those which had not yet done so to follow their example.

87/Document 116
See page 392

214    Meanwhile, the Special Committee against Apartheid actively promoted campaigns for economic measures against South Africa and against the involvement of transnational corporations and financial interests in the country. Other organs of the United Nations, especially the Economic and Social Council, the Commission on Transnational Corporations and the Commission on Human Rights, commissioned studies and called on transnational corporations to disengage from South Africa.

215    Revelations in the early 1970s about wages and working conditions in foreign-owned corporations in South Africa led to further actions. The Special Committee devoted particular attention at its con-

ferences and seminars to economic measures against South Africa and to the activities of transnational corporations doing business there. It encouraged trade unions, religious bodies, anti-apartheid movements and student and youth groups to take appropriate action.

216    By the late 1970s, a powerful movement had developed in the United States, the United Kingdom and other Western countries for disinvestment and divestment. Many state, city and local authorities refused contracts to corporations involved in South Africa. Trade unions withdrew their pension funds from such corporations, and many universities divested themselves of holdings in them. The issue of apartheid was often discussed at corporate shareholders' meetings. Opponents of apartheid exerted great pressure on banks and corporations, even in countries where national Governments took little action, and persuaded them, especially after 1984 when the crisis in South Africa escalated, to halt loans to South Africa and to end their operations in that country.

217    Beginning in 1985, most international banks ceased lending to South Africa and hundreds of transnational corporations began to divest themselves of their holdings in that country. The United States Congress passed the Comprehensive Anti-Apartheid Act of 1986. The European Community imposed significant measures. Members of the Commonwealth agreed on a series of steps, despite reservations by the United Kingdom. The Nordic countries prohibited trade with South Africa. The pressure became increasingly intense and effective.[88]

88/Document 126
See page 410;
Document 127
See page 411

## Release of political prisoners

218    The United Nations repeatedly emphasized the need for the release of political prisoners as essential to a peaceful resolution of the situation in South Africa. This focus became especially clear in 1963, after Nelson Mandela and other leaders were charged in the Rivonia trial. The General Assembly's 1963 resolution inspired worldwide demands for an amnesty in South Africa.[89]

89/Document 32
See page 267

219    The Special Committee against Apartheid stressed the issue. In 1964, it appealed to all Governments to intercede with the South African authorities to stop executions and to release political prisoners. In response, several Heads of State and Government acted promptly. The British Anti-Apartheid Movement set up the World Campaign for the Release of South African Political Prisoners, sponsored by several Members of Parliament and other public figures. In March 1964, it gave the Secretary-General a declaration signed by 143 eminent persons from around the world for the release of Nelson Mandela and other leaders. The signatories included some of the most renowned writers and artists, academics, political, trade union and religious leaders and jurists. Sub-

sequently, it presented petitions signed by over 185,000 people, as well as organizations representing some 250 million people. In addition, many groups and individuals around the world organized demonstrations, deputations and other actions.

220    The Security Council, in two resolutions in June 1964, called on South Africa to renounce the execution of any persons sentenced to death for their opposition to apartheid.[90] A number of Governments, trade unions and other organizations sent appeals for clemency. Thereafter, anti-apartheid movements and other organizations launched many campaigns on these issues, with the support of the Special Committee. As a result, the South African Government commuted some death sentences.

90/Document 41
See page 283

221    Beginning in 1963, the South African Government enacted a number of laws providing for the arbitrary and indefinite detention of persons suspected of political offences, and of potential witnesses. The detainees were held in solitary confinement for prolonged periods and denied access to families, lawyers or courts. Reports soon began to be received of maltreatment of political prisoners and other detainees contrary to international minimum standards—prolonged solitary confinement and denial of exercise, as well as brutal assaults and torture, including electric shocks. A large percentage of the detainees, so brutalized, were never charged in court. Those persons sentenced to imprisonment for political offences were automatically classified for a year or more as "D" category prisoners, a category created for hardened and dangerous criminals. They were allowed only one visit and one letter every six months. Moreover, they were frequently beaten, humiliated and punished. Numerous affidavits from former prisoners became available in 1964, and the Special Committee and many anti-apartheid groups organized vigorous protests.[91]

91/Document 50
See page 295

92/Document 51
See page 295

222    In February 1967, the Special Committee against Apartheid gave a hearing to Mr. Dennis Brutus, a poet and sports leader, who had spent 22 months in Robben Island prison.[92] It then asked the Commission on Human Rights to consider the situation and furnished affidavits and other evidence. The Commission expressed its serious concern and established a Working Group of jurists to undertake an international investigation. The subsequent outrage and criticism persuaded the South African Government to make some improvements in prisons and to invite a delegate of the International Committee of the Red Cross to visit the prisoners. However, it refused to allow visits to detainees or prisoners awaiting trial. The situation remained alarming, especially with the enactment of the stringent Terrorism Act in 1967. Meanwhile, legal assistance to political prisoners, provided and encouraged by the United Nations, helped curb the excesses of the South African Police and secure

the acquittal, or reduction of sentences, of thousands of persons charged with political offences.

223    In the following years, a particularly shocking development was the detention of thousands of children under the state of emergency after 1985. An International Conference on Children, Repression and Law in Apartheid South Africa (held in Harare in September 1987) was attended by many children, parents and lawyers from South Africa. It confirmed reports of systematic assaults and torture of children in detention. The outrage around the world persuaded the apartheid regime to release many children.

224    While campaigns and activities focused on specific aspects of apartheid, for the United Nations the basic issue was that an amnesty for political prisoners was essential to a negotiated and peaceful solution to the crisis. With the unanimous support of all Member States, the United Nations annually adopted resolutions calling for the release of South African political prisoners. In several resolutions after 1968, it declared that freedom fighters who were taken prisoner during the legitimate struggle for freedom "should be treated as prisoners of war under international law, particularly the Geneva Convention relative to the Treatment of Prisoners of War of 12 August 1949".

225    In 1975, in connection with the thirtieth anniversary of the United Nations, the General Assembly proclaimed that "the United Nations and the international community have a special responsibility . . . towards those imprisoned, restricted or exiled for their struggle against apartheid". It expressed its solidarity with all South Africans struggling against apartheid and for the principles enshrined in the Charter of the United Nations, and called upon the South African regime "to grant an unconditional amnesty to all persons imprisoned or restricted for their opposition to apartheid or acts arising from such opposition, as well as to political refugees from South Africa".[93]

226    Public pressure reflected the United Nations resolutions. Petitions for the release of Mr. Mandela and other political prisoners were drawn up and circulated by different groups following a recommendation of the World Conference for Action against Apartheid, held in Lagos in August 1977. In March 1978, for example, the British Anti-Apartheid Movement delivered petitions signed by about 45,000 persons in four countries; and petitions containing some 40,000 signatures came directly from seven other countries.

## The "Free Mandela" Campaign

227    The worldwide observance of the sixtieth birthday of Nelson Mandela on 18 July 1978, initiated by the Special Committee against Apartheid, demonstrated international solidarity with the struggle against apartheid and publicized the cause of political prisoners.

93/Document 78
*See page 335;*
Document 79
*See page 336*

Several parliaments referred to the observance and meetings were held in many cities. More than 10,000 letters and telegrams were sent by Governments, organizations and individuals to Mr. Mandela in prison or to his wife, Winnie Mandela, then confined to the remote town of Brandfort.

228    In 1980, Mr. Percy Qoboza, editor of the *Sunday Post* in Johannesburg, launched a campaign for the release of Mr. Mandela, and appealed in an editorial on 9 March: "For the sake of bringing about genuine peace and reconciliation in our troubled torn land, we ask you to join us in having Mr. Mandela released as soon as possible." A petition sponsored by the *Sunday Post* soon received over 86,000 signatures in South Africa and was supported by many organizations and leaders of opinion. A Release Nelson Mandela Committee was formed in that month with Mrs. Nokukhanya Luthuli, wife of the late ANC President, Chief Albert J. Luthuli, as patron. The release of Mr. Mandela became an issue uniting broad segments of the South African population.

229    In August 1981, the City of Glasgow, Scotland, awarded the Freedom of the City to Mr. Mandela. Later that year, the Lord Provost of Glasgow, The Right Honourable Michael Kelley, with the encouragement of the Special Committee against Apartheid, initiated a Declaration of Mayors for the immediate and unconditional release of Mr. Mandela and all other political prisoners in South Africa. A total of 2,264 mayors from 56 countries signed the Declaration.

230    On 5 August 1982, the twentieth anniversary of Mr. Mandela's arrest, the Chairman of the Special Committee called for an expansion of the campaign. Anti-apartheid movements and many other organizations supported his appeal. On 11 October, Archbishop Trevor Huddleston, President of the British Anti-Apartheid Movement, launched an international declaration, in cooperation with the Special Committee, for the release of Mr. Mandela and other imprisoned leaders. The declaration was signed by tens of thousands of persons from more than 70 countries, including numerous parliamentarians and other public figures.

231    While in prison, Mr. Mandela was accorded many prestigious awards and honorary degrees, and the freedom of many cities. Numerous institutions, buildings and streets around the world were named after him and he was elected an honorary member of many trade unions and other organizations. "Bicycle for Mandela" became an annual event in the United Kingdom on Mandela's birthday. In the Netherlands, the Holland Committee on Southern Africa issued a Mandela coin as part of its campaign against the krugerrand, and also as a means of fundraising for the freedom movement. No political prisoner in history had been so honoured all over the world.

232    The campaign for the release of prisoners took on a new sense of urgency with the mass resistance to the imposition of the new constitution in 1984, and the institution of a state of emergency in 1985 with the subsequent detention of tens of thousands of people and the constant killings of peaceful demonstrators by security forces. The demands of the United Democratic Front, trade unions and numerous other organizations—for the release of Mr. Mandela and other political prisoners, the unbanning of people's organizations, the ending of the state of emergency and the dismantling of apartheid—received strong support from the international community.

233    Various groups took imaginative initiatives to promote the campaign. In the United States, for instance, the Africa Fund started a campaign to "Unlock Apartheid's Jails" under the honorary chairman-ship of Bill Cosby, a popular TV personality. Supporters were invited to send keys as a demonstration of opposition to the detentions in South Africa. The campaign was launched at United Nations Headquarters on 28 September 1987. Mayors of six large cities in the United States attended the ceremony and presented the keys to their cities to the Chairman of the Special Committee against Apartheid.

## Information and promotion of public action

234    United Nations bodies recognized the importance of informed public opinion in facilitating effective international action against apartheid. The Special Committee against Apartheid repeatedly stressed that public information on apartheid was an essential component of United Nations efforts. It emphasized in particular the importance of informing the public in the countries which maintained close economic and other relations with South Africa, and of counteracting the propaganda of the South African Government and of business and other interests allied with it.

235    While the United Nations could not match the funds devoted by the South African Government to propaganda, or undertake secret projects as South Africa did, it could count on popular sentiment against racial discrimination and on the support of Governments and organizations committed to the struggle against apartheid. The General Assembly, in a number of resolutions from 1965 onward, requested the Secretary-General to take measures for the widest possible dissemination of information about apartheid and the struggle against it in South Africa, as well as the efforts of the United Nations and other groups, including non-governmental organizations for the elimination of apartheid.

*236*   In its resolution 2307 (XXII) of 13 December 1967, the General Assembly invited "all States to encourage the establishment of national organizations for the purpose of further enlightening public opinion on the evils of apartheid". As the international campaign developed, the Assembly called for activity to promote specific campaigns and reach various segments of opinion.

## Unit on Apartheid

94/Document 48
See page 293

*237*   Following a decision by the General Assembly in 1966, a Unit on Apartheid was established in the Secretariat, to ensure maximum publicity about apartheid.[94] The Unit, which subsequently became part of the Centre against Apartheid, established in January 1976, produced numerous studies—many of them prepared by the leaders of liberation movements and anti-apartheid movements, and by experts. The studies were disseminated through the United Nations Information Centres as well as anti-apartheid organizations.

*238*   In 1973, the General Assembly requested the Secretary-General to establish a fund, made up of voluntary contributions, to be used for the expansion of the Unit on Apartheid's activities. The Trust Fund for Publicity against Apartheid, created the next year, enabled the Unit (later the Centre against Apartheid) to publish documents and pamphlets in many languages; to produce posters, photographs, TV spots, slides, records of freedom songs and other audiovisual material; to arrange for the distribution of educational material in schools; to organize exhibits; and to distribute films on apartheid.

*239*   The Trust Fund made modest grants to anti-apartheid movements and other organizations for the production and distribution of material approved by the Centre, for the organization of essay and art competitions and for the production of posters, badges and other campaign items.

## Department of Public Information

*240*   At the request of the General Assembly, the Department of Public Information gave major importance to publicity on apartheid. Apart from providing coverage for meetings, conferences and other events of the United Nations organs concerned with apartheid, it published many pamphlets and produced films, radio programmes and exhibits. It ensured the widest dissemination of studies produced by United Nations organs on such subjects as violations of human rights in South Africa, the plight of women under apartheid, and activities of transnational corporations in South Africa. United Nations Information Centres, in cooperation with national Governments, non-governmental organizations, educational institutions and the media often took initiatives to promote the international campaign.

241    As repression and censorship increased in South Africa, where many United Nations publications were banned, the United Nations recognized the need to find ways to inform the people of South Africa about international action against apartheid. In 1977, the General Assembly requested the Secretary-General to undertake, in cooperation with Member States whose broadcasts could be heard in southern Africa, regular radio programmes directed at South Africa, concerned with United Nations efforts against apartheid and in support of the right of self-determination as well as related matters of interest to the peoples of southern Africa.[95] On 1 March 1978, the Radio Service of the United Nations Department of Public Information began producing daily programmes in several South African languages.

95/Document 91
See page 349

242    The programmes made extensive use of recorded material emanating from a great variety of sources, including the proceedings of United Nations organs concerned with apartheid; observances of International Days; interviews with leaders of liberation movements and individual experts, including many who were banned in South Africa; and reports of activities of non-governmental organizations involved in the campaign against apartheid such as anti-apartheid movements, trade unions, churches and student groups. Many prominent artists and writers contributed to the programmes.

243    The major theme of the programmes was the worldwide condemnation of apartheid, as well as the steady intensification of the international campaign against it. Within this framework, the programmes aimed at educating supporters of apartheid concerning their growing isolation, and at encouraging and reassuring the oppressed people and other opponents of apartheid about international solidarity with their cause. Well over 1,000 programmes were produced annually and sent to interested broadcasting organizations in many countries for broadcast to South Africa, where they could be heard throughout the country.

### Specialized agencies

244    The specialized agencies made many significant contributions to the dissemination of information on apartheid. UNESCO and the ILO, in particular, devoted great attention to public information about apartheid, in cooperation with the United Nations. UNESCO published a number of studies on the effects of apartheid on education, culture and science, and produced educational material for distribution to schools. The ILO Director-General's annual reports on apartheid were especially informative, for trade unions and others, about the situation in South Africa. FAO and WHO published authoritative special studies at the request of the Special Committee against Apartheid. UNICEF published

and widely disseminated a study on the destructive effects of apartheid on children in southern Africa, entitled "Children on the Front Line".

## Observance of International Days and Years

245    The observance of International Days and Years was another effective means of publicizing the situation in South Africa and promoting support for action against apartheid. The General Assembly proclaimed the following days relating to apartheid: International Day for the Elimination of Racial Discrimination (21 March, anniversary of the 1960 Sharpeville massacre), proclaimed by resolution 2142 (XXI) of 26 October 1966; International Day of Solidarity with the Struggling People of South Africa (16 June, anniversary of the 1976 uprising), proclaimed by resolution 31/6 I of 9 November 1976; International Day of Solidarity with the Struggle of Women in South Africa and Namibia (9 August, anniversary of a demonstration by women against the pass laws in Pretoria in 1956), proclaimed by resolution 36/172 K of 17 December 1981; Day of Solidarity with South African Political Prisoners (11 October, anniversary of General Assembly resolution 1881 (XVIII) calling for the release of political prisoners), proclaimed by resolution 31/6 C of 9 November 1976. It also proclaimed the following years: International Anti-Apartheid Year (year beginning 21 March 1978), proclaimed by resolution 32/105 B of 14 December 1977; and International Year of Mobilization for Sanctions against South Africa (1982), proclaimed by resolution 36/172 B of 17 December 1981.

246    Moreover, the General Assembly called for special attention to apartheid during the observance of the International Year for Action to Combat Racism and Racial Discrimination (1971), the Decade for Action to Combat Racism and Racial Discrimination (1973-1983) and the Second Decade for Action to Combat Racism and Racial Discrimination (1983-93).

247    The Special Committee against Apartheid also promoted the observance in various years of other days, such as the anniversaries of the founding of the South African liberation movements (8 January and 4 April), South Africa Freedom Day (26 June), the birthday of Nelson Mandela (18 July), the anniversary of the death of Steve Biko (12 September) and Heroes Day (16 December). The many conferences, seminars, missions and other activities organized by the Special Committee and other organs also provided occasions for publicity.

## Mobilization of personalities

248    With the development of the international campaign, the Special Committee against Apartheid encouraged prominent artists, writers, musicians and sportsmen not only to boycott South Africa but also to contribute their talents to mobilize world public opinion against

apartheid. Through them it became possible to reach tens of millions of people around the world with appeals for action.

249    In 1981, with the support of the Special Committee, a Committee of Artists of the World against Apartheid was established. Among the projects undertaken by this Committee was the Art contre/against Apartheid exhibit, to which 80 of the most prominent contemporary artists of the world made contributions. It was agreed that the exhibit would be donated to a free South Africa when apartheid was eliminated. Mr. Mandela, then in prison, was chosen as an honorary trustee of the Cultural Foundation against Apartheid, to which the exhibit was transferred. The exhibit was opened in Paris in 1983 by the Minister of Culture of France and the Chairman of the Special Committee against Apartheid. Thereafter, it was shown in 60 museums and galleries around the world and at United Nations Headquarters. Wherever it went it attracted great attention. Arrangements are now being made to transfer this valuable collection, demonstrating the solidarity of the great artists with the struggle of the South African people for liberation, to South Africa.

### Public action

250    An important aspect of the strategy of the international campaign against apartheid was to reach different segments of world public opinion, so as to make them aware of the effects of apartheid in areas of special concern to them, and to encourage them to take appropriate action. Against a background of international revulsion for apartheid, the United Nations sought to encourage a widening of the involvement of organizations and individuals in coordinated action. The resolutions of the General Assembly and other organs addressed specific appeals to trade unions, churches and other religious bodies, students, youth, women and their organizations, athletes and sports bodies, artists, writers, entertainers and other cultural figures, educational institutions, jurists, members of the medical profession and members of other professional groups.

251    Apartheid caused offence to many segments of the world's population. For example, in the area of labour relations, it denied recognition to African trade unions, reserved jobs by racial origin, prohibited strikes by African workers, banned multiracial trade unions and set up an inhuman migrant labour system reducing the status of African workers to semi-slavery. The international trade union movement, therefore, condemned apartheid and regularly called for sanctions against South Africa, even before the United Nations itself did so.

252    Organizations that were otherwise divided by serious ideological or other differences were united in taking action against apartheid. The Special Committee against Apartheid and other United Nations organs and agencies, as well as units in the United Nations

Secretariat, provided information to these organizations and encouraged them to take action appropriate to their own spheres of interest.

253   The Special Committee maintained contact with international and regional trade union confederations, the World Council of Churches, the International Commission of Jurists and numerous other international organizations. It promoted the establishment of bodies such as the World Campaign against Military and Nuclear Collaboration with South Africa, the Shipping Research Bureau, End Loans to South Africa, the Committee of Artists of the World against Apartheid and the Association of West European Parliamentarians against Apartheid. It organized many conferences and seminars where trade unionists, cultural figures, athletes, students and youth, women and others could hold consultations and plan actions in cooperation with the United Nations, the OAU and the liberation movements. The efforts of the United Nations to promote action by trade unions, students and youth, and women summarized below are illustrative of this aspect of the campaign against apartheid.

## Trade union action

254   The United Nations, in cooperation with the ILO, gave particular attention to promoting trade union action against apartheid in view of the opposition of the international trade union movement to apartheid and the effective role that trade unions could play in anti-apartheid action. In 1970, the General Assembly, in its resolution 2671 D (XXV) of 8 December, requested the Special Committee against Apartheid to consult on the holding of an international conference to promote concerted trade union action against apartheid. The following year the Assembly appealed to all national and international trade union organizations to intensify their action against apartheid.[96] It proposed: discouraging the emigration of skilled workers to South Africa; taking appropriate action in connection with the infringements of trade union rights and the persecution of trade unionists in South Africa; exerting maximum pressure on foreign economic and financial interests which were profiting from racial discrimination against non-White workers in South Africa, in order to persuade them to cease such exploitation; and cooperating with other organizations engaged in the international campaign against apartheid.

255   The Workers' Group of the ILO Governing Body convened an International Conference of Trade Unions against Apartheid in Geneva in June 1973 to work out a common programme of action.[97] It was attended by 380 delegates from more than 200 trade union organizations, representing 180 million workers from all over the world. The Conference proved particularly timely as there was a resurgence of strikes that year by Black South African workers defying

96/Document 63
See page 316

97/Document 66
See page 317;
Document 69
See page 323

repressive laws. The Conference urged all workers and their trade union organizations to give full support to the Black workers of South Africa by campaigning for the recognition of African trade unions, calling for an end to the system of contract or migrant labour and giving full financial, moral and material support to the workers and people of South Africa through their trade unions and political organizations. The General Assembly—in resolution 3151 A (XXVIII) of 14 December 1973—commended the resolution of the Conference to the attention of Governments, specialized agencies and intergovernmental and non-governmental organizations.

256    A Second International Trade Union Conference for Action against Apartheid took place in Geneva in June 1977 to review the implementation of the decisions adopted at the 1973 conference and to consider the most appropriate means to intensify worldwide action for the eradication of apartheid. Participants included representatives of 300 trade union organizations with a membership of about 200 million workers throughout the world. The Conference heard reports from the participants on actions taken by them against apartheid and noted with satisfaction that the 1973 conference had strengthened "solidarity actions by trade union organizations throughout the world in the interests of the workers and people suffering under racial discrimination and apartheid in southern Africa". The Conference unanimously adopted a resolution calling for specific actions by Governments, employers' associations and trade unions. The resolution provided for regular meetings of trade union representatives in Geneva to follow up on the decisions of the Conference, to review developments in southern Africa and to recommend further actions by trade union organizations. It asked them to hold annual meetings with the Special Committee against Apartheid.

257    A third conference—the International Conference of Trade Unions on Sanctions and Other Actions against the Apartheid Regime in South Africa—was organized in Geneva in June 1983 by the Workers' Group of the ILO Governing Body and the Special Committee, in cooperation with the OAU and the Organization of African Trade Union Unity. Its resolution called for stronger actions against apartheid.[98] The Conference led to an expansion of ILO activity against apartheid and increased assistance to the independent Black trade unions in South Africa.

98/Document 108
*See page 372*

258    The Special Committee against Apartheid held frequent consultations with international trade union confederations, the Organization of African Trade Union Unity, the South African Congress of Trade Unions and national trade union organizations in many countries. It encouraged the formation of the New York Area Labour Committee against Apartheid and assisted it in its activities. It also organized an

International Conference of Maritime Trade Unions on the Implementation of the United Nations Oil Embargo against South Africa in London in October 1985.

## Student and youth action

259   Students and youth were often in the forefront of the liberation struggle in South Africa. Especially after the Soweto uprising of 1976, their efforts inspired international student action in solidarity with the South African people. The General Assembly and other United Nations organs often drew attention to the plight of the South African students and encouraged international student solidarity with them. The Special Committee against Apartheid also took many initiatives to promote such solidarity actions.

**99/Document 13**
*See page 243*

260   Student solidarity had become a significant factor when Chief Albert J. Luthuli first appealed for a consumer boycott of South Africa in 1959,[99] and even more so when the 1960 Sharpeville massacre outraged world public opinion. At about that time, student resistance against segregation at South African universities had further encouraged international student action. Students and youth played a key role in initiating the boycott movement (later the anti-apartheid movement), especially in the United Kingdom, Ireland and the Nordic countries, and in developing mass action.

261   Student groups organized demonstrations against foreign tours by all-White South African sports teams. Their efforts developed into a mass movement by the late 1960s. There were huge demonstrations in the United Kingdom against the tour of the all-White South African rugby team from November 1969 to January 1970. The sports boycott became a major issue in Australia and New Zealand by 1970, and students played a key role in both countries. In Australia, students initiated the campaign for a sports boycott in 1970 and secured the support of churches, trade unions and public figures.

262   In the United Kingdom, the student campaign against Barclays Bank, the parent of South Africa's largest bank, began in the 1960s. It was carried on year after year, especially at the beginning of the academic year, to persuade students not to open accounts with that bank. The campaign against Barclays persisted until it eventually sold its shares in its South African affiliate in the late 1980s.

263   In the United States, students played an active role in the campaign against loans to South Africa which was begun in 1966 by a Committee of Conscience against Apartheid, established by the American Committee on Africa and the University Christian Movement. As a result, South Africa did not seek a renewal of a revolving credit it had previously used, and several banks announced that they would no longer make loans to the South African Government or its agencies.

264    Student actions in the United States were instrumental in inducing many academic institutions to divest themselves of investments in corporations involved in South Africa. They also helped to persuade state and city legislators to act against corporations involved in South Africa. Eventually, in the 1980s, a number of United States corporations withdrew from South Africa.

265    Students were also participants in other campaigns. In the United States, the Free South Africa Movement, launched mainly by African-American and church groups in November 1984, became a mass movement and was sustained over a long period largely because of the mobilization of students early in 1985. Thousands of students participated in demonstrations and risked imprisonment.

266    Student groups in several countries were active in collecting funds and supplies for assistance to the liberation movements in South Africa and Namibia. Runs and walks for the benefit of the liberation struggles attracted thousands of people. Student groups also sent volunteers to the front-line States and to institutions established by the liberation movements in exile. Students also publicized the cause of political prisoners and campaigned for their release.

267    In the 1960s, the Special Committee against Apartheid granted hearings to leaders of the Student Non-violent Coordinating Committee, Students for a Democratic Society and the University Christian Movement in the United States in order to publicize their activities against apartheid and to express appreciation to them. It established contact with the National Union of Students in the United Kingdom and many other international and national student and youth organizations. In subsequent years, it co-sponsored world conferences of students and youth against apartheid, held several consultations with student and youth groups on action against apartheid and invited those organizations to many of its conferences and special sessions.

## Women and children

268    After the Soweto uprising of 1976, the Special Committee against Apartheid decided to devote particular attention to the situation of children under apartheid, both as victims and as fighters against the system. It organized an International Seminar on Children under Apartheid, UNESCO House, Paris, 18-20 June 1979. The General Assembly, in its resolution 34/93 K of 12 December 1979 on "Women and children under apartheid", expressed concern about the special problems of women and children forced to flee South Africa and live as refugees, and recognized the urgent need for humanitarian and other assistance to women and children victimized by apartheid. It appealed to all Governments and organizations to contribute generously towards assistance for such women and children, including refugees.[100]

100/Document 101
*See page 355*

269   In order to publicize the role of women prior to the July 1980 World Conference of the United Nations Decade for Women in Copenhagen, the Special Committee organized and co-sponsored two seminars for that purpose: the Hemispheric Seminar on Women and Apartheid, Montreal, 9-11 May 1980; and the International Seminar on Women and Apartheid, Helsinki, 19-21 May 1980. These events brought together women's leaders from the South African liberation movements and representatives of a number of women's organizations and United Nations agencies. Their deliberations and declarations helped to focus attention on the situation of women and children in South Africa and to promote action by relevant United Nations organs.

270   Reports on women under apartheid were prepared for the Copenhagen Conference in 1980, and the Centre against Apartheid published several studies on the subject. The Copenhagen Conference recommended a series of measures to assist women suffering under apartheid. The General Assembly endorsed the recommendations of the Conference and asked Governments and organizations to give the highest priority to measures for the assistance of South African and Namibian women. It requested the Commission on Human Rights to investigate crimes against women and children in South Africa; it also invited women's organizations all over the world to intensify action in solidarity with the struggle for liberation in South Africa and to consider coordination of efforts in cooperation with the Special Committee against Apartheid.

271   In its resolution 36/172 K of 17 December 1981 on "Women and children under apartheid", the General Assembly invited all Governments and organizations to observe 9 August annually as the International Day of Solidarity with the Struggle of Women in South Africa and Namibia.

272   The question of women and children was pursued by the Commission on Human Rights, the Commission on the Status of Women and the Economic and Social Council. For its part, the Special Committee against Apartheid established a task force on women and children under apartheid. It encouraged and assisted in the establishment of an International Committee of Solidarity with the Struggle of Women in South Africa and Namibia in 1981, with Madame Jeanne Martin Cissé of Guinea as Chairperson.

273   The Special Committee, in cooperation with this International Committee, also organized an International Conference on Women in South Africa and Namibia in Brussels in May 1982. Prior to the Conference, the Special Committee sent a mission to southern Africa to consult with liberation movements and Governments on the need for assistance. About 300 participants from women's and other organizations, United Nations organs and agencies, member States of the Euro-

pean Communities and other States, and national liberation movements attended the Conference. The Conference adopted a comprehensive programme of action and asked that the Special Committee and the International Committee redouble their efforts to support the national liberation movements and the Front-line States.[101]

274    After 1984, the number of refugees from South Africa increased, as a consequence of the declaration of a state of emergency in parts of the country. In April 1986, the Special Committee sent a mission to Angola, Tanzania and Zambia to evaluate the needs of refugee women and children. It held consultations with the national liberation movements and visited various projects organized by them. It then reported to the International Conference on Women and Children under Apartheid, organized by the Special Committee in Arusha that May. The question of women and children under apartheid also received great attention at the World Conference to Review and Appraise the Achievements of the United Nations Decade for Women, held later that year.

275    United Nations organs encouraged international condemnation when thousands of children were detained in South Africa under emergency regulations. Meanwhile, UNICEF assisted South African refugee women and children, in consultation with the OAU and the national liberation movements, and publicized the destructive effects of apartheid on children in southern Africa.

276    In 1989, the Special Committee against Apartheid sent another delegation of eminent women, led by Mrs. Lisbet Palme of Sweden, to visit refugee areas in southern Africa and assess the needs of South African and Namibian refugee women and children. It held consultations with liberation movements, especially their women's sections, as well as Governments and agencies involved in assistance programmes, and made a number of recommendations. The Special Committee transmitted the findings of this mission to the special session of the General Assembly that December.

101/Document 105
See page 368

## Cultural, sports, and other boycotts

277    In 1968, the General Assembly, on the recommendation of the Special Committee against Apartheid, in its resolution 2396, asked all States and organizations to suspend cultural, educational, sporting and other exchanges with the racist regime and with organizations or institutions in South Africa which practised apartheid.[102] In 1973, the General Assembly also called for an end to civic contacts and exchanges.

278    Anti-apartheid movements had already promoted boycotts of South Africa. Father Trevor Huddleston had made an appeal for a cultural boycott of South Africa as early as 1954. At the request of the

102/Document 56
See page 308

ANC, movements were established in the United Kingdom and other countries from 1959 onward to organize consumer boycotts of South African wine, fruit and other products. These developed into anti-apartheid movements.

279   The boycott of apartheid sports teams began in earnest in 1963 with efforts to exclude South Africa from the Olympic Games. By 1964, many writers, artists, musicians and others in the United Kingdom and the United States had signed declarations announcing a boycott of South Africa. Several playwrights prohibited the staging of their works in South Africa. Unions of musicians, actors and others took action to persuade their members not to perform in South Africa.

280   The Special Committee took note of these actions and commended them. After 1965, when the South African regime enacted stringent regulations prohibiting multiracial performances or audiences and multiracial sports—segregation had generally been the "custom" earlier—the Special Committee held consultations with South African and international sports and cultural leaders, as well as with anti-apartheid movements, and became convinced that the United Nations should actively promote the boycotts. After the 1968 resolution of the General Assembly, the Special Committee encouraged public boycotts of South Africa even as it continued its efforts to secure sanctions and other measures by Governments.

### Cultural boycott

281   The Special Committee gave increased attention to the cultural boycott in the 1970s because of the persistence of several Governments in maintaining cultural agreements with South Africa and disclosures of secret operations by South African Government agencies aimed at promoting cultural exchanges and enticing musicians and other entertainers to South Africa. In 1980, the General Assembly adopted a separate resolution asking all States to take steps to prevent cultural, academic, sports and other exchanges with South Africa, to cancel all cultural agreements and similar arrangements entered into between their Governments and the racist regime of South Africa, to prevent any promotion of tourism to South Africa, and to terminate visa-free entry privileges to South African nationals.[103]

103/Document 100
See page 355

282   The Special Committee established extensive contacts with writers, artists and entertainers opposed to apartheid. In 1983, it began publication of a Register of Entertainers, Actors and Others Who Have Performed in Apartheid South Africa.[104] The Register was an effective instrument for inducing entertainers and others to refrain from performing in South Africa. The Committee also encouraged and assisted art competitions against apartheid (in the United States, India, the Netherlands and Bangladesh), art exhibits against apartheid (in France, the

104/Document 109
See page 375

German Democratic Republic, the United Kingdom and the United States), the production of anti-apartheid calendars (in the German Democratic Republic and the United States), recordings of anti-apartheid freedom songs (Germany, Nigeria, Sweden, the Union of Soviet Socialist Republics, the United Kingdom and the United States), and essay competitions against apartheid (Ireland). Books of poetry against apartheid were published in Bangladesh and the United Kingdom with the support of the Special Committee.

283    Following consultations at the International Conference on Sanctions against South Africa in Paris in 1981, the Special Committee encouraged the formation of a Committee of World Artists against Apartheid under the chairmanship of the Spanish artist Antonio Saura. That Committee, with the support of the Special Committee, organized the Art contre/against Apartheid exhibit, with contributions from over 80 of the world's most prominent contemporary artists. The Special Committee also supported Artists and Athletes against Apartheid, sponsored by Transafrica in the United States, under the leadership of the United States singer Harry Belafonte and the tennis player Arthur Ashe. In addition, it also backed a committee of community artists against apartheid in New York which organized a number of exhibits and other projects. Groups of artists against apartheid were formed in several other countries as well.

284    The Committee of World Artists against Apartheid organized a Symposium against Apartheid in Athens from 2 to 4 September 1988, in cooperation with the Ministry of Culture of Greece and the Hellenic Association for the United Nations. It brought together 36 artists—writers, actors, musicians, composers, directors, producers and others from around the world, including South Africa—to develop proposals for positive action against apartheid. It held another symposium in Los Angeles in May 1991 at which the participants agreed to promote appropriate assistance to anti-apartheid cultural structures in South Africa.

### Sports boycott

285    The movement for the international boycott of apartheid in sports was a powerful means of sensitizing world public opinion against apartheid and mobilizing millions to demonstrate their abhorrence of apartheid and their support of the freedom movement in South Africa. It effectively showed the people of South Africa—especially the Whites who were enthusiastic about sports—that world public opinion was against apartheid. Hundreds of thousands of people participated in demonstrations against all-White South African teams. Thousands of the participants risked imprisonment, especially in Western countries such as the United Kingdom, New Zealand, Australia and the United

States. Many athletes and sports bodies made sacrifices to show their solidarity with the Black South African athletes.

286    The South African Government enforced racial segregation in sports in flagrant violation of the Olympic principle of non-discrimination. The majority of the population had inadequate sports facilities and were denied equal opportunities to compete in national and international tournaments. When modern sports were organized in South Africa, Whites formed their own sports bodies which excluded Blacks. These White sports bodies secured affiliation to international sports federations. A few Black athletes managed to go abroad and gain international recognition, but they could not hope to become national champions in South Africa.

287    Resistance against discrimination in sports and the formation of non-racial sports bodies began with the development of the freedom movement in the 1950s. A Committee for International Recognition was formed by Black sportsmen in 1955. The following year it secured the recognition of the non-racial South African Table Tennis Board (SATTB) by the International Table Tennis Federation. The SATTB team participated in the world championships held in Stockholm in 1957. However, immediately thereafter, the South African Government ruled that no Black could compete internationally except through a White sports body, and began to refuse passports to Black table tennis team members.

288    The formation of the Committee for International Recognition was followed by the founding of the South African Sports Association (SASA) in 1958 and the South African Non-Racial Olympic Committee (SAN-ROC) in 1963. Their purpose was to oppose racism in sports and press for international recognition of the non-racial sports bodies in South Africa. The South African Council on Sport (SACOS) was established in 1973, uniting all the non-racial and anti-apartheid sports federations.

289    The efforts of SAN-ROC, which was obliged to operate from London from 1966 onwards, prompted sports organizations in many countries to press for the exclusion of segregated South African sports bodies from international sports. Successes were achieved with threats of boycotts of international sports events if South African athletes were invited. South Africa was excluded from the Tokyo Olympics in 1964 and expelled from the International Olympic Committee in 1970.

290    The United Nations General Assembly first called for a sports boycott of South Africa in 1968.[105] In 1971, it adopted a special resolution on apartheid in sports.[106] In it the Assembly called on all sports organizations to uphold the Olympic principle of non-discrimination, expressed regret that some sports organizations had continued exchanges with racially selected South African teams and commended the

105/Document 56
See page 308

106/Document 61
See page 314

international campaign against apartheid in sports. The Special Committee against Apartheid publicized and denounced all sports exchanges with South Africa, encouraged groups demonstrating against Whites-only teams and asked Governments and sports bodies to act.

291    Apartheid in sports became a public issue in every country with which South Africa sought sports exchanges. Indeed, by 1970 South Africa not only had been expelled from the Olympic movement but also had been excluded from most major world championships. South Africa's international contacts in amateur sports were reduced to tennis, golf, cricket and rugby, the latter two primarily with the United Kingdom, Australia and New Zealand.

292    In the United Kingdom, a "Stop the Seventy Tour" Committee was formed, with Mr. Peter Hain as Chairman, to oppose the planned 1970 tour of England by a White cricket team from South Africa. Although South Africa had banned an English cricket tour in 1968 when the Marylebone Cricket Club (MCC), the English cricket association, had included Mr. Basil d'Oliveira, a Coloured cricketer, on its team, the MCC persisted with its invitation to South Africa. Already in 1969, large demonstrations had taken place wherever a South African rugby team had gone, and matches had to be played behind barbed wire fences. Only after the expression of a public disapproval in the United Kingdom and indications by a number of Commonwealth countries that they would boycott the 1970 Commonwealth Games if the South African cricket team toured England did the British Government formally ask the MCC to rescind South Africa's invitation.

293    The following year, massive anti-apartheid demonstrations greeted the South African rugby tour of Australia. The South African team had to be transported in Australian Air Force planes as the trade unions refused to service planes or trains carrying them. Seven hundred people were arrested and many were injured in demonstrations. The State of Queensland declared a 10-day state of emergency during the tour, provoking a general strike by trade unions. The South African cricket tour scheduled for later that year was cancelled. A new Government subsequently came to power in Australia and announced an anti-apartheid sports policy in December 1972, a policy followed by all subsequent Governments.

294    In New Zealand, apartheid in sports was a national issue for many years. The New Zealand national rugby team, the All Blacks, toured South Africa in June and July 1970, despite protests from many groups in New Zealand and appeals from the United Nations. Three years later, the New Zealand rugby authorities invited the South African rugby team for a tour. Numerous organizations opposed the visit and some vowed non-violent disruption of the matches. African Commonwealth countries and India announced in April 1972 that they would

boycott the Commonwealth Games in Christchurch in 1974 if the tour went ahead. Soon after, a new Government came to power and decided to stop the tour "in the larger interests of New Zealand".

295    The New Zealand rugby federation then decided on a tour of South Africa in 1976, despite the opposition of the Government and the public. The tour happened to begin in late June, soon after the Soweto uprising. In protest, a number of Governments and sports organizations decided to boycott sporting events with New Zealand. African nations withdrew from the 1976 Montreal Olympics in protest against the participation of New Zealand; they were joined by Guyana and Iraq. This boycott did much to focus international attention on the issue of apartheid in sports.

296    The issue again came to the fore in 1981 when the South African Springbok rugby team toured New Zealand. There were mass demonstrations and non-violent disruption of matches all over the country and some 2,000 people were jailed. The Conservative Party was defeated in the next elections, held in 1983, and the new Labour Government took active steps to prevent sports exchanges with South Africa.

297    Meanwhile, the Commonwealth Heads of State and Government had adopted the Gleneagles Agreement in June 1977. The Agreement provided that they would take "every practical step to discourage contact or competition of their nationals with sporting organizations, teams or sportsmen from South Africa". The next year, Sports Ministers of the member States of the Council of Europe adopted a similar declaration. These declarations helped greatly to reduce sporting exchanges with South Africa.

298    As apartheid in sports became more isolated internationally, the South African Government tried to restore some contacts through propaganda and the expenditure of millions of rand to entice sportsmen from abroad and build pro-apartheid lobbies. In response, the campaign against apartheid focused on counteracting apartheid propaganda, upholding the Olympic principle of non-discrimination and confronting those who collaborated with apartheid in sports. The Special Committee against Apartheid endorsed the declaration of the South African Council on Sport in 1976 that "there can be no normal sport in an abnormal society".

299    To prevent South African athletes from visiting other countries for unpublicized events, the United Nations appealed to Governments to deny visa-free entry privileges to South African nationals; several countries took action. Even contacts with South African sports bodies that claimed to be non-racial were discouraged, so as to avoid the risk of any deception. Nevertheless, a number of sports bodies and athletes, especially from some Western countries, continued to play in

South Africa. Many English cricketers, for instance, spent their winter months in South Africa. Some international sports bodies, like the International Tennis Federation, not only rejected proposals to exclude South Africa but also tried to penalize countries which boycotted South Africa.

*300*   Many Governments and sports bodies therefore felt that boycott of apartheid teams alone was not enough, and that some action should be taken against those who violated the boycott. The United Nations responded with a proposal for an International Convention against Apartheid in Sports and a register of athletes playing in South Africa. Both involved a "third party boycott", i.e., a boycott not only of South Africa but also of those cooperating with apartheid in sports. In May 1976, a United Nations Seminar in Havana had endorsed a suggestion by Prime Minister Michael Manley of Jamaica for an international convention against apartheid in sports, which would provide for action against those maintaining contact with South African sports. The fifth Summit Conference of Non-Aligned Countries, held in Colombo in August 1976, endorsed the proposal. On a proposal by the non-aligned countries, the United Nations General Assembly, by its resolution 31/6 F of 9 November 1976, appointed a committee to draw up the convention and a draft declaration.

*301*   The General Assembly approved the International Declaration against Apartheid in Sports drawn up by the Committee on 14 December 1977. The drafting of the Convention, however, proved more problematic because of apprehension about a legally binding provision on a "third party boycott". After extensive consultations over several years, the Committee completed the draft Convention in 1985.[107] It was adopted by the General Assembly and opened for signature on 16 May 1986. Within one year the Convention was signed by 71 States and ratified by 21. The Convention required States to prohibit the entry into their country of athletes who participated in competitions in South Africa, or athletes or administrators who invited apartheid sports bodies or teams officially representing South Africa. Signatories also undertook to secure sanctions against them by the relevant international sports bodies.[108]

*302*   The United Nations Register of Sports Contacts with South Africa—a record of sports exchanges with South Africa and a list of athletes who participated in sporting events in South Africa—was initiated in 1980 by the Special Committee against Apartheid.[109] The Special Committee agreed to delete from the register the name of any athlete who undertook not to play in South Africa again. The register proved an effective instrument for discouraging collaboration with South Africa. Many African and other countries prohibited those on the register from playing in their countries. Hundreds of city councils and

107/Document 118
*See page 393*

108/Document 134
*See page 418;*
Document 144
*See page 433*

109/Document 102
*See page 356*

local authorities in the United Kingdom and other Western countries decided to deny the use of their sports facilities to persons on the register. The register also dissuaded many athletes from accepting invitations and lucrative offers from South Africa. The Special Committee presented citations to a number of athletes and sports administrators who promoted the boycott and rejected financial inducements to play in South Africa.

## Assistance for opponents of apartheid

*303* The United Nations first considered assistance to South Africans in 1963, on the recommendation of the Special Committee against Apartheid, following the arrest and trial of thousands of opponents of apartheid that year. In December, the General Assembly appealed to Governments to contribute funds for humanitarian assistance to political prisoners and their families. The Special Committee appealed to Governments through the Secretary-General in 1964, and by November 1965, 12 Governments had announced contributions totalling nearly $300,000 to the Defence and Aid Fund, London, and the World Council of Churches, Geneva. The General Assembly then decided, in December 1965, to establish a United Nations Trust Fund for South Africa to promote increased assistance. In the same year, at the request of the Security Council, the Secretary-General established an educational and training programme for South Africans.

*304* From 1966 onward, the General Assembly began to appeal to Governments and organizations for assistance to those struggling against apartheid in South Africa. In resolution 2202 A (XXI) of 16 December 1966, it appealed to all States "to consider effective political, moral and material assistance to all those combating the policies of apartheid". In resolution 2307 (XXII) of 13 December 1967, it called upon all States and organizations to provide "moral, political and material assistance to the people of South Africa in their legitimate struggle for the rights recognized in the Charter". Thereafter, it made similar appeals annually, referring specifically in the 1970s to assistance to the South African liberation movements recognized by the OAU, namely, the ANC and the PAC. However, no United Nations funds were created for direct assistance to liberation movements. To facilitate assistance by Governments, which found it difficult to provide aid directly to liberation movements recognized by the OAU, the General Assembly appealed, in its resolution 2775 F (XXVI) of 29 November 1971, for contributions to the OAU Assistance Fund for the Struggle against Colonialism and Apartheid. The Fund had been set up in 1971 to assist economic and social projects of the national liberation movements.

*305* The General Assembly also asked the specialized agencies and other institutions in the United Nations system "to consider appropriate assistance for the employment in their secretariats and programmes of qualified South Africans who are victims of apartheid", and later to initiate or expand programmes of assistance to the oppressed people of South Africa. With the encouragement of the General Assembly, the United Nations Development Programme (UNDP) and several specialized agencies of the United Nations, in consultation with the OAU, began programmes of economic and social assistance to the liberation movements. UNDP established the Trust Fund for Assistance to Colonial Countries and Peoples in 1974 to finance humanitarian assistance projects of national liberation movements recognized by the OAU. The Trust Fund provided assistance to a number of projects of the ANC and the PAC in fields such as education and manpower development, agricultural development, management training and training of health personnel, at a cost of nearly $20 million. In order to promote and coordinate assistance by the United Nations system, the General Assembly in 1979 requested that the Economic and Social Council "review annually, in consultation with the Special Committee against Apartheid, the assistance provided by agencies and institutions within the United Nations system".

*306* With the upsurge of resistance by trade unions and other organizations in South Africa and Namibia in the early 1970s, there was a growing need for appropriate assistance to such groups inside South Africa. United Nations organs encouraged assistance through voluntary agencies and in consultation with liberation movements.

*307* As a result of the efforts of the United Nations, Governments all over the world contributed hundreds of millions of dollars for assistance to victims of apartheid and the liberation movements. When South Africa resorted to acts of aggression aimed at destabilizing neighbouring independent African States, the United Nations recognized that assistance to those States was an essential component of international action against apartheid. The Security Council and the General Assembly repeatedly appealed for assistance to those States. The General Assembly also supported SADCC, from the time it was established in 1980, and the Africa Fund established by the Movement of Non-Aligned Countries in 1986.

### Trust Fund for South Africa

*308* The United Nations Trust Fund for South Africa was established by the General Assembly in a December 1965 resolution for: legal assistance to persons charged under repressive and discriminatory legislation in South Africa; relief for dependants of those persecuted for their opposition to apartheid; education of prisoners and their dependants; and relief for refugees from South Africa.[110] The Fund was conceived as a humanitarian component of the United Nations commitment to the elimination of apartheid, and was made up entirely of voluntary contributions from Governments, organizations and individuals. A Committee of Trustees—composed of the permanent representatives to the United Nations of Chile, Morocco, Nigeria, Pakistan and Sweden—decided on grants from the Trust Fund to organizations engaged in humanitarian assistance in South Africa.[111]

**110/Document 45**
*See page 290*

**111/Document 54**
*See page 303*

309    The Committee of Trustees, in its final report in June 1994, stated that since it was established in 1965, the Trust Fund had spent $50 million on programmes of humanitarian, legal and educational assistance within the purview of its mandate. Thousands of victims of apartheid owed their very survival and hopes for the future to the activities of the Trust Fund.[112]

**112/Document 214**
*See page 510*

310    The grants from the Trust Fund helped pay for the legal defence of a number of persons charged under apartheid laws, provided assistance to families in which the breadwinner was incarcerated, paid for the education of political prisoners and their dependants and provided modest assistance to refugees from South Africa, especially those in African countries.[113] With the encouragement of the United Nations and the Committee of Trustees, hundreds of millions of dollars were also contributed by Governments directly to voluntary agencies engaged in such humanitarian assistance, such as the International Defence and Aid Fund for Southern Africa.

**113/Document 132**
*See page 415;*
**Document 145**
*See page 434*

311    In December 1991, the General Assembly expanded the mandate of the Trust Fund to include assistance to facilitate the reintegration of released political prisoners and returning exiles into South African society, as well as legal assistance aimed at redressing the continuing adverse effects of apartheid laws.[114]

**114/Document 151**
*See page 441*

312    After 1991, in the light of positive developments in South Africa and the expanded mandate from the General Assembly, the Committee of Trustees provided assistance directly to South African voluntary agencies involved particularly in constitutional and human rights litigation, land and housing issues and legal representation for disadvantaged communities, children's rights, gender discrimination, needs of marginalized youths and environmental issues.[115]

**115/Document 197**
*See page 487*

313    On 23 June 1994, the General Assembly dissolved the Trust Fund and transferred the balance to the United Nations Educational and Training Programme for Southern Africa.[116] In view of the South African Government's ban on the Defence and Aid Fund, the Committee of Trustees withheld the publication of the names of the recipients of grants from the Trust Fund until its final report.

**116/Document 218**
*See page 538*

## Assistance for education and training

314    A United Nations Educational Programme for South Africans was established by the Secretary-General in 1965 on a recommendation of the Group of Experts on South Africa, which had been endorsed by the Security Council in 1964. It was combined, at the beginning of 1968, with similar programmes for other Territories in southern Africa into the United Nations Educational and Training Programme for Southern Africa and was financed by voluntary contributions from Governments, organizations and individuals. The General Assembly established a committee to advise the Secretary-General on the strengthening and expansion of the programme and on other policy matters, including the promotion of contributions.

315    The programme was set up to address the lack of educational opportunities for South African Blacks, as well as the needs of refugees from South Africa, and, as the Group of Experts stated, "for training abroad of a large number of South African lawyers, engineers, agronomists, public administrators, teachers at all levels and skilled workers, as well as training in such fields as labour education and business and industrial management . . . The purpose will be to enable as many South Africans as possible to play a full part as quickly as possible in the political, economic and social advance of the country." The programme provided education and training in institutions outside South Africa, with preference given to institutions in African countries. In 1992, however, in view of the changing situation in South Africa, the programme shifted the focus of its activities to education and training inside the country. Particular attention was devoted to enhancing institution-building and contributing to filling South Africa's human resource needs during the transition to democracy and beyond. Priority fields for study and training have included agriculture, computer science, economic and social development, education, engineering, medical and paramedical studies, public administration and finance, and sciences.

316    From the programme's inception in 1965 to 1 October 1993, it granted 7,216 scholarships to South Africans. UNDP and the specialized agencies also provided similar assistance. In December 1993, the General Assembly requested the Secretary-General to include the United Nations Educational and Training Programme for Southern Africa in the annual United Nations Pledging Conference for Development Activities.[117]

117/Document 198
See page 488

317    In 1976, when hundreds of students began to leave South Africa for neighbouring countries in the aftermath of the Soweto uprising, the General Assembly asked the Secretary-General to take immediate steps to provide emergency assistance to the student refugees. It invited United Nations agencies to lend their cooperation and urged Member States to respond generously to any appeals by the Secretary-

General for assistance. The Secretary-General sent a mission to investigate the needs of the student refugees and designated the Office of the United Nations High Commissioner for Refugees (UNHCR) as coordinator of United Nations assistance.

*318* In subsequent years, as the number of student refugees continued to increase, the General Assembly and the Economic and Social Council made further appeals for increased assistance and received annual reports from the Secretary-General on assistance provided to the student refugees. Contributions by Governments for assistance to student refugees from South Africa, in response to appeals by UNHCR, amounted to more than $5 million by 24 May 1980, in addition to general refugee assistance.

### Other assistance

*319* The United Nations and its agencies provided financial assistance for liberation movement representatives invited to their meetings, conferences, seminars and other events. Moreover, in 1977 the General Assembly—in resolution 32/105 I of 14 December—authorized the Special Committee against Apartheid to associate representatives of the South African liberation movements recognized by the OAU with its missions. And from 1979, the Assembly made financial provision in the United Nations budget for grants to the South African liberation movements to maintain offices in New York so that they could participate in the work of the Special Committee against Apartheid and other organs. This assistance, amounting to several million dollars, enabled the liberation movements to make effective contributions to the work of the United Nations and its agencies in the struggle against apartheid and to develop contacts with many Governments and organizations.

# IV  Towards a non-racial democratic government, 1990-1994

*320*    The changes in South Africa between 1990 and 1994 were testimony to a remarkable spirit of reconciliation and to the determination by leading political groups to bring about by peaceful means a free and united society based on the principles of equality for all. This period also witnessed the first direct involvement of the United Nations within South Africa, with the Secretary-General first given the mandate to follow and report on the situation in South Africa to the General Assembly, and then, in August 1992, being asked by the Security Council to deploy United Nations observers to assist in creating the conditions for peace.

*321*    But despite the rapid moves towards peace, years of apartheid had resulted in a deeply divided society in which fear and violence had become endemic. Opponents of negotiation in this period used this legacy to promote violence at all levels in order to block the road towards a peaceful settlement. In this climate, the good offices of the Secretary-General of the United Nations were, at critical times, crucial to the maintenance of the peace process.

*322*    In 1990, as the new Government of President F. W. de Klerk took conciliatory steps—by revoking the bans on the ANC, the PAC and other political organizations, and by releasing Nelson Mandela and other leaders—the United Nations sought to encourage the South African authorities to proceed with negotiations. The Declaration on South Africa adopted by the General Assembly in December 1989 set the tone for this process. The United Nations played a facilitating role in promoting the first negotiations in 1990 and 1991 through consultations by my predecessor, Mr. Javier Pérez de Cuéllar, who also used his good offices to have the United Nations High Commissioner for Refugees (UNHCR) play the central role in facilitating the return of refugees— the first time a United Nations agency functioned in the Republic of South Africa.

*323*    In difficult circumstances of mounting violence and considerable mistrust between the principal parties in this period, the United Nations sought the promotion of a climate conducive to negotiations and provided vital assistance in the process of negotiation itself when severe difficulties were encountered. After the suspension of negotiations amid renewed violence in mid-1992, I sent a Special Representative, whose efforts helped to overcome the differences concerning violence and the continued detention of political prisoners. In September

1992, with the endorsement of the Security Council, I sent the United Nations Observer Mission in South Africa (UNOMSA) to help strengthen the structures under the National Peace Accord. The Mission quickly helped to defuse tensions and improve the atmosphere. It therefore facilitated the resumption of talks between the Government and other parties, particularly the ANC. United Nations fact-finding missions had high-level discussions with representatives of the Government and the other parties.

324    After these and other efforts at mediation, the Multi-party Negotiating Council was convened in 1993 to prepare an interim constitution and organize elections for April 1994. As the negotiations progressed, the international community responded readily to the request of Mr. Mandela to terminate restrictions on economic relations with South Africa as from October 1993. The Transitional Executive Council, established in December 1993 for the first phase of the transition to majority rule, requested the United Nations both to observe the electoral process and to coordinate the deployment of other foreign observers. The United Nations responded promptly by greatly expanding UNOMSA and assisting the electoral authorities. UNOMSA played a key role in observing the April 1994 elections. There were more than 2,000 United Nations observers among the 6,000 foreign observers present for the elections, the conduct of which was a triumph for democracy.

325    Ultimately, with apartheid eliminated as a State policy, the South African people were able, in a remarkable spirit of reconciliation, to bury the past and establish a non-racial democratic State. South Africa has resumed its place as a full and active member of the United Nations system. The United Nations now stands ready to support South Africa and its efforts at reconstruction after the devastation and divisions brought about by four and a half decades of apartheid.


## South Africa isolated

326    By the end of 1989, South Africa was more than ready for change. Mass resistance to apartheid had spread after the introduction of the new constitution in 1984. The Government had resorted to increased repression but had proved unable to quell opposition other than temporarily, and its brutality had galvanized international public opinion against apartheid.

327    The persistent efforts to mobilize world public opinion for the elimination of apartheid, in which the United Nations played a key role, succeeded in enabling the people around the world to develop a new level of solidarity with those struggling for a non-racial democratic

society in South Africa. Governments began to break or reduce their economic relations with South Africa; some acted unilaterally and others collectively, on the recommendation of organizations such as the Commonwealth and the European Community. The Security Council for the first time encouraged such voluntary measures.

328    South Africa began to feel acutely the effects of these international measures. The Special Committee against Apartheid reported in 1989 that sanctions had imposed substantial constraints on the South African economy, primarily through the denial of loans and capital for investment. Estimates of the total cost imposed by economic sanctions varied significantly, but some studies had suggested that, without sanctions, South Africa's economy could have been 20 to 35 per cent larger than it was. The oil embargo, on its own, had cost the South African economy an estimated $22.1 billion in the period from 1979 to 1988.

329    Moreover, according to the United Nations Centre on Transnational Corporations, a total of 605 transnational corporations disinvested from South Africa between August 1985 and August 1990.

330    Sections of the White community, including business people, began to feel that the course followed by the Government would only lead to a protracted civil war and the devastation of the economy. A number of South African business and other delegations began to visit the exiled leadership of the ANC for consultations. The United Nations responded to these developments not only by calling for greatly increased pressure on the South African Government and assistance to the liberation struggle, but also by pointing the way to a peaceful solution. In resolutions in 1987 and 1988, the Assembly demanded that the South African Government take a series of steps which would "create the appropriate conditions for free consultations among all the people of South Africa with a view to negotiating a just and lasting solution to the conflict in that country".[118] The requisite actions included lifting the state of emergency, releasing political prisoners, ending the bans on political organizations and opponents of apartheid and withdrawing troops from Black townships.

118/Document 121
See page 407

## The turning-point

331    The possibility of moves towards a peaceful solution finally appeared in 1989. During that year, there was a resurgence of resistance by opponents of apartheid within South Africa, despite the state of emergency. More than 700 detainees went on a hunger strike early in the year. Community organizations launched a series of actions, in defiance of the law, against segregation, discrimination and repression. These culminated in a coordinated campaign of defiance led by the Mass

Democratic Movement on the eve of the racially exclusive general elections to be held on 6 September.

332    In addition, the South African Government and the White voters had begun to feel more acutely the effects of international ostracism. There was growing recognition in the ruling National Party that the resistance against apartheid could not be suppressed by military means. Meanwhile, an improvement in the international climate after the end of the cold war had facilitated cooperation by the major Powers in resolving conflicts in southern Africa.

333    In the light of these developments, the authorities in Pretoria reassessed their options. The National Party contested the September 1989 elections with proposals for a reform programme envisaging a new constitutional order with a bill of rights and a role for the Black majority in the Government. With the party's victory, its leader, Mr. F. W. de Klerk, who had been elected President, outlined a plan for change. This programme fell short of establishing a non-racial democratic society, but it represented a move away from apartheid and towards peaceful change. Following a suggestion by the ANC, the OAU Ad Hoc Committee on Southern Africa, composed of heads of State and Government, meeting in Harare, adopted a Declaration on the Question of South Africa on 21 August 1989. It expressed the belief that "as a result of the liberation struggle and international pressure against apartheid, as well as global efforts to liquidate regional conflicts, possibilities exist for further movement towards the resolution of the problems facing the people of South Africa".

334    The OAU Committee declared in a statement of principles: "We believe that a conjuncture of circumstances exists which, if there is a demonstrable readiness on the part of the Pretoria regime to engage in negotiations genuinely and seriously, could create the possibility to end apartheid through negotiations. Such an eventuality would be an expression of the long-standing preference of the majority of the people of South Africa to arrive at a political settlement. We support the position held by the majority of the people of South Africa that these objectives, and not the amendment or reform of the apartheid system, should be the aims of the negotiations."

335    The Harare Declaration added that the outcome of such a process should be a new constitutional order, "a united, democratic and non-racial State" in which all the people would "enjoy common and equal citizenship and nationality, regardless of race, colour, sex or creed" and "have the right to participate in the government and administration of the country on the basis of a universal suffrage, exercised through one person one vote, under a common voters' roll".

336    The Declaration supported the view of the South African liberation movement that the process of negotiations should begin with

discussions about a suspension of hostilities between the regime and the liberation movements. Negotiations should then proceed on the principles which should form the basis of a new Constitution, the role to be played by the international community in ensuring a successful transition to a democratic order, the formation of an interim government and the holding of elections.

337    On 9 December, a Conference for a Democratic Future in South Africa, with the participation of representatives from more than 2,000 organizations in South Africa, endorsed the Harare Declaration and called for a non-racial constituent assembly to draw up a new constitution.

338    The United Nations General Assembly met to discuss the situation at a special session in December 1989. The Special Committee against Apartheid held extensive consultations to secure a consensus and succeeded in formulating a draft based on the Harare Declaration which considered the views of all Member States of the United Nations. The General Assembly then adopted, by consensus, the Declaration on Apartheid and its Destructive Consequences in Southern Africa.[119] In the Declaration, the Assembly expressed its belief that, "as a result of the legitimate struggle of the South African people for the elimination of apartheid, and of international pressure against that system, as well as global efforts to resolve regional conflicts, possibilities exist for further movement towards the resolution of the problems facing the people of South Africa".

119/Document 135
See page 419

339    While reaffirming its support for those striving for a non-racial and democratic society in South Africa, "a point on which no compromise is possible", it recalled that the United Nations had repeatedly sought a peaceful solution. It noted that the people of South Africa and their liberation movements had also expressed, for many decades, their preference for a peaceful solution, and continued to do so. The General Assembly also encouraged the people of South Africa, as part of their legitimate struggle, to join together to negotiate an end to apartheid and agree on the measures necessary to transform their country into a non-racial democracy.

340    Affirming that the outcome of such a process should be a new constitutional order determined by the South African people and based on the Charter of the United Nations and the Universal Declaration of Human Rights, the General Assembly stressed the importance of some fundamental principles, including the following: that South Africa should be a united, non-racial and democratic State; that all its people should enjoy common and equal citizenship and nationality, regardless of race, colour, sex or creed; that there should be universal, equal suffrage, under a non-racial voters' roll, and by secret ballot, in a united and non-fragmented South Africa; and that all should enjoy universally

recognized human rights, freedoms and civil liberties, protected under an entrenched bill of rights.

341    The General Assembly also considered the steps needed to create a climate conducive to negotiations, and indicated that the parties concerned should negotiate the future of their country in an atmosphere which, by mutual agreement between the liberation movements and the South African Government, would be free of violence. It proposed that the process could commence with agreements on the mechanism for the drawing up of a new constitution; the role to be played by the international community in ensuring a successful transition to a democratic order; and the modalities for preparing and adopting a new constitution, and for the transition to a democratic order, including the holding of elections.

342    The General Assembly also agreed on a programme of action, including increased support to opponents of apartheid, and the use of concerted and effective measures for applying pressure to ensure a speedy end to apartheid.

343    Finally, the General Assembly requested the Secretary-General to transmit copies of the Declaration to the South African Government and the representatives of the oppressed people of South Africa, and to report on progress made in the implementation of the Declaration. Although the South African regime rejected the Declaration, it finally began to take steps to meet the demands of the international community.

## Creating a climate for negotiations

344    A prerequisite for a peaceful settlement in South Africa was the release of political prisoners and the taking of other steps to create the necessary climate for free political activity. In this connection, the

120/Document 135
See page 419

General Assembly said in its 1989 Declaration[120] that the South African regime should, at the least: release all political prisoners and detainees unconditionally and refrain from imposing any restrictions on them; lift all bans and restrictions on all proscribed and restricted organizations and persons; remove all troops from the townships; end the state of emergency and repeal all legislation, such as the Internal Security Act, designed to circumscribe political activity; and cease all political trials and political executions.

345    On 2 February 1990, President de Klerk declared that his final aim was a totally new and just constitutional dispensation in which "every inhabitant would enjoy equal rights, treatment and opportunity in every sphere of endeavour—constitutional, social and economic". He announced the lifting of the ban on the ANC, the PAC, the South

African Communist Party and other political organizations, and the removal of restrictions on the activities of 33 organizations. He also announced the suspension of the death penalty, the repeal of certain emergency regulations, including those restricting the media, and the withdrawal of banning orders on individuals and promised to release Nelson Mandela and other political prisoners. On 11 February, Mr. Mandela, who had been in prison for more than 27 years, was released unconditionally.

346    The international community warmly welcomed these actions and the ANC decided to begin talks with the Government. However, initial progress was slow and difficult, because of the reluctance of the Government to take immediate steps to implement all the measures suggested in the Declaration on Apartheid. There was also an upsurge of violence, much of it directed at ANC supporters.

347    Only persons serving sentences for membership in banned organizations or for activities furthering their aims were released; by June 1990 the number freed was only 104 and the great majority of political prisoners and detainees remained in prison. Political trials continued. While banning orders on persons were removed, some 300 persons convicted of various offences under the Internal Security Act continued to live under restriction and could not be quoted by the media.[121]

121/Document 138
*See page 426*

348    The elaborate repressive structures which had been created over the years, with the use of secret funds and operations, and the prevalence of racist elements in the security forces, proved difficult to dismantle. Troops were removed from the townships but continued to enter them. There was continued police violence against demonstrators, as well as acts of violence, including bombings and assassinations of anti-apartheid activists, by extremist White political groups bent on preventing or disrupting the negotiation process. Moreover, in Natal and elsewhere, violent incidents had been taking place for years between supporters of the Inkatha Freedom Party (IFP) and supporters of the United Democratic Front (UDF), the Congress of South African Trade Unions (COSATU) and the ANC. The strife continued to adversely affect the political atmosphere. Elements of the security forces were accused of favouring the IFP and of provoking violence.

349    The Human Rights Commission and the Independent Board of Enquiry into Internal Repression, two private bodies in South Africa, reported that at least 176 persons had been killed and 1,563 injured as a result of police action during some 70 demonstrations between 2 February and 2 June 1990. They observed that most of the Black vigilante activity had occurred in the context of the conflict in Natal, while White vigilantism had been carried out by covert death squads. The latter were found to be related to undercover operations of the Civil

Cooperation Bureau, a military unit alleged to have been involved in assassinations, and to acts of the right-wing extremists. The growth of far-right-wing intimidation and violence was attributed to tacit support and encouragement that were received from the local police and security forces.

350    There were complaints that the Government was unwilling to take firm action to stop the violence in Natal, the vigilante attacks in other areas and police actions against peaceful demonstrators. There were also demands that the Government should immediately disband the overt and covert units in the military and police establishments which had allegedly been involved in assassinations and violent acts against opponents of apartheid, as well as other violence against the Black people.

### First talks commence

351    The ANC decided in March 1990, after Mr. Mandela met with ANC leaders in exile in Lusaka, to hold talks with the Government, and the latter granted temporary immunity to several ANC representatives in exile to return to South Africa to participate in the talks. The talks, however, were delayed when, on 26 March, police fired at demonstrators in the township of Sebokeng in the Transvaal, killing at least 12 persons and wounding nearly 500.

352    President de Klerk and his delegation met with ANC leaders at Groote Schuur in Cape Town from 2 to 4 May to consider the removal of obstacles to the negotiation process. The parties adopted the Groote Schuur Minute, which established a Working Group to make recommendations on the definition of political offences applicable to those inside and outside South Africa, the release of political prisoners and the granting of immunity for political offences. The Government agreed to consider, on an urgent basis, temporary immunity for members of the ANC National Executive Committee. It also undertook to review the existing security legislation. Both parties pledged to seek an end to "the existing climate of violence and intimidation from whatever quarter", and reiterated their "commitment to stability and to a peaceful process of negotiations".

353    On 8 June, when the country-wide state of emergency lapsed, the Government reimposed it only in the province of Natal (where it was subsequently lifted on 18 October 1990). Also in June, the parliament in Cape Town decided to repeal, as of October 1990, the Reservation of Separate Amenities Act, which had mandated separate public facilities for members of different racial groups. The Government and the ANC then met in Pretoria on 6 August 1990 for talks that resulted in the adoption of the Pretoria Minute. Both sides accepted the report of the Working Group set up under the Groote Schuur Minute, agreed on a

timetable for the release of prisoners in various categories listed by the Working Group and set 30 April 1991 as the latest date for the completion of that provision. The Government undertook to review emergency and security matters. In the interest of moving speedily towards a negotiated settlement and in the context of the agreements reached, the ANC announced that it was suspending all armed actions immediately. The two parties also announced: "We are convinced that what we have agreed upon today can become a milestone on the road to true peace and prosperity for our country . . . The way is now open to proceed towards negotiations on a new constitution."

354    Subsequently, however, serious disagreements arose between the Government and the ANC concerning the release of political prisoners, the procedures for the granting of immunity to exiles and the measures needed to end the violence. The process of negotiations stalled. The United Nations, monitoring the situation, pressed the Government to take all the necessary steps to create a climate conducive to negotiations, appealed to all parties to end violence and encouraged the parties concerned to participate fully in the negotiations for the establishment of a united, non-racial and democratic South Africa.

## First report of the Secretary-General

355    A United Nations team, led by Under-Secretary-General Abdulrahim A. Farah, visited South Africa from 9 to 19 June 1990 and met with members of the Government as well as with a large number of organizations representing a wide cross-section of South African opinion. On the basis of the team's report, and of his own consultations with President de Klerk and Mr. Mandela, Secretary-General Javier Pérez de Cuéllar reported to the General Assembly on 1 July that the political process of dismantling the apartheid system was still at an early stage.[122] 122/Document 136
*See page 421* He said that he had been "greatly encouraged" by the positive developments that had taken place within South Africa, and added: "The bold and courageous policy to which President de Klerk has committed his Government opens up distinct possibilities for the dismantling of the apartheid system. Equally encouraging and statesmanlike has been the vision and forbearance displayed by the Black leadership which, despite long years of injustice and oppression, has renewed its commitment to a peaceful process for ending apartheid and building a non-racial and democratic society".

356    The Secretary-General indicated that, of the measures required by the Declaration on Apartheid to create a climate for free political activity, the lifting of the ban on political parties and movements had been implemented in full, while other measures had been implemented in part. He appealed to all parties to do whatever was

necessary to end the violence and to work together to build a peaceful South Africa.

357   The General Assembly considered the Secretary-General's report in September. It also took note of a report of the Monitoring Group of the OAU Ad Hoc Committee on Southern Africa and other information. In a resolution adopted on 17 September 1990, the Assembly indicated that while the regime had declared its commitment to abolish apartheid and had taken some significant steps in that direction, continued efforts were needed to establish a climate fully conducive to

123/Document 137
See page 425

negotiations and free political activity.[123] The Assembly also welcomed the ongoing talks between the ANC and the Government, and commended the ANC for having taken the initiative in calling for talks and for its landmark decision in August to suspend the armed struggle. The Assembly urged the South African authorities to end violence, by dismantling apartheid structures and ensuring effective and impartial action by the security forces. It called upon all parties concerned to contribute to the establishment of a climate free of violence. The General Assembly asked the Secretary-General, through the relevant United Nations agencies, to provide all necessary assistance for the voluntary repatriation of South African refugees and political exiles in safety and dignity.

358   On 19 December, after considering the report of the Special Committee against Apartheid as well as other developments, the General Assembly adopted a resolution on "International efforts to eradicate

124/Document 139
See page 427

apartheid",[124] in which it called upon the South African authorities to continue their efforts to foster a climate fully conducive to negotiations and free political activity, in particular by repealing all repressive legislation, by ending detentions without trial, by allowing the return of all political exiles without restrictions and by fully implementing all agreements reached with the ANC, including those regarding the release of all remaining political prisoners. The Assembly also asked the South African authorities to redouble their efforts to end violence, and called upon all parties concerned to contribute to the establishment of an atmosphere free of violence.

359   The General Assembly also encouraged all parties concerned, taking into account the guidelines on the process of negotiations contained in the Declaration, to participate fully in future negotiations, in order to secure the adoption of a new constitution and the establishment of a united, non-racial and democratic South Africa. It asked the Secretary-General to ensure the coordination of activities of the United Nations system in the implementation of the Declaration and to pursue initiatives to facilitate all efforts leading to the peaceful eradication of apartheid.

360   The process of removing the obstacles and initiating substan-

tive negotiations encountered serious difficulties. Anti-apartheid organizations in South Africa charged that the Government was not abiding by its undertakings on ending repression, releasing political prisoners and allowing the return of the exiles, and was not taking firm action to end the violence. Political parties and movements, as well as concerned organizations, conducted mass campaigns calling for the release of all political prisoners and the return of all exiles. They also called for an elected constituent assembly to draft a new constitution. Following revelations of secret funding of political organizations by the Government, and of covert security operations, there were increasing demands for an interim government. The Government, it was argued, could not be both a player and a referee in the democratization process.

361    At a national consultative conference in December 1990, held in Soweto, the ANC decided to suspend negotiations if all obstacles, including the violence, were not removed by the end of April 1991. On 5 April 1991, the ANC addressed an open letter to President de Klerk calling on the Government to fulfil a series of demands concerning political violence by 9 May, and stating that otherwise the ANC would suspend all discussions or exchanges with the Government. On 18 May, the ANC announced a plan of mass action to back the demands of the open letter.

### Three crucial issues

362    Despite these set-backs, a combination of public pressure in South Africa and international efforts helped to maintain momentum on the difficult questions of political prisoners, the return of refugees and the search for an end to the violence.

363    Political prisoners were a subject of great concern to the liberation movements. In accordance with the agreement in the Pretoria Minute, on 7 November 1990 the Department of Justice established the process of granting pardon and indemnity to political prisoners and exiles but it omitted one category, namely, common crimes which could be regarded as political offences. In April 1991, many political prisoners still remained in jail, and more than 200 went on a hunger strike. Some were hospitalized as a result.

364    There was progress in May 1991 when the International Committee of the Red Cross, at the invitation of the Government, brought the release programme to the attention of each prisoner. Thousands of applications were received, and by the end of that month over 1,000 political prisoners were released. On 30 June, the Government and the ANC agreed to set 15 July as the deadline for new applications. The Government indicated that it would grant special remission of sentences to some prisoners who did not qualify for release according to the categories and guidelines; a number of prisoners benefited from this

reduction of sentence. The ANC, the PAC and other organizations, however, claimed that political prisoners were still in detention, including a substantial number in the "independent homeland" of Bophuthatswana. The problem continued to plague the negotiations.

365    Equally troublesome was the issue of refugees. Some refugees and political exiles returned to South Africa after the unbanning of political organizations in February 1990 and the announcement of guidelines for the return of exiles issued by the South African Government on 1 November. But political organizations and exiles strongly criticized the procedures under the November guidelines, which required political exiles to apply for pardon or immunity by filling out questionnaires providing full details about the "offences" committed and giving an undertaking about peace which would be considered by the Government.

366    Following efforts by the United Nations, the South African Government in March 1991 approached UNHCR for assistance with the return of refugees and political exiles. UNHCR had already consulted with the ANC and the PAC concerning the matter. After protracted negotiations, the Government and UNHCR signed a Memorandum of Understanding on 4 September 1991; this formed the basis for UNHCR's involvement in the voluntary repatriation exercise.

367    UNHCR was charged with organizing the repatriation operation and was authorized to open temporary offices in South Africa to assist in the process. It would have free access to the returnees in South Africa, and the returnees themselves would enjoy complete freedom of movement. The Government agreed to grant amnesty to returnees for political offences which had been committed before 8 October 1990 and which qualified for indemnity in terms of the guidelines appended to the agreement. Persons granted indemnity could return without risk of arrest, detention, imprisonment or legal proceedings for those offences. UNHCR could make representations on behalf of returnees.

368    In accordance with the terms of the Memorandum, procedures and formalities for the readmission, reception and reintegration of returnees were established. Reintegration assistance in the form of cash grants was provided to returnees, including those who had arrived prior to the establishment of a UNHCR presence. UNHCR monitored the situation of returnees, many of whom had suffered harassment, detention and the adverse effects of the violence in the townships, and took appropriate action. By the end of May 1993, 10,957 South African refugees and exiles had registered for voluntary repatriation and the Government had cleared a total of 10,730; 6,604 had returned to South Africa under UNHCR auspices. Others returned earlier or independently. The international donor community contributed over $27 million through UNHCR to finance the South African repatriation and

reintegration operation. The assistance of UNHCR thus removed one of the serious impediments to negotiations.

369    The most alarming problem threatening the climate for negotiations was the escalating violence. The ANC and the IFP held a top-level meeting in Durban on 29 January 1991 to address the issue. Though they agreed on measures to end the violence, the results were disappointing. There were frequent complaints that the police were showing partiality or instigating killings. After disclosures by the media, several Government ministers acknowledged in July 1991 that public funds had been used secretly to assist the activities of some political organizations. Subsequently, the Government announced a set of measures to stop such use of public funds.

370    Meanwhile, on 22 June 1991 religious leaders, in cooperation with business leaders, facilitated the convening of a peace conference. As a result, a preparatory committee, including the Government, the ANC and the IFP, was established for what became known as the National Peace Initiative. The Initiative released a draft national accord on 14 August 1991 which provided codes of conduct for political parties, organizations and the security forces and a monitoring mechanism.

371    On 14 September 1991, in Johannesburg, the ANC, the IFP, the Government and a number of political parties, trade unions and religious and civic organizations signed the National Peace Accord (the PAC, the Conservative Party and the "homeland" governments of Transkei, Venda and Bophuthatswana did not sign it). The Accord provided for a code of conduct for the security forces and political parties and organizations, mechanisms to enforce these provisions and measures for the reconstruction and development of communities. A National Peace Committee was established to monitor the implementation of the Accord, and a National Peace Secretariat was set up to establish and coordinate regional and local dispute resolution committees.

372    A Commission of Inquiry regarding the Prevention of Public Violence and Intimidation, a statutory body, was set up to investigate violent incidents and to make recommendations on how violence and intimidation could be prevented. The Government appointed Justice Richard J. Goldstone as Chairman of the Commission, which came to be known as the Goldstone Commission.

373    An issue on which there was good progress was the repeal of discrimatory laws. A major pillar of apartheid was removed when the Discriminatory Legislation Regarding Public Amenities Repeal Act came into force in October 1990. Four of the other discriminatory laws were repealed on 5 June 1991—the Natives Land Act, No. 27 of 1913; the Development Trust and Land Act, No. 18 of 1936; the Group Areas Act,

No. 36 of 1966; and the Black Communities Development Act, No. 4 of 1984. The Population Registration Act, No. 30 of 1950, was cancelled on 17 June 1991. The Internal Security Act, No. 74 of 1982, was amended on 21 June, and the listing of persons under that Act was ended.

### Moves towards negotiations

*374* These developments—progress on the release of prisoners, the agreement with UNHCR on the return of refugees and exiles, the National Peace Accord and the repeal of discriminatory legislation—though they did not solve all the difficulties or result in an immediate end to violence, helped to create a new climate.

*375* On 27 October 1991, a Patriotic/United Front Conference was convened by the ANC and the PAC in Durban, and some 90 organizations attended. The participants adopted a Declaration which called for: a constituent assembly to draft and adopt a democratic constitution; a sovereign interim government or transitional authority; and an all-party congress or pre–constituent assembly meeting, brought together by independent and neutral convenors, to be held as soon as possible.

*376* Consultations followed and at a preparatory meeting held on 29 and 30 November—chaired by Judge Ismail Mohammed and Judge Petrus Schabort—19 political and other organizations decided unanimously or by "sufficient consensus" that the first meeting of a Convention for a Democratic South Africa (CODESA) would be held near Johannesburg on 20 and 21 December 1991. Participating delegations also agreed on a nine-point agenda for the Convention, on the establishment of a steering committee to facilitate its convening and on invitations to various international organizations to observe its proceedings.

*377* The PAC, however, dissociated itself from the final statement read by the two judges chairing the preparatory meeting, saying that it "did not reflect the PAC's position". Several PAC proposals, such as neutral international convenors, the holding of CODESA outside South Africa and the opening of CODESA's sessions to the media, had not been accepted by other parties.

*378* After discussing these developments, the General Assembly on 13 December 1991 adopted a resolution entitled "International efforts towards the total eradication of apartheid and support for the establishment of a united, non-racial and democratic South Africa".[125] The Assembly welcomed the National Peace Accord and the convening of the preparatory meeting for CODESA, including broad-based substantive negotiations towards an agreement on the basic principles of a new constitution. It also asked the international community, in view of

125/Document 147
*See page 436*

the progress made in overcoming obstacles to negotiation, "to resume academic, scientific and cultural links with democratic anti-apartheid organizations and the individuals in these fields, to resume sports links with unified non-racial sporting organizations of South Africa which have received endorsement by appropriate non-racial sporting organizations within South Africa and to assist disadvantaged athletes in that country".

## The negotiations

379    CODESA met in Johannesburg on 20 and 21 December 1991, with representatives from the Government and 19 political groups. (The IFP did not attend the meeting as the Steering Committee had not separately invited the Zulu King, Goodwill Zwelithini, to lead a delegation.) The United Nations, the OAU, the Movement of Non-Aligned Countries, the Commonwealth and the European Community were represented by observer delegations. Mrs. Sadako Ogata, United Nations High Commissioner for Refugees, and Professor Ibrahim Gambari, Nigeria's Permanent Representative to the United Nations and Chairman of the Special Committee against Apartheid, represented the United Nations.

380    At the first session of CODESA on 20 December, 17 of the 19 political groups signed a Declaration of Intent which stated:

"We, the duly authorized representatives of political parties, political organizations, administrations and the South African Government, coming together at this first meeting of the Convention for a Democratic South Africa, mindful of the awesome responsibility that rests on us at this moment in the history of our country, declare our solemn commitment:

"1. To bring about an undivided South Africa with one nation sharing a common citizenship, patriotism and loyalty, pursuing amid our diversity freedom, equality and security for all irrespective of race, colour, sex or creed; a country free from apartheid or any other form of discrimination or domination.

"2. To work to heal the divisions of the past, to secure the advancement of all and to establish a free and open society based on democratic values where the dignity, worth and rights of every South African are protected by law . . ."

381    The signatories agreed that South Africa would be a united, democratic, non-racial and non-sexist State, with an independent judiciary, universal suffrage and a bill of rights; and that South Africa would be a multi-party democracy in which the basic electoral system would be that of proportional representation. The Declaration also acknow-

ledged the diversity of languages, cultures and religions of the people whose human rights would be entrenched in the bill of rights. They solemnly committed themselves to be bound by the agreements of CODESA and to take steps to realize their implementation. (The PAC and the Conservative Party did not sign the Declaration.)

382    The following day, the Convention decided to set up five working groups to negotiate and report to the next CODESA plenary session on: political participation and the role of the international community; constitutional principles and the constitution-making body and process; transitional arrangements; the future of the "independent homelands" of Transkei, Bophuthatswana, Venda and Ciskei; and a time frame for implementation of decisions. The observer delegations from the United Nations and other international organizations said in a joint statement that "the broad objectives expressed in the Declaration of Intent are a most constructive and auspicious beginning for CODESA and give promise of attainment of true democracy for South Africa".

## Struggle for change

383    When I assumed the office of Secretary-General in January 1992, there were great hopes for a negotiated settlement in South Africa. At the same time there was little reason for euphoria. Violence was continuing on an alarming scale. Not all the requirements for a climate conducive to negotiations had been fully implemented.

384    There was a wide gulf between the positions of the parties, but CODESA had shown that there was also a keen desire for an agreement, a willingness to make accommodations in the interests of the future of the nation, and above all, there was a high degree of statesmanship.

385    I expressed my deeply held feelings in the light of my close interest in the South African situation over the years, when I addressed the Special Committee against Apartheid on 18 February 1992: "The system of apartheid in South Africa, which has rightly been on the agenda of the United Nations for many years, is crumbling under the combined pressure of internal and external forces. It is possible now to envisage a new society in South Africa—a society which respects human rights, a society which does not discriminate on grounds of colour, sex, political affiliation or creed; an undivided society in which economic wealth and opportunity are shared by all."[126]

126/Document 152
See page 442

386    I warned, however, of the need for vigilance and said that the Secretary-General and the Special Committee, in their mutually supportive roles, had the challenging duty to provide advice and assistance during the difficult transition.

387    The Government, concerned by the opposition of right-wing Whites to the negotiations, decided to hold a Whites-only referendum

on 17 March 1992 to determine support for the continuation of the negotiation process. About 86 per cent of the voters participated, with 68.7 per cent in favour of continuing with negotiations for a new constitutional dispensation and 31.3 per cent against. I welcomed the referendum results as a positive impetus for democratic reform, and said: "these results constitute a major step forward towards the eradication of apartheid and the creation of a new, non-racial society in South Africa, based on the respect of human rights".[127]

127/Document 153
*See page 443*

388    But hopes of greater progress after the referendum were not fulfilled. Although the CODESA working groups made great progress, some serious disagreements developed. Four of the groups reached consensus among the participants, subject to reservations, but the important Working Group 2 on constitutional principles and procedures was unable to reach any accord. There was consensus on a bill of rights, a governmental structure organized on a national, regional and local level, and effective participation by minority parties, but there was disagreement over the percentage of votes necessary for the adoption or amendment of the new constitution. The Government proposed that while the constitution as a whole, and each of its clauses, should be adopted by a majority of 66.7 per cent of the votes, the bill of rights and provisions dealing with the general constitutional principles should require a majority of 75 per cent for adoption, and provisions affecting the distribution of power between central, regional and local levels of government should require a special majority still to be agreed upon.

389    In March and April 1992, as the second plenary session of CODESA, or CODESA II, approached, there was an escalation of political violence. On 15 and 16 May 1992, CODESA II convened in Johannesburg to discuss the reports of the five working groups established by CODESA I. The United Nations was represented by an observer delegation led by Mr. Chinmaya R. Gharekhan, Permanent Representative of India to the United Nations. The ANC declined to accept a partial agreement, and since the issues addressed by the working groups were interrelated, none of the reports was considered at CODESA II. Participants mandated the Management Committee with resolving the outstanding issues and drafting legislation formalizing agreements reached thus far, so that a third session of CODESA could be convened.

390    After CODESA II ended in an impasse, the ANC and its allies decided on a four-phase plan of mass action, beginning on 16 June, which included marches, sit-ins and a general strike, to press for the establishment of an interim government and elections for a constituent assembly. On 17 June, the day after the mass action began, armed men attacked the township of Boipatong, leaving more than 40 people dead. Witnesses alleged that the violence had been perpetrated by residents of

a nearby hostel for migrant labourers and that members of the police had assisted them. Subsequently, the Goldstone Commission reported that there was no evidence of police collusion in the killings, but blamed the South African police for suffering from "organizational problems" such as inadequate command and control and lack of effective intelligence and contingency planning.

391    The ANC decided on 20 June to suspend its bilateral talks with the South African Government and its participation in the CODESA negotiations. It put forward 14 demands as preconditions to negotiations. They concerned the creation of an elected constituent assembly, the setting up of an interim government, the ending of all covert operations, the disbanding of all special forces and detachments made up of foreign nationals, the suspension and prosecution of all members of the security forces involved in the violence, the ending of repression in the homelands, the phasing out of hostels and the installation of fences around them, the banning of all dangerous weapons, the setting up of an international inquiry into acts of violence, the repeal of all repressive legislation and the release of all political prisoners.

## Causes and effects of violence

392    Violence in the country tended to disrupt the negotiations and create a crisis of confidence. Its increase, despite the National Peace Accord, was attributed by observers to several causes. There was violence by forces which opposed change, as well as by groups which had little confidence in obtaining sufficient support in democratic elections and, therefore, resorted to violence to gain attention and secure their objectives in talks prior to any elections. There was violence by some unpopular homeland governments to prevent campaigning, especially by the ANC, in areas under their control. There was also violence associated with unemployment and other socio-economic problems. As the Goldstone Commission pointed out in its interim report in May 1992: "the causes of the violence are many and complicated. They include economic, social and political imbalances among the people of South Africa. These are the consequences of three centuries of racial discrimination and over 40 years of extreme forms of racial and economic dislocations in consequence of the policy of apartheid."

393    While the cooperation of all political groups was essential to curb violence and ensure peaceful conditions, the primary responsibility for maintaining law and order remained with the Government. But there was widespread suspicion among anti-apartheid groups that the violence was also perpetrated, instigated, or condoned by secret agencies and elements in the security forces which had in the past been used to suppress resistance against apartheid and had resorted to assassinations and other crimes.

*394* Anti-apartheid groups accused the Government of reluctance or tardiness in addressing their concerns about the security forces. The complaints by the ANC and other anti-apartheid groups related particularly to secret agencies in the defence establishment, Battalions 31 and 32, the police unit Koevoet, which had been formed for the war in Namibia, and the Internal Stability Units of the South African Police. The ANC also complained of violence by the KwaZulu Police and the IFP in collusion with elements of the South African Police.

*395* President de Klerk announced in July 1992 that Battalions 31 and 32 would be disbanded and Koevoet dissolved, after the Goldstone Commission recommended that Battalion 32 "should not again be used for peace-keeping duties anywhere in South Africa" because of the violence it had committed against Africans. Even then there were long delays in the implementation of this announcement. Battalion 31 was disbanded only in March 1993 when its soldiers were transferred to other units in the northern Cape. Internal Stability Units were not replaced in the Johannesburg area, despite repeated complaints, until February 1994. When they were replaced, violence in the region declined sharply. In April 1994, after revelations by the Human Rights Commission, security forces raided a camp where thousands of IFP members received military training; they seized weapons and arrested persons suspected to be members of hit squads.

*396* Earlier, the Goldstone Commission had raided a military intelligence unit in November 1992 and seized files containing evidence of a campaign to discredit the ANC. On 19 December, President de Klerk announced that he was suspending or retiring 23 officers of the South African Defence Force (SADF), including two generals and four brigadiers, for illegal and unauthorized activities and misconduct.

*397* The Government took no action in KwaZulu until the Goldstone Commission released a report on 18 March 1994 disclosing the involvement of senior South African Police officers, senior officials of the KwaZulu Police and IFP officials in a conspiracy aimed at destabilizing the elections. The Goldstone report was widely seen as substantiating long-standing allegations of the involvement of members of the South African Police in the activities of a so-called "Third Force" which included assassinations of political opponents and organizing and training "hit squads".[128] Following the release of the report, President de Klerk suspended the officers named by the Commission from active duty. The Goldstone Commission also recommended prohibiting the carrying of dangerous weapons in public and the fencing off of hostels for migrant labourers. The IFP objected to these measures and, as a result, the Government took only partial action.

128/Document 215
*See page 511*

*398* Such tardiness by the authorities aroused suspicion that the Government was tolerating violence in order to prevent the formerly banned organizations from rebuilding their structures. Such concerns were deepened by a perception that elements of the ruling National Party were advocating partnership with the homeland governments and others to frustrate the demands for a united, non-racial democratic State and for genuine majority rule, thereby securing White minority rule in subtler forms through "group rights" and "power sharing" on racial lines.

399    By mid-1992, the ANC and its allies felt that their only recourse was to organize mass action at home and to seek international pressure on the regime. The ANC and the PAC appealed to both the OAU and the United Nations. The Assembly of Heads of State and Government of the OAU, meeting in Dakar from 29 June to 1 July, adopted a resolution condemning the escalation of violence in South Africa, especially the violence perpetrated against the population of Boipatong, and demanding a full and public investigation of that incident as well as other acts of violence. It called for the convening of an urgent meeting of the Security Council to consider the situation. It suggested that the United Nations become involved in exploring and creating conditions conducive to the resumption of negotiations.

400    The crisis posed a challenge which the United Nations was prepared to face. On my visit to the OAU session and to Nigeria during June, I had discussions with the Foreign Minister of South Africa, the Presidents of the ANC and the PAC and the Chairman of the IFP on the situation in South Africa and the constructive role the United Nations could play in facilitating an end to the violence and the resumption of negotiations.

401    In response to domestic and international pressure, the South African Government took some positive steps. Justice P. N. Bhagwati, former Chief Justice of India, was appointed to join the Goldstone Commission as an assessor. Mr. P. A. J. Waddington, Director of Criminal Justice Studies at Reading University, United Kingdom, was appointed to evaluate the police investigation of the Boipatong massacre. On 2 July, President de Klerk offered to lower the majority needed for changes in the constitution from 75 to 70 per cent.

402    Nevertheless, the situation remained grave and the Security Council met on 15 and 16 July 1992, at the request of African States, to consider "the question of South Africa", in particular the violence and the breakdown of negotiations. It heard representatives of the South African Government, the ANC and the PAC, and several other CODESA participants, including several representatives of homeland governments: Mr. Mangosuthu G. Buthelezi, Mr. Lucas M. Mangope, Brigadier Oupa J. Gqozo, Mr. J. N. Reddy, Mr. E. Joosab, Mr. Kenneth M. Andrew and Mr. E. E. Ngobeni at the request of the representative of South Africa; and Mr. Bantu Holomisa, Mr. Essop Pahad,

Mr. Philip Mahlangu and Mr. Manguezi Zitha at the request of the representative of India. After two days of deliberations, in which 48 Member States addressed the Council, the Security Council unanimously adopted resolution 765 (1992),[129] in which the Council emphasized the responsibility of the South African authorities to stop the violence and protect the life and property of all South Africans, and stressed the need for all parties to exercise restraint and cooperate in combating violence. It also underlined the importance of having all parties cooperate to resume the negotiating process as speedily as possible.

129/Document 156
See page 444

*403* In the same resolution the Security Council invited me to appoint a Special Representative to South Africa to recommend, after discussion with the relevant parties, "measures which would assist in bringing an effective end to the violence and in creating conditions for negotiations leading towards a peaceful transition to a democratic, non-racial and united South Africa". Finally, the Council decided to "remain seized of the matter until a democratic, non-racial and united South Africa is established".

## Mission of Mr. Cyrus Vance

*404* Immediately after the adoption of the resolution, I appointed Mr. Cyrus Vance, former United States Secretary of State, as my Special Representative to South Africa. Mr. Vance visited South Africa from 21 to 31 July, accompanied by Mr. Virendra Dayal, a former Under-Secretary-General of the United Nations. The two held discussions with the Government, representatives of all major parties, key politicians, church groups, business and trade union organizations, and leaders of structures set up by the National Peace Accord.

*405* While the mission was in South Africa, Mr. Vance arranged a meeting between the Justice Minister and the ANC on the problem of political prisoners. Also during the mission's presence, the ANC, the South African Communist Party and COSATU reached an agreement with the South African Police on the principles outlined by a panel of experts regarding the control of mass demonstrations. Nevertheless, several church leaders and others expressed concern that the general strike planned by the ANC and its allies for 3 and 4 August might lead to violence. At the suggestion of Mr. Mandela, and after discussions between Mr. Vance and the Government, I sent an appeal to the main parties to make every effort to stave off violence and, with their full approval, sent a team of 10 observers.[130] They were deployed in various provinces during the week of mass action, and it was generally agreed that their presence had a salutary effect.

130/Document 157
See page 445

*406* On 7 August, I submitted a report to the Security Council on Mr. Vance's mission.[131] I said that I had been profoundly impressed by the open and responsive manner in which the United Nations delegation

131/Document 158
See page 445

was received by all sectors of society. This was further evidence of a transformation taking place in South Africa as its leaders and peoples strove to create a democratic, non-racial and united country. I added, nevertheless, that decades of apartheid had left a painful legacy of distrust and anguish and that violence must be brought under control and conditions established to ensure the success of the negotiating process. To this end, the unanimous adoption of resolution 765 (1992) had "heightened expectations that the continuous involvement of the Security Council in this new phase of South Africa's evolution will be marked by understanding and a readiness to contribute constructively to the process of peaceful change."

407    I then made a series of recommendations to support the efforts of the Goldstone Commission and to strengthen the mechanisms created by the National Peace Accord, to deal with the problem of violence. In that context, I recommended that the United Nations make some observers available to serve in South Africa in close association with the National Peace Secretariat, which was overseeing the Accord.

408    Referring to the question of political prisoners who remained in detention, I said: "It is essential that this painful problem should be expeditiously resolved. If so handled, it would, in a bold and humane gesture, do much to bury the past and to clean the slate of distrust."

409    The Security Council, by its resolution 772 (1992), adopted unanimously on 17 August 1992, called upon the South African Government and all parties in South Africa to implement my recommendations.[132] It authorized me "to deploy, as a matter of urgency, United Nations observers in South Africa, in such a manner and in such numbers as he determines necessary to address effectively the areas of concern noted in his report, in coordination with the structures set up under the National Peace Accord". It invited me to assist in the strengthening of the structures set up under the National Peace Accord in consultation with the relevant parties, and requested me to report to the Security Council quarterly, or more frequently if necessary, on the implementation of the resolution. It also called upon international organizations such as the OAU, the Commonwealth and the European Community to consider deploying their own observers in South Africa in coordination with the United Nations and the structures set up under the National Peace Accord.

410    Thus began the active and coordinated involvement of three of the principal organs of the United Nations—the Security Council, the General Assembly and the Secretariat—working in harmony as catalysts in promoting peace and reconciliation in South Africa. The resolutions of the Security Council, as well as the principal resolutions of the General Assembly on the implementation of the 1989 Declaration against Apartheid were adopted unanimously, thus carrying great weight.

132/Document 160
See page 448

## United Nations Observer Mission in South Africa

*411* On 9 September 1992, in consultation with the Security Council, I issued a directive deploying 50 observers in South Africa and in a letter sent on 21 September to the Minister for Foreign Affairs I requested the Government of South Africa to extend all privileges and immunities necessary for the execution of their responsibilities.[133] I named Ms. Angela King, Director of the United Nations Office of Human Resource Management, Chief of the United Nations Observer Mission in South Africa (UNOMSA); she took up her post on 23 September.[134] By the end of October, UNOMSA observers were deployed in all 11 regions of South Africa designated in the National Peace Accord and the full complement of 50 observers was in the field by the end of November. In response to representations by parties in South Africa, the number of UNOMSA observers was increased to 60 in February 1993, and to 100 in October of that year.

*412* UNOMSA headquarters were in Johannesburg, with a regional office in Durban; deployment of observers was weighted towards the Witwatersrand and KwaZulu/Natal regions where 70 per cent of the political violence was occurring. The Mission's objective was to strengthen the structures of the National Peace Accord to end violence in the country. The Mission was to coordinate its work and cooperate with the National Peace Committee—composed of senior representatives of all the signatories to the Peace Accord—as well as regional and local peace committees, the National Peace Secretariat, and the Goldstone Commission.

*413* UNOMSA observers worked to ensure that demonstrations, marches, rallies, funerals and other forms of mass action were adequately planned and that the Goldstone Commission guidelines for marches and political gatherings were respected. They held hundreds of informal meetings and often acted as channels of communication between groups across the political and social spectrum. They attended meetings of the local and regional peace committees and other structures established under the National Peace Accord and lent full support to their activities. They attended the Goldstone Commission hearings at which a UNOMSA jurist participated as an objective commentator. Several members of the UNOMSA team with the requisite legal background were also assigned to the Commission, in addition to performing other duties. UNOMSA observers had attended more than 9,000 meetings and events by the end of 1993.

*414* They worked in close consultation with observers from the Commonwealth, the European Union and the OAU, and served as a channel of communication and coordination among international observer missions. The international observer teams established close working relationships, exchanged information and frequently observed

133/Document 164
See page 451

134/ Document 166
See page 452

events and meetings as mixed teams. UNOMSA observers were well received by the structures established under the National Peace Accord, as well as by the Government and major political parties; they frequently played an effective role in easing tensions.

415    The observers' field reports helped the Chief of Mission in her interventions with senior Government officials, the security forces, political organizations and other entities to bring potential flashpoints to the attention of decision-makers and help avert or defuse crises. As UNOMSA was a completely civilian mission, observers' personal security depended largely on their own good judgement and on the goodwill of the South African communities in which they worked. There was never a deliberate physical attack on any member of the international observer missions.

### Resumption of talks

416    United Nations intervention helped restore confidence that violence could be brought under control and facilitated the resumption of talks between the Government and the other parties, particularly the ANC. Representatives of the Government and the ANC—Mr. Roelf Meyer, Minister of Constitutional Development, and Mr. Cyril Ramaphosa, ANC Secretary-General—held a series of meetings beginning on 21 August 1992, with a view to removing obstacles to the resumption of negotiations and making way for a summit meeting between President de Klerk and Mr. Mandela. They agreed on the need for a democratically elected constituent assembly or constitution-making body, to be bound only by agreed-upon constitutional principles.

417    The Government and the ANC also agreed that during the interim or transitional period, the constituent assembly should also act as an interim or transitional parliament and that there should be an interim or transitional government of national unity. This government would function within a transitional constitutional framework which would provide for national and regional government and would incorporate guaranteed, justiciable rights and freedoms.

418    The two parties agreed that all those whose imprisonment was related to past political conflict and whose release could make a contribution to reconciliation should be freed by 15 November. Taking into account the reports of the Goldstone Commission, they also decided upon measures to deal with the problem of violence. Both sides then committed themselves to the strengthening of the Peace Accord process, to calm tensions and to promote reconciliation in South Africa.

419    Nevertheless, the ANC, while noting with satisfaction the Government's moves towards accepting the idea of a democratic constituent assembly, was concerned about repression in the homelands,

especially Ciskei and Bophuthatswana, and planned mass action there. On 7 September 1992, the Ciskeian security forces fired on demonstrators from the ANC and allied organizations who were marching on the homeland's capital, Bisho, killing at least 28 and wounding some 200 more. The President of the Security Council issued a statement on 10 September deploring the shootings, and urging everyone to exercise maximum restraint in order to help break the spiralling cycle of violence.[135]

135/Document 162
*See page 450*

420    After the shootings, I wrote to Justice Goldstone to convey my hope that the United Nations could contribute to a reduction of tensions, and to commend the important work being undertaken by his Commission.[136] The Goldstone Commission investigated the Ciskei killings and issued a report on 29 September in which it described the indiscriminate shooting of the demonstrators as "morally and legally indefensible". It called on the Ciskeian authorities to investigate criminal charges against the officials responsible for the massacre. It also invited the leaders of the ANC alliance to censure those members who had exposed the demonstrators to danger. Meanwhile, the ANC had deferred its planned march on Bophuthatswana.

136/Document 163
*See page 450*

421    I also addressed messages to President de Klerk and Mr. Mandela encouraging them to overcome any obstacles and meet.[137] I felt that such a meeting would be a source of immense relief to all South Africans. On 26 September 1992, three days before the Goldstone Commission issued its report, the two leaders did meet in Johannesburg. They approved a Record of Understanding reached in the talks between the representatives of the Government and the ANC. They agreed that this summit had laid a basis for the resumption of negotiations. They decided to hold further meetings in order to address matters which had not been resolved at the summit, namely: creating a climate of free political activity; repealing security and other repressive legislation; ending covert operations by special forces; and quelling violence.

137/Document 165
*See page 452*

422    That same day, the Government announced the immediate release of 150 political prisoners and indicated that the remaining political prisoners would be freed by 15 November, when 42 more were released. The National Council of Indemnity said that more information was needed about the circumstances of 22 other prisoners before it could determine if they qualified for release as those "who had committed crimes with political motivation and whose release could contribute to reconciliation and peace".[138]

138/Document 170
*See page 454*

423    Meanwhile, beginning in August, the Government and the PAC had held exploratory discussions. After a two-day summit on 24 October in Gaborone, they issued a joint statement of agreement on matters such as the peaceful resolution of political conflicts; the exertion of maximum efforts to end the violence; the need for a new, non-racial

constitution to be drawn up by a body elected from a common voters' roll; and the establishment of a more representative negotiating forum. A further meeting scheduled for 9 December was postponed, pending a clarification from the PAC on the stand of its military unit regarding violence against Whites.

424 Although the new agreements between the Government and the ANC were a breakthrough in the negotiating process, there were objections from some of the other parties. In particular, on 27 September, IFP President Chief Mangosuthu Gatsha Buthelezi denounced the agreements and again rejected the concept of a constituent assembly. In the following months, the Concerned South Africans Group (COSAG), composed of representatives from the IFP, the Conservative Party, the Afrikaner Volksunie and the homelands of KwaZulu, Bophuthatswana and Ciskei, was founded to express their concern at the agreements being reached, or likely to be reached, between the Government and the ANC.

139/Document 168
See page 453;
Document 169
See page 454

425 I appealed then to all leaders to make a renewed and determined effort to end the violence, move the peace process forward and set the tone for national reconciliation. In separate letters to Chief Buthelezi and Mr. Mandela in September, I suggested that a meeting between the two men could set the tone for national reconciliation.[139] I wrote to both leaders again in November.[140] President de Klerk, for his part, held several bilateral talks, and on 10 December met with the leaders of KwaZulu, Bophuthatswana and Ciskei, but no agreement was reached.

140/Document 173
See page 459;
Document 174
See page 459

### United Nations fact-finding missions

426 The United Nations followed developments closely. I designated two Special Envoys to South Africa after the Vance mission. Mr. Virendra Dayal, who had been part of Mr. Vance's mission in July, visited South Africa from 16 to 27 September 1992. Ambassador Tom Vraalsen, Assistant Secretary-General of the Ministry of Foreign Affairs of Norway and former Permanent Representative of Norway to the United Nations, was in the country from 22 November to 9 December 1992.

427 During their respective missions, the Special Envoys had discussions with senior Government officials and representatives of various political parties. They also met with officials of the National Peace Committee and Secretariat; representatives of non-governmental organizations and civic, religious, business, human rights and community groups; and other international observer teams. Their findings were incorporated into my report to the Security Council of 22 December 1992, in which I observed that there was substantial agreement on expediting arrangements for multi-party negotiations in South

Africa.[141] That trend, I said, should be encouraged by the international community. I reiterated my call to all South African political leaders to take immediate action to curb violence and cooperate fully with the Goldstone Commission.

428    In a resolution adopted on 18 December 1992—resolution 47/116 A—the General Assembly urged "the representatives of the people of South Africa to resume, without further delay, broad-based negotiations on transitional arrangements and basic principles for a process of reaching agreement on a new democratic and non-racial constitution and for its speedy entry into force".[142]

141/Document 176
*See page 462*

142/Document 175
*See page 460*

### Negotiations resume

429    There were extensive discussions in South Africa on the resumption of negotiations. A delegation of the Special Committee against Apartheid, led by its Chairman, Prof. Ibrahim Gambari, visited South Africa for 10 days in March 1993 and held broad-based consultations with high-ranking members of all the major parties in the political process. Representatives from 26 parties and organizations held a two-day, multi-party planning conference on 5 and 6 March, thus ending a 10-month deadlock. They agreed to start new multi-party negotiations. The planning conference also accepted a deadlock-breaking mechanism that was lacking in CODESA, i.e., all decisions would be taken by consensus, but if that could not be achieved, the conference would use "sufficient consensus". The Conservative Party abstained on the resolution incorporating the agreement. The Azanian People's Organization (AZAPO) and the Afrikaner Weerstandsbeweging (AWB) were not present and refused to participate in the multi-party talks.

430    I wrote to both President de Klerk and Mr. Mandela on 9 March to register the satisfaction of the United Nations at the successful conclusion of the multi-party conference and to express my confidence that the next round of meetings would be equally successful.[143] I assured them of the United Nations' continuing commitment to help South Africa's transition to non-racial democracy.

143/Document 178
*See page 471*

431    On 1 April 1993, delegations from the same 26 political parties and organizations began discussions. On 22 June, this Multi-party Negotiating Council, as it was called, adopted a Declaration on the cessation of hostilities, the armed struggle and violence, and a resolution on conditions necessary to eliminate violence.

432    On 2 July 1993, the Negotiating Council, meeting at a plenary session, adopted by consensus 27 constitutional principles which, along with a bill of rights, would be included in both the interim constitution and the final constitution to be adopted by an elected constituent assembly. It also decided, by sufficient consensus, that non-racial democratic elections for a constituent assembly would be

held on 27 April 1994. Representatives of Bophuthatswana, Ciskei, KwaZulu, the IFP and the Conservative Party opposed the date and withdrew from the talks. The process continued, however, while the Government and the ANC tried to engage them in bilateral talks. I wrote to Chief Buthelezi on 6 August urging him and the IFP to return to the negotiations so as to help move the peace process forward.[144] In October, however, the IFP, the Conservative Party and their allies formed a "Freedom Alliance" and remained outside the negotiating process.

144/Document 183
See page 475

433    The South African Parliament on 23 September passed a bill providing for the creation of a Transitional Executive Council (TEC) to oversee Government operations and preparations for elections. On the same day, in New York, I met President de Klerk and congratulated him on this historic decision.[145] I also informed him of my intention to increase the strength of UNOMSA. The next day, also in New York, at a meeting of the Special Committee against Apartheid, Mr. Mandela said: "The countdown to democracy in South Africa has begun. The date for the demise of the White minority regime has been determined, agreed and set." He appealed to the international community to lift economic sanctions against South Africa in response to these historic advances. The OAU supported his request.[146]

145/Document 185
See page 476

146/Document 186
See page 477

434    On my visit to Maputo from 18 to 20 October, I took the opportunity to meet South African political leaders, including Foreign Affairs Minister Roelof Botha and Chief Buthelezi of the IFP. In these discussions, I underlined the importance that the United Nations attached to the peace process and, in my meeting with Chief Buthelezi, I urged the Freedom Alliance to participate in the election process.[147]

147/Document 192
See page 482

435    On 18 November 1993, after protracted negotiations, the Multi-party Negotiating Council decided, at a plenary session, to establish several election-related institutions and adopted an Interim Constitution. The institutions included, in addition to the Transitional Executive Council, the Independent Electoral Commission (IEC), the Independent Media Commission (IMC) and the Independent Broadcasting Authority (IBA). The five parties of the Freedom Alliance, which had withdrawn from the Negotiating Council in July, did not attend the plenary session.

436    The TEC, which was to remain in existence until the Interim Constitution entered into force on 27 April 1994, was to facilitate, in conjunction with all existing legislative and executive governmental structures at the national, regional and local levels, the transition to, and preparation for, the implementation of a democratic system of government by holding free and fair elections. The Interim Constitution contained a Bill of Rights guaranteeing fundamental human rights such as equality of race and gender; freedom of speech, assembly and movement; the right to vote; the right to a fair trial; and the right not to be

## South Africa: new provinces

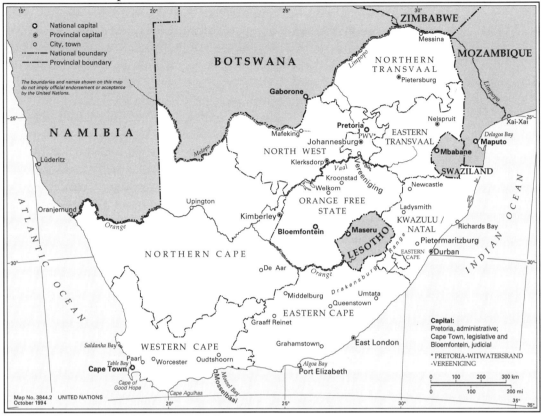

The Interim Constitution, agreed in November 1993, established nine provinces,
each of which has a legislature, administrative structures and an executive council.

exposed to torture or inhuman punishment. It stipulated that the new
South Africa would be divided into nine regions, each of which would
have a legislature, administrative structures and an executive council.

*437* The Interim Constitution also provided that Parliament
would consist of a 400-member National Assembly elected on the basis
of proportional representation and a 90-member Senate elected by the
nine regional legislatures. The Assembly and Senate, at a joint sitting,
would form the Constituent Assembly whose main task would be to
draft, during the first two years of a five-year transition period, a final
constitution for the country. The Head of State would be an Executive
President elected by the National Assembly. A Government of National
Unity would be composed, on the basis of proportional representation,
of nominees of political parties which had obtained 5 per cent or more
of the vote in the elections and which would remain in office until 1999.
Cabinet decisions would be made by consensus in a manner which

would give consideration to the spirit underlying the concept of a government of national unity as well as the need for the effective administration of the country. A Constitutional Court would have final jurisdiction in matters pertaining to the interpretation, protection and enforcement of the Interim Constitution. Constitutional Court decisions would be final.

*438*    The TEC began its work on 6 December 1993. Nine days later, the South African Parliament voted to restore citizenship to the estimated 10 million residents of the "independent homelands" of Transkei, Bophuthatswana, Venda and Ciskei. That same month, the South African Parliament adopted the Interim Constitution, as well as bills to enact the agreements reached by the Multi-party Negotiating Council.

*439*    Earlier, on 2 December, the South African Minister for Foreign Affairs, Mr. Roelof Botha had written to me suggesting that immediate consideration be given to advance planning in order to ensure that the United Nations would be in a position to mount an effective operation when the IEC and TEC became operational. In my reply of 3 December, I informed him of my decision, following consultations with the OAU, European Union and the Commonwealth, to send a survey mission to South Africa for a period of 10 days for consultations in order to facilitate preparatory arrangements for a United Nations role in the electoral process.[148]

148/Document 191
*See page 481*

## Embargoes lifted

*440*    During the latter months of 1993, the United Nations, welcoming the agreements reached in South Africa, began the process of ending the country's international isolation. A first step was the dismantling of the economic embargoes so arduously built up over the previous decades. The Special Committee against Apartheid had already discontinued the registers of sports and cultural boycotts of South Africa in February 1993. On 8 October, the General Assembly called upon States to terminate restrictions on economic relations with South Africa immediately, and end the oil embargo once the Transitional Executive Council in South Africa became operational.[149] On 23 November, the President of the Security Council issued a statement on the Council's behalf welcoming the successful completion of the Multi-party Negotiating Process and the conclusion of relevant agreements. It also invited me to accelerate contingency planning for a possible United Nations role in the South African electoral process.[150] On 9 December 1993, the General Assembly repealed its oil embargo.[151] On 20 December, it revoked the mandate of the Intergovernmental Group to Monitor the Supply and Shipping of Oil and Petroleum Products to South Africa.[152]

149/Document 187
*See page 480*

150/Document 190
*See page 481*

151/Document 193
*See page 484*

152/Document 196
*See page 487*

*441*    Also on 20 December 1993, the General Assembly adopted a resolution on "International efforts towards the total eradication of apartheid and support for the establishment of a united, non-racial and democratic South Africa".[153] The Assembly strongly urged the South African authorities to: exercise the primary responsibility in ending the ongoing violence; protect the lives, security and property of all South Africans; and promote and protect South Africans' right to participate in the democratic process, including the right to demonstrate peacefully in public, organize and participate in political rallies, run for election and participate in the elections without intimidation.

153/Document 194
See page 484

442    The General Assembly also urged all parties in South Africa, including those which had not participated fully in the multi-party talks, to respect agreements reached during the negotiations, recommit themselves to democratic principles, take part in the elections, and resolve outstanding issues by peaceful means.

443    The electoral process in South Africa commenced with the December 1993 inauguration of the TEC. The Government and the ANC, with the support of the United Nations, not only made preparations for free and fair elections, but also tried to persuade all other parties to cooperate in the process. The Freedom Alliance had decided not to participate in the TEC and to boycott the elections unless their demands for stronger powers for provincial governments, creation of an Afrikaner *volkstaat*, or separate region, and separate ballots for elections to the national and provincial legislatures were met. On 20 January 1994, Ciskei left the Freedom Alliance, joined the TEC and announced that it would take part in the elections. The PAC did not participate in the TEC because of the Government's continuing control over the security forces. However, the PAC announced the suspension of its armed struggle on 16 January 1994 and participated in the electoral process.

## National elections

444    At its first meeting, on 7 December 1993, the Transitional Executive Council endorsed a resolution adopted the previous day by the Multi-party Negotiating Council asking the United Nations to provide a sufficient number of international observers to monitor the electoral process. It appealed to the United Nations to coordinate, in close cooperation with the IEC, the deployment of international observers provided by the OAU, the European Union, the Commonwealth, Governments and non-governmental organizations.

445    On 9 December, I dispatched a survey team to South Africa to assess the needs of the United Nations in carrying out these requests. After consultation with the Security Council, I appointed Mr. Lakhdar Brahimi, former Minister for Foreign Affairs of Algeria, as my Special Representative for South Africa. The Special Representative's task was

to assist me in the implementation of relevant Security Council resolutions and decisions concerning South Africa and to coordinate the activities of other international observers, as requested by the TEC. Mr. Brahimi visited South Africa from 16 to 23 December 1993 and consulted extensively with the Government, the TEC, political parties, an IEC delegation—led by its Chairman, Judge Johann C. Kriegler—intergovernmental observer missions, leaders of the national peace structures, members of the diplomatic community in South Africa and leading individuals. He was also briefed by the United Nations survey team.

154/Document 199
*See page 489*

446    After considering Mr. Brahimi's findings, I submitted a detailed report to the Security Council on 10 January 1994.[154] It contained recommendations on United Nations assistance during the electoral process. I noted that, owing to the delay in the establishment of electoral structures, the elections would be organized under intense pressure of time. I proposed that the mandate of UNOMSA be expanded to include election observing. In this new context, UNOMSA would have a significant role not only in assessing the ultimate freedom and fairness of the elections, but also in monitoring the electoral process at every stage.

447    UNOMSA would establish a direct relationship with the IEC and offer constructive suggestions. It would report any irregularities to the electoral authorities and, when appropriate, ask the electoral authorities to take remedial action. UNOMSA would continue to cooperate with the structures established under the National Peace Accord, but its mandate would have to be expanded to include: observation of IEC activities and verification of the adequacy of voter education efforts; verification that qualified voters were not denied documents that would enable them to vote; and new responsibilities related to coordination. I suggested the creation of a coordinating committee comprising the chiefs of the four intergovernmental observer missions.

448    Efforts would be made to establish a cooperative relationship with foreign non-governmental organizations, which were expected to send a large number of observers, especially in the days prior to the elections. I indicated that I would create a special Trust Fund, made up of voluntary contributions, to finance the participation of observers from African and developing countries so that there would be a balance in the geographical distribution of foreign observers. As there would be a very large number of polling-stations, I suggested arrangements which would take into account the distances to be travelled in rural areas and the fact that violence was concentrated in certain places. Mobile teams of observers would cover several polling-stations in areas where expectations of violence were low. However, in districts with a history of violence, one observer would be assigned to each polling-station.

*449*    On 14 January 1994, the Security Council adopted resolution 894 (1994) welcoming my report of 10 January 1994 and endorsing my proposals.[155] The General Assembly then adopted resolution 48/233 on 21 January 1994.[156] It commended my prompt response to the request in resolution 48/159 A, noted with satisfaction Security Council resolution 894 (1994) and encouraged Member States to respond positively to my call for election observers. It again urged all parties in South Africa, including those which had not participated fully in the multi-party talks, to respect agreements reached during the negotiations, adhere to democratic principles and take part in the elections. It also called on them to promote the full participation of all South Africans in the democratic process by exercising restraint and by refraining from acts of violence and intimidation, and to respect the safety and security of the international observers. It requested the South African authorities to protect the rights of all South Africans to be able to participate in peaceful public manifestations and political rallies, run for election and vote in an atmosphere free of intimidation. The General Assembly approved an expenditure of $38.9 million for UNOMSA operations, to be financed from the regular budget of the United Nations.

155/Document 200
*See page 502*

156/Document 201
*See page 503*

## Role of UNOMSA in the election process

*450*    UNOMSA's mandate was expanded for electoral observing. Mr. Lakhdar Brahimi, my Special Representative for South Africa, directed UNOMSA during the election process. Ms. Angela King, who had served as UNOMSA's Chief of Mission from its initial deployment in 1992, was designated Deputy Special Representative.

*451*    The broader mandate required UNOMSA to: (*a*) observe the actions of the IEC and its organs, verifying their compatibility with the conduct of a free and fair election; (*b*) observe the extent of freedom of organization, movement, assembly and expression during the electoral campaign; (*c*) monitor the compliance of the security forces with the requirements of the relevant laws and decisions of the TEC; (*d*) verify the satisfactory implementation of the relevant parts of the Independent Media Commission and the Independent Broadcasting Authority Acts; (*e*) verify that the voter education efforts of the electoral authorities and other interested parties were sufficient; (*f*) verify that qualified voters were not denied the identification documents or temporary voter's cards that would allow them to exercise their right to vote; (*g*) verify that voting occurred on election days in an environment free of intimidation and in conditions which ensured free access to voting stations and the secrecy of vote, and verify that adequate measures were taken to ensure proper transport and custody of ballots, security of the vote count and timely announcement of the results; and (*h*) coordinate the activities of all election observers.

## UNOMSA: deployment of observers, as of 24 March 1994

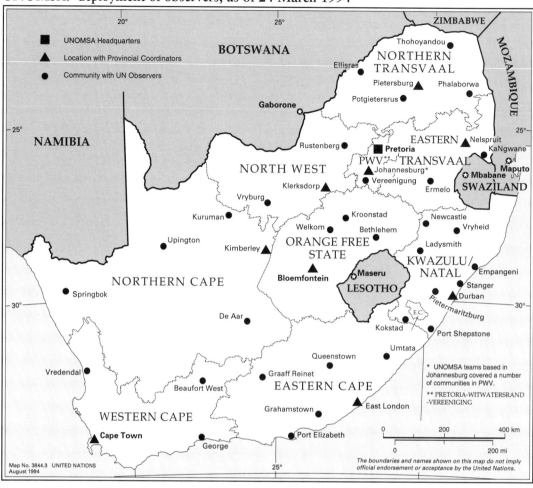

By March 1994, some 500 United Nations observers operated from more than 40 localities throughout the country, assisting in the implementation of the 1991 National Peace Accord. In April, they were joined by more than 1,600 additional international electoral observers.

452    UNOMSA thus had a significant role not only in assessing the ultimate freedom and fairness of the elections but also in monitoring the electoral process at every stage.

453    The deployment of the observers proceeded rapidly. By the end of March, 500 observers were in some 60 IEC operational locations. They included 200 United Nations volunteers from 44 countries who arrived on 18 March; 55 per cent of the volunteers were nationals of African countries. The United Nations also concluded bilateral agreements with the Governments of Finland, the Netherlands, Sweden and Switzerland regarding the provision of electoral observers for UNOMSA. In the final phase of deployment, from 17 April onward, over 1,600 additional international electoral observers joined UNOMSA, thus making a total of 2,120 United Nations observers. Other intergovernmental organizations provided 596 international elec-

toral observers—the OAU, 150, the Commonwealth, 120, and the European Union, 326. Individual Governments provided 600 observers and 97 non-governmental organizations provided about 3,000 observers. They included nearly 400 parliamentarians deployed by the Association of West European Parliamentarians for Action against Apartheid. UNOMSA shared briefing and logistical information with them.

454    UNOMSA had two operating arms—a Peace Promotion Division and an Electoral Division. Under the latter, three bodies were established to coordinate the activities of intergovernmental observer missions: a Coordinating Committee, composed of the heads of the four international observer missions; a Technical Task Force, to oversee all technical electoral matters; and a Joint Operations Unit, to coordinate logistical and training support for international observers.

455    Mr. Brahimi and his staff met regularly with representatives of virtually all political organizations, to impress upon them the importance the international community attached to achieving a peaceful transition to democracy. UNOMSA officials continued to interact with political parties, attend rallies and other public events, investigate instances of intimidation and related complaints and work closely with the IEC and national, regional and local peace structures. Information provided by UNOMSA to IEC observers and monitors, both before and during the elections, helped the IEC to address many problems.

456    As the election days approached, it became clear that South Africa's first non-racial democratic elections would be the most closely observed in history. Every stage of the process was to be subject to the fullest possible verification.

457    By 12 February 1994, 19 political parties had complied with the deadline for registration for the elections, but these did not include members of the Freedom Alliance. Since some political parties continued to oppose the elections, politically inspired violence continued to take a high toll in human lives. The Government, the ANC and public figures made concerted efforts, with the encouragement of the United Nations, to bring all parties into the democratic process, to avert the threat of violence and to ensure the success of the elections.

458    On 16 February 1994, Mr. Mandela announced that in order to avoid any postponement of the elections, ensure the integrity and sovereignty of South Africa and address the fears of those parties that felt left out of the process, the ANC had agreed to certain amendments to the Interim Constitution. These were: inclusion of a constitutional principle on self-determination, as well as provisions for a mechanism and process for the consideration of the issue of an Afrikaner *volkstaat*; amendment of the Electoral Act to enable voters to cast two ballots, one for national and one for provincial representatives; and amendment of the Interim Constitution to provide for:  provincial finances based on

agreements reached in negotiations with the Freedom Alliance; allowing provinces, in drafting provincial constitutions, to determine their own legislative and executive structures; ensuring that powers granted in the Interim Constitution were not substantially diminished when the Constituent Assembly drafted the final Constitution; authorizing the democratically elected provincial legislatures to decide on names for their provinces; and renaming the province of Natal "KwaZulu/Natal".

*459*  On 21 February, the Multi-party Negotiating Council approved these amendments to the Interim Constitution and the Electoral Act; they were enacted on 2 March by Parliament, which had been reconvened for that purpose. The deadline for registration was extended to 4 March to encourage more parties to take part. On 1 March, Mr. Mandela met Chief Buthelezi. They indicated that they would resolve their differences through international mediation, and the IFP agreed provisionally to register for the elections.[157] On 2 March, I congratulated both men on the initiatives they had taken to promote reconciliation and peace.[158] By midnight of 4 March, 10 additional parties had registered, including the IFP, bringing the total of registered parties to 29. Meanwhile, from 26 February to 6 March, a mission of the Special Committee against Apartheid, led by its Chairman, Prof. Ibrahim Gambari, again visited South Africa to encourage party leaders in their efforts to bring all parties into the process and to conduct the elections as scheduled in an atmosphere free from violence and intimidation.

157/Document 203
*See page 504*

158/Document 204
*See page 505*

*460*  The Freedom Alliance recognized the amendments to the Interim Constitution and Electoral Act as positive but rejected the package; it argued that too much power remained in the hands of the central Government and that the changes failed to guarantee the creation of an Afrikaner *volkstaat* after the elections. However, the Alliance soon began to disintegrate. General Constand Viljoen, co-leader of the Afrikaner Volksfront, resigned as Chairman of the Alliance and registered a new party, the Freedom Front, for the elections. Individual members of the Conservative Party were included in its list of candidates. On 23 April, Gen. Viljoen signed an accord with the South African Government and the ANC on behalf of the Freedom Front. The signatories agreed to address the idea of Afrikaner self-determination, including the concept of a *volkstaat*, through negotiations, and the Freedom Front undertook to seek a non-racial *volkstaat* based on democratic principles and human rights. The South African Government and the ANC agreed that votes cast for the Freedom Front in the elections would be considered to reflect a desire for Afrikaner self-determination.

*461*  Meanwhile, in cooperation with the South African Government, the TEC took a series of steps to reincorporate the homelands into

South Africa, to ensure that all political parties could campaign freely in those territories without intimidation and to enable the IEC to establish the necessary infrastructure for the holding of elections. In Bophuthatswana, the Chief Minister, Mr. Lucas Mangope, a member of the Freedom Alliance, had announced a boycott of the elections. Despite warnings from the TEC, he prevented the ANC from campaigning in the homeland and rejected a request by the IEC to allow campaigning and polling there.

462    Mr. Mangope's attitude provoked widespread protests in Bophuthatswana. In early March, following a strike by civil servants, huge demonstrations took place. Protesters demanded the immediate reincorporation of the territory into South Africa; many people were killed or injured. Some 3,000 heavily armed right-wing Whites entered the homeland to assist Mr. Mangope. They took over the air force base with his approval. However, disagreements arose between the leaders of two factions; one group killed or wounded a number of civilians before leaving the homeland in confusion. Mr. Mangope fled the capital. The South African Defence Force then intervened and escorted from the area some 2,000 right-wingers stranded at the air force base. Mr. Mangope was removed from office on 13 March. The next day, the TEC appointed an administrator to oversee the territory until the elections. A week later, South Africa assumed direct control of the administration of Ciskei following a mutiny by police and defence force members and the resignation of Ciskei leader Brigadier Oupa Gqozo.

463    The ANC and the Government made intensive efforts to persuade the IFP and the Zulu King, Goodwill Zwelithini, to join the electoral process so that elections could be held in KwaZulu/Natal in an atmosphere free of fear, intimidation and violence. These efforts were complicated when the King rejected the Interim Constitution and demanded sovereignty over the entire province of KwaZulu/Natal. Although the IFP had registered provisionally for the elections before the 4 March deadline, it did not submit a list of candidates by 16 March, a date established purposely to accommodate parties that registered late.

464    There was an escalation of violence in KwaZulu/Natal, with attempts to prevent voter education and electioneering. The number of deaths rose from 180 in February to 311 in March. Some electoral workers became the targets of attacks. On 18 March, the Goldstone Commission released a report asserting the complicity of senior South African, IFP and KwaZulu police officials in political violence aimed at destabilizing the elections. There was also violence in downtown Johannesburg on 28 March when several thousand armed supporters of the IFP and the Zulu King marched through the area. During clashes with ANC supporters and officials, 53 people were reported killed and several hundred more wounded.

465    The IFP demanded that the elections be postponed pending a negotiated settlement of the question of Zulu sovereignty. In the absence of such an agreement, it warned, South Africa would descend into "ungovernability and violence beyond control".

466    On 29 March, the President of the Security Council issued a statement on behalf of the Council's members. It deplored the violence as being clearly aimed at derailing the transition process, called upon all the people of South Africa to eschew violence and reiterated the importance the Council attached to "the holding of the first general, free and democratic elections in South Africa". That same day, my Special Representative and the heads of the missions of the OAU, the Commonwealth and the European Union called a press conference in Johannesburg. They issued a statement deploring the needless violence and loss of life and expressing their "deepening concern over the impact of 'war talk', threats and challenges that are calculated to unleash emotions in the population".

467    As tensions increased, President de Klerk, in consultation with the TEC, declared a state of emergency in KwaZulu/Natal on 31 March and deployed 3,000 troops in the region. At a peace summit held on 8 April and attended by Mr. Mandela, President de Klerk, Chief Buthelezi and King Goodwill Zwelithini, Mr. Mandela made several proposals aimed at satisfying the King. These proposals were not accepted by the King and Chief Buthelezi. An attempt at international mediation also proved abortive, when the ANC and the South African Government rejected a demand by Chief Buthelezi that the election dates be a topic of discussion.

468    On 19 April, the ANC, the IFP and the Government reached an agreement recognizing and protecting the institution, status and constitutional position of the Zulu monarchy, which would be provided for in the provincial constitution of KwaZulu/Natal. As a result, the IFP agreed to participate in both national and provincial elections. The King endorsed the agreement and called on his people to take part in the elections. I welcomed this breakthrough and expressed the hope that it would ensure that the elections would be peaceful.[159]

159/Document 207
See page 506;
Document 206
See page 506

469    The South African Parliament met in a special session on 25 April to enact the Constitution of the Republic of South Africa Second Amendment Bill, which incorporated the agreement. There followed a dramatic decline in violence in KwaZulu/Natal. Violence around Johannesburg had already diminished after the Internal Stability Units of the South African Police left the townships. However, there were several tragic incidents as right-wing Whites tried to destabilize the elections. In rural right-wing strongholds of the Western Transvaal and Orange Free State, there were 40 bombings of ANC offices, railway lines, power pylons and a shelter for deprived children. Between 25 and

29 April, 21 people died in bomb attacks allegedly perpetrated by right-wing groups in order to spread panic and fear among voters. These included the 25 April explosion of a powerful car bomb in downtown Johannesburg, just a block away from ANC headquarters, in which nine people died and over 100 were injured. In another bomb explosion, at a Germiston taxi stand, 10 people were killed and 41 injured. A bomb also went off at the country's main airport on 26 April, injuring several people. The security forces moved quickly and arrested 34 people in connection with these attacks, including leading members of the Afrikaner Weerstandsbeweging.

### The elections proceed

470    With the last-minute participation of the IFP, a total of 19 political parties contested the national election while 28 appeared on the provincial ballot in South Africa's first democratic non-racial elections. The Azanian People's Organization, the Black Consciousness Movement, the Conservative Party and the Afrikaner Volksfront did not participate. Out of a total estimated population of 40.3 million, approximately 22.7 million South Africans were eligible to vote. Over 70 per cent of the electorate had never voted before and many were functionally illiterate.

471    The IEC recruited, trained and deployed approximately 200,000 voting officers, enumerators and electoral officials to staff over 9,000 polling-stations across the country. It undertook a massive voter education campaign with assistance from a large number of non-governmental organizations, South African and international alike. In addition to the 9,000 South African monitors trained by the IEC, some 6,000 international observers monitored the elections.

472    The elections were scheduled for 26 to 28 April, but serious practical problems arose because of the short time the IEC had had to prepare and the late entry of the IFP into the elections. Voting hours were extended and a fourth day of voting was added for three of the nine voting regions of the country, namely, the Northern Transvaal (GazanKulu, Lebowa and Venda), the Eastern Cape (Ciskei and Transkei) and KwaZulu/Natal. The first day of voting was for the elderly and the infirm, and for South Africans resident abroad.

473    There were 190 overseas polling-stations, where some 300,000 South Africans resident abroad cast their votes. The Electoral Assistance Unit of the United Nations provided observers at 120 polling-stations in 57 countries. A polling-station was set up at United Nations Headquarters in New York, staffed by South Africans and United Nations personnel.

474    The vast majority of South Africans voted with great enthusiasm. Despite some serious organizational mix-ups and long queues,

there was a festive atmosphere and virtually no violence. The voter turnout was estimated at about 86 per cent.

475    On the election days, United Nations observers visited and reported on thousands of polling-stations. On 26 April, the special voting day set aside for the elderly and the infirm, the observers visited 2,960 polling places. On the next two days, the regular voting days, they visited 7,430 of 8,478 voting stations. UNOMSA observers also witnessed some of the vote counting.

476    The day after the voting ended, Mr. Brahimi and the heads of other international observer missions said in a joint statement that the people of South Africa had clearly demonstrated their commitment to the end of apartheid and the transformation to non-racial democracy by turning out in enormous numbers to vote—most for the first time in their lives. They expressed satisfaction that the people of South Africa had been able to participate freely in the voting. They said that what they had observed, over the four days of voting, had been a great achievement for South Africa: "A people who have, in the past, been systematically separated came together in an historic national expression of their determination to create a peaceful, non-racial and democratic South Africa."

477    In a final statement, on 5 May, the international observer missions said they shared the collective view that the outcome of the elections reflected the will of the people of South Africa. They added: "The tolerance and patience demonstrated by South Africans during the voting period, the dramatic drop in the level of political violence and the expressed commitment of the political parties to national reconciliation augur well for the new South Africa."[160]

160/Document 216
See page 515

478    According to the official final results, the ANC won 62.6 per cent of the vote, the National Party 20.4 per cent and the IFP 10.5 per cent. None of the other parties received the 5 per cent of the votes required for representation in the Government. The ANC obtained a majority of the seats in seven of the nine provincial legislatures, the National Party took the Western Cape and the IFP won in KwaZulu/Natal.

479    On 6 May, IEC Chairman Judge Johann Kriegler, announcing the final results, said that although the electoral process had been flawed, the elections were "sufficiently free and fair" and "we were able to establish the will of the people". That same day, I issued a statement conveying my warm congratulations to the people of South Africa and all their leaders.[161]

161/Document 209
See page 507

480    At its first session, held in Cape Town on 9 May, South Africa's newly elected National Assembly unanimously proclaimed Mr. Nelson Mandela as President of South Africa. Mr. Thabo Mbeki was elected First Deputy President, and Mr. F. W. de Klerk became

# Results of the National Assembly Elections, April 1994

| Party | Votes | National % | Seats |
|---|---|---|---|
| African National Congress (ANC) . . . . . | 12,237,655 | 62.65 | 252 |
| National Party (NP) . . . . . . . . . . . | 3,983,690 | 20.39 | 82 |
| Inkatha Freedom Party (IFP) . . . . . . . | 2,058,294 | 10.54 | 43 |
| Freedom Front (FF) . . . . . . . . . . . | 424,555 | 2.17 | 9 |
| Democratic Party (DP) . . . . . . . . . . | 338,426 | 1.73 | 7 |
| Pan Africanist Congress (PAC) . . . . . | 243,478 | 1.25 | 5 |
| African Christian Democratic Party (ACDP) | 88,104 | 0.45 | 2 |
| Africa Muslim Party (AMP) . . . . . . . . | 34,466 | 0.18 | 0 |
| African Moderates Congress Party (AMCP) | 27,690 | 0.14 | 0 |
| Dikwankwetla Party (DP) . . . . . . . . | 19,451 | 0.10 | 0 |
| Federal Party (FP) . . . . . . . . . . . . | 17,663 | 0.09 | 0 |
| Minority Front (MF) . . . . . . . . . . . | 13,433 | 0.07 | 0 |
| SOCCER Party . . . . . . . . . . . . | 10,575 | 0.05 | 0 |
| African Democratic Movement (ADM) . . | 9,886 | 0.05 | 0 |
| Women's Rights Peace Party (WRPP) . . . | 6,434 | 0.03 | 0 |
| Ximoko Progressive Party (XPP) . . . . . | 6,320 | 0.03 | 0 |
| Keep It Straight and Simple (KISS) . . . . | 5,916 | 0.03 | 0 |
| Workers List Party (WLP) . . . . . . . . | 4,169 | 0.02 | 0 |
| Luso South African Party . . . . . . . . | 3,293 | 0.02 | 0 |
| Total . . . . . . . . . . . . . . . . . . | 19,533,498 | 100.00 | 400 |

# Winners of the Elections for Provincial Assemblies

**Western Cape**

| Party | Votes | % of Votes |
|---|---|---|
| NP | 1,138,242 | 53.2 |

**Northern Cape**

| Party | Votes | % of Votes |
|---|---|---|
| ANC | 200,839 | 49.7 |

**Eastern Cape**

| Party | Votes | % of Votes |
|---|---|---|
| ANC | 2,453,790 | 84.4 |

**KwaZulu-Natal**

| Party | Votes | % of Votes |
|---|---|---|
| IFP | 1,844,070 | 50.3 |

**Orange Free State**

| Party | Votes | % of Votes |
|---|---|---|
| ANC | 1,037,998 | 76.6 |

**Pretoria/Witwatersrand/Vereeniging**

| Party | Votes | % of Votes |
|---|---|---|
| ANC | 2,418,257 | 57.6 |

**North West**

| Party | Votes | % of Votes |
|---|---|---|
| ANC | 1,310,080 | 83.3 |

**Eastern Transvaal**

| Party | Votes | % of Votes |
|---|---|---|
| ANC | 1,070,052 | 80.7 |

**Northern Transvaal**

| Party | Votes | % of Votes |
|---|---|---|
| ANC | 1,759,597 | 91.6 |

Second Deputy President. The following day, Nelson Rolihlahla Mandela took the oath of office as South Africa's first democratically elected President at a ceremony held at the Union Buildings in Pretoria. In his inaugural address, President Mandela called on the people of South Africa to act together for national reconciliation and nation-building. He thanked the international community and appealed for its continued support as South Africa faced the challenge of building peace, prosperity, sexual equality, non-racialism and democracy. A Government of National Unity was established the next day and Mr. Mandela was inaugurated as President in a ceremony I was privileged to attend.[162]

162/Document 210
See page 507

163/Document 213
See page 510

164/Document 215
See page 511

165/Document 218
See page 538

166/Document 220
See page 540

481    On 25 May, the Security Council terminated the arms embargo, the last remaining sanction against South Africa.[163] A mission of the Special Committee against Apartheid, led by its Chairman, visited South Africa from 6 to 10 June. This was a fact-finding mission to enable the Committee to incorporate its assessment of the situation in South Africa in its final report to the General Assembly. After considering the mission's findings, the Special Committee reported to the General Assembly and the Security Council that apartheid had been brought to an end and that the mandate of the Special Committee had been successfully fulfilled.[164]

482    On 23 June, the General Assembly accepted the credentials of the South African delegation led by the new Foreign Minister, Mr. Alfred Nzo. In resolution 48/258 A, adopted without a vote, it welcomed South Africa back into the community of nations as represented in the General Assembly and called upon the specialized agencies and related organizations of the United Nations system to take all necessary action to re-establish South Africa's full membership. It decided to remove from its agenda the item on "Elimination of apartheid and establishment of a united, democratic and non-racial South Africa".[165] On 27 June, the Security Council, in resolution 930 (1994),[166] adopted unanimously, noted with great satisfaction the establishment of a united, non-racial and democratic Government in South Africa and decided to remove the question of South Africa from the list of matters of which the Council was seized. South Africa had already resumed participation in the policy-making organs of the International Atomic Energy Agency after it signed the Safeguards Agreement in September 1991. It had been readmitted to the FAO in December 1993, to WHO on 2 May 1994 and to the ILO on 7 June 1994.

## The United Nations and the new South Africa

483    While apartheid and racial discrimination have been eliminated from the statute-books in South Africa, and a new, non-racial

democratic Government is committed to promoting equal rights and opportunities for all the country's people, there remain the daunting tasks of overcoming the long legacy of racial discrimination and segregation, and eradicating poverty and deprivation.

484    As the Special Committee against Apartheid pointed out: "Apartheid has not only bitterly divided a nation but has also resulted in glaring disparities in the socio-economic situation. Even after the adoption of a new Constitution, the dismantling of a system which has been so deeply embedded in the structure and everyday life of the country will not be without difficulties and pain. The legacy left behind by apartheid will be complex and will take long years to overcome."[167]

167/Document 172
*See page 457*

485    The Special Committee also noted that under apartheid an estimated 2.5 million people could not afford to satisfy their basic nutritional needs. Only 8 per cent of rural Blacks were self-sufficient; others had to rely on remittances from relatives working in the cities. Almost half the economically active African population were unemployed. Nearly a million and a half people were homeless. Four out of every 10 children died before they reached the age of five. The average pass rate of African students in matriculation examinations was about 40 per cent, compared to 95 per cent for White students; only about 10 per cent qualified for university admission. More than three quarters of the land was owned by the White minority.

486    After 1990, the South African Government began to increase allocations for the education, health and housing of the African people, but the problems were so vast that the measures were far from being sufficient. Already, from the beginning of the process of implementing the 1989 Declaration on Apartheid, the United Nations was concerned with the socio-economic situation in the country and its effect on the transitional phase as well as future democratic stability.[168]

168/Document 129
*See page 413;*
Document 142
*See page 431;*
Document 148
*See page 438;*
Document 195
*See page 486*

487    My predecessor, Mr. Pérez de Cuéllar, pointed out in his first progress report of July 1990 on the implementation of the Declaration: "The Secretary-General would strongly endorse any measures aimed at redressing the social and economic imbalances, particularly in the area of housing, education, employment and health. Such measures would go a long way towards effectively addressing glaring inequities and instilling public confidence in the democratic process and in national institutions."

488    In his second progress report of 4 September 1991, he indicated that the United Nations system was preparing a concerted response to requests for assistance, particularly from disadvantaged sectors of society. He added: "Furthermore, the Secretary-General stands ready, when requested by the South Africans themselves and the

international community, to help . . . in the provision of assistance during the transitional period and beyond."

*489* In resolutions in December 1990 and 1991, the General Assembly appealed for economic, humanitarian, legal, educational and other assistance and support to the victims of apartheid and to all those who opposed apartheid and promoted a united, non-racial and democratic society in South Africa.[169] It urged assistance by United Nations agencies to facilitate the re-establishment of previously banned organizations, as well as the reintegration of released political prisoners and returning South African refugees and exiles. In 1992, it also recommended assistance to South Africans "in their efforts to address the serious socio-economic problems of the disadvantaged people of South Africa, particularly in the areas of education, employment, health and housing".[170]

169/Document 139
*See page 427;*
Document 147
*See page 436*

170/Document 175
*See page 460*

*490* One of the main concerns of the United Nations was to focus international attention on the immediate requirements of the disadvantaged sectors in South Africa and plan for increased assistance after the establishment of a non-racial democratic Government.

*491* In June 1991, the Special Committee against Apartheid and the Advisory Committee of the United Nations Educational and Training Programme for Southern Africa (UNETPSA), in collaboration with UNESCO, organized an International Conference on Educational Needs of the Victims of Apartheid in South Africa at UNESCO House, Paris. The Conference called on the South African authorities to address urgently the educational crisis in South Africa by taking appropriate political, legal and financial steps. It also outlined ways in which the international community could provide assistance in order to help alleviate the crisis and contribute to the formulation and implementation of a human resource development strategy for the future.

*492* A Follow-up Conference on International Educational Assistance to Disadvantaged South Africans, organized by UNETPSA and its Advisory Committee, was held at United Nations Headquarters in New York on 8 and 9 September 1992, with more than 300 participants, including representatives of major donor countries, United Nations agencies and intergovernmental and non-governmental organizations, providing educational assistance to disadvantaged South Africans, as well as a number of South African experts on education.

*493* In May 1992, the Special Committee against Apartheid and the Centre against Apartheid organized a Seminar in Windhoek on "South Africa's Socio-economic Problems: Future Role of the United Nations System in Helping to Address Them". In attendance were about 20 representatives of various South African organizations and about 35 representatives of United Nations bodies, specialized agencies and other offices. The Seminar set out to identify the socio-economic needs of the new South Africa, to explore priority areas for development and to formulate guidelines for future assistance by various United Nations agencies and offices.

*494* The Special Committee co-sponsored, with the Centre for the Study of the South African Economy and International Finance of the London School of Economics and Political Science, a Seminar on "Sustainable Economic Growth and Development in South Africa: Policy Priorities for the Early Years of a Democratic Government", which was held in London from 22 to 24 January 1994. It focused on the marshalling of domestic resources through financial and fiscal planning, the mobilization of external resources and management of external finance and exchange rate policy, the restructuring of the domestic economy through labour-market policies, and trade and industrial strategies.

*495* Meanwhile, the Secretary-General, at the request of the General Assembly, had taken steps towards a concerted response by the United Nations system to current and future requests for assistance; he reported annually to the General Assembly. These reports revealed that, in order to assess the needs and prepare plans, many of the agencies had established contacts with the liberation movements, anti-apartheid bodies and other institutions concerned with assisting the disadvantaged South Africans. Others indicated readiness to provide assistance as soon as a democratic Government was established.

*496* UNDP, in consultation with other agencies, began to formulate policies for technical assistance to South Africa. The ILO held several consultations with representatives of trade unions and employers' organizations, as well as with liberation movements, in planning its technical cooperation and assistance. UNESCO organized three workshops to discuss issues concerning a post-apartheid South Africa. WHO, the United Nations Population Fund (UNFPA) and the United Nations Development Fund for Women (UNIFEM) sent missions to South Africa.

*497* UNETPSA initiated a number of educational and training programmes for the disadvantaged in South Africa. The United Nations University (UNU) began to analyse the technology policy implications of industrialization in the new South Africa and consider the role UNU might play with regard to university development. UNICEF helped promote the formation of a National Children's Rights Committee and undertook a study of the problems of children and women in South Africa as a basis for the formulation of a programme of action.

*498* The World Bank initiated studies on various sectors of the South African economy and began a programme to train South Africans in the fundamentals of economic policy and in management of urban development projects. It supported the creation of an independent Institute for Economic Research in Cape Town and started a programme of assistance to South African institutions to train South Africans in development. It indicated its willingness to resume lending now that there was a democratic Government in South Africa. In 1993, South Africa also received a loan from the International Monetary Fund, the first since 1982.

*499* All agencies followed the situation with a view to assisting in development, after the establishment of a democratic Government, especially to redress the gross economic and social inequalities created by apartheid. After the lifting of economic sanctions against South Africa, the General Assembly, in its resolution 48/159 A of 20 December 1993, strongly urged the international community "to respond to the appeal by the people of South Africa for assistance in the economic reconstruction of their country and to ensure that the new South Africa

171/Document 194
*See page 484*

begins its existence on a firm economic base".[171] It requested the Secretary-General to take the necessary measures for the initiation and coordination among the United Nations and its agencies of detailed planning for programmes of socio-economic assistance, particularly in the areas of human resource development, employment, health and housing; it also asked him to ensure that those programmes were coordinated with other international agencies and with legitimate non-racial structures in South Africa.

*500* The ANC's five-year Reconstruction and Development Programme, released in April 1994, pledged to build 1 million homes; provide clean water, sanitation and health care to all; redistribute 30 per cent of the farmland; develop an integrated system of education and training that would provide opportunities to all, including a 10-year compulsory education cycle; and launch a public works programme to create jobs.

*501* The way is now clear for the United Nations agencies, and the international community generally, to assist in the fulfilment of these goals and thereby help the South African people consolidate their democracy.

*502* The General Assembly, in its resolution 48/258 A of 23 June 1994, strongly appealed to Member States and the international community to provide generous assistance to the Government and people of South Africa in the implementation of their reconstruction and development programmes, and requested the Secretary-General to consider the appointment, in consultation with the Government of South Africa, of a high-level coordinator for United Nations development activities in that country. The United Nations, in cooperation with UNDP and the Commonwealth Secretariat, had already been coordinating, at the request of the TEC, preparations for the International Donors' Conference for Human Resources Development in a Post-Apartheid South Africa, held in October, to focus attention on the country's needs and encourage donor countries and agencies to provide concrete assistance.

503    As I pledged on the occasion of the inauguration of President Mandela on 10 May 1994, the United Nations, its agencies and programmes are ready to provide continued support for the achievement of dignity, equal rights and social progress for all the people of South Africa.[172] The goodwill that South Africa's democratic Government has already acquired in the international community, and the preparatory work undertaken by the United Nations agencies, provide an assurance of constructive cooperation in promoting the economic and social development of the new South Africa.

172/Document 210
*See page 507*

# Index

*[The numbers following the entries refer to paragraph numbers in the text.]*

Economic Commission for Africa.
see UN. ECA

Economic sanctions, 13, 22, 47,
55, 86, 132, 135, 137, 141,
160, 206, 207, 327, 328, 433,
499.
see also Economic boycotts
lifting, 324, 440

Education, 37, 491

Educational assistance, 92, 134

Educational institutions, 240, 250

Egypt, 25, 32

Election observers, 444, 448, 449,
451, 453
South African monitors, 471
Trust Fund, 448

Elections, 15, 73, 140, 324, 341,
392, 436, 441, 442, 443,
444-482.
see also Vote
racially exclusive, 331, 387

Electoral Act, 458, 459, 460

Electoral process, 324, 439, 440,
443, 444, 446, 452, 463, 479

Electoral structures, 446

Electoral system, 381

Embargoes.
see also Sanctions
arms, 13, 65, 66, 68, 92, 99, 101,
111, 135, 137, 178-192, 206
dismantling, 440
economic, 14, 99
oil, 14, 86, 99
skilled manpower, 86
trade, 86

Emergency laws
suspension, 345

End Loans to South Africa, 253

Entertainment industry, 100, 250,
281, 282, 284.
see also Actors; Musicians

European Community, 102, 209
217, 273, 327, 379, 409

European Governments, 121

European Union, 414, 439, 444,
453, 466

Exiles, 112, 311, 354, 357, 358,
360, 363, 365, 366, 368, 374,
489

Expert Committee [Security
Council], 83, 85-89

Expert Group on South Africa,
70-89

# F

Fact-finding missions
UN, 323

FAO, 39, 152, 154, 244, 482

Farah, Abdulrahim A., 355

Farah Report, 355

Finland, 453

Follow-up Conference on
International Educational
Assistance to Disadvantaged
South Africans
(1992 : New York), 492

Food and Agriculture
Organization of the
United Nations.
see FAO

Foot, Hugh, 70

Foreign investments
South Africa, 51, 94. 206, 208,
210, 211, 254

Foreign trade
South Africa, 94

France, 42, 66, 78, 94, 120, 132,
181, 192, 282

"Free Mandela" Campaign, 123,
227-233

Free South Africa Movement
(United States), 265

Freedom Alliance, 432, 434, 435,
443, 457, 458, 460, 461

Freedom fighters.
see National liberation
movements

Freedom Front, 460

Front-line States, 120, 266.
see also South Africa—
neighbouring States

# G

Gambari, Ibrahim, 379, 429,
459

Gazankulu, 472

General Assembly.
see UN, General Assembly

General Law Amendment Act,
52, 67

Geneva Convention relative to the
Treatment of Prisoners of
War (1949), 224

German Democratic Republic,
282

Germany, 282

Germany, Federal Republic of,
132, 192

Gharekhan, Chinmaya R., 389

Glasgow, Scotland
award to Mandela, 229

Goldstone, Richard J., 372, 420

Goldstone Commission, 372, 390,
392, 395, 396, 397, 401, 407,
412, 413, 418, 420, 421, 464

Golf.
see Sports

Good Offices Commission, 29

Government
central, 388, 436
interim, 336, 360, 375, 390,
391, 417
local, 388, 436
regional, 388, 417, 436, 437

Government of National Unity,
437, 480

Gqozo, Oupa, 402, 462

Greece, 284

Groote Schuur Minute (1990),
352, 353

Group Areas Act, No.36 (1966),
373

Group of African States.
see UN. Group of African
States

Guyana, 295

# H

Haekkerup, Per, 69

Hain, Peter, 292

Hambro, Edvard, 171

Hammarskjöld, Dag, 43

Hellenic Association for the
United Nations, 284

Hemispheric Seminar on Women
and Apartheid (1980 :
Montreal), 269

Heroes Day (16 Dec.), 247

Holland Committee on Southern Africa, 199, 200, 231

Holomisa, Bantu, 402

Homelands, 103, 104, 364, 371, 382, 391, 392, 398, 402, 419, 424, 438, 461, 462.
see also Bantustanization; Bophuthatswana; Ciskei; Transkei; Venda

independence, 104

reincorporation, into South Africa, 461

Hostels, 391, 397

Huddleston, Trevor, 230, 278

Human rights, 1, 17, 21, 25, 33, 34, 35, 36, 49, 68, 90, 98, 100, 143, 144, 146, 172, 183, 240, 312, 340, 381, 385, 387, 436, 460

Human Rights Commission (South Africa), 349, 395

Humanitarian assistance, 24, 63, 67, 91, 92, 268, 303, 309, 310, 484

# I

IAEA, 482

IAEA Safeguards Agreement, 482

IEC.
see Independent Electoral Commmission

IFP.
see Inkatha Freedom Party

ILO, 39, 143, 152, 154, 155, 244, 254, 255, 257, 482, 496
assistance to national liberation movements, 154

ILO. Governing Body. Worker's Group, 155, 255, 257

IMF, 152, 498

Immunity
ANC National Executive Committee, 352
exiles, 354
political prisoners, 352

Independent Board of Enquiry into Internal Repression (South Africa), 349

Independent Broadcasting Authority Acts, 451

Independent Broadcasting Authority (IBA), 435

Independent Electoral Commission (IEC), 435, 439, 444, 445, 447, 451, 453, 455, 461, 471, 472

Independent Media Commission (IMC), 435, 451

India, 21, 26, 27, 30, 32, 282, 294

Indian Organization of South Africa, 27

Indonesia, 32

Inkatha Freedom Party (IFP), 348, 369, 371, 379, 394, 395, 397, 400, 424, 432, 459, 463, 464, 465, 468, 470, 472, 478

Institute for Economic Research (South Africa), 498

Intergovernmental Group to Monitor the Supply and Shipping of Oil and Petroleum Products to South Africa, 200, 203, 205, 440

Intergovernmental organizations, 96

Interim Constitution, 435, 436, 437, 438, 458, 459, 460, 463

Interim government, 336, 360, 375, 390, 391, 417

Internal Security Act, No.74 (1982), 344, 347, 373

International Anti-Apartheid Year (1978), 245

International Atomic Energy Agency.
see IAEA 482

International banks, 102, 216, 217, 263

International Campaign against Apartheid, 96, 97-102, 106, 114, 133, 159, 163, 208, 230, 250, 254

International Commission of Jurists, 253

International Committee of the Red Cross, 145, 222, 364

International Conference for Sanctions against South Africa (London : 1964), 63

International Conference for Sanctions against South Africa (Paris : 1981), 283

International Conference of Experts for the Support of Victims of Colonialism and Apartheid in Southern Africa, 174

International Conference of Maritime Trade Unions on the Implementation of the UN Oil Embargo against South Africa (London : 1985), 202

International Conference of Trade Unions against Apartheid (Geneva : 1973), 255

International Conference of Trade Unions on Sanctions and Other Actions against the Apartheid Regime in South Africa (Geneva : 1983), 257

International Conference on Children, Repression and Law in Apartheid South Africa (Harare : 1987), 223

International Conference on Educational Needs of the Victims of Apartheid in South Africa (1991 : Paris), 491

International Conference on Women and Children under Apartheid (Arusha : 1986), 274

International Conference on Women in South Africa and Namibia (Brussels : 1982), 273

International Convention against Apartheid in Sports, 300

International Convention on the Suppression and Punishment of the Crime of Apartheid, 131, 146

International Day for an Oil
Embargo against South Africa
(20 May), 199
International Day for the
Elimination of Racial
Discrimination (21 March),
245
International Day of Solidarity
with South African
Political Prisoners (11 Oct.),
245
International Day of Solidarity
with the Struggle of Women
in South Africa and Namibia
(9 Aug.), 245
International Day of Solidarity
with the Struggling People
of South Africa (16 June), 245
International Declaration against
Apartheid in Sport (1977),
301
International Defence and Aid
Fund for Southern Africa,
63, 303, 313
International Donors' Conference
for Human Resources
Development in a
Post-Apartheid South Africa
(1994), 502
International Labour Organisation.
see ILO
International Monetary Fund.
see IMF
International observers, 449, 471.
see also Election observers;
Peace observers
International Seminar on an Oil
Embargo against South Africa
(Amsterdam : 1980), 199
International Seminar on
Children under Apartheid
(Paris : 1979), 268
International Seminar on
Women and Apartheid
(Helsinki : 1980), 269
International Table Tennis
Federation, 287, 299
International Trade Union
Conference for Action
against Apartheid
(2nd : Geneva : 1977), 256

International Year for Action to
Combat Racism and Racial
Discrimination (1971), 246
International Year of Mobilization
for Sanctions against South
Africa (1982), 245
Iran (Islamic Republic of), 32, 195
Iraq, 32, 295
Ireland, 260, 282
Israel, 132, 192
Italy, 132

# J

Jamaica. Prime Minister, 300
Japan, 132
Joosab, E., 402

# K

Kelly, Michael, 229
King, Angela, 411, 450
King, Coretta Scott, 186
King, Martin Luther, 63
Koevoet, 394, 395
Kriegler, Johann C., 445, 479
Krugerrands, 210, 213, 231
KwaZulu, 397, 424, 425, 432
KwaZulu/Natal, 458, 464, 467,
468, 469, 472, 478.
see also Natal
KwaZulu Police, 394, 397, 464

# L

Labour, 37, 155, 255, 390, 397
Labour Government
(New Zealand), 296
Land ownership, 27
Laugier, Henri, 36
Lebanon, 32
Lebowa, 472
Lestor, Joan, 186
Liberia, 61
Loans, 102, 136, 141, 209, 211,
212, 213, 263, 328, 498
London School of Economics, 494
Luthuli, Albert J., 47, 63, 66, 260
Luthuli, Nokukhanya, 228

# M

Madagascar, 61
Mahlangu, Philip, 402
Majority rule, 125, 130, 139,
152, 324, 398
Mandela, Nelson, 1, 5, 10, 17,
45, 51, 52, 58, 67, 72, 218,
219, 226, 247, 249, 324, 345,
351, 355, 405, 416, 421, 425,
430, 433, 459, 467, 480, 503
campaign, for release of, 123,
227-233
imprisonment, 81
release, 322, 345
trial, 71
Mandela, Winnie, 227
Mangope, Lucas, 402, 461, 462
Manley, Michael, 300
Marof, Achkar, 166
Marylebone Cricket Club (MCC),
292
Mass Democratic Movement
(South Africa), 331
Mass media, 124, 208, 210, 240,
242, 345, 369, 377, 435, 451
Mbeki, Thabo, 480
Media.
see Mass media
Mediation, 324
Memorandum of Understanding
(1991), 366
Meyer, Roelf, 416
Migrant labour, 37, 255, 390, 397
Military forces
South Africa, 50, 62, 106, 113,
191, 349, 350
Minty, Abdul, 187
Mitterrand, François, 120
Mohammed, Ismail, 376
Morocco, 308
Movement of Non-Aligned
Countries, 134, 136, 300,
379
Mozambique, 108, 116, 119, 120
Multi-Party Negotiating Council
(South Africa), 324, 431, 432,
435, 438, 440, 444, 459
Multi-Party Planning Conference
(1993), 429, 430

Musicians, 248, 279, 281, 284.
    *see also* Entertainment
    industry
Myrdal, Alva, 70

# N

Namibia, 107, 116, 148, 150, 245,
    266, 306, 394.
    *see also* Territory of South
    West Africa
Natal, 348, 349, 350, 353, 458.
    *see also* KwaZulu/Natal
National Children's Rights
    Committee (South Africa),
    497
National Council of Indemnity,
    422
National liberation movements,
    99, 106, 109, 116, 127, 129,
    158, 170-177, 237, 269, 273,
    274, 275, 276, 306, 339. 495.
    *see also* ANC; PAC;
    Zimbabwe African People's
    Union
    anniversaries, 247
    assistance to, 112, 266, 304
    institutions, 266
    leaders, assassination, 113
    participation in UN bodies,
    153, 175
    representatives of the people,
    11, 100, 174
    underground structures, 108
National Party (South Africa),
    21, 30, 332, 333, 398, 478
    reform programme, 333
National Peace Accord, 323,
    371, 374, 378, 392, 404, 407,
    409, 411, 412, 413, 414, 418,
    447
National Peace Committee, 371,
    412, 427
National Peace Initiative, 370
National Peace Secretariat, 371,
    407, 412
National reconciliation, 425
National Union of Students
    (United Kingdom), 267
Natives Land Act, No.27 (1913),
    373

Negotiations, 15, 102, 321, 322,
    323, 324, 334, 336, 341, 346,
    348, 350-354, 383, 387, 391,
    392, 399, 402, 403, 424, 427,
    428, 429, 432, 435, 442, 449,
    460, 421, 423
    climate, 334-378
    multi-party, 429
    suspension, 361
Neighbouring States
    South Africa, 98, 113, 118, 137
Netherlands, 199, 282, 453
Netherlands. Parliament, 200
New York Area Labour
    Committee against
    Apartheid, 258
New Zealand, 261, 285, 291, 294,
    295, 296
Ngobeni, E. E., 402
Nigeria, 195, 282, 308, 400
Nkomati Non-Aggression Treaty
    (1984) (Mozambique), 119
Non-governmental organizations,
    92, 96, 100, 164, 199, 210, 240,
    242, 255, 427, 444, 448, 471
Nordic countries, 112, 212, 217,
    260
Northern Transvaal, 472
Norway, 211
Nuclear capability
    South Africa, 149
Nuclear collaboration, 141, 182,
    191, 192, 213
Nzo, Alfred, 482

# O

OAU, 100, 127, 129, 135, 158,
    164, 174, 253, 257, 304, 305,
    319, 379, 399, 400, 409, 433,
    439, 444, 453, 466
OAU. Ad Hoc Committee
    on Southern Africa
    (1989 : Harare), 333
OAU. Ad Hoc Committee on
    Southern Africa. Monitoring
    Group
    report, 357
OAU. Assembly of Heads of State
    and Government (28th sess. :
    1992 : Dakar), 399

OAU Assistance Fund for the
    Struggle against Colonialism
    and Apartheid, 304
Ogata, Sadako, 379
Ogbu, Edwin Ogebe, 167
Oil embargo, 14, 86, 99, 135, 136,
    193-205, 209, 328
    repeal by General Assembly, 440
Oil sanctions, 193
Olympic Games, 64, 100
    Montreal, 295
    Tokyo, 289
Orange Free State, 469
Organization of African Trade
    Union Unity, 257, 258
Organization of African Unity.
    *see* OAU
Ould Sidi Baba, Dey, 70

# P

Paarl
    disturbances, 59
PAC, 106, 127, 305, 364, 366,
    371, 375, 377, 381, 399, 400,
    402, 423, 443
    banning, 44, 50
    detention of members, 44, 59
    military wing, 50
    participation in UN bodies, 175
    unbanning, 322, 345.
    *see also* National liberation
    movements
Pahad, E., 402
Pakistan, 32, 308
Palme, Olof, 186
Pan Africanist Congress of Azania.
    *see* PAC
Parliament (South Africa).
    *see* South Africa—Parliament
Pass laws, 37, 40, 41, 44, 60, 245
Passive resistance, 27, 32
Patriotic/United Front Conference
    (1991 : Durban), 375
Peace Accord.
    *see* National Peace Accord
Peace observers, 320, 324, 409,
    411, 412, 413, 414, 453
Pérez de Cuéllar, Javier, 322, 355,
    487

Workers.
  *see* Black South African workers

Working Group Kairos (Utrecht, Netherlands), 199, 200

World Bank, 152, 498

World Campaign against Military and Nuclear Collaboration with South Africa, 185, 186, 253

  hearings, 187

World Campaign for the Release of South African Political Prisoners, 219

World Conference for Action against Apartheid (Lagos : 1977), 226

World Conference of the United Nations Decade for Women (Copenhagen : 1980), 269

World Conference to Review and Appraise the Achievements of the UN Decade for Women: Equality, Development and Peace (1985 : Nairobi), 274

World Council of Churches, 253, 303

World Health Organization.
  *see* WHO

World Intellectual Property Organization.
  *see* WIPO

Writers, 219, 242, 248, 250, 279, 282, 284

# Y

Yemen, 32

Youth, 250

  public action, 259-267

# Z

Zambia, 120, 274

Zimbabwe, 116, 120

Zimbabwe African People's Union, 107, 116, 120

Zitha, Manguezi, 402

Zulu sovereignty, 465

Zwelithini, Goodwill, King of the Zulus, 379, 463, 464, 467

# Section Two
# Chronology and Documents

# I Chronology of events

## United Nations consideration of apartheid, 1946-1966

### 31 October 1946

The United Nations General Assembly, at the request of the Government of India, decides to include in its agenda an item entitled "Treatment of Indians in the Union of South Africa"; the Assembly rejects South Africa's contention that the matter is within the domestic jurisdiction of South Africa and that the United Nations is not competent to consider the matter.

### 19 November 1946

The General Assembly unanimously adopts resolution 103 (I) — proposed by Egypt — which declares that religious and racial discrimination should be brought to an end.

### 8 December 1946

The General Assembly expresses the opinion that the treatment of Indians in South Africa should be in conformity with the international obligations under the agreements concluded between the two Governments and with the relevant provisions of the Charter of the United Nations.
*See Document 1, page 221*

### 26 May 1948

General elections are held in South Africa; the National Party comes to power and institutes apartheid as a State policy; the Government soon enacts a series of racially discriminatory and repressive laws to impose racial segregation and perpetuate racial domination, such as the Prohibition of Mixed Marriages Act of 1949, and the Group Areas Act, the Population Registration Act, the Immorality Amendment Act and the Suppression of Communism Act of 1950.

### 12 July 1948

In a letter to the Secretary-General, marking the first formal reference at the United Nations to the policy of apartheid, the representative of India brings to his attention the continuing racial discrimination against South African nationals of Indian origin.
*See Document 2, page 221*

### 2 December 1950

The General Assembly states that a policy of racial segregation (apartheid) is necessarily based on doctrines of racial discrimination.
*See Document 3, page 223*

### 26 June 1952

A non-violent "Campaign of Defiance against Unjust Laws" is launched by the African National Congress of South Africa (ANC) and the South African Indian Congress; by contravening selected discriminatory laws and regulations, more than 8,000 persons of all racial origins court imprisonment.

### 12 September 1952

Thirteen African and Asian Member States request that the General Assembly consider "the question of race conflict in South Africa resulting from the policies of apartheid of the Government of the Union of South Africa".
*See Document 4, page 223*

### 5 December 1952

The General Assembly adopts its first resolutions on apartheid and establishes a three-member Commission to study the racial situation in South Africa.
*See Document 7, page 227; Document 8, page 228; Document 9, page 228; Document 10, page 231; and Document 11, page 233*

### 1953

The South African Government enacts the Criminal Law Amendment Act and the Public Safety Act to suppress peaceful protest against apartheid; the Criminal Law Amendment Act provides stiff penalties (fines, jail and lashes) for lawbreaking by way of protest or incitement to protest. This legislation succeeds in ending the defiance campaign and many of its leaders are subjected to "banning" (restriction) orders, including Chief Albert J. Luthuli, President of the ANC. The Government also enacts the Bantu Education Act to enforce racial segregation of schools.

### 1955

The South African Government withdraws from membership in the United Nations Educational, Scientific and Cultural Organization (UNESCO) to protest UNESCO's activities against racial discrimination.

### 26 June 1955

A multiracial "Congress of the People", convened by the ANC and other organizations in Kliptown and attended by 3,000 delegates, adopts the "Freedom Charter".
*See Document 12, page 241*

**28 February 1956**

The South African Parliament passes the Separate Representation of Coloured Voters Act, which removes Coloured voters from the common roll in Cape Province.

**March 1956**

South Africa's "pass laws", which hitherto have been used to control the movements of African men, are extended to include African women.

**7 May 1956**

Under the Industrial Conciliation Act, the Minister of Labour is empowered to reserve any job on a racial basis and to order the dissolution of racially mixed trade unions.

**9 August 1956**

Twenty thousand African women protest at the Prime Minister's office in Pretoria against the pass laws; the anniversary of this date began to be observed after 1981 as the International Day of Solidarity with the Struggle of Women in South Africa and Namibia.

**27 November 1956**

South Africa's Minister of External Affairs announces that the Government will in future maintain only token representation at meetings of the General Assembly and other meetings at United Nations Headquarters.

**December 1956**

One hundred and fifty-six leaders of the ANC and allied organizations are arrested throughout the country and charged with high treason. (After a trial lasting more than four years they are found not guilty and discharged in March 1961.)

**1958**

South Africa, having noted that a more conciliatory attitude was taken by the General Assembly during its twelfth session, resumes full participation in the United Nations.

**30 October 1958**

The General Assembly adopts resolution 1248 (XIII) on apartheid, expressing "regret and concern" that the South African Government has not yet responded to Assembly appeals to reconsider its policies.

**9 April 1959**

The Pan Africanist Congress of Azania (PAC) is established.

**20 June 1959**

The Promotion of the Bantu Self-Government Act revokes the limited African representation in the Union Parliament and divides Africans into eight national units, envisaging eventual self-government through tribal authorities.

**3 February 1960**

Addressing the Parliament in Cape Town, the Prime Minister of the United Kingdom, Mr. Harold Macmillan, declares that a "wind of change" is blowing through the African continent.

**21 March 1960**

In Sharpeville, police shoot at people demonstrating peacefully against the pass laws; 68 men, women and children are killed and about 200 are wounded.

**24 March 1960**

The Government bans all public meetings of more than 12 persons until 30 June.

**25 March 1960**

Representatives of 29 African and Asian Member States request an urgent meeting of the Security Council to consider the situation in South Africa.
*See Document 14, page 244*

**27 March 1960**

The Commissioner of Police announces that the pass laws are to be suspended until a normal situation is restored because the jails can no longer accommodate the many Africans who present themselves for arrest by openly violating the pass laws; the same day, Chief Albert J. Luthuli, President of the ANC, publicly burns his pass.

**28 March 1960**

The ANC calls for a nationwide stay-at-home in protest against the Sharpeville massacre; pass books are burned in countless bonfires.

**30 March 1960**

The Security Council begins consideration of the situation in South Africa. The Government declares a state of emergency, under which thousands of people are arrested.

**31 March 1960**

Four regiments of the Citizens' Force are mobilized; legal authorities in Johannesburg state that the emergency regulations create a situation of virtual martial law.

**1 April 1960**

The Security Council, in its first action on South Africa, deplores the policies and actions of the South African Government and calls upon the Government to abandon its policies of apartheid and racial discrimination.
*See Document 15, page 244*

**6 April 1960**

After a brief 10-day suspension, the pass system is re-instituted.

**8 April 1960**

The Unlawful Organizations Act is passed by Parliament, and the Government bans the ANC and the PAC.

**4 May 1960**

The President of the PAC, Mr. Robert Sobukwe, is sentenced to three years' imprisonment for incitement of Africans to urge the repeal of the pass laws.

**15-24 June 1960**

The Second Conference of Independent African States, held in Addis Ababa, calls for sanctions against South Africa.
*See Document 16, page 245*

**31 August 1960**

The state of emergency is lifted.

**5 October 1960**

In a referendum limited to White voters only, 52 per cent favour the establishment of a Republic.

**6-12 January 1961**

Secretary-General Dag Hammarskjöld visits South Africa; in his 23 January report to the Security Council, he says that in the course of his discussions with the Prime Minister of South Africa, "no mutually acceptable arrangement" has so far been found on racial policies in South Africa.
*See Document 18, page 246*

**15 March 1961**

Following strong opposition in the Conference of Commonwealth Prime Ministers, the South African Prime Minister, Mr. H. F. Verwoerd, announces that South Africa will withdraw from the Commonwealth in the interests of its "honour and dignity".

**25-26 March 1961**

The All-In African Conference, held in Pietermaritzburg, South Africa, is attended by 1,400 delegates from 145 religious, cultural and political bodies from around South Africa; the Conference calls upon the Government to organize a national convention of elected representatives without regard to race, colour or creed — failing which the people are asked to organize mass demonstrations on the eve of the proclamation of the Republic; Mr. Nelson Mandela is appointed Secretary of the National Action Committee.
*See Document 19, page 247*

**13 April 1961**

The General Assembly deplores racial discrimination in South Africa as "reprehensible and repugnant to human dignity".
*See Document 21, page 249*

**May 1961**

South Africa's security forces are ordered to prevent a nationwide strike that has been called to protest against the establishment of the Republic.

**31 May 1961**

South Africa proclaims itself a Republic and withdraws from the Commonwealth.

**11 October 1961**

The General Assembly censures the Foreign Minister of South Africa for a speech in the General Assembly that causes widespread offence.

**10 December 1961**

The Nobel Peace Prize is awarded to Chief Albert J. Luthuli, President of the ANC.

**16 December 1961**

*Umkhonto we Sizwe* (Spear of the Nation), an underground organization associated with the ANC, makes its appearance and distributes its manifesto; a series of explosions are set off near Johannesburg and Port Elizabeth, damaging a post office, several offices of the Department of Bantu Administration and Development and an electric power station.
*See Document 22, page 250*

**5 August 1962**

Mr. Mandela, who has been underground since 1961, is arrested near Durban.

**6 November 1962**

The General Assembly requests Member States to take specific measures to bring about the abandonment of apartheid, including breaking diplomatic, trade and transport relations with South Africa; it also establishes a Special Committee to follow developments and report to the General Assembly and the Security Council.
*See Document 23, page 251*

**7 November 1962**
Mr. Mandela is sentenced to five years' imprisonment; the following year he is tried again in the "Rivonia trial" (so called because several of the accused were arrested at a farm in Rivonia).

**2 April 1963**
The Special Committee on the Policies of Apartheid of the Government of the Republic of South Africa (later renamed the Special Committee against Apartheid), established by the General Assembly on 6 November 1962, holds its first meeting.
*See Document 25, page 253*

**7 August 1963**
The Security Council calls upon all States to cease the sale and shipment of arms, ammunition and military vehicles to South Africa.
*See Document 27, page 254; and Document 28, page 257*

**11 October 1963**
The General Assembly requests the Government of South Africa to abandon the Rivonia trial of Mr. Mandela and other leaders; this date is subsequently proclaimed the Day of Solidarity with South African Political Prisoners.
*See Document 32, page 267; and Document 33, page 267*

**4 December 1963**
The Security Council calls upon all States "to cease forthwith the sale and shipment of equipment and materials for the manufacture and maintenance of arms and ammunition in South Africa", and requests the Secretary-General to establish a small group of experts to examine methods of resolving the situation in South Africa.
*See Document 34, page 269*

**16 December 1963**
The General Assembly appeals for assistance to families of persons persecuted by the South African Government for their opposition to apartheid.
*See Document 35, page 270*

**14 March 1964**
South Africa announces its withdrawal from the International Labour Organisation.

**20 April 1964**
The Group of Experts on South Africa presents its report to the Secretary-General; its main conclusion is that "all the people of South Africa should be brought

into consultation and should thus be enabled to decide the future of their country at the national level".
*See Document 37, page 272*

After being sentenced to life imprisonment at the Rivonia trial in Pretoria, Mr. Mandela makes a statement declaring his belief in a "democratic and free society in which all persons live together in harmony and with equal opportunities".
*See Document 39, page 280*

**9 June 1964**
The Security Council urges the South African Government to end the Rivonia trial and grant an amnesty to all persons imprisoned or restricted for having opposed the policy of apartheid, and particularly to the defendants in the Rivonia trial (S/RES/190 (1964)).

**16 June 1964**
The Rt. Rev. Joost de Blank presents a petition to the Secretary-General on behalf of the World Campaign for the Release of South African Political Prisoners (sponsored by the British Anti-Apartheid Movement).

**18 June 1964**
The Security Council invites South Africa to accept the proposal of national consultations that was made in the report of the Group of Experts.
*See Document 41, page 283*

**9 November 1965**
The Secretary-General establishes a programme for the education and training abroad of South Africans, as requested by the Security Council on 18 June 1964.

**15 December 1965**
The General Assembly requests the Secretary-General to establish a United Nations Trust Fund for South Africa to provide humanitarian assistance to persons persecuted under discriminatory and repressive legislation in South Africa and to their dependants.
*See Document 45, page 290*

**18 March 1966**
The Defence and Aid Fund is declared an unlawful organization in South Africa.

**23 August - 4 September 1966**
The International Seminar on Apartheid, organized by the United Nations Special Committee against Apartheid, the United Nations Commission on Human Rights and the Government of Brazil, is held in Brasilia — the first of many conferences and seminars on apartheid organized or co-sponsored by the United Nations.
*For a chronology of United Nations conferences and seminars, see page 167.*

**26 October 1966**

The General Assembly proclaims 21 March, the anniversary of the Sharpeville massacre, as the International Day for the Elimination of Racial Discrimination.
*See Document 47, page 292; and Document 48, page 293*

## International campaign against apartheid, 1967-1989

**6 March 1967**

The United Nations Commission on Human Rights deplores the actions of the South African Government, which are "contrary to international law and international morality".
*See Document 52, page298*

**29 September 1967**

The Chairman of the Special Committee against Apartheid, Mr. Achkar Marof (Guinea), calls for a reassessment of the international measures being taken against apartheid.
*See Document 53, page 300*

**2 July 1968**

The Acting President of the ANC, Mr. Oliver Tambo, urges the international community to pursue a more comprehensive isolation of the South African regime.
*See Document 55, page 304*

**2 December 1968**

The General Assembly requests all States and organizations "to suspend cultural, educational, sporting and other exchanges with the racist regime and with organizations or institutions in South Africa which practise apartheid".
*See Document 56, page 308*

**16 April 1969**

The Lusaka Manifesto on Southern Africa, which asserts a commitment to human equality and dignity, is adopted by the Fifth Summit Conference of East and Central African States in Lusaka.
*See Document 57, page 309*

**20 November 1969**

The General Assembly recommends the Lusaka Manifesto to the attention of all States and peoples (A/RES/ 2505 (XXIV)).

**May 1970**

The International Olympic Committee expels South Africa for practising racial discrimination in sports.

**24 October 1970**

In a declaration on the occasion of the twenty-fifth anniversary of the United Nations, the General Assembly describes apartheid as "a crime against the conscience and dignity of mankind" (A/RES/2627 (XXV)).

**29 November 1971**

The General Assembly calls for a boycott of sports teams selected in violation of the Olympic principle of non-discrimination.The Assembly also condemns the South African Government's establishment of Bantu homelands (Bantustans) and the forcible removal of African people.
*See Document 61, page 314; and Document 62, page 315*

**15 November 1972**

The General Assembly states that "the United Nations has a vital interest in securing the speedy elimination of apartheid".
*See Document 65, page 317*

**30 November 1973**

The General Assembly adopts and opens for signature the International Convention on the Suppression and Punishment of the Crime of Apartheid.
*See Document 70, page 325*

**14 December 1973**

The General Assembly declares that the South African regime has "no right to represent the people of South Africa" and that the liberation movements recognized by the Organization of African Unity (OAU) are "the authentic representatives of the overwhelming majority of the South African people".
*See Document 71, page 328*

**30 September 1974**

The General Assembly decides not to accept the credentials of the representatives of South Africa.
*See Document 73, page 332; and Document 74, page 332*

**18 - 30 October 1974**

The Security Council receives a proposal to recommend to the General Assembly the immediate expulsion of South Africa from the United Nations in compliance with Article 6 of the Charter; the proposal receives 10 votes in favour but is not adopted because of the negative votes of three permanent members — France, the United Kingdom and the United States of America.

**12 November 1974**

The President of the General Assembly, Mr. Abdelaziz Bouteflika (Algeria), rules that the South African dele-

gation cannot participate in the work of the Assembly; the President's ruling is challenged but upheld.
*See Document 75, page 333*

**28 November 1975**
The General Assembly declares that the United Nations and the international community have "a special responsibility towards the oppressed people of South Africa and their liberation movements".
*See Document 79, page 336*

**1 January 1976**
The Centre against Apartheid is established in the United Nations Secretariat.

**16 June 1976**
Police fire at students in Soweto, near Johannesburg, who are protesting against "Bantu education" and the imposition of Afrikaans as a medium of instruction; during that demonstration and in the ensuing period of nationwide resistance by students, more than 1,000 are killed and many more are injured.
*See Document 82, page 339; and Document 83, page 340*

**18 July 1976**
The International Convention on the Suppression and Punishment of the Crime of Apartheid comes into force.

**26 October 1976**
South Africa proclaims the "independence" of one of the Bantustans, Transkei; on the same day, the General Assembly rejects the "independence" and declares it invalid.
*See Document 85, page 343*

**9 November 1976**
The General Assembly adopts a comprehensive Programme of Action against Apartheid by Governments, specialized agencies and other intergovernmental organizations, as well as trade unions, churches, anti-apartheid and solidarity movements and other non-governmental organizations (A/RES/31/6 J).

**12 September 1977**
Black Consciousness leader Steve Biko dies in detention.

**20 September 1977**
The Foreign Ministers of the European Community (EC), meeting in Brussels, adopt a code of conduct for corporations operating in South Africa.

**October 1977**
In a new wave of repression, the South African Government bans 17 organizations; the newspapers *World* and *Weekend World* are also banned.

**4 November 1977**
The Security Council imposes a mandatory arms embargo against South Africa.
*See Document 89, page348; and Document 90, page 348*

**6 December 1977**
The General Assembly denounces the declaration of the so-called "independence" of Bophuthatswana, as well as that of Transkei earlier, and declares them invalid.

**14 December 1977**
The General Assembly adopts the International Declaration against Apartheid in Sports and proclaims the period from 21 March 1978 to 20 March 1979 International Anti-Apartheid Year (A/RES/32/105 B and A/RES/32/105 M).

**11 October 1978**
At a special meeting of the General Assembly, the United Nations gives awards to personalities, some posthumously, in recognition of their contribution to the international campaign against apartheid; the recipients are the Reverend Canon L. John Collins (United Kingdom), Prime Minister Michael Manley (Jamaica), General Murtala Mohamed (Nigeria), President Gamal Abdel Nasser (Egypt), President Jawaharlal Nehru (India), Mr. Olof Palme (Sweden) and Mr. Paul Robeson (United States).

**28 March 1979**
The World Campaign against Military and Nuclear Collaboration with South Africa is launched in London with the support of the Special Committee against Apartheid.

**5 April 1979**
The Security Council calls on the South African Government to spare the lives of Mr. Solomon Mahlangu and other South African political prisoners under sentence of death. (Mr. Mahlangu is executed on 6 April.)

**21 September 1979**
The Security Council condemns and declares invalid the proclamation of the so-called "independence" of the Bantustan of Venda.

**26 October 1979**
The General Assembly requests the Secretary-General to conduct an investigation into reports concerning a

nuclear explosion by South Africa in the area of the Indian Ocean and the South Atlantic on 22 September 1979.

**5 December 1979**
South Africa is expelled from the General Conference of the International Atomic Energy Agency (IAEA) at its annual meeting held in New Delhi.

**March 1980**
Following the elections in Southern Rhodesia, leading to its independence as Zimbabwe, the *Sunday Post* of Johannesburg launches a campaign for the release of Mr. Mandela; the campaign receives wide support in the country.

**1 April 1980**
A summit meeting of nine southern African countries in Lusaka decides to form the Southern African Development Coordination Conference in order to promote regional development and lessen dependence on South Africa.

**13 June 1980**
Following police violence against a series of demonstrations by students and other groups, the Security Council strongly condemns the South African regime for further aggravating the situation and calls upon it to release Mr. Mandela and all other Black leaders "with whom it must deal in any meaningful discussions of the future of the country".
*See Document 97, page 352*

**15 May 1981**
The First Register of Sports Contacts with South Africa is published by the Special Committee against Apartheid.
*See Document 102, page 356*

**18 June 1981**
The ILO General Conference, meeting in Geneva, condemns apartheid as degrading, criminal and inhuman and decides that the ILO should give assistance to South African liberation movements; the Conference sets up a permanent committee to monitor South Africa's racial policies and approves ILO technical assistance to liberation movements through a voluntary fund.

**9 August 1981**
The International Day of Solidarity with the Struggle of Women in South Africa and Namibia is observed for the first time, on the twenty-fifth anniversary of the demonstration of South African women against the pass laws.

**4 December 1981**
The Bantustan of Ciskei is proclaimed "independent"; the Security Council condemns the purported proclamation and declares it invalid.
*See Document 104, page 367*

**10 December 1981**
The Committee of Artists of the World against Apartheid is established in Paris with the support of the Special Committee against Apartheid.

**1982**
International Year of Mobilization for Sanctions against South Africa, as proclaimed by the General Assembly in its resolution 36/172 B of 17 December 1981.

**21 March 1982**
The Special Committee against Apartheid publishes a declaration by some 1,500 mayors calling for the release of Mr. Mandela and all other South African political prisoners.

**5 November 1982**
The United Nations presents awards to seven personalities in recognition of their outstanding contribution to the international movement for sanctions against South Africa: the late President Houari Boumediene (Algeria), Mr. Romesh Chandra (India), Ms. Jeanne Martin-Cissé (Guinea), the Most Reverend Trevor Huddleston (United Kingdom), the late Reverend Dr. Martin Luther King, Jr. (United States), Prime Minister Olof Palme (Sweden) and Mr. Jan Nico Scholten (Netherlands).

**21 March 1983**
The Declaration for the Release of Nelson Mandela and All Other South African Political Prisoners, signed by over 4,000 public leaders, is published; the Declaration was initiated by Archbishop Trevor Huddleston in cooperation with the Special Committee against Apartheid.

**9 September 1983**
The South African Parliament approves a new constitution which envisages a tri-cameral parliament, with chambers for Whites, Coloured people and Indians, while denying representation for Africans; the constitution also allows for an executive presidency.

**26 October 1983**
The Special Committee against Apartheid publishes the First Register of Entertainers, Actors and Others Who Have Performed in Apartheid South Africa.
*See Document 109, page 375*

**2 November 1983**
A referendum of the White electorate approves the constitutional proposals for a tri-cameral parliament; the General Assembly later declares the new constitution to be contrary to the principles of the Charter of the United Nations.
*See Document 110, page 378*

**22 November 1983**
The Art contre/against Apartheid exhibit opens at the Fondation nationale des arts graphiques et plastiques, Paris, sponsored by the Committee of Artists of the World against Apartheid in cooperation with the Special Committee against Apartheid.

**5 December 1983**
The General Assembly adopts a new Programme of Action against Apartheid.
*See Document 111, page 379*

**16 March 1984**
The Governments of South Africa and Mozambique, meeting at Nkomati, Mozambique, sign an Agreement on Non-Aggression and Good Neighbourliness.

**29 May 1984**
The South African Prime Minister, Mr. P. W. Botha, flies to Europe to try to win support for the new constitution and other plans for reform but fails to secure any endorsement from Governments.

**17 August 1984**
The Security Council rejects the new constitution of 1983 and the validity of the elections that are about to be held.
*See Document 113, page 390*

**11 September 1984**
After two weeks of riots in Black townships, the South African Government issues a new order banning protest meetings.

**10 December 1984**
South African Bishop Desmond Tutu is awarded the Nobel Peace Prize.

**31 January 1985**
Mr. P. W. Botha, now President under the new constitution, offers to release Mr. Mandela, on condition that he renounce the use of violence; Mr. Mandela rejects the offer but indicates that he is prepared to negotiate with the Government if the ban on the ANC and other groups is lifted.

**7 February 1985**
One of the largest banks in the United States, Citibank, declares that it will make no more loans to the South African Government for the foreseeable future; the decision comes amid moves by the New York City government to cease to do business with banks and corporations maintaining links with South Africa; PepsiCo is the first of many large United States corporations to announce that it will divest its holdings in South Africa.

**8 March 1985**
A bill seeking to prevent new United States investment in South Africa is introduced in the United States Senate by Mr. Edward Kennedy and other senior Senators.

**22 March 1985**
The Security Council expresses grave concern over the killing and wounding of innocent people by the South African police in the town of Uitenhage the previous day, when 19 people died.
*See Document 115, page 391*

**5 June 1985**
The United States House of Representatives votes overwhelmingly in favour of economic sanctions against South Africa; the sanctions cover new bank loans, new commercial investments, imports of krugerrand gold coins, computer sales to the Government and sales of nuclear fuel, equipment and technology.

**11 July 1985**
The United States Senate votes to impose limited sanctions covering bank loans, computers and nuclear collaboration; it also calls upon United States companies to follow the so-called Sullivan Principles, which require them to offer Blacks the same treatment as Whites in housing and employment.

**21 July 1985**
The South African Government declares a state of emergency in parts of the most heavily populated areas of the country.

**24 July 1985**
France recalls its Ambassador to South Africa and announces a ban on all new investment in South Africa in protest against the Government's policies.

**26 July 1985**
The Security Council urges Member States to adopt a wide range of economic sanctions against South Africa.
*See Document 116, page 392*

**15 August 1985**
President Botha makes a policy statement in which he indicates that his Government will reject any dictation of policy from the outside world.

**9 September 1985**
United States President Ronald Reagan orders a series of limited economic sanctions against South Africa.

**10 September 1985**
Ministers of the EC demand the immediate and unconditional release of Mr. Mandela and a firm commitment from the South African Government to end apartheid.

**25 September 1985**
The 12 Governments of the EC agree on a number of sanctions against South Africa, although some Governments are unwilling to impose mandatory sanctions.

**9 October 1985**
The Government of Japan, which is South Africa's second-largest trading partner, announces a series of economic sanctions against South Africa.

**22 October 1985**
A summit meeting of the Commonwealth in Nassau, Bahamas, adopts an agreement regarding sanctions against South Africa; it also establishes a seven-member Group of Eminent Persons for the purpose of promoting a dialogue on constitutional reform in South Africa.

**25 October 1985**
The state of emergency is extended; it now covers an area inhabited by more than 9 million people.

**10 December 1985**
The General Assembly adopts and opens for signature the International Convention against Apartheid in Sports.
*See Document 118, page 393*

**4 February 1986**
Foreign Ministers from the EC meet their counterparts from the six Front-line States (Angola, Botswana, Mozambique, Tanzania, Zambia and Zimbabwe) and issue a joint communiqué calling upon South Africa to dismantle apartheid; the Foreign Secretary of the United Kingdom holds discussions with the ANC leadership in Lusaka.

**6 March 1986**
Barclays Bank of the United Kingdom declares that it will lend no new money to South Africa until the Government demonstrates that it can reduce its debts and abolish apartheid.

**23 April 1986**
The South African Government issues a White Paper with proposals to scrap the pass laws and influx control.

**May 1986**
The South African armed forces undertake raids in Botswana, Zambia and Zimbabwe.

**12 June 1986**
The South African Government declares a national state of emergency and orders the arrest of hundreds of anti-apartheid activists, including leaders of the United Democratic Front (UDF), the Azanian People's Organization (AZAPO), Anglican and Catholic bishops and community workers.

**16 - 20 June 1986**
The World Conference on Sanctions against Racist South Africa is held in Paris, organized by the United Nations in cooperation with the OAU and the Movement of Non-Aligned Countries.
*See Document 119, page 397*

**18 August 1986**
The South African Government acknowledges to Parliament that 8,501 people are in detention under the emergency regulations.

**29 September and 2 October 1986**
The United States House of Representatives and Senate vote to override a veto by the President on the Comprehensive Anti-Apartheid Act. The Act, which includes a number of sanctions against South Africa, becomes law; many large United States corporations announce their withdrawal from South Africa.

**16 April 1987**
The Security Council calls upon the South African authorities to revoke their decree of 10 April 1987, under which protests against detentions without trial or support for those detained are prohibited.
*See Document 120, page 406*

**20 November 1987**
The General Assembly reaffirms its full support for the struggle against apartheid by the people of South Africa, under the leadership of their national liberation movements.
*See Document 121, page 407*

**3 April 1988**
The International Convention against Apartheid in Sports enters into force.

**26 October 1988**

Segregated municipal elections are held in South Africa; the General Assembly overwhelmingly rejects the elections as a manoeuvre to further entrench White minority rule and apartheid.

**9 December 1988**

The International Olympic Committee asks the federations that govern worldwide sports to bar from the Olympic Games any athlete who competes in South Africa.

**22 December 1988**

Angola, Cuba and South Africa sign a treaty at United Nations Headquarters in New York that includes agreement by the parties on the implementation of the United Nations plan for the independence of Namibia contained in Security Council resolution 435 (1978).

**29 June 1989**

The National Party of South Africa adopts a five-year programme of objectives, including a political "reform" plan.

**5 July 1989**

Nelson Mandela is taken from prison to meet with South African President Botha at the latter's office in Cape Town.

**2 August 1989**

The Mass Democratic Movement launches a campaign of defiance of apartheid laws in advance of the racially exclusive general elections to take place on 6 September.

**14 August 1989**

South African President Botha resigns; Mr. F. W. de Klerk becomes leader of the National Party in advance of the elections due to be held in September.

**21 August 1989**

Meeting in Harare, the OAU Heads of State adopt a declaration on South Africa recognizing that possibilities exist for a resolution of South Africa's problems; the declaration is subsequently endorsed by a summit of the non-aligned countries in Belgrade.

**20 September 1989**

Mr. F. W. de Klerk is elected President of South Africa, following the general election held on 6 September.

**14 December 1989**

The General Assembly, building on the Harare Declaration of 21 August 1989, adopts at its sixteenth special session the Declaration on Apartheid and its Destructive Consequences in Southern Africa, which calls for negotiations to end apartheid and lays down steps needed to create a climate conducive to negotiations.
*See Document 135, page 419*

## Towards a non-racial democratic Government, 1990-1994

**2 February 1990**

President de Klerk announces, among other measures, the lifting of the 30-year ban on the ANC, the PAC and other anti-apartheid organizations, the release of some political prisoners and the lifting of restrictions on the media under emergency regulations.

**11 February 1990**

Mr. Mandela is released from prison unconditionally.

**20 March 1990**

Namibia gains its independence.

**2 - 4 May 1990**

The South African Government and the ANC hold preliminary talks, with both sides expressing hope for peace and for an end to apartheid.

**7 May 1990**

The Indemnity Bill, which allows exiles to be granted temporary immunity or permanent indemnity against arrest or prosecution, is passed by the South African Parliament at a joint sitting.

**16 May 1990**

The South African Government announces plans to abolish racial segregation in State hospitals.

**8 June 1990**

The nationwide state of emergency, in force since 1986, is lifted at midnight, except in Natal and in the "homeland" of KwaZulu.

**9 - 19 June 1990**

A United Nations team led by Under-Secretary-General Abdulrahim A. Farah (Somalia) visits South Africa on a fact-finding mission and meets representatives of the Government, political parties and organizations.

**22 June 1990**

Mr. Mandela, addressing the United Nations Special Committee against Apartheid in New York, urges the United Nations to do everything in its power to maintain its consensus on the ending of apartheid.
*See Document 136, page 421*

**1 July 1990**

In his first progress report on implementation of the 1989 Declaration on Apartheid, Secretary-General Javier Pérez de Cuéllar states that he is greatly encouraged by the positive developments that have taken place in South Africa.

*See Document 136, page 421*

**14 July 1990**

Chief Mangosuthu Gatsha Buthelezi, leader of the Inkatha Movement, announces the transformation of the movement into a multiracial political party, the Inkatha Freedom Party (IFP).

**22 July 1990**

After an IFP rally in Sebokeng, in the East Rand, members of the party clash with ANC supporters, leaving at least 27 people dead.

**6 August 1990**

The ANC and the South African Government hold further talks and issue a joint declaration, the Pretoria Minute; a timetable for the release of political prisoners is agreed and the ANC announces that it will immediately suspend all armed actions, while the Government undertakes to consider lifting the state of emergency in Natal "as early as possible" and to continue reviewing the security legislation and its application "in order to ensure free political activity".

**14 August 1990**

An estimated 143 people die in disturbances involving IFP and ANC supporters in the townships of Thokoza, Vosloorus and Katlehong.

**22 August 1990**

After 42 burnt or mutilated bodies are found in Vosloorus, the death toll from four weeks of violent incidents exceeds 500.

**1 - 14 September 1990**

Further violent incidents claim more than 225 lives, including those of a large number of train and bus commuters who are shot at random by unidentified armed men.

**15 October 1990**

The Discriminatory Legislation Regarding Public Amenities Repeal Act comes into effect.

**19 October 1990**

The National Party decides to open membership to all South Africans.

**28 October 1990**

At least 16 people are killed and 33 injured when a group of armed men carries out three separate attacks in Soweto.

**1 November 1990**

The Minister of Justice, Mr. Kobie Coetsee, announces guidelines that restrict the planned release of political prisoners and the return of exiles.

**18 November 1990**

Fighting in a squatter camp near Katlehong claims the lives of at least 20 people.

**16 December 1990**

The national consultative conference of the ANC mandates the National Executive Committee to serve notice on the regime that unless specific obstacles to negotiations are removed on or before 30 April 1991, the ANC will consider the suspension of the entire negotiation process.

**12 January 1991**

Unidentified gunmen kill 35 people and injure at least 50 at a funeral for an ANC organizer in Sebokeng.

**29 January 1991**

Chief Buthelezi and Mr. Mandela, leaders of the IFP and the ANC respectively, meet in Durban and issue a joint statement expressing their commitment to political tolerance and calling on the security forces to play an effective peace-keeping role.

**1 February 1991**

In a speech at the opening of the parliamentary session in Cape Town, President de Klerk announces that legislation will be submitted shortly for the repeal of the Land Acts of 1913 and 1936, the Population Registration Act of 1950, the Group Areas Act of 1966 and the Development of Black Communities Act of 1984.

**12 February 1991**

President de Klerk and Mr. Mandela announce, after a meeting at Cape Town, that they have resolved differences on the interpretation of the Pretoria Minute of 7 August 1990; under the new agreement, the authorities undertake to expedite the return of exiles and the release of political prisoners, while the ANC assents to end the recruitment and training of cadres for its armed wing, *Umkhonto we Sizwe.*

**21 March 1991**

South Africa and the Office of the United Nations High Commissioner for Refugees (UNHCR) agree that

UNHCR will assist with the process of the return to South Africa of refugees and political exiles.

**8 May 1991**
President de Klerk announces an immediate ban on "cultural weapons" "excluding at this stage spears" in townships declared "unrest areas"; he also says that the Government will upgrade the workers' hostels and convert some of them into family accommodations.

**12 May 1991**
At least 27 people are killed during an attack by IFP members on a squatter camp at Swanieville.

**5 - 21 June 1991**
The South African Parliament repeals a number of basic laws of apartheid, such as the Land Acts, the Group Areas Act and the Population Registration Act, and amends the Internal Security Act.

**22 June 1991**
A church-sponsored peace summit is attended by representatives of the Government, the ANC, the IFP, the PAC, AZAPO, the South African Communist Party (SACP) and other parties and trade unions; subjects of discussion include the mechanisms for enforcing a peace agreement, and the reconstruction of areas affected by violence.

**2 - 6 July 1991**
The ANC holds its forty-eighth national conference at Durban, the first time in 32 years that it has been held inside South Africa; the conference elects Mr. Mandela as the party's President and Oliver Tambo as National Chairman; it also elects a new National Executive Council.

**9 July 1991**
The International Olympic Committee recognizes the National Olympic Committee of South Africa, paving the way for that country's participation in the next Olympic Games.

**10 July 1991**
South Africa accedes to and signs the Treaty on the Non-Proliferation of Nuclear Weapons.

United States President George Bush announces that South Africa has met the conditions for lifting of the United States' trade and economic sanctions contained in the Comprehensive Anti-Apartheid Act of 1986.

**15 August 1991**
The South African Government, the ANC and the IFP agree on a draft National Peace Accord, including a code of conduct for the police and the security forces,

provisions for socio-economic development and a complex set of enforcement mechanisms.

**16 August 1991**
UNHCR and the South African Government initial a Memorandum of Understanding on the voluntary repatriation and reintegration of South African refugees and exiles.

**4 September 1991**
In his second progress report on implementation of the 1989 Declaration on Apartheid, the Secretary-General finds that "over the last 12 months the process towards the end of apartheid in South Africa, although halting, has remained on course".
*See Document 146, page 435*

UNHCR and the South African Government sign their Memorandum of Understanding.

**8 September 1991**
At least 42 people die and 50 are injured in political violence in Thokoza, Katlehong and Tembisa.

**14 September 1991**
The National Peace Accord is signed in Johannesburg by 23 political parties, trade unions, religious and civic organizations, and the Government; it includes a code of conduct for security forces and political parties and establishes a National Peace Committee and a Commission of Inquiry regarding the Prevention of Public Violence and Intimidation, chaired by Justice R. J. Goldstone, to monitor implementation of the Accord.

**16 September 1991**
South Africa signs a Safeguards Agreement with the IAEA, allowing the inspection of its nuclear facilities by the Agency.

**27 October 1991**
At the end of a Patriotic/United Front Conference held at Durban and attended by some 90 organizations, the participants adopt a Declaration in which they call for a constituent assembly to draft and adopt a democratic constitution; a sovereign interim government/transitional authority; and an all-party congress/pre-constituent assembly meeting, brought together by independent and neutral conveners, to be held as soon as possible.

**30 November 1991**
At the end of a two-day preparatory meeting chaired by Judges Ismail Mohammed and Petrus Schabort, 19 political and other organizations decide unanimously or by "sufficient consensus" that the first meeting of a

Convention for a Democratic South Africa (CODESA) will be held in December.

**13 December 1991**
The General Assembly calls upon the international community to resume academic, scientific and cultural links with democratic anti-apartheid organizations and sports links with unified non-racial sporting organizations of South Africa.
*See Document 147, page 436*

**17 December 1991**
The Secretary-General announces that Mrs. Sadako Ogata, United Nations High Commissioner for Refugees, and Prof. Ibrahim Gambari (Nigeria), Chairman of the Special Committee against Apartheid, will lead the United Nations observer delegation to CODESA.

**18 December 1991**
The Steering Committee of CODESA reaches an agreement whereby all parties will commit themselves "politically and morally" to put CODESA's decisions into effect. Chief Buthelezi announces that he will not attend the first session of CODESA, in view of the decision taken by its Steering Committee not to invite Zulu King Goodwill Zwelithini to lead a delegation separate from that of the IFP.

**20 December 1991**
The first plenary session of CODESA meets in Johannesburg; 19 organizations, as well as the Government, are represented; the United Nations, the OAU, the Movement of Non-Aligned Countries, the Commonwealth and the EC are represented by observer delegations; 17 participants (which do not include the PAC and the Conservative Party) sign a Declaration of Intent, whereby they commit themselves to "bring about an undivided South Africa free from apartheid" and to a number of constitutional principles.

**21 December 1991**
Participants in CODESA decide to set up five working groups to report to a second CODESA plenary session. The United Nations and other observer delegations declare, in a joint statement, that "the broad objectives expressed in the Declaration of Intent are a most constructive and auspicious beginning for CODESA and give promise of attainment of true democracy for South Africa".

**18 February 1992**
Boutros Boutros-Ghali, the newly elected Secretary-General of the United Nations, addressing the Special Committee against Apartheid, says it is possible to envisage a new society in South Africa, "an undivided society in which economic wealth and opportunity are shared by all".
*See Document 152, page 442*

**20 February 1992**
President de Klerk announces that a referendum for Whites only will be held on 17 March 1992 to determine their support for the continuation of the reform process aimed at drafting a new constitution through negotiations.

**17 March 1992**
Eighty-six per cent of the White voting population participate in the referendum: 68.7 per cent vote "Yes", compared with 31.3 per cent who vote "No".
*See Document 153, page 443*

**3 April 1992**
In an attack by a gang from an IFP stronghold in Katlehong, 23 people, including women and children, are killed.

**15 - 16 May 1992**
The second plenary session of CODESA (CODESA II) is held in Johannesburg; failure to resolve the deadlock in Working Group 2, especially over the percentage vote required for the adoption or amendment of the constitution, leads to an impasse and prevents the consideration of other reports; the ANC decides on mass action to press for the establishment of an interim government and elections for a constituent assembly.

**16 June 1992**
The ANC begins an open-ended campaign of public protest with a day of rallies and work stoppages.

**17 June 1992**
Armed attackers shoot and hack their way through the township of Boipatong, leaving more than 40 people dead and scores injured, including women and children.

**23 June 1992**
The ANC National Executive Committee decides, at an emergency meeting, to suspend bilateral talks with the Government and participation in CODESA negotiations.

**27 June 1992**
On a visit to Nigeria, Secretary-General Boutros-Ghali meets with South African Foreign Minister Roelof Botha to discuss the deteriorating situation in South Africa and the constructive role the United Nations could play; he also meets the Chairman of the IFP, who hands him a message from Chief Buthelezi.

**29 June - 1 July 1992**

Responding to requests from the ANC and the PAC, OAU heads of State at their summit in Dakar, Senegal, adopt a resolution calling for an urgent meeting of the Security Council to examine the issue of violence in South Africa and to take action to put an end to it. During the summit, Secretary-General Boutros-Ghali meets with ANC President Nelson Mandela and PAC President Clarence Makwetu and discusses the situation in South Africa and possible assistance by the international community.

**1 July 1992**

Justice P. N. Bhagwati, former Chief Justice of India, is appointed to join the Commission of Inquiry regarding the Prevention of Public Intimidation and Violence (Goldstone Commission) as an assessor in the investigation of the recent Boipatong massacre; Mr. P. A. J. Waddington, Director of Criminal Justice Studies of Reading University, United Kingdom, is appointed to evaluate the police investigation of that massacre.

**2 July 1992**

President de Klerk offers to lower the margin of approval needed for changes in South Africa's constitution from 75 per cent to 70 per cent.

**10 July 1992**

An international panel led by Mr. Philip Heymann, Director of the Harvard Law School Center for Criminal Justice, proposes changes in the way South African police deal with protesters, including the universal ban on demonstrators carrying weapons, timely notice by protest organizers and the prohibition of the use of lethal force to disperse a crowd.

**15 - 16 July 1992**

The Security Council meets to examine the issue of violence in South Africa and to take appropriate action; the representatives of almost 50 Member States, as well as the Presidents of the ANC and the PAC, make statements; the Council also hears nine representatives from other political parties in CODESA who speak in their personal capacity; the Council then unanimously adopts resolution 765 (1992), pursuant to which the Secretary-General appoints a Special Representative, Mr. Cyrus Vance, to visit South Africa.
*See Document 156, page 444*

**21 - 31 July 1992**

Mr. Vance visits South Africa and holds discussions with the Government and a wide range of political parties, as well as religious, business and other leaders.

**23 July 1992**

Agreement is reached between the South African Police, the ANC, SACP and the Congress of South African Trade Unions (COSATU) on the principles outlined by a panel of experts on how mass demonstrations should be controlled; the IFP says that it is unable to agree to terms restricting the carrying of "cultural weapons".

**31 July 1992**

At the request of Mr. Mandela, and after consultation with the South African Government and others, Secretary-General Boutros-Ghali assigns 10 United Nations observers to monitor events during the week of mass action by the ANC and allied organizations beginning on 3 August; they are immediately deployed in various provinces of the country.

**3 - 4 August 1992**

Millions of workers participate in a two-day nationwide strike called by the ANC.

**7 August 1992**

The Secretary-General submits to the Security Council a report based on the findings of his Special Representative and makes a number of recommendations, including a strengthening and reinforcement of the mechanisms established by the National Peace Accord.
*See Document 158, page 445*

**17 August 1992**

The Security Council approves the Secretary-General's report and authorizes the stationing of the United Nations Observer Mission in South Africa (UNOMSA) to work closely with the National Peace Secretariat to address the areas of concern noted in the report; the Council also invites the deployment of observers from the OAU, the Commonwealth and the EC.
*See Document 160, page 448*

**21 August 1992**

ANC Secretary-General Cyril Ramaphosa and Constitutional Affairs Minister Roelf Meyer begin discussions on a number of matters relating to the negotiations.

**7 September 1992**

Ciskei security forces fire on ANC demonstrators marching towards the capital of the homeland, killing 29 of them and wounding more than 200.
*See Document 161, page 449*

**10 September 1992**

The Security Council deplores the killing of demonstrators in Ciskei on 7 September and emphasizes the need to put an end to violence and create conditions for

negotiations leading to the establishment of a democratic, non-racial and united South Africa.
*See Document 162, page 450*

**16 September 1992**
The Secretary-General writes to Justice Goldstone to commend the work of his Commission.
*See Document 163, page 450*

**16 - 26 September 1992**
Mr. Virendra Dayal visits South Africa as the Special Envoy of the Secretary-General.
*See Document 165, page 452; and Document 167, page 453*

**23 September 1992**
Ms. Angela King, head of UNOMSA, arrives in Johannesburg with six observers, bringing the total number of United Nations observers in the country to 20.
*See Document 166, page 452*

**26 September 1992**
A bilateral meeting between delegations of the ANC and the South African Government, led respectively by Mr. Mandela and President de Klerk, is held in Johannesburg; agreement is reached on a number of issues.

**27 September 1992**
Chief Buthelezi, leader of the IFP, denounces the agreements between the Government and the ANC.

**30 September 1992**
The National Executive Committee of the ANC ratifies the party's agreements with the Government and agrees that it indicates sufficient movement to enable the ANC to return to negotiations.

**24 October 1992**
In a joint statement, the Government and the PAC say that they agree on the urgent need for the establishment of a more representative forum which would decide on transitional arrangements leading to a new constitution.

**6 November 1992**
In the third progress report on implementation of the 1989 Declaration on Apartheid, the Secretary-General reports that UNOMSA is proceeding to fulfil its mandate.
*See Document 171, page 455*

**15 November 1992**
Forty-two political prisoners are released in accordance with the agreements between the South African Government and the ANC.

**22 November - 9 December 1992**
Mr. Tom Vraalsen visits South Africa as Special Envoy of the Secretary-General.

**26 November 1992**
President de Klerk announces a proposed timetable for the transitional process in South Africa which envisages that a fully representative government of national unity would be in place no later than the first half of 1994.

**22 December 1992**
The Secretary-General submits a comprehensive report to the Security Council on the efforts to establish peace and to promote multi-party negotiations in South Africa. He notes that the goal of a democratic, non-racial and united South Africa must remain a high priority for the United Nations.
*See Document 176, page 462*

**1 - 10 March 1993**
A delegation of the Special Committee against Apartheid, headed by its Chairman, Prof. Ibrahim Gambari, visits South Africa; it holds consultations with high-ranking representatives of all the major parties.

**5 March 1993**
Ending a 10-month deadlock since the collapse of the CODESA II negotiations, delegations from 26 parties and organizations hold a two-day multi-party planning conference; in a resolution adopted by all the parties (except the Conservative Party, which abstains), they agree to start new multi-party negotiations.

**24 March 1993**
In a speech to Parliament, President de Klerk discloses that the South African Government has been engaged in a 15-year clandestine nuclear-weapon programme, leading to the production of six crude atomic bombs, and was at work on a seventh when it decided to dismantle its nuclear arsenal in 1989; IAEA welcomes the disclosure and declares that it intends to inspect the sites involved and to review records.

**1 April 1993**
Representatives from 26 South African political parties and organizations begin multi-party negotiations.

**10 April 1993**
The general secretary of the South African Communist Party, Mr. Chris Hani, is assassinated at his home in Boksburg.

**24 April 1993**
Mr. Oliver Tambo, National Chairman of the ANC, dies.
*See Document 181, page 474*

**2 July 1993**
The Plenary of the Multi-party Negotiating Process adopts by consensus 27 constitutional principles which, along with a Bill of Rights, would be included in both the interim constitution and the final constitution to be adopted by an elected constituent assembly.

**6 August 1993**
Secretary-General Boutros-Ghali contacts Chief Buthelezi to urge that the IFP participate in the negotiating process.

**24 August 1993**
Following an upsurge of violence in South Africa, and especially in the East Rand, the Security Council expresses concern and urges the political parties to reaffirm their commitment to the Multi-party Negotiating Process.
*See Document 184, page 476*

**23 September 1993**
The South African Parliament passes a bill establishing the Transitional Executive Council (TEC).

**24 September 1993**
Nelson Mandela, addressing the Special Committee against Apartheid, expresses his gratitude for the sustained support of the United Nations and calls for an end to economic sanctions.
*See Document 186, page 477*

**7 October 1993**
Parties opposed to the proposed election date of 27 April 1994 and to the constitutional arrangements under consideration form a "Freedom Alliance" and remain outside the negotiating process; they include the IFP, the Conservative Party, the Afrikaner Volksfront and the leaders of Bophuthatswana and Ciskei.

**8 October 1993**
The General Assembly requests States to terminate prohibitions or restrictions on economic relations with South Africa immediately and to terminate the oil embargo against South Africa when the TEC becomes operational.
*See Document 187, page 480*

**15 October 1993**
Nelson Mandela and President de Klerk are awarded the Nobel Peace Prize.
*See Document 188, page 480*

**18 - 20 October 1993**
During a visit to Maputo, Secretary-General Boutros-Ghali meets South African political leaders, including

Chief Buthelezi and Foreign Minister Roelof Botha, and underlines the importance the United Nations attaches to the peace process.
*See Document 192, page 482*

**18 November 1993**
Leaders of 20 political parties at the Multi-party Negotiating Process endorse an interim constitution and an electoral bill; they also formulate a package of agreements for the transition; the Secretary-General applauds the "historic agreement".
*See Document 189, page 480; and Document 190, page 481*

**6 December 1993**
In the fourth progress report on implementation of the 1989 Declaration on Apartheid, the Secretary-General urges all parties in South Africa to cooperate in the implementation of the transitional arrangements.
*See Document 192, page 482*

**7 December 1993**
At its first meeting, the TEC adopts a resolution of the Multi-party Negotiating Council requesting that the United Nations, the Commonwealth, the European Union, the OAU and individual Governments provide a sufficient number of international observers to monitor the electoral process; the TEC also appeals to the United Nations to coordinate all international observers and to ensure close cooperation with the Independent Electoral Commission.

**9 December 1993**
The United Nations Electoral Assistance Unit sends a "Needs Assessment Team" to South Africa. The President of the General Assembly announces the repeal of the oil embargo against South Africa in view of the TEC's becoming operational.
*See Document 193, page 484*

**15 December 1993**
The South African Parliament votes to restore citizenship to residents of "the independent" States of Bophuthatswana, Ciskei, Transkei and Venda.

**16 December 1993**
The Secretary-General appoints Mr. Lakhdar Brahimi (Algeria) as his Special Representative for South Africa; Mr. Brahimi visits South Africa from 16 to 23 December and holds extensive consultations.

**20 December 1993**
The General Assembly terminates the mandate of the Intergovernmental Group to Monitor the Supply

and Shipping of Oil and Petroleum Products to South Africa.
*See Document 196, page 487*

**22 December 1993**
The South African Parliament adopts the Constitution for the Transition Period, to come into force on 27 April 1994.

**10 January 1994**
The Secretary-General submits to the Security Council and the General Assembly a report based on the findings of the survey team and Mr. Brahimi's mission, with detailed recommendations for the observation of elections in South Africa, including an expansion of the mandate of UNOMSA.
*See Document 199, page 489*

**14 January 1994**
The Security Council unanimously approves the recommendations of the Secretary-General.
*See Document 200, page 502*

**16 January 1994**
The PAC announces the suspension of armed struggle.

**2 February 1994**
President de Klerk announces that South Africa's first non-racial democratic elections will be held from 26 to 28 April.

**12 February 1994**
Nineteen political parties register to participate in the first democratic elections in South Africa.

**14 February 1994**
At a meeting held in Durban City Hall, Zulu King Goodwill Zwelithini tells President de Klerk that he is prepared to set up a Zulu kingdom; in a memorandum which he presents to President de Klerk, the King rejects South Africa's Interim Constitution.

**16 February 1994**
Nelson Mandela announces constitutional concessions which would strengthen the power of the provinces under the country's post-apartheid constitution, including the power of taxation and a constitutional principle of "self-determination".
*See Document 202, page 504*

**21 February 1994**
The ANC and the South African Government make concessions in an attempt to draw all parties into an inclusive constitutional settlement; the Multi-party Negotiating Council agrees that provincial legislatures would in certain circumstances be competent to draw up laws for the provinces.

**7 March 1994**
General Constand Viljoen, co-leader of the Afrikaner Volksfront, registers a new party, the Freedom Front, for the elections; the Bophuthatswana cabinet, for its part, continues to oppose registration.

**14 March 1994**
Following a widespread revolt against the government of Bophuthatswana, the TEC Management Committee decides on a new administration for the territory.

**22 March 1994**
The TEC decides on a new administration in Ciskei, following a mutiny by the police and the defence forces and the resignation of the territory's ruler, Brigadier Oupa Gqozo.

**28 March 1994**
A march organized by IFP supporters in central Johannesburg results in clashes with ANC supporters; over 50 people are killed and 250 are injured; the Secretary-General strongly deplores the violence.

**31 March 1994**
President de Klerk declares a state of emergency in KwaZulu/Natal following an upsurge of violence in the province.

**19 April 1994**
The IFP agrees — following talks between President de Klerk, Mr. Mandela and Chief Buthelezi — to participate in the elections; King Goodwill Zwelithini calls on his subjects to take part in the elections; political violence drops dramatically in the country.
*See Document 207, page 506; and Document 208, page 506*

**23 April 1994**
The Government, the ANC and the Freedom Front sign an agreement establishing a framework for the consideration of a separate State for Whites.

**26 - 29 April 1994**
General elections are held in South Africa; they are extended by one day in some regions where practical difficulties are encountered.

**27 April 1994**
South Africa's Interim Constitution enters into force; South Africa's new six-colour flag is unfurled for the first time at United Nations Headquarters.

**6 May 1994**

Announcing the final results of the elections, Judge Johann Kriegler, Chairman of the Independent Electoral Commission, says that the elections were substantially free and fair and that "we were able to establish the will of the people with reasonable accuracy"; the ANC obtains 62.6 per cent of the vote, the National Party 20.4 per cent and the IFP 10.5 per cent; the ANC wins in seven of the nine provinces, the National Party wins in the Western Cape and the IFP wins in KwaZulu/Natal.

The Secretary-General applauds the election process as a peaceful expression of the people's aspiration to a better future and pledges continued United Nations commitment to South Africa.
*See Document 209, page 507*

**10 May 1994**

A democratic non-racial Government takes office in South Africa, with Mr. Mandela as President. At the inauguration, Secretary-General Boutros-Ghali states, "Today, South Africa regains its rightful place in Africa, in the United Nations and in the family of nations".
*See Document 210, page 507*

**23 May 1994**

South Africa is formally accepted as the fifty-third member of the OAU.

**24 May 1994**

President Mandela, in his state-of-the-nation address to Parliament, announces that South Africa will subscribe to the Universal Declaration of Human Rights and accede to other human rights conventions of the United Nations.

**25 May 1994**

The Security Council terminates the arms embargo against South Africa.
*See Document 212, page 508; and Document 213, page 510*

**31 May 1994**

South Africa joins the Movement of Non-Aligned Countries as a full member.

**1 June 1994**

South Africa resumes membership in the Commonwealth.

**14 June 1994**

The Special Committee against Apartheid adopts its final report to the General Assembly and the Security Council, declaring that the system of apartheid has been brought to an end and that the Committee has fulfilled its mandate.
*See Document 215, page 511*

**16 June 1994**

Secretary-General Boutros-Ghali issues his final report on the question of South Africa on the successful holding of South Africa's first democratic elections and congratulating the Independent Electoral Commission on its work.
*See Document 216, page 515*

**23 June 1994**

The General Assembly approves the credentials of the South African delegation, terminates the mandate of the Special Committee against Apartheid, discontinues the United Nations Trust Fund for South Africa and removes from its agenda the item on "Elimination of apartheid and establishment of a united, democratic and non-racial South Africa".
*See Document 217, page 537; Document 218, page 538; and Document 219, page 540*

**27 June 1994**

The Security Council notes "with great satisfaction" the establishment of a united, non-racial and democratic Government of South Africa and removes the item on "The question of South Africa" from its agenda.
*See Document 220, page 540*

**3 October 1994**

In his first address to the General Assembly as President of South Africa, Nelson Mandela states: "We therefore return to the United Nations to make the commitment that as we undertook never to rest until the system of apartheid was defeated, so do we now undertake that we cannot rest while millions of our people suffer the pain and indignity of poverty in all its forms."
*See Document 221, page 541*

# II Chronology of United Nations conferences and seminars

*The following chronology of conferences and seminars organized by the United Nations or its affiliated bodies also provides the symbol for United Nations documents that contain relevant resolutions, reports or other information about the proceedings. These documents can be found at the Dag Hammarskjöld Library at United Nations Headquarters in New York, at other libraries in the United Nations system or at libraries around the world which have been designated as depository libraries for United Nations documents. Some of these documents are reproduced in this book; in such cases the chronology entry includes the document number established for this book as well as a cross-reference to the page on which the text appears.*

**23 August - 4 September 1966**
International Seminar on Apartheid, Brasilia.
Organized by the Secretary-General of the United Nations in consultation with the Special Committee against Apartheid and the Commission on Human Rights and with the cooperation of the Government of Brazil.
*A/6412; ST/TAO/HR/27*

**25 July - 4 August 1967**
International Seminar on Apartheid, Racial Discrimination and Colonialism in Southern Africa, Kitwe, Zambia.
Organized by the Secretary-General of the United Nations in consultation with the Special Committee against Apartheid and the United Nations Special Committee on Decolonization.
*See Document 53, page 300*

**9 - 14 April 1973**
International Conference of Experts for the Support of Victims of Colonialism and Apartheid in Southern Africa, Oslo.
Organized by the United Nations in cooperation with the Organization of African Unity (OAU).
*See Document 68, page 319*

**15 - 16 June 1973**
International Conference of Trade Unions against Apartheid, Geneva.
Organized by the Workers' Group of the International Labour Organisation (ILO) Governing Body in cooperation with the Special Committee against Apartheid.
*See Document 66, page 317; Document 69, page 323; A/AC.115/L.238*

**28 April - 2 May 1975**
Seminar on South Africa, Paris.
Organized by the Special Committee against Apartheid.
*A/10103-S/11708; A/AC.115/L.402*

**24 - 28 May 1976**
International Seminar on the Eradication of Apartheid and in Support of the Struggle for Liberation in South Africa, Havana.
Organized by the Special Committee against Apartheid in cooperation with the Government of Cuba and the OAU.
*A/31/104-S/12092*

**10 - 11 June 1977**
Second International Trade Union Conference for Action against Apartheid, Geneva.
Organized by the Workers' Group of the ILO Governing Body in cooperation with the Special Committee against Apartheid.
*A/RES/31/6 G; A/32/22/Add.1 - S/12363/Add.1*

**22 - 26 August 1977**
World Conference for Action against Apartheid, Lagos.
Organized by the United Nations in cooperation with the OAU and the Federal Republic of Nigeria and in consultation with the South African liberation movements recognized by the OAU and the NGO Subcommittee on Racism, Racial Discrimination, Apartheid and Decolonization.
*See Document 87, page 344; A/CONF.91/9 and Corr.1*

**4-8 April 1978**
Conference on Migratory Labour in Southern Africa, Lusaka.
Organized by the Economic Commission for Africa and the International Labour Organisation in cooperation with the Government of Zambia and the liberation movements of southern Africa that are recognized by the OAU.
*A/RES/33/162*

**17 - 22 July 1978**
Symposium on the Exploitation of Blacks in South Africa and Namibia and on Prison Conditions in South African Jails, Maseru, Lesotho.
Organized by the Commission on Human Rights.
*ST/HR/SER.A/1*

**28 - 31 August 1978**
International NGO Conference for Action against Apartheid, Geneva.
Organized by the NGO Subcommittee on Racism, Racial Discrimination, Apartheid and Decolonization in cooperation with the Special Committee against Apartheid.
*A/AC.115/L.501*

**19 - 22 February 1979**
World Conference of Youth and Students on the Struggle of the Peoples, Youth and Students of Southern Africa, Paris.
Organized by youth and student organizations in cooperation with the Special Committee against Apartheid and the United Nations Educational, Scientific and Cultural Organization (UNESCO).
*UN Press Release GA/AP/885*

**24 - 25 February 1979**
United Nations Seminar on Nuclear Collaboration with South Africa, London.
Organized by the Special Committee against Apartheid in cooperation with the NGO Subcommittee on Racism, Racial Discrimination, Apartheid and Decolonization and the British Anti-Apartheid Movement.
*S/13157*

**18 - 20 June 1979**
International Seminar on Children under Apartheid, Paris.
Organized by the Special Committee against Apartheid in cooperation with the NGO Subcommittee on Racism, Racial Discrimination, Apartheid and Decolonization.
*A/34/512*

**2 - 4 November 1979**
International Seminar on the Role of Transnational Corporations in South Africa, London.
Organized by the British Anti-Apartheid Movement in cooperation with the Special Committee against Apartheid.
*A/34/655; A/AC.115/L.521*

**14 - 16 March 1980**
International Seminar on an Oil Embargo against South Africa, Amsterdam.
Organized by the Holland Committee on Southern Africa and Working Group KAIROS in cooperation with the Special Committee against Apartheid.
*A/AC.115/L.521; A/35/160-S/13869*

**9 - 11 May 1980**
Hemispheric Seminar on Women under Apartheid, Montreal, Canada.
Organized by the Ligue des femmes du Quebec and other Canadian organizations in cooperation with the Special Committee against Apartheid and the Secretariat of the World Conference of the United Nations Decade for Women.
*A/AC.115/L.525; A/CONF.94/BP/17*

**19 - 21 May 1980**
International Seminar on Women and Apartheid, Helsinki.
Organized by the NGO Subcommittee on Racism, Racial Discrimination, Apartheid and Decolonization in cooperation with the Special Committee against Apartheid, UNESCO and the Secretariat of the World Conference of the Decade for Women.
*A/35/286; A/AC.115/L.528; A/CONF.94/BP/17*

**23 - 26 May 1980**
International Seminar on Youth Solidarity with the People's Struggle in Southern Africa and Consultative Meeting with International Youth and Student Organizations, Sigtuna, Sweden.
Organized by the Special Committee against Apartheid with the assistance of the International Youth and Student Movement for the United Nations (ISMUN).
*A/AC.115/L.526; A/AC.115/L.529*

**30 June - 3 July 1980**
International NGO Action Conference for Sanctions against South Africa, Geneva.
Organized by the NGO Subcommittee on Racism, Racial Discrimination, Apartheid and Decolonization in cooperation with the Special Committee against Apartheid.
*A/35/439-S/14160*

**20 - 24 October 1980**
United Nations Institute for Training and Research (UNITAR) Colloquium on the Prohibition of Apartheid, Racism and Racial Discrimination and the Achievement of Self-determination in International Law, Geneva.
Organized by UNITAR.
*A/35/677-S/14281*

**6 - 7 November 1980**
Seminar on the role of transnational corporations in South Africa and Namibia, London.
Organized by the United Nations Department of Public Information.

**30 - 31 January 1981**
Conference of West European Parliamentarians on an Oil Embargo against South Africa, Brussels.
Organized by the Special Committee against Apartheid in cooperation with a committee of nine West European parliamentarians.
*UN Press Release GA/AP/1167*

**1 - 3 April 1981**
International Seminar on the Implementation and Reinforcement of the Arms Embargo against South Africa, London.
Organized by the Special Committee against Apartheid in cooperation with the World Campaign against Military and Nuclear Collaboration with South Africa and with the assistance of the British Anti-Apartheid Movement.
*A/RES/35/206 B; A/36/170-S/14442; A/AC.115/L.547*

**5 - 7 April 1981**
International Seminar on Loans to South Africa, Zurich, Switzerland.
Organized by the Special Committee against Apartheid in cooperation with the World Council of Churches, the NGO Subcommittee on Racism, Racial Discrimination, Apartheid and Decolonization, the Swiss Anti-Apartheid Movement and the Bern Declaration Group.
*A/AC.115/L.548; A/36/201-S/14443*

**20 - 27 May 1981**
First International Conference on Sanctions against South Africa, Paris.
Organized by the Special Committee against Apartheid in cooperation with the OAU.
*See Document 103, page 361; A/RES/34/93 C; A/36/319-S/14531*

**11 - 12 June 1981**
Symposium on the role of transnational corporations in South Africa and Namibia, Detroit, United States.
Organized by the United Nations Department of Public Information in cooperation with the Detroit City Council.
*A/AC.115/SR.478*

**29 June - 3 July 1981**
Seminar on Effective Measures to Prevent Transnational Corporations and Other Established Interests from Collaborating with the Racist Regime of South Africa, Geneva.
Organized by the Commission on Human Rights in cooperation with the Special Committee against Apartheid.
*ST/HR/SER.A/9*

**31 August - 2 September 1981**
International Seminar on Publicity and Role of the Mass Media in the International Mobilization against Apartheid, Berlin, German Democratic Republic.
Organized by the Special Committee against Apartheid in cooperation with the Government of the German Democratic Republic and the Solidarity Committee of the German Democratic Republic.
*A/36/496-S/14686; A/AC.115/L.555*

**13 - 15 November 1981**
International Conference of Youth and Students in Solidarity with the Peoples, Youth and Students of Southern Africa, Luanda.
Organized by international, African and Angolan youth and student organizations in cooperation with the Special Committee against Apartheid.
*A/AC.115/L.564*

**11 - 13 March 1982**
Conference on Southern Africa — "Time to Choose", London.
Organized by the British Anti-Apartheid Movement in cooperation with the Special Committee against Apartheid.
*A/AC.115/L.568*

**29 March - 2 April 1982**
International Seminar on the History of Resistance against Occupation, Oppression and Apartheid in South Africa, Paris.
Organized by the Special Committee against Apartheid in cooperation with UNESCO.
*A/AC.115/L.576*

**17 - 19 May 1982**
International Conference on Women and Apartheid, Brussels.
Organized by the Special Committee against Apartheid in cooperation with the International Committee of Solidarity with the Struggle of Women in South Africa and Namibia.
*See Document 105, page 368; A/37/261-S/15150*

**24 - 26 May 1982**
Asian Regional Conference for Action against Apartheid, Manila.
Organized by the Special Committee against Apartheid in cooperation with the Government of the Philippines.
*A/37/265-S/15157; A/AC.115/L.573*

**26 - 27 November 1982**
Conference of West European Parliamentarians on Sanctions against South Africa, The Hague.
Organized by five Netherlands parliamentarians in cooperation with the Special Committee against Apartheid.
*A/37/691-S/15508; A/AC.115/L.587*

**10 - 11 June 1983**
International Conference of Trade Unions on Sanctions and Other Actions against the Apartheid Regime in South Africa, Geneva.
Organized by the Workers' Group of the Governing Body of the ILO and the Special Committee against Apartheid in cooperation with the United Nations Council for Namibia, the OAU and the Organization of African Trade Union Unity.
*See Document 108, page 372; UN Press Release GA/AP/1455*

**27 - 29 June 1983**
International Conference on Sanctions against Apartheid in Sports, London.
Organized by the Special Committee against Apartheid in cooperation with the South African Non-Racial Olympic Committee (SAN-ROC).
*A/38/310-S/15882; A/AC.115/L.594*

**5 - 8 July 1983**
International NGO Conference of Action against Apartheid and Racism, Geneva.
Organized by the NGO Subcommittee on Racism, Racial Discrimination, Apartheid and Decolonization in cooperation with the Special Committee against Apartheid.
*A/38/309-S/15881; A/AC.115/L.596*

**11 - 13 July 1983**
International Conference on the Alliance between South Africa and Israel, Vienna.
Organized by the Special Committee against Apartheid in cooperation with the Afro-Asian Peoples' Solidarity Organization, the Organization of African Trade Union Unity and the World Peace Council.
*A/38/311-S/15883; A/AC.115/L.595*

**16 - 18 September 1983**
Latin American Regional Conference for Action against Apartheid, Caracas.
Organized by the Special Committee against Apartheid in cooperation with the Government of Venezuela.
*A/38/451-S/16009; A/AC.115/L.603;*

**5 - 7 March 1984**
Interfaith Colloquium on Apartheid, London.
Organized by the Most Reverend Trevor Huddleston in cooperation with the Special Committee against Apartheid.
*A/AC.115/L.605*

**18 - 21 June 1984**
North American Regional Conference for Action against Apartheid, New York.
Organized by the Special Committee against Apartheid.
*A/39/370-S/16686; A/AC.115/L.614*

**25 - 26 June 1984**
Consultative Meeting of Anti-Apartheid and Solidarity Movements, London.
Organized by the British Anti-Apartheid Movement with the support of the Special Committee against Apartheid.
*A/AC.115/L.613*

**2 - 5 July 1984**
International NGO Conference for the Independence of Namibia and the Eradication of Apartheid, Geneva.
Organized by the NGO Subcommittee on Racism, Racial Discrimination, Apartheid and Decolonization in cooperation with the Special Committee against Apartheid and the United Nations Council for Namibia.
*A/AC.115/SR.550*

**7 - 9 August 1984**
Conference of Arab Solidarity with the Struggle for Liberation in Southern Africa, Tunis.
Organized by the Special Committee against Apartheid in cooperation with the League of Arab States.
*A/39/450-S/16726; A/AC.115/L.615*

**13 - 16 August 1984**
Seminar on the Legal Status of the Apartheid Regime and Other Legal Aspects of the Struggle against Apartheid, Lagos.
Organized by the Special Committee against Apartheid in cooperation with the Government of Nigeria.
*A/39/423-S/16709 and Corr.1; A/AC.115/L.616*

**17 - 19 October 1984**
International NGO Seminar on Women and Children under Apartheid, Geneva.
Organized by the NGO Subcommittee on Racism, Racial Discrimination, Apartheid and Decolonization in cooperation with the Special Committee against Apartheid.

**7 - 10 May 1985**
International Conference on Women and Children under Apartheid, Arusha, Tanzania.
Organized by the Special Committee against Apartheid in cooperation with the OAU and the Government of the United Republic of Tanzania.
*A/40/319-S/17197; A/AC.115/L.623*

**16 - 18 May 1985**
Second International Conference on Sports Boycott against South Africa, Paris.
Organized by the Special Committee against Apartheid in cooperation with the Supreme Council on Sports in Africa and SAN-ROC.
*A/40/343-S/17224; A/AC.115/L.624 and Corr.1*

**20 - 22 May 1985**
Media Workshop on Countering Apartheid Propaganda, London.
Organized by the Commonwealth Secretariat in cooperation with the Special Committee against Apartheid.
*A/40/696-S/17511*

**9 - 11 September 1985**
International Seminar on Racist Ideologies, Attitudes and Organizations Hindering Efforts for the Elimination of Apartheid and Means to Combat Them, Siofok, Hungary.
Organized by the Special Committee against Apartheid in cooperation with the Hungarian Solidarity Committee.
*A/40/660-S/17477; A/AC.115/L.634*

**30 - 31 October 1985**
International Conference of Maritime Trade Unions on the Implementation of the United Nations Oil Embargo against South Africa, London.
Organized by the Maritime Trade Unions against Apartheid in cooperation with the Special Committee against Apartheid.
*A/40/892-S/17632; UN Press Release GA/AP/1684*

**28 April - 9 May 1986**
Seminar on International Assistance and Support to Peoples and Movements Struggling against Colonialism, Racism, Racial Discrimination and Apartheid, Yaoundé, Cameroon.
Organized by the United Nations Centre for Human Rights and the Government of Cameroon.
*A/41/571; ST/HR/SER.A/19*

**28 - 30 May 1986**
International Seminar on the United Nations Arms Embargo against South Africa, London.
Organized by the Special Committee against Apartheid in cooperation with the World Campaign against Military and Nuclear Collaboration with South Africa.
*S/RES/421 (1977); S/18288; A/41/388-S/18121*

**4 - 6 June 1986**
Seminar on Oil Embargo against South Africa, Oslo.
Organized by the Special Committee against Apartheid in cooperation with the Government of Norway.
*A/41/404-S/18141; A/AC.115/L.636*

**16 - 20 June 1986**
World Conference on Sanctions against Racist South Africa, Paris.
Organized by the United Nations in cooperation with the OAU and the Movement of Non-Aligned Countries.
*See Document 119, page 397; A/RES/40/64 C; A/41/434-S/18185 and Corr.1*

**31 July - 3 August 1987**
International Student Conference in Solidarity with the Struggle of the Students of Southern Africa, London.
Organized by the Special Committee against Apartheid in cooperation with the British Anti-Apartheid Movement, the National Union of Students (U.K.), the All African Students Union, the Indian Youth Congress and the International Union of Students.
*A/42/665-S/19218; A/AC.115/L.649*

**5 - 7 November 1987**
International Conference against Apartheid Sport, Harare.
Organized by the Special Committee against Apartheid in cooperation with the Government of Zimbabwe, the Supreme Council for Sport in Africa, the Association of National Olympic Committees of Africa, the Union of African Sports Confederations, SAN-ROC and the Zimbabwe National Olympic Committee.
*A/42/762-S/19266*

**7 - 9 March 1988**
Seminar on the Role of the Latin American and Caribbean Media in the International Campaign against Apartheid, Lima.
Organized by the Special Committee against Apartheid in cooperation with the Government of Peru.
*A/AC.115/L.651/Rev.1*

**2 - 4 September 1988**
Symposium on Culture against Apartheid, Athens.
Organized by the Special Committee against Apartheid in cooperation with the Government of Greece and the Hellenic Association for the United Nations.
*A/43/606-S/20184; A/AC.115/L.656; A/AC.115/ INF/8*

**7 - 9 November 1988**
International Conference on Apartheid, Lagos.
Organized by the Special Committee against Apartheid in cooperation with Nigeria's National Committee against Apartheid.
*A/43/854-S/20288*

**16 - 18 January 1989**
Seminar on the Special Needs of South African and Namibian Refugee Women and Children, Harare.
Organized by the Special Committee against Apartheid in cooperation with the Association of Women's Clubs of Zimbabwe.
*A/AC.115/L.659*

**4 - 6 September 1989**
International NGO Seminar on Education against Apartheid, Geneva.
Organized by the NGO Sub-Committee on Racism, Racial Discrimination, Apartheid and Decolonization in cooperation with the Special Committee against Apartheid.
*A/44/522-S/20844; A/AC.115/L.663*

**23 - 25 January 1990**
Regional Seminar on East Asian Action against Apartheid, Tokyo.
Organized by the Special Committee against Apartheid.
*A/AC.115/L.666; A/AC.115/INF/12/Rev.1; UN Centre against Apartheid Notes and Documents No. 2/90*

**4 - 6 September 1990**
Fourth International Conference against Apartheid in Sports, Stockholm.
Organized by SAN-ROC, the Supreme Council for Sport in Africa, the International Campaign against Apartheid in Sport and the Swedish National Olympic Committee in cooperation with the Special Committee against Apartheid.
*A/AC.115/L.670; UN Centre against Apartheid Notes and Documents No. 14/90*

**10 - 14 December 1990**
International Seminar on the Political, Historical, Economic, Social and Cultural Factors Contributing to Racism, Racial Discrimination and Apartheid, Geneva.
Organized by the United Nations Centre for Human Rights.
*E/CN.4/1991/63 and Add.1; ST/HR/PUB/91/3*

**11 - 12 May 1991**
Symposium on Cultural and Academic Links with South Africa, Los Angeles, United States.
Organized by the Special Committee against Apartheid in cooperation with the City of Los Angeles, the Screen Actors Guild and the Directors Guild of America.
*A/46/177; A/AC.115/L.677; UN Centre against Apartheid Information Note No. SCA/GE/91/3*

**18 - 21 June 1991**
Workshop on Human Rights Issues for a Post-Apartheid South Africa, Banjul, Gambia.
Organized by the UNESCO Division of Human Rights and Peace and the African Commission on Human and People's Rights.

**25 - 27 June 1991**
International Conference on the Educational Needs of the Victims of Apartheid in South Africa, Paris.
Organized by the Special Committee against Apartheid and the Advisory Committee of the United Nations Educational and Training Programme for Southern Africa.
*A/AC.115/L.678; A/AC.115/INF/17*

**22 - 24 May 1992**
Seminar on South Africa's Socio-economic Problems: Future Role of the United Nations System in Helping to Address Them, Windhoek, Namibia.
Organized by the Special Committee against Apartheid.
*A/AC.115/L.685*

**14 - 15 July 1992**
International Hearing on Political Violence in South Africa and the Implementation of the National Peace Accord, London.
Organized by Archbishop Trevor Huddleston, President of the British Anti-Apartheid Movement, in cooperation with the Special Committee against Apartheid.
*A/AC.115/L.687*

**8 - 9 September 1992**
Follow-up Conference on International Educational Assistance to Disadvantaged South Africans, New York.
Organized by the United Nations Educational and Training Programme for Southern Africa.
*A/RES/46/80*

**14 - 15 June 1993**
International Conference on Southern Africa: Making Hope a Reality, London.
Organized by the British Anti-Apartheid Movement and the Special Committee against Apartheid.
*A/48/255-S/26048*

**30 July - 1 August 1993**
Symposium on Political Tolerance in South Africa: Role of Opinion-makers and the Media, Cape Town.
Co-sponsored by the Special Committee against Apartheid, the Institute for a Democratic Alternative in South Africa (IDASA) and the Institute for Multiparty Democracy (MPD).
*A/AC.115/L.694*

**22 - 24 January 1994**
Seminar on Sustainable Economic Growth and Development in South Africa: Policy Priorities for the Early Years of a Democratic Government, London.
Organized by the Special Committee against Apartheid, the Centre for the Study of the South African Economy and the London School of Economics and Political Science.
*A/AC.115/L.696*

**8 - 10 February 1994**
Seminar on the Image of the United Nations in South Africa, Cape Town.
Organized by the United Nations Department of Public Information in cooperation with the University of the Western Cape, Cape Town.
*UN press releases PI/831-SAF/167 and SAF/169*

**28 February - 1 March 1994**
International Briefing on South Africa's First Democratic and Non-racial Elections, Brussels.
Organized by the Special Committee against Apartheid and the Liaison Group of the Anti-Apartheid Movements in the European Union.
*A/48/895-S/1994/261*

# III Bibliography of Documents

*The following bibliography contains a selection of United Nations resolutions, reports and other documents relating to the international struggle against apartheid in South Africa. A bullet (•) indicates that the text of a document has been reproduced in this book; a list of the reproduced documents, including the page numbers on which they can be found, appears on pages 205-219. Documents not reproduced in this book can be consulted at the Dag Hammarskjöld Library at United Nations Headquarters in New York, at other libraries in the United Nations system or at libraries around the world which have been designated as depository libraries for United Nations documents. This bibliography should be seen as an introduction to the vast of array of available materials; a complete listing of all the Organization's documentation concerning apartheid would run to several volumes.*

1.  ## General Assembly
    1.1    Resolutions
    1.2    Reports
    1.3    Other documents

2.  ## Security Council
    2.1    Resolutions
    2.2    Statements by the President of the
           Security Council on behalf of the Council
    2.3    Reports
    2.4    Other documents

3.  ## Economic and Social Council
    3.1    Resolutions
    3.2    Reports

4.  ## Other Documents and Materials
    4.1    Conference and seminar documents
    4.2    Correspondence of Secretaries-General
    4.3    Other documents and materials

Omnibus resolutions of the General Assembly, which contain more than one constituent resolution (e.g. A/RES/48/258 A, A/RES/48/258 B), are listed by the main title only (A/RES/48/258).

# 1. General Assembly

## 1.1 Resolutions

### Treatment of Indians in the Union of South Africa

- •A/RES/44 (I) .............................8 December 1946
- •A/RES/395 (V)...........................2 December 1950

### Policies of apartheid of the Government of South Africa

- •A/RES/616 (VII) ........................5 December 1952
- A/RES/721 (VIII) .......................8 December 1953
- A/RES/820 (IX).....................14 December 1954
- A/RES/917 (X)..........................6 December 1955
- A/RES/1016 (XI) ......................30 January 1957
- A/RES/1178 (XII....................26 November 1957
- A/RES/1248 (XIII)....................30 October 1958
- A/RES/1375 (XIV) ................17 November 1959
- •A/RES/1598 (XV)...........................13 April 1961
- A/RES/1663 (XVI) ...............28 November 1961
- •A/RES/1761 (XVII)...................6 November 1962
- •A/RES/1881 (XVIII ..................11 October 1963
- •A/RES/1978 (XVIII) ..............16 December 1963
- •A/RES/2054 (XX)...................15 December 1965
- •A/RES/2202 (XXI)..................16 December 1966
- A/RES/2307 (XXII)................13 December 1967
- •A/RES/2396 (XXIII) ...............2 December 1968
- A/RES/2506 (XXIV) ...........21 November 1969
- A/RES/2624 (XXV) ..................13 October 1970
- •A/RES/2671 (XXV) ................8 December 1970
- A/RES/2764 (XXVI) ..............9 November 1971
- •A/RES/2775 (XXVI) .............29 November 1971
- •A/RES/2923 (XXVII)..............15 November 1972 and 13 December 1972
- •A/RES/3151 (XXVIII)............14 December 1973
- A/R ES/3324 (XXIX) .............16 December 1974
- •A/RES/3411 (XXX) ...............28 November1975 and 10 December 1975
- •A/RES/31/6 ...............................26 October1976 and 9 November 1976
- •A/RES/32/105 .........................14 December 1977 and 16 December 1977

[contains International Declaration against Apartheid in Sports]

- •A/RES/33/183 ...........................24 January 1979
- •A/RES/34/93 ...............12 and 17 December 1979

[contains Declaration on South Africa]

- •A/RES/35/206 ........................16 December 1980
- A/RES/36/172 .........................17 December 1981
- •A/RES/37/69 .............................9 December 1982
- A/RES/38/39 .............................5 December 1983
- A/RES/39/72 ...........................13 December 1984
- •A/RES/40/64 ..........................10 December 1985

[contains International Convention against Apartheid in Sports]

- A/RES/41/35 ..........................10 November 1986
- •A/RES/42/23 .........................20 November 1987
- •A/RES/43/50 .............................5 December 1988
- •A/RES/44/27 .........................22 November 1989
- •A/RES/44/244 .......................17 September 1990
- •A/RES/45/176 ........................19 December 1990
- •A/RES/46/79 ...........................13 December 1991
- •A/RES/47/116 ........................18 December 1992

### Elimination of all forms of racial discrimination

- •A/RES/2142 (XXI) ...................26 October 1966
- A/RES/2438 (XXIII) ..............19 December 1968
- A/RES/2646 (XXV)...............30 November 1970
- A/RES/2647 (XXV)...............30 November 1970
- A/RES/2784 (XXVI) .................6 December 1971

[contains message from the President of the General Assembly on South Africa]

- A/RES/3057 (XXVIII) ..............2 November 1973
- A/RES/3223 (XXIX) ................6 November 1974
- A/RES/3377 (XXX) ...............10 November 1975
- A/RES/31/77 ...........................13 December 1976
- A/RES/32/10 ...........................7 November 1977
- A/RES/33/98 ...........................16 December 1978
- A/RES/33/99 ...........................16 December 1978
- A/RES/34/24 ...........................15 November 1979
- A/RES/35/33 ...........................14 November 1980
- A/RES/36/8 ................................28 October 1981
- A/RES/36/12 ..............................28 October 1981
- A/RES/37/40 .............................3 December 1982
- A/RES/37/41 .............................3 December 1982
- A/RES/38/14 ...........................22 November 1983
- A/RES/39/16 ...........................23 November 1984
- A/RES/39/21 ...........................23 November 1984
- A/RES/40/22 ...........................29 November 1985

• Text reproduced in this book; see list of reproduced documents pages 205-219

A/RES/40/28 .........................29 November 1985
A/RES/41/94 ...........................4 December 1986
A/RES/42/47 ........................30 November 1987
A/RES/43/91 ..........................8 December 1988
A/RES/44/52 ..........................8 December 1989
A/RES/45/105 .......................14 December 1990
A/RES/46/85 .........................16 December 1991
A/RES/47/77 .........................16 December 1992
A/RES/48/91 .........................20 December 1993

*Question of the violation of human
rights and fundamental freedoms,
including policies of racial discrimination and segregation and of apartheid*
•A/RES/2144 (XXI) ....................26 October 1966
A/RES/2714 (XXV) ...............15 December 1970

*United Nations Educational and
Training Programme for Southern Africa*
A/RES/2235 (XXI).................20 December 1966
A/RES/2349 (XXII)................19 December 1967
A/RES/2431 (XXIII) ..............18 December 1968
A/RES/2557 (XXIV) .............12 December 1969
A/RES/2706 (XXV) ...............14 December 1970
A/RES/2875 (XXVI) ..............20 December 1971
A/RES/2981 (XXVII)..............14 December 1972
A/RES/3119 (XXVIII)............12 December 1973
A/RES/3301 (XXIX) ..............13 December 1974
A/RES/3422 (XXX) .................8 December 1975
A/RES/31/31 ..........................29 November 1976
A/RES/32/37 ..........................28 November 1977
A/RES/33/42 ..........................13 December 1978
A/RES/34/31 ..........................21 November 1979
A/RES/35/30 ..........................11 November 1980
A/RES/36/53 ..........................24 November 1981
A/RES/37/33 ..........................23 November 1982
A/RES/38/52 ............................7 December 1983
A/RES/39/44 ............................5 December 1984
A/RES/40/54 ............................2 December 1985
A/RES/41/27 ............................31 October 1986
A/RES/42/76 ............................4 December 1987
A/RES/43/31 ..........................22 November 1988
A/RES/44/86 ..........................11 December 1989
A/RES/45/19 ..........................20 November 1990
A/RES/46/80 ..........................13 December 1991
A/RES/47/117 ........................18 December 1992
•A/RES/48/160........................20 December 1993

*Capital punishment in southern Africa*
A/RES/2394 (XXIII)..............26 November 1968

*United Nations Trust
Fund for South Africa*
(see also under: Policies of apartheid
of the Government of South Africa)
A/RES/2397 (XXIII) ................2 December 1968
A/RES/2774 (XXVI) .............29 November 1971

*Measures for effectively combating racial
discrimination and the policies of apartheid
and segregation in southern Africa*
A/RES/2439 (XXIII) ..............19 December 1968
A/RES/2547 (XXIV) ..............11 December 1969
                              and 15 December 1969

*Political prisoners in South Africa*
A/RES/2440 (XXII)................19 December 1968
A/RES/3055 (XXVIII)................26 October 1973
A/RES/32/65 ............................8 December 1977

*Measures to achieve the rapid and
total elimination of all forms of racial
discrimination in general and of the
policy of apartheid in particular*
A/RES/2446 (XXIII) ..............19 December 1968

*Manifesto on Southern Africa*
A/RES/2505 (XXIV) ..............20 November 1969

*Relationship between the United Nations
and South Africa and credentials of
representatives of South Africa*
A/RES/2636 (XXV)...............13 November 1970
A/RES/2862 (XXVI) ..............20 December 1971
A/RES/2948 (XXVII) ...............8 December 1972
•A/RES/3206 (XXIX) ..............30 September 1974
•A/RES/3207 (XXIX) ..............30 September 1974
•A/PV.2281.............................12 November 1974
[contains ruling by the President
of the General Assembly]

*International Convention on the
Suppression and Punishment
of the Crime of Apartheid*
A/RES/2786 (XXVI) ................6 December 1971

A/RES/2922 (XXVII) .............15 November 1972
•A/RES/3068 (XXVIII)...........30 November 1973
[contains Convention]
A/RES/3380 (XXX) ...............10 November 1975
A/RES/31/80 .........................13 December 1976
A/RES/32/12 .........................7 November 1977
A/RES/33/103 .......................16 December 1978
A/RES/34/27 ........................15 November 1979
A/RES/35/39 ........................25 November 1980
A/RES/36/13..........................28 October 1981
A/RES/37/47 ........................3 December 1982
A/RES/38/19 .......................22 November 1983
A/RES/39/19 .......................23 November 1984
A/RES/40/27 .......................29 November 1985
A/RES/41/103 ........................4 December 1986
A/RES/42/56 .......................30 November 1987
A/RES/43/97 ........................8 December 1988
A/RES/44/69 ........................8 December 1989
A/RES/45/90 .......................14 December 1990
A/RES/46/84 .........................16 December 1991
A/RES/47/81 .........................16 December 1992
A/RES/48/89 .........................20 December 1993

*Adverse consequences for the enjoyment
of human rights of political, military,
economic and other forms of assistance
given to colonial and racist regimes
in southern Africa*
A/RES/3383 (XXX) ...............10 November 1975
A/RES/31/33 ........................30 November 1976
A/RES/33/23 ........................29 November 1978
A/RES/35/32 ........................14 November 1980
A/RES/37/39 .........................3 December 1982
A/RES/39/15 .......................23 November 1984
A/RES/41/95 ..........................4 December 1986
A/RES/43/92 ..........................8 December 1988
A/RES/45/84 .......................14 December 1990

*Assistance to South African
student refugees
(1980-1990: Assistance to student
refugees in southern Africa)*
A/RES/31/126 ........................16 December 1976
A/RES/32/119 ........................16 December 1977
A/RES/33/164 .......................20 December 1978
A/RES/34/174 ........................17 December 1979

A/RES/35/184 ........................15 December 1980
A/RES/36/170 ........................16 December 1981
A/RES/37/177 ........................17 December 1982
A/RES/38/95 ........................16 December 1983
A/RES/39/109 ........................14 December 1984
A/RES/40/138 ........................13 December 1985
A/RES/41/136 ........................4 December 1986
A/RES/42/138 .........................7 December 1987
A/RES/43/149 ..........................8 December 1988
A/RES/44/157 ........................15 December 1989
A/RES/45/171 ........................18 December 1990

*Protection of persons detained or impris-
oned as a result of their struggle against
apartheid, racism and racial discrimination,
colonialism, aggression and foreign occupation and for self-determination, independence and social progress for their people*
A/RES/32/122 .........................16 December 1977

*Migratory labour in southern Africa*
A/RES/33/162...........................20 December 1978
[contains Charter of Rights]

*Status of persons refusing service in
the military or police forces used
to enforce apartheid*
A/RES/33/165 .........................20 December 1978

*Appeal for clemency in favour of
South African freedom fighters*
A/RES/37/1 ....................................1 October 1982
A/RES/37/68 ............................7 December 1982

*South Africa's application for credit
from the International Monetary Fund*
A/RES/37/2................................21 October 1982

*Proposed new racial
constitution of South Africa*
•A/RES/38/11 ........................15 November 1983

*Situation in South Africa*
A/RES/39/2 .............................28 September 1984

Measures of assistance provided
to South African and Namibian
refugee women and children
A/RES/41/123 ...........................4 December 1986

International Conference on the Plight
of Refugees, Returnees and Displaced
Persons in Southern Africa
A/RES/42/106 ...........................7 December 1987
A/RES/43/116 ...........................8 December 1988
A/RES/44/136 .......................15 December 1989
A/RES/45/137 .......................14 December 1990

Torture and inhuman treatment of
children in detention in South Africa
A/RES/42/124 ...........................7 December 1987
A/RES/43/134 ...........................8 December 1988
A/RES/44/143 .......................15 December 1989
A/RES/45/144 .......................14 December 1990

Pretoria's racial "municipal elections"
A/RES/43/13 ............................26 October 1988

Death sentence passed on a
South African patriot
A/RES/44/1 ...........................28 September 1989

Declaration on Apartheid and its
Destructive Consequences in
Southern Africa
•A/RES/S-16/1 ..........................14 December 1989

Lifting of sanctions against South Africa
•A/RES/48/1 ................................8 October 1993

Elimination of apartheid and
establishment of a united, democratic
and non-racial South Africa
•A/RES/48/159 .......................20 December 1993
•A/RES/48/258 ...............................23 June 1994

Democratic and non-racial elections
in South Africa
•A/RES/48/233 ............................21 January 1994

## 1.2 Reports

United Nations Commission on the Racial Situation in the Union of South Africa
•A/2505 (GAOR*, 8th session, Supplement No. 16) ...........................................................................1953
•A/2505/Add.1 (GAOR, 8th sess., Suppl. No. 16) .............................................................................1953
•A/2719 (GAOR, 9th sess., Suppl. No. 16) .......................................................................................1954
•A/2953 (GAOR, 10th sess., Suppl. No. 14) .....................................................................................1955

Special Committee against Apartheid
(1963-1970: Special Committee on the Policies of Apartheid of the
Government of the Republic of South Africa)
(1971-1974: Special Committee on Apartheid)
A/5418-S/5310 (GAOR, 18th sess., Annexes, agenda item 30) .........................................................1963
A/5453-S/5353 (GAOR, 18th sess., Annexes, a.i. 30) .....................................................................1963
•A/5497 (GAOR, 18th sess., Annexes, a.i. 30 ...............................................................................1963
A/5497/Add.1 (GAOR, 18th sess., Annexes, a.i. 30) ......................................................................1963
A/5692-S/5621 (GAOR, 19th sess., Annexes, a.i. 12) .....................................................................1964
A/5707-S/5717 (GAOR, 19th sess., Annexes, a.i. 12 ......................................................................1964
A/5825-S/6073 (GAOR, 19th sess., Annexes, a.i. 12) .....................................................................1964
A/5825/Add.1-S/6073/Add.1 (GAOR, 19th sess., Annexes, a.i. 12) ................................................1964
A/5932-S/6453 (GAOR, 20th sess., Annexes, a.i. 36) .....................................................................1965

*General Assembly Official Records

A/36/22/Add.1 (GAOR, 36th sess., Suppl. No. 22A)..............................................................1981
A/36/22/Add.2 (GAOR, 36th sess., Suppl. No. 22A)..............................................................1981
A/37/22 (GAOR, 37th sess., Suppl. No. 22) ........................................................................1982
A/37/22/Add.1 (GAOR, 37th sess., Suppl. No. 22A)..............................................................1982
A/37/22/Add.2 (GAOR, 37th sess., Suppl. No. 22A)..............................................................1982
A/38/22 (GAOR, 38th sess., Suppl. No. 22) ........................................................................1983
A/38/22/Add.1 (GAOR, 38th sess., Suppl. No. 22A)..............................................................1983
A/39/22 (GAOR, 39th sess., Suppl. No. 22) ........................................................................1984
A/39/22/Add.1 (GAOR, 39th sess., Suppl. No. 22A)..............................................................1984
A/40/22 (GAOR, 40th sess., Suppl. No. 22) ........................................................................1985
A/40/22/Add.1 (GAOR, 40th sess., Suppl. No. 22A)..............................................................1985
A/40/22/Add.2 (GAOR, 40th sess., Suppl. No. 22A)..............................................................1985
A/40/22/Add.3 (GAOR, 40th sess., Suppl. No. 22A)..............................................................1985
A/40/22/Add.4 (GAOR, 40th sess., Suppl. No. 22A)..............................................................1985
A/41/22 (GAOR, 41st sess., Suppl. No. 22) ........................................................................1986
A/41/22/Add.1-S/18360/Add.1 .........................................................................................1986
A/41/22/Add.1/Corr.1-S/18360/Add.1/Corr.1 ...................................................................1986
A/42/22 (GAOR, 42nd sess., Suppl. No. 22) .......................................................................1987
A/42/22/Add.1-S/19217/Add.1 .........................................................................................1987
A/43/22 (GAOR, 43rd sess., Suppl. No. 22) ........................................................................1988
A/44/22 (GAOR, 44th sess., Suppl. No. 22) ........................................................................1989
A/45/22 (GAOR, 45th sess., Suppl. No. 22) ........................................................................1990
A/46/22 (GAOR, 46th sess., Suppl. No. 22) ........................................................................1991
•A/47/22 (GAOR, 47th sess., Suppl. No. 22) .......................................................................1992
A/48/22 (GAOR, 48th sess., Suppl. No. 22) ........................................................................1993
•A/48/22/Add.1-S/26714/Add.1 ........................................................................................1994

*Report of the Special Committee against Apartheid on radio broadcasts directed at South Africa*
A/AC.115/L.505 ...........................................................................................8 November 1978
A/AC.115/L.515 ...........................................................................................2 November 1979

*Ad Hoc Committee on the Drafting of an International Convention against Apartheid in Sports*
A/32/36 (GAOR, 32nd sess., Suppl. No. 36) ......................................................................1977
A/33/36 (GAOR, 33rd sess., Suppl. No. 36) .......................................................................1978
A/34/36 (GAOR, 34th sess., Suppl. No. 36) .......................................................................1979
A/35/36 (GAOR, 35th sess., Suppl. No. 36) .......................................................................1980
A/36/36 (GAOR, 36th sess., Suppl. No. 36) .......................................................................1981
A/36/36/Corr.1 (GAOR, 36th sess., Suppl. No. 36, Corrigendum) ........................................1981
A/37/36 (GAOR, 37th sess., Suppl. No. 36) .......................................................................1982
A/38/36 (GAOR, 38th sess., Suppl. No. 36) .......................................................................1983
A/38/36/Corr.1 (GAOR, 38th sess., Suppl. No. 36, Corrigendum) ........................................1983
A/39/36 (GAOR, 39th sess., Suppl. No. 36) .......................................................................1984
A/40/36 (GAOR, 40th sess., Suppl. No. 36) .......................................................................1985

*Intergovernmental Group to Monitor the Supply and*
*Shipping of Oil and Petroleum Products to South Africa*

A/42/45 (GAOR, 42nd sess., Suppl. No. 45) ...............................................................................1987
A/43/44 (GAOR, 43rd sess., Suppl. No. 44)................................................................................1988
A/43/44/Corr.1 (GAOR, 43rd sess., Suppl. No. 44, Corrigendum)........................................1988
A/44/44  (GAOR, 44th sess., Suppl. No. 44) ...............................................................................1989
A/44/44/Add.1 (GAOR, 44th sess., Suppl. No. 44) .....................................................................1990
A/45/43 (GAOR, 45th sess., Suppl. No. 43) .................................................................................1990
A/46/44 (GAOR, 46th sess., Suppl. No. 44) .................................................................................1991
A/47/43 (GAOR, 47th sess., Suppl. No. 43) .................................................................................1992
A/48/43 (GAOR, 48th sess., Suppl. No. 43) .................................................................................1993

*Commission against Apartheid in Sports*

A/44/47 (GAOR, 44th sess., Suppl. No. 47)................................................................................1989
A/45/45 (GAOR, 45th sess., Suppl. No. 45) .................................................................................1990
A/47/45 (GAOR, 47th sess., Suppl. No. 45) .................................................................................1992

*Ad Hoc Committee of the Whole of the Sixteenth Special Session*

A/S-16/4 (GAOR, 16th special sess., Suppl. No. 1)...................................................................1989

*Report of the Secretary-General on the*
*United Nations Trust Fund for South*
*Africa*

A/6494...............................1 December 1966
A/6873 ................................23 October 1967
A/7270 .................................15 October 1968
A/7715 .................................17 October 1969
A/8109 .................................12 October 1970
A/8468 .................................15 October 1971
A/8822 ...................................5 October 1972
A/9235 .................................25 October 1973
A/9806 .................................16 October 1974
A/9806/Add.1 ...........................30 October 1974
A/10281 ....................................6 October 1975
A/31/277 ...............................22 October 1976
A/32/302 ...............................28 October 1977
A/33/313 ............................10 November 1978
A/33/313/Corr.1 .............................12 June 1979
A/34/661 .............................8 November 1979
A/35/509 ...................................9 October 1980
A/36/619 .................................30 October 1981
A/37/484 ...................................4 October 1982
A/38/455 .................................13 October 1983
A/39/605 .................................24 October 1984

A/40/780 ..................................21 October 1985
A/41/638 ..................................20 October 1986
A/42/659 ..................................15 October 1987
A/43/682 ....................................6 October 1988
A/44/556 ....................................5 October 1989
A/45/550 ...............................27 September 1990
A/46/507 ....................................8 October 1991
A/47/525 ..................................15 October 1992
A/48/523 ..................................25 October 1993
•A/48/523/Add.1 .............................13 June 1994

*Panel on the Hearings on the Oil Embargo*
*against South Africa*

A/44/279-S/20634 ..........................16 May 1989

*Report of the Secretary-General on the*
*International Conference of Experts for the*
*Support of Victims of Colonialism and*
*Apartheid in Southern Africa*

•A/9061...............................................7 May 1973

*Report of the Secretary-General on the implementation of national measures adopted against South Africa*
A/43/786 ....................................7 November 1988

*Report of the Secretary-General on restrictive measures affecting externally dependent areas of the South African economy*
A/44/555 ...................................11 October 1989
A/44/555/Corr.1 .......................7 November 1989

*Progress report of the Secretary-General on the implementation of the Declaration on Apartheid and its Destructive Consequences in Southern Africa*
•A/44/960 ..............................................1 July 1990
•A/45/1052 ...............................4 September 1991
•A/47/574 ................................6 November 1992
•A/48/691 .................................6 December 1993

*Report of the Secretary-General on measures to monitor sanctions against South Africa undertaken by the United Nations system, Governments and non-governmental agencies*
A/45/670 ..................................6 November 1990

*Report of the Secretary-General on a coordinated approach by the United Nations system on questions relating to South Africa*
A/46/648 ...............................25 November 1991
A/47/559 ..................................6 November 1992
A/48/467 .................................22 October 1993

*Report of the Secretary-General on the question of South Africa*
•A/48/845-S/1994/16 ..................10 January 1994
A/48/845/Add.1-S/1994/16/
   Add.1 ......................................17 January 1994

## 1.3 Other documents

*Letter from India requesting inclusion of treatment of Indians in South Africa in the agenda of the General Assembly*
•A/577 .............................................16 July 1948

*Letters from Member States requesting inclusion of apartheid in the agenda of the General Assembly*
•A/2183 ...................................12 September 1952
A/3190 ...................................13 September 1956
A/3190/Add.1 .............................1 October 1956
A/3190/Add.2 ...........................15 October 1956
A/3628 .........................................8 August 1957
A/3628/Add.1 .........................10 September 1957
A/3872 .......................................14 August 1958
A/4147 ...........................................15 July 1959
A/4147/Add.1 ................................22 July 1959
A/4419 ...........................................21 July 1960
A/4419/Add.1 ................................21 July 1960
A/4419/Add.2 ................................25 July 1960
A/4804 ..........................................20 July 1961
A/4804/Add.1 ................................22 July 1961
A/4804/Add.2 ................................24 July 1961
A/4804/Add.3 ................................26 July 1961
A/4804/Add.4 ................................29 July 1961
A/4804/Add.5 ...............................2 August 1961
A/5167 .......................................17 August 1962
A/5167/Add.1 .............................22 August 1962
A/5167/Add.2 .............................23 August 1962
A/5167/Add.3 .............................27 August 1962
A/5167/Add.4 .............................29 August 1962
A/5167/Add.5 .............................30 August 1962
A/5167/Add.6 .........................12 September 1962

*Statement by Mrs. Vijaya Lakshmi Pandit, Chairperson of the delegation of India, introducing the item on apartheid in the Ad Hoc Political Committee of the General Assembly*
•A/AC.61/SR.13 .......................12 November 1952

*Letter from Mr. Z. K. Matthews, representative of the African National Congress, to the chairman of the Ad Hoc Political Committee*
•A/AC.61/L.14 ........................19 November 1952

*Statement by Mr. Peter Smithers, representative of the United Kingdom, in the Special Political Committee of the General Assembly*
•A/SPC/SR.242 ...................................5 April 1961

*Statement by Secretary-General U Thant at the first meeting of the Special Committee on the Policies of Apartheid of the Government of the Republic of South Africa*
•UN Press Release SG/1453...............2 April 1963

*Statement by Mr. Per Haekkerup, Minister for Foreign Affairs of Denmark, in the General Assembly*
•A/PV.1215..............................25 September 1963

*Statement by Dr. Hermod Lanning, representative of Denmark, in the Special Political Committee*
•A/SPC/82.....................................9 October 1963

*Statement by Mr. Diallo Telli (Guinea), Chairman of the Special Committee on the Policies of Apartheid of the Government of the Republic of South Africa, at the plenary meeting of the General Assembly on a resolution concerning the trial of Mr. Nelson Mandela and others*
•A/PV.1238 ..................................11 October 1963

*Statement by Mr. Thabo Mbeki, son of Mr. Govan Mbeki, the African leader on trial in Pretoria, before a delegation of the Special Committee on the Policies of Apartheid of the Government of the Republic of South Africa in London, 13 April 1964*
•A/AC.115/L.65...............................23 April 1964

*Appeal to Member States by the Special Committee on the Policies of Apartheid of the Government of the Republic of South Africa for contributions to assist families persecuted by the South African Government for their opposition to apartheid*
•UN Press Release GA/AP/42......26 October 1964

*Statement by Mr. Dennis Brutus, Director of the Campaign for the Release of Political Prisoners in South Africa, in the Special Committee on the Policies of Apartheid of the Government of the Republic of South Africa*
•A/AC.115/L.194.......................27 February 1967

*Statement by Mr. Sverker C. Astrom (Sweden), Chairman of the Committee of Trustees of the United Nations Trust Fund for South Africa, in the Special Political Committee*
•A/SPC/PV.563 ..........................9 November 1967

*"The present stage of the struggle against apartheid in South Africa": paper prepared by Mr. Oliver Tambo, acting President of the African National Congress, at the request of the Special Committee on the Policies of Apartheid of the Government of the Republic of South Africa*
•A/AC.115/L.222 ................................2 July 1968

*Statement by Mr. Abdulrahim A. Farah (Somalia), Chairman of the Special Committee on the Policies of Apartheid of the Government of the Republic of South Africa, at the Committee's 138th meeting, held on 24 June 1970*
•A/AC.115/L.277.............................25 June 1970

*Statement by the President of the General Assembly, Mr. Edvard Hambro (Norway), concerning the credentials of the delegation of South Africa*
•A/PV.1901.............................11 November 1970

*Statement by Secretary-General Kurt Waldheim to the Special Committee on Apartheid at a meeting on the occasion of the Committee's tenth anniversary*
- UN Press Release SG/SM/1837 - GA/AP/317 .....................................2 April 1973

*Statement by Mrs. Jeanne Martin Cissé (Guinea), Chairperson of the Special Committee against Apartheid*
- UN Press Release GA/AP/523 ....21 January 1976

*Statement by Mr. Leslie O. Harriman (Nigeria), Chairman of the Special Committee against Apartheid, on the proposal to declare the "independence" of Transkei*
- UN Press Release GA/AP/596 21 September 1976

*Declaration on Apartheid, adopted by the Special Committee against Apartheid at its special session, Kingston, Jamaica, 22-25 May 1979*
A/34/313-S/13391 .............................13 June 1979

*Letter dated 29 July 1980 from Mr. O. R. Tambo, President of the African National Congress, to the Chairman of the Special Committee against Apartheid, Mr. B. A. Clark (Nigeria), concerning the anniversary of the Freedom Charter*
- A/AC.115/L.531.....................15 September 1980

*Declaration to Commemorate the Day of Solidarity with South African Political Prisoners, adopted by the Special Committee against Apartheid, New York, 12 October 1981*
A/36/592-S/14724 .......................14 October 1981

*Statement by Mr. Alhaji Yusuff Maitama-Sule (Nigeria), Chairman of the Special Committee against Apartheid, at the meeting of the Committee on 13 January 1983*
- Published by the United Nations Centre against Apartheid

*Programme of Action against Apartheid, adopted by the General Assembly on 5 December 1983 in A/RES/38/39 B*
- A/38/539-S/16102....................8 November 1983

*Appeal by the Special Committee against Apartheid to the cities of the world, issued on 21 March 1984*
- A/AC.115/L.606..............................4 April 1984

*Declaration adopted by the Special Committee against Apartheid at the conclusion of its special session in commemoration of the twenty-fifth anniversary of the Sharpeville massacre, New York, 28 March 1985*
A/40/213 and Corr.1 ....................29 March 1985

*Statement by Secretary-General Boutros Boutros-Ghali at the first meeting in 1992 of the Special Committee against Apartheid*
- UN Press Release SG/SM/4700 - GA/AP 2064 ..........................18 February 1992

*Statement by Secretary-General Boutros Boutros-Ghali at a meeting of the Special Committee against Apartheid for the observance of the International Day of Solidarity with South African Political Prisoners*
- UN Press Release SG/SM/4832 - GA/AP/2095 .............................12 October 1992

*Statement by Secretary-General Boutros Boutros-Ghali at the solemn meeting by the Special Committee against Apartheid in observance of the International Day for the Elimination of Racial Discrimination*
- UN Press Release SG/SM/4948- GA/AP/2118 ................................22 March 1993

*Statement by Mr. Nelson Mandela,*
*President of the African National Congress,*
*in the Special Committee against Apartheid*
*on 24 September 1993*
•A/AC.115/SR.668 and United Nations Centre
against Apartheid, Notes and Documents,
No.8/93, September 1993

*Statement by the President of the General*
*Assembly, Mr. S. R. Insanally (Guyana), on*
*the lifting of the oil embargo against South*
*Africa*
•A/48/PV.72 ...............................9 December 1993

*Statement by Secretary-General Boutros*
*Boutros-Ghali to the General Assembly ple-*
*nary meeting on the resumption of South*
*Africa's participation in the work of the*
*Assembly*
•A/48/PV.95 ......................................23 June 1994

*Address by President Nelson Mandela of*
*South Africa to the forty-ninth session of*
*the General Assembly*
•A/49/PV.14 .................................3 October 1994

# 2. Security Council

## 2.1 Resolutions

•S/RES/134 (1960).............................1 April 1960
Concerns the situation in the Union of South
Africa

•S/RES/181 (1963).........................7 August 1963
Concerns policies of apartheid in South Africa
and calls upon States to cease sales of arms to
South Africa

•S/RES/182 (1963) .....................4 December 1963
Concerns policies of apartheid in South Africa

S/RES/190 (1964).............................9 June 1964
Concerns policies of apartheid in South Africa

•S/RES/191 (1964)...........................18 June 1964
Concerns policies of apartheid in South Africa

S/RES/282 (1970)..........................23 July 1970
Concerns arms embargo against South Africa

•S/RES/311 (1972)......................4 February 1972
Concerns policies of apartheid in South Africa

•S/RES/392 (1976)..........................19 June 1976
Concerns killings and violence by the regime in
Soweto

•S/RES/417 (1977) ......................31 October 1977
Concerns policies of apartheid in South Africa

•S/RES/418 (1977) ....................4 November 1977
Imposes mandatory arms embargo against South
Africa

S/RES/421 (1977) ....................9 December 1977
Establishes the Security Council Committee concerning the Question of South Africa to monitor
the arms embargo

•S/RES/473 (1980)...........................13 June 1980
Concerns policies of apartheid in South Africa

S/RES/503 (1982) ...........................9 April 1982
Concerns death sentences imposed upon
members of the ANC

S/RES/525 (1982) ...................7 December 1982
Concerns death sentences imposed upon
members of the ANC

S/RES/533 (1983) .............................7 June 1983
Concerns death sentences imposed upon three
members of the ANC

S/RES/547 (1984)......................13 January 1984
Concerns death sentence imposed upon a
member of the ANC

•S/RES/554 (1984).........................17 August 1984
Rejects the so-called new constitution, and elections to be organized in August 1984 in South Africa

S/RES/556 (1984) ......................23 October 1984
Concerns policies of apartheid in South Africa

S/RES/558 (1984) ....................13 December 1984
Concerns application of arms embargo imposed by Security Council resolution 418 (1977) against South Africa

S/RES/560 (1985).........................12 March 1985
Concerns policies of apartheid in South Africa

•S/RES/569 (1985).............................26 July 1985
Concerns sanctions against South Africa

S/RES/581 (1986) .....................13 February 1986
Concerns South Africa's threats against States in southern Africa and eradication of apartheid

S/RES/591 (1986)...................28 November 1986
Concerns arms embargo against South Africa

S/RES/610 (1988).........................16 March 1988
Concerns death sentences imposed upon the Sharpeville Six

S/RES/615 (1988) ............................17 June 1988
Concerns death sentences imposed upon the Sharpeville Six

S/RES/623 (1988)...................23 November 1988
Concerns death sentence imposed upon an anti-apartheid activist in South Africa

•S/RES/765 (1992).............................16 July 1992
Concerns the situation in South Africa

•S/RES/772 (1992).......................17 August 1992
Concerns the situation in South Africa

S/RES/894 (1994).......................14 January 1994
Concerns participation of the United Nations and

international observers in the election process in South Africa

•S/RES/919 (1994)............................25 May 1994
Terminates the arms embargo and other restrictions related to South Africa imposed by resolution 418 (1977) and dissolves the Security Council Committee Established by Resolution 421 (1977)

•S/RES/930 (1994)............................27 June 1994
Terminates the mandate of the United Nations Observer Mission in South Africa and removes the item entitled "The question of South Africa" from the list of matters of which the Security Council is seized

## 2.2 Statements by the President of the Security Council on behalf of the Council

S/13226
Statement made at the 2140th meeting, 5 April 1979, containing an appeal for clemency for Solomon Mahlangu

S/13549
Statement made at the 2168th meeting, 21 September 1979, condemning the proclamation by South Africa of independence of the Bantustan, Venda

S/14361
Statement made at the 2264th meeting, 5 February 1981, expressing concern over death sentences against three members of the ANC

•S/14794
Statement made at the 2315th meeting, 15 December 1981, concerning proclamation by South Africa of independence of Ciskei

S/15444
Statement made on 4 October 1982, concerning the death sentences imposed on three members of the ANC

•S/17050
Statement made on 22 March 1985, expressing grave concern over the killing and wounding of innocent people by the South African police in the town of Uitenhage, 21 March

S/17408
Statement made on 20 August 1985, urging the South African authorities to commute the death sentence imposed upon Malesela Benjamin Moloise

•S/17413
Statement made at the 2603rd meeting, 21 August 1985, concerning the situation in South Africa since the imposition of the state of emergency on 21 July 1985

S/17575
Statement made at the 2623rd meeting, 17 October 1985, concerning the death sentence imposed on Benjamin Moloise

S/18157
Statement made at the 2690th meeting, 13 June 1986, concerning the observance of the 10th anniversary of the events in Soweto

•S/18808
Statement made on 16 April 1987, calling upon the South African authorities to revoke the decree of 10 April 1987, under which protest against detentions without trial or support for those detained are prohibited

S/24456
Statement made at the 3107th meeting, 17 August 1992, concerning the number of observers to be deployed in South Africa

•S/24541
Statement made on 10 September 1992, concerning the situation in South Africa

S/25578
Statement made at the 3197th meeting, 12 April

1993, concerning assassination of Chris Hani, a member of the National Executive Committee of the ANC and the Secretary-General of the South African Communist Party

•S/26347
Statement made at the 3267th meeting, 24 August 1993, concerning the upsurge in violence in South Africa, especially in the East Rand

•S/26785
Statement made at the 3318th meeting, 23 November 1993, welcoming the successful completion of the multiparty negotiating process, looking forward to the elections in South Africa in April 1994 and urging the early establishment of the Transitional Executive Council and Independent Electoral Commission

•S/PRST/1994/20
Statement made at the 3365th meeting, 19 April 1994, welcoming the agreement reached on 19 April between the Inkatha Freedom Party, the ANC and the Government of South Africa, following which the Inkatha Freedom Party decided to participate in the forthcoming elections

## 2.3 Reports

*Expert Committee Established by Resolution 191 (1964)*
•S/6210 ...........................................2 March 1965
(SCOR*, 20th year, Special Suppl. No. 2)
S/6210/Add.1 ...............................24 March 1965
(SCOR, 20th year, Special Suppl. No. 2)

*Reports of the Secretary-General*
•S/4635......................................23 January 1961
[pursuant to S/RES/134 (1960)]
S/5438 ......................................11 October 1963
[pursuant to S/RES/181 (1963)]
S/5438/Add.1.............................22 October 1963
S/5438/Add.2.............................30 October 1963

* Security Council Official Records

S/5438/Add.3 ............................8 November 1963
S/5438/Add.4 ........................20 November 1963
S/5438/Add.5 ........................26 November 1963
S/5438/Add.6 ..........................23 December 1963
•S/5658 ............................................20 April 1964
[pursuant to S/RES/182 (1963)]
[contains report of the Group of Experts]
S/5658/Add.1 .................................21 April 1964
S/5658/Add.2 ....................................6 May 1964
S/5658/Add.3 ....................................8 June 1964
S/5913 .........................................25 August 1964
[pursuant to S/RES/190 I(1964)]
S/5913/Add.1 .........................28 September 1964
S/5913/Add.2 .........................25 November 1964
S/6891.....................................9 November 1965
[pursuant to S/RES/191 (1964)]
S/10092 .....................................3 February 1971
[pursuant to S/RES/282 (1970)]
S/12673 ............................................28 April 1978
[pursuant to S/RES/418 (1977)]
S/14167.................................12 September 1980
[pursuant to S/RES/473 (1980)]
S/14167/Add.1 .........................18 December 1980
S/18961 ............................................30 June 1987
[pursuant to S/RES/591 (1986)]
S/18961/Add.1 ................................17 July 1987
S/18961/Add.2 ..............................5 August 1987
S/18961/Add.3 ............................26 August 1987
S/18961/Add.4 .......................22 September 1987
S/18961/Add.5 ...........................2 February 1988
•S/24389.........................................7 August 1992
[pursuant to S/RES/765 (1992)]
•S/25004 ....................................22 December 1992
[pursuant to S/RES/772 (1992)]
•S/1994/16-A/48/845 ...................10 January 1994
S/1994/16/Add.1-A/48/845/Add.1 17 January 1994
S/1994/435 .....................................14 April 1994
[pursuant to S/RES/772 (1992) and
S/RES/894(1994)]
•S/1994/717......................................16 June 1994
[pursuant to S/RES/772 (1992) and S/RES/894
(1994)]

*Security Council Committee Established by
Resolution 421 (1977) concerning the
Question of South Africa*
S/13708 ...................................26 December 1979
S/13721 .....................................31 December 1979
S/14179 .................................19 September 1980
S/21015 ...................................11 December 1989

*Panel on the Hearings on the Oil Embargo
against South Africa*
A/44/279-S/20634 ...........................16 May 1989

## 2.4 Other documents

*Letter from Member States to the President
of the Security Council requesting consideration of the situation in South Africa*
•S/4279 and Add.1 ........................25 March 1960

*Statement by Mr. Adlai Stevenson, represen-
tative of the United States of America, in the
Security Council, announcing the decision of
the United States to stop sales of arms to
South Africa*
•S/PV.1052......................................2 August 1963

*Statement by Chief Albert J. Luthuli,
President of the African National Congress,
in the Security Council, on the sentencing of
Mr. Nelson Mandela and others to life
imprisonment*
•S/PV.1130........................................12 June 1964

*Statement by Secretary-General Kurt
Waldheim in the Security Council after the
adoption of resolution 418 (1977) concern-
ing a mandatory arms embargo against
South Africa*
•S/PV.2046 ................................4 November 1977

•*Letter dated 10 July 1992 from Mr. L. M.
Mangope, Chief Minister of
Bophuthatswana, to the President
of the Security Council*
[Not issued as a United Nations document]

*Letter dated 18 May 1994 from President
Nelson Mandela of South Africa to the
President of the Security Council*
•S/1994/606....................................23 May 1994

*Statement by Mr. Thabo Mbeki, First
Deputy President of South Africa, in the
Security Council*
•S/PV.3379....................................25 May 1994

# 3.  Economic and Social Council

## 3.1 Resolutions

*Question of the violation of human rights
and fundamental freedoms, including the
policies of racial discrimination and segrega-
tion and of apartheid*
E/RES/1102 (XL)..........................4 March 1966
E/RES/1164 (XLI).........................5 August 1966
E/RES/1235 (XLII)........................6 June 1967
E/RES/1236 (XLII)........................6 June 1967
E/RES/1424 (XLVI)........................6 June 1969
E/RES/1501 (XLVIII) .....................27 May 1970

*Question of slavery and the slave trade in
all their practices and manifestations,
including the slavery-like practices of
apartheid and colonialism*
E/RES/1126 (XLI)..........................26 July 1966
E/RES/1232 (XLII)........................6 June 1967
E/RES/1330 (XLIV) .......................31 May 1968
E/RES/1331 (XLIV) .......................31 May 1968

E/RES/1419 (XLVI)........................6 June 1969
E/RES/1593 (L)...........................21 May 1971
E/RES/1695 (LII).........................2 June 1972

*Racism and racial discrimination*
E/RES/1146 (XLI) ........................2 August 1966
E/RES/1244 (XLII)........................6 June 1967
E/RES/1588 (L)...........................21 May 1971
E/RES/1863 (LVI) ........................17 May 1974
E/RES/1938 (LVIII).......................6 May 1975
E/RES/1989 (LX) .........................11 May 1976
E/RES/2056 (LXII)........................12 May 1977
E/RES/1978/7.............................4 May 1978
E/RES/1979/3.............................9 May 1979
E/RES/1980/7.............................24 April 1980
E/RES/1981/30 ...........................6 May 1981
E/RES/1982/31 ...........................5 May 1982
E/RES/1985/19 ...........................29 May 1985
E/RES/1988/6.............................24 May 1988
E/RES/1990/49 ...........................25 May 1990
E/RES/1991/2.............................29 May 1991
E/RES/1992/13 ...........................30 July 1992
E/RES/1993/8 ............................27 July 1993

*Infringements of trade union
rights in South Africa*
E/RES/1216 (XLII) .......................1 June 1967
E/RES/1302 (XLIV)........................28 May 1968
E/RES/1412 (XLVI) .......................6 June 1969
E/RES/1509 (XLVIII)......................28 May 1970
E/RES/1599 (L) ..........................21 May 1971
E/RES/1997 (LX) .........................12 May 1976
E/RES/2086 (LXII) .......................13 May 1977
E/RES/1978/21 ...........................5 May 1978
E/RES/1979/39 ...........................10 May 1979
E/RES/1980/33 ...........................2 May 1980
E/RES/1981/41 ...........................8 May 1981
E/RES/1982/40 ...........................7 May 1982
E/RES/1984/42 ...........................24 May 1984
E/RES/1985/43 ...........................30 May 1985
E/RES/1987/63 ...........................29 May 1987
E/RES/1988/41 ...........................27 May 1988
E/RES/1989/82 ...........................24 May 1989
E/RES/1990/44 ...........................25 May 1990
E/RES/1991/37 ...........................31 May 1991
E/RES/1992/12 ...........................20 July 1992

*Monitoring the transition to democracy in South Africa*

E/RES/1993/45 ...................................28 July 1993


## 3.2 Reports

*Ad Hoc Working Group of Experts on Southern Africa*

E/CN.4/950................................27 October 1967
E/4459 ......................................15 February 1968
E/CN.4/984................................19 February 1969
E/CN.4/984/Add.1 .....................19 February 1969
E/4646 .........................................22 April 1969
E/CN.4/984/Add.2/Rev.1 .................29 July 1969
E/CN.4/984/Add.3/Rev.1 .................29 April 1969
E/CN.4/984/Add.4 .....................20 February 1969
E/CN.4/984/Add.5 .....................26 February 1969
E/CN.4/984/Add.6/Rev.1 ...........1 December 1969
E/CN.4/984/Add.7/Rev.1 .................20 June 1969
E/CN.4/984/Add.8 .....................25 February 1969
E/CN.4/984/Add.9 .....................27 February 1969
E/CN.4/984/Add.10/Rev.1 ..........1 December 1969
E/CN.4/984/Add.11/Rev.1 ...............20 June 1969
E/CN.4/984/Add.12 ...................27 February 1969
E/CN.4/984/Add.13 ...................28 February 1969
E/CN.4/984/Add.14 ...................28 February 1969
E/CN.4/984/Add.15/Rev.1 ...............29 July 1969
E/CN.4/984/Add.16/Rev.1 ...............20 June 1969
E/CN.4/984/Add.17 ...................28 February 1969
E/CN.4/984/Add.18 ...................28 February 1969
E/CN.4/984/Add.19.........................4 March 1969
E/CN.4/1020 ...............................27 January 1970
E/CN.4/1020/Add.1 ...................30 January 1970
E/CN.4/1020/Add.2 ...................12 February 1970
E/CN.4/1020/Add.3 ...................16 February 1970
E/4791 ......................................26 February 1970
E/CN.4/1050................................2 February 1971
E/CN.4/1050/Corr.1 ........................2 March 1971
E/4953 ......................................19 February 1971
E/CN.4/1076............................15 February 1972
E/CN.4/1111............................1 February 1973
E/CN.4/1135.............................4 February 1974
E/CN.4/1159 ...............................27 January 1975
E/CN.4/1187 ...............................30 January 1976
E/5767 ......................................18 February 1976

E/CN.4/1222 ...............................31 January 1977
E/CN.4/1222/Corr.1...................22 February 1977
E/CN.4/1270 ...............................31 January 1978
E/1978/21 ................................28 February 1978
E/CN.4/1311 ...............................26 January 1979
E/CN.4/1365 ...............................31 January 1980
E/CN.4/1366 ...............................31 January 1980
E/CN.4/1429 ...............................28 January 1981
E/CN.4/1429/Corr.1 .....................26 March 1981
E/CN.4/1430 ...............................28 January 1981
E/CN.4/1485 .............................8 January 1982
E/CN.4/1486 .............................8 January 1982
E/CN.4/1497 .............................8 January 1982
E/CN.4/1983/10 ........................21 January 1983
E/CN.4/1983/37 .........................20 January 1983
E/CN.4/1983/38 .........................20 January 1983
E/CN.4/1984/8 .........................24 January 1984
E/CN.4/1985/8 .........................23 January 1985
E/CN.4/1986/9 .........................28 January 1986
E/CN.4/AC.22/1987/1 ................29 January 1987
E/CN.4/1988/8 .........................22 January 1988
E/CN.4/1989/8 .........................31 January 1989
E/CN.4/1990/7 ........................18 December 1989
E/CN.4/1990/7/Add.1 ...............20 February 1990
E/CN.4/1991/10 ...........................2 January 1991
E/CN.4/1992/8 ........................26 December 1991
E/CN.4/1993/14 ..........................8 January 1993
E/CN.4/1994/15 .........................11 January 1994


*Group of Three [on the Implementation of the International Convention on the Suppression and Punishment of the Crime of Apartheid]*

E/CN.4/1286...............................3 February 1978
E/CN.4/1328...............................2 February 1979
E/CN.4/1358...............................1 February 1980
E/CN.4/1417 ..............................30 January 1981
E/CN.4/1507 ..............................29 January 1982
E/CN.4/1983/25 .........................28 January 1983
E/CN.4/1984/48.............................3 February 1984
E/CN.4/1985/27.............................4 February 1985
E/CN.4/1986/30.............................31 January 1986
E/CN.4/1987/28.............................2 February 1987
E/CN.4/1988/32.............................2 February 1988
E/CN.4/1989/33.............................2 February 1989
E/CN.4/1990/35 .........................30 January 1990

E/CN.4/1991/42 ..........................25 January 1991
E/CN.4/1993/54 ..........................5 February 1993
E/CN.4/1993/54/Corr.1 .............15 February 1993

*Note by the Secretary-General on the*
*implementation of the International*
*Convention on the Suppression and*
*Punishment of the Crime of Apartheid*
E/CN.4/1327 ...........................20 December 1978
E/CN.4/1327/Add.1 ......................25 January 1979
E/CN.4/1327/Add.2 ..................27 February 1979
[contains report on cases of murder, torture and
deprivation of liberty in South Africa]

### Special Rapporteurs

*Special study of racial discrimination in*
*the political, economic, social and cultural*
*spheres: reports prepared by Hernán*
*Santa Cruz*
E/CN.4/Sub.2/267 .................17 November 1966
E/CN.4/Sub.2/276 ............................24 July 1967
E/CN.4/Sub.2/288 ............................25 July 1968
E/CN.4/Sub.2/301 ...........................24 June 1969
E/CN.4/Sub.2/307/Rev.1 ...............................1971
E/CN.4/Sub.2/370/Rev.1 ...............................1976

*Question of slavery and the slave trade in*
*all their practices and manifestations,*
*including the slavery-like practices of*
*apartheid and colonialism: reports pre-*
*pared by Mohamad Awad*
E/CN.4/Sub.2/304 ........................18 August 1969
E/CN.4/Sub.2/312 ...............................1 July 1970
E/CN.4/Sub.2/322 .............................16 July 1971

*Study of apartheid and racial discrimina-*
*tion in southern Africa: reports prepared*
*by Manouchehr Ganji*
E/CN.4/949 ............................22 November 1967
E/CN.4/949/Corr.1 .....................8 February 1968
E/CN.4/949/Add.1 ..................30 November 1967
E/CN.4/949/Add.1/Corr.1 ...........8 February 1968
E/CN.4/949/Add.2 ..................21 December 1967
E/CN.4/949/Add.3 ..................21 December 1967
E/CN.4/949/Add.4 ......................23 January 1968

E/CN.4/949/Add.5 ......................24 January 1968
E/CN.4/979 ............................18 December 1968
E/CN.4/979/Add.1 ...................30 December 1968
E/CN.4/979/Add.1/Corr.1 ...........13 January 1969
E/CN.4/979/Add.2 ......................21 January 1969
E/CN.4/979/Add.3 ......................24 January 1969
E/CN.4/979/Add.4 ...................12 February 1969
E/CN.4/979/Add.5 ...................12 February 1969
E/CN.4/979/Add.6 ......................20 January 1969
E/CN.4/979/Add.7 ......................6 February 1969
E/CN.4/979/Add.8 ...................13 February 1969

*Adverse consequences for the enjoyment of*
*human rights of political, military, econom-*
*ic and other forms of assistance given to*
*the racist and colonialist regime of South*
*Africa: reports prepared by Ahmed Khalifa*
E/CN.4/Sub.2/L.624 .........................23 July 1975
E/CN.4/Sub.2/371 ............................14 July 1976
E/CN.4/Sub.2/383/Rev.2 ...............................1979
E/CN.4/Sub.2/425 ............................12 July 1979
E/CN.4/Sub.2/425/Corr.1 ........14 December 1979
E/CN.4/Sub.2/425/Corr.2 ..............9 January 1980
E/CN.4/Sub.2/425/Corr.3 .............25 March 1980
E/CN.4/Sub.2/425/Add.1 ...............6 August 1979
E/CN.4/Sub.2/425/Add.2 .............15 August 1979
E/CN.4/Sub.2/425/Add.3 .............22 August 1979
E/CN.4/Sub.2/425/Add.4 .........14 September 1979
E/CN.4/Sub.2/425/Add.5 .........21 November 1979
E/CN.4/Sub.2/425/Add.6 .............23 January 1980
E/CN.4/Sub.2/425/Add.7 ...................3 April 1980
E/CN.4/Sub.2/469 ............................31 July 1981
E/CN.4/Sub.2/469/Corr.1 ...................31 July 1981
E/CN.4/Sub.2/469/Add.1 ...........6 November 1981
E/CN.4/Sub.2/1982/10 ...................30 June 1982
E/CN.4/Sub.2/1983/6 ....................20 July 1983
E/CN.4/Sub.2/1983/6/Add.1 .............20 July 1983
E/CN.4/Sub.2/1983/6/Add.2 .............20 July 1983
E/CN.4/Sub.2/1984/8/Rev.1 ...............................1985
E/CN.4/Sub.2/1985/8 .......................16 July 1985
E/CN.4/Sub.2/1985/8/Add.1 .............16 July 1985
E/CN.4/Sub.2/1985/8/Add.2 .............16 July 1985
E/CN.4/Sub.2/1987/8/Rev.1 ...............................1987
E/CN.4/Sub.2/1987/8/Rev.1/Add.1 ...29 May 1987
E/CN.4/Sub.2/1988/6 .......................15 June 1988
E/CN.4/Sub.2/1988/6/Add.1 ........18 August 1988

E/CN.4/Sub.2/1988/6/
    Add.1/Corr.1 .............................15 August 1988
E/CN.4/Sub.2/1989/9...........................11 July 1989
E/CN.4/Sub.2/1989/9/Add.1 ..............12 July 1989
E/CN.4/Sub.2/1989/9/Corr.1.........15 August 1989
E/CN.4/Sub.2/1990/13.....................8 August 1990
E/CN.4/Sub.2/1990/13/Add.1 ..............1 July 1990
E/CN.4/Sub.2/1991/13.......................18 July 1991
E/CN.4/Sub.2/1991/13/Add.1 ............18 July 1991
E/CN.4/Sub.2/1992/12.......................23 June 1992
E/CN.4/Sub.2/1992/12/Add.1 .............3 June 1992

*Monitoring the transition to democracy in*
*South Africa: reports prepared by Judith*
*Sefi Attah*
E/CN.4/Sub.2/1993/11..........................2 July 1993
E/CN.4/Sub.2/1993/11/Add.1 ......18 January 1994

### Reports of the Secretary-General submitted to the Commission on the Status of Women

*The effects of apartheid on the status of*
*women in South Africa, Namibia and*
*Southern Rhodesia*
E/CN.6/619 ....................................5 January 1978

*Measures of assistance provided to women*
*inside South Africa and Namibia and to*
*women in South Africa and Namibia who*
*have become refugees as the result of the*
*practice of apartheid*
E/CN.6/1986/5...........................18 February 1986

*New developments concerning the situation*
*of women under apartheid in South Africa*
*and Namibia and measures of assistance to*
*women from South Africa and Namibia*
*who have become refugees as a result of*
*the practice of apartheid*
E/CN.6/1988/2...........................15 October 1987

*New developments concerning the situation*
*of women under apartheid in South Africa*
*and Namibia and measures of assistance to*
*women in South Africa and Namibia*
E/CN.6/1989/3 ...........................30 January 1989

*Monitoring the implementation of the*
*Nairobi Forward-looking Strategies for the*
*Advancement of Women regarding women*
*and children living under apartheid in*
*South Africa*
E/CN.6/1990/9 ..........................5 December 1989

*Women and children living under apartheid*
E/CN.6/1991/8 ............................28 January 1991
E/CN.6/1993/11 ..........................21 January 1993
E/CN.6/1994/7...........................23 February 1994

### Reports of the Secretary-General submitted to the Commission on Transnational Corporations

*Policies and practices of transnational cor-*
*porations regarding their activities in South*
*Africa and Namibia*
E/C.10/1983/10 ..................................3 May 1983

*Activities of transnational corporations in*
*South Africa and Namibia and their collab-*
*oration with the racist minority regime in*
*that area*
E/C.10/1983/10/Add.1 ......................20 May 1983
E/C.10/1985/7 ............................30 January 1985
E/C.10/1985/7/Corr.1................12 February 1985
E/C.10/1986/8 ............................30 January 1986
E/C.10/1987/7.............................3 February 1987
E/C.10/1988/7.............................2 February 1988
E/C.10/1989/8...........................14 February 1989
E/C.10/1989/8/Corr.1 ...................22 March 1989

*Activities of transnational corporations and*
*measures being taken by Governments to*
*prohibit investments in South Africa and*
*Namibia*
E/C.10/1984/10 ..........................30 January 1984

*Responsibilities of home countries with respect to the transnational corporations operating in South Africa and Namibia in violation of the relevant resolutions and decisions of the United Nations*

E/C.10/1986/10............................4 February 1986
E/C.10/1987/8..............................4 February 1987
E/C.10/1988/8..............................9 February 1988
E/C.10/1989/9............................22 February 1989

*Public hearings on the activities of transnational corporations in South Africa and Namibia*

E/C.10/1986/9............................31 October 1985

*Measures relating to trade, finance, investment and technology transfers to South Africa*

E/C.10/1990/8..............................1 February 1990

*Transnational corporations with interests in South Africa*

E/C.10/1991/11 ..........................22 March 1991

*Role of transnational corporations in South Africa*

E/C.10/1992/6 ...................................2 May 1992
E/C.10/1992/6/Corr.1 ....................25 March 1992
E/C.10/1993/13 ...............................5 March 1993

*List of transnational corporations with interests in South Africa*

E/C.10/1992/7 ...............................30 March 1992
E/C.10/1993/13/Add.1...................30 March 1993

**Economic Commission for Africa (ECA)**

*The destabilization of the southern African (Front-line) States: cumulative impact on the current economic and social crisis: preliminary note of the ECA Secretariat*

E/ECA/CM.11/66 ..........................16 April 1985

*Towards socio-economic development of democratic South Africa: ECA's role in perspective*

E/ECA/CM.20/33 ..........................24 April 1994

# 4. Other Documents and Materials*

## 4.1 Conferences and seminars

•Resolution adopted by the Second Conference of Independent African States, Addis Ababa, 24 June 1960

•Resolutions of the All-In African Conference held in Pietermaritzburg, South Africa, 25-26 March 1961

•Resolution on Apartheid and Racial Discrimination adopted by the Conference of Heads of African States and Governments, Addis Ababa, 22-25 May 1963
A/AC.115/L.11

Declaration concerning the Policy of Apartheid of the Republic of South Africa, adopted by the International Labour Conference at its forty-eighth session, Geneva, 8 July 1964
International Labour Conference, Record of Proceedings, forty-eighth session, Appendix XVIII

Seminar on Apartheid, Brasilia, 23 August-4 September 1966
A/6412; ST/TAO/HR/27

•Paper by Mr. Achkar Marof (Guinea), Chairman of the Special Committee on the Policies of Apartheid of the Government of the Republic of South Africa, entitled "The crisis in southern Africa with special reference to South Africa and measures to be taken by the international community", presented to the International Seminar on Apartheid, Racial Discrimination and Colonialism in Southern Africa, held at Kitwe, Zambia, from 25 July to 4 August 1967
A/6818

* Many of the materials in this section have not been issued as United Nations documents; all such materials are reproduced in this book.

International Conference of Trade Unions against Apartheid, Geneva, 15-16 June 1973
•A/RES/2923 F; •A/9169; A/AC.115/L.238

•Statement by the Chairman of the Special Committee on Apartheid, Mr. Edwin Ogebe Ogbu (Nigeria), at a meeting of the Anti-Apartheid Committee of New Zealand, held at Victoria University in Wellington on 13 September 1974
UN Press Release GA/AP/413

Seminar on South Africa, Paris, 28 April-2 May 1975
A/10103-S/11708; A/AC.115/L.402

Declaration and Programme of Action adopted by the International Seminar on the Eradication of Apartheid and in Support of the Struggle for Liberation in South Africa, Havana, 24-28 May 1976
A/31/104-S/12092

Second International Trade Union Conference for Action against Apartheid, Geneva, 10-11 June 1977
A/RES/31/6 G; A/32/22/Add.1-S/12363/Add.1

World Conference for Action against Apartheid, Lagos, 22-26 August 1977
•S/12426; A/CONF.91/9 and Corr.1

Charter of Rights for Migrant Workers in Southern Africa, adopted by the Conference on Migratory Labour in Southern Africa, Lusaka, Zambia, 4-8 April 1978
A/RES/33/162

Report of the Symposium on the Exploitation of Blacks in South Africa and Namibia and on Prison Conditions in South Africa Jails, Maseru, Lesotho, 17-22 July 1978
ST/HR/SER.A/1

Declaration adopted by the International NGO Conference for Action against Apartheid, Geneva, 28-31 August 1978
A/AC.115/L.501

World Conference of Youth and Students on the Struggle of the Peoples, Youth and Students of Southern Africa, Paris, 19-22 February 1979
UN Press Release GA/AP/885

Declaration adopted by the United Nations Seminar on Nuclear Collaboration with South Africa, London, 24-25 February 1979
S/13157

Declaration adopted by the International Seminar on Children under Apartheid, Paris, 18-20 June 1979
A/34/512

International Seminar on the Role of Transnational Corporations in South Africa, London, 2-4 November 1979
A/34/655; A/AC.115/L.521

International Seminar on an Oil Embargo against South Africa, Amsterdam, 14-16 March 1980
A/35/160-S/13869; A/AC.115/L.521

Hemispheric Seminar of Women under Apartheid, Montreal, 9-11 May 1980
A/AC.115/L.525; A/CONF.94/BP/17

International Seminar on Women and Apartheid, Helsinki, 19-21 May 1980
A/35/286; A/AC.115/L.528; A/CONF.94/BP.17

Declaration and communiqué adopted by the International Seminar on Youth Solidarity with the People's Struggle in Southern Africa and Consultative Meeting with International Youth and Student Organizations, Sigtuna, Sweden, 23-26 May 1980
A/AC.115/L.526; A/AC.115/L.529

Declaration adopted by the International NGO Action Conference for Sanctions against South Africa, Geneva, 30 June - 3 July 1980
A/35/439-S/14160

United Nations Institute for Training and Research (UNITAR) Colloquium on the Prohibition of

Apartheid, Racism and Racial Discrimination and the Achievement of Self-determination in International Law, Geneva, 20-24 October 1980
A/35/677-S/14281

Declaration adopted by the Conference of West European Parliamentarians on an Oil Embargo against South Africa, Brussels, 30-31 January 1981
UN Press Release GA/AP/1167

International Seminar on the Implementation and Reinforcement of the Arms Embargo against South Africa, London, 1-3 April 1981
A/RES/35/206 B; A/36/190-S/14442;
A/AC.115/L.547
International Seminar on Loans to South Africa, Zurich, 5-7 April 1981
A/36/201-S/14443; A/AC.115/L.548

First International Conference on Sanctions against South Africa, Paris, 20-27 May 1981
A/RES/34/93 C; A/36/319-S/14531;
•A/CONF.107/8

Report on the mission of the Special Committee against Apartheid to the Symposium on Transnational Corporations, Detroit, United States of America, 11-12 June 1981
A/AC.115/SR.478

Declaration concerning the Policy of Apartheid in South Africa, adopted by the International Labour Conference, sixty-seventh session, twenty-third sitting, Geneva, 18 June 1981
International Labour Conference, Record of Proceedings, sixty-seventh session, pages LXXVIII-LXXXIV

Seminar on Effective Measures to Prevent Transnational Corporations and Other Established Interests from Collaborating with the Racist Regime of South Africa, Geneva, 29 June - 3 July 1981
ST/HR/SER.A/9

International Seminar on Publicity and Role of the Mass Media in the International Mobilization

against Apartheid, Berlin, German Democratic Republic, 31 August-2 September 1981
A/36/496-S/14686; A/AC.115/L.555

Declaration adopted by the International Conference of Youth and Students in Solidarity with the Peoples, Youth and Students of Southern Africa, Luanda, Angola, 13-15 November 1981
A/AC.115/L.564

Declaration adopted by the Conference on Southern Africa — "Time to Choose", London, 11-13 March 1982
A/AC.115/L.568
Declaration adopted by the International Seminar on the History of Resistance against Occupation, Oppression and Apartheid in South Africa, Paris, 29 March - 2 April 1982
A/AC.115/L.576

International Conference on Women and Apartheid, Brussels, 17-19 May 1982
A/37/261-S/15150; •A/AC.115/L.571

Asian Regional Conference for Action against Apartheid, Manila, 24-26 May 1982
A/37/265-S/15157; A/AC.115/L.573

Conference of West European Parliamentarians on Sanctions against South Africa, The Hague, 26-27 November 1982
A/37/691-S/15508; A/AC.115/L.587

International Conference of Trade Unions on Sanctions and Other Actions against the Apartheid Regime in South Africa, Geneva, 10-11 June 1983
•A/38/272-S/15832; UN Press Release GA/AP/1455

International Conference on Sanctions against Apartheid in Sports, London, 27-29 June 1983
A/38/310-S/15882; A/AC.115/L.594

International NGO Conference of Action against Apartheid and Racism, Geneva, 5-8 July 1983
A/38/309-S/15881; A/AC.115/L.59 6

International Conference on the Alliance between South Africa and Israel, Vienna, 11-13 July 1983
A/38/311-S/15883; A/AC.115/L.595

Latin American Regional Conference for Action against Apartheid, Caracas, 16-18 September 1983
A/38/451-S/16009; A/AC.115/L.603

Declaration adopted by the Interfaith Colloquium on Apartheid, London, 5-7 March 1984
A/AC.115/L.605

North American Regional Conference for Action against Apartheid, New York, 18-21 June 1984
A/39/370-S/16686; A/AC.115/L.614
Declaration adopted by the Consultative Meeting of Anti-Apartheid and Solidarity Movements, London, 25-26 June 1984
A/AC.115/L.613

Report on the mission of the Special Committee against Apartheid to the International NGO Conference for the Independence of Namibia and the Eradication of Apartheid, Geneva, 2-5 July 1984
A/AC.115/SR.550

Conference of Arab Solidarity with the Struggle for Liberation in Southern Africa, Tunis, 7-9 August 1984
A/39/450-S/16726; A/AC.115/L.615

Seminar on the Legal Status of the Apartheid Regime and Other Legal Aspects of the Struggle against Apartheid, Lagos, 13-16 August 1984
A/39/423-S/16709 and Corr.1; A/AC.115/L.616

International Conference on Women and Children under Apartheid, Arusha, Tanzania, 7-10 May 1985
A/40/319-S/17197; A/AC.115/L.623

Second International Conference on Sports Boycott against South Africa, Paris, 16-18 May 1985
A/40/343-S/17224; A/AC.115/L.624 and Corr.1

Report of the Media Workshop on Countering Apartheid Propaganda, London, 20-22 May 1985
A/40/696-S/17511

International Seminar on Racist Ideologies, Attitudes and Organizations Hindering Efforts for the Elimination of Apartheid and Means to Combat Them, Siofok, Hungary, 9-11 September 1985
A/40/660-S/17477; A/AC.115/L.634

International Conference of Maritime Trade Unions on the Implementation of the United Nations Oil Embargo against South Africa, London, 30-31 October 1985
A/40/892-S/17632; UN Press Release GA/AP/1684
Seminar on International Assistance and Support to Peoples and Movements Struggling against Colonialism, Racism, Racial Discrimination and Apartheid, Yaoundé, Cameroon, 28 April-9 May 1986
A/41/571; ST/HR/SER.A/19

International Seminar on the United Nations Arms Embargo against South Africa against South Africa, London, 28-30 May 1986
S/RES/421 (1977); S/18288; A/41/388-S/18121

Seminar on Oil Embargo against South Africa, Oslo, 4-6 June 1986
A/41/404-S/18141; A/AC.115/L.636

World Conference on Sanctions against Racist South Africa, Paris, 16-20 June 1986
A/RES/40/64 C; A/41/434-S/18185 and Corr.1;
•A/CONF.137/5

International Student Conference in Solidarity with the Struggle of the Students of Southern Africa, London, 31 July-3 August 1987
A/42/665-S/19218; A/AC.115/L.649

Declaration adopted by the International Conference against Apartheid Sport, Harare, Zimbabwe, 5-7 November 1987
A/42/762-S/19266

Report of the Seminar on the Role of the Latin American and Caribbean Media in the International Campaign against Apartheid, Lima, 7-9 March 1988
A/AC.115/L.651/Rev.1

Symposium on Culture against Apartheid, Athens, 2-4 September 1988
A/43/606-S/20184; A/AC.115/L.656; A/AC.115/INF/8

Declaration adopted by the International Conference on Apartheid, Lagos, 7-9 November 1988
A/43/854-S/20288
Report of the Seminar on the Special Needs of South African and Namibian Refugee Women and Children, Harare, Zimbabwe, 16-18 January 1989
A/AC.115/L.659

International NGO Seminar on Education against Apartheid, Geneva, 4-6 September 1989
A/44/522-S/20844; A/AC.115/L.663

Regional Seminar on East Asian Action against Apartheid, Tokyo, 23-25 January 1990
A/AC.115/L.666; A/AC.115/INF/12/Rev.1; United Nations Centre against Apartheid, Notes and Documents, No. 2/90

Fourth International Conference against Apartheid in Sports, Stockholm, 4-6 September 1990
A/AC.115/L.670; United Nations Centre against Apartheid, Notes and Documents, No. 14/90

International Seminar on the Political, Historical, Economic, Social and Cultural Factors Contributing to Racism, Racial Discrimination and Apartheid, Geneva, 10-14 December 1990
E/CN.4/1991/63 and Add.1; ST/HR/PUB/91/3

Symposium on Cultural and Academic Links with South Africa, Los Angeles, 12 May 1991
A/46/177; A/AC.115/L.677; United Nations Centre against Apartheid, Information Note No. SCA/GE/91/3

International Conference on the Educational Needs of the Victims of Apartheid in South Africa, Paris, 25-27 June 1991
A/AC.115/L.678; A/AC.115/INF/17

Report of the Seminar on South Africa's Socio-economic Problems: Future Role of the United Nations System in Helping to Address Them, Windhoek, Namibia, 22-24 May 1992
A/AC.115/L.685

Declaration adopted by the Follow-up Conference on International Educational Assistance to Disadvantaged South Africans, New York, 8-9 September 1992
A/RES/46/80

Declaration adopted by the International Conference on Southern Africa: Making Hope a Reality, London, 14-15 June 1993
A/48/255-S/26048

Report of the Symposium on Political Tolerance in South Africa: Role of Opinion-makers and the Media, Cape Town, South Africa, 30 July - 1 August 1993
A/AC.115/L.694

Report of the Seminar on Sustainable Economic Growth and Development in South Africa: Policy Priorities for the Early Years of a Democratic Government, London, 22-24 January 1994
A/AC.115/L.696

Seminar on the Image of the United Nations in South Africa, Cape Town, South Africa, 8-10 February 1994
UN press releases PI/831-SAF/167 and SAF/169

Declaration adopted by the International Briefing on South Africa's First Democratic and Non-racial Elections, Brussels, 28 February - 1 March 1994
A/48/895-S/1994/261

## 4.2 Correspondence
of Secretaries-General

•Telegram from Mr. W. B. Ngakane, on behalf of the Consultative Committee of African leaders (Johannesburg, 16-17 December 1960), to Secretary-General Dag Hammarskjöld

•Letter dated 9 March 1964 from Chief Albert J. Luthuli, President-General of the African National Congress, to Secretary-General U Thant

•Letter dated 3 February 1967 from the Chairman of the Special Committee on the Policies of Apartheid of the Government of the Republic of South Africa, Mr. Achkar Marof (Guinea), to Secretary-General U Thant concerning the treatment of political prisoners in South Africa
UN Press Release GA/AP/88

•Telegram dated 3 November 1975 from Mr. Oliver Tambo, President of the African National Congress, to Secretary-General Kurt Waldheim
A/AC.115/SR.973

•Letter dated 27 July 1992 from Secretary-General Boutros Boutros-Ghali to Mr. Nelson Mandela, President of the African National Congress

•Letter dated 13 August 1992 from Secretary-General Boutros Boutros-Ghali to Mr. Abdou Diouf, Acting President of the Organization of African Unity

•Letter dated 16 September 1992 from Secretary-General Boutros Boutros-Ghali to Justice R. J. Goldstone, Chairman of the Commission of Inquiry regarding the Prevention of Public Violence and Intimidation

•Letter dated 21 September 1992 from Secretary-General Boutros Boutros-Ghali to Mr. Roelof F. Botha, Minister for Foreign Affairs of the Republic of South Africa

•Letter dated 23 September 1992 from Secretary-General Boutros Boutros-Ghali to Mr. Frederik Willem de Klerk, President of South Africa

•Letter dated 29 September 1992 from Secretary-General Boutros Boutros-Ghali to Chief Mangosuthu Buthelezi, President of the Inkatha Freedom Party of South Africa

•Letter dated 29 September 1992 from Secretary-General Boutros Boutros-Ghali to Mr. Nelson Mandela, President of the African National Congress

•Letter dated 20 November 1992 from Secretary-General Boutros Boutros-Ghali to Mr. Nelson Mandela, President of the African National Congress

•Letter dated 20 November 1992 from Secretary-General Boutros Boutros-Ghali to Chief Mangosuthu Buthelezi, President of the Inkatha Freedom Party of South Africa

•Letter dated 18 January 1993 from Mr. Thabo Mbeki, Secretary for International Affairs of the African National Congress, to Secretary-General Boutros Boutros-Ghali

•Letter dated 9 March 1993 from Secretary-General Boutros Boutros-Ghali to President de Klerk of South Africa

•Letter dated 24 April 1993 from Secretary-General Boutros Boutros-Ghali to Mr. Nelson Mandela, President of the African National Congress

•Letter dated 6 August 1993 from Secretary-General Boutros Boutros-Ghali to Chief Mangosuthu Buthelezi, President of the Inkatha Freedom Party of South Africa

•Letter dated 3 December 1993 from Secretary-General Boutros Boutros-Ghali to Mr. Roelof Frederik Botha, Minister for Foreign Affairs of South Africa

•Letter dated 2 March 1994 from Secretary-General Boutros Boutros-Ghali to Mr. Nelson Mandela, President of the African National Congress

•Letter dated 11 March 1994 from Secretary-General Boutros Boutros-Ghali to Mr. André Ouellet, Minister for Foreign Affairs and International Trade of Canada

•Letter dated 19 April 1994 from Secretary-General Boutros Boutros-Ghali to Mr. Nelson Mandela, President of the African National Congress

## 4.3 Other documents and materials

•Freedom Charter, adopted by the Congress of the People, Kliptown (South Africa), 26 June 1955
S/12425

•Appeal by leaders of the African National Congress, the South African Indian Congress and the Liberal Party of South Africa for a boycott of South African produce by the British people, December 1959

•Manifesto of *Umkhonto We Sizwe* (Spear of the Nation), an underground organization associated with the African National Congress, 16 December 1961

•"Appeal for action against apartheid" issued jointly by Chief Albert J. Luthuli and the Reverend Dr. Martin Luther King, Jr., on 10 December 1962 Published by the United Nations at the request of the Special Committee on the Policies of Apartheid of the Government of the Republic of South Africa in a pamphlet in tribute to Dr. King

•Declaration signed by 143 international personalities in connection with the trials in South Africa of Mr. Nelson Mandela and others, March 1964
A/AC.115/L.60

•Statement by Mr. Nelson Mandela at his trial in Pretoria, 20 April 1964
A/AC.115/L.67

•Statement by Secretary-General U Thant at the Assembly of Heads of State and Government of the Organization of Africa Unity, 17 July 1964
UN Press Release SG/SM/112

Apartheid and the treatment of prisoners in South Africa: statements and affidavits
OPI/279

Repressive legislation of the Republic of South Africa
ST/PSCA/SER.A/7

•Manifesto on Southern Africa, adopted by the Leaders of East and Central African States, Lusaka, 16 April 1969
A/7754

•Paper presented by the Chairman of the Special Committee against Apartheid, Mr. Edwin Ogebe Ogbu (Nigeria), to the Extraordinary Session of the Council of Ministers of the Organization of African Unity, held at Dar es Salaam, April 1975
United Nations Unit on Apartheid, Notes and Documents No. 11/75

Declaration entitled "Southern Africa: Towards Economic Liberation", adopted by the Heads of Government of Nine Independent States of Southern Africa, Lusaka, 1 April 1980
TD/B/C.7/51(Pt.II)/Add.1(Vol.V), p. 234-238

•Message from the Chairman of the Special Committee against Apartheid, Mr. B. A. Clark (Nigeria), to the African National Congress on the twenty-fifth anniversary of the Freedom Charter, 26 June 1980

Resolution 26/5 on the Strengthening of the Oil Embargo against the South African Regime, adopted by the Council of Ministers of the Arab

Petroleum-Exporting Countries, Kuwait City, 6
May 1981
A/36/665-S/14750

•Introduction to the First Register of Sports
Contacts with South Africa, published by the
Special Committee against Apartheid
Uited Nations Centre against Apartheid, Notes and
Documents, No. 18/81

•Introduction to the First Register of Entertainers,
Actors and Others Who Have Performed in
Apartheid South Africa, published by the Special
Committee against Apartheid, October 1983
United Nations Centre against Apartheid, Notes
and Documents, No. 20/83

•Telegram dated 27 November 1984 from the
Chairman of the Special Committee against
Apartheid, Major-General J. N. Garba (Nigeria),
to Mr. Walter Fauntroy, Mrs. Mary Frances Berry
and Mr. Randall Robinson, Washington, D.C.,
commending non-violent direct action in support
of the oppressed people of South Africa
United Nations Centre against Apartheid,
Information Note No. 61/84

Communiqué on the Political Situation in Southern
Africa, issued by the Foreign Ministers of the
Front-Line States and the European Community,
Lusaka, 3-4 February 1986
A/41/154-S/17809

Declaration against Apartheid in Sports, adopted
by the International Olympic Committee,
Lausanne, Switzerland, 21 June 1988
A/43/543

Statement on the occasion of the seventieth birth-
day of Mr. Nelson Mandela, issued by the
European Community, 18 July 1988
A/43/468-S/20024

Declaration on the Question of South Africa,
adopted by the OAU Ad Hoc Committee on

Southern Africa, Harare, 21 August 1989
A/44/697

Kuala Lumpur Statement on Southern Africa: The
Way Ahead, adopted by the Commonwealth Heads
of Government Meeting, Kuala Lumpur, 21
October 1989
A/44/672-S/20914

Groote Schuur Minute, adopted by the South
African Government and the African National
Congress, Cape Town, 4 May 1990
A/45/268

Report issued by the Monitoring Group of the
OAU Ad Hoc Committee on Southern Africa,
Lusaka, 8 June 1990
A/44/963

•Statement by Secretary-General Javier Pérez de
Cuéllar on the occasion of the International Day
of Solidarity with South African Political Prisoners,
11 October 1990
UN Press Release SG/SM/4504-GA/AP/2001

Abuja Statement on South Africa, adopted by the
OAU Ad Hoc Committee on Southern Africa,
Abuja, Nigeria, 29 July 1991
A/46/450

•Statement by the Spokesman for Secretary-General
Boutros Boutros-Ghali concerning the results of
the referendum in South Africa, 18 March 1992
UN Press Release SG/SM/4717-SAF/131

•Statement by Secretary-General Boutros Boutros-
Ghali at a meeting on the occasion of the obser-
vance of the International Day for the Elimination
of Racial Discrimination, 20 March 1992
UN Press Release SG/SM/4720/Rev.1-
GA/AP/2070/Rev.1-RD/662/Rev.1

Five Working Group Reports submitted to the
Second Plenary Session of the Convention for a
Democratic South Africa (CODESA II), May 1992
A/47/215

Report of the International Hearing on Political Violence in South Africa and the Implementation of the National Peace Accord, London, 14-15 July 1992
A/AC.115/L.687

Second Interim Report issued by the Goldstone Commission of Inquiry regarding the Prevention of Public Violence and Intimidation, July 1992
A/46/950-S/24319

•Statement by the Spokesman for Secretary-General Boutros Boutros-Ghali concerning loss of life in Ciskei, and details on the United Nations Observer Mission in South Africa, 9 September 1992
UN Press Release SG/SM/4807-SAF/141

•Statement by the Spokesman for Secretary-General Boutros Boutros-Ghali concerning the arrival of Ms. Angela King, Chief of the UN Observer Mission in South Africa, in Johannesburg, 23 September 1992
UN Press Release SG/SM/4821-SAF/145

•Statement by the Spokesman for Secretary-General Boutros Boutros-Ghali concerning the forthcoming meeting between President de Klerk and Mr. Nelson Mandela, President of the African National Congress, 24 September 1992
UN Press Release SG/SM/4822-SAF/146

Joint Statement issued by the Government of South Africa and the Pan-Africanist Congress of Azania, Gaborone, Botswana, 23-24 October 1992
A/47/631

Resolution on the Need for the Resumption/ Commencement of Multi-Party Negotiations, adopted by the Multi-Party Planning Conference, Kempton Park, South Africa, 5-6 March 1993
A/48/114-S/25406

•Remarks by Secretary-General Boutros Boutros-Ghali at the annual ceremony to receive contributions and pledges to United Nations assistance

programmes and funds for Southern Africa, 22 March 1993
UN Press Release SG/SM/4947-SAF/155

•Statement by a Spokesman for Secretary-General Boutros Boutros-Ghali expressing "outrage" at right-wing Afrikaners' "brazen display" of force and intimidation against multi-party negotiations, 27 June 1993
UN Press Release SG/SM/5028

•Statement by the Spokesman for Secretary-General Boutros Boutros-Ghali concerning a meeting of the Secretary-General with President de Klerk of South Africa, 23 September 1993
UN Press Release SG/SM/5104-SAF/160

Statement on developments in South Africa, adopted by the OAU Ad Hoc Committee on Southern Africa, New York, 29 September 1993
A/48/461-S/26514

•Statement by the Spokesman for Secretary-General Boutros Boutros-Ghali congratulating President de Klerk of South Africa and ANC President Mandela on their being awarded the Nobel Peace Prize, 15 October 1993
UN Press Release SG/SM/5129

•Statement by the Spokesman for Secretary-General Boutros Boutros-Ghali applauding the "historic agreement" on an interim constitution for South Africa, 18 November 1993
UN Press Release SG/SM/5157-SAF/163

•Statement by the Spokesman for Secretary-General Boutros Boutros-Ghali concerning the declaration by Mr. Nelson Mandela offering new concessions to the Freedom Alliance in order to secure participation by all parties in the forthcoming elections, 17 February 1994
UN Press Release SG/SM/5228-SAF/170

•Joint statement by Mr. Nelson Mandela, President of the African National Congress, and Mr. Mangosuthu Buthelezi, President of the Inkatha Freedom Party, 1 March 1994

•Statement by the Spokesman for Secretary-General Boutros Boutros-Ghali welcoming the breakthrough agreement in South Africa, 19 April 1994
UN Press Release SG/SM/5268-SAF/172

•Statement by the Spokesman for Secretary-General Boutros Boutros-Ghali applauding the election process in South Africa, 6 May 1994
UN Press Release SG/SM/5282-SAF/176

•Statement by Secretary-General Boutros Boutros-Ghali in Pretoria at the luncheon following the inauguration of Mr. Nelson Mandela as President of South Africa, 10 May 1994
UN Press Release SG/SM/5286

# IV List of reproduced documents

*The documents reproduced on pages 221-544 include resolutions of the General Assembly and the Security Council, statements by the Presidents of the General Assembly and the Security Council, reports of the Secretary-General and United Nations bodies, correspondence of the Secretary-General, communications from Member States and other materials. Some texts appear in excerpted form. A more comprehensive bibliography of selected documents, which includes all of the documents on the list below, appears on pages 175-204.*

**Document 13**

Appeal by leaders of the African National Congress, the South African Indian Congress and the Liberal Party of South Africa for a boycott of South African produce by the British people, December 1959.
Not issued as a United Nations document
*See page 243*

**Document 14**

Letter dated 25 March 1960 from the representatives of Afghanistan, Burma, Cambodia, Ceylon, Ethiopia, the Federation of Malaya, Ghana, Guinea, India, Indonesia, Iran, Iraq, Japan, Jordan, Laos, Lebanon, Liberia, Libya, Morocco, Nepal, Pakistan, the Philippines, Saudi Arabia, Sudan, Thailand, Tunisia, Turkey, the United Arab Republic and Yemen to the President of the Security Council requesting consideration of the situation in South Africa.
S/4279 and Add.1, 25 March 1960
*See page 244*

**Document 15**

Security Council resolution: Question relating to the situation in the Union of South Africa.
S/RES/134 (1960), 1 April 1960
*See page 244*

**Document 16**

Resolution adopted by the Second Conference of Independent African States, Addis Ababa, 24 June 1960.
Not issued as a United Nations document
*See page 245*

**Document 17**

Telegram from Mr. W. B. Ngakane, on behalf of the Consultative Committee of African leaders (Johannesburg, 16-17 December 1960), to the Secretary-General.
Not issued as a United Nations document
*See page 246*

**Document 18**

Report of Secretary-General Dag Hammarskjöld on certain steps taken in regard to the implementation of Security Council resolution 134 (1960) including his visit to South Africa.
S/4635, 23 January 1961
*See page 246*

**Document 19**

Resolutions of the All-In African Conference held in Pietermaritzburg, South Africa, 25-26 March 1961.
Not issued as a United Nations document
*See page 247*

**Document 20**

Statement by Mr. Peter Smithers, representative of the United Kingdom, in the Special Political Committee of the General Assembly.
A/SPC/SR.242, 5 April 1961
*See page 248*

**Document 21**

General Assembly resolution: Question of race conflict in South Africa resulting from the policies of apartheid of the Government of the Union of South Africa.
A/RES/1598 (XV), 13 April 1961
*See page 249*

**Document 22**

Manifesto of *Umkhonto We Sizwe* (Spear of the Nation), an underground organization associated with the African National Congress, 16 December 1961.
Not issued as a United Nations document
*See page 250*

**Document 23**

General Assembly resolution: The policies of apartheid of the Government of the Republic of South Africa.
A/RES/1761 (XVII), 6 November 1962
*See page 251*

**Document 24**

"Appeal for action against Apartheid" issued jointly by Chief Albert J. Luthuli and the Reverend Dr. Martin Luther King, Jr., on 10 December 1962.
Published by the United Nations at the request of the Special Committee on the Policies of Apartheid of the Government of the Republic of South Africa in a pamphlet in tribute to Dr. King.
*See page 252*

**Document 25**

Opening statement by Secretary-General U Thant at the first meeting of the Special Committee on the Policies of Apartheid of the Government of the Republic of South Africa.
UN Press Release SG/1453, 2 April 1963
*See page 253*

**Document 26**

Resolution adopted by the Conference of Heads of African States and Governments, Addis Ababa, 22-25 May 1963, on apartheid and racial discrimination.
A/AC.115/L.11, 27 June 1963
*See page 253*

**Document 119**
Declaration adopted by the World Conference on Sanctions against Racist South Africa, Paris, 20 June 1986.
A/CONF.137/5, 1986
*See page 397*

**Document 120**
Statement by the President of the Security Council, on behalf of the Council, calling upon the South African authorities to revoke the decree of 10 April 1987, under which protests against detentions without trial or support for those detained are prohibited.
S/18808, 16 April 1987
*See page 406*

**Document 121**
General Assembly resolution: Policies of apartheid of the Government of South Africa—International solidarity with the liberation struggle in South Africa.
A/RES/42/23 A, 20 November 1987
*See page 407*

**Document 122**
General Assembly resolution: Policies of apartheid of the Government of South Africa—Imposition, coordination and strict monitoring of measures against racist South Africa.
A/RES/43/50 D, 5 December 1988
*See page 407*

**Document 123**
General Assembly resolution: Policies of apartheid of the Government of South Africa—Special session of the General Assembly on apartheid and its destructive consequences in southern Africa.
A/RES/43/50 G, 5 December 1988
*See page 408*

**Document 124**
General Assembly resolution: Policies of apartheid of the Government of South Africa—International solidarity with the liberation struggle in South Africa.
A/RES/44/27 A, 22 November 1989
*See page 409*

**Document 125**
General Assembly resolution: Policies of apartheid of the Government of South Africa—International support for the eradication of apartheid in South Africa through genuine negotiations.
A/RES/44/27 B, 22 November 1989
*See page 410*

**Document 126**
General Assembly resolution: Policies of apartheid of the Government of South Africa—Comprehensive and mandatory sanctions against the racist regime of South Africa.
A/RES/44/27 C, 22 November 1989
*See page 410*

**Document 127**
General Assembly resolution: Policies of apartheid of the Government of South Africa—Imposition, coordination and strict monitoring of measures against racist South Africa.
A/RES/44/27 D, 22 November 1989
*See page 411*

**Document 128**
General Assembly resolution: Policies of apartheid of the Government of South Africa—International financial pressure on the apartheid economy of South Africa.
A/RES/44/27 E, 22 November 1989
*See page 412*

**Document 129**
General Assembly resolution: Policies of apartheid of the Government of South Africa—Programme of work of the Special Committee against Apartheid.
A/RES/44/27 G, 22 November 1989
*See page 413*

**Document 130**
General Assembly resolution: Policies of apartheid of the Government of South Africa—Oil embargo against South Africa.
A/RES/44/27 H, 22 November 1989
*See page 413*

**Document 131**
General Assembly resolution: Policies of apartheid of the Government of South Africa—Military collaboration with South Africa.
A/RES/44/27 I, 22 November 1989
*See page 415*

**Document 132**
General Assembly resolution: Policies of apartheid of the Government of South Africa—United Nations Trust Fund for South Africa.
A/RES/44/27 J, 22 November 1989
*See page 415*

**Document 133**
General Assembly resolution: Policies of apartheid of the Government of South Africa—Concerted international action for the elimination of apartheid.
A/RES/44/27 K, 22 November 1989
*See page 416*

**Document 163**
Letter dated 16 September 1992 from the Secretary-General to Justice R. J. Goldstone, Chairman of the Commission of Inquiry regarding the Prevention of Public Violence and Intimidation.
Not issued as a United Nations document
*See page 450*

**Document 164**
Letter dated 21 September 1992 from the Secretary-General to Mr. Roelof F. Botha, Minister for Foreign Affairs of the Republic of South Africa.
Not issued as a United Nations document
*See page 451*

**Document 165**
Letter dated 23 September 1992 from the Secretary-General to Mr. Frederik Willem de Klerk, President of South Africa.
Not issued as a United Nations document
*See page 452*

**Document 166**
Statement by the Spokesman for Secretary-General Boutros Boutros-Ghali concerning the arrival of Ms. Angela King, the Chief of UNOMSA, in Johannesburg.
UN Press Release SG/SM/4821-SAF/145, 23 September 1992
*See page 452*

**Document 167**
Statement by the Spokesman for Secretary-General Boutros Boutros-Ghali concerning the forthcoming meeting between President de Klerk and Mr. Nelson Mandela, President of the African National Congress.
UN Press Release SG/SM/4822-SAF/146, 24 September 1992
*See page 453*

**Document 168**
Letter dated 29 September 1992 from the Secretary-General to Chief Mangosuthu Buthelezi, President of the Inkatha Freedom Party of South Africa.
Not issued as a United Nations document
*See page 453*

**Document 169**
Letter dated 29 September 1992 from the Secretary-General to Mr. Nelson Mandela, President of the African National Congress.
Not issued as a United Nations document
*See page 454*

**Document 170**
Statement by Secretary-General Boutros Boutros-Ghali at a meeting of the Special Committee against Apartheid for the observance of the International Day of Solidarity with South African Political Prisoners.
UN Press Release SG/SM/4832-GA/AP/2095, 12 October 1992
*See page 454*

**Document 171**
Third report of the Secretary-General on the implementation of the Declaration of Apartheid and its Destructive Consequences in Southern Africa.
A/47/574, 6 November 1992
*See page 455*

**Document 172**
Report of the Special Committee against Apartheid.
A/47/22-S/24663, 6 November 1992
*See page 457*

**Document 173**
Letter dated 20 November 1992 from the Secretary-General to Mr. Nelson Mandela, President of the African National Congress.
Not issued as a United Nations document
*See page 459*

**Document 174**
Letter dated 20 November 1992 from the Secretary-General to Chief Mangosuthu Buthelezi, President of the Inkatha Freedom Party of South Africa.
Not issued as a United Nations document
*See page 459*

**Document 175**
General Assembly resolution: Policies of apartheid of the Government of South Africa—International efforts towards the total eradication of apartheid and support for the establishment of a united, non-racial and democratic South Africa.
A/RES/47/116 A, 18 December 1992
*See page 460*

**Document 176**
Report of the Secretary-General on the question of South Africa.
S/25004, 22 December 1992
*See page 462*

**Document 177**
Letter dated 18 January 1993 from Mr. Thabo Mbeki, Secretary for International Affairs of the African National Congress, to the Secretary-General.
Not issued as a United Nations document
*See page 471*

**Document 192**
Fourth progress report of the Secretary-General on the implementation of the Declaration on Apartheid and its Destructive Consequences in Southern Africa.
A/48/691, 6 December 1993
*See page 482*

**Document 193**
Statement by the President of the General Assembly, Mr. S. R. Insanally (Guyana), on the lifting of the oil embargo against South Africa.
A/48/PV.72, 9 December 1993
*See page 484*

**Document 194**
General Assembly resolution: Elimination of apartheid and establishment of a united, democratic and non-racial South Africa—International efforts towards the total eradication of apartheid and support for the establishment of a united, non-racial and democratic South Africa.
A/RES/48/159 A, 20 December 1993
*See page 484*

**Document 195**
General Assembly resolution: Elimination of apartheid and establishment of a united, democratic and non-racial South Africa—Programme of work of the Special Committee against Apartheid.
A/RES/48/159 B, 20 December 1993
*See page 486*

**Document 196**
General Assembly resolution: Elimination of apartheid and establishment of a united, democratic and non-racial South Africa—Work of the Intergovernmental Group to Monitor the Supply and Shipping of Oil and Petroleum Products to South Africa.
A/RES/48/159 C, 20 December 1993
*See page 487*

**Document 197**
General Assembly resolution: Elimination of apartheid and establishment of a united, democratic and non-racial South Africa—United Nations Trust Fund for South Africa.
A/RES/48/159 D, 20 December 1993
*See page 487*

**Document 198**
General Assembly resolution: United Nations Educational and Training Programme for Southern Africa.
A/RES/48/160, 20 December 1993
*See page 488*

**Document 199**
Report of the Secretary-General concerning arrangements for United Nations monitoring of the electoral process in South Africa and coordination of activities of internal observers.
A/48/845-S/1994/16, 10 January 1994
*See page 489*

**Document 200**
Security Council resolution: The question of South Africa.
S/RES/894 (1994), 14 January 1994
*See page 502*

**Document 201**
General Assembly resolution: Elimination of apartheid and establishment of a united, democratic and non-racial South Africa—Democratic and non-racial elections in South Africa.
A/RES/48/233, 21 January 1994
*See page 503*

**Document 202**
Statement by the Spokesman for Secretary-General Boutros Boutros-Ghali concerning the declaration by Mr. Nelson Mandela offering new concessions to the Freedom Alliance in order to secure participation by all parties in the forthcoming elections.
UN Press Release SG/SM/5228-SAF/170, 17 February 1994
*See page 504*

**Document 203**
Joint statement dated 1 March 1994 by Mr. Nelson Mandela, President of the African National Congress, and Mr. Mangosuthu Buthelezi, President of the Inkatha Freedom Party.
Not issued as a United Nations document
*See page 504*

**Document 204**
Letter dated 2 March 1994 from the Secretary-General to Mr. Nelson Mandela, President of the African National Congress.
Not issued as a United Nations document
*See page 505*

**Document 205**
Letter dated 11 March 1994 from the Secretary-General to Mr. André Ouellet, Minister for Foreign Affairs and International Trade of Canada.
Not issued as a United Nations document
*See page 505*

# V Texts of documents

*The texts of the 221 documents listed on the preceding pages are reproduced below. The appearance of ellipses ( . . . ) in the text indicates that portions of the document have been omitted. A subject index to the documents appears on page 545.*

## Document 1

*General Assembly resolution: Treatment of Indians in the Union of South Africa*

A/RES/44 (I), 8 December 1946

*The General Assembly,*

*Having taken note* of the application made by the Government of India regarding the treatment of Indians in the Union of South Africa, and having considered the matter:

1. *States* that, because of that treatment, friendly relations between the two Member States have been impaired, and unless a satisfactory settlement is reached, these relations are likely to be further impaired;

2. *Is of the opinion* that the treatment of Indians in the Union should be in conformity with the international obligations under the agreements concluded between the two Governments, and the relevant provisions of the Charter;

3. *Therefore requests* the two Governments to report at the next session of the General Assembly the measures adopted to this effect.

## Document 2

*Letter dated 12 July 1948 from the representative of India to the Secretary-General concerning the treatment of Indians in South Africa*

A/577, 16 July 1948

It will be recalled that, in June 1946, the Government of India brought to your attention the racial discrimination to which the South African nationals of Indian origin are subjected by the Government of the Union of South Africa, and requested consideration of this question by the General Assembly of the United Nations. After full consideration of the matter and prolonged deliberations, the General Assembly adopted the following resolution on 8 December 1946:

"*The General Assembly,*

"*Having taken note* of the application made by the Government of India regarding the treatment of Indians in the Union of South Africa, and having considered the matter:

"1. *States* that, because of that treatment, friendly relations between the two Member States have been impaired and, unless a satisfactory settlement is reached, these relations are likely to be further impaired;

"2. *Is of the opinion* that the treatment of Indians in the Union should be in conformity with the international obligations under the agreements concluded between the two Governments and the relevant provisions of the Charter;

"3. *Therefore requests* the two Governments to report at the next session of the General Assembly the measures adopted to this effect."

2. Pursuant to paragraph 3 of this resolution, reports were submitted by the Governments of the Union of South Africa and of India for consideration by the second session of the General Assembly. These reports were first referred to the Political and Security Committee of the General Assembly; that Committee, after full discussion of the reports, adopted on 17 November 1947 the following resolution, by twenty-nine votes against fifteen with five abstentions:

"I. *Whereas* in resolution 44 (I) dated 8 December 1946 the General Assembly, taking note of an application made by the Government of India regarding the treatment of Indians in the Union of South Africa, observed that because of that treatment, friendly relations between the two Member States had been impaired, and unless a satisfactory agreement was reached, their relations were likely to be further impaired;

"II. *Whereas* after a careful consideration of the matter, the General Assembly was of the opinion that the treatment of Indians in the Union of South Africa should be in conformity with the international obligations under the agreements concluded between the two Governments and the relevant provisions of the Charter; and

"III. *Whereas* the General Assembly requested the two Governments to report at the next session of the General Assembly the measures adopted to that effect;

"IV. *The General Assembly,*

"*Having considered* the reports submitted by the Government of India and the Government of the Union of South Africa pursuant to the aforesaid resolution;

"*Reaffirms* its resolution dated 8 December 1946;

"V. *Requests* the two Governments to enter into discussions at a Round Table Conference on the basis of that resolution without any further delay and to invite the Government of Pakistan to take part in such discussions;

"VI. *Requests* that the result of such discussions be reported by the Governments of the Union of South Africa and India to the Secretary-General of the United Nations, who shall from time to time make enquiries from them and submit a report on the action taken on this resolution by the two Governments to the Assembly at its next session."

When the Committee's resolution came before the General Assembly in November 1947, it received a substantial measure of support; thirty-one Members voted in favour of the resolution, nineteen voted against, and six Members abstained. Owing, however, to a ruling that the adoption of this resolution required a two-thirds majority, it failed to be formally adopted by the General Assembly. The net result of the deliberations on this important question during the second session of the General Assembly thus was that the General Assembly failed to make any further recommendations on this subject.

3. The treatment of Indians in the Union of South Africa continues to be a serious violation of the purposes and principles of the Charter on which the United Nations is founded. The Government of the Union of South Africa has made no change whatever either in its discriminatory laws or in the practice of discrimination, on racial grounds alone, against its nationals of Indian origin. For example, the Asiatic Land Tenure and Indian Representation Act, 1946, enacted by the South African Government, which introduced a most severe measure of residential and economic segregation against Asians, still remains on the Statute Book. The continuation by the South African Government of the policy of racial discrimination against Asians and other non-Whites is clearly the result of an assumption by that Government that the failure of the General Assembly of the United Nations to adopt an effective resolution on this subject last year constitutes a tacit approval by the United Nations of that policy. The present Government in the Union of South Africa stands committed to the policy of "apartheid", or racial segregation, and the domination of all non-White peoples by the Europeans; this Government has proclaimed its intention of taking away whatever restricted political rights are at present enjoyed by Indians and other Asians, and of extending the policy of residential and commercial segregation to the Cape Province, the only part of the Union of South Africa which has been comparatively free from racial segregation and political discrimination.

4. The Government of India is of the opinion that the situation of Indians in South Africa is such that it calls for fresh and urgent consideration by the United Nations, in order to uphold the basic moral principles of its Charter and to prevent further deterioration in the already strained relations between India and the Union of South Africa. The Government of India does not believe that it could be the intention of the United Nations to continue to acquiesce in the refusal of the Union of South Africa to act on the General Assembly resolution of 8 December 1946. Such acquiescence would be a denial of human rights and fundamental freedoms, on purely racial grounds, to an important section of the population of the Union of South Africa, and would gravely undermine the prestige of the United Nations, which ultimately depends upon the effectiveness with which its Members carry out the obligations which they have assumed under the Charter. If the belief that there is to be one standard of treatment for the White races and another for the non-White continues to gain strength among the latter, the future for solidarity among the Members of the United Nations, and consequently, for world peace, will indeed be dark. The Government of India therefore earnestly desires that the United Nations will consider the question of the treatment of Indians in the Union of South Africa again, and take appropriate action under Articles 10 and 14 of its Charter; and requests that you will be so good as to place this subject on the provisional agenda of the forthcoming session of the General Assembly.

*(signed)* P. P. PILLAI
Representative of India to the United Nations

# Document 3

## General Assembly resolution: Treatment of people of Indian origin in the Union of South Africa

A/RES/395 (V), 2 December 1950

*The General Assembly,*

*Recalling* its resolutions 44 (I) and 265 (III) relating to the treatment of people of Indian origin in the Union of South Africa,

*Having considered* the communication by the Permanent Representative of India to the Secretary-General dated 10 July 1950,

*Having in mind* its resolution 103 (I) of 19 November 1946 against racial persecution and discrimination, and its resolution 217 (III) dated 10 December 1948 relating to the Universal Declaration of Human Rights,

*Considering* that a policy of "racial segregation" (Apartheid) is necessarily based on doctrines of racial discrimination,

...

---

# Document 4

## Letter dated 12 September 1952 addressed to the Secretary-General by the permanent representatives of Afghanistan, Burma, Egypt, India, Indonesia, Iran, Iraq, Lebanon, Pakistan, the Philippines, Saudi Arabia, Syria and Yemen

A/2183, 12 September 1952

On instructions from our respective Governments, we have the honour to request that the following item be included in the agenda of the seventh regular session of the United Nations General Assembly:

"The question of race conflict in South Africa resulting from the policies of apartheid of the Government of the Union of South Africa."

An explanatory memorandum in accordance with rule 20 of the rules of procedure of the General Assembly is enclosed.

(*signed*)
Sultan AHMED
for Permanent representative of Afghanistan

Fouad EL-PHARONY
Acting permanent representative of Egypt

L. N. PALAR
Permanent representative of Indonesia

A. KHALIDY
Permanent representative of Iraq

Ahmed S. BOKHARI
Permanent representative of Pakistan

Asad AL-FAQIH
Permanent representative of Saudi Arabia

Farid ZEINEDDINE
Permanent representative of Syria

BA MAUNG
Liaison officer of Burma to the United Nations

Rajeshwar DAYAL
Permanent representative of India

A. G. ARDALAN
Permanent representative of Iran

Karim AZKOUL
Acting permanent representative of Lebanon

Carlos P. ROMULO
Permanent representative of the Philippines

A. ABOUTALEB
Permanent representative of Yemen

### Explanatory Memorandum

The race conflict in the Union of South Africa resulting from the policies of apartheid of the South African Government is creating a dangerous and explosive situation, which constitutes both a threat to international peace and a flagrant violation of the basic principles of human rights and fundamental freedoms which are enshrined in the Charter of the United Nations.

Although Africa's importance in world affairs is

increasing rapidly, many parts of that continent still remain subject to racial discrimination and exploitation. The founding of the United Nations and the acceptance of the Member States of the obligations embodied in the Charter have given to the peoples of these areas new hope and encouragement in their efforts to acquire basic human rights. But, in direct opposition to the trend of world opinion, the policy of the Government of the Union of South Africa is designed to establish and to perpetuate every form of racial discrimination which must inevitably result in intense and bitter racial conflict. Apartheid, which is the declared objective of the Government of the Union of South Africa, implies a permanent White superiority over the non-Whites, who constitute the great majority of the Union's population. To achieve apartheid, the following measure are being taken:

(a) Under the notorious Group Area Act, non-Whites are compelled to abandon their present lands and premises and to move to new and usually inferior reserved areas without compensation or provisional alternative accommodation;

(b) Complete segregation is enforced in public services, such as railways, buses and post offices;

(c) The Suppression of Communism Act is being used to suppress democratic movements, especially of the non-Whites, for example, those which advocate racial equality or urge opposition to apartheid;

(d) Non-Whites are debarred from combat service in the armed forces;

(e) No voting or other political rights whatsoever are enjoyed by non-Whites, except in Cape Province, where Africans and the "Coloured" inhabitants have a limited franchise;

(f) Africans are confined to reserves, and their movements are restricted to certain places after specified hours under certain restrictive laws. The interprovincial movements of non-Whites are also restricted;

(g) Non-Whites are excluded under the Mines Works Amendment Act of 1926 from certain classes of skilled work and a systematic drive is in progress to replace them, even in the lower grades of the public services, by Whites;

(h) The education of non-Whites and their housing and living conditions are deplorable. Such facilities of this type as are available to non-Whites are vastly inferior to those offered to the White population.

As a result of these measures, a social system is being evolved under which the non-Whites, who constitute 80 per cent of the population of the Union of South Africa, will be kept in a permanently inferior state to the White minority. Such a policy challenges all that the United Nations stands for and clearly violates the basic and fundamental objectives of the Charter of the United Nations.

The Preamble and Article 1, paragraph 3, and Article 55 c of the Charter proclaim universal respect for, and the due observance of, human rights and fundamental freedoms, without distinction as to race, sex, language, or religion. Under Article 56, all Members have pledged themselves to take joint and separate action in cooperation with the United Nations for the achievement of these purposes.

Under resolution 103 adopted unanimously by the General Assembly in 1946, the United Nations called on governments to put an end to racial persecution and discrimination. Resolution 217 (III) proclaimed the Universal Declaration of Human Rights, and article 2 of the Declaration affirms the equal application of these rights without distinction as to colour, race or religion. Under resolution 395 (V), the United Nations held that the policy of apartheid was necessarily based on doctrines of racial discrimination and therefore called upon the South African Government not to implement or enforce the provisions of the Group Areas Act. These findings and this recommendation were repeated in resolution 511 (VI) adopted at the sixth session of the General Assembly.

It is recognized in all countries, as well as among liberal South African Europeans, that the solution of South Africa's racial problem lies not in any domination of one race by another, but in a partnership of races on a basis of equality and freedom.

Thus the apartheid policy of the Government of the Union of South Africa is contrary not only to the basic premises of the United Nations and to its specifics and repeated recommendations, but also to the trend of opinion all over the world.

Because they have been unable to secure redress by constitutional methods and because the South African Government has turned a deaf ear to the repeated appeals of the United Nations not to embark on a policy of racial discrimination, the non-Whites of the Union have been compelled to launch a completely non-violent resistance movement against the Government's unjust and inhuman racial policies. In their efforts to destroy this movement, the Government has so far arrested over 4,000 persons. Despite the non-violent character of the campaign, physical violence such as flogging is being used to suppress it. The South African Government's reaction to a movement of peaceful resistance against legislation which world opinion and the United Nations have repeatedly and emphatically condemned, is having wide repercussions. We are convinced that the continuance of such repression will only aggravate race conflict throughout Africa and arouse indignation elsewhere. A new tension is thus being created which is no less serious than others affecting world peace.

It is therefore imperative that the General Assembly give this question its urgent consideration in order to prevent an already dangerous situation from deteriorating further and to bring about a settlement in accordance with the Purposes and Principles of the United Nations Charter.

# Document 5

*Statement by Mrs. Vijaya Lakshmi Pandit, Chairperson of the delegation of India, introducing the item on apartheid in the Ad Hoc Political Committee of the General Assembly*

A/AC.61/SR.13, 12 November 1952

. . .

16. The 13 countries which had joined in placing the item on the agenda represented some 600 million people. They had felt that the deliberate attempt on the part of the South African Government to establish racial discrimination by a policy of apartheid, which implied permanent superiority of the White inhabitants over the non-White who comprised 80 per cent of the total population, had created a dangerous tension in South Africa with serious consequences for harmony among nations and peace in the world. They further considered that the objectives of South Africa's policy were to force the non-European population into perpetual economic and social servitude by racial discrimination and segregation in violation of basic human rights and fundamental freedoms and of the principles of the Charter, to which all States, including South Africa, had pledged adherence.

17. Mrs. Pandit reviewed the principal legislative acts adopted by the South African Government to implement its apartheid policy. The Group Areas Act, based on the complete segregation of racial groups, would, when implemented, involve the uprooting of thousands of non-Whites, depriving them of homes, property and business premises without compensation or provisional alternative accommodations. It divided the entire population into White, native and coloured groups and defined the characteristics of each. It would prevent any direct business relations among the three groups, and relegate the non-Whites to menial occupations. Under the Population Registration Act, identity cards defining his racial or ethnic group would be issued to each person over sixteen years of age, to be presented for inspection on demand by any member of the police force, which would consist entirely of Whites. The Mixed Marriages Act prohibited marriages between Whites and non-Whites, declared such marriages null and void and imposed penalties on persons performing them. It had been justified by pseudo-scientific theories and was an insult to the non-White population. The Separate Representation of Voters Act removed so-called coloured voters in the Cape Province from a common roll vote to a separate roll. They would be represented in Parliament by four Europeans. The act had been adopted by a narrow majority, consisting largely of the Nationalist Party, against strong opposition by both Europeans and non-Europeans. It was a

clear violation of one of the "entrenched" clauses of the Constitution, which required that amendment of franchise rights of the coloured population must be made by a two-thirds majority of both Houses of Parliament voting together. The Supreme Court had declared the Act *ultra vires* of Parliament, but the Government had overridden the Court's decision by enacting the High Court of Parliament Act. Thus, in pursuance of its racial policies, it had not hesitated to violate the Constitution. The Suppression of Communism Act had also been made a potential vehicle for the persecution of the non-White population in that it defined communism as any doctrine encouraging hostility between Europeans and non-Europeans. Finally, the Bantu Authorities Act relegated the African race to the ancient system of tribal rule for the express purpose of preventing their fusion into a modern nation. Apartheid was enforced even in the use of common public facilities, in trade unions and in the armed forces of the country. Non-Whites could not fight in defence of the nation, they had no opportunities for jobs as skilled workers or in government service and therefore no scope for their social and economic betterment. The Prime Minister, Mr. Malan, had recently reaffirmed his intention to effect no changes in the laws differentiating racial groups and to continue to bar Bantus and other non-Europeans from administrative, executive and legislative posts.

18. Deprived of constitutional and legal means to seek redress of its grievances against unjust racial laws, the non-White population of South Africa had begun a campaign of passive resistance, a technique first developed in 1915 by the young Gandhi. At that time, the British Viceroy of India had expressed his deepest sympathy with the movement started in South Africa. Gandhi's theory of passive resistance or *Satyagraha* was based on the concept that the dignity of man required obedience to the law of the spirit; consequently, that resistance, far from being an expression of submission or cowardice, was motivated by a strength derived from an indomitable will to defy evil. It expressed a moral protest against continuing injustice, as Professor Julius Lieuwen, a European professor in a South African university, had said, and was not intended to injure the White population. Professor Lieuwen had interpreted the feeling of an increasing number of Europeans when he had called upon the South African Government to desist from further repressive measures and upon the European population to make a moral

gesture of equal significance by expressing sympathy and solidarity with the resistance movement. In a statement issued jointly by the Bishop of Johannesburg and others, the wide response to the movement had been recognized, the courage and sacrifice it demanded had been emphasized and it had been described as a challenge to the entire White community as well as to all who participated in the exercise of political power in South Africa.

19. The decision to embark on a passive resistance campaign on a national scale had been taken out of desperation, but only after the Government had been given due warning and a final appeal had been made for a relaxation of repressive and discriminatory measures. When the Malan Government had replied with a threat to use the full power of governmental machinery against the alleged inciters to subversion, the resistance movement had no choice. Demonstrations had been held and volunteers selected who, after advance notice to the police authorities, had defied various laws and regulations deriving from the apartheid policy. To date, over 7,000 persons had sought arrest and been sentenced to imprisonment. It was a tribute to the discipline of the resisters that, despite great provocation by the police and fanatical White elements, they had maintained the peaceful character of the movement. Moreover, despite brutal treatment in the prisons, the resistance had not been broken and enjoyed widespread support among all sectors of the non-White population and among the liberal Whites. The Presbyterian Church of South Africa, for example, had condemned the Government's discriminatory policies, had urged tolerance of other racial groups and had exhorted its members to pursue the fight against repressive measures. The Chancellor of St. Paul's Cathedral in London likewise had called upon all Christians to support the liberal forces combating apartheid. The Archbishop of York had appealed to Christians to reject the master-race theory. The British Trade Union Congress, representing some eight million workers, had assured its full support to those fighting the South African Government's racial policies.

20. The international implications of South African racial policies were clear to all Member States which had pledged themselves to uphold the basic principles of the Charter, in particular those concerning the observance of human rights. Moreover, that pledge had been strengthened by the unanimous adoption of General Assembly resolution 103 (I) calling for an end to religious and racial persecution and discrimination and of resolution 377 (V), entitled "Uniting for Peace", urging an intensification of joint action to develop and stimulate respect for human rights if lasting peace was to be achieved. The Preamble of the Declaration of Human Rights further strengthened that pledge.

21. The situation in South Africa was imperilling the entire continent of Africa. Unless the United Nations acted rapidly to stir the conscience of men of goodwill everywhere to repudiate the South African Government's policies and actions, the world would be threatened with a new conflict. In his appeal, the Bishop of Johannesburg had called for a revival of the liberal tradition of the country, based on the principle of equal rights for all civilized peoples and equal opportunities for all to become civilized. He had urged a reasonable status for non-Europeans and a Government policy resting on a moral basis under which persons were evaluated by the tests of civilization and education rather than by race and colour.

22. The Bishop's statement implied that an attempt should be made to build a new pattern, which would, by providing equal opportunities for all groups, create a synthesis of cultures for the greatest benefit of the whole population. India would welcome a study of the situation in South Africa with a view to assisting the Government to resolve it on a rational and humanitarian basis of mutual toleration and understanding among all racial groups. The purpose of the Indian delegation in co-sponsoring the item under discussion was not to condemn South Africa; it harboured no rancour. Its only desire was to end a situation as degrading to those who enforced the discriminatory laws as to the victims.

# Document 6

*Letter dated 17 November 1952 from Mr. Z. K. Matthews, representative of the African National Congress, to the Chairman of the Ad Hoc Political Committee*

A/AC.61/L.14, 19 November 1952

In the course of a recent debate in the Ad Hoc Political Committee on the question of the race conflict in South Africa arising out of the apartheid policy of the Government of the Union of South Africa, it was suggested that I be invited to make a statement to the Committee on behalf of the African people whose views would not otherwise be available to the Committee, although they are vitally affected by the present trend of events in South Africa.

May I respectfully draw your attention to the fact that the request for a hearing by the United Nations comes from the African National Congress? In July 1952, before the item at present under discussion was placed on the agenda of the seventh session of the General Assembly, the African National Congress addressed a communication to Mr. Trygve Lie, Secretary-General of the United Nations, asking for an opportunity to put their grievances before the General Assembly. (See *The New York Times* report, 26 July 1952). I do not know whether this request has been brought to the attention of your Committee, but as far as I am aware that is the only official request which has been addressed to the United Nations on behalf of the African people.

As a member of the National Executive of the African National Congress I have received a cable from the General Secretary of the African National Congress, Mr. W. M. Sisulu, authorizing me to speak on behalf of that organization at the United Nations, should the occasion arise. I have also received from him a copy of a memorandum setting forth the views of that organization regarding the apartheid policy of the Government of the Union of South Africa, and the grievances of the people subject to it. I am forwarding this memorandum herewith.

I feel bound to point out that ever since it became known in South Africa that there was even a remote possibility that I might be invited to make a statement before the United Nations on this subject, considerable official pressure has been brought to bear upon me not to accept such an invitation in view of the action which the Union Government would feel compelled to take against me. The University College of Fort Hare, in South Africa, with which I am connected, has also been warned that the Government "will be reluctantly compelled to take a very serious view of the matter as he (i.e., myself) is employed by your college which receives a considerable subsidy from the State". The authorities of the college, in view of this direct threat, have instructed me not to accept any invitation to appear. It is in the face of such threats of victimization that I submit the enclosed document for your consideration. As the request of the African National Congress for a hearing has not yet been considered, I do not feel called upon to decide, at this stage, on the issue of a personal appearance.

*(signed)* Z. K. MATTHEWS
*Representative of the African National Congress (Cape)*

# Document 7

*General Assembly resolution: The question of race conflict in South Africa resulting from the policies of apartheid of the Government of the Union of South Africa*

A/RES/616 A (VII), 5 December 1952

*The General Assembly,*

. . .

*Considering* that one of the purposes of the United Nations is to achieve international cooperation in promoting and encouraging respect for human rights and fundamental freedoms for all, without distinction as to race, sex, language or religion,

*Recalling* that the General Assembly declared in its resolution 103 (I) of 19 November 1946 that it is in the higher interests of humanity to put an end to religious and so-called racial persecution, and called upon all governments to conform both to the letter and to the spirit of the Charter and to take the most prompt and energetic steps to that end,

*Considering* that the General Assembly has held, in its

resolutions 395 (V) of 2 December 1950 and 511 (VI) of 12 January 1952, that a policy of "racial segregation" (apartheid) is necessarily based on doctrines of racial discrimination,

1. *Establishes* a Commission, consisting of three members, to study the racial situation in the Union of South Africa in the light of the Purposes and Principles of the Charter, with due regard to the provisions of Article 2, paragraph 7, as well as the provisions of Article 1, paragraphs 2 and 3, Article 13, paragraph 1 b, Article 55 c, and Article 56 of the Charter, and the resolutions of the United Nations on racial persecution and discrimination, and to report its conclusions to the General Assembly at its eighth session;

. . .

# Document 8

*General Assembly resolution: The question of race conflict in South Africa resulting from the policies of apartheid of the Government of the Union of South Africa*

A/RES/616 B (VII), 5 December 1952

*The General Assembly,*

...

1. *Declares* that in a multi-racial society harmony and respect for human rights and freedoms and the peaceful development of a unified community are best assured when patterns of legislation and practice are directed towards ensuring equality before the law of all persons regardless of race, creed or colour, and when economic, social, cultural and political participation of all racial groups is on a basis of equality;

2. *Affirms* that governmental policies of Member States which are not directed towards these goals, but which are designed to perpetuate or increase discrimination, are inconsistent with the pledges of the Members under Article 56 of the Charter;

...

# Document 9

*Report of the United Nations Commission on the Racial Situation in the Union of South Africa*

A/2505 and Add.1, 1953

...

**The Commission's terms of reference in relation to certain Charter provisions and General Assembly resolutions (448)**

893. (i) When setting up the Commission and establishing its terms of reference, the Assembly affirmed its own competence in principle to study and act on problems of racial discrimination. Nevertheless, in inviting the Commission to have regard to various articles of the Charter, including Article 2, paragraph 7, in carrying out its terms of reference, the Assembly undoubtedly wished the Commission to study the extent to which those articles might determine, condition or restrict the competence of the United Nations.

The Commission therefore assumed that the Assembly had placed in its terms of reference a definite instruction to study this problem. The Commission carried out that study most carefully in chapter II of the report and reached a formal conclusion. The Assembly, assisted by the commissions which it establishes and authorizes, is permitted by the Charter to undertake any studies and make any recommendations to Member States which it may deem necessary in connection with the application and implementation of the principles to which the Member States have subscribed by signing the Charter. That universal right of study and recommendation is absolutely incontestable with regard to general problems of human rights and particularly of those protecting against discrimination for reasons of race, sex, language or religion.

The exercise of the functions and powers conferred on the Assembly and its subsidiary organs by the Charter does not constitute an intervention prohibited by Article 2 (7) of the Charter.

894. (ii) The Commission is convinced that this interpretation, which it believes to be legally correct and which has been confirmed by the invariable practice of the General Assembly, also serves the cause of peace and the legitimate aspirations of mankind. The study which it has carried out has enabled it to appreciate the serious dangers of a problem such as this, not only to the social equilibrium of the countries concerned, but also friendship and peace among nations. The Commission therefore considers that in such cases the Assembly is not merely exercising a right, but actually fulfilling a duty in using its functions and powers under the Charter.

...

**The substance of the question**

897. (v) Since the Nationalist Party came to power, it has systematically applied its apartheid doctrine. To that end it has enacted and intends to continue to enact a series of statutes, regulations and administrative measures. The most important aspects of that legislation are considered in chapter VI; an attempt has been made in

chapter VII to describe its effects on the various groups of the population, and in chapter VIII to compare its provisions with those of the United Nations Charter and the Universal Declaration of Human Rights.

In view of the differences observed between certain groups or specific geographic areas, these legislative and administrative measures affect to a greater or lesser degree nearly all aspects of the domestic, familial, social, political and economic life of the non-White population, who make up 79 per cent of the whole population of the country. They affect its most fundamental rights and freedoms: political rights, freedom of movement and residence, property rights, freedom to work and practise occupations, freedom of marriage and other family rights. They establish obvious inequality before the law in relation to the rights, freedoms and opportunities enjoyed by the 20 per cent of the population consisting of "Whites" or "Europeans", or of persons regarded as such.

For example, approximately 3 million Bantus live in Native "Reserves", which constitute a mere 9.7 per cent of the area of the Union; non-Europeans may not marry members of the White ethnic group; an Indian from Natal may not cross the frontier of his province to go to another province of the Union without previously obtaining a written authorization; no Bantu may buy a bottle of wine; no non-European may order a meal in a restaurant or spend a night in a hotel other than the few reserved for non-Europeans; no Bantu may move freely at night in the urban zones subject to curfew; no Bantu living on a Reserve may leave it to seek work in a town without previously obtaining a written authorization; no non-European may enroll as a student in the universities of Pretoria or Potchefstroom; no non-European may play on a Rugby football team consisting of Europeans; no non-European may operate a hoist in the gold mines of the Rand or drive a locomotive; a non-European may not be elected to Parliament, and his voting rights are restricted and are subject to different conditions from those of the Whites. Because of all kinds of restrictions, Bantus working in urban areas are obliged to live in communities where the proportion of men is nearly double that of women; in the gold-mining areas that disproportion is even greater.

898. (vi) These facts and situations constitute obvious racial discrimination. Four fifths of the population are thereby reduced to a humiliating level of inferiority which is injurious to human dignity and makes the full development of personality impossible or very difficult. . . .

899. (vii) The apartheid policy has given rise to the serious internal conflicts described in chapter VII, and maintains a condition of latent and ever-increasing tension in the country. . . .

900. (viii) Among the population subjected to discrimination in the Union of South Africa there are 365,000 persons of Indian origin, who either immigrated under contract by virtue of a treaty signed by the authorities which then administered India and the rulers of the territories now belonging to the Union of South Africa, or are descended from such immigrants. These thousands of persons, who belong to the most "developed" groups, maintain ties and relations with the citizens of their country of origin, which now consist of India and Pakistan. These countries are watching with increasing anxiety the development of the policy of discrimination against that part of the population; their persistent appeals to the General Assembly to deal with the question and help to find a solution show the extent of their anxiety.

The Commission also notes the profound alarm which is spreading in Africa, the Middle East and, generally speaking, wherever the spirit of solidarity among Coloured persons has resented the attack made upon it. Publications, statements and resolutions bear witness to that alarm. The Commission is convinced that the pursuit of this policy cannot fail immediately and seriously to increase the anti-White sentiment in Africa resulting from nationalist movements, the force of which must not be underestimated. This policy is therefore contrary to the efforts of the part of mankind which believes in the unity of the destiny of peoples and the necessity of the maintenance of peace and which aspires to use such aspirations through peaceful channels of international collaboration to carry out the purposes laid down in the United Nations Charter, including that of "the right of peoples to self-determination".

There can be no doubt, therefore, that the position in the Union of South Africa is, to say the least, "likely to impair the general welfare or friendly relations among nations", in the sense of Article 14 of the Charter.

901. (ix) The Commission considers that the doctrine of racial differentiation and superiority on which the apartheid policy is based is scientifically false, extremely dangerous to internal peace and international relations, as is proved by the tragic experience of the world in the past twenty years, and contrary to "the dignity and worth of the human person".

. . .

902. (x) All the previously-described discriminatory legislative and administrative measures, especially those laid down in pursuance of the apartheid policy, conflict with the solemn declaration in the Preamble of the United Nations Charter, in which the signatories state that they are determined to "reaffirm faith in fundamental human rights, in the dignity and worth of the human person, in the equal right of men and women and of nations large and small". They are also contrary to the

purpose of the Charter to "achieve international cooperation in ... encouraging respect for human rights and for fundamental freedoms for all without distinction as to race, sex, language or religion".

903. (xi) Those measures are also contrary to the purposes of international economic and social cooperation laid down in Article 55 of the Charter, which states that the United Nations should, "with a view to the creation of conditions of stability and well-being which are necessary for peaceful and friendly relations among nations", promote "universal respect for, and observance of, human rights and fundamental freedoms for all without distinction as to race, sex, language, or religion." Thus the measures taken in application of the apartheid policy constitute a failure by the Government of the Union of South Africa to observe the obligation undertaken by it under Article 56 of the Charter, "to take joint and separate action in cooperation with the Organization for the achievement of the purposes set forth in Article 55". This failure is clear to the Commission, because that Government has, after having signed the Charter, not pursued a policy for the progressive elimination of discriminatory measures contrary to the Charter, but has instead adopted new measures likely to aggravate the situation with regard to racial discrimination.

904. (xii) The Commission's study of previous General Assembly resolutions on racial persecution and discrimination showed that the racial policy pursued by the Government of the Union of South Africa is also contrary to the whole doctrine repeatedly and firmly upheld by the United Nations. ...

905. The members of the Commission are aware that prophecy is within neither their terms of reference nor their capacity. Nevertheless, they believe that it is their duty as free and responsible men to transmit to the Assembly a conviction which they bore in mind during their long work and which was strengthened daily. They wished to communicate their concern to the Assembly. They reached the following conclusions:

(a) It is highly unlikely, and indeed improbable, that the policy of apartheid will ever be willingly accepted by the masses subjected to discrimination;

(b) Efforts at persuasion, however powerful they may be or may become, by the Government and Europeans can never convince the non-Europeans that the policy is based on justice and a wish to promote their material and moral interests, and not on pride of race and a will to domination;

(c) As the apartheid policy develops, the situation it has made is constantly being aggravated and daily becomes less open to settlement by conciliation, persuasion, information or education, daily more explosive and more menacing to internal peace and to the foreign relations of the Union of South Africa. Soon any solution will be precluded and the only way out will be through violence, with all its inevitable and incalculable dangers. ...

906. The members of the Commission, faced with a situation which is so serious and which seems to them to be fraught with such grave and imminent threats, feel in duty bound to communicate to the Assembly for its consideration on certain suggestions which have occurred to them concerning the assistance which the community of peoples convened in the United Nations could, and therefore should, give to help a Member, the Union of South Africa, to solve those problems at a difficult moment in its history. The members of the Commission realize that the Commission was set up for inquiry and not as a commission of good offices, but are willing to risk reproach for an unduly wide interpretation of their terms of reference if they make the following suggestions: ...

908. (ii) Nevertheless, international cooperation has another duty as important if not more important: to face reality and seek by all peaceful means, not neglecting any, a manner in which to help to solve problems. Every Member State going through a serious and difficult period is entitled to receive aid and assistance. This aid must include all the friendly advice which the great family of the United Nations is able to give to one of its Members in a spirit of brotherhood. In the case of the Union of South Africa, there is a great opportunity to give both moral and material aid and assistance and thus to confirm international solidarity and co-operation by deeds.

The United Nations, in view of its serious anxiety at the development of ethnic tensions in South Africa and at the feelings which those tensions have aroused in other States and among other peoples, might *express the hope* that the Government of the Union of South Africa will be able to reconsider the components of its policy towards various ethnic groups. The United Nations might *suggest* ways and means in which the Union might draw up a new policy: for example, a round-table conference of members of different ethnic groups of the Union, which would, in an effort towards conciliation, make proposals to the Government to facilitate the peaceful development of the racial situation in the Union of South Africa. The United Nations might offer its help to that conference by sending a number of United Nations representatives, so that all parties might be sure that the principles of the Charter would guide the debates.

909. (iii) Nevertheless, the South African racial problem cannot be solved by the mere wish of a government which has decided to change its policy. In the course of its survey the Commission has stressed the multiple and complex factors from which the problem has arisen and which the apartheid policy has systematized and coordi-

nated. These historical, religious, social and economic factors have played and will continue to play an active part in South African life, and their effects, even in the most favourable circumstances, can only disappear gradually. Obviously, the economic and social factors are especially important.

The non-European groups, especially the Natives, constitute the major part of the proletariat of the Union of South Africa, which suffers not only from discriminatory measures but also from those conditions which affect the proletariat of any economically under-developed country. The economic development of the whole country, the actual diminution of the social inequality which is now so great, and the opening of real opportunities and openings for individual and collective progress, together with the sincere wish of the Government and of the European population progressively to eliminate discrimination must be combined if the situation is to be appreciably improved.

The Commission therefore considers that the best course of international cooperation would be to offer the Government of the Union of South Africa at an opportune moment all the material and intellectual assistance which an international organization should and can give to one of its Members in difficulty. This assistance, if it were requested and accepted, might take the form of carrying out studies, setting up conciliation machinery, or lending, through technical, financial, economic and social assistance, the Organization's effective support to a policy and projects aimed at facilitating, in education, health, housing, agriculture, industry and public works, the maintenance of peaceful relations among the ethnic groups of the Union of South Africa and the progressive development of their collaboration in the life of the community.

910. In conclusion, the Commission considers it fitting to recall the words of a man who gave evidence before it and who, after describing and censuring the apartheid policy, pointed out that the campaign of resistance in South Africa was directed against injustice but had not yet developed into hatred among men. The Commission welcomed that testimony as a ray of hope and hoped that its optimism would be confirmed by events. In any case, the Commission was convinced that if the South African Government merely indicated its wish to review its racial policy and to accept spontaneously, in complete sovereignty and independence, the fraternal collaboration of the community of nations in solving that problem, a simple gesture of that kind might even now clear the air and open a new path of justice and peace to the development of the Union of South Africa within the United Nations.

# Document 10

*Second report of the United Nations Commission on the Racial Situation in the Union of South Africa*

A/2719, 1954

. . .

### Suggestion I. Interracial contacts; interracial conference

370. Considering that the greatest contribution to harmony and understanding among the various groups could be made by frequent and repeated contacts between the individuals of which they are composed, the Commission *suggests* that serious and sustained efforts in that direction should be made by all the parties concerned. In particular, the Commission wishes to draw attention to the statement made in its first report that "the United Nations might *express the hope* that the Government of the Union of South Africa will be able to reconsider the components of its policy towards various ethnic groups. The United Nations might *suggest* ways and means in which the Union might draw up a new policy: for example, a round-table conference of members of different ethnic groups of the Union, which would, in an effort towards conciliation, make proposals to the Governments to facilitate the peaceful development of the racial situation in the Union of South Africa. The United Nations might offer help to that conference by sending a number of United Nations representatives, so that all parties might be sure that the Principles of the Charter would guide the debates".

. . .

### Suggestion II. Basic ideas for a peaceful settlement

372. The Commission has stated on a previous occasion that it is for the South African people themselves to solve their problem. It wishes, however, to set out a number of basic ideas derived from plans or projects originating in the Union of South Africa which it believes to be consistent with the United Nations Charter and the Universal Declaration of Human Rights. These ideas

should be taken into consideration in any discussion of the solution of the racial problem. In setting them out, the Commission is fully aware of the fact that they can be put into effect only gradually and over a long period. They are as follows:

373. (A) In view of the wretched economic and social conditions in which the non-White peoples live, any steps to raise their standard of living will help to reduce internal tension in the Union. The Commission has no hesitation in stating this obvious fact. . . We must add that the Commission would hesitate to urge the leaders of a Member State to accept painful sacrifices had it not already expressed the opinion in its previous Report that the State could appeal for international cooperation in a task of such importance to mankind. . . .

374. (B) In view of the predominant part undoubtedly played by economic and technical factors in inter-group tensions in the Union of South Africa, the Commission believes that it will be difficult for the Government to postpone without risk steps towards an *"economic" integration* designed to alleviate the serious suffering caused to the Bantu people by the *dispersal* and *inadequacy* of the reserves, the *over-population* in relation to their *natural resources*, the *quality of their soil* and their economic and technical development and also by the *discriminatory measures* against Bantu workers employed in industry in the European areas. Reemphasizing its inability to present a coordinated plan with priorities owing to the conditions under which it has worked, the Commission can only draw attention to some of the many areas in which a re-direction of policy might make an effective contribution to the relaxation of tension.

375. (a) *Announcement of a policy for the progressive reduction, with a view to the ultimate abolition, of the system of migrant labour.*

The Commission's previous report contains references to the harmful effects of the system of migrant labour, while the annex to the present report describes the serious limitations it places on the productivity of human labour and on economic, industrial and agricultural development. The Commission believes it to be an incontrovertible fact that neither the system, which is degrading to human dignity, causes a vast amount of individual and collective human suffering and disrupts family life, nor the working conditions it involves, will ever be accepted by those subjected to them and will never be regarded by an aroused world conscience as an inevitable necessity. Clearly, however, any policy directed towards the progressive eradication of this serious cause of tension implies *the gradual removal of the statutory restrictions of the settlement of non-Whites in urban centres, the recognition of the Bantus' right to become permanent city-dwellers, and the genuine acceptance by* *the Europeans of a non-White population settled in the cities and having the right to own urban property.*

376. (b) *The organization of a continuous programme of fundamental adult education,* with the assistance of the United Nations and UNESCO, if required, for the purpose of creating in the reserves agricultural communities receiving the maximum practical advice, information and equipment as speedily as circumstances permit, in order to ensure first the conservation and then the development of the known resources of the Reserves and the surveying and exploration of their unknown or potential resources.

377. (c) *Execution of a long-term* (but not too long) *plan for the organization of general education* or, at the very least, for the accelerated development of a system of universal education for the non-Europeans in order to give all children the greatest possible opportunities to develop their aptitudes and their ability to serve the community, and to train the non-Europeans and qualify them for genuine full employment within their country's economy. The Commission believes that the Union of South Africa should be able to count upon moral—and material—support for such a long-term plan from all Members of the United Nations and upon its machinery for technical and financial assistance.

378. (d) *Elimination of the colour bar and recognition of the principle of "equal pay for equal work".* Many voices of protest have been raised in the Union of South Africa itself not only against the legislative measures establishing a colour bar and driving the non-Whites into inferior and badly-paid employment, but also against the administrative measures to the same end: the so-called "Civilized Labour Policy", the policy governing the issue of licences for carrying on commercial, industrial or craft undertakings, the conditions imposed on parties tendering for contracts for public works of supplies, etc. Contrary to what has been claimed, the establishment of equal opportunities would not lead to a sharp fall in the White population's standard of living, because the Union is suffering from a shortage of manpower, which is acute in certain branches, and because, owing to their educational level, the Europeans possess a considerable advantage over the other groups, in particular the Bantus. But the proclamation of the principle that all men, whatever the colour of their skin, have equal access to all employment, and that there is equal pay for equal work would, in itself, effect an easing of tension.

379. (e) In close connection with the foregoing, *the reorganization of the apprenticeship system* so that it constitutes the normal means of access to specialized and better-paid employment and is thus open to children with the necessary aptitude.

380. (f) *The progressive enactment of new legisla-*

*tion recognizing the right of Bantus, Coloureds and non-Europeans in general to become members of trade unions* and to participate with full rights and complete equality in all arbitration proceedings and negotiations for the peaceful settlement of labour disputes.

381. (g) *Abolition, by rapidly succeeding stages, of the pass laws* which are clearly inconsistent with most of the measures and efforts suggested above and result in restrictions and disabilities in the daily lives of non-Europeans, which are incompatible with the conception of freedom and the dignity of the human person held by the United Nations.

. . .

383. Although the Commission appreciates the importance of securing equal economic opportunities for all, regardless of differences in race, colour or belief, it feels bound to state its conviction that *steps to achieve political equality among ethnic groups are of prime importance and cannot be continually* deferred without serious danger. . . .

## Suggestion III.  Possible assistance by the United Nations

384. Should the General Assembly take the view that all or part of the programme outlined above could provide a provisional basis for possible cooperation with the Government of the Union of South Africa, the Commission would suggest that an offer might be made to that Government to set up at its request a committee of technical experts specializing in the planning of economical and social development, particularly in multi-racial societies, who might be asked to catalogue all the various forms of assistance which the United Nations and the specialized agencies can supply. Such a proposal might doubtless strike many persons as incompatible with the timidity or caution usually associated with international operations. But while caution may be justified, timidity is not. It should be borne in mind that similar action and on an extensive scale has been taken by the United Nations in the reconstruction and rehabilitation of countries *after* they had suffered the consequences of a dispute; why then should it hesitate to take such action when it involves the *preventing* a threatened dispute? The latter is the type of situation with which the international community is confronted in South Africa.

For the Union of South Africa the road towards eventual reconciliation and willing collaboration among the ethnic groups is assuredly a long and arduous one, blocked by many obstacles. *The essential thing, however, is the right road should be taken.* The Commission sincerely believes that the road of *apartheid* leads to inevitable deadlock and to the threat of disputes. Despite all the difficulties inherited from the past and still acute today, Europeans, Bantus and Coloureds must necessarily wend their way together; we might almost go so far as to say that they are doomed to live together and together to build an organic community. The road of gradual integration is the only one that seems to be open and it alone is likely to lead to a peaceful future acceptable to all parties. To travel that road will require a steadfast, persevering and tenacious will, renewed from day to day, to collaborate, to negotiate and to compromise, a will to give and take. This partnership will be difficult; one side will have to jettison theories of racial superiority which give a semblance of legality to political supremacy but are in reality based on obsolete ideas to which modern science gives not a shred of confirmation; the other will have to realize that the ideas of fraternal equality and collaboration enshrined in the United Nations Charter and deep in the hearts of men cannot become reality at the stroke of a magic wand, without passing through many successive stages. Both will often have to moderate, for a time, the force of their claims and aspirations in order to fulfil their duty towards the community which is to be built up in peace. We repeat that the essential thing is that the right road should be taken. . . .

---

# Document 11

*Third report of the United Nations Commission on the Racial Situation in the Union of South Africa*

A/2953, 1955

. . .

## Concluding observations

306. In view of the special nature of this report the Commission considers that this is hardly the occasion for offering any fresh conclusions in the proper sense of the term.

The conclusions contained in the first report (A/2505 and Add.1) to the General Assembly concerning the effects of the policy of apartheid on economic and social life and on internal tensions between groups of human beings in the territories of the Union, concerning the dangers of isolation or dispute which, as a consequence, beset the Union's foreign relations, and concerning the conflict between the principles of apartheid, on the one hand, and the provisions of the United Nations Charter and the principles of the Universal Declaration of Human Rights, on the other—all these conclusions are still valid.

Next, the Commission's second report (A/2719) had set forth various general and specific suggestions for dealing with the racial difficulties of the Union of South Africa by peaceful and non-violent means. The Commission considers that these suggestions are now as sound as when they were made and cannot honestly say that by reason of the lapse of time they should be modified in any way.

Hence the remarks which follow, in the manner of a conclusion, are intended essentially to convey supplementary information; they add certain further particulars and reflections concerning points which, in the Commission's view, should engage the attention of the General Assembly. Because these remarks supplement the previous report in certain respects, they should, it is felt, enable everybody to gain a more comprehensive and more accurate insight into the racial situation in the Union of South Africa as it appears at the end of this year of observation.

For the sake of a better understanding of these remarks, the paragraphs immediately below briefly recapitulate the principal features of the Commission's first and second reports and describe concisely the features of the present report. An interpretation of the year's developments follows thereafter, and the report closes with a section entitled "Present thoughts on past suggestions".

### 1. Principal features of the Commission's first and second reports

307. In its first report (A/2505 and Add.1) the Commission had:

(a) Given the General Assembly a short account of the geography, history, demographic situation, ethnic composition and government of the Union of South Africa which the Commission thought was indispensable to a fair appreciation of an extraordinarily complex racial situation;

(b) Defined the doctrine and programme of apartheid;

(c) Analysed and described the racial situation in South Africa, particularly as it resulted from the legislation enacted and promulgated by a Parliament representing, almost exclusively, the minority of European origin;

(d) Compared this legislation with the principles of the Charter, the provisions of the Universal Declaration

of Human Rights and certain important resolutions of the principal United Nations organs and found it to be utterly at variance with those principles;

(e) Offered some preliminary and tentative suggestions for the future.

In its second report (A/2719), the Commission:

(a) Supplemented its previous report by giving fuller particulars of the country's economic structure and development, for undoubtedly economic reality is the factor which, in a particular racial situation, exerts the most direct influence, the influence most heavily charged with individual or collective emotion or resentment and hence often the most decisive influence;

(b) Made further comparative analyses on the lines described above;

(c) Gave an account of one year of life in the Union of South Africa (1953-54) under apartheid;

(d) Studied the various solutions to the racial problem which had been proposed in the Union of South Africa itself by institutions, political parties or persons directly concerned and particularly qualified;

(e) As expressly requested in its terms of reference, offered carefully considered suggestions which, it believed, could "alleviate the situation and promote a peaceful settlement".

### 2. Features of the present report

308. In the present report, the Commission:

(a) Continues its custom of analysing and studying the implications of new legislation and regulations;

(b) Presents a methodical and descriptive account of events of some significance which occurred between August 1954 and July 1955 and which affected or threw fresh light on the racial situation in South Africa.

It was not without some hesitation that the Commission entitled the second part of its report "Development of the situation", for a racial situation which is the product of 300 years of local history, of traditional customs and behaviour and, inevitably, of collective emotions attributable to some extent to special (but ever-present) circumstances can hardly develop perceptibly in the space of 12 months. The Commission's function, in formulating its conclusions, is, however, precisely to discuss, behind the imperceptible or the barely perceptible, some faint signs or clues which may herald a new trend in events or in thinking.

The Commission approached its task not less humbly but a little more confidently than before. Having been an objective observer of the Union of South Africa for almost three years it has been able gradually to accumulate a wider selection of documents, to draw on more varied sources of information, to acquire a more thorough knowledge of the factors which motivate the Afrikaner population, the descendants of the Voortrekkers and Boers whose past was both arduous and heroic.

In its conclusions the Commission has ventured to attempt an interpretation of the events recounted above and also of some other facts and imponderables, which will be discussed later, because it has been encouraged, however paradoxical this may appear at first sight, by the very fact of its remoteness from the scene. Naturally, it does not claim that there can be any substitute for the personal contact which it would have desired, and the absence of which it deplores, with the realities, complexities, disconcerting primitiveness and unexpected ultra-modernism of South Africa. Yet, by reason of its knowledge of crises and occurrences of the more or less recent past which, in some respects, present an analogy with the multiracial situation in South Africa, the Commission believes that precisely this perspective of distance—which it would not enjoy at Pretoria or the Cape—offers certain advantages. In a world where strictly local problems no longer exist, far less solutions which depend exclusively on local factors, this perspective and this distance make it possible to adopt an objective approach which is sometimes difficult to achieve in a field where emotional factors play a considerable part. The Commission trusts that it has achieved this objectivity in the pages which follow.

### 3. *Interpretation of the year's events*

309. In the first place, the Commission considers that the general lines of the policy of apartheid have not changed in the year which has elapsed since it wrote its second report. Indeed, the new Government under Mr. Strijdom has announced its intention of carrying out this policy of apartheid to its full extent.

Secondly, as indicated in part II, chapter I, of the present report, during the year a series of legislative measures were enacted which, like those mentioned in the Commission's previous reports, are consistent neither with the obligations assumed by the Union of South Africa under the Charter nor with certain provisions of the Universal Declaration of Human Rights.

Thirdly, certain discriminatory legislation which had been enacted in earlier years and which the Commission had analysed at the time became operative or continued in operation during the year. The Commission would draw particular attention to the Bantu Education Act, which is discussed in the present report. Not only does this Act imply a negation of the principles of human rights—an aspect considered by the Commission in its second report (A/2719, paras. 110-111)—but also its application will, in the Commission's opinion, invite other dangers to which it wishes to draw the Assembly's attention.

(*a*) Apartheid in education, symbolized by the words "Bantu education"—a term detested by all the non-Europeans, who demand, according to their slogan, not education "made to measure" but "universal" education—is liable to accentuate even more and to spread among the entire Native population a Bantu nationalism with a strong anti-White orientation. The Commission believes that the Nationalist Government, in carrying its policy of school segregation to extremes, may receive some sad surprises, including a stiffening in the anti-European attitude of the Bantu population. Should this occur, apartheid in this as no doubt in other fields would produce an effect very contrary to the pacification and reduced friction which its proponents say they hope to achieve.

(*b*) As indicated in the section relating to Bantu education, Afrikaans is being introduced somewhat prematurely and very extensively side by side with English in school curricula. This means that children under 10 years of age will have to study three different languages (every Bantu child speaks one of the seven vernacular idioms), which will certainly overtax their minds and memories to the detriment of other possibly more useful and more necessary subjects.

The Commission further considers that the effect of this measure will be to weaken among the Natives the influence and spread of the English language which, because of its universality, is a cultural asset of great importance and a closer link with their racial brethren of Africa and America whose social, economic and cultural progress they watch with pride.

Fourthly, the Commission reaffirms what it had said in its earlier reports: the continuation of the policy of apartheid constitutes a serious threat to national life within the Union of South Africa. The reactions, described in the present report, of the various social groups to the legislation passed or to the measures enacted merely confirm this view.

Fifthly, the material assembled by the Commission, especially that mentioned in the section dealing with the "international repercussions of the race problem" likewise confirms the Commission in yet another opinion (stated elsewhere), viz., that the policy of apartheid is a seriously disturbing factor in international relations, and the least that can be said of it is that it is "likely to impair the general welfare or friendly relations among nations". This, then, is one of those situations which, under Article 14 of the Charter, may form the subject of recommendations by the General Assembly.

The material also shows that the attention of the world, particularly of the Coloured world, is firmly focused on South Africa disapprovingly and often with a resentment which sometimes distorts the view and may even lead to extreme opinions and may finally become a potential source of international disputes.

Sixthly, despite what has been said under points one to three above, despite the declarations of responsible members of the Government, in which they invariably profess their explicit and unequivocal adherence to the principles of apartheid and their intention of translating it into reality, nevertheless the policy of apartheid, so far as it has been possible to observe its operation in law and in practice during the year under review, seems still to be characterized mainly by gradualism and flexibility. That had also been the Commission's observation in its first report (A/2505 and Add.1, para. 423). Indeed, this gradualism seems to have become more marked in recent times, in other words the pace at which the apartheid programme is being carried into effect has been slowed even further.

In July 1955, at the end of the parliamentary session, the objective appeared almost as far away as one year before.

Another noteworthy point is that the Government apparently recognizes more or less explicitly and discreetly that complete territorial separation might well be a theoretical objective unattainable in practice.

Last year, one chapter in the Commission's report was entitled "One year of life in South Africa under apartheid". The Commission would hesitate to give this title to its report today. The title should rather be "One year of life in a country proceeding towards apartheid", but proceeding slowly, extremely slowly, cautiously and carefully. At the rate at which the Government is promoting each day a fuller measure of apartheid, it may well take many years before the theories of the new apartheid bear even a modest resemblance to actual fact. By then, the succession of generations, White and Black, will have changed the course of events.

Seventhly, there is ample evidence of the flexibility of apartheid already mentioned by the Commission; this flexibility is somewhat unexpected on the part of political leaders who remain firm in their statements of principle. It is to be found mainly in the form of exceptions to traditional segregation, or to discrimination as prescribed by regulations, whenever some overriding interest makes an exception desirable in the eyes of the Government.

Eighthly, the Commission also notes a significant hesitancy in the application of the policy of apartheid, for example the notable delay in "proclaiming" the principal group areas, although the Minister of Native Affairs had announced, on 23 March 1955, that these areas would be proclaimed in quick succession; the delay in reaching a decision on the Holloway Commission's report on the feasibility of actually introducing complete apartheid in higher education; and the Government's delay in publishing the voluminous report on the social and economic development of the Native reserves, of capital importance so far as the policy of apartheid is concerned, which was completed almost a year ago by the Tomlinson Commission.

Ninthly, the Commission cannot avoid asking in public the questions which it asked itself. Is this slowness to act the sign of mere caution or discretion on the part of the Government, in anticipation of possible national and international repercussions? Is it the sign of intellectual hesitation regarding the methods to be employed in guiding the South African nation towards future structural patterns which are still considered realizable? Or is it not rather the sign of certain nascent misgivings about the legitimacy, or the attainability, of the proposed objectives?

The Commission cannot supply the answers. It sincerely hopes that this year, when action to promote apartheid was, if not almost at a standstill, at least very slow, marks the beginning of a change of mind in favour of the principles upheld by the United Nations.

310. The Commission considers, however, that it should mention certain factors which, in its opinion, may have influenced the trend thought to be discernible and which may have affected, in the manner indicated, the rate and intensity of implementation of the policy of apartheid.

The Commission believes that this flexibility, this delay, these misgivings, not to mention the countless new obstacles which arise unexpectedly on the way however clearly it may be drawn on the theoretical map of apartheid, may have been influenced by the following facts:

(a) On the strength of the information classified and analysed in the body of the present report, the Commission continues to believe, as it had stressed in its second report (A/2719, para. 177), that, so far as the economy of South Africa is concerned, despite the attempts to brake the employment of Native workers in industry, despite the drive for increased mechanization in European factories designed to replace part of the hitherto indispensable Bantu labour, despite the theoretical limitation of the number of Bantus admitted to live in locations "in the sky" in Johannesburg apartment buildings, nevertheless the integration of Native workers in "European" industry, commerce, agriculture and domestic service continues unabated.

In other words the trend towards greater apartheid desired by the present Government is counter-balanced by a trend in the exactly opposite direction, an insidious, slow, but continuous and apparently irreversible, trend towards integration.

(b) The increasing demand for manpower, the steady influx of unskilled or semi-skilled workers to the constantly more numerous mines or factories and the settlement of both non-Europeans and Europeans in urban areas have encouraged the trend towards detribalization, a trend which conflicts with the Government's efforts to consolidate or even to re-establish the tribal system in the Native reserves, hostels, compounds or reserved quarters of urban and rural areas.

(c) The internal reactions of important "social" groups which the Commission has studied in detail in the body of its report.

These groups have steadfastly opposed the policy of apartheid, arguing cogently that this policy is irreconcilable with the moral principles and the respect for human dignity which the civilized world has accepted as standards of national and international conduct, and stressing that the policy has no chance of being translated into reality.

In this connection, the Commission would refer to the statements of certain Members of Parliament and to the attitude of the churches and certain scientific institutions.

(d) The moral force of international public opinion. The Commission is convinced that the Union Government must have given serious and careful consideration to the remarkable fact that year after year, and during the last session even more forcefully than before, the General Assembly, by a more than two-thirds majority, has proclaimed that this racial policy is contrary to the principles of the Charter and has suggested that it should be reconsidered.

The Government of the Union of South Africa must also have been aware of the moral force of the other great expressions of world opinion which the Commission describes in its report and others which the Commission did not mention but which must certainly have come to the knowledge of the South African Government: the opinion of most of the world's leading periodicals which have discussed racial tension in the Union and which are unanimous in their judgment of the policy of apartheid.

(e) Another factor closely connected with the above which the Commission mentioned in its first report is the fact that, in this century of extensive and rapid communication, it is impossible to prevent the groups against whom discrimination is practised in the Union of South Africa from "catching" the idea of aspiring to a better, more humane and more equalitarian life, with the full enjoyment of the political, social, economic and cultural rights which millions of human beings in other countries enjoy. These include millions of persons of African descent, a circumstance which confirms the belief that colour differences cannot exclude the non-Europeans of South Africa from the enjoyment of any of the rights guaranteed by law or custom to other citizens.

Every day more and more non-Europeans are confronted with some basic facts of international life: for example, they have now become aware that there is not another country in any of the five continents that has set up racial segregation as an absolute and eternal principle or what might even be called a principle of divine right. In no other country of the world is there an ethnic minority labouring to clear up to its own advantage a racial muddle which it has itself created. The South African Government is the only Government in the world which believes that it can carry out such a fabulous experiment successfully and, to quote a familiar metaphor frequently used by Bantu preachers and journalists, that it can "unscramble a plate of scrambled eggs". South Africa is the only country in the British Commonwealth which does not accept universal suffrage even as an objective to be achieved gradually in the distant future. South Africa is the only country in Africa where the Natives are not represented by their own kind in any legislative or consultative assembly. South Africa is the only country in the world where the Natives are rigorously excluded from certain categories of employment by the legislation of a minority intent on reserving them for itself.

Yet at the same time—a phenomenon which is, as it were, on the other side of the balance—the South Africans, all South Africans, both European and non-European, watch with something like fascination the peaceful conquests and progress of the Negroes north of the Limpopo, variously deploring or welcoming, as the case may be, the latter's advancement.

We could quote many more such extracts. Every issue of the *Bantu World* (Johannesburg) has a special column entitled "Those Near Us, but Far Away" which makes a point of reporting such news items.

It is also noteworthy that America in general holds a kind of fascination for non-Europeans in the Union of South Africa. This is particularly true of the United States whose present experiment in racial desegregation is being followed with rapt attention. This is evident from a mere perusal of the Bantu Press. The South African Negroes are proud of the amazing progress of their overseas brethren of African origin; they are proud of their economic progress, proud of their continuously more brilliant social victories and proud of their eminent cultural achievements. They aspire to closer links with them and the English language is the first and most indispensable of these links.

An educated South African Native, Selby Bangani Ngcobo, M.A., B. Econ., has said that the progress of Negroes in the United States was being closely observed by the Bantu patriot, who regarded it as proof that it was possible for a people of African origin to reach the highest levels of civilization in a relatively short time (*La Nation sud-africaine*, Collection "Profil des Nations," Editions du Rocher, Monaco, p. 69).

In the Commission's opinion this situation—in which the emotions of the century and the great currents of world thought penetrate the most tightly closed frontiers, while the non-Europeans of South Africa are aware that they are denied the opportunities, progress and the rights that, at least in principle, are held to be the due of all human beings in other African territories and in other continents—such a situation has distressing implications for the future. Its effect is to stir up latent discontent and to prompt painful and irritating comparisons; in short, it adds to interracial tension.

### 4. *Present thoughts on past suggestions*

(a) *Interracial contacts and the United Nations*

311. The Commission considers that a solution of the problems arising out of the relationships between the White minority and the Bantu majority should be sought in more and more frequent interracial contacts, conferences and round-table discussions between men of good will, White and non-White.

The Commission is becoming more and more deeply convinced, however, that these inter-governmental or inter-group contacts should take place in the presence of proper and very high-ranking representatives of the United Nations (the President or Vice-Presidents of the General Assembly, the Presidents of the Security Council, of the Economic and Social Council, of the Trusteeship Council, the Secretary-General, or their qualified representatives) so that the principles of the Charter and of the Universal Declaration of Human Rights should be effectively represented at the discussion and planning of solutions.

In these days, the United Nations is bringing its influence to bear—with difficulty perhaps, even laboriously, but nevertheless effectively—to secure the cessation of conflicts and a reconciliation between nations which are at odds. Some day—and it is hoped that the day will come soon—this influence will be regarded as necessary to facilitate the settlement of "threatening racial conflicts or deteriorating colonial disputes" (A/2719, para. 355).

(b) *Technical assistance by the United Nations*

312. The Commission draws the General Assembly's attention once again to a suggestion made in its second report (A/2719, para. 384) entitled "Suggestion III. Possible assistance by the United Nations", namely that the United Nations should offer its cooperation to the Union of South Africa including, as special technical assistance, the intellectual and material resources which the United Nations and the specialized agencies can command, for the purpose of promoting international studies and contacts and carrying out economic and social measures conducive to a peaceful settlement of the racial tension in the Union in the spirit of the Charter and of the Universal Declaration of Human Rights.

In its previous report the Commission offered this suggestion quite explicitly but at the same time very discreetly and cautiously. It would be extremely gratified if a discussion on this suggestion were to be held in the General Assembly.

The Commission realizes that this proposal may come as a surprise. The Economic and Social Council and the General Assembly, in the rules which they have drawn up for technical assistance, have stipulated that every assistance project must be preceded by a specific application from the Member State concerned. These rules, undoubtedly wise in most cases, were drawn up by the United Nations itself; accordingly, if it so desires, it can certainly make changes or variations therein or permit exceptions thereto, as circumstances or particular cases may require.

There is no reason why the United Nations should not decide that it is itself prepared to *offer* assistance to a Member State which is experiencing difficulties threatening both the stability of its national life and the continuance of its peaceful relations with outside communities.

The Union of South Africa cannot of course be likened in any respect to an under-developed country like those for which technical assistance is intended within the limited meaning of the term as now interpreted in the United Nations. The Union of South Africa is a country whose natural resources, and the enterprising spirit of whose leading minority, guarantee growing economic prosperity; but the authorities of the Union are faced, in their relations with a Native majority indispensable to the very life of the nation and an integral part of its structure, by social problems of such magnitude and scope that the disinterested assistance of the international community is undeniably justified by the principles of solidarity which the assembled peoples have incorporated in the Charter.

Nor does the Commission fail to appreciate that such assistance projects, if agreed upon, would have little chance of immediate acceptance by the Government of the Union of South Africa. But the fact that such assistance, in its general lines, would be planned by United Nations experts; the assurance that the offer of such assistance would always be open to any Government of the Union disposed to accept it; and the very existence of such projects—all these would certainly have a beneficial (even though long-range) effect on the development of the situation in South Africa.

Such an offer of assistance and good offices on the part of the United Nations would clearly have much to commend it: first, the most diverse circles are becoming more and more convinced that hardly any national problem is without its international implications and repercussions, which means that every such problem concerns the bodies set up by man to further peace and social progress. It is also coming to be realized that the problems of South Africa are among those whose international implications are most obvious.

Secondly, an atmosphere of *détente* and international cooperation, particularly noticeable now at Geneva [at the time of the Commission's session] has spread throughout the world after the Four-Power Conference and makes it incumbent on all Governments and international agencies to do everything in their power and to use all their imagination to settle all disputes.

It seems to us impossible that the Government of the Union of South Africa can remain for ever deaf to the appeal and to the generous and disinterested offers of good offices tendered by all mankind in its earnest desire to promote the implementation of the principles of the Charter and of the Universal Declaration of Human Rights.

(c) *Technical assistance and human rights*

313. Lastly, a new development has occurred this year which would justify, if justification were needed, such an offer of assistance by the United Nations to the Union of South Africa. It was with deep satisfaction that our Commission noted that another United Nations Commission, the Commission on Human Rights—an inter-governmental body—adopted a resolution of considerable implications, with great boldness of thought and in equally forceful language, giving universal application to the principle of United Nations technical assistance for the promotion of human rights. We had formulated this same principle last year in our own report, within the limitations of our terms of reference. By adopting this resolution, the Commission on Human Rights has opened to the United Nations a new field of action for the promotion of human rights, the possibilities of which are immense but the effectiveness of which will depend on the willingness of the United Nations to take practical steps.

The suggestions we made last year in our report are so obviously allied to the resolution of the Commission on Human Rights that we feel we should reproduce the gist of the resolution as adopted by the Economic and Social Council at its twentieth session (resolution 586 (XX)), together with the paragraph of our previous report containing our proposals which are still valid in respect of the Union of South Africa (A/2719, para. 384).

"Advisory services in the field of human rights

"*The Economic and Social Council,*

"*Recommends* to the General Assembly the adoption of the following draft resolution:

"*The General Assembly,*

"*Considering* that by Articles 55 and 56 of the United Nations Charter the States Members of the United Nations have pledged themselves to promote universal respect for, and observance of, human rights and fundamental freedoms for all without distinction as to race, sex, language or religion.

"*Recognizing* that technical assistance, by the international interchange of technical knowledge through international cooperation among countries, represents one of the means by which it is possible to promote the human rights objectives of the United Nations as set forth in the Charter and the Universal Declaration of Human Rights,

"...

"*Taking note* of resolution 730 (VIII) of the General Assembly authorizing the Secretary-General to render, at the request of any Member State, technical advice and other services which do not fall within the scope of existing technical assistance programmes, in order to assist the Government of that State within its territory in the eradication of discrimination or in the protection of minorities, or both,

"...

"1. *Decides* to consolidate the technical assistance programmes already approved by the General Assembly (relating to the promotion and safeguarding of the rights of women, the eradication of discrimination and protection of minorities, and the promotion of freedom of information) with the broad programme of assistance in the field of human rights proposed in this resolution, the entire programme to be known as 'Advisory services in the field of human rights';

"2. *Authorizes* the Secretary-General:

"(*a*) Subject to the directions of the Economic and Social Council, to make provision at the request of Governments, and with the cooperation of the specialized agencies where appropriate and without duplication of their existing activities, for the following forms of assistance with respect to the field of human rights:

   (i) Advisory services of experts;
   (ii) Fellowships and scholarships;
   (iii) Seminars;

"(*b*) To take the programme authorized by this resolution into account in preparing the budgetary estimates of the United Nations."

"Suggestion III. Possible assistance by the United Nations

"384. Should the General Assembly take the view that all or part of the programme outlined above could provide a provisional basis for possible cooperation with the Government of the Union of South Africa, the Commission would suggest that an offer might be made to that Government to set up at its request a committee of technical experts specializing in the planning of economic and social development, particularly in multi-racial societies, who might be asked to catalogue all the various forms of assistance which the United Nations and the specialized agencies can supply. Such a proposal might doubtless strike many persons as incompatible with the timidity or caution usually associated with international operations. But while caution may be justified, timidity is not. It should be borne in mind that similar action and on an extensive scale has been taken by the United Nations in the reconstruction and rehabilitation of countries *after* they had suffered the consequences of a dispute; why then should it hesitate to take such action when it involves the *preventing* of a threatened dispute? The latter is the type of situation with which the international community is confronted in South Africa."

It is to be hoped that this resolution of the Commission on Human Rights, which has already been approved by the Economic and Social Council, will be accepted by the General Assembly and be more than a pious wish, more than a well-meaning—but completely ineffectual—token of good intentions.

The Union of South Africa, it seems to us, might be a field where this resolution could be applied. That is why we think it our duty to reaffirm here that this possibility for United Nations action could and, in our view, should be used. The only difference between our suggestions and the resolution adopted by the Commission on Human Rights is this: in our suggestions technical help is *offered* by the United Nations; in the resolution such help is to be *requested* by the Government concerned. We have already indicated why and how the United Nations can remove this minor difficulty created by the Organization's own procedures.

In any case, it is our firm belief that if the United Nations were to adopt the principle embodied in our suggestions, were to enter resolutely upon the course of action recommended by the Commission on Human Rights and the Economic and Social Council, and were to decide, with all the caution that wisdom dictates and after making all the prerequisite studies, to undertake this new kind of technical assistance, it would be opening in the field of its supreme responsibilities new, unexplored channels for United Nations activity; it would be a decision to discharge one of the most noble tasks entrusted to the United Nations by the Charter of the peoples, that of dealing with racial tensions and finding peaceful solutions in keeping with the high purpose of the Universal Declaration of Human Rights to safeguard the dignity of man.

### 5. The Union of South Africa and international solidarity

314. The deeper one delves into the human problems of South Africa the more strongly one gains the conviction that the situation in that country is historically and sociologically unique.

The situation may be summed up as that of a colony without a mother country, and hence very different from the situation in most colonial countries. In the latter the White minority becomes conscious again of the fact that it is a majority and powerful when it considers itself in association and identifies itself with the mother country. This association and this solidarity with the mother country give the White element a feeling of security with which to face the course of events and relieve it of the anxieties that cloud a minority's view of an uncertain future.

That was still the position of the descendants of the English or Scottish settlers in South Africa under the Botha, Hertzog and Smuts Governments, and so it remained, with some modifications of course, after the Nationalist Government's advent to power in 1948. The Union's membership of the British Commonwealth reassures them and gives them a sense of security. Should circumstances in South Africa deteriorate beyond repair, they have the comforting feeling that they could withdraw to the old country with which they have kept very strong sentimental ties.

The Afrikaners have no similar consolation. They are, among the White minority, the majority at present in power; they feel isolated, they feel no solidarity with a distant mother country and they are confronted with a growing majority of Negroes and Coloureds. This no doubt explains, at least partly, some reactions of the leaders of the Union of South Africa.

The Commission takes the view that this isolation (which it realizes and which, it knows, is such a great strain that the White minority is often on the point of faltering under the burden and takes refuge in questionable gestures) ought to influence the Union to seek the solidarity which the United Nations endeavours to create among its Members. What is meant here is not, of course, racial solidarity but that human solidarity which transcends the ties that history, geography, tradition and biological appearances have forged between man and man. We mean a solidarity which is based on a common striving towards justice and social progress according to common and generally accepted principles, a solidarity which should become daily more intimate, more urgent and more effective. This solidarity, in which the Union of South Africa may share actively, if it so desires, and from which it may derive great benefit progressively, will become, because of its material strength and moral authority, the most effective guarantee of the security so anxiously sought by minorities such as the White minority in South Africa against the threats which, rightly or wrongly, they discern in the future.

Surely this is the basis for the solutions to the problems of the future, not solutions gratifying the vain and dangerous aspirations of some threatened and sensitive national prestige but, we think the only solutions which offer any chance of success and peace in the treatment of racial disputes as in the conduct of colonial conversations.

Accordingly we sincerely hope and wish that the Union of South Africa may reconsider its policy towards the United Nations and enter into close and extensive cooperation with the Organization in the various fields where this cooperation is possible, and in particular that it may accept, in a spirit of solidarity, the numerous and varied forms of help and assistance which the United Nations can offer to it in the treatment of the Union's problems.

This hope is strengthened by a perusal of recent issues of the newspaper *Die Transvaler*, hitherto regarded as the bulwark of South African isolationism. The Commission cannot think of more fitting words with which to close this report than those used in an editorial which appeared in that newspaper and which said:

> "The factor which in the past so powerfully contributed to the formation of Afrikanerdom may prove to be fatal in the future: this factor is isolation."

To this opinion the Commission subscribes wholeheartedly.

# Document 12

*The Freedom Charter adopted by the Congress of the People, Kliptown, South Africa, 26 June 1955*

S/12425, 25 October 1977

*We, the People of South Africa, declare for all our country and the world to know:*

that South Africa belongs to all who live in it, Black and White, and that no Government can justly claim authority unless it is based on the will of all the people;

*that* our people have been robbed of their birthright to land, liberty and peace by a form of government founded on injustice and inequality;

*that* our country will never be prosperous or free until all our people live in brotherhood, enjoying equal rights and opportunities;

*that* only a democratic State, based on the will of all the people, can secure to all their birthright without distinction of colour, race, sex or belief;

*And therefore*, we, the people of South Africa, Black and White together—equals, countrymen and brothers—adopt this Freedom Charter. And we pledge ourselves to strive together, sparing neither strength nor courage, until the democratic changes here set out have been won.

THE PEOPLE SHALL GOVERN!

Every man and woman shall have the right to vote for and to stand as a candidate for all bodies which make laws;

All people shall be entitled to take part in the administration of the country;

The rights of the people shall be the same, regardless of race, colour or sex;

All bodies of minority rule, advisory boards, councils and authorities shall be replaced by democratic organs of self-government.

ALL NATIONAL GROUPS SHALL HAVE EQUAL RIGHTS!

There shall be equal status in the bodies of state, in the courts and in the schools for all national groups and races;

All people shall have equal right to use their own languages, and to develop their own folk culture and customs;

All national groups shall be protected by law against insults to their race and national pride;

The preaching and practice of national, race and or colour discrimination and contempt shall be a punishable crime;

All apartheid laws and practices shall be set aside.

THE PEOPLE SHALL SHARE IN THE COUNTRY'S WEALTH!

The national wealth of our country, the heritage of all South Africans, shall be restored to the people;

The mineral wealth beneath the soil, the banks and

monopoly industry shall be transferred to the ownership of the people as a whole;

All other industry and trade shall be controlled to assist the well-being of the people;

All people shall have equal rights to trade where they choose, to manufacture and to enter all trades, crafts and professions.

## THE LAND SHALL BE SHARED AMONG THOSE WHO WORK IT!

Restrictions of land ownership on a racial basis shall be ended, and all the land redivided amongst those who work it, to banish famine and land hunger;

The State shall help the peasants with implements, seed, tractors and dams and to save the soil and assist the tillers,

Freedom of movement shall be guaranteed to all who work on the land;

All shall have the right to occupy land wherever they choose;

People shall not be robbed of their cattle, and forced labour and farm prisons shall be abolished.

## ALL SHALL BE EQUAL BEFORE THE LAW!

No one shall be imprisoned, deported or restricted without a fair trial;

No one shall be condemned by the order of any government official;

The courts shall be representative of all the people;

Imprisonment shall be only for serious crimes against the people, and shall aim at re-education, not vengeance;

The police force and army shall be open to all on an equal basis and shall be the helpers and protectors of the people;

All laws which discriminate on grounds of race, colour or belief shall be repealed.

## ALL SHALL ENJOY EQUAL HUMAN RIGHTS!

The law shall guarantee to all their right to speak, to organize, to meet together, to publish, to preach, to worship and to educate their children;

The privacy of the house from police raids shall be protected by law;

All shall be free to travel without restriction from countryside to town, from province to province, and from South Africa abroad;

Pass Laws, permits and all other laws restricting these freedoms shall be abolished.

## THERE SHALL BE WORK AND SECURITY!

All who work shall be free to form trade unions, to elect their officers and to make wage agreements with their employers;

The State shall recognize the right and duty of all to work, and to draw full unemployment benefits;

Men and women of all races shall receive equal pay for equal work;

There shall be a 40-hour working week, a national minimum wage, paid annual leave, and sick leave for all workers, and maternity leave on full pay for working mothers;

Miners, domestic workers, farm workers and civil servants shall have the same rights as all others who work;

Child labour, compound labour, the tot system and contract labour shall be abolished.

## THE DOORS OF LEARNING AND OF CULTURE SHALL BE OPENED!

The Government shall discover, develop and encourage national talent for the enhancement of our cultural life;

All the cultural treasures of mankind shall be open to all, by free exchange of books, ideas and contract with other lands;

The aim of education shall be to teach the youth to love their people and their culture, to honour human brotherhood, liberty and peace;

Education shall be free, compulsory, universal and equal for all children;

Higher education and technical training shall be opened to all by means of state allowances and scholarships awarded on the basis of merit;

Adult illiteracy shall be ended by a mass state education plan;

Teachers shall have all the rights of other citizens;

The colour bar in cultural life, in sport and in education shall be abolished.

## THERE SHALL BE HOUSES, SECURITY AND COMFORT!

All people shall have the right to live where they choose, to be decently housed, and to bring up their families in comfort and security;

Unused housing space to be made available to the people;

Rent and prices shall be lowered, food plentiful and no one shall go hungry;

A preventive health scheme shall be run by the State;

Free medical care and hospitalization shall be provided for all, with special care for mothers and young children;

Slums shall be demolished, and new suburbs built where all have transport, roads, lighting, playing fields, creches and social centres;

The aged, the orphans, the disabled and the sick shall be cared for by the State;

Rest, leisure and recreation shall be the right of all;

Fenced locations and ghettoes shall be abolished, and laws which break up families shall be repealed.

THERE SHALL BE PEACE AND FRIENDSHIP!

South Africa shall be a fully independent State, which respects the rights and sovereignty of all nations;

South Africa shall strive to maintain world peace and the settlement of all international disputes by negotiation—not war;

Peace and friendship amongst all our people shall be secured by upholding the equal rights, opportunities and status of all;

The people of the protectorates—Basutoland, Bechuanaland and Swaziland shall be free to decide for themselves their own future;

The right of all the peoples of Africa to independence and self-government shall be recognized, and shall be the basis of close co-operation.

*Let all who love their people and their country now say, as we say here*: "THESE FREEDOMS WE WILL FIGHT FOR, SIDE BY SIDE, THROUGHOUT OUR LIVES, UNTIL WE HAVE WON OUR LIBERTY."

---

# Document 13

*Appeal by leaders of the African National Congress, the South African Indian Congress and the Liberal Party of South Africa for a boycott of South African produce by the British people, December 1959*

Not issued as a United Nations document

In May, 1960, the Union of South Africa will be 50 years old. The Government is preparing to celebrate this jubilee with great enthusiasm, but most South Africans see no cause for celebration. During this 50 years Non-White South Africans have almost completely lost their rights to be represented in Parliament, their right to take any job for which they are fitted, their right to hold land in freehold; their school education is now to be of a specific kind, the open universities of Cape Town and Witwatersrand are to be closed to them, they cannot move about freely within the country of their birth. At the same time these White South Africans who believed in these rights and freedoms have seen them destroyed one by one.

What has been the response of Non-White South Africans to these attacks on them? They have sent deputations and submitted petitions to the authorities and they have tried to influence the course of events through their meager Parliamentary representation. When these approaches were unsuccessful they turned to passive resistance and then boycott. They have consistently forsworn violence and pledged themselves to non-violence. But with trade unions frowned upon, strikes illegal and their buying power limited, Non-White South Africans face real problems in mounting sufficiently effective internal pressures to be able to influence the South African Government. They look for assistance abroad and particularly to the people of Britain, by whose Parliament the original Act of Union was approved.

Next year it is proposed to conduct a limited boycott of South African produce in Britain for a period of one month. The boycott is a protest against apartheid, the removal of political rights, the colour bar in industry, the extension of passes to African women and the low wages paid to Non-White workers. In the towns and cities of South Africa over half the African families live below the breadline.

It has been argued that Non-White people will be the first to be hit by external boycotts. This may be so, but every organization which commands any important Non-White support in South Africa is in favour of them. The alternative to the use of these weapons is the continuation of the status quo and a bleak prospect of unending discrimination. Economic boycott is one way in which the world at large can bring home to the South African authorities that they must either mend their ways or suffer for them.

This appeal is therefore directed to the people of Great Britain to strike a blow for freedom and justice in South Africa and for those whom the state would keep in continuing subjection in the Union. If this boycott makes the South African authorities realise that the world outside will actively oppose apartheid it will have struck that blow for freedom and justice in our country.

The statement is signed by:

Albert J. LUTHULI
President-General, African National Congress
Groutville Mission,
P.O. Groutville,
Natal, South Africa.

G. M. NAICKER
President, South African Indian Congress

Peter BROWN
National Chairman, Liberal Party of South Africa

# Document 14

*Letter dated 25 March 1960 from the representatives of Afghanistan,
Burma, Cambodia, Ceylon, Ethiopia, the Federation of Malaya, Ghana,
Guinea, India, Indonesia, Iran, Iraq, Japan, Jordan, Laos, Lebanon,
Liberia, Libya, Morocco, Nepal, Pakistan, the Philippines, Saudi
Arabia, Sudan, Thailand, Tunisia, Turkey, the United Arab Republic
and Yemen to the President of the Security Council requesting
consideration of the situation in South Africa*

S/4279 and Add.1, 25 March 1960

Under instructions from our Governments and in accordance with Article 35, paragraph (1) of the United Nations Charter, we have the honour to request an urgent meeting of the Security Council to consider the situation arising out of the large-scale killings of unarmed and peaceful demonstrators against racial discrimination and segregation in the Union of South Africa. We consider that this is a situation with grave potentialities for international friction, which endangers the maintenance of international peace and security.

The representatives of the following States Members of the United Nations:

(*signed*)
A. R. PAZHWAK (Afghanistan)
U. THANT (Burma)
Caimerom MEASKETH (Cambodia)
Alfred EDWARD (Ceylon)
Tesfaye GEBRE-EGZY (Ethiopia)
Dato' Nik Ahmed KAMIL (Federation of Malaya)
Alex QUAISON-SACKEY (Ghana)
CABA Sory (Guinea)

C. S. JHA (India)
E. J. LAPIAN (Indonesia)
M. VAKIL (Iran)
Adnan PACHACHI (Iraq)
Koto MATSUDAIRA (Japan)
A. M. RIFA'I (Jordan)
Thephathay VILAIHONGS (Laos)
Georges HAKIM (Lebanon)
John COX (Liberia)
Mohieddine FEKINI (Libya)
El Mehdi Ben ABOUD (Morocco)
Rishikesh SHAHA (Nepal)
Aly S. KHAN (Pakistan)
L. D. CAYCO (Philippines)
Jamil M. BAROODY (Saudi Arabia)
Omar ADEEL (Sudan)
Jotisi DEVAKUL (Thailand)
Mongi SLIM (Tunisia)
Seyfullah ESIN (Turkey)
Rafik ASHA (United Arab Republic)
Kamil A. RAHIM (Yemen)

# Document 15

*Security Council resolution: Question relating to the situation in the
Union of South Africa*

S/RES/134 (1960), 1 April 1960

*The Security Council,*

*Having considered* the complaint of twenty-nine Member States contained in document S/4279 and Add.1 concerning "the situation arising out of the large-scale killings of unarmed and peaceful demonstrators against racial discrimination and segregation in the Union of South Africa",

*Recognizing* that such a situation has been brought about by the racial policies of the Government of the Union of South Africa and the continued disregard by that Government of the resolutions of the General Assembly calling upon it to revise its policies and bring them into conformity with its obligations and responsibilities under the Charter of the United Nations,

*Taking into account* the strong feelings and grave concern aroused among Governments and peoples of the world by the happenings in the Union of South Africa,

1. *Recognizes* that the situation in the Union of South Africa is one that has led to international friction and if continued might endanger international peace and security;

2. *Deplores* that the recent disturbances in the Union of South Africa should have led to the loss of life of so many Africans and extends to the families of the victims its deepest sympathies;

3. *Deplores* the policies and actions of the Government of the Union of South Africa which have given rise to the present situation;

4. *Calls upon* the Government of the Union of South Africa to initiate measures aimed at bringing about racial harmony based on equality in order to ensure that the present situation does not continue or recur, and to abandon its policies of apartheid and racial discrimination;

5. *Requests* the Secretary-General, in consultation with the Government of the Union of South Africa, to make such arrangements as would adequately help in upholding the purposes and principles of the Charter and to report to the Security Council whenever necessary and appropriate.

# Document 16

*Resolution adopted by the Second Conference of Independent African States, Addis Ababa, 24 June 1960*

Not issued as a United Nations document

*The Conference of Independent African States meeting in Addis Ababa,*

*Having learned with indignation* of the death of many African political leaders in the prisons of the Union of South Africa, thus adding to the already long list of victims of the shameful policy of racial discrimination;

*Recalling* resolution No. 1375 (XIV), adopted by the United Nations General Assembly, condemning the policy of apartheid and racial discrimination practised by the Government of the Union of South Africa;

*Recalling further* the Security Council's Resolution of April 1, 1960, recognizing the existence of a situation in South Africa which, if continued, might endanger international peace and security;

*Reaffirming* the declaration of Bandung and the resolutions adopted by the United Nations, the Government of the Union of South Africa still persists in its evil policy of apartheid and racial discrimination;

1. *Desires* to pay homage to all victims of the shameful policy of apartheid and racial discrimination;

2. *Decides* to assist the victims of racial discrimination and furnish them with all the means necessary to attain their political objectives of liberty and democracy;

3. *Calls upon* Member States to sever diplomatic relations or refrain from establishing diplomatic relations, as the case may be, to close African ports to all vessels flying the South African flag, to enact legislation prohibiting their ships from entering South African ports, to boycott all South African goods, to refuse landing and passage facilities to all aircraft belonging to the Government and companies registered under the laws of the Union of South Africa and to prohibit all South African aircraft from flying over the airspace of the Independent African States;

4. *Invites* the Arab States to approach all petroleum companies with a view to preventing Arab oil from being sold to the Union of South Africa and recommends that the African States refuse any concession to any company which continues to sell petroleum to the Union of South Africa;

5. *Invites* the Independent African States which are members of the British Commonwealth to take all possible steps to secure the exclusion of the Union of South Africa from the British Commonwealth;

6. *Recommends* that appropriate measures be taken by the United Nations in accordance with Article 41 of the Charter;

7. *Appeals* to world public opinion to persevere in the effort to put an end to the terrible situation caused by apartheid and racial discrimination;

8. *Decides* to instruct the Informal Permanent Machinery to take all steps necessary to secure that effect shall be given to the above recommendations and to furnish full information on cases of racial discrimination in the Union of South Africa, so that the outside world may be correctly informed about such practices.

# Document 17

*Telegram from Mr. W. B. Ngakane, on behalf of the Consultative Committee of African leaders (Johannesburg, 16-17 December 1960), to the Secretary-General*

Not issued as a United Nations document

Conference of African leaders welcomes Security Council Resolution on South Africa and proposed visit of Secretary-General. Firmly urge get true picture of South Africa by meeting African leaders.

Pondoland situation alarming. Military operations against unarmed Africans. Recommend UNO send commission of observers.

Support demand South West African people for independence. Nationalist government no moral nor legal right to rule.

W. B. NGAKANE
Johannesburg

---

# Document 18

*Report of Secretary-General Dag Hammarskjöld on certain steps taken in regard to the implementation of Security Council resolution 134 (1960) including his visit to South Africa*

S/4635, 23 January 1961

1. By the resolution which the Security Council adopted on 1 April 1960, it requested the Secretary-General in consultation with the Government of the Union of South Africa, "to make such arrangements as would adequately help in upholding the purposes and principles of the Charter and to report to the Security Council whenever necessary and appropriate".

2. In his interim report of 19 April 1960, the Secretary-General informed the Security Council that after an exchange of communications between the Minister of External Affairs of the Union of South Africa and himself, through the Permanent Representative of the Union Government, he had accepted a proposal of the Union Government that preliminary consultations between the Prime Minister and Minister of External Affairs and himself should be held in London after the conclusion of the Commonwealth Prime Ministers' Conference, probably in early May 1960.

3. It will be recalled that paragraph 5 of the interim report stated that:

"The consultations rendered necessary by the provisions of paragraph 5 of the Security Council's resolution of 1 April 1960 will be undertaken on the basis of the authority of the Secretary-General under the Charter. It is agreed between the Government of the Union of South Africa and myself that consent of the Union Government to discuss the Security

Council's resolution with the Secretary-General would not require prior recognition from the Union Government of the United Nations authority."

4. In his second interim report of 11 October 1960, the Secretary-General informed the Security Council that during the preliminary discussions which took place in London on 13 and 14 May 1960 between the Secretary-General and the Minister of External Affairs of the Union of South Africa, it was agreed that the basis for future discussions would flow from paragraph 5 of the first interim report and that agreement had also been reached on the character and course of the further consultations to take place in Pretoria. It was also stated that "during the contemplated visit to the Union of South Africa, while consultation throughout would be with the Union Government, no restrictive rules were to be imposed on the Secretary-General".

5. In paragraphs 5 and 6 of the second interim report, the Secretary-General explained that:

"Due to circumstances resulting from the mandate given to me by the Security Council by resolutions S/4387, S/4405 and S/4426 dated 14 and 22 July and 9 August 1960 in connection with the United Nations operation in the Republic of the Congo (Leopoldville), I have been unable to visit the Union of South Africa as envisaged in the interim report. On four occasions, precise plans were made for the visit but on each occasion it became necessary first to postpone, then to cancel those plans owing to developments in the Republic of the Congo.

"During a meeting at Headquarters with the Minister of External Affairs of the Union of South Africa on 28 September 1960, a new invitation was extended to me by the Prime Minister of the Union Government to visit the Union early in January 1961."

6. It will be recalled that I stated in the same report that it would be my hope to arrange for the visit at the time suggested for the purpose of the requested consultations with the Prime Minister of the Union of South Africa and that it would be my intention to explore with the Prime Minister the possibility of arrangements which would provide for appropriate safeguards of human rights, with adequate contact with the United Nations.

7. Accordingly I visited the Union of South Africa between 6 and 12 January 1961. It had been my plan to stay two additional days, but due to the convening of the Security Council on a question relating to the mandate given to me by the Council, I felt it necessary to hold myself available to members of the Council when the United Nations operation in the Republic of the Congo was being discussed.

8. While in the Union of South Africa, consultations took place between the Secretary-General and the Prime Minster of the Union at six meetings on 6, 7, 10 and 11 January 1961. In Cape Town, Umtata (Transkei), Johannesburg and Pretoria, the Secretary-General had opportunities to have unofficial contacts with members of various sections of the South African community.

9. Having regard to paragraph 5 of Security Council resolution S/4300, the Secretary-General wishes to state that during the discussions between the Secretary-General and the Prime Minister of the Union of South Africa so far no mutually acceptable arrangement has been found. In the view of the Secretary-General this lack of agreement is not conclusive and he wishes to give the matter his further consideration.

10. The exchange of views in general has served a most useful purpose. The Secretary-General does not consider the consultations as having come to an end, and he looks forward to their continuation at an appropriate time with a view to further efforts from his side to find an adequate solution for the aforementioned problem.

11. The Prime Minister of the Union of South Africa has indicated that further consideration will be given to questions raised in the course of the talks and has stated that "the Union Government, having found the talks with the Secretary-General useful and constructive, have decided to invite him at an appropriate time, or times, to visit the Union again in order that the present contact may be continued".

---

# Document 19

*Resolutions of the All-In African Conference held in Pietermaritzburg, South Africa, 25-26 March 1961*

Not issued as a United Nations document

A grave situation confronts the people of South Africa. The Nationalist Government after holding a fraudulent referendum among only one-fifth of the population, has decided to proclaim a White Republic on May 31st, and the all White Parliament is presently discussing a Constitution. It is clear that to the great disadvantage of the majority of our people such a Republic will continue even more intensively the policies of racial oppression, political persecution and exploitation and the terrorization of the non-White people which have already earned South Africa the righteous condemnation of the entire world.

In this situation it is imperative that all the African people of this country, irrespective of their political, religious or other affiliations, should unite to speak and act with a single voice.

For this purpose, we have gathered here at this solemn All-In Conference, and on behalf of the entire African nation and with a due sense of the historic responsibility which rests on us. . .

1. *We declare* that no Constitution or form of Government decided without the participation of the African people who form an absolute majority of the population can enjoy moral validity or merit support either within South Africa or beyond its borders.

2. *We demand* that a *National Convention* of elected representatives of all adult men and women on an equal basis irrespective of race, colour, creed or other limitation, be called by the Union Government not later than May 31st, 1961; that the Convention shall have sovereign powers to determine, in any way the majority of the representatives decide, a new non-racial democratic Constitution for South Africa.

3. *We resolve* that should the minority Government ignore this demand of the representatives of the

united will of the African people—

(a) We undertake to stage country-wide demonstrations on the eve of the proclamation of the Republic in protest against this undemocratic act.

(b) We call on all Africans not to cooperate or collaborate in any way with the proposed South African Republic or any other form of Government which rests on force to perpetuate the tyranny of a minority, and to organize and unite in town and country to carry out constant actions to oppose oppression and win freedom.

(c) We call on the Indian and Coloured communities and all democratic Europeans to join forces with us in opposition to a regime which is bringing disaster to South Africa and to win a society in which all can enjoy freedom and security.

(d) We call on democratic people the world over to refrain from any cooperation or dealings with the South African government, to impose economic and other sanctions against this country and to isolate in every possible way the minority Government whose continued disregard of all human rights and freedoms constitutes a threat to world peace.

4. *We further decide* that in order to implement the above decisions, Conference —

(a) Elects a National Action Council;

(b) Instructs all delegates to return to their respective areas and form local Action Committees.

---

# Document 20

*Statement by Mr. Peter Smithers, representative of the United Kingdom, in the Special Political Committee of the General Assembly*

A/SPC/SR.242, 5 April 1961

Mr. Smithers (United Kingdom) said that his delegation had not participated in the general debate, since its views on the general issue were well known. The policies of the United Kingdom Government, both in its former African territories which were now independent and in those progressing rapidly towards independence, proved more eloquently than words the gulf separating those policies from the system of apartheid practised in the Union of South Africa.

His delegation had always attached the greatest importance to the observance of Article 2, paragraph 7, of the Charter, which assured Member States, especially those which found themselves in a minority, of reasonable immunity from interference in their internal affairs. Some representatives maintained that the General Assembly had established the fact that Article 2, paragraph 7, did not apply to the question of apartheid; but that would mean that the General Assembly could amend the Charter. The paragraph was an indispensable part of the Charter, and it was in the interest of all Member States to abide by it. However, the question of apartheid was unique in that it involved the deliberate adoption, retention and development of policies based entirely on racial discrimination. Moreover, those policies were directed amongst and against the permanent inhabitants of the territory concerned. The problem caused grave international repercussions, in Africa mainly, but also in other continents, as events at the recent Commonwealth Conference had shown. While the importance attached by the United Kingdom to Article 2, paragraph 7, of the Charter remained undiminished, it regarded apartheid as being now so exceptional as to be *sui generis*, and his delegation felt able to consider the three-Power draft resolution (A/SPC/L.59/Rev.1) on its merits.

There was a serious reservation to be made in connection with operative paragraph 5. It was true that the policies of the Union Government had led to international friction, but his delegation could not agree that, at present at least, they endangered international peace and security. There was some danger that such phrases might become a kind of standard incantation introduced, almost as a matter of routine, into General Assembly resolutions. Hence it was not desirable for the words "and that their continuance endangers international peace and security" to form part of the resolution, and in a separate vote on those words his delegation would abstain.

Apartheid was an essay in folly. It was, however, easier to recognize folly than to find wisdom and to prescribe it for others. As the Defence Minister of India had pointed out (241st meeting), one State had no right to prescribe what others should do. The word "collective" in operative paragraph 3 might give rise to considerable difficulties, and his delegation would therefore abstain on that paragraph. With those two exceptions, his delegation would vote in favour of the three-Power draft resolution.

The draft resolution (A/SPC/L.60/Corr.1) purported to advise States the course of action they should take, and he shared the misgivings expressed by the Defence Minister of India concerning operative paragraph 5. It might be argued that the use of the word "consider" in the first line left States free to do as they pleased, but the operative word was "*recommends*". It was inconceivable that any delegation voting in favour of such a recommendation should not be prepared itself to implement it, and such delegations would, in fact, be committing their Governments to breaking off diplomatic relations with the Union Government and imposing economic sanctions.

To break off diplomatic relations was a perfectly legal and proper procedure, but the question was whether it would have the desired effect. The establishment of diplomatic relations was not a kind of prize conferred on Governments whose policies a country approved or tolerated. Its purpose was not to pay a compliment to a Government, but to secure certain conveniences. The first task of a diplomatic mission was to supply its own Government with accurate information and wise advice concerning the country and Government to which it was accredited, and without such information and advice it would be difficult to form a policy. Its second duty was to carry out the instructions of its own Government and to seek to influence the Government to which it was accredited. It would be ludicrous to sacrifice one of the few remaining means of influencing the Union Government when the avowed intent of the co-sponsors was to influence that Government.

Regarding the imposition of economic sanctions, it had been pointed out that such punitive measures were unprecedented in the history of the United Nations. It was true that the Committee was dealing with an unprecedented problem, but Member States might one day face similar action in other circumstances. Such measures would certainly do most harm to those whom the Committee wished to help; many people in South Africa and other countries would be thrown out of work. It was easy to sneer at the power of "commercial interests", but in the free world these meant the jobs of ordinary men and women. To add to the sum of human misery in many lands could be justified only if it were likely to achieve the desired end, but such action would make a change in the policies of the Union Government less, rather than more, probable. Past experience showed that such action greatly strengthened the position of a Government; it would cause many patriotic South Africans who opposed the policies of apartheid to rally to the support of the Government. There were many moderate and liberal-minded White people in South Africa, and economic sanctions would have an adverse effect on their prospects, which appeared to be increasing at present, of bringing about a change in their Government's policies. No boycott in the past had ever attained its object, and surely no delegation really expected that the draft resolution would achieve what had never been achieved before; on the contrary, it would bring the United Nations into ridicule and contempt.

The representative of the Ukrainian SSR had made great play at the 241st meeting with the economic interests of the United Kingdom in South Africa. The United Kingdom thought it desirable to make investments and develop industries in other countries, and it welcomed similar activities by others in the United Kingdom. The promotion of international trade improved relations between countries; he had the impression that the Government of the Soviet Union took the same view, and was sorry that the outlook of the Ukrainian SSR was so reactionary.

He urged the co-sponsors of the draft resolution (A/SPC/L.60/Corr.1) to turn back from the dangerous course on which they had embarked and to withdraw the draft resolution; if that were not done, his delegation would be obliged to vote against it.

---

# Document 21

*General Assembly resolution: Question of race conflict in South Africa resulting from the policies of apartheid of the Government of the Union of South Africa*

A/RES/1598 (XV), 13 April 1961

*The General Assembly,*

Recalling its previous resolutions on the question of race conflict in South Africa resulting from the policies of apartheid of the Government of the Union of South Africa,

. . .

*Recalling also* that the Government of the Union of South Africa has failed to comply with the repeated requests and demands of the United Nations and world public opinion and to reconsider or revise its racial policies or to observe its obligations under the Charter,

1. *Deplores* such continued and total disregard by

the Government of the Union of South Africa and furthermore its determined aggravation of racial issues by more discriminatory laws and measures and their enforcement, accompanied by violence and bloodshed;

2. *Deprecates* policies based on racial discrimination as reprehensible and repugnant to human dignity;

3. *Requests* all States to consider taking such separate and collective action as is open to them, in conformity with the Charter of the United Nations, to bring about the abandonment of these policies;

4. *Affirms* that the racial policies being pursued by the Government of the Union of South Africa are a flagrant violation of the Charter of the United Nations and the Universal Declaration of Human Rights and are inconsistent with the obligations of a Member State;

5. *Notes with grave concern* that these policies have led to international friction and that their continuance endangers international peace and security;

6. *Reminds* the Government of the Union of South Africa of the requirement in Article 2, paragraph 2, of the Charter that all Members shall fulfil in good faith the obligations assumed by them under the Charter;

7. *Calls upon* the Government of the Union of South Africa once again to bring its policies and conduct into conformity with its obligations under the Charter.

---

# Document 22

## *Manifesto of* Umkhonto We Sizwe *(Spear of the Nation), an underground organization associated with the African National Congress, 16 December 1961*

Not issued as a United Nations document

Units of *Umkhonto We Sizwe* today carried out planned attacks against Government installations, particularly those connected with the policy of apartheid and race discrimination.

*Umkhonto We Sizwe* is a new, independent body, formed by Africans. It includes in its ranks South Africans of all races.

. . .

*Umkhonto We Sizwe* will carry on the struggle for freedom and democracy by new methods, which are necessary to complement the actions of the established national liberation organizations. *Umkhonto We Sizwe* fully supports the national liberation movement, and our members, jointly and individually, place themselves under the overall political guidance of that movement.

It is however, well known that the main national liberation organizations in this country have consistently followed a policy of non-violence. They have conducted themselves peaceably at all times, regardless of Government attacks and persecutions upon them, and despite all Government-inspired attempts to provoke them to violence. They have done so because the people prefer peaceful methods of change to achieve their aspirations without the suffering and bitterness of civil war. But the people's patience is not endless.

The time comes in the life of any nation when there remain only two choices: submit or fight. That time has now come to South Africa. We shall not submit and we have no choice but to hit back by all means within our power in defence of our people, our future and our freedom.

The Government has interpreted the peacefulness of the movement as weakness: the people's non-violent policies have been taken as a green light for Government violence. Refusal to resort to force has been interpreted by the Government as an invitation to use armed force against our people without any fear of reprisals. The methods of *Umkhonto We Sizwe* mark a break with that past.

We are striking out along a new road for the liberation of the people of this country. The Government policy of force, repression and violence will no longer be met with non-violence resistance only! The choice is not ours; it has been made by the Nationalist Government which has rejected every peaceable demand by the people for rights and freedom and answered every such demand with force and yet more force! Twice in the past 18 months, virtual martial law has been imposed in order to beat down peaceful, non-violent strike action of the people in support of their rights. It is now preparing its forces—enlarging and rearming its armed forces and drawing White civilian population into commandos and pistol clubs—for full-scale military actions against the people. The Nationalist Government has chosen the course of force and massacre, now, deliberately, as it did at Sharpeville.

*Umkhonto We Sizwe* will be at the front line of the people's defence. It will be the fighting arm of the people against the Government and its policies of race oppression. It will be the striking force of the people for liberty, for rights and for their final liberation! Let the Government, its supporters who put it into power, and those whose passive toleration of reaction keeps it in power, take note of where the Nationalist Government is leading the country.

We of *Umkhonto We Sizwe* have always sought—as the liberation movement has sought—to achieve liberation, without bloodshed and civil clash. We do so still. We hope—even at this late hour—that our first actions will awaken everyone to a realization of the disastrous situation to which the Nationalist policy is leading. We hope that we will bring the Government and its supporters to theirs senses before it's too late, so that both Government and its policies can be changed before matters reach the desperate stage of civil war. We believe our actions to be a blow against the Nationalist preparations for civil war and military rule.

In these actions, we are working in the best interests of all people of this country—Black, Brown and White— whose future happiness and well-being cannot be attained without the overthrow of the Nationalist Government, the abolition of White supremacy and the winning of liberty, democracy and full national rights and equality for all the people of this country.

We appeal for the support and encouragement of all South Africans who seek the happiness and freedom of the people of this country.

*Afrika Mayibuye!*

---

# Document 23

*General Assembly resolution: The policies of apartheid of the Government of the Republic of South Africa*

A/RES/1761 (XVII), 6 November 1962

*The General Assembly,*

. . .

1. *Deplores* the failure of the Government of the Republic of South Africa to comply with the repeated requests and demands of the General Assembly and of the Security Council and its flouting of world public opinion by refusing to abandon its racial policies;

2. *Strongly deprecates* the continued and total disregard by the Government of South Africa of its obligations under the Charter of the United Nations and, furthermore, its determined aggravation of racial issues by enforcing measures of increasing ruthlessness involving violence and bloodshed;

3. *Reaffirms* that the continuance of those policies seriously endangers international peace and security;

4. *Requests* Member States to take the following measures, separately or collectively, in conformity with the Charter, to bring about the abandonment of those policies:

(a) Breaking off diplomatic relations with the Government of the Republic of South Africa or refraining from establishing such relations;

(b) Closing their ports to all vessels flying the South African flag;

(c) Enacting legislation prohibiting their ships from entering South African ports;

(d) Boycotting all South African goods and refraining from exporting goods, including all arms and ammunition, to South Africa;

(e) Refusing landing and passage facilities to all aircraft belonging to the Government of South Africa and companies registered under the laws of South Africa;

5. *Decides* to establish a Special Committee consisting of representatives of Member States nominated by the President of the General Assembly, with the following terms of reference:

(a) To keep the racial policies of the Government of South Africa under review when the Assembly is not in session;

(b) To report either to the Assembly or to the Security Council or to both, as may be appropriate, from time to time;

. . .

8. *Requests* the Security Council to take appropriate measures, including sanctions, to secure South Africa's compliance with the resolutions of the General Assembly and of the Security Council on this subject and, if necessary, to consider action under Article 6 of the Charter.

# Document 24

*"Appeal for action against Apartheid" issued jointly by Chief Albert J. Luthuli and the Reverend Dr. Martin Luther King, Jr., on 10 December 1962*

Published by the United Nations at the request of the Special Committee on the Policies of Apartheid of the Government of the Republic of South Africa, in a pamphlet in tribute to Dr. King

[Editor's note: This joint statement, initiated by Chief Luthuli and the Rev. Dr. Martin Luther King, Jr., was signed by many prominent Americans and promoted the public campaign for sanctions against South Africa.]

In 1957, an unprecedented Declaration of Conscience was issued by more than 100 leaders from every continent. That Declaration was an appeal to South Africa to bring its policies into line with the Universal Declaration of Human Rights adopted by the General Assembly of the United Nations.

The Declaration was a good start in mobilizing world sentiment to back those in South Africa who acted for equality. The non-Whites took heart in learning that they were not alone. And many White supremacists learned for the first time how isolated they were.

## Measures of Desperation

Subsequent to the Declaration, the South African Government took the following measures:

* BANNED the African National Congress and the Pan Africanist Congress, the principal protest organizations, and jailed their leaders;

* COERCED the press into strict pro-government censorship and made it almost impossible for new anti-apartheid publications to exist;

* ESTABLISHED an arms industry, more than tripled the military budget, distributed small arms to the White population, enlarged the army, created an extensive White civilian militia;

* ACTIVATED total physical race separation by establishing the first Bantustan in the Transkei—with the aid of emergency police regulations;

* LEGALLY DEFINED protest against apartheid as an act of "sabotage"—an offence ultimately punishable by death;

* PERPETUATED its control through terrorism and violence:

* Human Rights Day (December 10), 1959 - 12 South West Africans killed at Windhoek and 40 wounded as they fled police

* March 21, 1960 - 72 Africans killed and 186 wounded at Sharpeville by police

* Before and during the two-year "emergency" in the Transkei - 15 Africans killed by police, thousands arrested and imprisoned without trial.

## The Choice

The deepening tensions can lead to two alternatives:

### Solution 1

Intensified persecution may lead to violence and armed rebellion once it is clear that peaceful adjustments are no longer possible. As the persecution has been inflicted by one racial group upon all other racial groups, large-scale violence would take the form of a racial war.

This "solution" may be workable. But mass racial extermination will destroy the potential for interracial unity in South Africa and elsewhere.

Therefore, we ask for your action to make the following possible:

### Solution 2

"Nothing which we have suffered at the hands of the government has turned us from our chosen path of disciplined resistance," said Chief Albert J. Luthuli at Oslo. So there exists another alternative—and the only solution which represents sanity—transition to a society based upon equality for all without regard to colour.

Any solution founded on justice is unattainable until the Government of South Africa is forced by pressures, both internal and external, to come to terms with the demands of the non-White majority.

The apartheid republic is a reality today *only* because the peoples and governments of the world have been unwilling to place her in quarantine.

## Translate public opinion into public action

We, therefore, ask all men of goodwill to take action against apartheid in the following manner:

Hold meetings and demonstrations on December 10, Human Rights Day;

Urge your church, union, lodge, or club to observe this day as one of protest;

Urge your Government to support economic sanctions;

Write to your mission to the United Nations urging adoption of a resolution calling for international isolation of South Africa;

Don't buy South Africa's products;

Don't trade or invest in South Africa;

Translate public opinion into public action by explaining facts to all peoples, to groups to which you belong, and to countries of which you are citizens until AN EFFECTIVE INTERNATIONAL QUARANTINE OF APARTHEID IS ESTABLISHED.

# Document 25

*Opening statement by Secretary-General U Thant at the first meeting of the Special Committee on the Policies of Apartheid of the Government of the Republic of South Africa*

UN Press Release SG/1453, 2 April 1963

I welcome you to the first meeting of the Special Committee on the policies of apartheid of the Government of Republic of South Africa, established by General Assembly resolution 1761 (XVII).

The General Assembly has asked this Committee to keep the racial policies of the Government of South Africa under review when the Assembly is not in session, and to report either to the General Assembly or to the Security Council, or to both, as may be appropriate from time to time.

It may be recalled that the question of racial policies of the Government of South Africa has been before the United Nations, in one form or another, since 1946. The General Assembly has adopted altogether 28 resolutions on the subject. The Security Council also adopted a resolution on 1 April 1960 after the serious incident at Sharpeville.

In these circumstances, the General Assembly and the Security Council expressed their serious concern that the racial policies of the South African Government were not only not in conformity with its obligations and responsibilities under the Charter of the United Nations, but that they were also a source of international friction and a danger to the maintenance of international peace and security.

The lack of response on the part of the Government of South Africa to the repeated recommendations and decisions of the United Nations organs has given rise to increasing concern among Member States, a concern which I share.

I wish to add, on this occasion, that the attitudes of the South African Government and its leaders, as disclosed in recent statements concerning the role of the United Nations, is also a matter of serious concern to us.

Finally, I wish to express the hope that your deliberations will be constructive and fruitful. The Secretariat will provide all the assistance it can to facilitate the discharge of your responsibilities.

# Document 26

*Resolution adopted by the Conference of Heads of African States and Governments, Addis Ababa, 22-25 May 1963, on apartheid and racial discrimination*

A/AC.115/L.11, 27 June 1963

*The Summit Conference of Independent African States meeting in Addis Ababa, Ethiopia, from 22 May to 25 May 1963*

Having considered all aspects of the questions of apartheid and racial discrimination,

*Unanimously convinced* of the imperious and urgent necessity of coordinating and intensifying their efforts to put an end to the South African Government's criminal policy of apartheid and wipe out racial discrimination in all its forms,

*Have agreed unanimously* to concert and coordinate their efforts and action in this field, and to this end have decided on the following measures:

1. *To grant* scholarships, educational facilities and possibilities of employment in African government service to refugees from South Africa;

2. *To support* the recommendations presented to the Security Council and the General Assembly by the special Committee of the United Nations on the apartheid policies of the South African Government;

3. *To dispatch* a delegation of Foreign Ministers to inform the Security Council of the explosive situation existing in South Africa. (The Conference has decided the members of the delegation to be: Liberia, Tunisia, Madagascar and Sierra Leone.);

4. *To coordinate* concerted measures of sanction against the Government of South Africa;

5. *Appeals* to all States, and more particularly to those which have traditional relations and cooperate with the Government of South Africa, to strictly apply United Nations resolution 1761 (XVII) of 6 November 1962 concerning apartheid;

6. *Appeals* to all Governments who still have diplomatic, consular and economic relations with the Government of South Africa to break off those relations and to cease any other form of encouragement for the policy of apartheid;

7. *Stresses* the great responsibility incurred by the colonial authorities administering territories neighbouring South Africa in the pursuit of the policy of apartheid;

8. *Condemns* racial discrimination in all its forms in Africa and all over the world;

9. *Expresses* the deep concern aroused in all African peoples and Governments by the measures of racial discrimination taken against communities of African origin living outside the continent and particularly in the United States of America; expresses appreciation for the efforts of the Federal Government of the United States of America to put an end to these intolerable malpractices which are likely seriously to deteriorate relations between the African peoples and Governments on the one hand and the people and Government of the United States of America on the other.

---

# Document 27

*Statement by Mr. Adlai Stevenson, representative of the United States, in the Security Council, announcing the decision of the United States to stop sales of arms to South Africa*

S/PV.1052, 2 August 1963

. . .

48. We all suffer from the disease of discrimination in various forms, but at least most of us recognize the disease for what it is: a disfiguring blight. The whole point is that, in many countries, governmental policies are dedicated to rooting out this dread syndrome of prejudice and discrimination, while in South Africa we see the anachronistic spectacle of the Government of a great people which persists in seeing the disease as the remedy, prescribing for the malady of racism the bitter toxic of apartheid.

49. Just as my country is determined to wipe out discrimination in our society, it will support efforts to bring about a change in South Africa. It is in the United States' interest to do this; it is in the interest of South Africa; it is in the interest of a world which has suffered enough from bigotry, prejudice and hatred.

50. The past two decades have seen an explosion of nationhood unequalled in history. Certainly, the pace of decolonization in Africa has been nothing less than phenomenal, and it offers a record of progress far beyond what the most optimistic among us could have expected in 1945. The new States of Africa are gaining strength, resolutely fighting to build prosperous, dynamic societies, and to do this in cooperation with other Africa States.

51. But, as this meeting of the Security Council so graphically emphasizes, the full potential of this new era cannot be realized because of South Africa's self-chosen isolation. Worse yet, progress in Africa is overshadowed by the racial bitterness and resentment caused by the policies of the South African Government; and it is the duty of this Council to do what it can to ensure that this situation does not deteriorate further, and that the injustice of apartheid comes to an end, not in blood and bondage, but in peace and freedom.

52. What we see and hear, however, offers us at present little hope. Indeed, the situation is worse than it was three years ago, when the Council first met on the question of apartheid. Speakers before me have reviewed the record of previous discussions of apartheid by this Council and the General Assembly. As they have pointed out, we have called repeatedly upon the Government of South Africa to consider world opinion, to cooperate with the United Nations, and to set in motion some meaningful steps toward ending discrimination and the policies and practices that would offend the whole world, wherever they were pursued.

53. Outside this Organization, many Members— not the least of which is my own Government—have attempted repeatedly to persuade the South African Government to begin moving along the lines of these resolutions. I myself have had something emphatic to say on this score, on two occasions, in the Republic of South Africa—things that it grieved me to say after enjoying so much courtesy and hospitality from the friendly and gracious people of the lovely land. But it is only stating a

fact of life to say that the visible result of all these discussions and resolutions here in the United Nations, and all the diplomatic activities so far, is zero. It is only stating the obvious to say that, up until this time, our efforts have yielded no tangible results. It is only calling things by their right name to say that we are confronted for the moment with a deadlock between the overwhelming majority of mankind and the Republic of South Africa. There has been no forward motion; indeed, there has been retrogression—calculated retrogression.

54. Need I read the bill of particulars? For the past fifteen years, the Government of South Africa has built a barrier between the races, piling new restrictions upon old: all South Africans must carry identity cards indicating racial ancestry; segregation in religion, education and public accommodation is virtually total; freedom of employment is limited; wages rates for the same work and the same responsibility are different, according to the colour of one's skin; freedom of movement is inhibited; strikes by Africans in South Africa are illegal; Africans in South Africa are prohibited from residing, from doing business, or acquiring real property, in most cities and in large areas of the countryside; voters are registered on separate rolls according to race. This is not the whole story; but the point is that these and other measures of discrimination, aimed at the total separation of races into privileged and underprivileged segments of society, do not represent inherited social defects for which remedies are being sought: but injustices, deliberately and systematically imposed, in the recent past.

55. We are all agreed, and we have proclaimed again and again, in this body and in the General Assembly, and in many other forums of the United Nations, certain basic views about the issue before us. However, we must restate them again and again so that we can sum up where we stand, and deliberate with clarity and with candour on how to move forward.

56. First, we have affirmed and reaffirmed that apartheid is abhorrent. Our belief in the self-evident truths about human equality is enshrined in the Charter. Apartheid and racism, despite all of the tortured rationalizations that we have heard from the apologists, are incompatible with the moral, social, and constitutional foundations of our societies.

57. A second basic principle on which we are agreed is that all Members of the Organization have pledged themselves to take action, in cooperation with the Organization, to promote observance of human rights, without distinction as to race.

58. Thirdly, we continue to believe that this matter is of proper and legitimate concern to the United Nations. We have often stated, in the General Assembly, our belief that the Assembly can properly consider questions of racial discrimination and other violations of human rights where they are a Member's official policy and are inconsistent with the obligations of that Member, under Articles 55 and 56 of the Charter, to promote observance of human rights, without distinction as to race.

59. Moreover, the apartheid policy of South Africa has clearly led to a situation the continuance of which is likely to endanger international peace and security. We also believe that all Members, in the words of the resolution passed almost unanimously by the sixteenth General Assembly, should take such separate and collective action as is open to them in conformity with the Charter to bring about an abandonment of those policies. The United States supported that resolution and has complied with it.

60. I should like to take this occasion to bring up to date the record of the measures the United States has taken to carry out this purpose. First, we have continued and indeed have accelerated our official representations to the Government of South Africa on all aspects of apartheid in that country. We have done this through public words and private diplomacy, expressing our earnest hope that the South African Government would take steps to reconsider and to revise its racial policies and to extend the full range of civic rights and opportunities to non-Whites in the life of their country. And we have observed to the South African Government that in the absence of an indication of change, the United States would not cooperate in matters that would lend support to South Africa's present racial policies.

61. We have utilized our diplomatic and our consular establishments in South Africa to demonstrate by words and by deeds our official disapproval of apartheid and, as the United States representative informed the Special Political Committee of the General Assembly on 19 October last, the United States has adopted and is enforcing the policy of forbidding the sale to the South African Government of arms and military equipment whether from Government or commercial sources, which could be used by that Government to enforce apartheid either in South Africa or in the Administration of South West Africa. We have carefully screened both government and commercial shipments of military equipment to make sure that this policy is rigorously enforced.

62. But I am now authorized to inform the Security Council of still another important step which my Government is prepared to take. We expect to bring to an end the sale of all military equipment to the Government of South Africa by the end of this calendar year, in order further to contribute to a peaceful solution and to avoid any steps which might at this point directly contribute to international friction in the area. There are existing contracts which provide for limited quantities of strategic equipment for defence against external threats, such as

air-to-air missiles and torpedoes for submarines. We must honour these contracts. The Council should be aware that in announcing this policy the United States, as a nation with many responsibilities in many parts of the world, naturally reserves the right in the future to interpret this policy in the light of requirements for assuring the maintenance of international peace and security.

63. If the interests of the world community require the provision of equipment for use in the common defence effort, we would naturally feel able to do so without violating the spirit and the intent of this resolution. We are taking this further step to indicate the deep concern which the Government of the United States feels at the failure of the Republic of South Africa to abandon its policy of apartheid. In pursuing this policy the Republic of South Africa, as we have so often said, is failing to discharge its obligations under Articles 55 and 56 of the Charter, whereby Members pledge themselves to take joint and separate action in cooperation with our Organization for the achievement, among other things, of "universal respect for, and observance of, human rights and fundamental freedoms for all without distinction as to race, sex, language, or religion".

64. Stopping the sale of arms to South Africa emphasizes our hope that the Republic will now reassess its attitude towards apartheid in the light of the constantly growing international concern at its failure to heed the numerous appeals made to it by various organs of the United Nations, as well as appeals of Member States such as my Government.

65. As to the action of the Council in this proceeding, we are prepared to consult with other members and with the African Foreign Ministers present at the table and we will have some suggestions to make. It is clear to my delegation that the application of sanctions under Chapter VII in the situation now before us would be both bad law and bad policy. It would be bad law because the extreme measures provided in Chapter VII were never intended and cannot reasonably be interpreted to apply to situations of this kind. the founders of the United Nations were very careful to reserve the right of the Organization to employ mandatory coercive measures in situations where there was an actuality of international violence or such a clear and present threat to the peace as to leave no reasonable alternative but resort to coercion.

66. We do not have that kind of a situation here. Fortunately for all of us, there is still some time to work out a solution through measures of pacific settlement, and any solution adopted by this Council must be reasonably calculated to promote such settlement. It is bad policy because the application of sanctions in this situation is not likely to bring about the practical result that we seek, that is, the abandonment of apartheid. Far from encour-

aging the beginning of a dialogue between the Government of South Africa and its African population, punitive measures would only provoke intransigence and harden the existing situation. Furthermore, the result of the adoption of such measures, particularly if compliance is not widespread and sincere, would create doubts about the validity of, and diminish respect, for the authority of the United Nations and the efficacy of the sanction process envisioned in the Charter.

67. Also, views on this matter differ so widely that we cannot hope to agree on the necessary consensus to make such action effective even if it were legitimate and appropriate. And as for suggestions of diplomatic isolation, persuasion cannot be exercised in a vacuum. Conflicting views cannot be reconciled *in absentia*. Instead, we believe that still further attempts should be made to build a bridge of communication, of discussion and of persuasion. If the human race is going to survive on this earth wisdom, reason and right must prevail. Let us not forget that there are many wise and influential people in that great country who share our views. It is regrettable that the accomplishments in so many fields of human endeavour in South Africa are being obscured by a racial policy repugnant to Africa and to the world. Certainly, one ultimate goal for all of us is to assist South Africa to rejoin the African continent and to assist in the development of all the peoples of Africa. And that is why my Government has looked with such favour on the idea of appointing special representatives of the Security Council who can work energetically and persistently and be free to exercise their own ingenuity and to pursue every prospect and every hint of a useful opening.

68. We cannot accept the proposition that the only alternative to apartheid is bloodshed. We cannot accept the conclusion that there is no way out, no direction in which to go except the present collision course towards ultimate disaster in South Africa. Certainly there are alternatives and they must be identified and they must be explored before it is too late.

69. It is a matter of considerable regret to my delegation that the Government of South Africa has chosen to absent itself from these proceedings. But aside from regrets, it is exceedingly difficult in this shrunken interdependent world to live in self-ostracism from international society. In this world of instant communication, it is progressively more hazardous to fly in the face of world opinion. And certainly the obligation to talk about dangerous disputes is too solemn to be ignored by even the most stubborn of leaders today.

70. There is nothing inherently immutable in any impasse in human affairs. Many a seemingly hopeless cause has prevailed in the course of history. I had occasion just last week to recall here that negotiations over the testing of nuclear weapons looked hopeless for five

long, dreary, frustrating years, until the impasse was broken suddenly, to the vast relief of an anxious world. And, as I said, the stalemate was broken because men refused to give up hope, because men declined to give in to despair, because men worked consistently and doggedly to break the deadlock. Manifestly this treaty does not solve all of the problems in connection with nuclear armaments. But every long journey begins with a single step, and this is a beginning.

71. So I should like to suggest very emphatically that we approach the problem of apartheid in South Africa as a similar challenge to ingenuity, to the instinct for survival for humankind. As President Kennedy said with reference to the atomic treaty, "We must not be afraid to test our hopes". It is in the spirit of testing our hopes that this sad episode will end in reason and not in flame that I, on behalf of my Government, solemnly and earnestly appeal to the Government of South Africa to change course and to embark on a policy of national reconciliation and emancipation.

# Document 28

*Security Council resolution: Question relating to the policies of apartheid of the Government of the Republic of South Africa*

S/RES/181 (1963), 7 August 1963

*The Security Council,*

*Having considered* the question of race conflict in South Africa resulting from the policies of apartheid of the Government of the Republic of South Africa, as submitted by the thirty-two African Member States,

. . .

*Taking into account* that world public opinion has been reflected in General Assembly resolution 1761 (XVII) of 6 November 1962, and particularly in its paragraphs 4 and 8,

. . .

*Noting with concern* the recent arms build-up by the Government of South Africa, some of which arms are being used in furtherance of that Government's racial policies,

*Regretting* that some States are indirectly providing encouragement in various ways to the Government of South Africa to perpetuate, by force, its policy of apartheid,

. . .

*Being convinced* that the situation in South Africa is seriously disturbing international peace and security,

1. *Strongly deprecates* the policies of South Africa in its perpetuation of racial discrimination as being inconsistent with the principles contained in the Charter of the United Nations and contrary to its obligations as a Member of the United Nations;

2. *Calls upon* the Government of South Africa to abandon the policies of apartheid and discrimination, as called for in Security Council resolution 134 (1960), and to liberate all persons imprisoned, interned or subjected to other restrictions for having opposed the policy of apartheid;

3. *Solemnly calls upon* all States to cease forthwith the sale and shipment of arms, ammunition of all types and military vehicles to South Africa;

. . .

# Document 29

*Report of the Special Committee on the Policies of Apartheid of the Government of the Republic of South Africa*

A/5497, 16 September 1963

. . .

**Conclusions and recommendations**

A. *Racial policies of the Republic of South Africa and their repercussions*

434. In the discharge of its mandate under operative paragraph 5 of General Assembly resolution 1761 (XVII), the Special Committee has carefully reviewed the racial policies of the Government of the Republic of South Africa; taken note of numerous communications from Governments, non-governmental organizations and individuals; heard a number of petitioners; and studied official statements and documents of the South African Government, as well as reports in the Press.

435. The results of the Committee's study, as indi-

cated in the two interim reports and the present report, make it clear that the Government of the Republic of South Africa has not only not complied with the General Assembly resolution, but has taken further measures to aggravate the situation. It has likewise not complied with the provisions of the Security Council resolutions of 1 April 1960 (for the text, see annex II) and 7 August 1963 (for the text, see paragraph 57).

436. The Special Committee notes that the Government of the Republic of South Africa continues to implement the mass of discriminatory and repressive legislation, and has added to it serious new measures such as the Transkei Constitution Act, 1963, the Bantu Laws Amendment Act, 1963, and the General Law Amendment Act, 1962.

437. During the period since 6 November 1962, the Government has uprooted thousands of families from their homes in the urban areas and expelled many thousands of persons from these areas. Hundreds of thousands of persons have been arrested under pass laws and other racially discriminatory measures. The non-Whites have been excluded from new categories of employment. A reign of terror has been instituted against opponents of apartheid: the leaders of the non-Whites have been jailed or restricted, and thousands of persons have been thrown in jail for opposition to apartheid, with no certainty of ever being set free. Harsh penalties have been imposed on members of the major non-White organizations. Simultaneously, efforts are being made to set up colonial enclaves in the African reserves as a means to consolidate White supremacy.

438. The Government has openly relied on its political, military and economic power to defy the will of the great majority of the people of South Africa, as well as that of the United Nations. With ruthless measures of repression, it has denied all avenues for peaceful change, greatly increased tension within the country and has created the grave danger of a violent conflict which cannot but have serious international repercussions.

439. The Special Committee notes that, far from pausing to consider means of complying with the provisions of the resolutions of the General Assembly and the Security Council, the Government of the Republic of South Africa has reacted to these resolutions by new and harsher measures of repression against its opponents. The hastening of apartheid measures, and attempts to rally its supporters to mere stubborn resistance to the legitimate and urgent demands of the international community. The unrepresentative and minority Government of the Republic of South Africa continues thus to pursue an increasingly isolationist course and policy, dragging the overwhelming majority of the inhabitants against their wishes away from the mainstream of international life and cooperation and from the benefits and advantages deriving therefrom.

440. The Special Committee notes that the attitude of the Government of the Republic of South Africa to the Security Council resolution of 7 August 1963, described in the previous chapter, deserves particular condemnation in the light of Article 25 of the United Nations Charter. In calling for a report by the Secretary-General by 30 October 1963, the Security Council gave sufficient time for the South African Government to reconsider its position and take meaningful steps towards compliance so that additional measures may be avoided. The Special Committee feels that the utterly negative reaction of the South African Government makes it essential to consider, with no further delay, possible new measures in accordance with the Charter which provides for stronger political, diplomatic and economic sanctions, suspension of the rights and privileges of the Republic of South Africa as a Member State, and expulsion from the United Nations and its specialized agencies.

### Certain aspects of the situation in the Republic of South Africa

441. Before discussing such measures, the Special Committee wishes to submit certain observations on the salient aspects of the problem.

442. First, the Special Committee wishes to emphasize that the problem in South Africa is not merely the perpetuation of inequalities arising from historic developments or the continued existence of such inequities as the denial of franchise to a majority of the population, the separation of peoples by race or the discrimination in the sharing of the fruits of labour. Such terms as segregation and discrimination can hardly describe the humiliation and oppression to which millions of people, who constitute a large majority of the population of the country, have been subjected by the policies of its Government.

443. Second, the Special Committee considers that the problem is not one of a peculiar political or social system which democratic-minded peoples find objectionable, but of an official policy of a State, a tyrannical policy imposed for purposes which are repugnant to the fundamental principles of the United Nations Charter. The racist creed that the policies of apartheid are based on is not only unjust, but is the very antithesis of the concept of international cooperation which is at the root of the existence of the United Nations.

444. Third, the Special Committee rejects the claims of the Government of the Republic of South Africa that it is, by its policy, defending the Western or Christian civilization in its territory or that it is the victim of attacks led by one of the protagonists of the cold war. The Special Committee notes that the policies of the Republic of South Africa are a matter of concern to all States and to all peoples. They have been denounced almost unanimously by Member States and by world public opinion.

It is the responsibility of all Member States, irrespective of other differences, to cooperate in an endeavour to put an end to the dangerous situation in the Republic of South Africa, in the interests solely of the people of South Africa and the maintenance of international peace and security.

445. Fourth, the Special Committee reiterates its view, stated in its first interim report (see annex III), that the problem in the Republic of South Africa is not one of colour or race but "the consequence of a racialist ideology enshrined as State policy and implemented by force against the majority of the people of the country, despite the obligations of the Government of the Republic of South Africa under the United Nations Charter" (annex III, para. 22).

446. The hearings of the petitioners and the review of the developments have underscored the Committee's view that the policies of apartheid are detrimental to the interests of all sections of the population of the Republic of South Africa. These policies cannot be implemented without undermining the freedom and human rights of all persons, Whites and non-Whites alike. Indeed, as the Committee stated in the declaration issued by its Chairman and Rapporteur on the occasion of the publication of its second interim report, which appeared in United Nations Press Release GA/AP/13:

"The present Government of the Republic of South Africa offers for all time no other future to its non-White population than perpetual subordination. Though it describes itself as engaged in a struggle for the survival of the White population, it deliberately imperils their own safety and offers them no other destiny than a hopeless struggle for domination."

447. The Special Committee rejects as unfounded the claim of the Government of South Africa that the choice in South Africa is between White domination and the end of the White community in the country. It feels that the White community cannot ensure its survival by seeking perpetual domination over the non-Whites, and that efforts to that end can only lead to catastrophic consequences.

448. Contrary to the assertions of the Government of the Republic of South Africa, the Special Committee noted that the major non-White organizations favour equality of all citizens, irrespective of race, and that they have repeatedly expressed a desire for discussions to ensure progress towards equality. It has also noted with great satisfaction that among those who oppose the policies of apartheid, despite severe repression, are members of all racial groups in the country, including many Whites.

449. The United Nations has already made clear in General Assembly resolution 616 B (VII), reaffirmed in subsequent resolutions, that the peaceful development of a unified community in multiracial societies such as the Republic of South Africa would best be assured "when patterns of legislation and practice are directed towards ensuring equality before the law of all persons regardless of race, creed or colour, and when economic, social, cultural and political participation of all racial groups is on a basis of equality". The Special Committee feels that this is the only course which can serve the true interests of all the peoples of the Republic of South Africa, irrespective of race or colour.

450. Fifth, the Special Committee notes that the harsh repressive measures instituted by the Government frustrate the possibilities for peaceful settlement, enhance hostility among the racial groups, and precipitate a violent conflict with incalculable harm to persons of all racial groups in the country, to friendly relations among States and to the maintenance of peace in Africa and the world.

451. The Special Committee, therefore, attaches the utmost importance to the release of political prisoners, withdrawal of orders of banishment and other restraints against political leaders and the abolition of repressive legislation. Moreover, it takes note of the serious and special hardship faced by the families of persons persecuted only because of their opposition to the policies of apartheid and considers that the international community, for humanitarian reasons, should provide them with relief and other assistance.

452. Sixth, it is the duty and in the interest of the leaders and people of the Republic of South Africa to seek the aid and support of the United Nations to help them overcome the burdensome legacy of inequality, prejudice, tension and fear.

453. The present Government, however, has aggravated the tensions in the country and attempted to entrench itself in power by utilizing the fears and prejudices of the White population. The Special Committee feels, therefore, that in order to put an end to the explosive situation in the country, it is essential that the White community in South Africa should be made to realize that the Government's plans to reinforce White supremacy cannot succeed and will only lead to needless suffering for all concerned.

454. Seventh, the Special Committee notes that the racial policies of the Government of the Republic of South Africa have long been matters of international concern. The General Assembly has dealt with this problem at every session since 1946 and adopted numerous resolutions with a view to dissuading the South African Government from its racial policies. The Security Council has twice considered the matter and adopted resolutions on 1 April 1960 and 7 August 1963.

455. The Special Committee recalls that, as early as the first session in 1946, the General Assembly noted that friendly relations between South Africa and India had been impaired because of the treatment of people of Indian origin

in South Africa. It notes that the refusal of the South African Government to implement the recommendations of the General Assembly led to further aggravation of its relations with the Governments of India and Pakistan.

456.    The Special Committee also recalls that the General Assembly and the Security Council have repeatedly recognized that the continuance of the racial policies of the Government of South Africa has led to international friction and seriously endangered international peace and security.

457.    It recalls further that the Government of South Africa has extended its racial policies to the mandated Territory of South West Africa, and has refused to fulfil its obligation towards that Territory, defying numerous resolutions of the General Assembly. The report on South West Africa by the Special Committee on the Situation with regard to the Implementation of the Declaration on the Granting of Independence to Colonial Countries and Peoples (A/5446/Rev.1, chap. IV), and recent statements of the Government of the Republic of South Africa concerning South West Africa, indicate the grave dangers created by the policies of apartheid, as the South African Government threatens to prevent by force the fulfilment of the responsibilities of the United Nations towards the people of South West Africa.

458.    Further, the recent developments in the colonial territories in southern Africa indicate that the racial policies of the South African Government are a grave hindrance to the peaceful and speedy development of the neighbouring colonial territories to independence and prosperity.

459.    The Special Committee wishes to emphasize that, in the context of the historic developments in Asia and Africa since the establishment of the United Nations, the policies and actions of the Republic of South Africa have increasingly serious international repercussions. They have become a constant provocation to peoples beyond the borders of the Republic who feel an affinity with the oppressed people of South Africa, and to all opponents of racism everywhere. They have compelled many States to break relations with the Republic of South Africa or to refrain from establishing relations. They have caused friction between African and other States on the one hand, and Governments which, these States feel, have not taken adequate measures to dissuade the Government of the Republic of South Africa from its present policies. Finally, they constitute a serious threat to the maintenance of international peace and security.

B.  *Measures to dissuade the Government of South Africa from its present policies*

460.    The General Assembly and the Security Council have repeatedly appealed to the Government of South Africa since 1946 to modify its policies in order to conform with its obligations under the Charter. As these appeals were not heeded, it became essential that effective measures be taken to induce that Government to recognize the folly of its policies and fulfil its obligations. General Assembly resolution 1761 (XVII) of 6 November 1962 represented a new stage in the United Nations consideration of the matter as it recommended specific measures for implementation by all Member States.

461.    In operative paragraph 4 of that resolution, the General Assembly

"Requests Member States to take the following measures, separately or collectively, in conformity with the Charter, to bring about the abandonment of those policies:

"(a)    Breaking off diplomatic relations with the Government of the Republic of South Africa or refraining from establishing such relations;

"(b)    Closing off their ports to all vessels flying the South African flag;

"(c)    Enacting legislation prohibiting their ships from entering South African ports;

"(d)    Boycotting all South African goods and refraining from exporting goods, including all arms and ammunition, to South Africa;

"(e)    Refusing landing and passage facilities to all aircraft belonging to the Government of South Africa and companies registered under the laws of South Africa."

462.    The Security Council, in its resolution of 7 August 1963, taking note of General Assembly resolution 1761 (XVII) and the interim reports of the Special Committee, again called upon the Government of South Africa to abandon its policies of apartheid and discrimination; called for the liberation of all persons imprisoned, interned or subjected to other restrictions for having opposed the policy of apartheid; and solemnly called upon all States to cease forthwith the sale and shipment of arms, ammunition of all types and military vehicles to South Africa (see paragraph 57).

463.    The Special Committee considers that these resolutions represent important steps in the efforts of the United Nations to dissuade the Government of South Africa from its disastrous policies and deserve full support by all Member States. In this connection, the Special Committee wishes to make the following observations.

464.    The Special Committee notes the increasing abhorrence by world public opinion of the racial policies of the Government of the Republic of South Africa and the growing recognition that the continuation of these policies would seriously endanger the maintenance of international peace.

465.    Member States of the United Nations have condemned the racial policies of the Republic of South

Africa by ever-increasing majorities, and recognized that effective and prompt measures need to be taken by the international community to deal with the problem. No Member State has condoned or defended these policies.

466. A number of United Nations bodies have been obliged to take action in view of the effects of the policies of apartheid in their fields of competence.

467. The sixteenth World Health Assembly in May 1963 adopted a resolution noting that the conditions imposed upon the non-White population of South Africa seriously prejudiced their physical, mental and social health, and was contrary to the principles of the Organization; inviting the Government of the Republic of South Africa to renounce the policy of apartheid, and take appropriate measures so that all populations of South Africa would benefit by the public health services of that country; undertaking, within the provisions of the Constitution of the Organization, to support all measures that may be taken to contribute towards the solution of the problem of apartheid; and requesting the Director-General to transmit the resolution to the Special Committee (see A/AC.115/L.13).

468. The Governing Body of the International Labour Office adopted three resolutions in June 1963 deciding *inter alia* that the Republic of South Africa be excluded from meetings of the International Labour Organisation, the membership of which is determined by the Governing Body; that the Director-General be invited to provide the full cooperation of the Organisation in United Nations action relating to the Republic of South Africa; and that the Director-General, accompanied by a tripartite delegation of the Governing Body, should meet the Secretary-General of the United Nations to express the grave concern of the forty-seventh International Labour Conference and the Governing Body on the subject of apartheid and jointly seek a solution of the problems posed by the membership of the Republic of South Africa so long as it continues to maintain its present policy (see A/AC.115/L.12).

469. The Economic and Social Council decided by resolution 974 D (XXXVI), part IV, adopted on 30 July 1963 that, in accordance with the recommendation of the Economic Commission for Africa, the Republic of South Africa, "shall not take part in the work of the Economic Commission for Africa, until the Council, on the recommendation of the Economic Commission for Africa, shall find that conditions for constructive cooperation have been restored by a change in its racial policy".

470. The Special Committee has, moreover, taken note of the condemnation of the racial policies of South Africa by numerous non-governmental organizations which represent great segments of humanity, and of concrete measures taken by many organizations and individuals, despite serious sacrifices, to assist in the solu-

tion of the problem (see paragraph 26).

471. The Special Committee attaches great significance to the moral isolation of the Government of the Republic of South Africa which these developments represent. However, in view of the failure of efforts at persuasion to dissuade the Government of the Republic of South Africa from pursuing its disastrous course, the implementation of the concrete measures recommended by the General Assembly and the Security Council has become imperative.

472. The Special Committee draws the attention of the General Assembly and the Security Council to the replies received from Member States to the letter dated 11 April 1963 by the Chairman of the Special Committee, which are annexed to this report (see annex V).

473. The Special Committee notes with great satisfaction that a number of Member States have reported effective measures taken by them in accordance with the provisions of General Assembly resolution 1761 (XVII). It notes that a number of other States have taken similar measures and awaits reports from them in due course. It recognizes that the adoption of such measures represents a substantial sacrifice for many Member States.

474. The Special Committee wishes to express its great appreciation to all Member States which have thus given concrete evidence of their attachment to international solidarity and their abhorrence of racial discrimination. It has noted with satisfaction the fact that many developing countries have made great sacrifices and have thereby shown their determination to contribute to the speedy solution of the problem.

475. The Special Committee notes in connection with operative paragraph 4 (a) of General Assembly resolution 1761 (XVII), that States other than those which maintained diplomatic representatives in the Republic of South Africa on 6 November 1962, have refrained from establishing diplomatic relations with the Republic. A number of States have taken effective action in pursuance of operative paragraph 4 (b) to (e) concerning trade, and the landing and passage rights of South African ships and aircraft.

476. Moreover, the Special Committee notes that in the light of the conclusions of its first interim report (see annex III), supported unanimously by the Summit Conference of Independent African States, a number of countries have broken off consular relations or have refrained from establishing such relations, and have denied use of their air space to the aircraft of the Republic of South Africa.

477. The Committee notes, however, that a number of countries continue to maintain diplomatic relations with the Republic of South Africa, and some have substantially increased their trade with the Republic of South

Africa. The colonial powers have granted new passage and overflight facilities to provide alternate routes to South African aircraft, while various non-African States continue to grant landing and passage rights.

478. The Special Committee feels, therefore, that the United Nations must insist that all Member States should adopt the measures recommended in General Assembly resolution 1761 (XVII) and the Security Council resolution of 7 August 1963. Further, in view of the rapid deterioration of the situation in the Republic of South Africa and in order to ensure effective international action, the Special Committee feels that consideration should be given to appropriate additional measures.

479. The Special Committee is convinced that the Government of the Republic of South Africa could not have continued its disastrous policies and cannot continue them further, in opposition to world opinion, if the international community had not been patient and refrained from effective economic and other measures to induce it to abandon its policies.

480. The crucial aspect of the present system in the Republic of South Africa, defended by the power of its Government, is the appropriation of a disproportionate share of the fruits of labour of all racial groups for the benefit of the White minority. Political rights are restricted to the Whites and a tyranny imposed over the country to ensure a perpetuation of this inequity. The Government appeals to the material interests of the Whites, and to the very dangers and fears generated by its policies, to ensure the support of the White electorate and remain in power.

481. The international community, however, has adequate means to disabuse the Government of South Africa and its supporters of their short-sighted and dangerous calculations.

482. Foreign trade plays a great role in the economy of the Republic of South Africa which depends largely on the export of a few commodities. The international community can show its determination to end the policies of apartheid by a boycott of these exports. Moreover, as the Special Committee suggested in its second interim report (annex IV), an effective embargo on petroleum and on the means to manufacture arms would have a decisive effect on South Africa.

483. Foreign investments—mainly from a few countries—have contributed greatly to the economic development of the Republic and continue to play a significant role. A freeze on such investments can have a serious effect on the economy of South Africa.

484. The Government of the Republic of South Africa realizes its vulnerability to international action, but has persisted in its course in the belief that effective measures to dissuade it from pursuing its policies of apartheid would not be taken in the near future. The Special Committee considers that South African statements in this connection deserve serious consideration.

485. Spokesmen of the South African Government express confidence that the moral isolation of the Republic of South Africa with respect to its racial policies will not lead to isolation in other fields. They claim that measures recommended by the United Nations will remain ineffective as they will not be implemented by Member States which have the closest relations with the Republic. They note that the Member States which voted for General Assembly resolution 1761 (XVII) accounted for less than one sixth of the foreign trade of the Republic of South Africa, while the Member States opposed to it accounted for nearly two thirds. They claim, moreover, that South Africa's strategic position is so important and South Africa's role in the "cold war" so significant that the Western Powers could not accept and implement effective measures against the Republic of South Africa.

486. The Special Committee reiterates its view that the question of the policies of apartheid of the Government of the Republic of South Africa is not an aspect of the cold war (see paragraph 444). It feels, however, that the small number of States on whose cooperation the Government of the Republic of South Africa counts have a special responsibility to implement effective measures to disabuse that Government and its supporters of its hopes of continuing its policies.

487. In this connection, the Special Committee recalls its recommendation, in the first and second interim reports (annexes III and IV), that a special appeal be addressed to the Governments of (a) the States with traditional relations with South Africa; (b) the small number of States which account for most of the foreign trade of, and foreign investment in, the Republic of South Africa and which are the principal suppliers of arms and equipment to that country; and (c) the colonial powers responsible for the administration of territories neighbouring South Africa.

488. The Special Committee wishes to reiterate and emphasize the importance of effective measures by these States, for, without the cooperation of these States, the practical effect of the sacrifices being made at present by many others towards promoting a solution of the problem would be limited.

489. The Special Committee draws the attention of these States to the negative response of the Government of the Republic of South Africa to all efforts at persuasion by the United Nations and by Member States, and to the appeals of the major non-White organizations in South Africa for effective measures despite the temporary sacrifices which they might entail for the people of South Africa.

490. The Special Committee feels that the geographical position or strategic value of the Republic of South Africa cannot justify policies and actions which tend to permit perpetuation of racial oppression and thereby aggravate international friction and the threat to international peace and security. It notes, moreover, that the policies of the present Government of South Africa have evoked such abhorrence that any recognition of a community of interest with it tends to be regarded by large segments of world public opinion as an encouragement to that Government in its oppressive policies. Countries which claim to have special interests in the area should bear a special responsibility for taking all measures to end the present dangerous situation and ensure the speedy implementation of the decisions of the United Nations.

491. The Special Committee feels that all Member States have an obligation to respect the decisions and recommendations of the General Assembly and the Security Council, to attempt to implement them in good faith and to bring any difficulties of implementation to the attention of the United Nations, if necessary.

492. The Special Committee, however, cannot but express its regret at the actions of certain States which have increased their trade with and investment in, the Republic of South Africa, signed new trade agreements with it, provided new facilities for South African aircraft, or continue to supply military equipment to the Republic of South Africa.

493. The Special Committee feels, moreover, that special attention should be devoted to the attitudes and actions of Member States which administer colonial territories neighbouring the Republic of South Africa.

494. It notes with regret that the Government of Portugal has provided new facilities for South African aircraft and has entered into agreements for greater co-operation with the Government of the Republic of South Africa.

495. The Special Committee has watched with serious anxiety the treatment of South African nationals opposed to the policies of apartheid in the colonial territories administered by the United Kingdom.

496. In the first three months of 1963, forty-six South Africans were arrested in Southern and Northern Rhodesia by the authorities of the Federation of Rhodesia and Nyasaland and handed over to the South African police.

497. On 1 April 1963, Basutoland police arrested eleven persons, at the offices of the Pan-Africanist Congress in Maseru (six were subsequently reported to have been released). Mr. Potlako Leballo was reported to have disappeared mysteriously during the raid.

498. On 23 May, twelve South African refugees were arrested as prohibited immigrants in Lusaka, Northern Rhodesia, by the immigration authorities of the Fed-

eration of Rhodesia and Nyasaland. They were released on 4 June after strong protests by Northern Rhodesia authorities and a successful *habeas corpus* action by one of the prisoners.

499. Sir John Maud, United Kingdom Ambassador to the Republic of South Africa, stated on 15 May 1963 that there could be "no question" of the United Kingdom refusing political asylum to South African refugees in the three High Commission territories of Basutoland, Swaziland and Bechuanaland, but that the United Kingdom was "against the territories being used for fomenting violence in the Republic".

500. But complaints have been made by South African refugees that the authorities in these territories have denied political asylum even within the limits of that policy statement. A number of South African refugees have been declared prohibited immigrants in the High Commission territories—among them Mr. Patrick Duncan, a petitioner before the Special Committee.

501. The Special Committee noted with grave anxiety the reports that Dr. Kenneth Abrahams and three other South African political refugees had been kidnapped in Bechuanaland by South African authorities on 11 August 1963.

502. It has, further, noted with grave anxiety that an aircraft chartered to fly South African political refugees to Tanganyika was destroyed by explosion and fire at the Francistown airport, Bechuanaland, on 29 August. It has noted reports that Bechuanaland authorities suspected sabotage and that the South African Press had hinted that unorthodox methods might be used by the South African Government to deprive the refugees of their sense of security in neighbouring territories.

503. The Special Committee considers it essential that the General Assembly and the Security Council should insist that the colonial powers concerned provide asylum and other facilities to South African refugees and should take no action to assist the Government of the Republic of South Africa in the pursuit of its policies of apartheid.

504. Finally, the Special Committee recalls that, in its two interim reports, it reviewed the rapid expansion of the military and police forces in the Republic of South Africa and noted with grave anxiety that this expansion not only reflects the gravity of the present situation in the country but is likely to have serious international repercussions. It provided information on the main sources of arms (see paragraphs 408-413 and annex IV, appendix II) and recommended that the General Assembly and the Security Council call upon the States concerned to halt forthwith all assistance to the Government of South Africa in strengthening its armed forces. It emphasized the importance of the provision in paragraph 4 (*b*) of

General Assembly resolution 1761 (XVII) requesting Member States to refrain from exporting any arms or ammunition to South Africa.

505. The Special Committee has noted with great satisfaction the provision in the Security Council resolution of 7 August 1963 solemnly calling upon "all States to cease forthwith the sale and shipment of arms, ammunition of all types and military vehicles to South Africa". It has also noted with satisfaction the declaration by the United States of America that the sale of all military equipment to the Government of South Africa would be brought to an end by the end of 1963 (see paragraph 410 and annex V). It has also taken note of the declaration made by a number of other Member States concerning the measures taken by them in this respect. The Special Committee, however, cannot but express its regret that certain main suppliers of arms have not taken requisite action.

506. In connection with the question of arms supplies, the Special Committee wishes to reiterate its conclusion that the provision in paragraph 4 (d) of General Assembly resolution 1761 (XVII) "covers the supply of all material, from government or private sources, which can be used for military purposes or for the suppression of resistance to the policies and practice of apartheid, as well as assistance, direct or indirect, for the manufacture of such material in the Republic of South Africa". It recalls, further, the following observations made by it in paragraphs 22 and 23 of its second interim report (see annex IV):

> ". . . the Special Committee wishes to emphasize that Member States, in taking appropriate measures, should note that there is not merely the danger of a racial conflict within the Republic of South Africa, but that the present situation constitutes a threat to international peace and security. They should refrain from supplying not merely the small arms and ammunition, but any means to increase the mobility of the security forces, as well as material which can be used by the Government of South Africa to perpetuate by force the policies of apartheid.

> "The Special Committee also notes, in this connection, that the Government of the Republic of South Africa has continued to refuse to fulfil its obligations with respect to the mandated Territory of South West Africa."

507. The Special Committee wishes to emphasize that any distinction between equipment for external defence and that for internal security purposes is bound to be illusory and devoid of any practical interest, as the Government of the Republic of South Africa has viewed the two aspects as complementary and regards the defence forces as intended, in the first place, for the maintenance of internal security.

## C. Recommendations

508. In the light of the foregoing observations and conclusions, the Special Committee wishes to submit the following recommendations to the General Assembly and the Security Council for their consideration.

509. First, in view of the non-compliance of the Government of the Republic of South Africa with the provisions of General Assembly resolution 1761 (XVII) and its defiance of the Security Council resolutions of 1 April 1960 (see annex II) and 7 August 1963 (see paragraph 57), the Special Committee feels that the situation should be considered without delay and with particular reference to the obligations of the Republic of South Africa under Article 25 of the Charter.

510. Second, the Special Committee deems it essential that the General Assembly and the Security Council should: (a) take note of the continued deterioration of the situation in the Republic of South Africa, in consequence of the continued imposition of discriminatory and repressive measures by its Government in violation of its obligations under the United Nations Charter, the provisions of the Universal Declaration of Human Rights and the resolutions of the General Assembly and the Security Council; (b) affirm that the policies and actions of the Republic of South Africa are incompatible with membership in the United Nations; (c) declare the determination of the Organization to take all requisite measures provided in the Charter to bring to an end the serious danger to the maintenance of international peace and security; (d) call upon all United Nations organs and agencies and all States to take appropriate steps to dissuade the Republic of South Africa from its present racial policies.

511. Third, the Special Committee deems it essential that all Member States be called upon to take requisite measures speedily to implement the relevant provisions of General Assembly resolution 1761 (XVII) and the Security Council resolution of 7 August 1963. It feels that Member States which have taken effective measures in this respect should be commended, and that an urgent invitation should be addressed to all others to take action and report without delay. It feels, moreover, that the General Assembly and the Security Council should express disapproval at the actions of certain States which have taken measures contrary to the provisions of the resolutions of the General Assembly and the Security Council on the policies of apartheid of the Government of the Republic of South Africa (see paragraphs 472-478 and 492-505).

512. Fourth, the Special Committee feels that the States responsible for the administration of territories adjacent to the Republic of South Africa should be called upon to provide asylum and relief to South African nationals who are obliged to seek refuge because of the policies of apart-

heid and to refrain from any action which may assist the South African authorities in the continued pursuit of their present racial policies (see paragraphs 495-503).

513.    Fifth, in view of the persecution of thousands of South African nationals for their opposition to the policies of apartheid and the serious hardship faced by their families, the Special Committee considers that the international community, for humanitarian reasons, should provide them with relief and other assistance. It recommends that the Secretary-General should be requested, in consultation with the Special Committee, to find ways and means to provide such relief and assistance through appropriate international agencies (see paragraph 451).

514.    Sixth, with regard to the request to the Member States by the General Assembly that they refrain from exporting all arms and ammunition to South Africa, and by the Security Council that they cease forthwith the sale and shipment of arms, ammunition of all types and military vehicles to South Africa, the Special Committee submits the following supplementary recommendations: (*a*) Member States should be requested not to provide any assistance, directly or indirectly in the manufacture of arms, ammunition and military vehicles in South Africa, including the supply of strategic materials, provision of technical assistance, or the granting of licences; (*b*) Member States should be requested to refrain from providing training for South African military personnel; and (*c*) Member States should be requested to refrain from any form of cooperation with South African military and police forces.

515.    Seventh, the Special Committee suggests that the General Assembly and the Security Council give consideration to additional measures, including the following, to dissuade the Government of the Republic of South Africa from its racial policies: (*a*) recommendation to all international agencies to take all necessary steps to deny economic or technical assistance to the Government of the Republic of South Africa, without precluding, however, humanitarian assistance to the victims of the policies of apartheid; (*b*) recommendation to Member States to take steps to prohibit or discourage foreign investments in South Africa and loans to the Government of the Republic of South Africa or to South African companies; (*c*) recommendation to Member States to consider denial of facilities for all ships and aircraft destined to or returning from the Republic of South Africa; (*d*) recommendation to Member States to take measures to prohibit, or at least discourage, emigration of their nationals to the Republic of South Africa, as immigrants are sought by it to reinforce its policies of apartheid; and (*e*) study of means to ensure an effective embargo on the supply of arms and ammunition, as well as petroleum, to the Republic of South Africa, including a blockade if necessary under the aegis of the United Nations.

516.    Finally, the Special Committee feels that Member States should be urged to give maximum publicity to the efforts of the United Nations with respect to this question and take effective steps to discourage and counteract propaganda by the Government of the Republic of South Africa, its agencies and various other bodies which seek to justify and defend its policies.

517.    Considering the extreme gravity of the situation in the Republic of South Africa, and its serious international repercussions, the Special Committee deems it essential that the General Assembly and the Security Council should keep the matter under active consideration in order to take timely and effective measures to ensure the fulfilment of the purposes of the Charter in the Republic of South Africa. The Special Committee feels that they should consider, with no further delay, possible new measures in accordance with the Charter, which provides for stronger political, diplomatic and economic sanctions, suspension of rights and privileges of the Republic of South Africa as a Member State, and expulsion from the United Nations and its specialized agencies. The Special Committee will actively pursue its task of assisting the principal organs in connection with this problem, and to this end invites the continued cooperation of the Member States and specialized agencies, as well as all organizations and individuals devoted to the principles of the Charter.

# Document 30

*Statement by Mr. Per Haekkerup, Minister for Foreign Affairs of Denmark, in the General Assembly*

A/PV.1215, 25 September 1963

. . .

67.    This leads me directly to the question of the policies of apartheid in South Africa which once again weighs heavily on our agenda. The United Nations has by now dealt with this question for a good many years. You may know how deep it has gone to the heart of everybody in Denmark. Numerous manifestations of one kind or another bear witness to the intense preoccupation

of the Danish people with the question of apartheid.

68. The approach of the United Nations to the question of apartheid in South Africa has so far been, and rightly so, that apartheid must be abolished as contrary to the principles of the Charter and to human rights. Recently most of us have felt that if persuasion was not sufficient to induce the South African Government to change its policy, other means would have to be adopted. A most important step in this direction was banning exports of arms to South Africa. Other steps will undoubtedly have to follow.

69. The Danish Government is in agreement with this policy. I repeat: Denmark supports this line of action and feels that it should be pursued and pressure gradually increased. What we desire is not mere words or recommendations of a general nature, but measures the effects of which have been carefully studied beforehand and discussed thoroughly with a view to providing sufficient support from Member States. We recognize that the African countries have special interests in this matter, interests which naturally lead them to advocate an unconditional policy of sanctions. This special position also carries special responsibilities. It might be useful to initiate within a small group a dialogue between representatives of these specially interested countries and the major commercial partners of South Africa, which eventually will have to carry the main burden of such a policy of sanctions.

70. I repeat once again that we think such a policy of pressure necessary and justified. I must, however, ask myself and ask you a question which many Members of the Assembly have certainly for some time been asking themselves quietly. That crucial question is this: Is that limited line of action through pressure sufficient in itself to bring about peaceful developments towards a solution of all aspects of the South African question? I am very much afraid that that is not so. I am very much afraid that a policy of sanctions alone—I repeat alone—may well defeat its own ends, aggravate the present state of tension in the area and bring the possibility of tragic events closer.

71. Apartheid today causes misery to millions of people. Its abolition will, however, pose other problems. It is the duty of the United Nations to show the way forward in solving these problems in accordance with the basic principles of the Charter. We must face the fact that the great majority of the European population in South Africa wrongly assume that abandonment of White domination means abandonment of their own existence. It is our duty to prove to them that that is not so. It is our duty to demonstrate that there is an alternative to catastrophe and that the only way towards this alternative is through the abolition of apartheid. It is our duty to give all groups in South Africa hope and confidence that, after abolition of those inhuman and abhorrent principles by which the Republic of South Africa is now guided, there will be a happy and prosperous future for everybody who has his roots and wishes to continue his life in South Africa.

72. In other words, if the approach of the United Nations has so far followed a single line, we feel that it has now become necessary for the Assembly to formulate a supplementary policy, to make clear to the world what we would like should take the place of the present set-up—a truly democratic, multiracial society of free men, with equal rights for all individuals, irrespective of race.

73. Changing a society so deeply rooted in apartheid and dominated by a minority into such a free democratic, multiracial society may well prove to be a task which cannot be solved by the people of South Africa alone. I feel convinced that in such a process of development the United Nations will have to play a major role if we are to avoid disaster. We must consider how, if necessary, we can, in a transitional period, contribute to the maintenance of law and order and the protection of the life and civil rights of all individuals. We must likewise consider how the United Nations can best assist South Africa in laying the foundation of its new society.

74. In our opinion it is high time for the Assembly to give thought to the positive policy to be pursued in South Africa and to the role which the United Nations should play in coming developments. Careful studies to this end should be initiated now. If not, we may one day be taken by surprise and have reason to regret it.
. . .

---

# Document 31

*Statement by Dr. Hermod Lanning, representative of Denmark, at a meeting of the Special Political Committee*

A/SPC/82, 9 October 1963

. . .
In our search for the basis of a new modern society in South Africa to replace apartheid, political and humanitarian ideals have by necessity led us to the concept of a

truly democratic, multiracial society with equal rights for all individuals irrespective of colour and race. There have been many signs, and we have felt most encouraged by them, that this concept is shared by the African States and indeed by the great majority of the South African population.

I want, however, to take this opportunity to make it quite clear what we mean by the word "multiracial": By that we simply mean a society in which men and women of two or several races live together. It is exactly in that sense that the word is used in General Assembly resolution 616 B which was adopted by the General Assembly and which, by the way, was based on a Nordic initiative. That resolution, which is mentioned in paragraph 119 of the report of the Special Committee, declares, and I quote: "that in a multiracial society harmony and respect for human rights and freedoms and the peaceful development of a unified community are best assured when patterns of legislation and practice are directed towards ensuring equality before the law of all persons regardless of race, creed or colour". I hope that this makes it quite clear that in using the word "multiracial" we are not implying the concept of special protection for racial minorities. Any true democracy does by definition offer protection to minorities. But in our view it would be contrary to the very concept of multiracialism to give special protection to minorities just on the basis of race.

. . .

# Document 32

*General Assembly resolution: Release of political prisoners in South Africa*

A/RES/1881 (XVIII), 11 October 1963

*The General Assembly,*

. . .

*Considering* reports to the effect that the Government of South Africa is arranging the trial of a large number of political prisoners under arbitrary laws prescribing the death sentence,

*Considering* that such a trial will inevitably lead to a further deterioration of the already explosive situation in South Africa, thereby further disturbing international peace and security,

1. *Condemns* the Government of the Republic of South Africa for its failure to comply with the repeated resolutions of the General Assembly and of the Security Council calling for an end to the repression of persons opposing apartheid;

2. *Requests* the Government of South Africa to abandon the arbitrary trial now in progress and forthwith to grant unconditional release to all political prisoners and to all persons imprisoned, interned or subjected to other restrictions for having opposed the policy of apartheid;

3. *Requests* all Member States to make all necessary efforts to induce the Government of South Africa to ensure that the provisions of paragraph 2 above are put into effect immediately;

. . .

# Document 33

*Statement by Mr. Diallo Telli (Guinea), Chairman of the Special Committee on the Policies of Apartheid of the Government of the Republic of South Africa, at the plenary meeting of the General Assembly on a resolution concerning the trial of Mr. Nelson Mandela and others*

A/PV.1238, 11 October 1963

. . .

9. The Pretoria Government yesterday began the trial of eleven South African leaders, well known for their opposition to apartheid, on a trumped-up charge of sabotage which arbitrarily carries the death penalty.

10. The South African Minister of Justice had already announced that 165 prisoners would be charged with acts of sabotage and that inquiries were in progress in connection with similar charges against a further eighty-five prisoners.

11. The fact is that there are at this moment over 5,000 political prisoners in South African gaols and that the Government is constantly carrying out wholesale arrests of those who oppose its policy of racial discrimination. Over 300 leaders, well known for their struggle against apartheid, have now been taken into custody, without being brought before a court, under the recent law on imprisonment without trial.

12. These political prisoners are subjected to the most inhumane conditions: a number of them have been tortured, and some recently died in prison.

13. The South African Government's decision to proceed with this mass trial is a clear and direct challenge to the United Nations, and more particularly to the Security Council which on 7 August 1963 expressly called upon the Government of South Africa to liberate all political prisoners and all persons imprisoned, interned or subjected to other restrictions for having opposed apartheid.

14. The aim and the consequence of the new wave of repression are to make the possibility of a peaceful settlement more and more remote, to enhance hostility among the racial groups and to precipitate a violent conflict in which all the country's inhabitants without distinction, whether White or non-White, will suffer. These consequences, it must be pointed out, will necessarily affect peace in Africa and throughout the world.

. . .

16. The defendants now on trial include the most influential leaders of the African, Asian and European communities, who are fighting side by side for racial harmony and who are certainly the ones whom the majority of the people will call upon tomorrow to govern the country.

17. It is clear that any action placing in jeopardy the life of these revered leaders in the South African people's rightful struggle will create an irreparable situation that may destroy once and for all any chance for the various ethnic groups in South Africa to live in harmony under a regime of freedom, justice and democracy.

18. In the circumstances, the commission of the major crimes now in preparation must be prevented at all costs. On moral, political and humanitarian grounds the General Assembly should discharge its august duty in the manifest interest of all those who, on any terms whatsoever, live in South Africa, by unanimously adopting the draft resolution recommended to it by the Special Political Committee.

19. The General Assembly could thus save the lives of South Africa's best sons who alone are capable of promoting the conditions of racial harmony that the United Nations has been urging in vain for the past eighteen years.

20. The trial staged before the Supreme Court at Johannesburg is beyond all question a further manifestation of the attitude of contemptuous defiance constantly shown by the South African leaders towards the United Nations in general and towards all the repeated decisions of the Security Council and General Assembly in particular.

21. But that is not all. To make their defiance all the sharper, the *de facto* authorities at Pretoria have cynically timed the start of the scandalous trial at Johannesburg to coincide with the opening of our debates on the policy of apartheid, so as to make quite clear how little they think of the United Nations. The General Assembly cannot remain indifferent to such contempt, insolence and disrespect. If we do not react in a fitting manner, history will irrevocably convict us of failure to discharge our most sacred obligations.

22. In the face of this situation the United Nations must react vigorously and resolutely to save the last chance of finding a peaceful solution and of preserving the security and interests of the White minority in South Africa. It is the only way to prevent a fresh triumph for the hatred fanned by the representatives of the racist minority who solemnly proclaim themselves the sworn enemies of the United Nations.

23. A great crime—perhaps the greatest yet ascribable to the supporters of apartheid—is being openly prepared in South Africa: a crime which, if carried through, could spark the powder keg and thus touch off the much-feared racial conflict. Since the historic Addis Ababa Conference it has been common knowledge that, in that tragic event, all the African States and all the African peoples would stand beside their oppressed brothers of South Africa.

24. As we have already said, the best sons of South Africa are today implicated in this bogus trial, staged under arbitrary legislation, which deprives the accused of any possibility of legal defence and exposes them, without protection or safeguard, to the bloodthirsty executioners who control the country.

25. The accused, we repeat, represent the last chance for stability, peace and harmony in South Africa. Their names are: Nelson Mandela, a lawyer and acknowledged leader of the African National Congress, known to the Heads of most independent African States as one of the great leaders in the struggle for racial equality in South Africa; Walter Sisulu, another active leader of the African National Congress, of which he was Secretary-General; Govan Mbeki, another leader of the Congress and of the Transkei; and Ahmed Mohamed Kathrada, a leader of the Indian community who was convicted at the age of seventeen at the time of the resistance movement in 1946.

26. Whites have not been overlooked on the list. Lionel Bernstein; Bob Hepple; James Cantor, a lawyer; Dennis Goldberg, an engineer; and many others, are also implicated. Faithful to the memory of their friends who have died in prison in many cases beside them, after enduring unspeakable suffering—which the United Na-

tions should investigate diligently, for otherwise the Africans will set about doing so tomorrow—the alert and steadfast leaders of South Africa accept any and every sacrifice in order not to abandon the sacred struggle. How can we fail to salute their courage, their radiant vision of a future of understanding, reconciliation and friendship for which they are preparing, by their own suffering, for the benefit of all ethnic groups living on South African soil?

27. These men have had recourse to all peaceful means to put an end to racial oppression, but in vain; it is worth recalling in this connection that South Africa was for a long time the cradle of non-violence. It was there that Gandhi began his heroic struggle, over fifty years ago. But let this be clearly remembered: Gandhi himself declared that it was better to resort to violence than to submit in cowardly fashion to the oppressors. The African peoples and Governments consider that the criminals are not those who fight for their right to justice and equality but the oppressors who precipitate violence, repression and injustice.

. . .

32. Nelson Mandela, the great South African leader known the world over for his courage and lucidity, very eloquently summed up the philosophy and basic tenets of African nationalism during his last trial at Johannesburg, in which he was arbitrarily sentenced to imprisonment for five years at forced labour. The declaration of faith of Nelson Mandela, who is today the leading defendant in the infamous new trial, has become a veritable breviary for all South African nationalists. Listen to this extract from his celebrated address to the court—a moving document from beginning to end:

"I hate the practice of race discrimination and in my hatred I am sustained by the fact that the overwhelming majority of mankind hates it equally. I hate the systematic inculcation of children with colour prejudice, and I am sustained in that hatred by the fact that the overwhelming majority of mankind ... are with me in that. I hate racial arrogance which decrees that the good things of life shall be retained as the exclusive right of a minority of the population, and which reduces the majority of the population to a position of subservience and inferiority and maintains them as voteless chattels to work where they are told and behave as they are told by the ruling minority. . .

"Nothing that this Court can do to me will change in any way that hatred in me, which can only be removed by the removal of the injustice and the inhumanity which I have sought to remove from the political, social and economic life of this country.

"Whatever sentence [the Court] sees fit to impose upon me . . . may it rest assured that when my sentence has been completed I will still be moved . . . by [my conscience]; I will still be moved by my dislike of the race discrimination against my people . . . to take up again . . . the struggle for the removal of those injustices until they are finally abolished."

He added in conclusion:

"I have done my duty to my people and to Africa. I have no doubt that posterity will pronounce that I was innocent and that the criminals . . . are the members of the Verwoerd Government."

33. Are we to let a man of such stature—a leader so deeply conscious of his historic mission in the service of his country, his people and mankind—die for nothing, unjustly struck down through our inaction? We hope our Assembly will unanimously answer "No".

34. All the representatives of Africa and Asia have taken the initiative in what is now presented for our consideration. In their name, we address to all members of the Assembly a final friendly and trustful appeal that the last lingering hesitations should be overcome and that the General Assembly of the United Nations, confronted with this grave situation with its incalculable moral, political and human implications, should signify by its unanimous vote its will for a peaceful settlement of the explosive situation that exists in South Africa today.

# Document 34

*Security Council resolution: Question relating to the policies of apartheid of the Government of the Republic of South Africa*

S/RES/182 (1963), 4 December 1963

*The Security Council,*

. . .

*Being strengthened* in its conviction that the situation in South Africa is seriously disturbing international peace and security, and strongly deprecating the policies of the Government of South Africa in its perpetuation of racial discrimination as being inconsistent with the principles contained in the Charter of the United Nations and with its obligations as a Member of the United Nations,

*Recognizing* the need to eliminate discrimination in regard to basic human rights and fundamental freedoms for all individuals within the territory of the Republic of South Africa without distinction as to race, sex, language or religion,

*Expressing the firm conviction* that the policies of apartheid and racial discrimination as practised by the Government of the Republic of South Africa are abhorrent to the conscience of mankind and that therefore a positive alternative to these policies must be found through peaceful means,

1. *Appeals* to all States to comply with the provisions of Security Council resolution 181 (1963) of 7 August 1963;

2. *Urgently requests* the Government of the Republic of South Africa to cease forthwith its continued imposition of discriminatory and repressive measures which are contrary to the principles and purposes of the Charter and which are in violation of its obligations as a Member of the United Nations and of the provisions of the Universal Declaration of Human Rights;

3. *Condemns* the non-compliance by the Government of the Republic of South Africa with the appeals contained in the above-mentioned resolutions of the General Assembly and the Security Council;

4. *Again calls upon* the Government of the Republic of South Africa to liberate all persons imprisoned, interned or subjected to other restrictions for having opposed the policy of apartheid;

5. *Solemnly calls upon* all States to cease forthwith the sale and shipment of equipment and materials for the manufacture and maintenance of arms and ammunition in South Africa;

6. *Requests* the Secretary-General to establish under his direction and reporting to him a small group of recognized experts to examine methods of resolving the present situation in South Africa through full, peaceful and orderly application of human rights and fundamental freedoms to all inhabitants of the territory as a whole, regardless of race, colour or creed, and to consider what part the United Nations might play in the achievement of that end;

7. *Invites* the Government of the Republic of South Africa to avail itself of the assistance of this group in order to bring about such peaceful and orderly transformation;

. . .

# Document 35

*General Assembly resolution: The policies of apartheid of the Government of the Republic of South Africa*

A/RES/1978 B (XVIII), 16 December 1963

*The General Assembly,*

*Taking note* of the report of the Special Committee on the Policies of Apartheid of the Government of the Republic of South Africa, in which the Committee drew attention to the serious hardship faced by the families of persons persecuted by the Government of South Africa for their opposition to the policies of apartheid, and recommended that the international community, for humanitarian reasons, provide them with relief and other assistance,

*Considering* that such assistance is consonant with the purposes and principles of the United Nations,

*Noting* that those families continue to suffer serious hardship,

1. *Requests* the Secretary-General to seek ways and means of providing relief and assistance, through the appropriate international agencies, to the families of all persons persecuted by the Government of the Republic of South Africa for their opposition to the policies of apartheid;

2. *Invites* Member States and organizations to contribute generously to such relief and assistance;

. . .

# Document 36

*Letter dated 9 March 1964 from Chief Albert J. Luthuli,*
*President-General of the African National Congress, to*
*Secretary-General U Thant*

Not issued as a United Nations document

I address myself to you on an impending crisis in South Africa. The United Nations has, through the years, made valiant efforts to stave off disastrous race war in South Africa; to put pressures on the South African Government to give rights to the African and other non-White people of our country in accordance with the universally accepted principles of human dignity and justice. We are most deeply appreciative of the efforts made by the nations of the world, through your world organization, to counter and defeat the forces of racialism.

You no doubt know that my organization, the African National Congress, for close on half a century, and until it was declared unlawful, sought to achieve its objectives by strictly peaceful and non-violent methods, ranging from representations and protests made to the Government and its representatives in the early years, to mass demonstrations and defiance campaigns and strikes in the later years.

All these endeavours were to no avail. In fact, during the past half century oppression and racial discrimination have increased to such an extent that no one could at this juncture be morally blamed for resorting to violent methods in order to achieve racial equality and freedom from oppression.

I write to you most urgently today to stress that whatever hope there still remains for a negotiated and peaceful settlement of the South African crisis, will be lost, possibly for all time, if the United Nations does not act promptly and with firmness on the vital matter which has moved me to make this urgent appeal.

You will be aware that during this last year our movement has been subjected to relentless persecution. Our organization has been harried without respite. Our members have been arrested in huge numbers in every corner of the country. If not held on serious political charges, they have been detained under the barbaric "90 Day" detention law under which men and women and youths have been confined indefinitely, in solitary confinement, and physically tortured in attempts to extort confessions and false evidence from them. In numerous trials that took place in various courts throughout the country, some were sentenced to death and others to long terms of imprisonment.

You will also be aware that the last months of the year saw the bringing to trial of nine of the country's foremost liberation leaders, in the so-called Rivonia trial in which the leaders are charged with allegedly plotting a war of liberation against the government. The nine include Nelson Mandela, who was arrested shortly after his return from a tour of independent African States in 1962, and who was taken from his prison cell, where he was serving a five-year prison sentence, for leading the 1961 general strike of the African people and leaving South Africa without a passport. Also on trial is Walter Sisulu, formerly Secretary-General of the African National Congress, who was arrested while working underground in the freedom struggle.

The Rivonia trial, it is estimated, will continue for perhaps a further four to six weeks from the time of writing. It could be completed earlier. *There is the grave danger that all or some of the nine leaders on trial will receive the death sentence.* Such an outcome would be an African tragedy. It would be judicial murder of some of the most outstanding leaders on the African continent. It would have disastrous results for any prospects of a peaceful settlement of the South African situation and could set in motion a chain of actions and counter-actions which would be tragic for everyone in South Africa as they would be difficult to contain.

I address myself to you with the utmost urgency to urge that you use your good offices to avert the tragic crisis threatening South Africa. It is of the utmost importance that the United Nations Expert Group on South Africa bring its work to a rapid conclusion and leave the way open for measures to be adopted to ensure that a fast worsening race situation here does not explode into open violence. It is above all imperative that United Nations action be devised to compel compliance with UN resolutions and in particular to save the lives of the nine Rivonia trial leaders; for with them are arraigned, in the dock, all hopes of a peaceful settlement of the crisis in our country.

A. J. LUTHULI
President-General

# Document 37

*Report of the Group of Experts established in pursuance of Security Council resolution 182 (1963)*

S/5658, 20 April 1964

. . .

8. We feel that the growing gravity of the situation increases the need to point the way to an alternative course which could provide an escape from utterly calamitous consequences, and it is accordingly with a sense of critical urgency that we now submit our recommendations.

We wish to state at once a primary principle of first importance.

The future of South Africa should be settled by the people of South Africa—all the people of South Africa—in free discussion. There can be no settlement and no peace while the great majority of the people are denied the fundamental freedom to participate in decisions on the future of their country. We are convinced that a continuation of the present position including a denial of just representation must lead to violent conflict and tragedy for all the people of South Africa. We wish, therefore, to emphasize the first and basic principle that all the people of South Africa should be brought into consultation and should thus be enabled to decide the future of their country at the national level.

In order to give effect to this essential principle, we consider that all efforts should be directed to the establishment of a National Convention fully representative of the whole population. Such a representative National Convention would consider the views and proposals of all those participating and set a new course for the future.

We believe that the mounting condemnation by world opinion and the growing insistence on positive action should now be directed to the achievement of this purpose. It is only on the road of free and democratic consultation and cooperation and conciliation that a way can be found towards a peaceful and constructive settlement. Only thus can all people of South Africa be saved from catastrophe and the world from a conflagration of incalculable consequences.

. . .

## II. Principal Factors in the Present Situation

10. We wish to draw special attention to two main factors in the present situation. On one side is the mounting international condemnation of the racial policy of the South African Government and the growing determination of the African States, in particular, to take positive action against South African racial discrimination and domination. On the other side is the increased persistence and military preparation of the South African Government, coupled with repressive action and legislation which leave many South Africans with the conviction that they have no means of resistance other than violence. These forces are set on a collision course. They approach the crash at accelerating pace. As the explosion grows nearer the need to endeavour to prevent it becomes ever more urgent.

. . .

### D. *International Dangers*

31. These forces of conflict cannot be disregarded or minimized. Only when the extent of the danger is fully realized is there any hope that action sufficiently drastic will be taken to prevent it. Violence and counter-violence in South Africa are only the local aspects of a much wider danger. The coming collision must involve the whole of Africa and indeed the world beyond. No African nation can remain aloof. Moreover a race conflict starting in South Africa must affect race relations elsewhere in the world, and also, in its international repercussions, create a world danger of the first magnitude.

32. As the Secretary-General warned in addressing the Algerian House of Assembly on 3 February 1964:

> "There is the clear prospect that racial conflict, if we cannot curb and finally, eliminate it, will grow into a destructive monster compared to which the religious or ideological conflicts of the past and present will seem like small family quarrels. Such a conflict will eat away the possibilities for good of all that mankind has hitherto achieved and reduce men to the lowest and most bestial level of intolerance and hatred. This for, the sake of all our children, whatever their race and colour, must not be permitted to happen."

## III. The Need for a National Convention

33. It is against this background of mounting crisis and threatening conflict that we wish to state the case for conciliation and consultation, and to urge the need for an early National Convention.

34. The conception of a National Convention is far from novel in South Africa. The Union itself had its origin in the National Conventions of 1908 and 1909 (from which, however, all but White South Africans were

excluded). But the constitution which emerged from these conventions has been wholly unacceptable to the great bulk of the population, and for long past a principal objective of the national movement amongst the majority of South Africans has been a fully representative National Convention as the doorway to democracy. The unenfranchised people of South Africa, throughout long years of subjection, claimed the right to be consulted. They campaigned not for revolution but for representation. Such has been the moderation of the movement.

35. Even in December 1960, after the massacres at Sharpeville and Langa and the imprisonment of thousands of persons had greatly heightened tension and bitterness, thirty-six prominent African leaders, meeting in Johannesburg, called for the establishment of a non-racial democracy through a National Convention representing all the people of South Africa.

36. This meeting was followed by the All-In African Conference at Pietermaritzburg on 25-26 March 1961 attended by 1,400 delegates, including many from rural areas. While denouncing the establishment of a republic by decision of the White voters alone, this Conference unanimously demanded that "a National Convention of elected representatives of all adult men and women on an equal basis—irrespective of race, colour, creed or other limitations—be called not later than May 31, 1961".

37. This call for a National Convention was supported not only by the Indian and Coloured Congresses, but also by leaders of the Progressive and Liberal parties, and by other organizations and a number of persons prominent in academic, religious and public life.

38. All these pleas were rejected. The Government, in disregard of all attempts to achieve consultation, persisted in its policies; the non-White majority was left thereby with no constitutional means of seeking freedom and justice.

39. The conclusion might have been that when consultation and representation had been so flatly rejected there was no hope for the future. But we believe that the dangers are so great that there may yet be a desire, and consequently there may still be time, to avoid a vast and bloody collision. We are convinced that the way to do so, indeed we believe the only way, is to turn to the means of consultation for which the movement for emancipation has struggled so patiently and persistently for so long.

40. The question of the form and composition of a National Convention is open for discussion: it is a question which should be for South Africans to decide. There are many different processes and patterns which might be adopted. Once a Convention has set the general course to be followed and made a new start in constructive cooperation, it might decide to create a Constituent Assembly charged with the task of drawing up a detailed constitution, thus opening the way to the election of a representative Parliament. For a Constituent Assembly elections might well be required, perhaps undertaken with United Nations assistance and supervision.

41. But these are questions which should be considered and settled by the National Convention. The first and vital step is to start discussions on the formation of an agenda for the Convention.

42. Accordingly we make the specific recommendation that the South African Government should be invited at once to send its representatives to the United Nations to carry out discussions to that end. The United Nations on its part should, we propose, appoint a special body to undertake these discussions, and this special body would bring into consultation representatives of the opposition and leaders of the unenfranchised majority to ensure that the composition and agenda of the Convention are satisfactory to all concerned.

43. We do not wish to suggest stipulations and prior conditions. Nothing should be done to prejudice or delay the discussions we propose.

44. There is, however, one prerequisite which is essential if the discussions are to proceed and if the Convention is to be successful. The Convention must be fully representative, and it cannot be so unless all representative leaders can freely participate. For this purpose an amnesty for all opponents to apartheid, whether they are under trial or in prison or under restriction or in exile, is essential and we add our urgent appeal to those already made by the General Assembly and the Security Council that an immediate amnesty should be declared.

45. The amnesty for political prisoners would enable the National Convention to be fully representative. That is of great importance. But even more important for the future is the new spirit which the amnesty could create. Fear and bitterness could be set aside. The amnesty could mark a new start. Violence and capital punishment would in effect be renounced, and a new confidence created that the aims of "human rights and fundamental freedoms" will in fact be attainable. So would the situation be transformed, and all would enter the Convention in a spirit of reconciliation and genuine cooperation.

. . .

## V. The Role of the United Nations

80. In accordance with the Security Council resolution of 4 December 1963, setting out our terms of reference, we were required to consider what part the United Nations might play "in resolving the present situation in South Africa through full, peaceful and orderly application of human rights and fundamental freedoms".

81. We are limiting our comments to the early stages of the "peaceful and orderly" transformation; we are confident that when the transformation is started and a fully representative system of government is introduced a wide range of international assistance can be readily made available at the request of the Government of South Africa.

82. In the immediate task of initiating the transformation, how can the United Nations assist a new effort of constructive cooperation, and how, more particularly, can United Nations action facilitate the new start to be made through a National Convention?

83. We have already proposed that the United Nations should initiate action by inviting the South African Government to send representatives to the United Nations to carry out discussions on the formation of and the agenda for a National Convention, and that a special body should be appointed for these discussions. In these discussions the good offices of the United Nations could assist in several ways, and at the Convention itself the United Nations could, if so requested, provide expert advice on constitutional, economic and social problems.

84. At a later stage the United Nations could help in administrative reorganization and in particular could help to meet any request for the organization and supervision of elections. If the necessity should arise, the United Nations could also, as suggested by the Danish Foreign Minister in his speech to the General Assembly on 25 September 1963 "contribute to the maintenance of law and order and the protection of life and civil rights" and thus both allay fears and secure confidence.

85. There is one important task which could be put in hand by the United Nations and its specialized agencies at once. This would be in the vital field of education and training. The need for very large numbers of non-Whites to be qualified for the professions and for the civil service and for teaching is acute now. It will become quickly far greater. We consequently recommend that a United Nations South African Education and Training Programme should be prepared in consultation with the United Nations specialized agencies, the first purpose being to plan educational and training scholarship schemes and then to supervise and administer these schemes. UNESCO might accept responsibility for the project in cooperation with other specialized agencies (in particular the ILO), or it might be considered preferable to set up new and separate machinery for the administration of the programme including the control of funds provided by contributing nations and dealings with students and colleges and training centres participating in the programme. Useful experience in planning such assistance for South African students can be gained from the training schemes initiated by Scandinavian Governments.

86. Once preliminary plans have been drawn up we suggest that the United Nations should call on all Member States to make financial contributions to this programme for training abroad of a large number of South African lawyers, engineers, agronomists, public administrators, teachers at all levels and skilled workers, as well as training in such fields as labour education and business and industrial management. Much of the education and training programme could be undertaken in other African States. The purpose will be to enable as many South Africans as possible to play a full part as quickly as possible in the political, economic and social advance of their country.

87. This is a task to which the Member States can contribute and in which the specialized agencies can participate. It also offers a wider opportunity for concerted action by international organizations and other foundations whether associated with the United Nations or not. Each in its own field can play a part in helping South Africans who have been deprived of their rights and denied opportunities of education and professional, vocational and scientific training. Thus governments, specialized agencies of the United Nations, universities and training colleges and public and private organizations throughout the world can come together to assist in bringing influence to bear on the South African Government by positive action. An international effort of this constructive kind will at the same time illustrate international concern, show the general desire to give immediate practical assistance and give new hope to people who want to see some immediate evidence of a new start.

88. This would be a practical means of giving expression to world opinion, and we reaffirm our conviction that only by concerted international pressure can the new start be made. Every country and every organization and every individual who realizes the suffering which the present situation causes and the dangers which now threaten has an opportunity and an obligation to participate in that pressure. Nations can increase diplomatic pressure; churches can do more to make their views known and felt. Organizations and groups of many kinds, both international and national, can exert their influence in the closing circle of world opinion.

89. We emphasize the special importance of world opinion. Many countries, particularly African countries, are directly identifying themselves with the cause of the oppressed people of South Africa, but there is a wider international concern. The conscience of the world has been stirred, and there is a recognition in world opinion generally that the South African problem is unique, demanding exceptional treatment. There is an international crisis of conscience; it arises from the fact that in South Africa there is a government professing to speak in the

name of Christianity and the "European race" which is the only government in the world which chooses as its guiding policy not a striving to attain justice, equality and safeguards for human rights, but a determination to preserve privileges, defend discrimination and extend domination to such a degree that it amounts to the organization of a society on principles of slavery. In South Africa the denial of human rights and fundamental freedoms is openly pursued as an avowed policy. There are many in the Christian churches and amongst those who can claim to speak for European civilization who can be expected to feel an exceptional responsibility in regard to developments in South Africa. Their influence in many ways and through many channels might be more effectively deployed.

90.   There is another major international interest involved. That is the interest of commerce, industry and banking, often acting through great business concerns and organized on an international basis, which draws high profits and special benefits from investments in and trade with South Africa. They too should feel an exceptional responsibility, for it is largely from the cheap labour maintained by the policies of apartheid that their profits derive. These business interests and financial houses together with Chambers of Commerce and industrial trading concerns and associations could exercise effective influence on the South African Government, and specially might make a constructive contribution by demanding and putting into effect a "fair employment policy".

91.   The situation can also be influenced by voluntary action undertaken by trade unions and other such cooperative groups in many countries. The protests of these groups have occasionally been expressed in the form of a boycott of South African goods. Though the direct economic results of such boycotts have been limited, their psychological effect is valuable.

92.   While we emphasize the great and growing importance of international opinion, and while we recognize too that diplomatic pressure should be consistently maintained and increased, we also recognize that in the sphere of pressure for achieving a new start in South Africa in consultation and cooperation the United Nations itself should have a vital and central role of initiative and leadership.

93.   We have consequently studied what has been said and written in the records of United Nations discussions and elsewhere about various forms of strategic and economic pressure.

. . .

103.   We do not propose in this report to pursue a discussion on the economic and strategic aspects of sanctions, but we wish to record certain general conclusions which arise from our study of this problem.

104.   As to the argument that sanctions should not be imposed because they would harm the non-White population of South Africa, it should be noted that the African leaders have vigorously rejected any such contention. As Oliver Tambo of the African National Congress said when he was making his statement in the United Nations on 29 October 1963:

"This is a type of pity and paternalism which hurts us even more than sanctions would hurt us."

105.   It is true that sanctions would cause hardship to all sections of the population, particularly if they had to be long maintained, but for the supporters of apartheid to use this argument to oppose sanctions would lay them open to a charge of hypocrisy.

106.   Secondly, it is clear that if sanctions are to be effective they must be put into effect with the cooperation of South Africa's principal trading partners, particularly the United Kingdom and the United States.

107.   Thirdly, as South Africa is specially dependent on imports of petroleum and rubber there is a case for a ban on exporting these products to South Africa, on the ground that an embargo on these supplies could be more easily and quickly decided and enforced than a general ban on all imports into South Africa. The application of economic sanctions even if limited to petroleum (and possibly rubber) might act as a sufficient warning and deterrent.

108.   On the other hand, we recognize the force of the argument that any concerted plan for sanctions would be better directed not to one or two commodities but to all; that piecemeal and progressive application of sanctions might defeat its purpose and lead to a hardening of South Africa's determination to resist pressure from the outside world, whereas the object is of course to achieve a change in South African policy.

109.   Fourthly, the tests to be applied in deciding these questions are the tests of speedy decision, full cooperation and effective implementation, the overriding purpose being to achieve a rapid transformation with the minimum of suffering and dislocation.

110.   With these considerations in view we recommend that use should be made of the interval before a final reply is required from the South African Government on the proposal for a National Convention to enable an expert examination to be made of the economic and strategic aspects of sanctions. There seems to us to be urgent need for a further practical and technical study of the "logistics" of sanctions by experts in the economic and strategic field, particularly in international trade and transport.

111.   It is obviously of great importance to keep constantly in mind the purpose of sanctions. That purpose is not to cripple the South African economy, but to save it. If the decision to impose sanctions is universal then the threat of

sanctions will be compelling. The period of imposition will be reduced thus lessening hardship, and indeed if the threat is universal and complete the actual imposition of sanctions might in fact become unnecessary.

112. Our conclusion is that it can only be by United Nations action, in the form of a unanimous decision of the Security Council, that the weapon of sanctions can be rapidly effective. Only if action is agreed and complete can the threat of sanctions achieve its purpose. Only by this drastic means can material loss and trade dislocation and hardship to many innocent people both in South Africa and elsewhere be avoided.

## VI. Recommendations for Action by the Security Council

113. Our conclusion is that all efforts should be urgently directed to the formation of a National Convention fully representative of all the people of South Africa, and we therefore urge that, as a first step, our recommendation for such a Convention should be endorsed by the Security Council.

114. We propose that, at the same time, support be given to our recommendation in regard to the establishment of a United Nations South African Education and Training Programme.

115. We further propose that these decisions be referred to the South African Government, with an invitation to send its representatives to take part in discussions under the auspices of the United Nations on the formation of the National Convention.

116. We emphasize the need for a renewed and urgent appeal for an immediate amnesty for opponents of apartheid.

117. We recommend that the Security Council should fix an early date by which a reply to the invitation would be required from the South African Government.

118. We recommend, moreover, that the Security Council should invite all concerned to communicate their views on the agenda for the Convention before the date for the reply of the South African Government.

119. Such an invitation should be addressed to all representative groups including political parties, Congresses at present banned under the Unlawful Organizations Act, and other South African organizations such as the Churches, Universities, Trade Unions, Associations of Employers, Chambers of Commerce, Bar Associations, Institutes of Race Relations, the Press and all other representative groups.

120. We recommend that the interval pending the reply of the South African Government should be utilized by the Security Council for the urgent examination of the logistics of sanctions which we have recommended in paragraph 110 above.

121. The Security Council in December 1963 ex-pressed its strong conviction that "the situation in South Africa is seriously disturbing international peace and security". This situation has deteriorated further due to the actions of the South African Government. If no satisfactory reply is received from the South African Government by the stipulated date, the Security Council, in our view, would be left with no effective peaceful means for assisting to resolve the situation, except to apply economic sanctions. Consequently, we recommend that the Security Council should then take the decision to apply economic sanctions in the light of the result of the examination recommended in paragraphs 110 and 120 above.

## VII. Conclusion

122. Some may think that the time is past when there is any hope of avoiding the collision which is now approaching, and that the recent declarations and actions of the South African Government rule out any possibility of negotiation. Certainly time is short, and the dangers grow rapidly nearer and greater.

123. Nevertheless, there is some ground for hope that the point of no return has not yet been reached and that fruitful dialogue may yet take place among the different sections of the South African population.

124. Chief amongst the encouraging factors is the insistence on constitutional measures and methods advocated over many years by the parties and organizations opposing apartheid. Their leaders have displayed outstanding political responsibility and have throughout emphasized that all South Africans of whatever race should enjoy equal rights.

125. Chief Luthuli, in his Nobel lecture delivered in December 1961, made his famous declaration:

"The true patriots of South Africa, for whom I speak, will be satisfied with nothing less than the full democratic rights. In government, we will not be satisfied with anything less than direct individual adult suffrage and the right to stand for and be elected to all organs of government. In economic matters, we will be satisfied with nothing less than equality of opportunity in every sphere, and the enjoyment by all of those heritages which form the resources of the country which up to now have been appropriated on a racial 'White only' basis. In culture, we will be satisfied with nothing less than the opening of all doors of learning to non-segregatory institutions on the sole criterion of ability. In the social sphere, we will be satisfied with nothing less than the abolition of all racial bars. *We do not demand these things for people of African descent alone. We demand them for all South Africans, White and Black.*"

126. At the Conference at which the Pan-Africanist Congress was established in 1959, Robert Sobukwe said that everybody who owes his only loyalty to Africa should be regarded as an African; and that there is only one race, the human race.

127. Nelson Mandela of the African National Congress when on trial in 1962 before being sentenced to five years imprisonment told the court:

"I am no racialist, and I detest racialism because I regard it as a barbaric thing, whether it comes from a Black man or from a White man."

128. The struggle in South Africa is not a struggle between two races for domination; it is a struggle between the protagonists of racial domination and the advocates of racial equality.

129. We believe that if a new course is set now it is still possible to envisage all South Africans enjoying political justice and freedom under a constitution guaranteeing human rights and providing for a democratic system of government. Removal of the restrictions on employment and residence and movement will open up possibilities for far greater industrial and agricultural prosperity. The economy of South Africa can surge forward if the barrier of discrimination is removed. Reduction of expenditure on military and repressive measures will free large sums for development and welfare. And if equal opportunities for education are granted a great new reservoir of human capacity and skill will be created to contribute to fruitful and peaceful progress. When the burdens of oppression and discrimination and isolation are lifted all South Africans will benefit.

130. We have no doubt that the cause of emancipation will prevail in South Africa. The great majority of the population cannot be forced back into already overcrowded reserves constituting less than 13 per cent of the country. The right of the human person, the right of each individual to live and work and move freely in his own country cannot long be denied. A political, economic and social system built on the domination of one race by another by force cannot survive.

131. What is now at issue is not the final outcome but the question whether, on the way, the people of South Africa are to go through a long ordeal of blood and hate. If so all Africa and the whole world must be involved.

132. We believe that the course of reason and justice which we have advocated—a course which could be promptly and honourably accepted by all—offers the only way and the last chance to avoid such a vast tragedy.

Alva MYRDAL, *Chairman*
Edward ASAFU-ADJAYE
Hugh FOOT
Dey OULD SIDI BABA

# Document 38

*Statement by Mr. Thabo Mbeki, son of Mr. Govan Mbeki, the African leader on trial in Pretoria, before a delegation of the Special Committee on the Policies of Apartheid of the Government of the Republic of South Africa in London, 13 April 1964*

A/AC.115/L.65, 23 April 1964

Mr. Chairman, esteemed members: first of all, may I express my humble gratitude to you for allowing me to take your time in an attempt to add yet another voice in the fight against the evil and insane policies of persecution pursued so relentlessly and so brazenly by the South African Government. I might also, with your permission, Mr. Chairman, use this opportunity to voice my deep-felt appreciation of the contribution which you and your colleagues are making to the success of the South African struggle, in the name of all humanity. Here I feel justified in claiming further to represent not only my feelings but also my father's, Govan Mbeki, and his comrades now interned in the Pretoria Local Prison, South Africa, and appearing again before the Judge this Monday, 20 April, for what seems the last leg of what has come to be known as the Rivonia Trial. Free South Africa will remember your efforts dearly; for the moment, I for one offer to do whatever I can to help to bring the apartheid monster to heel. This is my dedication to your efforts. Thank you, Sir, and through you, I thank the other members of your Special Committee, both present and absent.

I feel it my duty to introduce myself to you, Mr. Chairman, inasmuch as this might help you in your task. Born on 18 June 1942, I was christened Thabo Mbeki. Since starting school at the age of five, the rest of my life has been taken up with acquiring education of one sort or another. During that time I have been at schools in the Transkei and in the Ciskei in the Cape Province. Expelled from school in 1959, I finished my secondary school education as a private student and qualified at the end of the year for entry into any South African University. As the system of Bantu Education had been introduced, however, after consultation with my father, I felt obliged to seek a university place outside South Africa. For this purpose I took my General Certificate of Education examinations in Johannesburg in 1961, with a first class pass in economics, and qualified for a place in any British university.

After staying for another year in Johannesburg studying as an external student of the University of London, I left South Africa in September 1962, together with and leading twenty-seven other African students who were going out to study overseas. Owing to the delay occasioned by our arrest in Southern Rhodesia, we finally reached Dar es Salaam in November through the efforts of the African National Congress.

While I was in South Africa I had participated extensively in anti-apartheid youth activities, during which time I had the fortune of enjoying constant contact with, among others, Nelson Mandela, Walter Sisulu and Duma Nokwe, who already has had occasion to meet this esteemed Committee in New York. When I left the country I held, among others, the position of National Secretary of the African Students Association. It was for these reasons that I thought it unwise for me to apply for a passport to leave South Africa. It is my sincere wish that this information about myself will help the Committee to appreciate even more the appeal which I shall make, with your permission, Sir, through you to the nations of the world gathered at the United Nations.

My father, Govan Mbeki, now in the Rivonia Trial, on whose behalf I am here primarily, was, by some curious coincidence, born on 4 July 1910, the year that South Africa became the Union of South Africa and the date of the Independence of America. Born of a family of peasant farmers in the Transkei, he went to school in his village and later to the Healdtown High School were he matriculated. After this he went to the University College of Fort Hare, the only institution of higher education in South Africa which took considerable numbers of African students, not only from South Africa but also from as far afield as Uganda. Working as newspaper seller during holidays in Johannesburg, he went through his B.A. degree and then took up teaching in Durban. He was later to be awarded a B. Econ. degree by the University of South Africa, after he had studied as an external student for a number of years.

From his early years my father took an interest in the welfare of his people, finally getting elected to the Transkei Territorial General Council in the early 1940s. He was not to stay long, however, as soon afterwards the

Government of the day began taking unto itself the tasks that the Council had previously regarded as falling under its jurisdiction. After a spirited fight he felt obliged to go back to his constituents to tell them that as the character of the Council had changed he felt he could not claim that he was representing the people by attending it, and therefore was obliged to resign and call on the people to resist the gradual whittling away of their rights by the Government. That fight met with an intransigent Government, but it heightened the respect of the people for his courage.

In 1943 he was to sign the document "The African Claims"—the African version of the Atlantic Charter— together with such distinguished African leaders as Moses Kotane, now in the team of ANC leaders overseas, ex-presidents of the ANC, Doctors A. B. Xuma and J. S. Moroka and Professor Z. K. Matthews, now Secretary of the World Council of Churches and a distinguished scholar. In later year he continued to work with these renowned leaders and others, gradually emerging as a man of powerful intellect and absolute dedication to the cause of freedom. After a number of business ventures by which he tried to secure his independence from a Government salary, he was forced to go back to teaching in 1954. He was expelled at the end of the year for his hostility to Government policies. He then joined the staff of the newspaper New Age which, together with its predecessors and its followers, acted as the newspaper of the liberation struggle.

In 1957 he played a prominent part in a national conference called by African Ministers to discuss the Tomlinson report, the Government's bantustan blueprint. In 1960 he attended the meeting of African leaders called to discuss the then plans of the South African Government to declare South Africa a Republic. The Committee elected at that meeting, of which he was a member, was later to organize the Conference that elected Nelson Mandela as its leader, which action has subsequently led to his being sentenced to five years' imprisonment. During this time he had become one of the prominent leaders of the African National Congress and recognized by his colleagues as an expert on the problems of the reserves, the so-called bantustans.

At the beginning of 1962 he was arrested and detained for five months on a charge of sabotage. The case was, however, withdrawn and he was released to be arrested again, this last time at Rivonia. If he is hanged he will leave behind his wife, whom he married in 1939, three sons and a daughter; the two boys at school in Basutoland, their mother and sister still in South Africa and myself in my second year at the University of Sussex in this country.

It has been necessary that this introduction be made

so as to explain the calibre of one of the men whom the South African Government seeks to hang today. I believe that the years of his political activity have derived their inspiration from his love for his people. During these years, as his older associates would testify, he has earned the respect of his people and his colleagues. Not a single one of the many South African courts has found him guilty of a petty or indictable crime. Yet today he stands accused, and his accusers, who only yesterday found glory in Nazi Germany, stand in full twilight of their cynical and inhuman power. For decades he, together with the rest of the African people, has appealed to the White Governments of South Africa, not for the exaltation of the African people to a position of dominance over the White, but for equality among the peoples. The only reward he has earned, that we have all earned, is the brutal might of South African law which has sought to bend human reason and feeling to the barbarity of madmen. By the profane and demented reasoning of the Government, Dr. Percy Yutar, well known for the murderers and thieves that he has sent to prison or to the gallows, is now prosecuting in the Rivonia trial.

Though much has been said on this subject I should also like to add my testimony about the character of the men that the South African Government would have the world believe are criminals. They are not only men of the greatest integrity that responsibility to their families and friends would demand, men who would be welcomed by any civilized country, but also men who would grace any Government in which they served. Activated by the noblest of motives, they have acquired through the years an understanding of leadership that would be a valuable contribution to the common human experience.

Today these men stand accused of treason, of plotting to overthrow the Government by violent means. If it is so, they have acted in defence of the people that the Government has sought to silence and subjugate with a whip and the instruments of war. The fact is inescapable that the trial is not only their trial as individuals, but it is a trial of all that they have stood for, which was not and is not war but peace among free and equal men. The Government has replied with more brutality, sentencing only last month three respected African National Congress leaders to death. By so doing that Government has declared freedom from poverty, from suffering and from degradation, and human equality without discrimination on grounds of colour or race, to be illegal and criminal in its eyes. And by the Rivonia trial, the Government intends to make ten times more its case that freedom is illegal.

The crimes that the South African Government has committed are of a magnitude that baffles the human mind. The continued existence of apartheid with the support of the Governments of, particularly, the United Kingdom, the United States, France and West Germany, cannot but be seen as an act of violence, not only against the whole African people but also against that portion of humanity which is trying so hard to remove racialism in the intercourse between men. Anybody therefore who, having the power to stop the decapitation of the men on trial in Pretoria, fails to use that power to the fullest extent is by omission an accomplice in the act.

Having said so much, Mr. Chairman, I wish again to thank you and your colleagues for giving me this audience. If, Sir, I may be so presumptuous as to seize the opportunity, I beg to ask you humbly, and in awareness of the immodesty of the request, to be so kind as to take this message to the nations of the world from one who may be about to lose a noble father and a noble leader.

He acted in defence of the principles on which the civilized human community so firmly stands, and so did his brothers who stand together under the sinister noose of the hangman. They were spurred on by the inspiration of the victorious struggles to their North, no less sacred among these the Algerian revolution. They drew strength from the respect accorded them by their people and the example that their forefathers had set them. For our part, if the butchers will have their way, we shall draw strength even from the little crosses that the kind may put at the head of their graves. In that process we shall learn. We shall learn to hate evil even more, and in the same intensity we shall seek to destroy it. We shall learn to be brave and unconscious of anything but this noblest of struggles. Today we might be but weak children, spurred on by nothing other than the fear and grief of losing our fathers. In time yet we shall learn to die both for ourselves and for the millions. Mr. Chairman, through you and through the esteemed members of your Committee, I wish, in the name of my mother, my brothers, my sister and myself, in the name of Mandela's, Sisulu's, Mhlaba's, Goldberg's and the others' families, and in the name of the South African people, to make this appeal to the world.

In the name of humanity the South African Government must be stopped. That Government has criminally taken up arms against my people. Was any gang of butchers so powerful as to defy the whole world? The leaders at the Rivonia trial cannot be allowed to die at the hands of the South African Government.

# Document 39

*Statement by Mr. Nelson Mandela at his trial in Pretoria, 20 April 1964*

A/AC.115/L.67, 6 May 1964, and OPI/279, 1967

. . .

Our fight is against real, and not imaginary, hardships, or to use the language of the State Prosecutor, "so-called hardships." Basically, we fight against two features which are the hallmarks of African life in South Africa and which are entrenched by legislation which we seek to have repealed. These are poverty and lack of human dignity, and we do not need Communists or so-called "agitators" to teach us about these things.

South Africa is the richest country in Africa, and could be one of the richest countries in the world. But it is a land of extremes and remarkable contrasts. The Whites enjoy what may well be the highest standard of living in the world, whilst Africans live in poverty and misery. Forty per cent of the Africans live in hopelessly over-crowded and, in some cases, drought-stricken reserves where soil erosion and the overworking of the soil make it impossible for them to live properly off the land. Thirty per cent are labourers, labour tenants and squatters on White farms and work and live under conditions similar to those of the serfs of the Middle Ages. The other 30 per cent live in towns where they have developed economic and social habits which bring them closer in many respects to White standards. Yet most Africans, even in this group, are impoverished by low incomes and the high cost of living.

The highest-paid and the most prosperous section of urban African life is in Johannesburg. Yet their actual position is desperate. The latest figures were given on 25 March 1964, by Mr. Carr, Manager of the Johannesburg Non-European Affairs Department. The poverty datum line for the average African family in Johannesburg (according to Mr. Carr's department) is R42.84 per month. He showed that the average monthly wage is R32.24 and that 46 per cent of all African families in Johannesburg do not earn enough to keep them going.

Poverty goes hand in hand with malnutrition and disease. The incidence of malnutrition and deficiency diseases is very high amongst Africans. Tuberculosis, pellagra, kwashiorkor, gastro-enteritis and scurvy bring death and destruction of health. The incidence of infant mortality is one of the highest in the world. According to the Medical Officer of Health for Pretoria, tuberculosis kills forty people a day (almost all Africans), and in 1961 there were 58,491 new cases reported. These diseases not only destroy the vital organs of the body, but they result in retarded mental conditions, lack of initiative, and reduced powers of concentration. The secondary results of such conditions affect the whole community and the standard of work performed by African labourers.

The complaint of Africans, however, is not only that they are poor and Whites are rich, but that the laws which are made by the Whites are designed to preserve this situation. There are two ways to break out of poverty. The first is by formal education, and the second is by the worker acquiring a greater skill at his work and thus higher wages. As far as Africans are concerned, both these avenues of advancement are deliberately curtailed by legislation.

The present Government has always sought to hamper Africans in their search for education. One of their early acts, after coming into power, was to stop subsidies for African school feeding. Many African children who attended schools depended on this supplement to their diet. This was a cruel act.

There is compulsory education for all White children at virtually no cost to their parents, be they rich or poor. Similar facilities are not provided for the African children, though there are some who receive such assistance. African children, however, generally have to pay more for their schooling than Whites. According to figures quoted by the South African Institute of Race Relations in its 1963 journal, approximately 40 per cent of African children in the age group between 7 to 14, do not attend school. For those who do attend school, the standards are vastly different from those afforded to White children. In 1960-61 the per capita Government spending on African students at State-aided schools was estimated at R12.46. In the same years, the per capita spending on White children in the Cape Province (which are the only figures available to me) was R144.57. Although there are no figures available to me, it can be stated, without doubt, that the White children on whom R144.57 per head was being spent all came from wealthier homes than African children on whom R12.46 per head was being spent.

The quality of education is also different. According to the Bantu Education Journal, only 5,660 African children in the whole of South Africa passed their J.C. in 1962, and in that year only 362 passed matric. This is presumably consistent with the policy of Bantu education about which the present Prime Minister said, during the debate on the Bantu Education Bill in 1953:

"When I have control of Native education I will reform it so that Natives will be taught from childhood to realise that equality with Europeans is not for them. . . . People who believe in equality are not desirable teachers for Natives. When my Department controls Native education it will know for what class of higher education a Native is fitted, and whether he will have a chance in life to use his knowledge."

The other main obstacle to the economic advancement of the African is the industrial colour bar under which all the better jobs of industry are reserved for Whites only. Moreover, Africans who do obtain employment in the unskilled and semi-skilled occupations which are open to them are not allowed to form trade unions, which have recognition under the Industrial Conciliation Act. This means that strikes of African workers are illegal, and that they are denied the right of collective bargaining which is permitted to the better-paid White workers. The discrimination in the policy of successive South African Governments towards African workers is demonstrated by the so-called "civilized labour policy" under which sheltered, unskilled Government jobs are found for those White workers who cannot make the grade in industry, at wages which far exceed the earnings of the average African employee in industry.

The Government often answers its critics by saying that Africans in South Africa are economically better off than the inhabitants of the other countries in Africa. I do not know whether this statement is true and doubt whether any comparison can be made without having regard to the cost-of-living index in such countries. But even if it is true, as far as the African people are concerned it is irrelevant. Our complaint is not that we are poor by comparison with people in other countries, but that we are poor by comparison with the White people in our own country, and that we are prevented by legislation from altering this imbalance.

The lack of human dignity experienced by Africans is the direct result of the policy of White supremacy. White supremacy implies Black inferiority. Legislation designed to preserve White supremacy entrenches this notion. Menial tasks in South Africa are invariably performed by Africans. When anything has to be carried or cleaned the White man will look around for an African to do it for him, whether the African is employed by him or not. Because of this . . . attitude, Whites tend to regard Africans as a separate breed. They do not look upon them as people with families of their own; they do not realize that they have emotions— that they fall in love like White people do; that they want to be with their wives and children like White people want to be with theirs; that they want to earn enough money to support their families properly, to feed and clothe them and send them to school. And what "house-boy" or "garden-boy" or labourer can ever hope to do this?

Pass Laws, which to the Africans are amongst the most hated bits of legislation in South Africa, render any African liable to police surveillance at any time. I doubt whether there is a single African male in South Africa who has not at some stage had a brush with the police over his pass. Hundreds and thousands of Africans are thrown into gaol each year under Pass Laws. Even worse than this is the fact that Pass Laws keep husband and wife apart and lead to the breakdown of family life.

Poverty and the breakdown of family life have secondary effects. Children wander about the streets of the townships because they have no schools to go to, or no money to enable them to go to school, or no parents at home to see that they go to school, because both parents (if there be two) have to work to keep the family alive. This leads to a breakdown in moral standards, to an alarming rise in illegitimacy and to growing violence which erupts, not only politically, but everywhere. Life in the townships is dangerous. There is not a day that goes by without somebody being stabbed or assaulted. And violence is carried out of the townships into the White living areas. People are afraid to walk alone in the streets after dark. Housebreakings and robberies are increasing, despite the fact that the death sentence can now be imposed for such offences. Death sentences cannot cure the festering sore.

Africans want to be paid a living wage. Africans want to perform work which they are capable of doing, and not work which the Government declares them to be capable of. Africans want to be allowed to live where they obtain work, and not be endorsed out of an area because they were not born there. Africans want to be allowed to own land in places where they work, and not be obliged to live in rented houses which they can never call their own. Africans want to be part of the general population, and not confined to living in their own ghettos. African men want their wives and children to live with them where they work, and not be forced into an unnatural existence in men's hostels. African women want to be with their men folk and not be left permanently widowed in the reserves. Africans want to be allowed out after 11 o'clock at night and not be confined to their rooms like little children. Africans want to be allowed to travel in their own country and to seek work where they want to and not where the Labour Bureau tells them to. Africans want a just share in the whole of South Africa; they want security and a stake in society.

Above all, we want equal political rights, because without them our disabilities will be permanent. I know this sounds revolutionary to the Whites in this country, because the majority of voters will be Africans. This makes the White man fear democracy.

But this fear cannot be allowed to stand in the way

of the only solution which will guarantee racial harmony and freedom for all. It is not true that the enfranchisement of all will result in racial domination. Political division, based on colour, is entirely artificial and, when it disappears, so will the domination of one colour group by another. The African National Congress has spent half a century fighting against racialism. When it triumphs it will not change that policy.

This then is what the ANC is fighting. Their struggle is a truly national one. It is a struggle of the African people, inspired by their own suffering and their own experience. It is a struggle for the right to live.

During my lifetime I have dedicated myself to this struggle of the African people. I have fought against White domination, and I have fought against Black domination. I have cherished the ideal of a democratic and free society in which all persons live together in harmony and with equal opportunities. It is an ideal which I hope to live for and to achieve. But if need be, it is an ideal for which I am prepared to die.

---

# Document 40

*Statement by Chief Albert J. Luthuli, President of the African National Congress, in the Security Council, on the sentencing of Mr. Nelson Mandela and others to life imprisonment*

S/PV.1130, 12 June 1964

[Editor's note: This statement was issued by Chief Luthuli on 12 June 1964, when Nelson Mandela, Walter Sisulu and six other leaders were sentenced to life imprisonment in the "Rivonia trial". It was read at the meeting of the United Nations Security Council on the same day by the representative of Morocco.]

Sentences of life imprisonment have been pronounced on Nelson Mandela, Walter Sisulu, Ahmed Kathrada, Govan Mbeki, Dennis Goldberg, Raymond Mhlaba, Elias Motsoaledi and Andrew Mlangeni in the "Rivonia trial" in Pretoria.

Over the long years these leaders advocated a policy of racial cooperation, of goodwill, and of peaceful struggle that made the South African liberation movement one of the most ethical and responsible of our time. In the face of the most bitter racial persecution, they resolutely set themselves against racialism: in the face of continued provocation, they consistently chose the path of reason.

The African National Congress, with allied organizations representing all racial sections, sought every possible means of redress for intolerable conditions, and held consistently to a policy of using militant, nonviolent means of struggle. Their common aim was to create a South Africa in which all South Africans would live and work together as fellow-citizens, enjoying equal rights without discrimination on grounds of race, colour or creed.

To this end, they used every accepted method: propaganda, public meetings and rallies, petitions, stay-at-home strikes, appeals, boycotts. So carefully did they educate the people that in the four-year-long Treason Trial, one police witness after another voluntarily testified to this emphasis on nonviolent methods of struggle in all aspects of their activities.

But finally all avenues of resistance were closed. The African National Congress and other organizations were made illegal, their leaders jailed, exiled or forced underground. The government sharpened its oppression of the peoples of South Africa, using its all-White Parliament as the vehicle for making repression legal, and utilising every weapon of this highly industrialized and modern state to enforce that "legality". The stage was even reached where a White spokesman for the disenfranchised Africans was regarded by the Government as a traitor. In addition, sporadic acts of uncontrolled violence were increasing throughout the country. At first in one place, then in another, there were spontaneous eruptions against intolerable conditions; many of these acts increasingly assumed a racial character.

The African National Congress never abandoned its method of a militant, nonviolent struggle, and of creating in the process a spirit of militancy in the people. However, in the face of the uncompromising White refusal to abandon a policy which denies the African and other oppressed South Africans their rightful heritage—freedom—no one can blame brave just men for seeking justice by the use of violent methods; nor could they be blamed if they tried to create an organized force in order to ultimately establish peace and racial harmony.

For this, they are sentenced to be shut away for long years in the brutal and degrading prisons of South Africa.

With them will be interred this country's hopes for racial cooperation. They will leave a vacuum in leadership that may only be filled by bitter hate and racial strife.

They represent the highest in morality and ethics in the South African political struggle; this morality and ethics has been sentenced to an imprisonment it may never survive. Their policies are in accordance with the deepest international principles of brotherhood and humanity; without their leadership, brotherhood and humanity may be blasted out of existence in South Africa for long decades to come. They believe profoundly in justice and reason; when they are locked away, justice and reason will have departed from the South African scene.

This is an appeal to save these men, not merely as individuals, but for what they stand for. In the name of justice, of hope, of truth and of peace, I appeal to South Africa's strongest allies, Britain and America. In the name of what we have come to believe Britain and America stand for, I appeal to those two powerful countries to take decisive action for full-scale action for sanctions that would precipitate the end of the hateful system of apartheid.

I appeal to all governments throughout the world, to people everywhere, to organizations and institutions in every land and at every level, to act now to impose such sanctions on South Africa that will bring about the vital necessary change and avert what can become the greatest African tragedy of our times.

# Document 41

## Security Council resolution: Question relating to the policies of apartheid of the Government of the Republic of South Africa

S/RES/191 (1964), 18 June 1964

*The Security Council,*

. . .

*Taking note with appreciation* of the reports of the Special Committee on the Policies of Apartheid of the Government of the Republic of South Africa and the report of the Group of Experts appointed by the Secretary-General pursuant to Security Council resolution 182 (1963) of 4 December 1963,

. . .

3. *Notes* the recommendations and the conclusions in the report of the Group of Experts;

4. *Urgently appeals* to the Government of the Republic of South Africa to:

(*a*) renounce the execution of any persons sentenced to death for their opposition to the policy of apartheid;

(*b*) grant immediate amnesty to all persons detained or on trial, as well as clemency to all persons sentenced, for their opposition to the Government's racial policies;

(*c*) abolish the practice of imprisonment without charges, without access to counsel or without the right of prompt trial;

5. *Endorses* and subscribes in particular to the main conclusion of the Group of Experts that "all the people of South Africa should be brought into consult-

ation and should thus be enabled to decide the future of their country at the national level";

6. *Requests* the Secretary-General to consider what assistance the United Nations may offer to facilitate such consultations among representatives of all elements of the population in South Africa;

7. *Invites* the Government of the Republic of South Africa to accept the main conclusion of the Group of Experts referred to in paragraph 5 above and to cooperate with the Secretary-General and to submit its views to him with respect to such consultations by 30 November 1964;

8. *Decides* to establish an expert committee, composed of representatives of each present member of the Security Council, to undertake a technical and practical study and report to the Council as to the feasibility, effectiveness and implications of measures which could, as appropriate, be taken by the Council under the Charter of the United Nations;

. . .

11. *Invites* the Secretary-General, in consultation with appropriate United Nations specialized agencies, to establish an educational and training programme for the purpose of arranging for education and training abroad for South Africans;

. . .

# Document 42

## Statement by Secretary-General U Thant to the Heads of State and Government of the Organization of African Unity

UN Press Release SG/SM/112, 17 July 1964

I may perhaps say a few words on two questions in which the African States have shown great concern: colonialism and racial discrimination. The attitude of the United Nations on these matters—laid down in the Charter and elaborated by the historic Declarations on Human Rights, Colonialism and Racial Discrimination—is unequivocal. The United Nations stands for the self-government and independence of all peoples, and the abolition of racial discrimination without reservations. It can never afford to compromise on these basic principles.

The United Nations has been acutely concerned with these problems since its inception. Today, respect for the right of peoples to self-determination and affirmation of racial equality are not only the principles of the Charter but are embodied in the very composition of the United Nations, half of whose member are newly-independent States from Asia and Africa. The United Nations may be proud of its contribution, however modest or seemingly hesitant at times, to the progress which has been made. We can feel gratified at the evolution of the attitudes of all but one or two of the colonial Powers. The colonial Powers and remaining defenders of racial discrimination are increasingly isolated and can less and less count on the acquiescence and patience of other States. This isolation of the colonialists has itself contributed to the fulfilment of the desire of African States to keep the colonial and racial problems out of the cold war. We can only hope that good sense and realism prevail so that resistance to change by a few die-hards will not lead to dangerous conflict on this continent.

I must emphasize that universality is an essential, although implicit, goal of the United Nations. The Organization cannot have full authority and cannot achieve maximum effectiveness until all the peoples who subscribe to its purposes and principles are represented in it. The independence of African States was a source of strength for the United Nations. In my view, this goal of universality required an end to colonialism and an end to the denial of fundamental rights to persons on the grounds of race, religion, language or sex. Thus, the problems that I have referred to are not only problems of which the United Nations is seized, but problems which affect the status of the Organization itself.

---

# Document 43

## Appeal to Member States by the Special Committee on the Policies of Apartheid of the Government of the Republic of South Africa for contributions to assist families persecuted by the South African Government for their opposition to apartheid

UN Press Release GA/AP/42, 26 October 1964

The Special Committee on the Policies of Apartheid of the Government of the Republic of South Africa has been concerned for some time with the urgent need for relief and legal assistance to persons persecuted in the Republic of South Africa for acts arising from their opposition to the Government's racial policies which have been repeatedly condemned by competent organs of the United Nations.

The Special Committee felt that these victims of persecution are entitled to assistance by the peoples of the world, not only because of humanitarian reasons, but also because they have faced persecution in the struggle for racial equality which is enshrined in the United Nations Charter as a fundamental purpose of the Organization. Indeed, assistance by the peoples of the world would be an effective means to express solidarity with the opponents of racial discrimination and to counter growth of racial bitterness in South Africa.

It may be recalled that, on the recommendation of the Special Committee, the General Assembly adopted resolution 1978 B (XVIII) on 16 December 1963 requesting the Secretary-General to seek ways and means of providing relief and assistance, through the appropriate international agencies, to the families of all persons persecuted by the Government of the Republic of South Africa for their opposition to the policies of apartheid.

In view of the acute and urgent need for assistance, and after consultation with the Secretary-General, the Special Committee has decided that an appeal should immediately be addressed to Member States and organizations to contribute urgently and generously to existing relief organizations, pending the conclusion of other appropriate arrangements.

In spite of all Security Council and General Assembly resolutions demanding the abandonment of the policies of apartheid, the Government of the Republic of South Africa has continued to implement its repressive laws providing extremely harsh penalties for belonging to or furthering the aims of the major African political organizations and for acts of protest and resistance against the Government's racial policies. The implementation of these laws has resulted in the detention of thousands of persons, many of whom are being tried or awaiting trial, thus facing long periods in prison or life imprisonment or even death sentences.

Hundreds of persons have been imprisoned under Section 17 of the General Law Amendment Act of 1963, which provides for the detention of persons without trial for periods of 90 days at a time. Numerous persons have been subjected to banishment, house arrest, banning orders and other restrictions which often prevent them from pursuing their occupations. The distress and misery caused by these repressive actions to the families may easily be imagined. Numerous families have been deprived of their breadwinners. Children have been separated from one or both of their parents.

When brought to trial, many an opponent of the policies of apartheid faces financial difficulties and has to rely on benevolent organizations for legal assistance, support of families and payment of bail.

It appears from communications received by the Special Committee from organizations concerned with relief and assistance to the victims of repression in South Africa that they are in urgent need of funds to provide even minimum legal assistance and relief to numerous persons who have been gaoled or brought to trial under repressive laws.

The Special Committee is attaching herewith communications received by it from three organizations— Amnesty International, Defence and Aid Fund (International) and Joint Committee on the High Commission Territories—which have been engaged in relief and assistance for the victims of persecution by the Republic of South Africa and which offer their services in implementing the purposes of General Assembly resolution 1978 B (XVIII).

The Special Committee notes that Amnesty International, sponsored by eminent personalities from many countries, "adopts" prisoners and detainees in South Africa who do not advocate violence and also assists refugees from South Africa. The Defence and Aid Fund, established in the United Kingdom in 1956, with Canon L. John Collins as Chairman, has so far contributed about £300,000 to the victims of the policies of apartheid and maintains contact with South Africa through local committees. Its efforts have been appreciated by prominent South African opponents of apartheid, including Chief Albert Luthuli, winner of the Nobel Peace Prize. The Joint Committee on the High Commission Territories, representative of a number of voluntary organizations, is concerned with the relief and assistance of South African refugees in the High Commission Territories and in Northern Rhodesia.

The Special Committee also notes that the World Council of Churches has, in July 1964, earmarked $60,000 for legal aid for political prisoners in South Africa and for assistance to their dependants, and is seeking further contributions for this purpose.

The Special Committee wishes to make an urgent appeal to Member States to contribute generously to the fulfilment of the purposes of General Assembly resolution 1978 B (XVIII) through these voluntary organizations or through other appropriate channels of their choice, and to give the widest publicity to this appeal in order to encourage charitable foundations, organizations and individuals in their countries to make generous contributions.

# Document 44

*Report of the Expert Committee established in pursuance of Security Council resolution 191 (1964)*

S/6210, 2 March 1965

1. On 18 June 1964, the Security Council adopted resolution S/5773 [S/RES/191] in connection with the question of race conflict in South Africa resulting from the policies of apartheid of the Government of South Africa, brought to the attention of the Security Council by fifty-eight Member States.

2. The Security Council, in operative paragraph 8 of the above resolution, decided "to establish an Expert Committee, composed of representatives of each present member of the Security Council, to undertake a technical and practical study, and report to the Security Council as to the feasibility, effectiveness and implications of measures which could, as appropriate, be taken by the Security Council under the United Nations Charter".

3. The Expert Committee held its first meeting on 21 July 1964 and decided that the Chairmanship of the Committee should rotate among its members on a monthly basis in alphabetical order beginning with Bolivia. The representative of Bolivia was also elected Rapporteur of the Committee. France did not participate in the meetings of the Committee. The members of the Expert Committee were Bolivia, Brazil, China, Czechoslovakia, France, Ivory Coast, Morocco, Norway, Union of Soviet Socialist Republics, United Kingdom of Great Britain and Northern Ireland and United States of America.

4. At its second meeting on 10 August 1964, the Committee agreed that in regard to decisions of the Committee, every effort should be made to achieve unanimity but if unanimity could not be achieved, decisions of the Committee would be taken by a majority of the members present and voting, on the understanding that the opinion of the minority would be recorded in the report.

5. At the same meeting, the Committee took up the question of the publicity of its meetings and decided that the meetings should normally be held in closed session. The representative of the USSR felt that the Committee should adhere to the usual procedure of the other United Nations bodies of meeting in public and should meet in private only if it decided to do so at the request of one of its members. The representative of Czechoslovakia felt that the Committee would work more effectively if it met in public so that other delegations could also attend. However, the representatives of the USSR and Czechoslovakia explained that they would not oppose the majority view in favour of private meetings.

6. In conformity with its mandate under operative paragraph 10 of Security Council resolution S/5773 [S/RES/191], the Chairman of the Expert Committee wrote to all Member States on 20 August 1964, informing them of the establishment of the Committee and expressing the hope that Member States would let the Committee "have the benefit of their views on issues which it will refer to the Governments of Member States in the course of its work". Fourteen replies were received from Member States. The Committee followed up this letter by a more specific request in a communication from the Chairman to Member States dated 30 October 1964. To this letter was attached a questionnaire to which the Committee wanted replies from Member States by 30 November 1964. The representative of the USSR expressed serious doubts as to the advisability of sending the questionnaire which in some respects cast doubt on the effectiveness of sanctions against South Africa and also because the majority of States had furnished such information in replies to earlier inquiries in connection with previous resolutions of the Security Council and of the General Assembly. Subsequently, the Committee also decided to send that letter, as well as the questionnaire, to those non-Member States with whom the Secretary-General had been in communication in carrying out his functions under Security Council resolution S/5471 of 4 December 1963. Thirty-four replies were received to this communication.

7. The Expert Committee had before it a list of measures referred to in previous resolutions of the Security Council and of the General Assembly, in the various reports of the Special Committee on the Policies of Apartheid of the Government of South Africa, as well as in the resolutions adopted by the Organization of African Unity and the Conference of Non-Aligned Countries. In addition, the Expert Committee had before it documents prepared by the Secretariat containing various statistical and other information relevant to the work of the Committee.

8. In all, the Expert Committee held thirty-eight meetings between 21 July 1964 and 27 February 1965. The summary records of the meetings are annexed to this report.

9. At the 33rd meeting of the Committee on 24 February 1965, the following three sets of draft conclusions were submitted:

(a) Draft conclusions, jointly sponsored by Czechoslovakia and the USSR.

(b) Draft conclusions, jointly submitted by the Ivory Coast and Morocco.

(c) Draft conclusions submitted by the United States of America.

10. At the 35th meeting of the Committee on 25 February 1965, the representatives of Bolivia and Brazil jointly submitted draft conclusions.

11. At the 37th meeting of the Committee on 26 February 1965, the representative of the United States of America indicated that he would not press the draft conclusions submitted by his delegation to a vote.

12. At the same meeting, the Committee voted upon the three draft resolutions before it:

(a) The draft conclusions submitted by Czechoslovakia and the USSR were rejected by 4 votes in favour (Czechoslovakia, Ivory Coast, Morocco, USSR), and 6 votes against (Bolivia, Brazil, China, Norway, United Kingdom, United States of America), with no abstentions.

(*b*) The draft conclusions submitted by the Ivory Coast and Morocco were rejected by 4 votes in favour (Czechoslovakia, Ivory Coast, Morocco, USSR), 5 votes against (Bolivia, Brazil, Norway, United Kingdom, United States of America) and 1 abstention (China).

(*c*) The draft conclusions submitted by Bolivia and Brazil were adopted by 6 votes in favour (Bolivia, Brazil, China, Norway, United Kingdom, United States of America) and 4 votes against (Czechoslovakia, Ivory Coast, Morocco and USSR) with no abstentions.

13. The Committee, therefore, submits to the Security Council, the following conclusions:

Pursuant to resolution S/5773 [S/RES/191] of the Security Council, the Expert Committee undertook a technical and practical study of the feasibility, effectiveness and implications of measures which could, as appropriate, be taken under the United Nations Charter against the Republic of South Africa.

The Expert Committee is of the view that while it is the prerogative of the Security Council to decide on the imposition of measures against the Republic of South Africa, it is essential that the Committee assist the Council by making available a study of the question under the provisions of its mandate.

The Committee had before it detailed information regarding the economy of the Republic of South Africa, as well as the information provided by a number of States concerning their economic relations with South Africa, special attention being given to possible implications of economic measures upon their own economies. Emphasis was also given by the Committee to the recommendations made in the past by the United Nations as well as by regional and other organizations and conferences on the question of economic and other measures against the Republic of South Africa.

Taking into account this detailed information, the Expert Committee reached the following general conclusions as to South Africa's economy and the effectiveness, feasibility and implications of economic measures against South Africa.

The Committee agreed that South Africa's economic strength, diversity and prosperity have been due in large part to: (a) its varied and abundant natural resources (both agricultural and mineral, with the exception of oil); (b) its rapidly developing industrial base; (c) the high degree of technical and managerial skill available; (d) foreign trade and investment; and (e) the exploitation of non-White labourers. Although it was pointed out that South Africa would not be readily susceptible to economic measures, the Committee agreed that South Africa was not immune to damages from such measures.

On the question of effectiveness of economic measures, it became apparent to the Committee that the degree of effectiveness of such measures would directly depend on the universality of their application and on the manner and the duration of their enforcement. While some members of the Committee disagreed on the degree of severity of the effects that such measures might have on the economy of South Africa, the Committee agreed that there were several areas of vulnerability in the economy of that country. In fact, from the discussions in the Committee, it became apparent that South Africa's economy would be susceptible to the effects of a total blocking of trade, both exports and imports, and to an interdiction of communications. Among other measures which could have appreciable effects, particular emphasis was given in the Committee to an embargo on petroleum and petroleum products and to a cessation of emigration into South Africa. Furthermore, some members considered that appreciable effects would also be caused by a banning of financial transactions. Similarly, it was also noted in the Committee that some means of alleviation, such as substitution, rationing and redeployment of resources could have significant results and that it was not possible to draw precise conclusions as to the degree to which these measures or a combination of them might affect South Africa's economic activity, or as to the length of time it would take for their effects to be felt. The susceptibility of the South African economy to measures would vary from case to case, effectiveness being largely dependent upon the availability of measures of alleviation on the part of South Africa on the one side and an organized and co-operative effort, including present and potential suppliers, on the other. As for an embargo on arms and ammunition, although it might not be considered an economic measure, if universally applied, it could have an important effect within the framework of a trade embargo, since military industries would make demands on resources that would otherwise be used to alleviate the effects of a trade embargo.

The consideration of these measures raised the problem of an adequate international machinery which could be set up under the aegis of the United Nations in order to prevent the circumvention of the measures by States and individuals, as well as problems arising from the non-cooperation of any State.

The Expert Committee is of the view that, while many measures are feasible, their effectiveness depends to a great extent on the degree of collective willingness, universality of application and genuine desire from those imposing measures, special attention being given to the States maintaining close economic relations with South Africa. Great emphasis was also given in the Committee to the psychological effects of these measures along with South Africa's present economic capacity to withstand such measures and the will of its people to do so.

In regard to implications, the Committee agreed that an international effort should be made to mitigate the hardships caused by such measures on economies of some Member States. There could be serious dislocations in world markets and in individual countries, varying with the type of measures chosen, for example, Basutoland, if an embargo on labour were in question, or the United Kingdom, if a general embargo were imposed by decision of the Security Council. While special consideration was given to the importance of these facts, they might not be of a nature, having regard to the possibility of mitigation, to prevent the application of measures against South Africa.

Taking into account the preceding considerations, emphasis was placed in the Committee on the importance of the following measures:

(a) total trade embargo;

(b) embargo on petroleum and petroleum products;

(c) embargo on arms, ammunition of all types, military vehicles and equipment and materials for the manufacture and maintenance of arms and ammunition in South Africa;

(d) cessation of emigration of technicians and skilled manpower to South Africa;

(e) interdiction of communications with South Africa;

(f) political and diplomatic measures as referred to in the resolutions already adopted by the Security Council and the General Assembly.

Similarly, emphasis was placed by the Committee on the varying effects of such measures and on the necessity of solving certain problems of implementation in order to judge the practicability and the effectiveness of these measures. In this connection, certain members pointed out the necessity of a total blockade to make such measures effective, as well as the great costliness of mounting such an operation. Consequently, in the event of a total blockade, consideration should be given to a proportionate sharing of costs. Other members, however, emphasized that measures affecting vulnerable sectors of the South African economy might constitute an effective action for their practical effects on the economy of that country, as well as for the political and psychological repercussions that they would entail on the White minority. In this connection, they pointed out the importance of a partial blockade. Furthermore, in taking a decision to apply measures against South Africa, it would be essential to set up a committee for the necessary coordination of action. The same committee should also coordinate action to mitigate proportionally the major hardships eventually caused on the economies of Member States.

Finally, it was emphasized that while these measures could prove feasible under conditions enumerated in the preceding paragraphs, the evaluation of their applicability and effectiveness in the political and psychological context lies solely within the province of the Security Council.

14. The delegations of Czechoslovakia and the USSR submitted the following dissenting note:

The representatives of the USSR and Czechoslovakia categorically opposed the above conclusions, which not only distort the true situation but may harm the cause of the struggle against apartheid in the Republic of South Africa. After a comprehensive and detailed examination of the question of application of economic and political sanctions against the Republic of South Africa, the Expert Committee had every ground for arriving at the following conclusions and recommendations.

Sanctions of an economic and political nature against the Republic of South Africa are undoubtedly feasible and their application will have the necessary effect on the authorities, legislative bodies and leading economic circles of the Republic of South Africa in inducing them to abandon the racist policy of apartheid.

The following set of measures, to be undertaken simultaneously on the basis of a decision of the Security Council, would be the most effective and fruitful:

(a) A total embargo on trade with the Republic of South Africa, including an embargo on the export to South Africa of goods and especially arms, ammunition, military equipment of all types and materials for their manufacture, and petroleum and petroleum products, and including also a boycott of South African goods.

(b) Cessation of all military and economic assistance to the Republic of South Africa and also of foreign investment in the Republic of South Africa and of loans to the South African authorities or to South African companies.

(c) Cessation of export of any qualified or specialized labour to the Republic of South Africa.

(d) Severance of diplomatic, consular and other relations with South Africa, including complete interruption of rail, sea, air, postal, telegraphic and radio communications.

(e) Prohibition on the establishment of new ties or agreements mentioned in sub-paragraphs (a), (b), (c) and (d).

As the representatives of the USSR and Czechoslovakia pointed out, the Expert Committee had every ground for saying that the implementation of the above-mentioned measures would be effective in inducing the South African authorities to abolish the racist policy of apartheid and comply with the decisions of various United Nations organs, it naturally being the prerogative of the Security Council to choose the best methods of implementing the above-mentioned sanctions.

These conclusions and recommendations of the representatives of the USSR and Czechoslovakia were fully supported in the Committee by the representatives of Morocco and the Ivory Coast.

The representatives of the USSR and Czechoslovakia pointed out that it was only because of the opposition of the Powers which are the principal economic and trading partners of the racist authorities of the Republic of South Africa that the Committee failed to carry out the task entrusted to it by the Security Council.

15. The views of the Ivory Coast and Morocco regarding the proper conclusions of the Committee are contained in the draft conclusions which they submitted to the Committee, the text of which reads as follows:

Pursuant to resolution S/5773 [S/RES/191] of the Security Council, the Expert Committee undertook a technical and practical study of the feasibility, effectiveness and implications of measures which could, as appropriate, be taken under the United Nations Charter against the Republic of South Africa.

The Expert Committee is of the view that while it is the prerogative of the Security Council to decide on the imposition of measures against the Republic of South Africa, it is essential that the Committee assist the Council by making available a study of the question under the provisions of its mandate.

The Committee had before it detailed information regarding the economy of the Republic of South Africa, as well as the information provided by a number of States concerning their economic relations with South Africa, special attention being given to the possible effects of economic measures on their own economies. Special attention was also given by the Committee to the recommendations made in the past by the United Nations as well as by regional organizations and conferences and other bodies on the question of economic and other measures against the Republic of South Africa.

Taking into account this detailed information, the Expert Committee reached the following general conclusions as to South Africa's economy and the feasibility, effectiveness and implications of economic measures against South Africa.

It is the view of the Committee that South Africa's economic prosperity has been due in large part to the following factors:

(a) its varied and abundant natural resources (both agricultural and mineral, with the exception of oil);

(b) the rapid development of its basic industries;

(c) the high degree of its technical capacity owing to intensive recruitment of skilled labour from certain countries;

(d) foreign trade and investment; and

(e) the exploitation of non-White labourers. Although it was pointed out that the application of economic measures against South Africa might not immediately paralyse its economy, the Committee felt that it could not be immune to the far-reaching repercussions which such measures were bound to have.

On the question of the effectiveness of economic measures, it became apparent to the Committee that the degree of effectiveness of such measures would be in direct proportion to the universality and to the manner and duration of their application. While some members of the Committee expressed different views as to the magnitude of the adverse effect that such measures might have on the economy of South Africa, the Committee was of the opinion that it contained several areas of vulnerability. What emerged from the Committee's discussions was that South Africa's economy would suffer from the effects of a total commercial blockade applying to both exports and imports, and from an interdiction of communications. Among other measures which could have appreciable effects, particular emphasis was given in the Committee to an embargo on petroleum and petroleum products and to a cessation of emigration to South Africa. Furthermore, some members considered that very appreciable effects would result from a ban on financial and monetary operations. It was also noted in the Committee that counter-measures aimed at mitigating the effects of the embargo, such as the replacement of certain products by others, rationing and redeployment of resources, might temporarily lessen the impact of the measures envisaged. The effects of those measures on the South African economy would vary from case to case, their effectiveness being largely dependent on the counter-measures which South Africa might take to deal with the situation and on the concerted effort made in a spirit of cooperation by present and potential suppliers. As regards an embargo on arms and ammunition, which might not be regarded as a strictly economic measure, if universally applied it could have considerable effect as part of a trade embargo, since the South African industries manufacturing military equipment would have to utilize resources that would otherwise be employed to lessen the effects of a trade embargo. The consideration of these measures raised the problem of establishing adequate international machinery, possibly under the auspices of the United Nations, to prevent circumvention of the measures by States or individuals, and to deal with difficulties resulting from lack of cooperation by any State.

The Expert Committee is of the view that, while measures are possible, the effectiveness of any Security Council decision along these lines will depend on the degree of sincere collective determination of those imposing the measures, and especially of the States which have close economic relations with South Africa. Great emphasis was also given in the Committee to the importance of the psychological effect of such measures, stress being laid on the fact that the present leaders and the inhabitants of South Africa would find it difficult to withstand their effects.

With regard to economic implications, the Committee, while believing that a spirit of sacrifice should prevail in a matter so important to the international community as that of eliminating apartheid, was of the opinion that an international effort should be made to mitigate the hardships which such measures would impose on the economies of some Member States. These might take the form of dislocations in certain markets and in particular countries, depending on the kind of measures applied. While special importance was attached to these factors, they should not by their nature prevent the application of measures against South Africa.

Having regard to the foregoing considerations, the Committee recognized the importance to be given to the following measures:

(a) embargo on the supply of petroleum and petroleum products;

(b) embargo on the supply of arms, ammunition of all types, military vehicles, and strategic equipment and materials for the manufacture and maintenance of arms and ammunition in South Africa;

(c) embargo on trade with South Africa;

(d) cessation of the emigration of technicians and skilled labour to South Africa;

(e) interdiction of communications with South Africa;

(f) application of political and diplomatic measures as mentioned in the various resolutions already adopted by the Security Council and the General Assembly.

The Committee also stressed the necessity of solving certain problems of implementation in order to judge the practical scope and the effectiveness of the above measures. Emphasis was placed on the necessity of a total blockade to make the measures effective and on the considerable costs involved in mounting such an operation. At the same time, it was pointed out that measures affecting vulnerable sectors of the South African economy might constitute an effective undertaking both in their practical impact on the country's economy and in the political and psychological repercussions they would have on the White minority. The possible importance of a partial blockade in the cases mentioned in paragraph 9 (a) and (b) above was pointed out in this connection. Furthermore, in a decision to apply measures against South Africa it would be useful to set up a committee to coordinate their implementation. The same committee could, if necessary, coordinate action to mitigate proportionally the hardships that might be suffered by the economies of Member States.

Finally, the Expert Committee is of the view that, while these measures could prove effective and would be feasible under the conditions enumerated in the preceding paragraphs, it should be stressed that the imposition of such measures involves political and psychological considerations which are matters for the Security Council.

16.   The Committee wishes to place on record its great appreciation of the cooperation and assistance it received from the Secretary and from his colleagues, who made a significant contribution to facilitating the Committee's work and understanding of the highly complex subject-matter under study.

# Document 45

*General Assembly resolution: The policies of apartheid of the Government of the Republic of South Africa*

A/RES/2054 B (XX), 15 December 1965

*The General Assembly,*

. . .

*Deeply concerned* at the plight of numerous persons persecuted by the Government of South Africa for their opposition to the policies of apartheid and repression, and at the plight of their families,

*Considering* that humanitarian assistance to such persons and their families is in keeping with the purposes of the United Nations,

1.   *Expresses its great appreciation* to the Governments which have made contributions in response to General Assembly resolution 1978 B (XVIII) and to the appeal made on 26 October 1964 by the Special Committee on the Policies of Apartheid of the Government of the Republic of South Africa;

2.   *Requests* the Secretary-General to establish a United Nations Trust Fund for South Africa, made up of voluntary contributions from States, organizations and

individuals, to be used for grants to voluntary organizations, Governments of host countries of refugees from South Africa and other appropriate bodies, towards:

(a) Legal assistance to persons charged under discriminatory and repressive legislation in South Africa;

(b) Relief for dependants of persons persecuted by the Government of South Africa for acts arising from opposition to the policies of apartheid;

(c) Education of prisoners, their children and other dependants;

(d) Relief for refugees from South Africa;

3. *Requests* the President of the General Assembly to nominate five Member States, each of which should appoint a person to serve on a Committee of Trustees of the United Nations Trust Fund for South Africa, which will decide on the uses of the Fund;

4. *Authorizes and requests* the Committee of Trustees to take steps to promote contributions to the Fund, and to promote cooperation and coordination in the activities of voluntary organizations concerned with relief and assistance to the victims of the policies of apartheid of the Government of South Africa;

. . .

---

# Document 46

*Report of the Special Committee on the Policies of Apartheid of the Government of the Republic of South Africa (extract from Conclusions and Recommendations)*

A/6486-S/7565, 25 October 1966

. . .

## A programme of action by the United Nations

Faithful to its mandate from the General Assembly the Special Committee has attempted to promote a comprehensive programme of action, under the auspices of the United Nations, to solve the problem of apartheid.

It has given primary importance to economic sanctions and related measures designed to secure the speedy eradication of apartheid and the development of a non-racial society in South Africa. It has suggested measures to persuade the main trading partners of South Africa to cooperate in facilitating universal economic sanctions.

It has suggested the arms embargo and various other partial steps to secure certain minimum but vital objectives.

It has emphasized the importance of public opinion in reinforcing and supporting United Nations action and suggested various measures to inform world opinion of the dangers of apartheid and of the United Nations efforts to solve the problem. In this connection, it emphasized the particular importance of informing opinion in the countries which maintain close economic and other relations with South Africa and of counteracting the deceitful propaganda by the South African Government and by business and other interests collaborating with it.

While constantly concerned with efforts to secure a solution, and without diverting attention from the need for urgent action for that purpose, the Special Committee has also given attention to various humanitarian, cultural

and other programmes. It made it clear that these programmes should in no way be regarded as alternatives for action to solve the problem.

In this connection, the Special Committee has been concerned with programmes and measures by which the international community can prevent serious aggravation of the situation and the growth of racial bitterness and hatred, and can help alleviate distress among the victims of apartheid. It encouraged various initiatives to save the lives of opponents of apartheid threatened with execution and to prevent the torture and brutal ill-treatment of prisoners. It encouraged programmes to provide for legal defence of persons accused under arbitrary laws, aid to families of political prisoners and education of their dependants, and relief to refugees. By emphasizing the humanitarian nature of these programmes, and keeping them distinct from efforts to secure an end to apartheid, the Special Committee has sought to enable wide segments of the international community to demonstrate, by action, their concern for a peaceful solution of the problem in South Africa.

In the same spirit, the Special Committee commended the United Nations Programme for the Education and Training Abroad of South Africans, designed to assist South Africans to receive higher education and technical training and enable them to contribute effectively to the progress of their country in accordance with the purpose of the Charter.

The Special Committee is awaiting a report, being

prepared at its request by the United Nations Educational, Scientific and Cultural Organization, on the effects of the policies of apartheid in the fields of education, science, culture and information in South Africa. It feels that such a report will provide authoritative information to non-governmental organizations and interested individuals and enable them to provide appropriate assistance to the millions who are denied equal opportunities because of racial discrimination.

The Special Committee has commended the efforts of the International Labour Organisation in pursuance of its declaration on the policy of apartheid of the Republic of South Africa and its programme for the elimination of apartheid in labour matters in the Republic of South Africa.

The Special Committee has encouraged various ameliorative measures without diverting attention from the primary task of contributing to the eradication of apartheid. It has maintained contact with other United Nations organs, as well as specialized agencies and non-governmental organizations, in order to promote meaningful action at all levels. It has thus sought to play a helpful role in promoting a comprehensive approach to deal with various aspects of the apartheid policy and its ill-effects, with emphasis on action rather than mere condemnation of apartheid. It has been gratified by the endorsement of its recommendations by the General Assembly, as well as the Seminar on Apartheid held at Brasilia in 1966 and by the responses from States and numerous non-governmental organizations concerned with this problem.

These efforts of the Special Committee demonstrated its intense concern to do all in its power, in accordance with its mandate from the General Assembly and the needs of the situation, to promote all possible peaceful measures towards a solution of the problem of apartheid during a period when the actions of the South African Government were precipitating a conflict. While the Special Committee had no doubt that the hopes of the South African Government that an armed racist minority can for ever dominate the country would fail, and that non-racialism and justice would triumph, it was always anxious to promote the widest international support and understanding of the struggle against apartheid, especially in the predominantly "White" and "Christian" nations, in order to promote the most peaceful transition and to mitigate the dangers of racial bitterness.

While the Special Committee respects the right of the oppressed people to liberate themselves by means of their own choice, and recognizes that avenues for peaceful change are increasingly closed by the Government, it may well be that the constant concern of the Special Committee, and the support it received from the Member States and public opinion, has helped to contribute toward mitigating violence and racial bitterness and hatred. It recognizes, however, that the danger of violent conflict cannot be eliminated unless decisive steps are taken to eradicate apartheid.

The Special Committee feels that, in view of the aggravation of the situation in South Africa and neighbouring territories, these many-sided efforts should be redoubled in a comprehensive international campaign against apartheid under the auspices of the United Nations. It has attempted to ensure that the Seminar on Apartheid would give particular attention to concrete measures for a programme of action and has noted with satisfaction that the Seminar has made a number of recommendations which deserve consideration and endorsement by the competent United Nations organs.

. . .

# Document 47

*General Assembly resolution: Elimination of all forms of racial discrimination*

A/RES/2142 (XXI), 26 October 1966

*The General Assembly*

. . .

8.  *Proclaims* 21 March as International Day for the Elimination of Racial Discrimination;

. . .

# Document 48

*General Assembly resolution: Question of the violation of human rights and fundamental freedoms, including policies of racial discrimination and segregation and of apartheid, in all countries, with particular reference to colonial and other dependent countries and territories*

A/RES/2144 A (XXI), 26 October 1966

*The General Assembly,*

...

*Taking note* of the conclusions and recommendations of the Seminar on Apartheid, organized under the programme of advisory services in the field of human rights and held at Brasilia in 1966,

...

7. *Appeals* to all States, governmental and non-governmental organizations, and individuals:

(*a*) To support the United Nations Trust Fund for South Africa and voluntary organizations engaged in providing relief and assistance to victims of colonialism and apartheid;

(*b*) To encourage judicial associations and other appropriate organizations, and the public in general, to provide such relief and assistance;

8. *Urges* Member States to take all necessary measures, in accordance with their domestic laws, against the operations of propaganda organizations of the Government of South Africa and of private organizations which advocate apartheid and policies of racial discrimination and domination;

...

13. *Requests* the Secretary-General to establish a unit within the Secretariat of the United Nations to deal exclusively with policies of apartheid, in consultation with the Special Committee on the Policies of Apartheid of the Government of the Republic of South Africa, in order that maximum publicity may be given to the evils of those policies;

...

# Document 49

*General Assembly resolution: The policies of apartheid of the Government of the Republic of South Africa*

A/RES/2202 A (XXI), 16 December 1966

*The General Assembly,*

...

*Taking note* of the reports of the Special Committee on the Policies of Apartheid of the Government of the Republic of South Africa and endorsing its proposals for an international campaign against apartheid under the auspices of the United Nations,

*Taking note with satisfaction* of the report of the Seminar on Apartheid, held at Brasilia from 23 August to 4 September 1966,

*Gravely concerned* at the intensification of the policies of apartheid in South Africa and the direct support given by the Government of South Africa to the colonialist and racist regimes on its borders, thus aggravating the situation in southern Africa,

*Noting with concern* that the policies of the Government of South Africa aim at perpetuating apartheid in South Africa, that they strengthen the colonialist and racist regimes on its borders and that they threaten the integrity and sovereignty of the neighbouring independent States,

1. *Condemns* the policies of apartheid practised by the Government of South Africa as a crime against humanity;

2. *Reaffirms* that the situation in South Africa and the resulting explosive situation in southern Africa continue to pose a grave threat to international peace and security;

3. *Deplores* the attitude of the main trading partners of South Africa, including three permanent members of the Security Council, which, by their failure to cooperate in implementing resolutions of the General Assembly, by their refusal to join the Special Committee on the Policies of Apartheid of the Government of the Republic of South Africa and by their increasing collaboration with the Government of South Africa, have encouraged the latter to persist in its racial policies;

4. *Draws the attention* of the main trading partners

of South Africa to the fact that their increasing collaboration with the Government of South Africa despite repeated appeals by the General Assembly has aggravated the danger of a violent conflict, and requests them to take urgent steps towards disengagement from South Africa and to facilitate effective action, under the auspices of the United Nations, to secure the elimination of apartheid;

5. *Appeals* to all States:

(*a*) To comply fully with the decisions duly taken by the Security Council which solemnly call on them to cease forthwith the sale and delivery to South Africa of arms, ammunition of all types, military vehicles and equipment and materials intended for their manufacture and maintenance;

(*b*) To discourage immediately the establishment of closer economic and financial relations with South Africa, particularly in investment and trade, and also to discourage loans by banks in their countries to the Government of South Africa or South African companies, and to submit reports to the Secretary-General on steps taken in this respect, such reports to be transmitted by the Secretary-General to the General Assembly and the Special Committee;

(*c*) To consider effective political, moral and material assistance to all those combating the policies of apartheid, in the light of the recommendations of the Seminar on Apartheid;

(*d*) To make adequate and generous contributions to humanitarian programmes designed to assist the victims of apartheid;

(*e*) To endeavour to grant asylum and extend travel facilities and educational and employment opportunities to refugees from South Africa;

6. *Requests* the Secretary-General:

(*a*) To organize as soon as possible, in consultation with the Special Committee on the Policies of Apartheid of the Government of the Republic of South Africa and the Special Committee on the Situation with regard to the Implementation of the Declaration on the Granting of Independence to Colonial Countries and Peoples, an international conference or seminar on the problems of apartheid, racial discrimination and colonialism in southern Africa, and to transmit the report of that conference or seminar to the General Assembly at its twenty-second session;

(*b*) To take steps, in consultation with the Special Committee on the Policies of Apartheid of the Government of the Republic of South Africa, for the periodic publication of statistics on South Africa's international trade;

(*c*) To provide all the necessary assistance to the Special Committee on the Policies of Apartheid of the

Government of the Republic of South Africa in publicizing and reporting on any tightening of economic and financial relations between other States and South Africa;

(*d*) To consult with the International Bank for Reconstruction and Development in order to obtain its compliance with the provisions of General Assembly resolutions 2105 (XX) of 20 December 1965 and 2107 (XX) of 21 December 1965 and with those of the present resolution, and to report to the General Assembly at its twenty-second session;

(*e*) To provide the Special Committee on the Policies of Apartheid of the Government of the Republic of South Africa with all the necessary means, including appropriate financial means, for the effective accomplishment of its task;

7. *Once again draws the attention* of the Security Council to the fact that the situation in South Africa constitutes a threat to international peace and security, that action under Chapter VII of the Charter of the United Nations is essential in order to solve the problem of apartheid and that universally applied mandatory economic sanctions are the only means of achieving a peaceful solution;

8. *Invites* the Special Committee on the Policies of Apartheid of the Government of the Republic of South Africa to continue to take all steps to discharge its mandate more effectively and, to that end, authorizes it:

(*a*) To hold sessions away from Headquarters or to send a sub-committee on a mission to consult specialized agencies, regional organizations, States and non-governmental organizations on ways and means to promote the international campaign against apartheid and to investigate various aspects of the problem of apartheid;

(*b*) To continue and to increase cooperation with the Special Committee on the Situation with regard to the Implementation of the Declaration on the Granting of Independence to Colonial Countries and Peoples with a view to the consideration of the activities of foreign economic interests in southern Africa which impede the efforts to eliminate apartheid, racial discrimination and colonialism in the region;

9. *Requests* the Secretary-General and the specialized agencies to consider appropriate assistance for the employment in their secretariats and programmes of qualified South Africans who are victims of apartheid;

10. *Invites* the specialized agencies, regional organizations, States and non-governmental organizations to cooperate with the Secretary-General and the Special Committee on the Policies of Apartheid of the Government of the Republic of South Africa in the accomplishment of their tasks under the present resolution.

# Document 50

*Letter dated 3 February 1967 from the Chairman of the Special Committee on the Policies of Apartheid of the Government of the Republic of South Africa, Mr. Achkar Marof (Guinea), to Secretary-General U Thant concerning the treatment of political prisoners in South Africa*

UN Press Release GA/AP/88, 3 February 1967

. . .

I have the honour, on behalf of the Special Committee, to request you to draw the urgent attention of the Commission on Human Rights to the continuing ill-treatment of prisoners, detainees and persons in police custody in the Republic of South Africa, particularly the numerous opponents of apartheid who have been imprisoned under arbitrary laws.

The Special Committee has always been gravely concerned over this matter and has reported on it to the General Assembly and the Security Council. A number of documents of the Special Committee, a list of which is attached, contain alarming evidence of ill-treatment of such persons in prisons and police stations.

In its reports of 30 November 1964 and 10 August 1965, the Special Committee suggested the establishment of an international commission composed of eminent jurists and prison officials to investigate the charges of torture and ill-treatment of prisoners in South Africa. The suggestion was not pressed in the General Assembly because it was hoped that the expression of international concern might persuade the South African Government to improve conditions so as to conform with civilized standards and the regulations in South Africa itself.

However, evidence of the continuing ill-treatment of prisoners, detainees and persons in police custody is still being received. Those being subjected to this ill-treatment include not only acknowledged leaders of the people and opponents of apartheid who have been persecuted under legislation which violates the fundamental principles of human rights, but also thousands who have been imprisoned for the infringement of apartheid laws.

As the Special Committee observed in its report of 21 October 1966, the ruthless measures of the South African Government seem to be increasingly designed to wreak vengeance against the opponents of apartheid. In the view of the Special Committee, such measures contravene international standards of behaviour and the Universal Declaration of Human Rights.

The Special Committee, therefore, hopes that the Commission on Human Rights will consider the matter urgently and take steps to secure an international investigation with a view to ameliorating the conditions of these victims.

# Document 51

*Statement by Mr. Dennis Brutus, Director of the Campaign for the Release of Political Prisoners in South Africa, in the Special Committee against Apartheid*

A/AC.115/L.194, 27 February 1967

. . .

I am especially grateful for this opportunity since I am speaking also as the Director of a Campaign launched by the International Defence and Aid Fund, under the presidency of Canon L. John Collins, for the release of all political prisoners in South Africa.

I cannot claim any professional training or expertise which would specially fit me for the task of testifying on conditions under which political prisoners are kept in South Africa, but I can refer to a record of more than twenty years of sustained opposition to apartheid in various fields, especially those of housing, education and sport, as well as in broader political issues, which opposition culminated in my being subjected to a series of restrictions and bans and finally in my imprisonment and subsequent placing under house-arrest for five years.

It is of my twenty-two months in prison and my experiences there that I wish especially to speak, and of the conditions as they applied to other prisoners. It is my conviction and that of those associated with me in the current campaign, that if the world can be brought to the knowledge of these conditions, there would be a strong and sincere demand for the release of all political prisoners, and that this demand could be backed by the moral, political and other pressures which would make it a meaningful reality.

We are especially heartened by the knowledge that the demand of our Campaign for an investigation of prison conditions in South Africa is made also by this Special Committee, as well as by a host of other organizations. We are particularly encouraged by the knowledge that this Committee, in its February meeting, has renewed this demand in very explicit terms to the Commission on Human Rights, asking:

> "that the Commission on Human Rights would consider this matter urgently and take steps to secure an international investigation with a view to ameliorating the conditions of these victims" (of apartheid).

I have had personal experience of prison conditions in South Africa, particularly at the Fort, Johannesburg, Leeukop (Bryanston, Johannesburg) and Robben Island Prison. In addition, I spent some days in the prisons at Pollsmoor and Roeland Street, Capetown, and passed through the prisons at Kroonstad, Bloemfontein, Colesberg, George and Port Elizabeth. This is apart from the days spent in a Portuguese prison in Lourenço Marques, Mozambique.

I propose to give some details of my experience in these prisons, and of what I observed of the treatment of others, and to refer briefly to the Red Cross Report on South African Prisons before going on to discuss our *Campaign for the Release of Political Prisoners*: its aims, methods and the manner in which it can, in conjunction with the Special Committee, contribute to the achievement of its purposes and the ultimate overthrow of apartheid which this implies.

I hope it is not necessary to stress that my ultimate aim can only be, as it is for the men who are imprisoned, the complete overthrow of apartheid and its replacement by a just social system.

Any campaign which does not set as its final goal the overthrow of apartheid can only be regarded as trifling, and as failing to come to grips with the realities of the South African situation.

The South African situation is one in which men are today being tried and imprisoned for their opposition to racist domination; it was this system which imprisoned me. In May of 1963, then under a ban, I was arrested at the offices of the South African Olympic Association and charged with attending a gathering. For this offence, and others related to it, I was eventually sentenced to eighteen months imprisonment with hard labour: sixteen months of this I served on Robben Island. In all I spent twenty-two months in various prisons.

I am still, to the best of my knowledge, the only prisoner who can come to you with first-hand information from Robben Island. I have also checked my information with those having served time in other prisons and who have left South Africa more recently than I (July 1966). These people have amply confirmed my facts, so that I am satisfied that the information which I place before this Committee is as up to date and accurate as it is possible to give at the present time.

...

After being sentenced to eighteen months imprisonment in Johannesburg, I was taken to the Fort, Johannesburg, and on the following day in chains to Leeukop Prison.

At Leeukop, after we had complained that we were not being given exercise for weeks, the group of about thirty-five in my cell were forced to run in circles in a quadrangle.

We were forced to run until we were exhausted, in the presence of a Lieutenant van Zyl. I had at that time not yet recovered completely from the effects of the bullet injury I had suffered when being shot by a member of the Security Police, and so asked that I be allowed to stop running. But this was refused me, and I was forced to run until at the point of collapse.

An even worse experience was had by a group of prisoners from Durban, who were made to run naked for almost an hour in a quadrangle—being continuously beaten by warders as they ran, and many of them falling and being beaten and made to rise.

Two months later a group of 120 of us—all political prisoners—were removed, again in chains, at night in three large trucks. Half of us were left the next day in Kroonstad, at the prison there, and the rest of us were brought down to Robben Island, still in chains.

On the day after our arrival in Robben Island, in March 1964, we saw a large number of prisoners, including Andrew Masondo, being assaulted indiscriminately by a group of warders in what was known as a "carry-on". This was a command given by a Lieutenant Fraser which allowed the warders to hit the prisoners—numbering perhaps sixty—at will.

Later the same day my own outfit of about sixty was taken to work with the Masondo group carrying stones at a quarry or building site. Here we were all continuously assaulted and beaten by warders armed with sticks, batons, straps and builders' planks. Most of us were covered with bruises, some were bleeding, and some collapsed but were made to rise and continue working.

On the Monday after our arrival, we were made to work in a quarry near the beach. Here we were again continuously assaulted and beaten throughout the day. In addition to being beaten by warders, I was also kicked in the stomach by one of the criminal boss-boys. It was as a result of this injury that I was later placed in the prison hospital and subsequently sent in June of 1964 to Pollsmoor Prison near Capetown for treatment at Victoria Hospital, Wynberg.

During my period on Robben Island I frequently saw prisoners, both political and criminal, being assaulted, and furthermore saw them exposed to additional punishments ranging from deprivation of three meals to periods of spare diet or lashes given while strapped to a metal frame.

One instance I remember especially is of a young political prisoner who was beaten because he would not submit to the homosexual embraces of the criminals. For this he was repeatedly beaten and at the time I made contact with him he was brought into the segregation section because he was alleged to be mad. It is true that his behaviour at this time suggested that he was deranged. He was subsequently taken out of segregation and I heard nothing more about him.

In addition to these incidents there were many others that I heard of by report, but since I did not have direct experience of these, I prefer to limit myself to those I know of: but I have not given all such instances here.

I am satisfied from my experience, however, that the two worst features of life in prison were:

(a)   the harshness and barrenness of the life which prisoners had to live, particularly under the hostility of warders and some of the criminal prisoners;

(b)   that men who had acted in conscience against an evil system should be punished by imprisonment—in many instances life.

For the greater part of my sentence, I was kept in the segregation section—also called, in one report, the "leadership" section, where I worked breaking stones alongside men like Nelson Mandela, Walter Sisulu, Ahmed Kathrada, Govan Mbeki, Andrew Mlangeni and Elias Matsoaledi—all of them sentenced for life imprisonment after the Rivonia trial. Also serving a life sentence was Jeff Mazemola; other prisoners with me were Andrew Masondo, George Peake, Lallo Chiba, Mac Maharaj, Eddie Daniels, Dr. Neville Alexander, Don Davis, Les van der Heyden and Zeph Mothupin.

Most of these men, at some time, broke stones with me in the enclosure of the segregated section, but the majority of them were later removed to the much harder work at the lime-pits—going out each day from our section to dig blocks of lime in the quarry.

Shortly before I left, a few of them had come in for brief periods because of some illness to work at breaking stones; these included Raymond Mhlaba and Billy Nair. Indres Naidoo and Jonas Mlambo were men I saw briefly when they had been brought into our section for a special purpose: both of them were tried on various charges and sentenced to lashes. I saw the scars thereafter, when the flesh was still cut open and raw. The scars will be with them for life.

. . .

This is only a brief and very sketchy account of what happened in prison in the time that I was there; I propose to provide your Committee with a much more detailed and fully documented account as well.

This testimony, however, should be sufficient to indicate the conditions under which political prisoners are kept. I hope that it will be useful to strengthen the demand made by the Special Committee as well as by International Defence and Aid and other organizations, that there should be an investigation into prison conditions in South Africa.

I should like to refer at this point to some attempts at investigation of prison conditions. While I was in prison, together with the rest of my group in the segregation section, one day we were given needles and thread and some old uniforms and told to mend them. We did this for a short time. Then a press photographer turned up and we were photographed at work. The very next day we were again given a load of stones and a hammer and instructed to reduce the stones to gravel. This incident can be vouched for by a number of prisoners. The picture of us mending uniforms has since been widely published— I have seen it—but is a completely false and misleading image of what we were required to do.

In May of 1964 we heard of the visit of an investigator—we believed from the United Nations. My personal knowledge of it came when it was decided to issue me with shoes—in case I should be called for by the visitor. I had previously been given sandals, but for some time had been going barefoot with large blisters on my feet—in addition to the cuts and sores I had sustained on the rocks while working in the quarry on the beach immediately after my arrival. At the time of this visit—by Dr. Hoffman, as I learned later—I saw for the first time—and it was a surprise also to criminals who had served many years—the convicts in hospitals wearing brown pajamas. These they wore—just as others who told Dr. Hoffman that they had been issued with new uniforms—until the visit was over. The most dishonest thing I saw, however, was the sight of sick prisoners lying in beds in the prison hospital—for the duration of this visit. Normally the beds were "for inspection only"—I had myself lain on the floor while in the prison hospital—and the sick prisoners were told to get back on the floor after the visit was over.

It should be understood that Dr. Hoffman did not know the extent to which he was being deceived—indeed his visit had real value in that it led to a few small improvements in treatment for a short while—but the Red Cross report is misleading and gives no indication of the real hardship endured by the prisoners. Subsequent to the release of the Red Cross report—and some comments by the South African Government attempting to white-wash facts given in the report which hint at how dreadful the real position is—there has been a statement made on behalf of the Government which denies that there are any political prisoners at all, conceding only that there might "possibly" be *one*—Mr. Robert Sobukwe.

. . .

Two things are certain: that there is a considerable amount of brutality and cruelty in the South African prisons where political prisoners are held, and that these men ought not to be in prison at all, for they have fought on the side of justice against injustice. These two points are the basis of the Campaign which has been launched by International Defence and Aid.

Originally called the Campaign for Release of Imprisoned Politicians in South Africa, the name has just been changed to the *Campaign for the Release of Political Prisoners in South Africa*, since it is now pooling resources with the *World Campaign for the Release of Political Prisoners in South Africa*—a Committee initiated by the Anti-Apartheid Movement. These bodies work together for their common goal, along with several others.

Two major bodies supporting the Campaign are the African National Congress and the Pan-Africanist Congress of South Africa. In addition, the Campaign has the formal support of the Organization of African Unity, as expressed in a letter from its Secretary-General, Mr. Diallo Telli.

. . . the principal aims of the Campaign are to seek an investigating commission to go to South Africa to look into prison conditions, and to make a demand for the release of all political prisoners. We seek, as a subsidiary aim, the amelioration of conditions for the prisoners, and we also urge an investigation on behalf of those who are held as 180-day detainees, without charge or trial.

The above request for the release of the political prisoners is based on the resolution adopted by the United Nations in 1964, by 106 votes to 1. I was in prison at the time but heard of the resolution: that all South African political prisoners should be released, and that all political trials should cease.

It is our hope, and the aim of this Campaign, that the United Nations will in time come to make this resolution not only meaningful, but a reality; we see the sending of an investigating commission as a preliminary step. It is quite possible that the South African Government will elect to defy the world and to refuse admission to such a commission. It is our hope that the world will be sufficiently resolute to impose its will against apartheid.

It is clear that mere resolutions are not likely to change the situation in my country. While conditions become increasingly intolerable, the prospect of peaceful change vanishes, and that of change by any means becomes increasingly distant. But it is imperative to create constantly fresh pressures for change as the prospect of disaster looms ever closer.

Ultimately there can be only one objective for all pressures against apartheid: the complete destruction of the system.

---

# Document 52

*Resolution adopted by the United Nations Commission on Human Rights*

E/CN.4/RES/2 (XXIII), 6 March 1967

*The Commission on Human Rights,*

*Considering* that the General Assembly by its resolution 2144 A (XXI), paragraph 12, invited the Commission to give urgent consideration to ways and means of improving the capacity of the United Nations to put a stop to violations of human rights wherever they may occur,

*Having considered and examined* the communication from the Secretary-General transmitting a letter from the Acting Chairman of the General Assembly's Special Committee on the Policies of Apartheid of the Government of the Republic of South Africa (E/CN.4/935) together with its enclosures (A/AC.115/L.53, 73, 87, 106, 116, 123 and 181),

*Deeply disturbed* by the evidence in those documents of continuing torture and ill-treatment of persons in the Republic of South Africa who have been detained by the police or imprisoned for opposition to, or infringement of, apartheid laws,

*Strongly deploring* the continued flagrant violation of the provisions of the Charter of the United Nations by the Government of the Republic of South Africa and the actions of that Government which are contrary to international law and international morality,

*Determined* to protect human rights and fundamental freedoms, and desirous of an urgent and immediate stop of violations of human rights and fundamental freedoms in the Republic of South Africa,

*Having heard* the statement of the Observer of the Republic of South Africa in connection this question,

*Noting* with appreciation the proclamation of the General Assembly in its resolution 2142 (XXI) of the annual commemoration of the massacre of Sharpeville, 21 March, as International Day for the Elimination of Racial Discrimination,

1. *Condemns* the practices described and complained of in the above-cited documents as constituting a double injury against the victims of the inhuman policies of apartheid of the Government of the Republic of South Africa, who are imprisoned or detained for opposing and violating those policies;

2. *Requests* the Secretary-General immediately to address, on behalf of the Commission, a telegram to the Government of the Republic of South Africa conveying the deep distress and serious concern of the Commission at this situation and requesting that Government to take positive action so that its treatment of political prisoners shall conform with civilized standards of penal law and practice;

3. *Decides* to establish, in accordance with resolution 9 (II) of 21 June 1946 of the Economic and Social Council, an ad hoc working group of experts composed of eminent jurists and prison officials to be appointed by the Chairman of the Commission to:

(*a*) investigate the charges of torture and ill-treatment of prisoners, detainees or persons in police custody in South Africa;

(*b*) receive communications and hear witnesses and use such modalities of procedure as it may deem appropriate;

(*c*) recommend action to be taken in concrete cases;

(*d*) report to the Commission on Human Rights at the earliest possible time;

4. *Calls upon* the Government of the Republic of South Africa to cooperate with the ad hoc working group of experts, providing it with the necessary facilities for the discharge of its task within South Africa;

5. *Requests* the Secretary-General to give the widest possible publicity, as soon as possible, to the documents received from the Acting Chairman of the Special Committee containing the testimony of political prisoners, victims of torture and ill-treatment in the prisons of South Africa, as well as the statements of Nelson Mandela and Abram Fischer in their recent court trials in South Africa;

6. *Calls upon* all Member States of the United Nations to give the widest national publicity, through all available information media, to the substance of the contents of these documents;

7. *Draws attention* of all international humanitarian organizations to these documents and appeals to them to take, as a matter of urgency, any appropriate action in their power to help alleviate the inhuman situation described therein;

8. *Appeals* to all Member States, governmental, non-governmental and private organizations, as well as private individuals, to support the United Nations Trust Fund for South Africa through financial and other aids;

9. *Requests* the Secretary-General to circulate this resolution to the members of the Security Council;

10. *Further requests* the Secretary-General to convey to the Special Committee on the Policies of Apartheid of the Government of the Republic of South Africa the desire of the Commission on Human Rights to maintain close collaboration with it in achieving their common objectives;

11. *Requests* its Chairman to maintain contact with the Secretary-General and to report before the end of the present session the progress of the implementation of this resolution;

12. *Recommends* that the Secretary-General, in consultation with Member States, arrange to provide facilities whereby Registers for the receipt of contributions from all sources, private and public, for the victims of the policies of apartheid and racism in South Africa may be opened in each country;

13. *Requests* the Secretary-General to report to the General Assembly the degree of cooperation he has received from the various Member States;

14. *Decides* to review the situation at its twenty-fourth session.

# Document 53

*Paper by Mr. Achkar Marof (Guinea), Chairman of the Special Committee on the Policies of Apartheid of the Government of the Republic of South Africa, "The crisis in southern Africa with special reference to South Africa and measures to be taken by the international community", presented to the International Seminar on Apartheid, Racial Discrimination and Colonialism in Southern Africa, held at Kitwe, Zambia, from 25 July to 4 August 1967*

A/6818, 29 September 1967

...

*The situation in southern Africa*

11.    I need hardly elaborate on the situation in southern Africa, as it is described in grim detail in numerous documents of the United Nations and will be dealt with in several papers of the Seminar. I will merely draw attention to a few main aspects of this situation.

12.    First, the situation in southern Africa today is not only intolerable for the oppressed peoples of that area, but constitutes a grave threat to international peace and security. There are already raging deadly wars in Mozambique and Angola where the forces of liberation are confronting colonial armies whose strength and whose equipment, obtained from NATO, are an indication of their intention to crush all resistance. Numerous incidents in Southern Rhodesia, South West Africa and South Africa point to the determination of the peoples of these countries to secure their liberation at all cost. If these incidents have not yet developed into large-scale combat, and the massive military forces of the racist regimes seem to be able to maintain control, that should not lead to miscalculations. The rulers of South Africa, who have increased their military budget sixfold since 1960, know and admit by their acts, which are even more eloquent than their words, the existence of an explosive situation. The history of liberation of colonial peoples in recent decades shows that the people will find ways to overcome reverses, to regroup and resist even the mightiest of the armies of the oppressors and win the battle of liberation.

13.    Second, a violent conflict in southern Africa cannot remain local but is bound to have grave international repercussions. It will undermine the efforts of African States to build non-racial societies and will damage prospects of international cooperation, an essential factor for peace and progress in the world. African and other States will inevitably be forced to intervene in various ways according to the needs of the African and Asian masses of South Africa. There is also reason to fear that certain Western Powers and other Powers which have been collaborating with the racist-colonialist forces face strong pressures by vested interests to induce them to intervene in one way or another against the liberation force on the fallaciously humanitarian pretence of protecting their nationals or economic interests.

14.    Third, it must be recalled that the responsibility for the constant deterioration of the situation in southern Africa rests largely with the Western Powers which have always resisted all effective international measures which have been suggested to solve the problem. There is doubt that the consensus which has developed in the United Nations against apartheid and colonialism remains rather hollow so long as meaningful action is not taken. The Western Powers (and Japan) bear a special responsibility for the serious crisis of southern Africa because of the dependence of the racist and colonial regimes in southern Africa on continued economic relations with them. The cooperation of these Powers is indispensable for the imposition and implementation of international economic sanctions which remain the only peaceful means for a solution. These Powers, however, have greatly increased their economic involvement in this area. Even the arms embargo, a very first step which they ostensibly supported, has not had much effect because of contravention by some Powers, such as France, loop-holes in the embargoes by others and open cooperation lent by several Powers toward the development of an arms industry inside South Africa. In these circumstances, it is essential to conclude that the only peaceful solution, which could have been achieved by mandatory economic sanctions, has become increasingly utopian and unrealizable.

15.    Fourth, among the forces which play the inglorious role of resisting the liberation of southern Africa, a prominent place is occupied by the numerous international corporations which have become involved in the area in the search for quick and exorbitant profits. They assist the racist and colonial regimes by loans and investments. They help develop arms and strategic industries to enable these regimes to resist sanctions. They help build

oil refineries in the area in order to circumvent the oil embargo against the regime in Southern Rhodesia.

16. Beneath the "unholy alliance", there is the giant economic complex, the "Cape to Katanga axis", which dominates the entire area. The big corporations of South Africa play a prominent role in this axis and international corporations participate in it, to a great extent, through subsidiaries and affiliates in South Africa.

17. Fifth, the continuance of the reign of apartheid and terror in South Africa, where the racist regime utilizes the country's immense wealth for military and political efforts to perpetuate racism constitutes the bulwark of reaction in the whole of southern Africa. The Pretoria regime is now openly challenging the United Nations all over southern Africa. It is illusory to expect that there can be substantial progress of liberation in that area so long as the South African regime is not neutralized. As I stated at the last session of the General Assembly:

> "The South African regime has been the main source of support for the Ian Smith clique in Southern Rhodesia and the principal obstacle to the implementation of the resolutions of the Security Council. It is in open rebellion against the United Nations in South West Africa. It has increasingly collaborated with the Portuguese colonialists who are carrying on colonial wars in Mozambique, Angola and so-called Portuguese Guinea. The sovereignty and independence of Lesotho and Botswana are threatened by the existence of this racist regime in South Africa.

> "There is a theory in some quarters that, in considering the liberation of southern Africa, South Africa should come last. According to this theory, we should deal first with Southern Rhodesia and the Portuguese territories and give full attention to the problems of South Africa only after these other territories are liberated. This theory, which superficially seems sound on geographical and logistical grounds, is misleading. So long as the regime in South Africa is secure, and feels itself to be secure, it would be idle to expect the liberation of other territories in southern Africa. The Pretoria regime has made it clear that it would sustain the Smith regime, whatever the next step in the United Nations. South Africa has also proclaimed that it will lend its support to the Portuguese colonialists in their war against the liberation movements. And in South West Africa, the United Nations and the liberation movement will face the full might of the Pretoria regime, which has been aided by the Powers of Western Europe and North America. When it threatens war against the United Nations if the United Nations seeks to fulfil its obligations to the people of South West Africa, its threats are backed by the planes, ships and guns supplied by the United Kingdom, the United States, France and Italy.

> "Of course, as I said recently, the war for South Africa has started in Angola and Mozambique and will soon move on to Southern Rhodesia, heading irresistibly towards Cape Town. This does not preclude the possibility of an explosion with South Africa itself, making easier the liberation of the whole of southern Africa."

*Measures to be taken by the international community*

18. The Seminar has been convened in the hope that it will thoroughly examine and reassess the situation in southern Africa, and formulate proposals for further action by the international community.

19. Before dealing with the possible measures, it may be useful to refer briefly to certain general considerations.

20. Some circles abroad, and even a handful of people in Africa, are overawed by the ostensible military strength of the regimes in South Africa and Southern Rhodesia, and the military forces that Portugal has been able to mobilize for its colonial wars. They argue that these regimes cannot be overthrown. They consequently propose the search for a solution through the grant of meagre concessions, which are in any case dictated by the economic development needs of these racist bastions and the determination of the racists to have it believed that they have succeeded in breaking the political and diplomatic ostracism to which they are subjected by establishing relations with some African States which are, for various reasons, submissive to them.

21. The Seminar will no doubt take account of the military aspect, but there is little need to try to refute these defeatists. It is quickly forgotten that mightier nations have been defeated by forces of liberation in colonial wars of an unprecedented barbarism in this generation. Moreover, the apparent strength of the racial and colonial regimes is built on insecure foundations of oppression of the great majority: it can make the struggle bloodier but can never achieve the final victory.

22. On the other hand, it should be recalled that the main role in the liberation of southern Africa should rightfully go first to the oppressed people themselves. The international community can assist them and help create the conditions in which they can secure the liberation with the least possible violence and delay, but it cannot aspire to deliver liberation to them. The efforts of the international community should only complement the efforts of the oppressed peoples. As I stated in my address to the European Conference against Apartheid in Paris on 6 May 1967:

"The struggle for freedom in South Africa is certainly the right, the responsibility and the privilege of the people of South Africa. They have not abdicated their struggle or asked for freedom as a gift from the rest of the world. Whatever we do at the international level—whether Governments or in anti-apartheid movements and other popular organizations—we need to recognize in all humility that our role is but secondary. We do not aspire to liberate—which would be tantamount to substituting ourselves to the South African people—but to assist the liberation, as that is our duty if we are loyal to our own convictions. We can discharge this duty only if we avoid any pity or paternalism and remain at all times responsive to the needs and desires of the liberation movement."

23. Frustrated and apathetic, the liberals abroad do not believe any more in the illusion that liberation in southern Africa would be achieved by painless efforts of persuasion of the oppressors and that the international opinion would be decisive. It is essential to recognize that popular revolutions take their time, face reverses and even lose battles but will ultimately succeed. The international community cannot formulate the methods of the liberation struggle or determine its timetable. Perseverance and determination are essential if it is to play a helpful role.

24. Third, while the United Nations can play a significant role in the international field, its role is not exclusive. States individually, as well as collectively through the Organization of African Unity and other inter-governmental organizations, can make additional contributions. Non-governmental organizations of various sectors of public opinion can also play an important role. It is essential to coordinate these efforts in order to promote maximum effectiveness or the totality of international effort. The Special Committee on Apartheid, in proposing an international campaign against apartheid, therefore, suggested a many-sided effort to mobilize all these forces in order to help eradicate apartheid.

25. The efforts in the United Nations on the problems of apartheid, racial discrimination and colonialism in southern Africa have so far been directed on several fronts:

(a) The political isolation of the racist and colonial regimes, and the imposition of universal economic sanctions against them, has been the primary objective of these efforts. These efforts have apparently been effective in terms of overwhelming votes for condemnation of apartheid and colonialism, for a total arms embargo against South Africa, for a limited arms embargo against Portugal and for selective mandatory sanctions against Southern Rhodesia. But the progress has been largely illusory, as recommendations for sanctions have not been accepted or implemented by the main trading partners of the racist and colonial regimes which have, in fact, increased their collaboration and more than nullified the effect of boycotts instituted by other States at substantial sacrifice.

(b) Exposure of collaboration by States with the racist and colonial regimes, and of the activities of foreign economic and other interests which support these regimes.

(The activities of foreign economic and other interests in colonial territories will be on the agenda of the twenty-second session of the General Assembly in 1967.)

(c) Dissemination of information on the situation in southern Africa in order to counteract the propaganda of the racist and colonial regimes, and encourage world public opinion to support international efforts toward a solution of the problems. Encouragement to anti-apartheid movements and other non-governmental organizations to play a more effective role in opposition to racism and colonialism.

(d) Humanitarian assistance to the victims of apartheid and colonialism.

26. The establishment of the United Nations Trust Fund for South Africa, the support to voluntary organizations such as the International Defence and Aid Fund for southern Africa, provision of relief to refugees from South Africa and colonial territories, and special educational and training programmes for inhabitants of these territories fall in this category.

27. The Seminar will no doubt discuss the progress made on all these measures which have been taken, draw up a balance sheet and consider means by which they can be made more effective.

28. It has become increasingly evident, however, that a reassessment is essential and that the focus of international effort should be reconsidered. While universal economic sanctions remain the most appropriate peaceful measures under the United Nations Charter for a solution of the problems, and pressure for such sanctions should continue, it is unrealistic to ignore the fact that the main trading partners of southern Africa, including three permanent members of the Security Council, are unwilling to implement these measures (except to a limited extent in the case of Southern Rhodesia where the measures are ineffective because of the refusal to take any action against violations by South Africa and Portugal).

29. The attitude of these Powers, despite numerous appeals by an overwhelming majority of States, has largely paralysed the United Nations with respect to southern Africa. It leaves violence as the only alternative. The liberation movements, for their part, have decided on a violent struggle as the only means of salvation left to them by their oppressors and a certain international conspiracy.

30. As I stated recently in the Special Committee

on Apartheid, there is developing a new trend of thinking about the focus of international effort:

"The future is likely to be difficult as the apartheid regime, taking advantage of the inaction of various Powers concerned, is launching a counter-offensive against African liberation—making use of its economic and military power . . .

"For the last two decades, the anti-apartheid movements were largely on the humanitarian level, exposing to the public opinion in their countries the inhumanity of apartheid and seeking to mobilize public opinion to exercise its influence on South Africa and on various Governments to reverse the trend of increasing racism.

"These efforts have not succeeded for reasons which are well-known to this Committee. Today, the people of South Africa and of southern Africa as a whole are forced to embark on efforts to overthrow the racist regimes by force and establish non-racial societies.

"It is no more sufficient for the world to sympathize with the victims of apartheid. We can no more speak in the United Nations, as was done before, of persuading the South African regime to abandon apartheid or dissuading it from racialism. That has proved to be impossible. We need to encourage world opinion to support democratic changes in South Africa and a reconstruction of its society by a revolutionary process. The role of the United Nations and of world opinion has to become more positive.

"The liberation of South Africa will have to be achieved by the people of South Africa. But they should be able to count on the support and solidarity of the rest of the world."

31. A beginning has already been made in the United Nations. The General Assembly of the United Nations has recognized—in resolutions 2189 (XX) and 2202 (XX), for instance—that the struggle of the peoples under colonial rule, and under the regime of apartheid, to exercise their right to independence and equality is a legitimate struggle and that all States should provide moral and material assistance to the liberation movements. This question of aid to the liberation movements should be thoroughly discussed at the Seminar with a view to the adoption of concrete recommendations.

32. It is to be hoped that the Seminar will bring forth an unequivocal declaration recognizing the legitimacy of the struggle for liberation and the duty of the international community to support that struggle and that it will formulate concrete proposals to encourage and enable the international community to provide the most effective assistance to that struggle.

# Document 54

*Statement by Mr. Sverker C. Astrom (Sweden), Chairman of the Committee of Trustees of the United Nations Trust Fund for South Africa, in the Special Political Committee*

A/SPC/PV.563, 9 November 1967

With your permission, Mr. Chairman, I should like to draw the attention of the members of the Committee to the report of the Committee of Trustees for help to the victims of apartheid (A/6873). I shall be very brief and I shall not go into details which are already stated in the report.

First of all, on behalf of the Committee of Trustees, I wish to express our sincere appreciation of the generous contributions to the Trust Fund from Governments and others during the past year. . . . The need for financial support of the victims of apartheid in South Africa continues to be great and it is the hope of the Committee of Trustees that new substantial contributions will be forthcoming. May I say also that the Committee of Trustees has been gratified to note the expressions of support from the General Assembly, the Commission on Human Rights, the Organization of African Unity and many others.

It should perhaps be recalled that the Trust Fund is concerned exclusively with humanitarian work. Under the terms of reference given in resolution 2054 B (XX), its activities include provision of funds for legal aid to persons on trial in South Africa for acts arising from opposition to apartheid, relief for dependants of persecuted persons, education of prisoners and their dependants and relief for refugees from South Africa. In adopting this resolution in 1965 the General Assembly recognized almost unanimously that humanitarian assistance of this nature is appropriate and worthy of support and encouragement.

The Committee of Trustees, may I mention in passing, has five members, nominated on an individual basis by the five Member States chosen by the General Assembly. Due regard was taken of the principle of a just geographical distribution within the limitations imposed by the Committee's membership. The Committee has been entrusted with an important and delicate task, and its members are deeply aware of their responsibility to ensure that contributions to the Trust Fund are utilized strictly for the purposes indicated by the General Assembly.

As appears from the first report of the Committee of Trustees in 1966 (A/6494), the Committee has followed the practice of deciding in principle to recognize certain voluntary organizations as possible recipients of grants after taking into account their sponsorship, their performance with regard to relief and assistance in South Africa, and their accounting and other procedures. Before accepting an organization as recipient, the Committee has requested it to make the following commitments:

"(a) To use the grants for the purpose indicated by the Committee of Trustees in the light of the provisions of operative paragraph 2 of General Assembly resolution 2054 B (XX);

"(b) To report to the Committee of Trustees on the use of the grants; and

"(c) To provide such financial statements as the United Nations Secretary-General and the Board of Auditors may require in order to satisfy the provisions of the Financial Regulations of the United Nations relating to financial review and external audit of Trust Fund operations."

I wish to say that the Trustees feel that, through this procedure, they have done everything possible in order to ensure that the grants given are being used for the purposes stipulated by the Committee in each case, under the overall mandate decided upon by the General Assembly.

Members of this Committee are aware that work in this field has been made difficult by the attitude of the South African Government. Organizations engaged in assistance to the victims of apartheid have been subjected to various pressures and administrative measures. The Committee of Trustees feels that its work in supporting the humanitarian activities of voluntary organizations should be conducted in such a way, with regard to publicity, etc., that it is not rendered more difficult.

May I be allowed to recall here that members of the General Assembly and, I may add, the Special Committee on Apartheid have recognized that this humanitarian work should be kept distinct from the political and other measures taken by the General Assembly with regard to the political problems in South Africa.

In this context I would like to stress again that the Committee of Trustees has been constantly aware that its work cannot, and is not intended to, resolve the political and social problems with which other organs of the United Nations are concerned. Its purpose is to meet a limited, albeit urgent, humanitarian need. There is no doubt, however, that if assistance is given to the victims of apartheid by the joint efforts of the international community, this provides moral support to all those, inside or outside South Africa, who work for racial equality and social justice. As I had occasion to state last year in this Committee, it is important that this bond of human solidarity be preserved.

# Document 55

*"The present stage of the struggle against apartheid in South Africa": paper prepared by Mr. Oliver Tambo, Acting President of the African National Congress, at the request of the Special Committee on the Policies of Apartheid of the Government of the Republic of South Africa*

A/AC.115/L.222, 2 July 1968

Twenty years ago last month, a minority of the White minority in South Africa, steeped in the doctrines Hitler sought to impose by force on mankind, seized political power from another section of the White minority and immediately embarked on a vicious offensive against basic human rights. Later that year, the accredited representatives of the world's Governments, filled with the horror of nazism and fascism, assembled at the United Nations and adopted the Universal Declaration of Human Rights.

Thus the year 1948 witnessed the crystallization of two opposing forces: the one, resting on an international base, seeking to advance human rights in all parts of the world and the other, aiming at a studied destruction of human rights for all Black people, and spearheaded by a clique of White-skinned men and women in South Africa.

It is fair to say that both forces have made great strides since that eventful year. On the one hand, hundreds of millions of people spread over Africa, Asia and the Caribbean Islands have won their independence and regained their human dignity. A new Africa is being built on the ruins of a colonial era, and a once dominated, oppressed and humiliated two thirds of the world now forms an integral and acknowledged part of the international community of peoples. This is an indisputable triumph of the principles enshrined in the Universal Declaration of Human Rights.

On the other hand, the bonds of bondage that bound millions of Black people in South Africa twenty years ago have since been tightened to the absolute limit, the screws of oppression and exploitation have been driven in without mercy and racial discrimination permeates every sphere of South African life. Basic freedoms, few and far between in 1948, have been ruthlessly whittled away until today there are none worth mentioning. This, also, is an indisputable achievement for the doctrines of *baaskap*, superiority of the White skin and colonial domination, and is the more sinister because victory for reactionary forces is by definition the defeat of the forces for progress.

These achievements of twenty years of effort in two opposite directions lend special significance to the International Year for Human Rights proclaimed by the General Assembly and underscore the historic importance which the African National Congress of South Africa, together with its allies and sister political organizations and all genuine opponents of nazism, attach to General Assembly resolution 2307 (XXII), adopted on 13 December 1967, authorizing the Special Committee on the Policies of Apartheid of the Government of the Republic of South Africa "to intensify its efforts to promote an international campaign against apartheid".

In view of the oft-repeated claim by the Fascist Government of South Africa that there is peace and calm in that country, and by the big Western Powers that the situation in South Africa in no way constitutes a threat to international peace and security—claims persisted in despite constant warnings not only by the liberation movement in South Africa but also by the vast majority of United Nations Member States—it might be useful to refer to some of the developments in and around South Africa during the past five years.

## Recent developments in South Africa

The South African delegate to the General Assembly in 1963 presented South Africa as an island of peace in a turbulent world, with great strides being made not only in the general welfare of what are contemptuously termed "Bantu" but also in the direction of "Bantu self-government", the Transkei being cited as an example of guided progress towards independence.

Since then, however, the racist regime has had to present the world with the barbarous 90-day and 180-day Detention Acts invoked to legalize police torture and secret murder, in a desperate bid to suppress the liberation movement; there have been more political hangings and life imprisonments, as well as the greatest number of long-term political prisoners than during any corresponding period in the twenty years of Fascist rule in South Africa; the State of Emergency in the Transkei, first proclaimed in 1960, is still in force in this so-called self-governing territory; the much-publicized policy of creating more bantustans in South Africa has ground to a halt in the face of the stubborn resistance of the people; to the unprecedented collection of draconian laws that besmirch the South African Statute Book, and despite the notorious Sabotage Act, there has now been added the infamous Terrorism Act.

These measures are not consistent with the prevalence of a state of cordial relations between a White master and his Black servant. Nor are they adopted merely to maintain a *status quo ante* or destroy a subversive liberation movement. They seek to contain a swelling tide of revolution and revolt by the masses of the people against the entire system represented by White racist minority rule. These measures are as inevitable in the short term as they are valueless and even disastrous in the long term—inevitable because those who set out to reverse the course of human history and change the basic nature of living man must need resort to methods that are increasingly offensive and intolerable to man; valueless because these methods must fail and are failing; disastrous because by their racialist orientation, purpose and brutality, their growing effect is to bedevil the future for the very White minority whose interests they purport to serve and protect.

Thus predictably, the logic of an economic policy founded on racial discrimination has forced the South African regime to further tighten the iniquitous Pass Laws by enacting legislation such as the Bantu Laws Amendment Act, more completely condemning the African population to the status of cheap migrant labour for White-owned industries. This law, the Suppression of Communism Act, the Sabotage Act, the 90-day and 180-day Detention Laws, the Terrorism Act and numerous sections and sub-sections all combine to form a repressive umbrella under cover of which a reign of police terror has been unleashed and is sweeping through the towns and rural areas of South Africa. The people are being hunted and hounded out of their homes, from one segregated ghetto to another, deported from towns and cities to the countryside, and in the country subjected to house-to-house raids in the course of which weapons of every description are seized and confiscated. Intimidation and victimization of opponents of apartheid has mounted. In the meantime, the exploitation of people has become more ruthless as the economy flourishes in an unprecedented boom. While such diseases as tuberculosis are being eliminated among the Whites in South Africa, they are taking a heavy toll of life among the Africans and other victims of White minority rule, and nowhere is this more evident than in the bantustan territory of the Transkei.

## Armed struggle for freedom

It is these and similar conditions, *inter alia*, that are at once the cause and the effect of the escalating racial conflict between the ruling White minority and the ruled Black majority in South Africa, and it is important to warn again and again that this escalation, born of a policy that is strictly inhuman, can only be accelerated, far from being slowed down, by lapse of time. By the year 1961, it had reached a level which led the African National Congress and the oppressed population of South Africa to decide on armed struggle as the next phase of the fight for freedom. That decision which, it can now be said, will always constitute an important chapter in any analysis of the current political situation in the whole of southern Africa, was not taken lightly. The massive loss of life it entailed, the destruction of property, its implication for individual African independent States and for the peace and security of the whole of Africa and the world were not lost to the African National Congress and its leaders. But no one familiar with the struggles of oppressed peoples against colonialism and racial discrimination, particularly in the period since World War II, no one conversant with the long struggle of the South African people, and no one who believes whole-heartedly in the Universal Declaration of Human Rights can seriously question the decision of the oppressed people of South Africa and their allies to embark on a national revolutionary armed struggle for freedom. For any who may still be in doubt, it is necessary only to refer to the countless resolutions condemning and demanding the abandonment of the policies of apartheid which have been adopted over a period of at least two decades by the United Nations, by its many committees and agencies, by individual Governments, organizations, conferences and groups of men and women in every quarter of the world; to the numerous times that the apartheid regime has ignored and defied these resolutions and appeals; to the mountains of documents and paper work embodying studies revealing the horrors of White rule in South Africa, all of which make our freedom struggle one of the most thoroughly documented in history; finally, we need only refer to the sustained and mounting violence with which our peaceful and non-violent struggles were treated, including the series of massacres inflicted on our people when they sought, unarmed, the restoration of their human dignity.

Mahatma Gandhi, the great apostle of non-violence who founded and perfected his methods of struggle in South Africa, often said that he preferred violence to cowardice, and we may here recall the words of Chief Luthuli in 1964, from the isolation of Groutville, Natal, when he explained the new phase of the freedom struggle:

> "However, in the face of an uncompromising White refusal to abandon a policy which denies the African and other oppressed South Africans their rightful heritage—FREEDOM—no one can blame brave and just men for seeking justice by the use of violent methods; nor can they be blamed if they tried to create organized force in order ultimately to establish peace and racial harmony".

## Conflict in southern Africa

There have been other developments in the past few years bearing directly on the struggle against apartheid. The attainment of independence by Zambia, Malawi, Botswana and Lesotho has occurred side by side with the implementation of an expansionist policy by the Pretoria regime, which has for its aim the establishment of an empire ruled over by the White master-race, and consisting of a large number of small Black bantustans extending over the whole of southern Africa from the Atlantic to the Indian Ocean. Zambia refused to be part of this empire or to stoop to the status of a glorified bantustan. Instead she threw her weight behind the liberation struggle in Zimbabwe and the rest of southern Africa. This led the South African regime to strengthen its ties with the other members of the unholy alliance, particularly Rhodesia. Ian Smith admitted last year that if the South African Government had not given him assurances of support, he would not have proceeded with UDI [Unilateral Declaration of Independence]. In fact South Africa can be expected to have encouraged UDI to ensure the existence of a neighbouring White minority regime to which she is now in the process of exporting apartheid.

The rest of the independent African States bordering on South Africa are faced with a choice between supporting the racist regime and supporting the liberation movement and little evidence of neutrality. The masses of the people throughout southern Africa, however, remain totally opposed to White minority rule and fully support the struggle of their brothers in South Africa. The attempts by the South African racist regime to blackmail and bully neighbouring African Governments into allying themselves with it is a mean and selfish move to involve these Governments in a bloody defence of its inhuman policies in the same manner that it has driven 200,000 Whites in Zimbabwe into an unequal war with 4,000,000 Africans.

With the growing scope and intensity of the struggle against the apartheid regime and other members of the unholy alliance of Vorster, Smith and Salazar, the pressure on neighbouring States to become actively involved increases, and the conflict progressively takes on the character of a confrontation between colonial and White minority rule on the one side, and on the other, the combined numerical might of the supporters of majority rule in southern Africa. In this sense the armed struggle against apartheid is the struggle against White minority rule everywhere, and has become inseparable from the struggle of the people of Zimbabwe as well as being an essential part of the struggle for freedom from Portuguese colonialism.

It is these factors, among others, which explain the alliance that has been forged between the African National Congress of South Africa and the Zimbabwe African People's Union.

The armed struggle launched by these two liberation movements in Zimbabwe has exposed not only the deep involvement of the Pretoria regime in the internal affairs of Rhodesia, but also its sinister designs against African States. Already the South African Prime Minister has repeated wild threats against Zambia. These threats have been followed up by the derailment of trains in Zambia, the blowing up of a bus, the bombing of civilians and very recently the blowing up of an important bridge. The existence of an active unholy alliance of which Vorster is a key member makes it unimportant which member of the unholy alliance is responsible for the attacks.

It is clear therefore that even at this very early stage of the armed conflict the situation in southern Africa, precisely because it now directly involves South Africa, is beginning to have serious international repercussions. When the conflict springs up and spreads, as it soon must, over South African territory, the desperation of the apartheid regime can be expected to make itself felt in the rest of Africa. But let it be emphasized that having started the armed struggle, we shall pursue it with increasing ferocity until the monster of racism and exploitation has been completely destroyed. The probability of an international crisis resulting from our struggle will not deter us.

Vorster's threats have been triggered off by the fact that already the South African regime is paying heavily in blood for the crimes it has perpetrated against our people under its apartheid policies. Scores of South African troops have been killed by ZAPU-ANC guerrilas in what are merely preliminary encounters in Rhodesia.

## Isolate the South African regime

So far we have omitted reference to the role of foreign capital and other financial interests of Western countries in the South African situation. This question, however, has been thoroughly canvassed in statements, memoranda and reports now in the possession of the United Nations. What remains to be considered is action which must be taken to induce these countries to withdraw their support for the apartheid regime.

We in the African National Congress have always believed that the honourable task of freeing South Africa rested firmly with the people of South Africa themselves. The task of international organizations was to assist the liberation movement. This still remains the fundamental position of principle from which all international action should be appraised.

We have in the past insisted on sanctions being imposed on South Africa. We believe this demand is more valid now when the armed struggle is in progress than at any previous time. We interpret United Nations resolutions acknowledging the legitimacy of our struggle and calling for moral and material support for it as meaning, *inter alia*, that member Governments should honour and carry out United Nations decisions on South Africa, including termination of trade links with that country. The least the United Nations can do is to enforce compliance with its resolutions by all Member States and to consider appropriate action against those countries which undermine these decisions.

Trade with South Africa by Britain, France, West Germany, United States of America, Italy and Japan is no moral and material support for the liberation movement but a deliberate act designed to perpetuate a racist regime in southern Africa. As such, it is a gross violation of the United Nations Charter and the Universal Declaration of Human Rights.

Other international pressures have been enforced in the past. It would be absurd for these to be in any way reduced at a time when the armed struggle of our people requires that they be considerably increased. The impression that South Africa has been totally unaffected by international pressures is one which the well-financed information service of that Government has spent millions to induce. It is a massive international whistling in the dark which South Africa must not be allowed to get away with. The recent hullabaloo over the exclusion of South Africa from the Mexico Olympic Games is an indication of how much the advocates of White supremacy feel international pressure. Therefore the demands for political, military, social and cultural isolation of the present regime remain valid and must be pursued with greater effort, organization and skill. Such pressures are now an important part of the armed struggle for the overthrow of apartheid by the people of South Africa and are a form of support for our people.

The South African Information Service has vast resources at its disposal and is supported by powerful lobbies in various key countries, through the radio, by means of glossy well-produced magazines distributed free, by means of films shown free whenever requested and, above all, by extolling an economy whose benefits are derived from the brutal exploitation of our people. It is essential that there should always be a world-wide campaign to win the masses of the people to the struggle for the complete eradication of racialism and apartheid.

*Struggle will grow until victory*

Any measures carried out by the international community are, however, only supplementary to the efforts of the oppressed people and their allies. The burden of conquering freedom is theirs. Our armed struggle begins, as always in such struggles, with the oppressed people weak materially, although powerful in the justice of their cause. But it will grow in strength like the triumphant struggle of the great and heroic people of Viet Nam. Already in the armed clashes that have taken place, the White Fascists have taken a severe beating from the ZAPU-ANC guerillas. A worse fate awaits them in the coming years. The price to be paid in South Africa and far beyond its borders will be enormously high, but final victory will go to the defenders of peace and human dignity.

# Document 56

*General Assembly resolution: The policies of apartheid of the Government of South Africa*

A/RES/2396 (XXIII), 2 December 1968

*The General Assembly,*

. . .

*Noting with concern* that the Government of South Africa continues to intensify and extend beyond the borders of South Africa its inhuman and aggressive policies of apartheid and that these policies have led to a violent conflict, creating a situation in the whole of southern Africa which constitutes a grave threat to international peace and security,

*Recognizing* that the policies and actions of the Government of South Africa constitute a serious obstacle to the exercise of the right of self-determination by the oppressed people of southern Africa,

*Convinced* that the international campaign against apartheid must be intensified urgently in order to assist in securing the elimination of these inhuman policies,

*Considering* that effective action for a solution of the situation in South Africa is imperative in order to eliminate the grave threat to the peace in southern Africa as a whole,

. . .

1. *Reiterates* its condemnation of the policies of apartheid practised by the Government of South Africa as a crime against humanity;

2. *Condemns* the Government of South Africa for its illegal occupation of Namibia and its military intervention and for its assistance to the racist minority regime in Southern Rhodesia in violation of United Nations resolutions;

3. *Reaffirms* the urgent necessity of eliminating the policies of apartheid so that the people of South Africa as a whole can exercise their right to self-determination and attain majority rule based on universal suffrage;

4. *Draws the attention* of the Security Council to the grave situation in South Africa and in southern Africa as a whole and requests the Council to resume urgently the consideration of the question of apartheid with a view to adopting, under Chapter VII of the Charter of the United Nations, effective measures to ensure the full implementation of comprehensive mandatory sanctions against South Africa;

5. *Condemns* the actions of those States, particularly the main trading partners of South Africa, and the activities of those foreign financial and other interests, all of which, through their political, economic and military collaboration with the Government of South Africa and contrary to the relevant General Assembly and Security Council resolutions, are encouraging that Government to persist in its racial policies;

6. *Reaffirms* its recognition of the legitimacy of the struggle of the people of South Africa for all human rights, and in particular political rights and fundamental freedoms for all the people of South Africa irrespective of race, colour or creed;

7. *Calls upon* all States and organizations to provide greater moral, political and material assistance to the South

African liberation movement in its legitimate struggle;

8. *Expresses its grave concern* over the ruthless persecution of opponents of apartheid under arbitrary laws and the treatment of freedom fighters who were taken prisoner during the legitimate struggle for liberation, and:

(*a*) Condemns the Government of South Africa for its cruel, inhuman and degrading treatment of political prisoners;

(*b*) Calls once again for the release of all persons imprisoned or restricted for their opposition to apartheid and appeals to all Governments, organizations and individuals to intensify their efforts in order to induce the Government of South Africa to release all such persons and to stop the persecution and ill-treatment of opponents of apartheid;

(*c*) Declares that such freedom fighters should be treated as prisoners of war under international law, particularly the Geneva Convention relative to the Treatment of Prisoners of War of 12 August 1949;

(*d*) Requests the Secretary-General to establish and publicize as widely as possible:

(i) A register of persons who have been executed, imprisoned, placed under house arrest or banning orders or deported for their opposition to apartheid;

(ii) A register of all available information on acts of brutality committed by the Government of South Africa and its officials against opponents of apartheid in prisons;

9. *Commends* the activities of anti-apartheid movements and other organizations engaged in providing assistance to the victims of apartheid and in promoting their cause, and invites all States, organizations and individuals to make generous contributions in support of their endeavours;

10. *Urges* the Governments of all States to discourage in their territories, by legislative or other acts, all activities and organizations which support the policies of apartheid, as well as any propaganda in favour of the policies of apartheid and racial discrimination;

11. *Requests* all States to discourage the flow of immigrants, particularly skilled and technical personnel, to South Africa;

12. *Requests* all States and organizations to suspend cultural, educational, sporting and other exchanges with the racist regime and with organizations or institutions in South Africa which practise apartheid;

. . .

---

# Document 57

*Manifesto on Southern Africa adopted by Leaders of East and Central African States, Lusaka, 14-16 April 1969*

A/7754, 7 November 1969

1. When the purpose and the basis of States' international policies are misunderstood, there is introduced into the world a new and unnecessary disharmony, disagreements, conflicts of interest, or different assessments of human priorities, which provoke an excess of tension in the world, and disastrously divide mankind, at a time when united action is necessary to control modern technology and put it to the service of man. It is for this reason that, discovering widespread misapprehension of our attitudes and purposes in relation to southern Africa, we the leaders of East and Central African States meeting at Lusaka, 16th April 1969, have agreed to issue this Manifesto.

2. By this Manifesto we wish to make clear, beyond all shadow of doubt, our acceptance of the belief that all men are equal, and have equal rights to human dignity and respect, regardless of colour, race, religion, or sex. We believe that all men have the right and the duty to participate, as equal members of the society, in their own government. We do not accept that any individual or group has any right to govern any other group of sane adults without their consent, and we affirm that only the people of a society, acting together as equals, can determine what is, for them, a good society and a good social, economic, or political organization.

3. On the basis of these beliefs we do not accept that any one group within a society has the right to rule any society without the continuing consent of all the citizens. We recognize that at any one time there will be, within every society, failures in the implementation of these ideals. We recognize that for the sake of order in human affairs, there may be transitional arrangements while a transformation from group inequalities to individual equality is being effected. But we affirm that without an acceptance of these ideals—without a commitment to these principles of human equality and self-determination—there can be no basis for peace and justice in the world.

4. None of us would claim that within our own States we have achieved that perfect social, economic, and political organization which would ensure a reasonable standard of living for all our people and establish individual security against avoidable hardship or miscarriage of justice. On the contrary, we acknowledge that within our own States the struggle towards human brotherhood and unchallenged human dignity is only beginning. It is on the basis of our commitment to human equality and human dignity, not on the basis of achieved perfection, that we take our stand of hostility towards the colonialism and racial discrimination which is being practised in southern Africa. It is on the basis of their commitment to these universal principles that we appeal to other members of the human race for support.

5. If the commitment to these principles existed among the States holding power in southern Africa, any disagreements we might have about the rate of implementation, or about isolated acts of policy, would be matters affecting only our individual relationships with the States concerned. If these commitments existed, our States would not be justified in the expressed and active hostility towards the regimes of southern Africa such as we have proclaimed and continue to propagate.

6. The truth is, however, that in Mozambique, Angola, Rhodesia, South-West Africa, and the Union of South Africa, there is an open and continued denial of the principles of human equality and national self-determination. This is not a matter of failure in the implementation of accepted human principles. The effective Administrations in all these territories are not struggling towards these difficult goals. They are fighting the principles; they are deliberately organizing their societies so as to try to destroy the hold of these principles in the minds of men. It is for this reason that we believe the rest of the world must be interested. For the principle of human equality, and all that flows from it, is either universal or it does not exist. The dignity of all men is destroyed when the manhood of any human being is denied.

7. Our objectives in southern Africa stem from our commitment to this principle of human equality. We are not hostile to the Administrations of these States because they are manned and controlled by White people. We are hostile to them because they are systems of minority control which exist as a result of, and in the pursuance of, doctrines of human inequality. What we are working for is the right of self-determination for the people of those territories. We are working for a rule in those countries which is based on the will of all the people, and an acceptance of the equality of every citizen.

8. Our stand towards southern Africa thus involves a rejection of racialism, not a reversal of the existing racial domination. We believe that all the peoples who have made their homes in the countries of southern Africa are Africans, regardless of the colour of their skins; and we would oppose a racialist majority government which adopted a philosophy of deliberate and permanent discrimination between its citizens on grounds of racial origin. We are not talking racialism when we reject the colonialism and apartheid policies now operating in those areas; we are demanding an opportunity for all the people of these States, working together as equal individual citizens, to work out for themselves the institutions and the system of government under which they will, by general consent, live together and work together to build a harmonious society.

9. As an aftermath of the present policies it is likely that different groups within these societies will be self-conscious and fearful. The initial political and economic organizations may well take account of these fears, and this group self-consciousness. But how this is to be done must be a matter exclusively for the peoples of the country concerned, working together. No other nation will have a right to interfere in such affairs. All that the rest of the world has a right to demand is just what we are now asserting—that the arrangements within any State which wishes to be accepted into the community of nations must be based on an acceptance of the principles of human dignity and equality.

10. To talk of the liberation of Africa is thus to say two things. First, that the people in the territories still under colonial rule shall be free to determine for themselves their own institutions of self-government. Secondly, that the individuals in southern Africa shall be freed from an environment posed by the propaganda of racialism, and given an opportunity to be men—not White men, Brown men, Yellow men, or Black men.

11. Thus the liberation of Africa—for which we are struggling—does not mean a reverse racialism.

. . .

12. On the objective of liberation as thus defined, we can neither surrender nor compromise. We have always preferred, and we still prefer, to achieve it without physical violence. We would prefer to negotiate rather than destroy, to talk rather than kill. We do not advocate violence; we advocate an end to the violence against human dignity which is now being perpetrated by the oppressors of Africa. If peaceful progress to emancipation were possible, or if changed circumstances were to make it possible in the future, we would urge our brothers in the resistance movements to use peaceful methods of struggle even at the cost of some compromise on the timing of change. But while peaceful progress is blocked by actions of those at present in power in the States of southern Africa, we have no choice but to give to the

peoples of those territories all the support of which we are capable in their struggle against their oppressors. This is why the signatory states participate in the movement for the liberation of Africa under the aegis of the Organization of African Unity. However, the obstacle to change is not the same in all the countries of southern Africa, and it follows therefore, that the possibility of continuing the struggle through peaceful means varies from one country to another.

. . .

20. *The Union of South Africa* is itself an independent sovereign State and a Member of the United Nations. It is more highly developed and richer than any other nation in Africa. On every legal basis its internal affairs are a matter exclusively for the people of South Africa. Yet the purpose of law is people and we assert that the actions of the South African Government are such that the rest of the world has a responsibility to take some action in defence of humanity.

21. There is one thing about South African oppression which distinguishes it from other oppressive regimes. The apartheid policy adopted by its Government, and supported to a greater or lesser extent by almost all its White citizens, is based on a rejection of man's humanity. A position of privilege or the experience of oppression in the South African society depends on the one thing which it is beyond the power of any man to change. It depends upon a man's colour, his parentage, and his ancestors. If you are Black you cannot escape this categorization; nor can you escape it if you are White. If you are a Black millionaire and a brilliant political scientist, you are still subject to the pass laws and still excluded from political activity. If you are White, even protests against the system and an attempt to reject segregation will lead you only to the segregation, and the comparative comfort, of a White jail. Beliefs, abilities, and behaviour are all irrelevant to a man's status; everything depends upon race. Manhood is

irrelevant. The whole system of government and society in South Africa is based on the denial of human equality. And the system is maintained by a ruthless denial of the human rights of the majority of the population—and thus, inevitably, of all.

22. These things are known and are regularly condemned in the Councils of the United Nations and elsewhere. But it appears that to many countries international law take precedence over humanity; therefore no action follows the words. Yet even if international law is held to exclude active assistance to the South African opponents of apartheid, it does not demand that the comfort and support of human and commercial intercourse should be given to a government which rejects the manhood of most humanity. South Africa should be excluded from the United Nations agencies, and even from the United Nations itself. It should be ostracized by the world community. It should be isolated from world trade patterns and left to be self-sufficient, if it can. The South African Government cannot be allowed both to reject the very concept of mankind's unity and to benefit by the strength given through friendly international relations. And certainly Africa cannot acquiesce in the maintenance of the present policies against people of African descent.

23. The signatories of this Manifesto assert that the validity of the principles of human equality and dignity extend to the Union of South Africa just as they extend to the colonial territories of southern Africa. Before a basis for peaceful development can be established in this continent, these principles must be acknowledged by every nation, and in every State there must be a deliberate attempt to implement them.

24. We reaffirm our commitment to these principles of human equality and human dignity, and to the doctrines of self-determination and non-racialism. We shall work for their extension within our own nations and throughout the continent of Africa.

# Document 58

*Statement by Mr. Abdulrahim A. Farah (Somalia), Chairman of the Special Committee on the Policies of Apartheid of the Government of the Republic of South Africa, at the Committee's 138th meeting, held on 24 June 1970*

A/AC.115/L.277, 25 June 1970

The statement of our distinguished rapporteur on the arms build-up in South Africa and on continued violations of the embargo by several Western Powers reflects the serious and distressing nature of the two long-stand-

ing and gross violations of the United Nations Charter: the use of arms by the South African Government to deny people their fundamental human rights, and the equally unpardonable act of some States which involve themselves in arms trafficking in support of that regime and which put material gain ahead of the principles of international morality they are pledged to support.

In 1963 and 1964 when the Security Council adopted resolutions calling for the imposition of an arms embargo against the Government of South Africa, great hope was attached to the role which the four permanent members of the Council had pledged themselves to play. We realized that if those four Powers lent their full cooperation, other States would follow their example and the embargo would have a considerable chance of succeeding.

The Soviet Union gave its unqualified support to the proposal. The United States pledged itself to "a policy forbidding the sale to the South African Government of arms and military equipment, whether from Government or commercial sources, which could be used to enforce apartheid". The French delegation declared that its Government "would take all the steps they considered necessary to prevent the sale to the South African Government of weapons which could be used for purposes of repression". The British representative announced that it was the position of his Government "that no arms should be exported to South Africa which would enable the policy of apartheid to be enforced". He reserved the British position regarding the supply of equipment to South Africa for purposes of self-defence under Article 51 of the Charter.

Briefly, let us recount what has happened since the adoption of the arms embargo resolution. The Soviet Union is the only State that has discharged its responsibility fully. France has honoured the arms embargo more in the breach than in the observance and by its actions has encouraged several other Western European States to break the embargo. Almost every report on the arms situation issued by this Committee since its inception has contained evidence of the supply of French arms and military equipment to South Africa in defiance of the Security Council resolution.

In all fairness to the United Kingdom and the United States we must state that considerable efforts have been made by those two States to honour their commitment, although at times we have had reason to point out discrepancies in their performance. These discrepancies arise from the extremely loose interpretation which they place on certain arms and military equipment as falling within the category of arms for external defence, and on arms contracts entered into before the arms embargo was instituted. It cannot be denied that arms and military equipment supplied ostensibly for purposes of external defence have been used extensively for internal security.

Yet despite these lapses, we must concede that the public commitment of the Soviet Union, the United States

and the United Kingdom to honour the arms embargo has had a restraining influence on the supply of arms to South Africa. The problem now is this: how can the Security Council persuade those few States who continue to supply arms to South Africa in defiance of the arms embargo to refrain from doing so, and how can we induce others to continue faithful compliance with the embargo. Whatever measures are adopted by the Security Council, the outcome in reality will depend on the action of the permanent members.

In recent weeks, and particularly since the elections in the United Kingdom, considerable speculation has been aroused about the attitude which the new Government is likely to adopt towards the arms embargo. Many of us have been alarmed at some statements, which have been attributed in the Press to leading personalities of the Conservative Party, about the stand they would take on the arms embargo against South Africa and on the type of relations they would wish to establish with the rebel regime of Ian Smith in Southern Rhodesia. On the other hand, we have noted the restraining influence which the new British Prime Minister—the Right Honourable Edward Heath—has tried to exercise on racist and other extremist groups within his country. We trust this to be a clear indication that the policies of his Government will in no way give in to racism. In our opinion it would be racism to reopen the flow of arms to South Africa, to assume a negative position in the international scene against the South African racist policies and to give some form of recognition to the racist regime in Salisbury.

Apart from the verbal condemnations of the policies of apartheid, and a hesitant and unconvincing response to the humanitarian needs of the situation, the arms embargo, for what it is worth, represents the only tangible measure taken by the international community to countermand the criminal and sustained aggression of the South African Government against the rights of the non-White people of South Africa.

Any weakening of the embargo will affect adversely not only the struggle of the oppressed in South Africa, but also the struggle of the populations of Southern Rhodesia, Namibia and the Portuguese-occupied territories of Angola and Mozambique. It is no secret that sanctions against Southern Rhodesia have been frustrated because of the open trade which South Africa freely conducts with the rebel regime. The extensive arms and military equipment which the South African Government has been able to procure from abroad, has enabled that Government to station its units on Southern Rhodesian territory, and its air force to carry out military reconnaissance and offensive operations against liberation movements in territories beyond the frontiers of South Africa. Should South Africa be permitted to increase its purchase of arms from abroad, or be provided with the means to increase its manufacture of them at home, the international community can be certain that those arms will find their way to the rebel regime of Southern Rhodesia, further undermining the international commitment to sanctions.

This then is the position: I suggest for the consideration of this Committee that in the light of evidence that has been collected over the years and in consideration of new developments that are taking place, we ask that the whole position be reviewed by the Security Council and that it take measures to strengthen the embargo.

# Document 59

*Statement by the President of the General Assembly, Mr. Edvard Hambro (Norway), concerning the credentials of the delegation of South Africa*

A/PV.1901, 11 November 1970

[Editor's note: This statement was made in reply to a question by the representative of Saudi Arabia as to the implications of the adoption of a proposal by a number of States that the General Assembly approve the report of the Credentials Committee "except with regard to the credentials of the representative of South Africa".]

... It is a very difficult question to answer now, but still, out of respect both for him and for the Assembly, I will try to give an answer. But I want to state in advance that that answer is not a ruling of the President. I do not think that the President has the power to make a ruling which will give a legally binding interpretation of a resolution of this kind. But if the time should come, as it undoubtedly must, later in the Assembly where I have to make a ruling on the basis of what has happened here today I believe that my opinion would be the following.

After listening very carefully to this extremely important and at times passionate debate, after having read and reread several times the text of the amendment proposed, and after having studied very carefully the opinion given by my learned friend here on the rostrum, I reach the conclusion that a vote in favour of the amendment would mean, on the part of this Assembly, a very strong condemnation of the policies pursued by the Government of South Africa. It would also constitute a warning to that Government as solemn as any such warning could be. But that, apart from that, the amendment as it is worded at present would not seem to me to mean that the South African delegation is unseated or cannot continue to sit in this Assembly; if adopted it will not affect the rights and privileges of membership of South Africa. That is my understanding.

# Document 60

*General Assembly resolution: The policies of apartheid of the Government of South Africa*

A/RES/2671 F (XXV), 8 December 1970

*The General Assembly,*

...

*Gravely concerned* over the aggravation of the situation in South Africa and in southern Africa as a whole, because of the inhuman and aggressive policies of apartheid pursued by the Government of South Africa in defiance of United Nations resolutions, in violation of the Universal Declaration of Human Rights and in contravention of its obligations under the Charter of the United Nations,

*Expressing deep concern* over the increasing mili-

tary build-up of South Africa, which constitutes a grave danger to the cause of peace and security on the African continent,

*Noting with indignation* the continued persecution and torture of African patriots and other opponents of apartheid by the Government of South Africa under the Terrorism Act of 1967 and other ruthless repressive legislation,

*Convinced* that the establishment of "bantustans" in South Africa is designed to deprive the majority of the people of their inalienable rights and to destroy the unity of the South African people,

. . .

1. *Declares* that the policies of apartheid of the Government of South Africa are a negation of the Charter of the United Nations and constitute a crime against humanity;

2. *Reaffirms* its recognition of the legitimacy of the struggle of the people of South Africa to eliminate, by all means at their disposal, apartheid and racial discrimination and to attain majority rule in the country as a whole, based on universal suffrage;

3. *Condemns* the establishment by the racist minority Government of South Africa of "bantustans" in so-called African reserves as fraudulent, a violation of the principle of self-determination and prejudicial to the territorial integrity of the State and the unity of its people;

4. *Again calls upon* the Government of South Africa to end all repressive measures against African patriots and other opponents of apartheid and to liberate all persons imprisoned, interned or subjected to other restrictions for their opposition to apartheid;

5. *Strongly deplores* the continued cooperation by certain States and foreign economic interests with South Africa in the military, economic, political and other fields, as such cooperation encourages the Government of South Africa in the pursuit of its inhuman policies;

6. *Again draws the attention* of the Security Council to the grave situation in South Africa and in southern Africa as a whole and recommends that the Council resume urgently the consideration of effective measures, in the light of relevant General Assembly resolutions, including those under Chapter VII of the Charter;

7. *Urges* all States:

(a) To terminate diplomatic, consular and other official relations with the Government of South Africa;

(b) To terminate all military, economic, technical and other cooperation with South Africa;

(c) To end tariff and other preferences to South African exports and facilities for investment in South Africa;

(d) To ensure that companies registered in their countries and their nationals comply with the United Nations resolutions on this question;

8. *Requests* all States and organizations to suspend cultural, educational, sporting and other exchanges with the racist regime and with organizations or institutions in South Africa which practise apartheid;

9. *Commends* the international and national sporting organizations for their contribution to the international campaign against apartheid by their boycott of South African teams selected under apartheid policies;

. . .

# Document 61

*General Assembly resolution: The policies of apartheid of the Government of South Africa—Apartheid in sports*

A/RES/2775 D (XXVI), 29 November 1971

*The General Assembly,*

*Recalling* that Member States have pledged themselves, under Article 1 of the Charter of the United Nations, to promote and encourage respect for human rights and for fundamental freedoms for all without distinction as to race, sex, language or religion,

*Recalling further* its requests to all States and national and international sports organizations to suspend exchanges of sporting events with South African teams selected under apartheid policies,

*Bearing in mind* that 1971 was designated as the International Year for Action to Combat Racism and Racial Discrimination, to be observed in the name of the ever-growing struggle against racial discrimination in all its forms and manifestations and in the name of international solidarity with those struggling against racism,

1. *Declares* its unqualified support of the Olympic principle that no discrimination be allowed on the grounds of race, religion or political affiliation;

2. *Affirms* that merit should be the sole criterion for participation in sports activities;

3. *Solemnly calls upon* all national and international sports organizations to uphold the Olympic principle of non-discrimination and to discourage and deny support to sporting events organized in violation of this principle;

4. *Calls upon* individual sportsmen to refuse to participate in any sports activity in a country in which there is an official policy of racial discrimination or apartheid in the field of sports;

5. *Urges* all States to promote adherence to the Olympic principle of non-discrimination and to encourage their sports organizations to withhold support from sporting events organized in violation of this principle;

6. *Requests* national and international sports organizations and the public to deny any form of recogni-

tion to any sports activity from which persons are debarred or in which they are subjected to any discrimination on the basis of race, religion or political affiliation;

7. *Condemns* the actions of the Government of South Africa in enforcing racial discrimination and segregation in sports;

8. *Notes with regret* that some national and international sports organizations have continued exchanges with teams from South Africa that have been selected for international competition on the basis of competition closed to otherwise qualified sportsmen solely on the basis of their race, colour, descent or national or ethnic origin;

9. *Commends* those international and national sports organizations that have supported the international campaign against apartheid in sports;

10. *Requests* all States to urge their national sports organizations to act in accordance with the present resolution;

11. *Requests* the Secretary-General:

(*a*) To bring the present resolution to the attention of international sports organizations;

(*b*) To keep the Special Committee on Apartheid informed on the implementation of the present resolution;

(*c*) To submit a report on this matter to the General Assembly at its twenty-seventh session.

---

# Document 62

*General Assembly resolution: The policies of apartheid of the Government of South Africa—Establishment of bantustans*

A/RES/2775 E (XXVI), 29 November 1971

*The General Assembly,*

. . .

*Noting* that the Government of South Africa, while treating the White inhabitants of that country, irrespective of their national origins, as constituting one nation, seeks artificially to divide the African people into "nations" according to their tribal origins and justifies the establishment of non-contiguous Bantu homelands (bantustans) on that basis,

*Recognizing* that the real purpose of the establishment of bantustans is to divide the Africans, setting one tribe against the other with a view to weakening the African front in its struggle for its inalienable and just rights,

*Having regard* to the subsequent resolutions adopted by the General Assembly and the Security Council on the policies of apartheid of the Government of South Africa, and in particular General Assembly resolution 2671 (XXV) of 8 December 1970,

*Recalling* its resolution 95 (I) of 11 December 1946, in which it affirmed the principles of international law recognized by the Charter of the International Military Tribunal, Nuremberg, and the judgement of the Tribunal,

*Bearing in mind* the obligations of all States under international law, the Charter of the United Nations, the human rights principles and the Geneva Conventions of 12 August 1949,

*Noting further* that under the aforementioned resolution crimes against humanity are committed when enslavement, deportation and other inhuman acts are enforced against any civilian population on political, racial or religious grounds,

*Noting* that many African communities have been uprooted and that large numbers of Africans have been forcibly removed from their homes in pursuance of the policies of apartheid,

*Considering* that the establishment of bantustans and other measures adopted by the Government of South Africa in pursuance of apartheid are designed to consolidate and perpetuate domination by a White minority and the dispossession and exploitation of the African and other non-White people of South Africa, as well as of Namibia,

1. *Again condemns* the establishment by the Government of South Africa of Bantu homelands (bantustans) and the forcible removal of the African people of South Africa and Namibia to those areas as a violation of their inalienable rights, contrary to the principle of self-determination and prejudicial to the territorial integrity of the countries and the unity of their peoples;

2. *Declares* that the United Nations will continue to encourage and promote a solution to the situation in South Africa through the full application of human rights and fundamental freedoms, including political rights, to all inhabitants of the territory of South Africa as a whole, regardless of race, colour or creed;

. . .

# Document 63

*General Assembly resolution: The policies of apartheid of the Government of South Africa—Trade union activities against apartheid*

A/RES/2775 H (XXVI), 29 November 1971

*The General Assembly,*

. . .

*Noting* the opposition of the international trade union movement to apartheid and racial discrimination,

*Convinced* of the need to promote concerted action by the trade union movement at the national and international levels in the campaign against apartheid,

. . .

1. *Appeals* to all national and international trade union organizations to intensify their action against apartheid, in particular by:

(*a*) Discouraging the emigration of skilled workers to South Africa;

(*b*) Taking appropriate action in connection with the infringements of trade union rights and the persecution of trade unionists in South Africa;

(*c*) Exerting maximum pressure on foreign economic and financial interests which are profiting from racial discrimination against non-White workers in South Africa, in order to persuade them to cease such exploitation;

(*d*) Cooperating with other organizations engaged in the international campaign against apartheid;

. . .

---

# Document 64

*Security Council resolution: The question of race conflict in South Africa resulting from the policies of apartheid of the Government of the Republic of South Africa*

S/RES/311 (1972), 4 February 1972

*The Security Council,*

*Noting with grave concern* the aggravation of the situation in South Africa resulting from the continued intensification and expansion of the policies of apartheid and repression by the Government of South Africa,

. . .

*Convinced* that urgent measures must be taken by the Security Council to secure implementation of its resolutions and thereby promote a solution to the grave situation in South Africa and southern Africa,

1. *Condemns* the Government of South Africa for continuing its policies of apartheid in violation of its obligations under the Charter of the United Nations;

2. *Reiterates* its total opposition to the policies of apartheid of the Government of South Africa;

3. *Recognizes* the legitimacy of the struggle of the oppressed people of South Africa in pursuance of their human and political rights, as set forth in the Charter and the Universal Declaration of Human Rights;

4. *Urgently calls upon* the Government of South Africa to release all persons imprisoned, interned or subjected to other restrictions as a result of the policies of apartheid;

5. *Calls upon* all States to observe strictly the arms embargo against South Africa;

6. *Urges* Governments and individuals to contribute generously and regularly to the United Nations funds which are used for humanitarian and training purposes to assist the victims of apartheid;

7. *Commends* the intergovernmental organizations, non-governmental organizations and individuals for assisting in the education and training of South Africans and urges those who do not to begin and those who do to expand their efforts in this field;

8. *Decides*, as a matter of urgency, to examine methods of resolving the present situation arising out of the policies of apartheid of the Government of South Africa.

# Document 65

*General Assembly resolution: Policies of apartheid of the Government of South Africa—Situation in South Africa resulting from the policies of apartheid*

A/RES/2923 E (XXVII), 15 November 1972

*The General Assembly,*

. . .

*Strongly convinced* that the United Nations has a vital interest in securing the speedy elimination of apartheid,

. . .

1. *Condemns* the racist Government of South Africa for continuing and intensifying the implementation of its inhuman policy of apartheid, and subjecting the opponents of apartheid to ruthless repression, in violation of its obligations under the Charter of the United Nations, thereby creating a grave threat to the peace;

. . .

11. *Appeals* to Governments, specialized agencies, national and international organizations and individuals to provide greater assistance, directly or through the Organization of African Unity, to the national movement of the oppressed people of South Africa;

12. *Requests* the specialized agencies and other organizations within the United Nations system to discontinue all collaboration with the Government of South Africa until it renounces its policies of apartheid in accordance with the relevant resolutions of the General Assembly;

13. *Requests* States members of international agencies and organizations, particularly the members of the European Economic Community, the General Agreement on Tariffs and Trade and the International Monetary Fund, to take the necessary steps to deny all assistance and commercial or other facilities to the Government of South Africa so long as it pursues its policies of apartheid and racial discrimination and continues to defy the resolutions of the General Assembly and the Security Council;

14. *Requests* all States to take appropriate steps, in accordance with General Assembly resolution 2775 D (XXVI), to uphold the Olympic principle of non-discrimination in sports and to withhold any support from sporting events organized in violation of this principle, particularly with the participation of racially selected teams from South Africa;

15. *Commends* the activities of anti-apartheid movements, trade unions, student organizations, churches and other groups which have promoted national and international action against apartheid;

16. *Invites* all organizations, institutions and information media to organize in 1973, in accordance with the relevant resolutions adopted by the United Nations, intensified and coordinated campaigns with the following goals:

(*a*) Discontinuance of all military, economic and political collaboration with South Africa;

(*b*) Cessation of all activities by foreign economic interests which encourage the South African regime in its imposition of apartheid;

(*c*) Condemnation of torture and ill-treatment of prisoners and detainees in South Africa;

(*d*) Discouragement of emigration to South Africa, especially of skilled workers;

(*e*) Boycott of South Africa in sports and in cultural and other activities;

(*f*) World-wide collection of contributions for assistance to the victims of apartheid and support to the movement of the oppressed people of South Africa for freedom;

. . .

# Document 66

*General Assembly resolution: Policies of apartheid of the Government of South Africa—International Conference of Trade Unions against Apartheid*

A/RES/2923 F (XXVII), 13 December 1972

*The General Assembly,*

. . .

1. *Again appeals* to all national and international trade union organizations to intensify their action against apartheid;

2. *Welcomes* the decision taken by the Workers'

Group at the International Labour Conference to convene at Geneva, in 1973, an international conference of trade unions to work out a common programme of action against apartheid;

3. *Notes with satisfaction* the constructive attitude of the main international trade union organizations in regard to the convening of the International Conference of Trade Unions against Apartheid;

4. *Commends* the Special Committee on Apartheid for its efforts in helping to promote action by the workers of the world against apartheid;

5. *Requests and authorizes* the Special Committee on Apartheid to participate effectively in the proposed International Conference of Trade Unions against Apartheid and in the meeting of the Preparatory Committee for the Conference;

6. *Requests* the Secretary-General to provide appropriate assistance to facilitate the holding of the Conference;

7. *Authorizes* the Secretary-General to reimburse the costs necessary to enable up to five representatives of trade union organizations from southern Africa to participate in the Conference, as shall be decided by the Special Committee on Apartheid, on the proposal of the Preparatory Committee for the Conference and in consultation with the Organization of African Unity;

. . .

---

# Document 67

*Statement by Secretary-General Kurt Waldheim to the Special Committee on Apartheid, at a meeting on the occasion of the Committee's tenth anniversary*

UN Press Release SG/SM/1837 - GA/AP/317, 2 April 1973

. . .

The General Assembly established this Committee to enable the situation in southern Africa to be followed continuously by the United Nations, and not only during the annual sessions of the Assembly. It was rightly felt that attention on developments in South Africa must be constant. This Committee has played an important role in this vital activity, and its work has made a major contribution to the ever-increasing public awareness of conditions which, unhappily, still exist more than 10 years after Sharpeville.

I should like to repeat to you words which I used on the International Day for the Elimination of Racial Discrimination:

"Discrimination based on race is cruel, squalid, and contemptible, and discredits all who engage in it. So long as it persists, the rancour and bitterness which it engenders will imperil the fragile peace which we now have."

The most important aspect of the work of this Committee over the past 10 years has been its determination to make positive proposals for the elimination of apartheid. It has actively and successfully urged the implementation of United Nations resolutions by a great number of Member States and organizations; it promoted the movement towards the arms embargo against South Africa; it has repeatedly drawn public attention to repressive policies and the ill-treatment of prisoners; it has initiated discussion and action in the human rights field; it was the driving force behind the United Nations Trust Fund for South Africa, and it is concerned with the work of the Advisory Committee on the United Nations Educational and Training Programme for South Africa; it has stimulated action in the specialized agencies; it proposed the establishment of the Unit on Apartheid whose work has been of such significance; and it has conduced conferences and seminars which have further attracted international attention to this subject.

This is not, of course, a comprehensive list of the activities of this Committee over the past 10 years, but it indicates the vigour and imagination with which the Committee has undertaken its important task. The forthcoming International Trade Union Conference against Apartheid, to be held in Geneva in June, is another example of the Special Committee's policy of bringing all groups of concerned citizens into the world-wide campaign against apartheid.

I know that the Committee would like me to make particular reference to the contribution which has been made by non-governmental organizations and individuals who have personal experience of, and are deeply concerned about, the policies of apartheid. The Secretariat's Unit on Apartheid has also benefited greatly from this assistance and advice. I very much hope that the Committee will continue to have this assistance which we deeply appreciate. It emphasizes the major role of non-governmental organizations in the humanitarian and political fields, and reminds us that the Charter opens with the words, "We the peoples of the United Nations". The endeavours of representatives of governments or liberation movements, of the Organization of African Unity, of the United Nations specialized agencies, and non-governmental organizations and individual experts, have given this Committee not only much vital information but have also established its important role in the struggle against apartheid.

We are about to enter the Decade to Combat Racism and Racial Discrimination. There are those who are sceptical about the proclamation of special years and decades for particular causes. Certainly, they alone cannot achieve our objective. But when they are used effectively to harness world opinion, to educate, and to promote not only concern but positive attitudes—then they have a vital role.

The International Conference for the Support of Victims of Colonialism and Apartheid in Southern Africa will be held in Oslo on 9 to 14 April. I hope that this very important Conference will lead to constructive proposals for greater action at all levels, both for assistance to the victims of colonialism and apartheid, and for the elimination of the policies that create these victims. The Oslo Conference, to which I attach great importance, could be a most significant step in the struggle against apartheid.

I know that there are many people who are discouraged by the continued persistence of policies of apartheid in spite of all the endeavours of the United Nations. But I do not feel that we need be disheartened. The steadily increasing international awareness and condemnation of apartheid has given the oppressed people of southern Africa real hope, and has encouraged them in their struggle. This year, government contributions for United Nations funds for our activities in this field have been greater than ever before. It is now, more than ever, imperative that we institute more effective international action to eliminate apartheid.

The situation in southern Africa has been one of my dominant concerns since I took office as Secretary-General. In this task I have had the full cooperation of the OAU and the various United Nations committees, including the Special Committee on Apartheid, led by Ambassador Ogbu of Nigeria. In the Secretariat, I have also had the invaluable and devoted assistance of Mangalam Chacko, whom many of you knew well. His sudden death has been a profound blow to the United Nations, to the international community at large, and to me personally. I cannot think of a better memorial to his life and work than the elimination of the evil disease of racial discrimination, and, in particular, of apartheid. All of us in the United Nations family honour his memory and will continue his work.

So long as apartheid remains, this Committee will continue to play a crucial role in the endeavours of the United Nations to eliminate this evil.

I thank you for giving me the opportunity to address you, and I wish you well in your vitally important work.

---

# Document 68

*Programme of action adopted by the International Conference of Experts for the Support of Victims of Colonialism and Apartheid in Southern Africa (Oslo, 9-14 April 1973)*

A/9061, 7 May 1973

. . .

### General assessment of the situation

(1)   Participants at the International Conference of Experts for the Support of Victims of Colonialism and Apartheid in Southern Africa, held in Oslo from 9 to 14 April 1973 under the auspices of the United Nations and the Organization of African Unity, share the grave concern of the international community about the present situation in South Africa, Namibia, Zimbabwe (Southern Rhodesia), Angola, Guinea (Bissau) and Cape Verde, Mozambique, and Sao Tomé and Príncipe.

(2)   The peoples of these Territories are carrying forward their struggle for freedom and independence through new victories on an unprecedented scale and intensity. In all parts of the world, and in growing numbers, freedom-loving States and peoples stand together in support of that struggle.

(3)   Yet the colonial and apartheid regimes of Lisbon, Pretoria and Salisbury remain stubbornly determined to maintain their domination. Their response to the peoples' struggle is desperately to perpetrate more savage repression and warfare. They also carry out acts of aggression against independent African States. These regimes are sustained only by the collaboration of certain Governments and major economic interests, without whose aid they would be impotent.

(4)   The conscience of the world demands as never before that the colonial and apartheid regimes be liquidated so that peace may be achieved and the dignity of man preserved.

(5)   The struggle of the peoples of these Territories is entirely just and legitimate, deserving the complete support of the world community. The liberation movements which lead that struggle are the authentic representatives of their peoples and should receive full international recognition.

(6)   It is thus the solemn duty of international organizations, Governments and peoples to accelerate the isolation of the colonial and apartheid regimes and channel massive assistance to the liberation movements. For it is the liberation movements which are leading the struggle, regaining and reconstructing their territories and shaping afresh the destinies of their peoples in dignity and freedom.

(7)   The proposals emanating from the International Conference of Experts for the Support of Victims of Colonialism and Apartheid in Southern Africa require the most serious and urgent consideration from the United Nations, Organization of African Unity, Governments, organizations and peoples all over the world. They form a programme of action for concerted international efforts to hasten the eradication of the scourge of colonialism and apartheid, thereby promoting international peace and security.

. . .

D. *Proposals for action in regard to South Africa*

(59)   The policy of apartheid, which is a crime against humanity, a flagrant violation of the principles of the United Nations and a massive and ruthless denial of human rights, constitutes a threat to peace. It amounts to a serious and grave threat to the peace and security of Africa and the world and requires urgent action by the Security Council under Chapter VII of the Charter of the United Nations because of the following:

(a)   South Africa's central role in helping to maintain and perpetuate colonial and racist rule in southern Africa;

(b)   Its continued illegal occupation of the international Territory of Namibia;

(c)   Its deliberate and systematic violation of international mandatory sanctions against Southern Rhodesia;

(d)   The illegal intervention of its armed units in defence of the racist minority regime in Southern Rhodesia;

(e)   Its military intervention in Angola and Mozambique;

(f)   Its acts of aggression against independent African States;

(g)   Its military build-up and threatening posture towards the rest of the continent.

(60)   The United Nations should adopt a programme of international economic and other mandatory sanctions to counteract the growing aggressive role of South Africa and ask all States to provide material and moral support to the liberation movement.

(61)   The collaborative role of international investment in, and trade and other relations with, South Africa should be exposed and the false claim that such supportive links can act as agents for change should be condemned and rejected. Investigations and studies of these links should take place in full consultation with the liberation movement.

(62)   Action should be taken by the United Nations and the organizations of the United Nations system, by States as well as by national and international bodies, governmental and non-governmental, in full support of campaigns conducted by anti-apartheid movements and other solidarity organizations to promote international disengagement from and an end to all collaborative links with South Africa.

(63)   Investments should be withdrawn; all new investment programmes should be stopped; no loans or any other assistance should be provided either to the White racist regime or to corporations operating in South Africa.

(64)   All economic and scientific support of, collaboration with, and assistance to South Africa should be stopped, in particular by:

(a)   Terminating the purchase of gold;

(b)   Terminating the purchase of platinum and other minerals;

(c)   Discontinuing all scientific collaboration, in particular nuclear cooperation;

(d)   Refusing to grant patents and licences to the Government of South Africa and its institutions, as well as to corporations and other bodies which operate in South Africa.

(65)   The flow of immigrants should be stopped; States should prohibit special recruiting organizations from operating in their countries and prevent, or at least dissuade, their citizens from migrating to South Africa; trade unions should take special measures to prevent their members from migrating to South Africa.

(66)   The European Economic Community should end all special terms and concessions already granted to South Africa, undertake to have no further dealings with its regime and its mission in Brussels and pledge that it will not enter into any special agreements or arrangements with South Africa in the future.

(67)   The Simonstown Agreements between the United Kingdom of Great Britain and Northern Ireland and South Africa should be terminated and no military arrangements should be made by any State with South Africa.

(68) The international arms embargo should be fully implemented by all States, and the Security Council should expose those States which violate it, especially France, and secure their compliance. The Security Council should take further action to prevent the importation of arms from South Africa by other States. The Security Council should also examine all other forms of military cooperation with South Africa and take appropriate action.

(69) International and national trade union movements and other organizations should take action to prevent the production of arms and other military equipment for and their supply to South Africa.

(70) The United Nations and the organizations of the United Nations system should work closely with anti-apartheid movements and provide them with full support. Where such movements do not exist, their establishment should be encouraged.

(71) The United Nations Special Committee on Apartheid should work closely with anti-apartheid movements to help promote a joint programme of conferences in support of the policies of the United Nations and the Organization of African Unity.

(72) Action should be taken by States, organizations and the international community to isolate South Africa from all athletic competitions and to end all cultural links with South Africa as long as the practice of apartheid is continued.

(73) The international boycott of South African goods and campaigns against corporations which have links with South Africa should be intensified.

(74) States should adopt the Convention on the Suppression and Punishment of the Crime of Apartheid.

E. *Proposals for general action in support of the liberation movements*

(75) Action should be taken by all United Nations bodies, the organizations of the United Nations system, the specialized agencies and other international organizations to ensure full representation and participation by liberation movements as the authentic representatives of their peoples and countries.

(76) All Governments and organizations should deal directly with the liberation movements recognized by the Organization of African Unity on all questions concerning their countries.

(77) The specialized agencies should discontinue all collaboration with the racist minority regime of Southern Rhodesia and the Governments of South Africa and Portugal.

(78) The right of the people of southern Africa to strive for their liberation by all appropriate means, including armed struggle against the oppression and bru-

tality of the colonial and racist regimes, should be fully recognized and supported.

(79) The United Nations and the Organization of African Unity should keep close contacts with all non-governmental organizations supporting the liberation struggle in southern Africa and cease all collaboration with those non-governmental organizations which are opposed to that struggle.

(80) The United Nations should collaborate more closely with intergovernmental and regional organizations and with non-governmental groups which mobilize public action in support of liberation movements.

(81) Governments should be encouraged to give financial support to non-governmental action groups working for the support of liberation movements in southern Africa.

(82) Non-governmental organizations should publicize the activities of companies involved in southern Africa and organize public campaigns for their withdrawal. Full information on these campaigns should be circulated all over the world in order to promote concerted campaigns in all countries where those companies have interests.

(83) The participation in international sports by the racist and colonial regimes is a direct affront to the international community as a whole and should be subject to boycott until such regimes are replaced by independent democratic governments.

(84) Governments and organizations should be encouraged to set up anti-colonial and anti-apartheid centres for the purpose of mobilizing public opinion in support of the liberation struggle.

(85) The United Nations should take further steps and more adequate measures to disseminate information widely through the press, radio, television and other media, especially in Western Europe, the Americas and Japan, in support of the national liberation struggle being waged by the people in southern Africa and to expose the crimes of the colonial and racist regimes and their accomplices.

. . .

Part Two. Proposals for action on assistance in southern Africa

A. *Reasons for assistance*

(90) The struggle of the people of southern Africa for freedom and independence is a legitimate struggle, and the international community has a duty to provide moral and material assistance to the liberation movements recognized by the Organization of African Unity.

(91) Assistance to the liberation movements in southern Africa is appropriate and desirable since they are engaged in a struggle for a just cause, consistent with

the purposes and principles of the United Nations, the Organization of African Unity and other organizations, while the colonial and racist regimes resort to colonial wars and oppressive measures in defiance of the United Nations, the Organization of African Unity and other organizations.

(92)  The colonial and racist regimes could not have continued to defy United Nations resolutions and world opinion but for the attitude of some Governments allied to them, which prevent effective international action and assist these regimes. Foreign economic interests, in their exploitation of the resources of southern Africa, continue to assist these regimes and profit from the oppression of the African peoples. It is, therefore, imperative that African peoples of these Territories receive all necessary assistance in their difficult struggles against the criminal oppressors and their accomplices.

(93)  It should be recognized that the liberation movements have been forced to embark on armed struggles because of the intransigence and brutality of the colonial and racist regimes. All countries and peoples who love freedom and peace and uphold justice should give assistance to the liberation movements in their just struggle, including armed struggle.

(94)  The needs of the liberation movements for international assistance have greatly grown in recent years because of their success in liberating large areas in Angola, Mozambique and Guinea (Bissau), because of the resort by the Portuguese forces to the use of defoliants and other barbarous methods of warfare, and because of the intensified struggle by the liberation movements in South Africa, Namibia, Zimbabwe (Southern Rhodesia) and the areas still under Portuguese colonial control.

(95)  There is increasing need for direct assistance to the oppressed peoples in southern Africa and their liberation movements in order to support the movements in the conduct of their legitimate struggle for freedom, to help in the reconstruction of the liberated areas and to alleviate the suffering occurring in the course of their struggle.

(96)  There is a need to continue and increase humanitarian assistance to refugees and persons persecuted for their opposition to colonialism and apartheid. There is a need to continue and increase educational and training facilities in order to build up cadres for the promotion of the liberation struggle and for the administration and development of these Territories.

(97)  There is a need for much greater assistance in the task of reconstructing the liberated areas which now have a population of over three million. There is a need for much greater support for the political and information activities of the liberation movements and for the various organizations involved in the struggle for freedom in the areas under colonial and racist control, such as labour and student organizations.

(98)  At this stage, greater moral and material assistance to the liberation movements is among the most effective ways to secure peace in the region by hastening the completion of the process of decolonization and elimination of apartheid.

(99)  In providing assistance to the oppressed peoples in southern Africa and their liberation movements, it should be recognized that this is not charity but an act of solidarity with peoples engaged in a just struggle.

(100)  The primary responsibility for the struggle for freedom and independence belongs to the oppressed people themselves and to their liberation movements. The role of the international community is supportive and complementary.

(101)  Governments and organizations providing assistance to liberation movements should avoid paternalism. They should, as far as possible, provide direct assistance to the liberation movements to be administered by the movements themselves as the authentic representatives of the people of these Territories.

. . .

C.  *Ways and means of assistance*

(107)  International assistance should be provided, as much as possible, directly to the liberation movements in southern Africa. In cases where the assistance is administered by other organizations, the Organization of African Unity and the liberation movements should be consulted on all aspects of the operations.

(108)  Direct assistance to the liberation movements reflects confidence in the movements. It ensures that assistance is utilized most effectively and is relevant to the needs of the Territories and to the struggle for freedom in southern Africa.

(109)  The United Nations and other international organizations should contribute a share of their budgets for assistance to the liberation movements in order to demonstrate full solidarity with and support of the struggles.

. . .

(117)  The United Nations organs dealing with development should allot sufficient funds for the programmes drawn up by the specialized agencies in consultation with the Organization of African Unity and the liberation movements. The specialized agencies should also, after consultation with the Organization of African Unity and the liberation movements, actively seek voluntary contributions from Governments and foundations.

. . .

# Document 69

*Statement by Mr. Edwin Ogebe Ogbu (Nigeria), Chairman of the Special Committee on Apartheid, at the opening meeting of the International Conference of Trade Unions against Apartheid, Geneva, 15 June 1973*

A/9169, 1 October 1973

. . .

The international trade union movement is centrally placed to play a significant role in the world-wide campaign against racism and the evil system of apartheid which can only be compared to nazism. It is everybody's hope that your deliberations will lead to the elaboration of a sustained and cohesive programme of action which will constitute a turning point in this common struggle of the masses and the oppressed workers of southern Africa.

I may perhaps note that you are holding this Conference 25 years after the apartheid regime came to power in South Africa with the votes of a minority of the White minority and 10 years after the Summit Conference of Independent African States proclaimed that the cause of the oppressed people of South Africa is the cause of all African Governments and peoples. It was exactly 10 years ago, at the general conference of the ILO, that the African delegations and the great majority of the workers joined together to press for more vigorous action by the ILO, including the expulsion of the South African racist regime and the racist trade unions. The present conference is, in a sense, a move to formulate further action which has become imperative in the light of the experience of the past decade.

. . .

Apartheid is an extremely devious and perfected system devised to impose segregation among people while perpetuating exploitation by the White minority of the masses of Black workers in South Africa. It includes geographical segregation in the form of bantustans and "separate development" of the White industrialized areas, using the hard work and labour of the Blacks. What is even more intolerable is the fact that the perpetrators of this crime pose as benefactors and pretend to work for the welfare and advancement of their hapless victims. The picture is dismal: tens of thousands of African workers have gone on strike against starvation wages and tragic working conditions, in spite of the great risks involved for themselves and their families; unprecedented amounts of capital, technology and weapons are pouring into South Africa every year; a well-orchestrated campaign is waged by the South African Government and its support-ers in order to convince the world that economic changes are or will occur, which will eventually change the whole system. This is an utterly false and debasing lie.

The system of exploitation and oppression of the Black South Africans has been codified and ruthlessly implemented. Millions of African workers have been jailed for contravening the so-called "pass laws"; thousands have been tortured or executed and many have died in detention; tens of thousands of families have been forcibly removed to impoverished "reserves" where malnutrition and high mortality rates prevail, real income for Africans has steadily diminished and unemployment is increasing. The trade union movement cannot and should not tolerate this situation if it wants to remain faithful to its fundamental principles of justice and equality for the worker.

A whole paraphernalia of so-called legal texts is used by South Africa to impose the system. The tool of "communist threat" is used by Vorster and his regime, in the same way as McCarthyism was used in the United States 20 years ago. A person is declared a communist in South Africa, at any time and under any pretext. The Suppression of Communism Act and its inhumaneness are surpassed only by the Terrorism Act. Under this Act, anyone suspected of the slightest opposition to the Government can be arrested and detained indefinitely. No court of law can intervene and no lawyer, relative or even clergyman has access to the detainee.

The apartheid situation has become one of the major problems facing the international community. Its implications for peace are far-reaching and incalculable. It has long been proved that this situation constitutes not only a breach of the United Nations Charter but a threat to international peace and security. Apartheid is a crime against humanity.

. . .

The trade unions of the world cannot in any way be a party to this crime of apartheid which is based on efforts to perpetuate the system of slave labour of the Black people. They cannot afford to condone this system or to acquiesce in it, if they are faithful to the principles of trade unionism.

. . .

International action against apartheid began with the establishment of the United Nations. The General Assembly of the United Nations, as is well known, has adopted a great number of resolutions and has recommended specific measures to deal with the situation in the Republic of South Africa. The Assembly has requested Member States to break off diplomatic relations with South Africa, to close their ports to vessels of South Africa, to prohibit their ships from entering South African ports, to boycott all South African goods and refrain from trading with that country, to refuse landing and passage facilities to all aircraft belonging to the Government and companies registered under the laws of South Africa, etc.

The long list of resolutions call for the release of political prisoners and for assistance to the organizations and individuals supporting the victims of apartheid. The General Assembly has appealed to all States to provide political, moral and material assistance to the national liberation movement of the oppressed people of South Africa. It has appealed to all States to discourage the flow of immigrants, particularly skilled and technical personnel, to South Africa. It has requested all States and organizations to suspend cultural, educational, sporting and other exchanges with the racist regime and its institutions. It has asked all States to refrain from extending loans, investments and technical assistance to South Africa.

In the Security Council, where the major Powers have permanent seats, several resolutions condemning the policies of apartheid have been adopted. The South African regime has been called upon to abandon its policies and to abolish the measures of repression against the people. The General Assembly has declared itself opposed to economic collaboration with the South African Government and has expressed itself in favour of an economic boycott of South Africa.

The Security Council has called upon all States to cease the sale and shipment to South Africa of arms, ammunition of all types, military vehicles, and equipment or materials for the manufacture and maintenance of arms and ammunition in South Africa.

This type of action cannot be implemented without the active support of the people, and particularly where collaboration with South Africa is strong. Action by non-governmental organizations is one of the main pillars on which the anti-apartheid campaign has to rest. Greater coordination between the United Nations and its agencies, on the one hand, and non-governmental organizations, on the other, is essential. In the face of Government inertia, the action of workers, students and church groups becomes extremely significant. Severance of trade relations with South Africa and the disengagement of foreign business cannot be promoted without the effective support of the workers of the world. Many countries in Africa, Asia, Eastern Europe and other areas are in fact enforcing sanctions against South Africa, some of them at great sacrifice. There are boycotts by anti-apartheid movements, cooperatives and some trade unions in Western countries, but the companies in Western countries and in Japan continue to increase their trade and investment.

It is for the trade union movement itself to decide what action it is prepared to take to answer the appeal of the United Nations. The realities of the situation should be recognized; the power in South Africa is in the hands of the White minority interests which, with foreign capital, own and control the mines, the banks, the finance houses and most of the farms and industries. The struggle to release the Black workers from slavery, to put an end to the torture, harassment and oppression, cannot be ignored by you. The Black people of South Africa are looking to you for help. The evidence clearly establishes that the Government of the Republic of South Africa has violated and continues to violate the principles of international law and morality. Therefore the responsibility of the United Nations to take severe action and to punish South Africa is clear and beyond any doubt. However, what we have come to discuss here today is the role of the workers. I recall, at this juncture, the recent decision by the World Council of Churches to liquidate its financial holdings in corporations doing business with South Africa and to withdraw all funds deposited in banks that maintain operations in countries where racist regimes dominate. This is one type of concrete action which can and has been taken by non-governmental organizations.

The Special Committee on Apartheid has followed closely this type of action taken by organizations and has given it its blessing and support. It wishes to emphasize the role which trade unions can play by boycotting shipments to and from South Africa and by refusing to load vessels travelling to and from South Africa. Measures could also be applied against air transport, where the workers could show their solidarity by boycotting aircraft carrying goods from South Africa. Pressure should be exercised on banks and companies to withdraw funds and to disengage from South Africa. The immigration of workers to South Africa should be completely halted. Trade union organizations may establish information committees which would act in close cooperation with anti-apartheid movements in countries from which workers emigrate to South Africa and where collaboration exists with South Africa. The phenomenon of the migration of workers from neighbouring countries into South Africa should also be halted. It may be necessary for a standing working body to be established among your organizations to draw the attention of the international trade union movement to violations of the embargo on shipments of arms to South Africa and of the economic boycott of South Africa. The trade union movement may also be in a position to provide financial aid to the victims of South Africa's policies. Certainly no trade union organization should be willing to invest its funds or to have holdings in companies which are involved in the exploitation of South African labour. It was estimated last year that in the United Kingdom alone, 18 trade unions had between them over £12 million invested in firms with South African interests.

. . .

I wish to emphasize that the United Nations needs the active and continuing support of the trade unions and other organizations all over the world if its resolutions on South Africa or Namibia are to be effective. Such support has become crucial because of the uncooperative attitude of some States which constitute the major trading partners of South Africa. The Security Council Committee on sanctions against Rhodesia has recognized that even the implementation of mandatory sanctions against the Smith regime requires the cooperation of trade unions and other organizations.

. . .

This Conference has a commitment which will grow steadily and which will change in a fundamental way the existing conditions of slave labour in South Africa. A united workers' movement in opposition to apartheid can deliver a mortal blow to the system of exploitation and oppression in that country. I therefore appeal to you, on behalf of the United Nations Special Committee on Apartheid and in the name of the suffering Black workers of South Africa, to consider concrete action which can be taken by the workers everywhere and as a common front. It may well be considered necessary to have a follow-up after three, four or six months to review progress. The decision will be yours to make. My Committee will cooperate with you. The approach to this matter which will be given by organizations in countries trading and cooperating with South Africa will be of special importance, and may well be the determining factor for the ultimate success or failure of the International Trade Union Conference against Apartheid.

# Document 70

*General Assembly resolution: International Convention on the Suppression and Punishment of the Crime of Apartheid*

A/RES/3068 (XXVIII), 30 November 1973

[Editor's note: The International Convention on the Suppression and Punishment of the Crime of Apartheid entered into force on 18 July 1976. As at 15 July 1994, 36 States had signed the Convention and 96 had ratified it or acceded to it.]

*The States Parties to the present Convention,*

*Recalling* the provisions of the Charter of the United Nations, in which all Members pledged themselves to take joint and separate action in cooperation with the Organization for the achievement of universal respect for, and observance of, human rights and fundamental freedoms for all without distinction as to race, sex, language or religion,

*Considering* the Universal Declaration of Human Rights, which states that all human beings are born free and equal in dignity and rights and that everyone is entitled to all the rights and freedoms set forth in the Declaration, without distinction of any kind, such as race, colour or national origin,

*Considering* the Declaration on the Granting of Independence to Colonial Countries and Peoples, in which the General Assembly stated that the process of liberation is irresistible and irreversible and that, in the interests of human dignity, progress and justice, an end must be put to colonialism and all practices of segregation and discrimination associated therewith,

*Observing* that, in accordance with the International Convention on the Elimination of All Forms of Racial Discrimination, States particularly condemn racial segregation and apartheid and undertake to prevent, prohibit and eradicate all practices of this nature in territories under their jurisdiction,

*Observing* that, in the Convention on the Prevention and Punishment of the Crime of Genocide, certain acts which may also be qualified as acts of apartheid constitute a crime under international law,

*Observing* that, in the Convention on the Non-Applicability of Statutory Limitations to War Crimes and Crimes Against Humanity, "inhuman acts resulting from the policy of apartheid" are qualified as crimes against humanity,

*Observing* that the General Assembly of the United Nations has adopted a number of resolutions in which the policies and practices of apartheid are condemned as a crime against humanity,

*Observing* that the Security Council has emphasized that apartheid and its continued intensification and expansion seriously disturb and threaten international peace and security,

*Convinced* that an International Convention on the Suppression and Punishment of the Crime of Apartheid would make it possible to take more effective measures at the international and national levels with a view to the suppression and punishment of the crime of apartheid,

*Have agreed* as follows:

### Article I

1. The States Parties to the present Convention declare that apartheid is a crime against humanity and that inhuman acts resulting from the policies and practices of apartheid and similar policies and practices of racial segregation and discrimination, as defined in article II of the Convention, are crimes violating the principles of international law, in particular the purposes and principles of the Charter of the United Nations, and constituting a serious threat to international peace and security.

2. The States Parties to the present Convention declare criminal those organizations, institutions and individuals committing the crime of apartheid.

### Article II

For the purpose of the present Convention, the term "the crime of apartheid", which shall include similar policies and practices of racial segregation and discrimination as practised in southern Africa, shall apply to the following inhuman acts committed for the purpose of establishing and maintaining domination by one racial group of persons over any other racial group of persons and systematically oppressing them:

(*a*) Denial to a member or members of a racial group or groups of the right to life and liberty of person:

(i) By murder of members of a racial group or groups;

(ii) By the infliction upon the members of a racial group or groups of serious bodily or mental harm, by the infringement of their freedom or dignity, or by subjecting them to torture or to cruel, inhuman or degrading treatment or punishment;

(iii) By arbitrary arrest and illegal imprisonment of the members of a racial group or groups;

(*b*) Deliberate imposition on a racial group or groups of living conditions calculated to cause its or their physical destruction in whole or in part;

(*c*) Any legislative measures and other measures calculated to prevent a racial group or groups from participation in the political, social, economic and cultural life of the country and the deliberate creation of conditions preventing the full development of such a group or groups, in particular by denying to members of a racial group or groups basic human rights and freedoms, including the right to work, the right to form recognized trade unions, the right to education, the right to leave and to return to their country, the right to a nationality, the right to freedom of movement and residence, the right to freedom of opinion and expression, and the right to freedom of peaceful assembly and association;

(*d*) Any measures, including legislative measures, designed to divide the population along racial lines by the creation of separate reserves and ghettos for the members of a racial group or groups, the prohibition of mixed marriages among members of various racial groups, the expropriation of landed property belonging to a racial group or groups or to members thereof;

(*e*) Exploitation of the labour of the members of a racial group or groups, in particular by submitting them to forced labour;

(*f*) Persecution of organizations and persons, by depriving them of fundamental rights and freedoms, because they oppose apartheid.

### Article III

International criminal responsibility shall apply, irrespective of the motive involved, to individuals, members of organizations and institutions and representatives of the State, whether residing in the territory of the State in which the acts are perpetrated or in some other State, whenever they:

(*a*) Commit, participate in, directly incite or conspire in the commission of the acts mentioned in article II of the present Convention;

(*b*) Directly abet, encourage or cooperate in the commission of the crime of apartheid.

### Article IV

The States Parties to the present Convention undertake:

(*a*) To adopt any legislative or other measures necessary to suppress as well as to prevent any encouragement of the crime of apartheid and similar segregationist policies or their manifestations and to punish persons guilty of that crime;

(*b*) To adopt legislative, judicial and administrative measures to prosecute, bring to trial and punish in accordance with their jurisdiction persons responsible for, or accused of, the acts defined in article II of the present Convention whether or not such persons reside in the territory of the State in which the acts are committed or are nationals of that State or of some other State or are stateless persons.

### Article V

Persons charged with the acts enumerated in article II of the present Convention may be tried by a competent tribunal of any State Party to the Convention which may acquire jurisdiction over the person of the accused or by an international penal tribunal having jurisdiction with respect to those States Parties which shall have accepted its jurisdiction.

## Article VI

The States Parties to the present Convention undertake to accept and carry out in accordance with the Charter of the United Nations the decisions taken by the Security Council aimed at the prevention, suppression and punishment of the crime of apartheid, and to cooperate in the implementation of decisions adopted by other competent organs of the United Nations with a view to achieving the purposes of the Convention.

## Article VII

1. The States Parties to the present Convention undertake to submit periodic reports to the group established under article IX on the legislative, judicial, administrative or other measures that they have adopted and that give effect to the provisions of the Convention.

2. Copies of the reports shall be transmitted through the Secretary-General of the United Nations to the Special Committee on Apartheid.

## Article VIII

Any State Party to the present Convention may call upon any competent organ of the United Nations to take such action under the Charter of the United Nations as it considers appropriate for the prevention and suppression of the crime of apartheid.

## Article IX

1. The Chairman of the Commission on Human Rights shall appoint a group consisting of three members of the Commission on Human Rights, who are also representatives of States Parties to the present Convention, to consider reports submitted by States Parties in accordance with article VII.

2. If, among the members of the Commission on Human Rights, there are no representatives of States Parties to the present Convention or if there are fewer than three such representatives, the Secretary-General of the United Nations shall, after consulting all States Parties to the Convention, designate a representative of the State Party or representatives of the States Parties which are not members of the Commission on Human Rights to take part in the work of the group established in accordance with paragraph 1 of this article, until such time as representatives of the States Parties to the Convention are elected to the Commission on Human Rights.

3. The group may meet for a period of not more than five days, either before the opening or after the closing of the session of the Commission on Human Rights, to consider the reports submitted in accordance with article VII.

## Article X

1. The States Parties to the present Convention empower the Commission on Human Rights:

(a) To request United Nations organs, when transmitting copies of petitions under article 15 of the International Convention on the Elimination of All Forms of Racial Discrimination, to draw its attention to complaints concerning acts which are enumerated in article II of the present Convention;

(b) To prepare, on the basis of reports from competent organs of the United Nations and periodic reports from States Parties to the present Convention, a list of individuals, organizations, institutions and representatives of States which are alleged to be responsible for the crimes enumerated in article II of the Convention, as well as those against whom legal proceedings have been undertaken by States Parties to the Convention;

(c) To request information from the competent United Nations organs concerning measures taken by the authorities responsible for the administration of Trust and Non-Self-Governing Territories, and all other Territories to which General Assembly resolution 1514 (XV) of 14 December 1960 applies, with regard to such individuals alleged to be responsible for crimes under article II of the Convention who are believed to be under their territorial and administrative jurisdiction.

2. Pending the achievement of the objectives of the Declaration on the Granting of Independence to Colonial Countries and Peoples, contained in General Assembly resolution 1514 (XV), the provisions of the present Convention shall in no way limit the right of petition granted to those peoples by other international instruments or by the United Nations and its specialized agencies.

## Article XI

1. Acts enumerated in article II of the present Convention shall not be considered political crimes for the purpose of extradition.

2. The States Parties to the present Convention undertake in such cases to grant extradition in accordance with their legislation and with the treaties in force.

## Article XII

Disputes between States Parties arising out of the interpretation, application or implementation of the present Convention which have not been settled by negotiation shall, at the request of the States parties to the dispute, be brought before the International Court of Justice, save where the parties to the dispute have agreed on some other form of settlement.

### Article XIII

The present Convention is open for signature by all States. Any State which does not sign the Convention before its entry into force may accede to it.

### Article XIV

1. The present Convention is subject to ratification. Instruments of ratification shall be deposited with the Secretary-General of the United Nations.

2. Accession shall be effected by the deposit of an instrument of accession with the Secretary-General of the United Nations.

### Article XV

1. The present Convention shall enter into force on the thirtieth day after the date of the deposit with the Secretary-General of the Untied Nations of the twentieth instrument of ratification or accession.

2. For each State ratifying the present Convention or acceding to it after the deposit of the twentieth instrument of ratification or instrument of accession, the Convention shall enter into force on the thirtieth day after the date of the deposit of its own instrument of ratification or instrument of accession.

### Article XVI

A State Party may denounce the present Convention by written notification to the Secretary-General of the United Nations. Denunciation shall take effect one year after the date of receipt of the notification by the Secretary-General.

### Article XVII

1. A request for the revision of the present Convention may be made at any time by any State Party by means of a notification in writing addressed to the Secretary-General of the United Nations.

2. The General Assembly of the United Nations shall decide upon the steps, if any, to be taken in respect of such request.

### Article XVIII

The Secretary-General of the United Nations shall inform all States of the following particulars:

(*a*)   Signatures, ratifications and accessions under articles XIII and XIV;

(*b*)   The date of entry into force of the present Convention under article XV;

(*c*)   Denunciations under article XVI;

(*d*)   Notification under article XVII.

### Article XIX

1. The present Convention, of which the Chinese, English, French, Russian and Spanish texts are equally authentic, shall be deposited in the archives of the United Nations.

2. The Secretary-General of the United Nations shall transmit certified copies of the present Convention to all States.

---

# Document 71

*General Assembly resolution: Policies of apartheid of the Government of South Africa—Situation in South Africa resulting from the policies of apartheid*

A/RES/3151 G (XXVIII), 14 December 1973

*The General Assembly,*

. . .

11.   *Declares* that the South African regime has no right to represent the people of South Africa and that the liberation movements recognized by the Organization of African Unity are the authentic representatives of the overwhelming majority of the South African people;

12.   *Authorizes* the Special Committee on Apartheid, in consultation with the Organization of African Unity, to associate the South African liberation movements closely with its work;

13.   *Requests* all specialized agencies and other intergovernmental organizations to deny membership or privileges of membership to the South African regime and to invite, in consultation with the Organization of African Unity, representatives of the liberation movements of the South African people recognized by that organization to participate in their meetings;

. . .

# Document 72

*Statement by the Chairman of the Special Committee against Apartheid, Mr. Edwin Ogebe Ogbu (Nigeria), at a meeting of the Anti-Apartheid Committee of New Zealand, held at Victoria University in Wellington on 13 September 1974*

UN Press Release GA/AP/413, 16 September 1974

I am delighted at this opportunity personally to convey the greetings of the United Nations Special Committee on Apartheid to the National Anti-Apartheid Committee of New Zealand and to all the organizations which are associated with it as sponsors.

What you have done in the past few years in informing the people of this country of the inhumanity of apartheid in South Africa, and in enabling the nation to pronounce itself against collaboration with racism in South Africa, especially in sport, has been a source of great satisfaction and, indeed, encouragement to us at the United Nations. It reinforced our conviction that when people know the truth—even in countries where the people are mostly of European origin—they will reject apartheid and will join in efforts to eradicate it. This conviction was also put to the test in Australia and other countries and prevailed.

This conviction is precious because if it is proved wrong, humanity can look forward to nothing better than a permanent division across racial or colour barriers.

The actions of the Governments of New Zealand and Australia have also been a source of great comfort to the people in South Africa who have been struggling for decades for freedom and now face difficult days in their march towards the inevitable triumph of their just cause.

We greatly appreciate what the New Zealand Government has done, under the leadership of the late Mr. Norman Kirk, in dissociating this country from apartheid, especially in the important area of sport, and in affirming its faith in the oneness of humanity. I have been assured that the present Government, under the leadership of Mr. Wallace Rowling, will continue the same course. In fact, I would like to believe that this has now become the irrevocable national commitment of New Zealand.

If giving up rugby with the South African Whites is a sacrifice—and I know that New Zealanders are devoted to rugby—I would like to assure you that your action has raised the esteem for New Zealand in Africa and all over the world.

I would like also to take this opportunity, as we are so close to the Commonwealth of Australia—which I am regrettably unable to visit at this time because of the session of the United Nations General Assembly—to reaffirm the great appreciation of the Special Committee for the steps taken by the Australian Government, under the leadership of Mr. Gough Whitlam, to dissociate Australia from apartheid. I would particularly like to refer to its recent decision to send home the military attaché of the Pretoria regime.

On behalf of the Special Committee, I would ask all other countries which have exchanged military attachés with the Pretoria regime to follow the example of Australia if they want us to believe their protestations of opposition to apartheid or of friendship with Africa or of loyalty to the United Nations.

Without in any way detracting from our appreciation for the actions of the Governments of New Zealand and Australia, I would like to acknowledge the commendable role played by the anti-apartheid movements and other non-governmental organizations in bringing about these welcome developments. The anti-apartheid movements have often acted, especially in the countries which have maintained relations with the South African regime, as the conscience of the nation.

Here in New Zealand, even a few years ago, you were a very small group—small in numbers though big in conviction and perseverance. You continued your efforts, in spite of attacks against you, to defend one of the fundamental principles of the United Nations, the Olympic principle of non-discrimination and the very soul of decent sport. You pressed that the nation face its conscience.

I am glad that people from various sectors of public life—churchmen, trade unionists, students and others—joined in reaffirming opposition to racism at home and abroad.

As a Christian, I am not in the least surprised that some churchmen have opposed apartheid and even faced persecution because of that opposition. How can any true Christian act otherwise? Could Jesus Christ, who was himself born in Asia, condone the oppression and humiliation of human beings, especially the great majority of people in South Africa and the world, for the colour of their skin? Could He remain unconcerned when the Gospel is cited to justify such oppression and humiliation?

And how can any trade unionist be unconcerned about the situation in South Africa? The struggle against apartheid is essentially a struggle of the working people against the denial of elementary trade union rights—indeed, against the imposition of forced labour and slavery—on the basis of colour. The struggle of the South African people for liberation is partly the struggle of the workers for their rights.

I am glad that the trade union movement in New Zealand has taken action in accordance with the decisions of the International Conference of Trade Unions against Apartheid, held in Geneva in June 1973.

But I would like to say that I am particularly heartened by the involvement of students and youth here in the struggle against apartheid and racism.

When you oppose apartheid, you are not merely showing sympathy with people suffering from poverty and oppression. You are not merely demonstrating solidarity with those struggling for a righteous cause.

You are contributing to the elimination of one of the scourges of our time and one of the major impediments to genuine cooperation between broad segments of humanity. You are helping to remove a cancer that can destroy our hopes for the future of humanity, in the next generation if not in the present.

The struggle in South Africa, let us be very clear, is not a struggle of the African people against the Whites, but a struggle of humanism against racism.

If it were a mere revolt of the slaves or a race war by Blacks against Whites, the situation would be very different. In the South African society where the Whites live in comfort on the labour of the Blacks, all that is needed to spread panic in the whole White community, as some one said, is a conspiracy of a few cooks and domestic servants.

But the African people, and their liberation movement, have shown the utmost restraint and attachment to humanism in refusing to meet terrorism with terrorism. They have suffered because they are struggling for the principle that South Africa belongs to all the people who live in it—Black, Brown or White. Their struggle is a struggle for all men and women, for the survival of Whites as much as for the freedom of the Blacks.

Just as the liberation movement of the African people of Angola, Guinea-Bissau and Mozambique fought for the liberation of the African people, and thereby also for the liberation of the Portuguese, the liberation movement of South Africa is struggling for the liberation of the Blacks as well as the Whites in South Africa. The true friends of the Whites of South Africa are those who prevent that minority from its march to suicide under its present racist leadership.

As you know, the present regime in South Africa has not only committed crimes against the Black people of South Africa, but has jailed and persecuted many Whites who have opposed racism. It is now threatening the White

students of the National Union of South African Students because they upheld the Universal Declaration of Human Rights and disclosed the miserable conditions to which African workers are subjected. In opposing apartheid, we declare our solidarity not only with the oppressed Black people but also with those Whites who espouse human dignity.

I have come here, as I said, on a friendly visit to this country, at the invitation of the Government, to convey our appreciation to the Government and people of New Zealand. It is not my intention to criticize anyone—even those few who are misguided and who are still advocating that this country, which has rejected racism at home, should fraternize with racists in southern Africa. It is my hope that they will see the light and join the mainstream of New Zealand, a country which we respect for its integrity.

But I must confess that I could hardly believe my eyes when I read in a paper that there is a group here which opposes the sports boycott against South Africa on the grounds that the world is discriminating against South Africa for its policies when other countries practise discrimination—and, I read to my amazement, including countries in Africa.

By refusing to play ball with the racists, it seems we are discriminating against the racists of South Africa, the one country in the world where racial discrimination is enshrined in the Constitution itself, not to mention hundreds of laws and in daily practice.

This group, I read, is apparently associated with some people in South Africa who call themselves, of all things, the "Committee for Fairness in Sport". That Committee, we know, is, in fact, a committee to defend the system under which 15 million Africans have never had fairness in sport or in anything else in life.

The present regime in South Africa has shown great inventiveness in giving misleading and utterly false titles to its acts. There is a Suppression of Communism Act under which numerous non-Communists and even opponents of Communism are persecuted—including Chief Albert Luthuli, the winner of the Nobel Peace Prize, and scores of churchmen. It passed an Abolition of Passes Act under which it reinforced the pass laws which prevent the free movement of Africans and made the passes more complicated. It has an Extension of University Education Act under which it prohibited Blacks from attending the established universities. It has an Immorality Act under which making love to one's sweetheart is a punishable crime if the skin colours of the couple are not the same. It set up a Republic which is the opposite of a Republic as defined in any dictionary.

I hope New Zealanders will never be taken in by such false names, or copy the South African example and lose their integrity.

Let me also, as an African, be very frank about the gratuitous reference to independent African countries. Africa is a continent which has just emerged into freedom—and it is not yet fully free. We are not perfect but we are trying hard to build our nations with the hope that we can forget the past and establish true international cooperation, even with our erstwhile oppressors. We hope we will succeed by our efforts, aided by the understanding, goodwill and cooperation of the rest of the world.

But before anyone tries to attack us for any real or imaginary mistakes we make during this period—in order to defend the humiliation of Africans and to undermine cooperation between Africa and the world—let him recall a bit of history.

In the centuries when Europe was developing its trade and industry, our continent suffered the ravages of the slave traders from which tens of millions of the sons and daughters of Africa perished—and whole regions of our continent, especially my part of Africa, were depopulated. Our continent suffered the pillages of the colonialists who took the rich natural wealth of our continent and left the people poor, sick and illiterate.

We have been independent nations for much less than a generation under difficult international conditions —facing inequalities in international trade and the remnants of prejudice in Europe and North America, as well as plots and conflicts instigated by the colonial and racist Powers and other vested interests.

We may have made mistakes—which nation didn't? —but in these few years the independent African States have made more progress in education, health and the enjoyment of human rights than perhaps any other continent has done in a comparable period to time. Despite the tragic past, we have opposed racism and stretched our hand of friendship to all the Whites who settled in Africa —on only one condition, that they accept that they are fellow human beings, fellow Africans, and not people destined to lord it over and humiliate Africans.

We seek friendship. We welcome friendly advice. But we will not tolerate inequality and humiliation. If this is discrimination, we do discriminate and we ask all our true friends to discriminate—against the racists.

We are grateful to New Zealand and we are grateful to all of you in the Anti-Apartheid Committee and the associated organizations because you have made your choice. You have chosen the friendship of the people of Africa as against the enticements of those who oppress the African people and whose policies and actions are an affront to humanity.

I would like to say a few words about one matter which seems not to have been fully understood in New Zealand.

The United Nations General Assembly, at its last session in 1973, declared that the liberation movements recognized by the Organization of African Unity are the authentic representatives of the overwhelming majority of the South African people, and reiterated that "the struggle of the oppressed people of South Africa by all available means for the total eradication of apartheid is legitimate and deserves the support of the international community".

Perhaps we had not adequately explained these provisions and some friends in New Zealand, I understand, have expressed apprehensions that they may imply an encouragement of violence.

Let me make it perfectly clear that the Special Committee on Apartheid—there is no doubt that Africa shares its view—is most anxious to promote a peaceful solution of the situation in South Africa. We have again and again warned of the dangers of conflict in South Africa—where it may develop into a race conflict with incalculable consequences—and pressed constantly for economic and other action by the international community to avert a tragedy.

Let me also recall that the people of South Africa have struggled for many decades by non-violent means, at great sacrifice, to secure their legitimate rights. They have been the pioneers and the most persistent practitioners of non-violent passive resistance. To tell them about the virtues of non-violence is as ludicrous as carrying coals to Newcastle.

But at the same time, it is imperative that the world should recognize that the struggle in South Africa is a struggle between right and wrong, and all nations, organizations and individuals must make a choice. It is equally important to recognize that the South African regime has been closing every possibility for a peaceful solution, by ruthlessly suppressing all non-violent and peaceful protest. It has been provoking the people to meet violence with violence, to meet massacres by armed self-defence.

Neither the United Nations nor Africa has tried to prescribe to the African people of South Africa the means of their struggle, nor have they encouraged one form of struggle against another. The form of struggle is for the South African people to decide according to their circumstances.

What the United Nations has done is to affirm the legitimacy of the struggle of the oppressed people by means of their own choice. It has thereby rejected the right of the oppressors in South Africa to tell the African people what kind of servile status they should aspire to—the bantustans, for instance—and how they should go about it. It has rejected the efforts of some foreign vested interests to find "solutions" convenient for themselves— "solutions" which are a compromise with racism and a continuation of racism, to enable these interests to go on making profits from injustice.

We reject and condemn the efforts of anyone who

attempts to limit the right of the people of South Africa to fight for their freedom, or to seek total eradication of apartheid and racial discrimination. We cannot accept that people of other countries have a right to resort to violence, but African people, because they are Black, are denied that right. At the same time, we will do everything possible, by international action, to spare the South African people the suffering and the agonies of a violent conflict. That is precisely why we are appealing for support from all countries and peoples.

Those of you who have followed recent events in Africa know that the African people have not resorted to violence in their struggle for freedom until their peaceful protests were met by ruthless massacres. Today, as we celebrate the confirmation of the freedom of the people of Guinea-Bissau, and look forward to the freedom of Angola and Mozambique, the people of Portugal share with the African people the fruits of the heroic armed struggle which the liberation movements were obliged to undertake in the African Territories. You are no doubt aware that the leaders of the independent African States have lent their good offices to secure settlements.

When the White minority in South Africa abandons its dream of perpetual domination over the Africans, and when it is ready to seek, hopefully by concerted international action, to negotiate, with the genuine representatives of the overwhelming majority of the people, the destiny of the nation as a whole, I have no doubt that the African people of South Africa will show their traditional tolerance and magnanimity. I have no doubt that independent Africa will do all it can to facilitate a solution, as it has pledged many times—for instance, in the Lusaka manifesto which was adopted by the Organization of African Unity and endorsed, almost unanimously, by the United Nations General Assembly.

That is the day we look forward to—that is the outcome towards which we are striving. And I want to thank all of you in joining in this international effort.

# Document 73

*General Assembly resolution: Credentials of representatives to the twenty-ninth session of the General Assembly*

A/RES/3206 (XXIX), 30 September 1974

*The General Assembly*
*Approves* the first report of the Credentials Committee.

# Document 74

*General Assembly resolution: Relationship between the United Nations and South Africa*

A/RES/3207 (XXIX), 30 September 1974

*The General Assembly,*

*Recalling* its resolutions 2636 A (XXV) of 13 November 1970, 2862 (XXVI) of 20 December 1971 and 2948 (XXVII) of 8 December 1972 and its decision of 5 October 1973, by which it decided to reject the credentials of South Africa,

*Recalling* that South Africa did not heed any of the aforementioned decisions and has continued to practise its policy of apartheid and racial discrimination against the majority of the population in South Africa,

*Reaffirming,* once again, that the policy of apartheid and racial discrimination of the Government of South Africa is a flagrant violation of the principles of the Charter of the United Nations and the Universal Declaration of Human Rights,

*Noting* the persistent refusal of South Africa to abandon its policy of apartheid and racial discrimination in compliance with relevant resolutions and decisions of the General Assembly,

*Calls upon* the Security Council to review the relationship between the United Nations and South Africa in the light of the constant violation by South Africa of the principles of the Charter and the Universal Declaration of Human Rights.

# Document 75

*Ruling by the President of the General Assembly, Mr. Abdelaziz Bouteflika (Algeria), concerning the credentials of the delegation of South Africa*

A/PV.2281, 12 November 1994

Today, for the first time, I am asked to state here my interpretation of the General Assembly's decision to reject the credentials of the delegation of South Africa. In that connection, I must say that the General Assembly, at its 2248th meeting on 30 September 1974, took two decisions. First, it approved the report of the Credentials Committee rejecting the credentials of the delegation of South Africa (*resolution 3206 (XXIX)*). Secondly, it adopted resolution 3207 (XXIX), in which it called upon the Security Council to review the relationship between the United Nations and South Africa in the light of the constant violation by South Africa of the principles of the Charter and the Universal Declaration of Human Rights.

In his letter of 31 October 1974 (*A/9847*), the President of the Security Council informed the General Assembly that the Council had not been able to adopt a resolution on this item and accordingly remained seized of the matter.

However, the absence of a decision by the Security Council in no way affects the General Assembly's rejection of the credentials of the delegation of South Africa. Since its twenty-fifth session the General Assembly has been regularly rejecting, each year, the credentials of that delegation. It did so until last year by adopting an amendment to the report of the Credentials Committee.

In 1970, Mr. Hambro, who was then President of the Assembly, stated the following after the adoption of the amendment rejecting the credentials of the delegation of South Africa:

"... the amendment as it is worded at present"—and I emphasize "as it is worded at present"—"would not seem to me to mean that the South African delegation is unseated or cannot continue to sit in this Assembly."

It is clear that the opinion of Mr. Hambro, a legal authority to whom I wish to pay tribute, was based above all on the exact words of the decision adopted by the General Assembly in the form of an amendment. That opinion did not mean that if the amendment had been worded in some other way it might not have had different consequences for the legal position of the South African delegation in this Assembly.

The question is all the more worthy of consideration because rule 29 of our rules of procedure states:

"Any representative to whose admission a Member has made objection shall be seated provisionally with the same rights as other representatives until the Credentials Committee has reported and the General Assembly has given its decision".

That text perhaps does not indicate with sufficient clarity what should happen once the General Assembly has taken a decision confirming the objection to the admission of a representative or a delegation. Now, year after year, the General Assembly has decided, by ever-larger majorities, not to recognize the credentials of the South African delegation, and during this session the Credentials Committee itself took the initiative of rejecting those credentials. It has not been necessary for the Assembly to adopt an amendment along these lines to the report submitted by the Credentials Committee.

It would therefore be a betrayal of the clearly and repeatedly expressed will of the General Assembly to understand this to mean that it was merely a procedural method of expressing its rejection of the policy of apartheid. On the basis of the consistency with which the General Assembly has regularly refused to accept the credentials of the South African delegation, one may legitimately infer that the General Assembly would in the same way reject the credentials of any other delegation authorized by the Government of the Republic of South Africa to represent it, which is tantamount to saying in explicit terms that the General Assembly refuses to allow the South African delegation to participate in its work.

Thus it is, as President of the twenty-ninth session of the General Assembly, that I interpret the decision of the General Assembly, leaving open the question of the status of the Republic of South Africa as a Member of the United Nations which, as we all know, is a matter requiring a recommendation from the Security Council. My interpretation refers exclusively to the position of the South African delegation within the strict framework of the rules of procedure of the General Assembly. That is my belief.

[Editor's note: The ruling of the President was challenged and upheld by 91 votes to 22, with 19 abstentions .]

# Document 76

*Paper presented by the Chairman of the Special Committee against Apartheid, Mr. Edwin Ogebe Ogbu (Nigeria), to the Extraordinary Session of the Council of Ministers of the Organization of African Unity, held at Dar es Salaam, April 1975*

United Nations Unit on Apartheid Notes and Documents No. 11/75

## Common position of the United Nations and OAU

. . .

As regards South Africa, both the United Nations and OAU are dedicated to the principle of full equality for all the people of the country, irrespective of race or colour. They oppose the regime in South Africa, not because it is White, but because it denies and fights against the principles of human equality and national self-determination.

Both the United Nations and OAU have recognized that the future of South Africa is a matter for decision by the people of South Africa—Black and White—on the basis of equality. The main parties to the dispute are the racist regime and its supporters, on the one hand, and the oppressed people and other opponents of racism, led by the liberation movements, on the other. The key to a peaceful solution is negotiation between the two parties to enable the people of South Africa as a whole to determine the destiny of the country.

At the same time, the United Nations and OAU have a vital interest in the situation because the policy and practice of apartheid have created a threat to the peace. They have, indeed, a duty to eliminate this threat to the peace and to assist the oppressed people in their legitimate struggle against the crime of racism so long as the regime refuses to accept the principle of human equality.

Both the United Nations and OAU have repeatedly declared their desire and willingness to promote a peaceful solution of the situation in South Africa.

. . .

It may be recalled that it was the South African regime which chose violence, by closing all avenues for peaceful change and resorting to ruthless repression against opponents of racism. It was only after decades of non-violent struggle, culminating in the Sharpeville massacre and the banning of liberation movements, that the liberation movements were forced to go underground and give up their adherence to non-violence. It was only then, and after repeated appeals to the Pretoria regime, that other African States called for sanctions against that regime and for moral and material support to the liberation movements.

Despite the intransigence of the South African regime, the United Nations and the OAU have continued constantly to call on it to choose the path of peaceful solution, and offered their assistance and good offices.

Their only demands have been that it accept the principle of human equality, release the political prisoners and seek negotiations with the genuine leaders and representatives of the great majority of the people.

## Apartheid—a matter of universal concern

The correctness of the position of the United Nations and the OAU is reflected in growing support in all regions of the world. Apartheid in South Africa has become a matter of universal concern. Many Governments have imposed sanctions against South Africa at some sacrifice, and are giving substantial assistance to the victims of apartheid and to their liberation movements. Many public organizations, especially in Western countries, have devoted commendable efforts in support of African aspirations. This world-wide support is of crucial importance for the Black people of South Africa in their struggle for liberation.

In order to maintain and strengthen this unity against apartheid it is essential that the United Nations and OAU should constantly reiterate and defend the fundamental principles of their common policy. Any action which will create confusion and divide their ranks—especially any action which will confuse the many States and organizations which have made sacrifices in defence of these principles—must be resisted.

. . .

The latest move for "detente" and "dialogue" was initiated by the South African regime because of its growing isolation. As shown in this paper, there has been no evidence however, of a meaningful change in its policy and actions. It has shown no willingness to abandon racial discrimination nor to release the political prisoners nor to negotiate with the genuine representatives of the people.

The purposes of the current South African moves are clearly to divert attention from the problem of apartheid, to counteract its growing isolation, to disrupt the United Nations efforts for concerted international action against apartheid, and to gain time in order to build up its military arsenal, to repress the resurgent resistance against apartheid in South Africa and enforce its plans for bantustans.

As the United Nations and OAU have already made it clear the South African regime must be told in clear terms that any meaningful "detente" or "dialogue" with respect to apartheid in South Africa should begin with the oppressed people and their liberation movements. Negotiations on Namibia can only be undertaken with the United Nations, which has assumed responsibility for the Territory, and the liberation movement, which has been recognized by the world as the authentic representative of the people.

### Co-operation between the United Nations and OAU on further action

In the absence of meaningful change in the situation, the United Nations is committed to intensifying its efforts—with the co-operation of Governments, and inter-governmental organizations—for the eradication of apartheid. Close co-operation between the United Nations and OAU is vital for the success of these efforts.

. . .

In pursuance of its mandate, the Special Committee has been engaged in contacts with many Governments and public organizations in the world. It has maintained close cooperation with OAU and the South African liberation movements which participate in all its meetings as observers. It greatly appreciates the invitations to attend sessions of appropriate OAU organs for an exchange of information and views.

The Special Committee would welcome any proposals for even closer cooperation with OAU in the present stage of the common struggle against apartheid. Attention may perhaps be given to means for consultation and coordination with respect to: (*a*) missions to governments, inter-governmental organizations and conferences to promote action against apartheid; (*b*) encouragement of public campaigns against apartheid in all regions of the world; and (*c*) dissemination of information on the inhumanity of apartheid, the legitimate struggle of the oppressed people and their liberation movements for freedom and equality, and international action for the eradication of apartheid.

The Special Committee would appreciate OAU action with respect to States which have continued and increased military, economic and diplomatic collaboration with the South African regime despite the appeals of the Special Committee.

It would, moreover, welcome urgent OAU action to persuade all States to cooperate in securing a mandatory arms embargo against South Africa, and to prohibit or discourage emigration to South Africa.

# Document 77

## *Telegram from Mr. Oliver Tambo, President of the African National Congress, to the Secretary-General*

A/AC.115/SR.973, 3 November 1975

All victims and genuine opponents of South Africa inhuman policies warmly acclaim UN resolution rejecting bantustans and so-called Transkei independence STOP Decision justifies vast majority of world peoples' faith in UN as promoter of just causes and defender of human rights STOP

# Document 78

## *General Assembly resolution: Policies of apartheid of the Government of South Africa—Solidarity with the South African political prisoners*

A/RES/3411 B, 28 November 1975

*The General Assembly,*

*Deeply concerned* over the ruthless repression of the opponents of apartheid and racism in South Africa, including the recent persecution of numerous student, cultural and other leaders,

*Reaffirming* its resolutions calling for an end to repression and unconditional amnesty for all persons imprisoned or restricted for their opposition to apartheid or acts arising from such opposition,

*Taking note* of the refusal of the racist regime of South Africa to heed these resolutions,

*Reaffirming* the legitimacy of the struggle of the South African people for the total eradication of apartheid and the exercise of the right of self-determination by all the inhabitants of South Africa,

*Reaffirming its conviction* that the release of the oppressed people of South Africa and other opponents of apartheid from imprisonment and other restrictions is an essential factor for the eradication of apartheid,

*Recognizing* the contribution of the liberation movements and other opponents of apartheid in South Africa to the purposes of the United Nations,

1. *Condemns* the ruthless repression by the racist regime of South Africa against the leaders of the oppressed people of South Africa and other opponents of apartheid;

2. *Strongly condemns* the Terrorism Act and other repressive legislation designed to suppress the legitimate struggle of the South African people for freedom and self-determination;

3. *Expresses its solidarity* with all South Africans struggling against apartheid and for the principles enshrined in the Charter of the United Nations;

4. *Again calls upon* the racist regime of South Africa to grant an unconditional amnesty to all persons imprisoned or restricted for their opposition to apartheid or acts arising from such opposition, as well as to political refugees from South Africa, and to repeal all repressive laws and regulations restricting the right of the people to strive for an end to the apartheid system;

5. *Requests* the Special Committee against Apartheid and the Unit on Apartheid of the Secretariat to redouble their efforts to publicize the cause of all those persecuted for their opposition to apartheid in South Africa.

# Document 79

*General Assembly resolution: Policies of apartheid of the Government of South Africa—Special responsibility of the United Nations and the international community towards the oppressed people of South Africa*

A/RES/3411 C (XXX), 28 November 1975

*The General Assembly,*

*Recalling* its numerous resolutions condemning the policies of apartheid of the racist regime of South Africa,

*Aware* of its responsibility of upholding the principles enshrined in the Charter of the United Nations and the Universal Declaration of Human Rights,

*Commending* the courageous struggle of the oppressed people of South Africa under the leadership of their liberation movements supported by the United Nations and the international community,

*Taking note* of the heavy sacrifices made by the people of South Africa in their legitimate struggle for self-determination,

*Meeting* on the occasion of the thirtieth anniversary of the United Nations,

1. *Proclaims* that the United Nations and the international community have a special responsibility towards the oppressed people of South Africa and their liberation movements, and towards those imprisoned, restricted or exiled for their struggle against apartheid;

2. *Reiterates* its determination to devote increasing attention and all necessary resources to concert international efforts, in close cooperation with the Organization of African Unity, for the speedy eradication of apartheid in South Africa and the liberation of the South African people.

# Document 80

*General Assembly resolution: Policies of apartheid of the Government of South Africa—Situation in South Africa*

A/RES/3411 G (XXX), 10 December 1975

*The General Assembly,*

. . .

11. *Appeals* to all States concerned to take the necessary measures to impose an effective embargo on the supply of petroleum, petroleum products and strategic raw materials to South Africa;

12. *Requests* the Special Committee against Apartheid to hold consultations with Governments and organizations, as necessary, to promote the implementation of the measures indicated in paragraph 11 above;

. . .

# Document 81

*Statement by Mrs. Jeanne Martin Cissé (Guinea), Chairperson of the Special Committee against Apartheid*

UN Press Release GA/AP/523, 21 January 1976

This year it will .be 30 years since the United Nations became seized of the problem of racist domination in South Africa.

In 1946, when the Government of India brought this problem to the attention of the General Assembly, at the request of the South African liberation movement, it was difficult to obtain sufficient votes even for a discussion of the item. The delegation of the South African liberation movement, led by the late Dr. Xuma, could best hope for a place in the visitor's gallery.

Since then, there has been a radical change because of the struggle of the oppressed people of South Africa, the emergence of the new States out of the colonial revolution, the ever increasing brutality of the racist regime, and the greater awareness of the inhumanity of apartheid and its dangers. The United Nations is now firmly committed to support the struggle of the oppressed people of South Africa for freedom and self-determination.

The South African liberation movement is no more on the sidelines in the United Nations. The African National Congress of South Africa and the Pan Africanist Congress of Azania are with us here, after being recognized as the authentic representatives of the great majority of the people of South Africa. The Pretoria regime is isolated from the deliberations in this Organization, as an illegitimate regime practising a criminal policy.

At its last session, on the thirtieth anniversary of the United Nations, the General Assembly proclaimed that the United Nations and the international community have a special responsibility towards the oppressed people of South Africa and their liberation movements, and towards those imprisoned, restricted or exiled for their struggle against apartheid. It has pledged all necessary efforts to secure the speedy eradication of apartheid in South Africa and the liberation of the South African people.

The primary duty of the Special Committee is to assist the international community in discharging the special responsibility towards the oppressed people of South Africa, in redeeming the pledge to assist them in their struggle until victory. This is a challenging task which we accept, with modesty but with determination.

. . .

I referred earlier to the thirty-year story of the consideration of racism in South Africa by the United Nations because I believe that we should always keep in mind the experience of the past in charting our course to the future.

I would like to recall that every advance that has been made in international action against apartheid arose from the struggle of the South African people—supported by the African, Asian and Non-aligned States, and the Socialist States—and despite the resistance of governments and interests which profit from collusion with the racist regime.

I might recall that in 1952 when the South African people launched "the campaign of defiance against unjust laws", the General Assembly began to consider the problem of apartheid as a whole. The newly-independent Arab and Asian countries helped to bring up the matter in the General Assembly. At that time, Western countries and their allies opposed any action—even the establishment of a Commission to study the situation. They were able to force the disbandment of the Commission in 1955.

In 1960, following the positive action campaign launched by the Pan Africanist Congress of Azania, the Sharpeville massacre and the nation-wide defiance which shook the foundations of the racist regime, the Security Council began consideration of the situation for the first time. But though the South African regime defied the Security Council and detained thousands of people under the State of Emergency, the friends of that regime made it impossible to obtain further action by the Council.

The racist regime proceeded in May 1961 to proclaim a so-called "republic" on the basis of a referendum of White voters. This sham republic—as illegitimate as the regime established by Ian Smith in Rhodesia in 1965— could only be launched by a massive show of force because of rejection by the Black people. Because it was illegitimate, the African States decided to break relations with South Africa and impose sanctions against it. The only African mission to South Africa, the legation of Egypt, was closed on 31 May 1961. The Commonwealth decided, on the initiative of Ghana and Malaysia, supported by other members including Canada, to exclude South Africa.

Looking back, 1961 is not only a mid-point in the United Nations discussion of racism in South Africa, but also a major turning point. On the one hand, the liberation movements were obliged to give up finally their adherence to non-violence in the face of racist violence. On the other hand, apartheid came to be unanimously condemned, though the Western Powers continued to resist concrete measures against South Africa. Even the United Kingdom, which had so far defended South Africa, joined in the condemnation, declaring that South Africa was a special case.

The Special Committee was established a year later, by General Assembly resolution 1761 (XVII) of 6 November 1972, to keep the situation under constant review. It began its work at a time when the crisis had deepened in South Africa and when thousands of South African patriots were being thrown into jail for their resistance against oppression and torture.

Since its inception, and despite the boycott by the Western Powers, the Special Committee has tried to do all in its power to secure wider international recognition and support for the struggle of the South African people for liberation.

We have stressed that apartheid in South Africa is not only a crime against the South African people or an affront to Africa, but also a grave threat to the peace which is of concern to all humanity. We have emphasized that condemnation is not enough, but that concrete action must be taken to isolate the racist regime and assist the oppressed people and their liberation movement.

We have tried to persuade all countries, including the Western countries, and all organizations concerned, to forget their differences on other matters and join in concerted action against apartheid, this universally-recognized menace and crime. We have appealed to the Western countries to abandon "cold war" thinking in dealing with South Africa and warned that freedom-loving governments and peoples of the world cannot but view with hostility any "bloc" allied with the apartheid regime.

We can perhaps recount some achievements in the course of our efforts.

Apartheid has come to be universally condemned, as a unique and most abhorrent crime. It has been recognized that the problem in South Africa is not a problem of a mere violation of human rights or arbitrary imprisonment of a few people but the oppression of the great majority of the people by the racist regime. There have been resolutions and declarations, with overwhelming majorities, committing the United Nations and Member States to the struggle of the South African people. There is an arms embargo which is not without significance, despite the regrettable violations by some Powers. Funds have been established to assist the oppressed people of South Africa, and substantial contributions have been made by States all over the world.

With the collapse of Portuguese colonialism, the boundaries of freedom moved to the borders of South Africa. The Special Committee reported in 1974 that a new stage had arrived in the struggle of the South African people and the efforts of the international community to eradicate apartheid. It warned of the manoeuvres of the South African regime and declared that it had become imperative to step up concerted international action to promote liberation.

Since then, the Special Committee has devoted more efforts than ever to secure concerted action, especially by frank consultations with the Western Powers.

It is, in this context, that we are concerned over the recent attitudes of some States towards the South African regime and its aggression in Angola. There is an attempt to undo the advances which have been made in these 30 years in international action against apartheid.

One great Power has even tried to weaken the action against the South African regime by describing it as "selective condemnation", using a phrase from South African propaganda. An organization in New York, which has arrogated to itself the role of judging freedom, has claimed that South Africa has more freedom than some independent African countries. They may perhaps soon find that there was more freedom under slavery in the United States than after the Civil War!

A high official of the United States of America recently asked that we should consider the pluses and minuses of the withdrawal of South African aggressors from Angola.

One would have thought that after all these years of United Nations consideration, it was agreed that the racist regime must be made to withdraw not only from Angola, but also from Namibia and from South Africa itself—in fact, from the face of this earth!

If I have been constrained to refer specifically to the United States of America, it is with distress because we have a right to expect cooperation from this country which has repeatedly protested its abhorrence of apartheid.

. . .

As regards South African aggression in Angola, the facts are absolutely clear. The racist regime, which is denounced by the international community, has launched military aggression against an African people on the eve of their hard-won independence. It has launched this aggression from the Territory of Namibia which it is occupying illegally—a Territory under the special responsibility of the United Nations. It has crossed the borders of Namibia to attack the militants of SWAPO, a liberation movement recognized by the United Nations as the authentic representative of the Namibian people, and threatened to launch similar aggression against other States which provide hospitality to SWAPO.

But to our astonishment and regret, some Powers, which have special responsibility for international peace, suggest that there should be a bargain over South African aggression. It looks as if the troops of the racist regime are the dogs unleashed by some external Power which then offers to leash them at a price.

We cannot but declare again categorically: the South African forces must be forced to withdraw unconditionally. There can be no ransom to the racist regime, but only retribution for this new crime of aggression.

We are, of course, aware of the propaganda by the Pretoria regime concerning the alleged danger of communism. Many years ago, it launched brutal repression against the South African liberation movements claiming that it was suppressing communism. It then proceeded to attack SWAPO claiming that SWAPO is "communist" and that its freedom fighters have Soviet weapons. It now uses the same slogan in committing aggression against the people of Angola.

The calculations of the South African racists are no mystery.

They have been trying constantly to break out of isolation by persuading Western countries that they have a common interest —whether it is the defence of the Cape route or the security of the Indian Ocean or the "cold war". They think that they can use Angola for this purpose.

I believe that the South African racists have an even more ambitious plan. They are nostalgic for the old days when they were admitted to the counsels of the colonial Powers in Africa to discuss how to retard freedom in Africa. They are anxious to secure recognition as a junior imperialist power dominating southern Africa. For this purpose, they have invested heavily in armaments and in propaganda.

It seems to me that the Special Committee and all opponents of apartheid must denounce and frustrate the moves to reinforce the links between South Africa and the Western Powers.

The Special Committee, for its part, will need to intensify its efforts to publicize the manoeuvres of the racist regime and its collaborators. It must analyse the new situation arising from the desperate adventures by the racist regime, far beyond the borders of South Africa. It must continue and intensify consultations with Governments and organizations, especially the Governments of the main trading partners of South Africa, to secure more concerted action. It must—in close cooperation with the liberation movements, the OAU, the Non-aligned movement, and all friends of freedom —contribute its utmost to the emancipation of the South African people. This challenge we accept as our duty.

---

# Document 82

*Security Council resolution: Situation in South Africa—Killings and violence by the apartheid regime in South Africa in Soweto and other areas*

S/RES/392 (1976), 19 June 1976

*The Security Council,*

. . .

*Deeply shocked* over large-scale killings and wounding of Africans in South Africa, following the callous shooting of African people including schoolchildren and students demonstrating against racial discrimination on 16 June 1976,

*Convinced* that this situation has been brought about by the continued imposition by the South African Government of apartheid and racial discrimination, in defiance of the resolutions of the Security Council and the General Assembly,

1. *Strongly condemns* the South African Government for its resort to massive violence against and killings of the African people including schoolchil-

dren and students and others opposing racial discrimination;

2. *Expresses* its profound sympathy to the victims of this violence;

3. *Reaffirms* that the policy of apartheid is a crime against the conscience and dignity of mankind and seriously disturbs international peace and security;

4. *Recognizes* the legitimacy of the struggle of the South African people for the elimination of apartheid and racial discrimination;

5. *Calls upon* the South African Government urgently to end violence against the African people and to take urgent steps to eliminate apartheid and racial discrimination;

. . .

# Document 83

*Special report of the Special Committee against Apartheid on "The Soweto massacre and its aftermath"*

A/31/22/Add.1, 3 August 1976

## I. Introduction

1. The uprising in South Africa since 16 June 1976 against apartheid and racial discrimination and the brutal massacres perpetrated by the South African regime against African schoolchildren and others represent a new stage in the struggle of the South African people for freedom and an inescapable challenge to the international community.

2. Though the immediate cause of demonstrations by the African students was the arbitrary imposition by the apartheid regime of Afrikaans as the second language of instruction in African secondary schools, they reflect, in fact, African resistance to apartheid in all its aspects.

3. As the Security Council recognized in resolution 392 (1976), adopted by consensus on 19 June, the present situation "has been brought about by the continued imposition by the South African Government of apartheid and racial discrimination, in defiance of the resolutions of the Security Council and the General Assembly". . . .

4. Numerous Governments and public organizations all over the world have expressed shock at the callous killing of Africans, demanded that the Pretoria regime abandon apartheid and repression, and called for more energetic international action to eradicate apartheid.

5. The Pretoria regime, however, has scorned the resolution of the Security Council. While making partial concessions on the issue of Afrikaans instruction, it resorted to massive repression against the African people and all opponents of apartheid, thereby aggravating the situation.

6. The Special Committee considers that the General Assembly and the Security Council, in particular, and the international community, generally, must urgently take further action to put an end to this increasingly grave situation, which is likely to lead to even more brutal repression and violence against innocent people and a consequent threat to the peace in a wider international context.

## II. The unfolding crisis

7. Since its inception in 1963, the Special Committee has repeatedly drawn attention to the constant aggravation of the situation in South Africa as a result of the imposition of apartheid by the racist White minority regime and its brutal repression against opponents of apartheid. In its annual and special reports to the General Assembly and the Security Council, it has shown that the Pretoria regime has resorted to ever-increasing repression to enforce apartheid as resistance to its policies continued unabated. ; . . .

8. In these 13 years, the racist regime has caused enormous suffering to the Black people by forcible removal of hundreds of thousands of families, arrests of millions of people under discriminatory laws and deprivation of elementary human rights. It has enacted a series of repressive laws which violate all canons of justice; it has imprisoned and restricted thousands of leaders of the Black people and other opponents of apartheid and subjected them to ill-treatment and torture, resulting in over a score of deaths in detention. It has resorted to police shootings against peaceful demonstrators on several occasions in incidents described as "mini-Sharpevilles".

9. Despite all this brutality, however, there has been ever-increasing resistance against apartheid by the oppressed people of South Africa. The legitimacy of their struggle for freedom has received growing international recognition.

. . .

15. These policies and actions of the South African racist regime have created a highly explosive situation, which has led to the recent ghastly massacre of African children in Soweto and other areas. The wide popular support for African student demonstrations against the imposition of Afrikaans as a medium of instruction in segregated secondary schools reflects a seething resentment against the diabolical plans of the regime for the perpetuation of White domination. The inhuman brutality of the regime in resorting to wanton killings of African children underlines its determination to continue on its present course, which can only be catastrophic.

## III. The Soweto massacre and its aftermath

16. On 16 June 1976, 10,000 African students in Soweto, the segregated African township of Johannesburg, joined a peaceful demonstration against the arbitrary decision imposed by the "Bantu education" authorities that Afrikaans should be used as the medium of instruction for several subjects in secondary schools. The police opened fire at the demonstrators, killing several children. A special police squad trained to combat urban terrorism was brought into Soweto by helicopters, which were also used to drop tear-gas canisters. In the ensuing confrontations between the police

and Africans, mainly students, large numbers of persons were killed and wounded. The Africans destroyed a number of buildings —notably the offices of the West Rand Bantu Administration Board, liquor stores and beer halls— which, to them, were symbols of racial discrimination and oppression.

17. Eyewitness accounts of the events of 16 June indicated that the police had shot and killed schoolchildren indiscriminately. A senior police officer told the press: "We fire into them. It is no good firing over their heads." The dispatch of large contingents of the police into the township tended to provoke African anger.

18. Several hundred White students from the University of Witwatersrand held demonstrations in Johannesburg on 17 June in sympathy with the Black students of Soweto and were joined by Black workers. They were brutally attacked by White vigilantes and by the police, resulting in serious injuries to scores of persons.

19. Demonstrations against "Bantu education" and in solidarity with the African students in Soweto soon spread to numerous African townships near Johannesburg, Pretoria, Krugersdorp, Germiston, Benoni, Boksburg, Klerksdorp and Nelspruit—indeed, to most townships in the Witwatersrand-Pretoria area, as well as parts of Northern Transvaal, the Orange Free State and Natal. Students at the University of the North at Turfloop and the University of Zululand in Ngoya also demonstrated in sympathy and both institutions were closed.*

20. According to official figures, 176 persons were killed and 1,139 wounded, many of whom were small children. Over 1,300 persons were arrested. There is reason to believe that the total was actually much higher.

21. The immediate cause of the student demonstration in Soweto, as noted earlier, was the imposition of Afrikaans as a medium of instruction in secondary schools.

22. It may be recalled that the South African regime segregated education in 1954 and instituted a "Bantu education" system for the Africans, based on the philosophy of the then Minister of Native Affairs, Mr. H. F. Verwoerd, that "there is no place for the Bantu in the European community above the level of certain forms of labour". The Africans were subjected to gross discrimination in education.

. . .

30. The Pretoria regime has gone through the pretence of consultations with members of the Urban Bantu Council, an apartheid institution scorned by the African people, and announced that the decision as to the medium of instruction would be left to the principals of schools, acting in consultation with their school boards and school committees. It also announced plans to provide electricity to all homes in Soweto in five to seven years and to grant greater powers to the Urban Bantu Councils.

31. While making these minor concessions in the hope of defusing resistance, the regime has categorically rejected demands for an end to apartheid and embarked on massive repression against the Black people, as well as against Whites who have called for an end to apartheid.

32. On 15 July, it put into force the indefinite detention provisions of the Internal Security Act and detained a large number of leaders of the South African Students Organization and the Black People's Convention. It gave formal warnings to several opponents of apartheid not to involve themselves in the situation.

## IV. Need for urgent efforts to isolate the racist regime and assist the oppressed people

33. The massacre in Soweto and related events demonstrate once again the inhumanity of the South African racist regime. They have shown that the Black people of South Africa, who constitute the great majority of the population of the country, cannot secure attention to a solution of their day-to-day grievances, let alone attain their inalienable rights, by appeals and representations to the racist regime. The callousness of the Government to repeated appeals by African educators and parents to heed the demands of students and the massive violence against the student demonstrators have reinforced the conviction of the African people that peaceful protests are ineffective, and that they need to resort to all other necessary means of liberation from racist oppression and tyranny.

34. The recent events have demonstrated that the racist regime is incapable of moving away from apartheid and racial discrimination, as its representative promised before the Security Council in October 1974, and of seeking a solution based on the principles enshrined in the United Nations Charter and the Universal Declaration of Human Rights.

35. They have shown that there can be no solution to the grave situation in South Africa without the replacement of the minority racist regime by a Government based on the principle of equality and the exercise of the right of self-determination by all the people of South Africa.

36. The Special Committee takes note of a resolution on the Soweto massacre adopted by the Organization of African Unity (OAU) at the twenty-seventh ordinary session of the Council of Ministers at the end of June 1976, that "the only effective guarantee for the African people of South Africa against the repetition of the massacres is the launching of an armed struggle for the seizure of power by the people".

*The third segregated tribal university for Africans—the University of Fort Hare—was on vacation in June. A solidarity demonstration was held by the students at that University on 17 and 18 July 1976 and the University was immediately closed.

37. The Special Committee considers that all those opposed to apartheid should abandon their vain efforts to persuade the criminal racist regime to abandon racism and should take firm action to isolate the racist regime and assist the oppressed people and their liberation movements in the struggle for the total eradication of apartheid and the exercise of the right of self-determination.

. . .

## V. Action taken by the Special Committee

43. Since the events of 16 June 1976, the Special Committee has attempted, in accordance with its mandate, to publicize the situation in South Africa and promote effective international action against apartheid.

44. In a statement on 17 June 1976, the Acting Chairman and the Rapporteur of the Committee pointed out that the events in Soweto were yet another example of the brutality of the Pretoria regime, and demonstrated the growing militancy of the oppressed people and their courage in the face of inhuman repression. They emphasized that the conflict in South Africa was a conflict between racism and non-racialism and added:

> "In resolution 3411 C (XXX) of 28 November 1975, the General Assembly proclaimed that the United Nations and the international community have a special responsibility towards the oppressed people of South Africa and their liberation movements, and towards those imprisoned, restricted or exiled for their struggle against apartheid. Every crime committed by the Vorster regime against Black people is, therefore, a direct affront to the United

Nations and the international community. The killing of the Black schoolchildren of Soweto is such a crime.

> "On behalf of the Special Committee against Apartheid, we appeal to all Governments and organizations to denounce this new crime of the Vorster regime.

> "We appeal again for a total embargo on all supplies for the armed forces and police in South Africa, and for the total isolation of the South African racist regime."

. . .

## VI. Recommendations for action

49. The Special Committee considers it imperative that the United Nations and the international community take urgent and effective action in the light of the present grave situation in South Africa, and in southern Africa as a whole, to secure the total eradication of apartheid and assist the South African people to exercise their right to self-determination. They must recognize that the South African racist regime, by its practice of the criminal policy of apartheid, continues to pose an ever-increasing grave threat to the peace in the area. They must recognize further the legitimacy of the struggle of the oppressed people of South Africa to secure their inalienable rights and must provide all necessary assistance to them in their struggle for liberation.

50. This has now become an urgent and inescapable task of the international community.

. . .

---

# Document 84

*Statement by Mr. Leslie O. Harriman (Nigeria), Chairman of the Special Committee against Apartheid, on the proposal to declare the "independence" of Transkei*

UN Press Release GA/AP/596, 21 September 1976

According to press reports, the Prime Minister of the apartheid regime in South Africa, Balthazar John Vorster, and the Chief Minister of the bantustan administration in the Transkei, "Paramount Chief" Kaiser Matanzima, signed agreements on 17 September as a prelude to the "independence" of Transkei on 26 October.

As Chairman of the Special Committee against Apartheid, I wish to declare that the agreements between these two men can have no validity. They are not agreements for the granting of the right of self-determination or independence to the African people, but a fraud

perpetrated by the racist rulers and the Government-appointed chiefs who act as their accomplices.

The sham "independence" of the Transkei is a step in the implementation of the diabolical scheme of the apartheid regime to deprive the African people—who constitute 70 per cent of the population of South Africa —of their rights of citizenship by relegating them to seven or eight bantustans to be established in 200 scattered reserves covering less than 13 per cent of the area of the country.

In the case of Transkei, the regime has decreed that not only the 1.7 million residents of the territory, but more than a million people of Xhosa origin in the rest of South Africa will become "citizens" of this phantom State on 26 October. The White Parliament in Cape Town has already enacted a law depriving all the people of Transkeian origin of citizenship. There is no parallel for this mass deprivation of citizenship except in Nazi Germany.

The African people have always fought against the manoeuvres of the apartheid regime to divide them arbitrarily into so-called ethnic groups, and establish bantustans as reservoirs of labour, and appropriate the rest of South Africa, whose economy has been built by the African labour for the ruling White minority.

The regime, however, proceeded to impose the bantustan scheme by resorting to brutal repression. Already six million people have been forcibly moved from their homes, and millions more are due to be moved.

In 1960, after the banning of the African National Congress of South Africa and the Pan Africanist Congress of Azania, the South African regime instituted a reign of terror in the Transkei under Proclamation 400 which provides for indefinite detention without trial. That Proclamation still remains in force.

While the leaders of the African people were imprisoned or forced into exile, the regime instituted so-called "self-government" in the Transkei in 1963. Despite banning of meetings and other acts of repression, the people voted against the supporters of bantustans led by Chief Kaiser Matanzima. But the so-called "legislative assembly" was stacked with a majority of government-appointed chiefs who elected him as Chief Minister. The regime made him a "paramount chief" in recognition of his services to the regime and his betrayal of the aspirations of the African people.

The "independence" which Vorster has now arranged with Matanzima does not in any way represent the will of the African people.

The Transkei, which consists of three isolated pieces of land, is not economically viable. Most of the able-bodied men in the territory are obliged to go to the White-owned mines, factories and farms in the rest of South Africa to find employment. The "independent" Transkei will remain totally dependent on South Africa.

Kaiser Matanzima has already declared that he would continue to enforce Proclamation 400 after "independence". He has assured investors that no African trade unions would be allowed in the territory. In July–August the entire leadership of the Transkei Democratic Party was detained for opposing "independence": the party was thus prevented from contesting the elections on 29 September. (The "parliament" of Transkei is to be composed of 75 elected members and 75 appointed chiefs.) Hundreds of African students have been arrested for opposing "independence" and Matanzima has threatened to deport anyone opposing independence.

The United Nations, the Organization of African Unity and the Conference of Non-aligned Countries have denounced bantustans and called on all States to refrain from recognition of Transkei's sham "independence". This position has been supported by the World Council of Churches and numerous non-governmental organizations.

Any recognition of the Transkei, and any dealings with the authorities in the Transkei, would constitute a hostile act against the oppressed people of South Africa and, indeed, against the United Nations which has declared special responsibility for them.

On behalf of the Special Committee against Apartheid, I invite all States which have not yet done so to declare categorically that they will refrain from any form of recognition to the Transkei.

I appeal to all governments and organizations to observe 26 October 1976 as a day of solidarity with the peoples of South Africa and Namibia in their struggle against bantustans and for the territorial integrity of their nations.

The destiny of South Africa shall be determined, not by the illegitimate racist regime and its accomplices among tribal chiefs, but by the people of South Africa and their genuine representatives—above all, the leaders of the liberation movement who are now in prison and in exile or underground in South Africa.

# Document 85

*General Assembly resolution: Policies of apartheid of the Government of South Africa—The so-called "independent" Transkei and other bantustans*

A/RES/31/6 A, 26 October 1976

*The General Assembly,*

. . .

*Taking note* that the racist regime of South Africa declared the sham "independence" of the Transkei on 26 October 1976,

. . .

1. *Strongly condemns* the establishment of bantustans as designed to consolidate the inhuman policies of apartheid, to destroy the territorial integrity of the country, to perpetuate White minority domination and to

dispossess the African people of South Africa of their inalienable rights;

2. *Rejects* the declaration of "independence" of the Transkei and declares it invalid;

3. *Calls upon* all Governments to deny any form of recognition to the so-called independent Transkei and to refrain from having any dealings with the so-called independent Transkei or other bantustans;

4. *Requests* all States to take effective measures to prohibit all individuals, corporations and other institutions under their jurisdiction from having any dealings with the so-called independent Transkei or other bantustans.

# Document 86

### General Assembly resolution: Policies of apartheid of the Government of South Africa—Investments in South Africa

A/RES/31/6 K, 9 November 1976

*The General Assembly,*

...

*Noting* the increase of foreign investments in South Africa which abets and encourages the apartheid policies of that country,

*Welcoming* as a positive step the decision of some Governments to achieve the cessation of further investments in South Africa,

*Considering* that a cessation of new foreign investments in South Africa would constitute one important step in the struggle against apartheid,

*Urges* the Security Council, when studying the problem of the continued struggle against the apartheid policies of South Africa, to consider steps to achieve the cessation of further foreign investments in South Africa.

# Document 87

### The Lagos Declaration for Action against Apartheid, adopted by the World Conference for Action against Apartheid, Lagos, 22-26 August 1977

S/12426, 28 October 1977

The World Conference for Action against Apartheid organized by the United Nations, in cooperation with the Organization of African Unity and the Federal Government of Nigeria, met in Lagos, Nigeria, from 22 to 26 August 1977, with the participation of representatives of 112 Governments, 12 intergovernmental organizations, 5 liberation movements, 51 non-governmental organizations and a number of prominent individuals.

1. The Conference heard keynote speeches from the Head of State of Nigeria, the President of Zambia and the Prime Minister of Norway, as well as other prominent personalities.

2. After a full discussion of the items on its agenda, the Conference adopted the following Declaration.

### I.

3. The Conference reiterates the universal abhorrence of apartheid and racism in all its forms and manifestations and the determination of the international community to secure its speedy elimination.

4. The Conference reaffirms support and solidarity for the oppressed peoples of southern Africa and their national liberation movements, and the commitment of Governments and peoples of the world to take actions to contribute towards the eradication of apartheid.

5. Apartheid, the policy of institutionalized racist domination and exploitation, imposed by a minority regime in South Africa, is a flagrant violation of the Charter of the United Nations and the Universal Declaration of Human Rights. It rests on the dispossession. plunder, exploitation and social deprivation of the African people since 1652 by colonial settlers and their descendants. It is a crime against the conscience and dignity of mankind. It has resulted in immense suffering and involved the forcible moving of millions of Africans under special laws restricting their freedom of movement; and the denial of elementary human rights to the great majority of the population, as well as the violation of the

inalienable right to self-determination of all of the people of South Africa. This inhuman policy has been enforced by ruthless measures of repression and has led to escalating tension and conflict.

6. The apartheid regime in South Africa is the bastion of racism and colonialism in southern Africa and is one of the main opponents of the efforts of the United Nations and the international community to promote self-determination and independence in the area.

7. It has continued illegally to occupy the Territory of Namibia, for which the United Nations has a special responsibility, and extended apartheid to that international Territory.

8. It has sustained and supported the illegal racist minority regime in Southern Rhodesia, and has constantly resorted to threats against neighbouring independent African States and violations of their sovereignty. Since the end of colonial rule in Angola and Mozambique it has engaged in a series of acts of aggression against neighbouring States and has connived at acts of aggression by the illegal regime in Southern Rhodesia. Its massive invasion of Angola and constant violations of the territorial integrity of Zambia have been condemned by the United Nations Security Council. It continues to violate the territorial integrity of neighbouring independent African States.

9. The policies and actions of the South African regime have already created an explosive situation in the whole of southern Africa and events have moved into a phase of an acute crisis. The apartheid regime has intensified its military activities along the borders of independent African States and is constructing and expanding new military bases. It is reinforcing its enormous military arsenal and the production of nuclear weapons is within its reach. The possession of this arsenal and the acquisition of nuclear weapon by this racist and aggressive regime constitutes a menace to all independent African States and the whole world.

## II.

10. The World Conference recalls with admiration the valiant efforts of the South African people for many decades for an end to racial discrimination and for the establishment of a non-racial society. By their courageous struggle at heavy sacrifice, the South African people, under the leadership of their national liberation movement, have made a significant contribution to the purposes of the United Nations.

11. The United Nations has solemnly recognized the legitimacy of the struggle of the South African people for freedom and human equality, and for enabling all the people of the country irrespective of race, colour or creed, to participate as equals in the determination of the destiny of the nation. It has proclaimed that the United Nations and the international community have a special responsibility towards the oppressed people of South Africa and their national liberation movement, and towards those imprisoned, restricted or exiled for their struggle against apartheid.

12. The World Conference pledges its full support to the legitimate aspirations of the South African people and urges Governments, organizations and individuals to provide all appropriate assistance to the oppressed people of South Africa and their national liberation movement in their just struggle for freedom and human equality.

13. The Conference rejects all aspects of the apartheid system, including the imposition of "bantustans", which divide the population, deprive the African people of their citizenship and inalienable right to self-determination, and deny them a just share of the wealth of the country. There can be no international co-operation with bantustans and other entities based on racism.

14. The Conference condemns all manoeuvres by the South African regime aimed at preserving racist domination and the system of exploitation and oppression in South Africa, and in southern Africa as a whole.

15. It calls upon all Governments to enact legislation declaring the recruitment, assembly, financing and training of mercenaries in their territories to be punishable as a criminal act and to do their utmost to discourage and prohibit their nationals from serving as mercenaries.

16. It declares that South Africa belongs to all its people irrespective of race, colour or creed and that all have the right to live and work there in conditions of full equality. The system of racist domination must be replaced by majority rule and the participation of all the people on the basis of equality in all phases of national life, in freely determining the political, economic and social character of their society and in freely disposing of their natural resources.

## III.

17. The Conference calls upon Governments, intergovernmental and non-governmental organizations to intensify the campaign for the further isolation of the apartheid regime with a view to complementing the efforts of the South African people and their national liberation movement and to ensure:

(a) The immediate and total elimination of the policy and practice of apartheid and granting equal rights to all its inhabitants, including equal political rights;

(b) The termination of all measures, under whatever name, which forcibly separate elements of the population on the basis of race;

(c) The dismantling of the system of apartheid and the policy of bantustanization, and abrogation of all racially discriminatory laws and measures;

(*d*) The ending of repression against the opponents of apartheid, and the immediate and unconditional release of all persons, imprisoned, detained, restricted or exiled for their opposition to apartheid;

(*e*) The exercise, freely and on the basis of equality, of the inalienable right to self-determination of the people of South Africa as a whole;

(*f*) The removal of the illegal South African forces of occupation in Namibia and compliance by the apartheid regime with the relevant Security Council resolutions, particularly resolution 385 (1976);

(*g*) Compliance by the South African regime with Security Council resolutions on the question of Southern Rhodesia, and full implementation of sanctions against the illegal racist minority regime, including the oil embargo;

(*h*) The immediate cessation by the apartheid regime of all aggressive acts and threats against the independence, sovereignty and territorial integrity of African States; and

(*i*) The immediate cessation by the apartheid regime of the military and nuclear build-up which constitutes a serious danger to international peace and security.

18. The World Conference recognizes that the continuation of the prevailing situation in South Africa, and in southern Africa as a whole, will inevitably lead to greater conflict in Africa with enormous repercussions to international peace and security.

19. The World Conference condemns the South African regime for its ruthless repressive measures which are designed to perpetuate White racist domination. It recognizes and respects the inalienable right of the oppressed South African people and their national liberation movement to resort to all available and appropriate means of their choice to secure their freedom, and the need to assist them to achieve freedom. It declares that the international community has an inescapable duty to take all necessary measures to ensure the triumph of freedom and human equality in South Africa.

20. It further calls upon the international community to assist States which have been subjected to pressure, threats and acts of aggression by the South African regime because of their opposition to apartheid and implementation of United Nations resolutions for action against apartheid.

21. Governments and organizations participating in the World Conference pledge to use their separate and collective efforts forthwith, and on a continuing basis, to bring about the elimination of apartheid, to provide assistance to the victims of oppression, and to lend appropriate support to their national liberation movements, in consultation with the United Nations and the OAU, in their legitimate struggle to eliminate apartheid, and to attain the inalienable right to self-determination of the South African people as a whole.

22. The Conference commends those States and organizations which have provided assistance to the oppressed people and their national liberation movements, and appeals to all States and organizations to increase such assistance.

23. It draws attention to the International Convention on the Suppression and Punishment of the Crime of Apartheid.

24. The Conference calls upon all States for the cessation of any assistance or co-operation enabling South Africa to obtain nuclear capability. It further calls upon all States to prevent companies or institutions within their jurisdiction, from any nuclear co-operation with South Africa.

25. The Conference solemnly calls upon all States to cease forthwith all sales and supplies of arms and military equipment, spare parts and components thereof; to withdraw all licences for the manufacture of arms and military equipment in South Africa and to refrain from assistance to the South Africa regime in its military build-up or any military co-operation with that regime. It further recommends the setting up of a watchdog committee to follow up the observance of the arms embargo.

26. It calls on the United Nations Security Council to take all necessary measures, under Chapter VII of the Charter, to ensure the full implementation of the arms embargo against South Africa.

27. The Conference recognizes the urgent need for economic, and other measures, universally applied, to secure the elimination of apartheid. It commends all Governments which have taken such measures in accordance with United Nations resolutions. It calls upon the United Nations and all Governments, as well as economic interests, including transnational corporations, urgently to consider such measures, including the cessation of loans to, and investments in, South Africa. It requests the Special Committee against Apartheid, in cooperation with the OAU and all other appropriate organizations, to promote the implementation of the above recommendations.

28. The Conference urges States, and international and national sporting bodies to take all appropriate steps within their jurisdiction to bring about the termination of all sporting contacts with South Africa.

29. It commends all public organizations which have taken actions in accordance with United Nations resolutions and in support of the legitimate struggle of the suppressed people of South Africa.

### IV.

30. The World Conference calls on all the Governments and peoples of the world to lend their full support to international efforts, under the auspices of the United Nations and in co-operation with the Organization of African Unity and the liberation movements recognized by it, to eliminate apartheid and enable the South African people as a whole to attain their inalienable right to self-determination.

31. The Conference expresses its solidarity with the oppressed people of South Africa and with all political prisoners and detainees in South Africa, and pledges the total support of all participants to continue and intensify their campaign for the immediate and unconditional release of all political prisoners and detainees. It further pledges its unswerving support to all efforts to end arbitrary arrests, detentions and political trials in South Africa.

32. It endorses the proposal to proclaim 1978 as the International Anti-Apartheid Year and appeals to all Governments and organizations to observe it in the spirit of this Declaration.

33. The liberation of southern Africa as a whole from colonial and racist rule will be the final step in the emancipation of the continent of Africa from centuries of domination and humiliation. It will be a major contribution to the elimination of racism and racial discrimination in the world, and to the strengthening of international peace and security.

34. The World Conference calls on all Governments and peoples to make their fullest contribution in this historic and crucial effort for freedom, peace and international co-operation.

---

# Document 88

*Security Council resolution: The question of South Africa*

S/RES/417 (1977), 31 October 1977

*The Security Council,*

...

*Noting* with deep anxiety and indignation that the South African racist regime has continued violence and massive repression against the Black people and all opponents of apartheid in defiance of the resolutions of the Security Council,

*Gravely concerned* over reports of torture of political prisoners and the deaths of a number of detainees, as well as the mounting wave of repression against individuals, organizations and the news media since 19 October 1977,

*Convinced* that the violence and repression by the South African racist regime have greatly aggravated the situation in South Africa and will certainly lead to violent conflict and racial conflagration with serious international repercussions,

*Reaffirming* its recognition of the legitimacy of the struggle of the South African people for the elimination of apartheid and racial discrimination,

*Affirming* the right to the exercise of self-determination by all the people of South Africa as a whole, irrespective of race, colour or creed,

*Mindful* of its responsibilities under the Charter of the United Nations for the maintenance of international peace and security,

1. *Strongly condemns* the South African racist regime for its resort to massive violence and repression against the Black people, who constitute the great majority of the country, as well as all other opponents of apartheid;

2. *Expresses* its support for, and solidarity with, all those struggling for the elimination of apartheid and racial discrimination and all victims of violence and repression by the South African racist regime;

3. *Demands* that the racist regime of South Africa:

(a) End violence and repression against the Black people and other opponents of apartheid;

(b) Release all persons imprisoned under arbitrary security laws and all those detained for their opposition to apartheid;

(c) Cease forthwith its indiscriminate violence against peaceful demonstrators against apartheid, murders in detention and torture of political prisoners;

(d) Abrogate the bans on organizations and the news media opposed to apartheid;

(e) Abolish the "Bantu education" system and all other measures of apartheid and racial discrimination;

(f) Abolish the policy of bantustanization, abandon the policy of apartheid and ensure majority rule based on justice and equality;

4. *Requests* all Governments and organizations to take all appropriate measures to secure the implementation of paragraph 3 of the present resolution;

...

# Document 89

*Security Council resolution: The question of South Africa*

S/RES/418 (1977), 4 November 1977

*The Security Council,*

. . .

*Recognizing* that the military build-up by South Africa and its persistent acts of aggression against the neighbouring States seriously disturb the security of those States,

*Further recognizing* that the existing arms embargo must be strengthened and universally applied, without any reservations or qualifications whatsoever, in order to prevent a further aggravation of the grave situation in South Africa,

. . .

*Gravely concerned* that South Africa is at the threshold of producing nuclear weapons,

*Strongly condemning* the South African Government for its acts of repression, its defiant continuance of the system of apartheid and its attacks against neighbouring independent States,

*Considering* that the policies and acts of the South African Government are fraught with danger to international peace and security,

. . .

*Convinced* that a mandatory arms embargo needs to be universally applied against South Africa in the first instance,

*Acting* therefore under Chapter VII of the Charter of the United Nations,

1. *Determines*, having regard to the policies and acts of the South African Government, that the acquisition by South Africa of arms and related *matériel* constitutes a threat to the maintenance of international peace and security;

2. *Decides* that all States shall cease forthwith any provision to South Africa of arms and related *matériel* of all types, including the sale or transfer of weapons and ammunition, military vehicles and equipment, paramilitary police equipment, and spare parts for the aforementioned, and shall cease as well the provision of all types of equipment and supplies and grants of licensing arrangements for the manufacture or maintenance of the aforementioned;

3. *Calls upon* all States to review, having regard to the objectives of the present resolution, all existing contractual arrangements with and licences granted to South Africa relating to the manufacture and maintenance of arms, ammunition of all types and military equipment and vehicles, with a view to terminating them;

4. *Further decides* that all States shall refrain from any cooperation with South Africa in the manufacture and development of nuclear weapons;

5. *Calls upon* all States, including States non-members of the United Nations, to act strictly in accordance with the provisions of the present resolution;

. . .

# Document 90

*Statement by Secretary-General Kurt Waldheim in the Security Council after the adoption of resolution 418 (1977) concerning a mandatory arms embargo against South Africa*

S/PV.2046, 4 November 1977

We have today clearly witnessed a historic occasion. The adoption of this resolution marks the first time in the 32-year history of the Organization that action has been taken under Chapter VII of the Charter against a Member State. It is not my purpose to seek to determine whether the Council's decision by itself is adequate to secure its objective. However, it is abundantly clear that the policy of *apartheid* as well as the measures taken by the South African Government to implement this policy are such a gross violation of human rights and so fraught with danger to international peace and security that a response commensurate with the gravity of the situation was required. It is also significant that this momentous step is based on the unanimous agreement of the Council members. Thus we enter a new and significantly different phase of the long-standing efforts of the international community to obtain redress of these grievous wrongs.

I note that the Council requests me to report within the next six months on the progress of the implementation of the mandatory arms embargo which it has decided to impose. To fulfil this task, I shall obviously need, and I am confident I shall receive, the whole-hearted co-operation of all States, Members and non-members of the United Nations. I would ask all Governments to provide me with the most complete information as quickly as possible on the measures which they take to comply with this binding decision of the Council.

It is, of course, unfortunate that the situation in South Africa should have deteriorated to such a point that the Council felt compelled to take this extraordinary measure.

However, this should come as no surprise to the Government of South Africa when it considers how long the world has appealed in vain for the abandonment of its apartheid policies.

We can only hope that the gravity of the Council's decision will be fully recognized by the Government of South Africa and that it will therefore begin without delay the process of restoring fundamental human rights to all the people in South Africa, without which there can be no peace.

# Document 91

*General Assembly resolution: Policies of apartheid of the Government of South Africa—Dissemination of information on apartheid*

A/RES/32/105 H, 14 December 1977

*The General Assembly,*

. . .

4. *Requests* the Secretary-General to undertake, in cooperation with Member States whose transmitters can be heard in southern Africa, a regular programme of radio broadcasts directed at South Africa and concerned with United Nations efforts against apartheid

and in support of the right of self-determination, as well as with related matters of interest to the peoples of southern Africa;

5. *Urges* Member States whose radio transmitters can reach South Africa and adjacent territories to make available transmission facilities for these broadcasts;

. . .

# Document 92

*General Assembly resolution: Policies of apartheid of the Government of South Africa—International mobilization against apartheid*

A/RES/33/183 B, 24 January 1979

*The General Assembly,*

*Recalling* its numerous resolutions on the policies of apartheid of the Government of South Africa and the relevant resolutions of the Security Council,

*Recalling,* in particular, its resolution 3411 C (XXX) of 28 November 1975 proclaiming that the United Nations and the international community have a special responsibility towards the oppressed people of South Africa and their liberation movements,

*Further recalling* its resolution 32/105 B of 14 December 1977 proclaiming the year beginning on 21 March 1978 International Anti-Apartheid Year,

*Considering* that the United Nations has an important and vital role in the promotion of international

action for the elimination of apartheid,

*Reaffirming* its full commitment to the eradication of apartheid and the elimination of the threat to international peace and security caused by the apartheid regime,

*Reaffirming* that apartheid is a crime against the conscience and dignity of mankind,

*Aware* that the righteous struggle of the oppressed people of South Africa has led to an international consensus against apartheid and to growing support for the struggle for freedom and human dignity in South Africa,

*Considering* that the observance of the International Anti-Apartheid Year must lead to acceleration of concerted international action towards the eradication of apartheid and the liberation of the South African people,

*Taking note* of the recommendations of the Special Committee against Apartheid for an international mobilization against apartheid,

1. *Calls upon* all Governments and intergovernmental and non-governmental organizations to join in the international mobilization against apartheid;

2. *Authorizes* the Special Committee against Apartheid, with the assistance of the Centre against Apartheid of the Secretariat and in cooperation with the liberation movements recognized by the Organization of African Unity, to promote the international mobilization against apartheid and to facilitate coordination of action;

3. *Appeals* to anti-apartheid movements, solidarity committees, trade unions, churches, youth organizations and all other non-governmental organizations to participate in the international mobilization against apartheid by appropriate action.

# Document 93

*General Assembly resolution: Policies of apartheid of the Government of South Africa—Nuclear collaboration with South Africa*

A/RES/33/183 G, 24 January 1979

*The General Assembly,*

*Taking note* of Security Council resolution 418 (1977) of 4 November 1977, in which the Council decided, *inter alia*, that all States should refrain from any cooperation with South Africa in the manufacture and development of nuclear weapons,

*Recalling* its resolutions concerning the denuclearization of the continent of Africa,

. . .

*Noting with great concern* that the racist regime of South Africa has intensified its nuclear capability,

*Considering* that the acquisition of nuclear-weapon capability by the racist regime of South Africa would constitute a grave threat to international peace and security,

1. *Requests* the Security Council to consider measures aimed at effectively preventing South Africa from developing nuclear weapons;

. . .

# Document 94

*General Assembly resolution: Policies of apartheid of the Government of South Africa—The situation in South Africa*

A/RES/34/93 A, 12 December 1979

*The General Assembly,*

. . .

7. *Reaffirms* the commitment of the United Nations to the total eradication of apartheid and the destruction of the racist regime, rather than so-called reforms by the apartheid regime;

. . .

13. *Requests* all States which have not yet done so to terminate visa-free entry privileges to South African nationals;

. . .

17. *Appeals* to the youth of South Africa to refrain from enlisting in the South African armed forces, which are designed to defend the inhuman system of apartheid, to repress the legitimate struggle of the oppressed people and to threaten, and commit acts of aggression against, neighbouring States;

18. *Invites* all Governments and organizations to assist, in accordance with General Assembly resolution 33/165 of 20 December 1978, persons compelled to leave South Africa because of a conscientious objection to assisting in the enforcement of apartheid through service in military or police forces;

. . .

# Document 95

*General Assembly resolution: Policies of apartheid of the Government of South Africa—Assistance to the oppressed people of South Africa and their national liberation movement*

A/RES/34/93 I, 12 December 1979

*The General Assembly,*

...

1. *Appeals* to all States to provide increased humanitarian, educational, economic and other forms of assistance to the oppressed people of South Africa, as well as all appropriate assistance to the national liberation movement of South Africa in its legitimate struggle for the exercise of the right of self-determination by the people of South Africa as a whole;

2. *Draws attention*, in particular, to the necessity of assisting the educational and self-help projects of the liberation movements recognized by the Organization of African Unity and of meeting the special and pressing needs of refugee women and children;

3. *Requests and authorizes* the Special Committee against Apartheid, with the assistance of the Centre against Apartheid of the Secretariat, to take all appropri-ate steps to promote greater assistance to the oppressed people of South Africa and their national liberation movement;

4. *Decides* to concretize its resolution 31/6 I of 9 November 1976, in which it declared that the South African people and their liberation movements were a special responsibility of the United Nations and the international community, by authorizing adequate financial provision in the budget of the United Nations for the purpose of maintaining the offices in New York of the national liberation movements recognized by the Organization of African Unity—the African National Congress of South Africa and the Pan Africanist Congress of Azania—in order to ensure the due and proper representation of the South African people through their national liberation movement;

...

---

# Document 96

*General Assembly resolution: Policies of apartheid of the Government of South Africa—Declaration on South Africa*

A/RES/34/93 O, 12 December 1979

*The General Assembly,*

*Reaffirming* that apartheid is a crime against the conscience and dignity of mankind,

*Convinced* that the United Nations must take the lead in concerted international action for the elimination of apartheid,

*Noting with concern* the continued intransigence of the South African regime, which has defied and disre-garded numerous resolutions of organs of the United Nations for a just, peaceful and lasting resolution of the situation, including unanimous resolutions of the General Assembly and the Security Council,

*Noting* that the South African regime, by its arbitrary laws and repression, has deprived the oppressed people of avenues of peaceful and legal action to secure their inalienable rights,

*Condemning* the military build-up of South Africa and the series of acts of aggression committed by the South African regime against neighbouring States,

*Gravely concerned* about the plans of the South African regime to divide and dispossess the African people through "bantustanization" in order to perpetuate apartheid and deprive the African people of their citizenship,

*Denouncing* all plans for the dismemberment of South Africa through "bantustanization" as invalid,

*Recognizing* the significant contribution of the struggle for freedom and equality in South Africa to the purposes and principles of the Charter of the United Nations,

*Recalling* that the great majority of the South African people have been deprived of the right to participate in the determination of the destiny of the country,

*Reaffirming* that all the people of South Africa, irrespective of race, colour or creed, should be enabled to exercise their right of self-determination,

*Convinced* that the establishment of a non-racial society in South Africa, based on the Universal Declaration of Human Rights, would be a significant contribution to international peace, security and cooperation,

*Adopts* the following Declaration:

### Declaration on South Africa

1. All States shall recognize the legitimacy of the struggle of the South African people for the elimination of apartheid and the establishment of a non-racial society guaranteeing the enjoyment of equal rights by all the people of South Africa, irrespective of race, colour or creed.

2. All States shall recognize the right of the oppressed people of South Africa to choose their means of struggle.

3. All States shall solemnly pledge to refrain from overt or covert military intervention in support of defence of the Pretoria regime in its effort to repress the legitimate aspirations and struggle of the African people of South Africa against it in the exercise of their right of self-determination, as enshrined in the Charter of the United Nations and the Declaration on Principles of International law concerning Friendly Relations and Cooperation among States in accordance with the Charter of the United Nations, or in its threats or acts of aggression against the African States committed to the establishment of a democratic government of South Africa based on the will of the people as a whole, regardless of race, colour or creed, as the imperative guarantee to lasting peace and security in southern Africa.

4. All States shall take firm action to prevent the recruitment, financing, training or passage of mercenaries in support of the apartheid regime of South Africa or the bantustans created by it in South Africa.

5. All States shall take appropriate measures to discourage and counteract propaganda in favour of apartheid.

6. All States shall respect the desire of African States for the denuclearization of the continent of Africa and refrain from any cooperation with the South African regime in its plans to become a nuclear Power.

7. All States shall demonstrate international solidarity with the oppressed people of South Africa and with the independent African States subjected to threats or acts of aggression and subversion by the South African regime.

---

# Document 97

## Security Council resolution: The question of South Africa

S/RES/473 (1980), 13 June 1980

*The Security Council,*

. . .

*Gravely concerned* by the aggravation of the situation in South Africa, in particular the repression and the killings of schoolchildren protesting against apartheid, as well as the repression against churchmen and workers,

*Noting also with grave concern* that the racist regime has intensified further a series of arbitrary trials under its racist and repressive laws providing for death sentences,

. . .

*Reaffirming* its recognition of the legitimacy of the struggle of the South African people for the elimination of apartheid and the establishment of a democratic society in accordance with their inalienable human and political rights as set forth in the Charter of the United Nations and the Universal Declaration of Human Rights,

*Taking note* of the extensive demands within and outside South Africa for the release of Nelson Mandela and other political prisoners,

*Gravely concerned* about reports of supply of arms and military equipment to South Africa in contravention of resolution 418 (1977),

. . .

*Mindful* of its responsibilities under the Charter for the maintenance of international peace and security,

1. *Strongly condemns* the racist regime of South Africa for further aggravating the situation and its massive repression against all opponents of apartheid, for killings of peaceful demonstrators and political detainees and for its defiance of General Assembly and Security Council resolutions, in particular resolution 417 (1977);

2. *Expresses its profound sympathy* with the victims of this violence;

3. *Reaffirms* that the policy of apartheid is a crime against the conscience and dignity of mankind and is incompatible with the rights and dignity of man, the Charter of the United Nations and the Universal Decla-

ration of Human Rights, and seriously disturbs international peace and security;

4. *Recognizes* the legitimacy of the struggle of the South African people for the elimination of apartheid and for the establishment of a democratic society in which all the people of South Africa as a whole, irrespective of race, colour or creed, will enjoy equal and full political and other rights and participate freely in the determination of their destiny;

5. *Calls upon* the Government of South Africa urgently to end violence against the African people and to take urgent measures to eliminate apartheid;

6. *Expresses its hope* that the inevitable change in the racial policies of South Africa can be attained through peaceful means and declares, however, that the violence and repression by the South African racist regime and its continuing denial of equal human and political rights to the great majority of the South African people greatly aggravate the situation in South Africa and will certainly lead to violent conflict and racial conflagration with serious international repercussions and the further isolation and estrangement of South Africa;

7. *Calls upon* the South African regime to take measures immediately to eliminate the policy of apartheid and grant to all South African citizens equal rights, including equal political rights, and a full and free voice in the determination of their destiny; these measures should include:

(a) Granting of an unconditional amnesty to all persons imprisoned, restricted or exiled for their opposition to apartheid;

(b) Cessation forthwith of its indiscriminate violence against peaceful demonstrators against apartheid, murders in detention and torture of political prisoners;

(c) Abrogation of the bans on political parties and organizations and the news media opposed to apartheid;

(d) Termination of all political trials;

(e) Provision of equal education opportunities to all South Africans;

8. *Urgently calls upon* the South African regime to release all political prisoners, including Nelson Mandela and all other Black leaders with whom it must deal in any meaningful discussions of the future of the country;

9. *Demands* that the South African racist regime should refrain from committing further military acts and subversion against independent African States;

10. *Calls upon* all States strictly and scrupulously to implement resolution 418 (1977) and enact, as appropriate, effective national legislation for that purpose;

11. *Requests* the Security Council Committee established by resolution 421 (1977) concerning the question of South Africa, in pursuance of resolution 418 (1977), to redouble its efforts to secure full implementation of the arms embargo against South Africa by recommending by 15 September 1980 measures to close all loop-holes in the arms embargo, reinforce and make it more comprehensive;

. . .

# Document 98

*Message from the Chairman of the Special Committee against Apartheid, Mr. B. A. Clark, to the African National Congress on the twenty-fifth anniversary of the Freedom Charter*

26 June 1980

I have great pleasure in sending you my greetings, on behalf of the United Nations Special Committee against Apartheid, on the occasion of the South Africa Freedom Day which coincides this year with the 25th anniversary of the adoption of the Freedom Charter.

The Freedom Charter, I may recall, was adopted by the Congress of the People in 1955, seven years after the apartheid regime came to power in South Africa and enacted a series of Draconian measures to institutionalize racist domination and to suppress by force the legitimate aspirations of the Black people in violation of the United Nations Charter and the Universal Declaration of Human Rights.

It is to its great credit that when the apartheid regime was provoking bitterness and hatred along racial lines and particularly against the Black majority of the population of the Republic, the African National Congress of South Africa convened a conference to adopt a Charter for the rights of all the people of South Africa, irrespective of race, colour or creed. It thereby proved that the struggle of the African people is indeed for the liberation of all the people of South Africa from racist tyranny and for the establishment of a genuinely democratic State.

The Freedom Charter assisted world public opinion to understand and admire the righteous struggle of the oppressed people of South Africa. In the hard and difficult struggle against a ruthless regime backed by greedy and powerful forces from abroad, the Charter has enabled the liberation struggle to increasingly obtain the solidarity and support of the great majority of humanity.

I note with great appreciation that in spite of the increasing savagery of the racist regime, the African National Congress and its allied organizations have continued to uphold the principles of the Freedom Charter.

Today, as the South African people enter the final and decisive stage of their struggle for emancipation, it is only right that their legitimate aspirations should be made clear to the entire world.

In its determination to fulfil those aspirations—in peace if possible and by armed resistance if necessary—the national liberation movement deserves the unequivocal support of all men and women of conscience.

I wish you success.

---

# Document 99

*Letter dated 29 July 1980 from Mr. Oliver R. Tambo, President of the African National Congress, to the Chairman of the Special Committee against Apartheid, Mr. B. A. Clark, concerning the anniversary of the Freedom Charter*

A/AC.115/L.531, 15 September 1980

I have the honour to present to Your Excellency and the United Nations Special Committee Against Apartheid the compliments of our National Executive Committee and my own fraternal greetings.

We write, Your Excellency, to thank you and your esteemed Committee most sincerely for your letter to us on the occasion of this year's South Africa Freedom Day and the twenty-fifth anniversary of the adoption of the Freedom Charter. We are deeply moved by the noble sentiments which the letter conveys.

The African National Congress and the vast majority of our people are convinced, and committed to the position, that our reply to the rabid racism represented by the apartheid system must be to sue for a non-racial and democratic South Africa. Centuries of conflict, bitterness and suffering must give way to a new era of peace and friendship among all the people of our country.

We consider ourselves particularly fortunate that we have the Freedom Charter as a statement of objectives to which the majority of our people adhere. That very fact imposes upon us the obligation to educate in the spirit of the Charter even the younger generations who were not there when it was freely available.

We are indebted to the Special Committee for the sterling work it has done over the years to bring the Freedom Charter to the attention of the international community. We are certain that this has helped to expose the bankruptcy of the policies pursued by the South African regime and the criminality of the apartheid design that it has imposed on our people.

We look forward to ever closer cooperation between ourselves, Your Excellency and the Special Committee which has established itself as a steadfast ally of our struggling people and a militant combatant for justice, liberty and peace in our country and in southern Africa.

We thank Your Excellency for your good wishes. I take this opportunity to assure Your Excellency that the will to be free among our people has never been stronger than it is today. The brutality which the Pretoria regime continues to mete out to our people serves only as confirmation that the sooner this regime is destroyed and power transferred to the people the better.

The African National Congress and our people's army, *Umkhonto We Sizwe*, are bending every effort to achieve this result. We are strengthened by the knowledge that we enjoy the continuing support of the Special Committee and the United Nations as a whole in the struggle for the realization of the objectives contained in the Freedom Charter.

(*signed*)
O. R. TAMBO
President, African National Congress

# Document 100

*General Assembly resolution: Policies of apartheid of the Government of South Africa—Cultural, academic and other boycotts of South Africa*

A/RES/35/206 E, 16 December 1980

*The General Assembly,*

*Having considered* the reports of the Special Committee against Apartheid,

*Considering* that the suspension of cultural, academic, sports and other contacts with South Africa is an important measure in the international campaign against apartheid,

*Commending* writers, musicians, artists, sportsmen and others who have boycotted South Africa because of their opposition to apartheid,

*Commending also* those States and non-governmental organizations, in particular anti-apartheid movements, student organizations, academic institutions and sports organizations, which have promoted the boycott of South Africa,

*Noting* that the racist regime of South Africa is using cultural, academic, sports and other contacts to promote its propaganda for the inhuman policies of apartheid and "bantustanization",

1. *Requests* all States to take steps to prevent all cultural, academic, sports and other exchanges with South Africa;

2. *Also requests* States which have not yet done so:

(a) To abrogate and cancel all cultural agreements and similar arrangements entered into between their Governments and the racist regime of South Africa;

(b) To cease any cultural and academic collaboration with South Africa, including the exchange of scientists, students and academic personalities, as well as cooperation in research programmes;

(c) To prevent any promotion of tourism to South Africa;

(d) To terminate visa-free entry privileges to South African nationals;

(e) To prohibit emigration to South Africa;

3. *Appeals* to writers, artists, musicians and other personalities to boycott South Africa;

4. *Urges* all academic and cultural institutions to terminate all links with South Africa;

5. *Encourages* anti-apartheid and solidarity movements in their campaigns for cultural, academic and sports boycotts of South Africa;

6. *Requests* the Special Committee against Apartheid to promote such boycotts against South Africa.

# Document 101

*General Assembly resolution: Policies of apartheid of the Government of South Africa—Women and children under apartheid*

A/RES/35/206 N, 16 December 1980

*The General Assembly,*

*Recalling* its resolutions 34/4 of 18 October 1979 and 34/93 K of 12 December 1979,

*Taking note* of the *Report of the World Conference of the United Nations Decade for Women: Equality, Development and Peace,* particularly its recommendations on assistance to women in southern Africa,

*Taking note also* of the Declaration and Recommendations of the International Seminar on Women and Apartheid, held at Helsinki from 19 to 21 May 1980,

*Noting with admiration* the great sacrifices of the women and children in South Africa in the struggle for their inalienable rights and their national liberation,

*Affirming* its full solidarity with the women of South Africa in their struggle for liberation under the leadership of their national liberation movement,

*Considering* that international efforts should be greatly intensified to publicize the plight of women and children in South Africa and to promote greater solidarity with and assistance to them in the context of their heroic struggle for the liberation of South Africa,

1. *Commends* the Special Committee against apartheid for giving special attention to the plight of women and children under Apartheid;

2. *Endorses* the Declaration and Recommendations of the International Seminar on Women and Apartheid and the relevant recommendations of the World Conference of the United Nations Decade for Women,

and commends them to the attention of Governments and organizations;

3. *Urges* all organizations of the United Nations system, Governments, international and regional inter-governmental organizations, women's organizations and anti-apartheid groups, non-governmental organizations and other groups to give the highest priority to the question of measures of assistance to women in South Africa and Namibia during the second half of the United Nations Decade for Women;

4. *Appeals* to all Governments and organizations to support the various projects of the national liberation movements and front-line States designed to assist refugee women and children from South Africa and Namibia;

5. *Requests* the Commission on Human Rights to investigate crimes against women and children in South Africa;

6. *Encourages* women's organizations and other organizations concerned with women in South Africa, in consultation with the Organization of African Unity, to proclaim an International Day of Solidarity with the

Struggle of Women of South Africa and Namibia in order to promote the widest mobilization of world public opinion in support of the righteous struggle of the women of South Africa and their national liberation movement, as well as to provide all necessary assistance to them to ensure the speedy triumph of that struggle;

7. *Invites* women's organizations all over the world to intensify action in solidarity with the struggle for liberation in South Africa and to consider greater coordination of their efforts in cooperation with the Special Committee;

8. *Requests* the Special Committee and its Task Force on Women and Children:

(*a*) To promote and monitor the implementation of the relevant recommendations of the World Conference of the United Nations Decade for Women;

(*b*) To publicize the plight of women and children under apartheid and their struggle for liberation;

(*c*) To encourage national, regional and international conferences on women and children under apartheid and to co-sponsor such conferences, as appropriate.

# Document 102

*Introduction to the First Register of Sports Contacts with South Africa, published by the Special Committee against Apartheid*

United Nations Centre against Apartheid, Notes and Documents, No. 18/81, May 1981

## Introduction

The Special Committee against Apartheid has for many years given special attention to the campaign for the boycott of apartheid sport in South Africa, as part of the international campaign against apartheid. The sports boycott merited special attention for several reasons.

1. Sport has been described as a sort of second religion of the White minority community in South Africa. A boycott of South African sportsmen and teams, therefore, effectively demonstrates to them the universal abhorrence of apartheid.

2. Apartheid has been enforced in sport in South Africa, ever more rigorously since the National Party regime came to power in 1948, by a variety of laws and regulations, as well as intimidation. It is still being enforced, despite superficial adjustments made in recent years to deceive world opinion.

Racial discrimination in sport is directly related to numerous oppressive measures imposed by the racist regime, such as: residential segregation; separation and inequality in education; unequal allocation of resources for sporting activities; bantustanization and the system of migrant labour; White control over all urban areas and

facilities; inadequate health services; ruthless exploitation of the Black people who are thereby destined to malnutrition and disease, and, indeed, all the deprivations to which the Black people are subjected under the system of racist domination and exploitation.

That is why the non-racial sports federations in South Africa have declared that there can be "no normal sport in an abnormal society".

3. The practice of sport is governed by a spirit of fair play as well as a set of principles, among which the foremost is the Olympic principle of non-discrimination.

The General Assembly of the United Nations, in resolution 2775 D (XXVI) adopted on 29 November 1971, during the "International Year for Action to Combat Racism and Racial Discrimination" declared its unqualified support of the Olympic principle that no discrimination be allowed on the grounds of race, religion or political affiliation."

This principle is flagrantly violated in South Africa.

4. The movement for elimination of apartheid in sport and for the boycott of apartheid sport was begun in South Africa by Black sportsmen as well as others opposed to racism. They appealed for the expulsion of

the Whites-only sports bodies from international sports federations.

The non-racial South African Sports Association was formed as early as 1955. Non-racial sports bodies have tens of thousands of members, despite denial of facilities and intimidation by the apartheid regime and its institutions. They are now grouped under the South African Council on Sport (SACOS), which has borne the brunt of the struggle against apartheid in sports. SACOS is a member of the Supreme Council for Sport in Africa.

The international sports boycott is, therefore, a response to the appeals of the oppressed people and the sportsmen of South Africa.

5. Because of the efforts of many organizations and individuals, the campaign against apartheid sport has attracted wide public support all over the world. This is a campaign to which all men and women of conscience can make a personal contribution.

Hundreds of thousands of sportsmen and spectators in several countries have participated in boycott actions against apartheid sports which have, in turn, helped to educate millions of others to the truth about apartheid. The struggle against apartheid in sport became a national issue in some countries—especially countries where the governments professed their abhorrence of apartheid but continued to collaborate with the apartheid regime—and confirmed the conviction of the Special Committee that when the facts about apartheid are made known, the great majority of the people would not fail to oppose it.

Of particular significance has been the fact that the young people have been in the forefront of the movement against apartheid sport.

## Progress of the campaign against apartheid sport

The international campaign against apartheid sport registered significant achievements in the past two decades.

The most notable victory was the suspension of South Africa from the Olympics in 1964 and expulsion in 1970. Over the years, South Africa has also been suspended or expelled from a series of codes of sports including: amateur boxing, athletics, badminton, basketball, canoeing, chess, cricket, cycling, football (soccer), swimming, table tennis, water-skiing, weightlifting and wrestling. In sports like judo and handball, South Africa's application for affiliation has been rejected.

In some sports federations, where a few Western countries dominate through a system of weighted votes, or in sports in which the African and non-aligned countries are not significant participants, and the votes of Socialist countries are small, it has not so far been possible to obtain the required majorities to exclude South Africa. Examples are: archery, fencing, gymnastics, modern pentathlon, rowing, shooting and yachting.

Even in those sports, there have been a series of boycotts by individual countries, teams or sportsmen in protest against the participation of apartheid South African teams and the pressures for exclusion of South Africa have been growing.

The boycott of apartheid sports, moreover, received support from the overwhelming majority of Governments of the world. While a majority of the Governments—particularly from African, non-aligned and Socialist States—took firm measures to prevent sports competitions with apartheid teams, several others, especially from the West, took partial measures to discourage such competitions. Special reference may be made in this connection to the actions recently taken by Australia, Canada, Denmark, France, Japan, and Sweden to bar South African sports teams.

The Irish Government has made its strong and uncompromising opposition to apartheid sport known to all her nationals. It banned the South African Barbarians rugby team in 1979, and vehemently opposed the visit of the Irish rugby team to South Africa in May 1981.

The Argentine Government decided on 30 September 1980 that South Africans visiting the country must declare that they will not participate in any sports event or be associated with other sports activities, such as technical advice and training.

The opposition of Governments to sports contacts with South Africa has also been expressed in international declarations. In the aftermath of the boycott of the Montreal Olympics by African States, Guyana and Iraq, the heads of Government of the Commonwealth Countries announced the "Gleneagles Agreement" of 1977, "to take every practical step to discourage contact or competition by their nationals with sporting organizations, teams or sportsmen from South Africa." The joint Nordic programme of actions against South Africa, announced in March 1978, included a recommendation that contacts with the apartheid regime in the field of sport be discontinued. The West European Sports Ministers, at their meetings in 1979 and 1981, called on sports organizations and sportsmen not to allow themselves to be used by countries which practise racial discrimination.

These advances in the isolation and boycott of apartheid sport were achieved by the sacrifices of many.

In South Africa itself, non-racial sports leaders have constantly been subjected to imprisonment, restriction, denial of passports, intimidation and harassment.

Outside South Africa, numerous sportsmen have had to give up precious opportunities for international competition because certain sports bodies insisted on allowing the participation of apartheid teams. The sacrifice of sportsmen from Africa, Guyana and Iraq who were obliged to boycott the Montreal Olympics is but one of many examples. Some sports federations even took punitive action against sportsmen who refused, on grounds of principle, to play against South African sportsmen and teams.

Tens of thousands of people, especially the youth in Western countries, have devoted their time and energy to demonstrate their opposition to tours by apartheid teams; many have suffered imprisonment and assaults during such demonstrations.

Mention must also be made of the heavy financial sacrifices of professional sportsmen like Mr. Muhammed Ali, Mr. John McEnroe, Mr. Vivian Richards, Mr. John Conte and others who refused on grounds of principle to play in apartheid South Africa.

### Manoeuvres of the apartheid regime

Faced with the growing boycott of apartheid sports, the apartheid regime in South Africa, its sports administrators and friends abroad began to engage in a series of manoeuvres and despicable practices in order to deceive the world and break out of isolation.

The sports administrators in South Africa who have been implementing gross racial discrimination, as well as administrators and promoters abroad who had organized sports exchanges with South Africa in defiance of all protests and appeals, have now come to claim that they are against apartheid in sport and that increased sports contacts with South Africa would be the best means for that purpose. The apartheid regime has encouraged and assisted them by a series of purported changes in sport policy which are designed to persuade the uninformed that sport is being freed from the shackles of apartheid.

The Special Committee, as well as the non-racial sports federations in South Africa and the Supreme Council on Sport in Africa, have analysed these so-called changes and pointed out that they are fraudulent manoeuvres by a regime that is irrevocably committed to racist domination.

The changes consist mainly of special dispensations to allow the inclusion of a few Blacks in some "national" teams, the attendance of multi-racial audiences at some sports fixtures and the entry of Black sportsmen into some clubs during certain sports events. The practice of sport, for the most part, remains racially segregated. Merit selection of sportsmen is not practised. The special dispensations are ended immediately after the particular sports events. The entire system of racist domination, which prevents equality in sport, is being streamlined and consolidated.

The non-racial sports bodies in South Africa have completely rejected the humiliating dispensations offered by the apartheid regime and its sports administrators, since they are aimed specifically at enabling the racist sports bodies to re-enter international sport.

Mr. Tony Ward, a rugby player who refused to join the Irish rugby team which went to South Africa in May 1981, expressed appreciation of their position. He said:

"But at the end of the day you and I play a game and then we go to the bar for a pint. If you are Black in South Africa that is not possible. I go to the bar and you go to your township or whatever. . .and I'm alone in the bar with my pint. That's neither rugby, sporting nor moral."

But a number of sports administrators in a few countries have shown utter insensitivity to the feelings of the oppressed people of South Africa, and have cooperated with the apartheid regime in its manoeuvres. While pretending to be interested only in sport, they have become instruments of the propaganda of the apartheid regime.

They have sent missions to South Africa to fraternize with the apartheid regime and its sports administrators, as well as a few dependent stooge bodies established by them. These missions claim that there is progress towards multi-racialism in South Africa and that greater contact rather than isolation would promote that trend. Their conclusions are then highly publicized to promote sports events in South Africa.

The apartheid regime for its part has spent public and secret funds to promote visits by such sports administrators, and to discredit the campaign against apartheid sport. It has, in collaboration with South African business interests, devoted large sums of money to entice sportsmen to participate in fixtures in South Africa. Some television networks have assisted them in this respect, not only by providing massive publicity but also by generous payments for broadcasting rights.

It must be emphasized that no credence can be given to the conclusions of the so-called "fact-finding" missions organized by certain Western sports bodies in cooperation with the apartheid regime and its sports federations. The Black sportsmen who suffer discrimination and their non-racial sports bodies, as well as the national liberation movement, have clearly stated their positions. They alone can provide authoritative testimony on the situation and indicate the means to eliminate apartheid in sport.

### Recent sports exchanges with South Africa

With the collaboration of a number of sports personalities and administrators in a few countries, the apartheid regime has been able to organize several major sports events in South Africa and send some of its teams on international tours.

These sports exchanges have been largely in professional boxing, golf and tennis where the players were mainly attracted by the enormous financial rewards offered by South Africa. In addition, there have been exchanges in rugby due to the intimate collaboration of the administrators in a few countries where rugby is a popular sport.

In these cases, the promoters and administrators of sport have not only defied the United Nations resolutions and protests by numerous national and international organizations, but spurned the representations of their own Governments and peoples. In their anxiety to play with apartheid South Africa, they have not hesitated to endanger the reputations of their countries and the interests of other sports codes in their countries.

Financial rewards have been a major consideration in their disregard for the Olympic principle, their contempt for the aspirations of the oppressed majority of the population in South Africa and their defiance of African and world public opinion.

Some of the major sports exchanges may be noted.

The World Boxing Association heavyweight championship fight between Mr. John Tate of the United States of America and Mr. Gerrie Coetzee of South Africa was held in Pretoria in October 1979. Emboldened by this, the United States promoter, Bob Arum proceeded to organize the next championship between Mr. Michael Weaver of the United States and Mr. Gerrie Coetzee in the so-called "independent" state of Bophuthatswana in October 1980.

The British and Irish Lions rugby team toured South Africa in June 1980. At a time when the apartheid regime was indiscriminately killing and maiming Black students protesting against inequality and segregation in education, this tour evoked particularly strong resentment in the Black community.

The South African Springbok rugby team toured Paraguay, Uruguay and Chile in October 1980 and the French national rugby team toured South Africa in November. These tours were to be preludes to the Irish rugby tour of South Africa in May 1981 and the Springbok rugby tour of New Zealand in July 1981.

South Africa was allowed to participate in the World Golf Championships in the United States in October 1980.

Such events, though limited to a few sports, were highly publicized and tended to overshadow the steady progress in the exclusion of South Africa from international sport. The apartheid regime and its supporters were greatly encouraged and looked forward to further breaches in the sports boycott.

## Some of the main collaborators with apartheid sport

Reference should be made to some sports bodies, promoters and administrators who have been flagrantly violating United Nations resolutions, including the International Declaration against Apartheid in Sport, and providing comfort to the apartheid regime.

The International Rugby Board (IRB) has been most active in promoting and facilitating exchanges with South Africa, despite the fact that racial discrimination is most glaring in the practice of rugby in South Africa. The IRB is made up of eight full members—the rugby unions of Australia, England, France, Ireland, New Zealand, Scotland, South Africa and Wales. All these members—with the exception of the rugby union from Australia—have supported exchanges with South Africa, defying numerous representations by their respective Governments, as well as public organizations.

In France, Mr. Albert Ferrasse, President of the French Rugby Federation, defied advice by the Government and protests by many organizations, to organize a tour of South Africa in 1980.

In Ireland, Mr. Robert (Bobby) Ganly, President of the Irish Rugby Football Union (IRFU), and Mr. Ronald Dawson, Vice-President of IRFU, have ignored repeated appeals by the Government, Parliament and the overwhelming majority of public opinion in organizing the Lions rugby tour of South Africa in 1980 and the Irish rugby tour of South Africa in May 1981.

Mr. Paddy Madigan, the manager of the Irish rugby team touring South Africa in 1981, has been another active proponent of sports links with South Africa.

In New Zealand, Mr. J. G. Fraser, President of the New Zealand Rugby Football Union (NZRFU), Mr. Ces Blazey, Chairman of RFU, and Mr. Ron Don, Chairman of the Auckland Rugby Union and a member of the council of NZRFU, have been the most active promoters of the South African Springbok rugby tour of South Africa. They have defied the appeals of the Government, political parties, churches, anti-apartheid groups, student and youth organizations and indeed the great majority of public opinion in New Zealand.

In Great Britain, the Welsh Rugby Union, under the leadership of Cliff W. Jones, its President, has been particularly active in collaboration with South Africa. He included three South Africans in the Welsh team at the tournament to commemorate the centenary of the Union on 25 April 1981.

The World Boxing Association (WBA) is another international sports federation which has actively assisted the apartheid regime in sports exchanges. The WBA has many South Africans on its committees.

Mr. Bob Arum, a boxing promoter in the United States of America, has ignored numerous protests to organize several world title fights involving South Africans, not only in South Africa and the United States of America, but also in the so-called "independent" state of Bophuthatswana.

The following are some of the other leading sports administrators who have been actively involved in promoting sports exchanges with South Africa.

-Mr. Richard (Dick) Jeeps, Chairman of the British Sports Council (BSC). At the beginning of 1980, he led the BSC "fact-finding" mission to South Africa which favoured sports exchanges with South Africa. He also visited South Africa to address a sports function and to attend a rugby match between South Africa and the British Lions. He has frequently called for sports exchanges with South Africa and in October 1980 even defended the action of the South African regime in refusing to allow Mr. Paul Stephenson, a member of the British Sports Council, to visit South Africa.

-Mr. William (Bill) Hicks, Chairman of the Information Committee of the British Sports Council, has been another active advocate of sports contacts with South Africa.

He visited South Africa in March 1981 and said:

"I believe that the Sports Council should try to persuade the Government to try to persuade the Commonwealth Prime Ministers' conference in August to loosen the Gleneagles Agreement's grip on sport, rather than tighten it."

-Mr. Harm Hendricks, Manager of the Netherlands Veterans' Athletics Team at the World Veterans Games, held in Christchurch, New Zealand, in January 1981. He entered ten South Africans as members of the team from the Netherlands in order to circumvent the ban on South Africans.

-Mr. John H. Macdonald of New Zealand, Chairman of the Organizing Committee for the World Veterans Games held in Christchurch, New Zealand, in January 1981. He helped facilitate the participation of South African athletes.

-Mr. Walter Hadlee, former chairman of the New Zealand Cricket Council and now a member of its Board of Control. He has been active in efforts to re-admit South Africa into the International Cricket Conference.

-Mr. P. J. Boatwright, President, Golf Association of the United States of America. Ignoring numerous protests, he enabled the South African teams to participate in the World Golf Tournament in Pinehurst, North Carolina, in October 1980.

### Decision of the Special Committee to initiate a register

In all the cases cited above, the Special Committee repeatedly appealed to the sports bodies, sportsmen and others concerned to desist from collaboration with apartheid, and requested their governments to take firm action to prevent the exchanges. But the promoters and sports bodies spurned all appeals. Some governments took no action, on the grounds that the practice of sport in their countries is independent, or limited themselves to mere expressions of opposition.

Meanwhile, the South African regime increased repression against non-racial sports bodies. An example was the seizure of the passport of Mr. M. N. Pather, secretary of the South African Council on Sport, in June 1980 on the eve of his departure from Durban for consultations with the Special Committee.

In the light of this situation, the Special Committee considered it essential to intensify its efforts to publicize the sports exchanges with South Africa so that the international community may concert its efforts to secure a total cessation of all such exchanges. Towards this end, it decided to undertake, in co-operation with all organizations concerned, the preparation of a register of sports contacts with South Africa, as well as a periodic list of sportsmen, administrators and promoters involved in such exchanges so that the violators of the United Nations resolutions may be widely made known.

The initiation of a register was enthusiastically supported by the Supreme Council on Sport in Africa, the South African Non-Racial Olympic Committee (SAN-ROC), and many other organizations. It was also welcomed by organizations inside South Africa which decided to prepare "boycott lists" to facilitate national and international action.

At its executive meeting held in Freetown, Sierra Leone, 17-20 December 1980, the Supreme Council for Sport in Africa urged all its member countries to take action against collaborators with apartheid sport, identified by the United Nations register, and in particular to deny them entry into their respective countries. The SAN-ROC proceeded to compile quarterly lists of sportsmen competing in South Africa in order to assist the Special Committee and the Supreme Council, as well as other interested organizations.

The circulation of the SAN-ROC lists led to prompt action by several countries. Kenya banned four tennis players from participating in events in that country. Nigeria banned several players from participating in the Nigerian Grand Prix Tennis Tournament. The Senegal Government refused to allow a French university club, Toulouse, an affiliate of the French Rugby Federation, from playing in Dakar. The Zimbabwe Government instructed the Zimbabwe Rugby Union not to invite the Greystones Club of Ireland because of Irish collaboration with apartheid rugby. A number of African sports organizations announced that they would take action.

British rugby players Bill Beaumont and John Carlton, tennis players Tim Gullickson and Jimmy Connors and golfer Nick Faldo have cancelled plans to go to South Africa on further tours.

Several sports events in South Africa have found it difficult to attract overseas entrants.

Sportsmen and sports administrators who had been insensitive to the issue of apartheid or were enticed by financial rewards offered by apartheid sport have found it essential to weigh the consequences. They have been warned that if they fraternize with and profit from apartheid, they cannot expect to fraternize with the sportsmen of many other countries nor make money in those countries.

### Conclusion

In publishing the first issue of the "Register of Sports Contacts with South Africa", the Special Committee reiterates the importance of the cessation of all exchanges with apartheid sport as a contribution to the international efforts for the elimination of apartheid and in support of freedom in South Africa.

It hopes that the register will facilitate appropriate action by Governments, organizations and individuals in the campaign for the boycott of apartheid sport.

The Special Committee invites the co-operation of all Governments, inter-governmental and non-governmental organizations, as well as information media, to publicize the register and exert their influence to secure the total isolation of apartheid sport.

In view of the fact that many of the persons involved in sports contacts with South Africa are enticed by the apartheid regime and institutions through monetary rewards—derived from the inhuman exploitation of the Black people—the Special Committee invites all Governments and sports bodies committed to freedom in South Africa to consider appropriate action to prevent such persons from benefiting from sports fixtures in their countries. Such action would effectively demonstrate the revulsion of the international community at the crime of apartheid, as well as collaboration with apartheid.

# Document 103

*Declaration of the International Conference on Sanctions against South Africa, Paris, 27 May 1981*

A/CONF.107/8, 1981

. . .

200. The International Conference on Sanctions against South Africa, organized by the United Nations in co-operation with the Organization of African Unity, was held at UNESCO House, Paris, from 20-27 May 1981.

201. The Conference was attended by representatives of 122 Governments, the United Nations organs, Organization of African Unity, Movement of Non-aligned Countries, specialized agencies of the United Nations, intergovernmental organizations, national liberation movements, international and national non-governmental organizations as well as a number of experts and leading statesmen. The national liberation movements of South Africa and Namibia—the African National Congress of South Africa, the Pan Africanist Congress of Azania and the South West Africa People's Organization—were represented by high-level delegations led by their respective Presidents.

202. The Conference reviewed the situation in South Africa, and in southern Africa as a whole. There was also an extensive exchange of views on the feasibility of sanctions and other means as credible measures not involving force, which the world community can employ to exert diplomatic, economic and other pressures against the racist regime of South Africa. Such measures could avert the grave danger to international peace and security arising from the policy and action of the racist regime of South Africa. The International Conference then adopted the following declaration which it commends for the earnest and urgent attention of all Governments, organizations and peoples for appropriate action to secure the expeditious eradication of apartheid and liberation of Namibia from illegal occupation by South Africa's racist regime.

### Grave situation

203. The Conference expresses its profound concern over the situation in South Africa, and in southern Africa as a whole, resulting from the policies and actions of the South African regime of racism, repression and terrorism.

204. The stubborn efforts of that regime to perpetuate racist domination by an ever-increasing dependence on violence and repression and to continue its illegal occupation of Namibia, in defiance of repeated appeals

by the international community and in flagrant contravention of the United Nations Charter, the Universal Declaration of Human Rights and the Declaration on the Granting of Independence to Colonial Countries and Peoples, have created an explosive situation in southern Africa and constitute no longer a threat to, but a manifest breach of international peace and security.

205. The Pretoria regime is, moreover, continuing its illegal occupation of Namibia in defiance of the United Nations and the advisory opinion of the International Court of Justice, thereby undermining the authority of the United Nations and violating the principles of the Charter of the United Nations. It has resorted to the militarization of the Territory, for which the United Nations has assumed direct responsibility, and to brutal repression of the Namibian people. It has frustrated the implementation of the United Nations plan for the independence of Namibia through free and fair elections. To this end, the South African racist regime deliberately caused the collapse of the pre-implementation meeting held at Geneva from 7 to 19 January 1981. The result has been a continuing and escalating armed conflict against the people of Namibia and its sole and authentic representative—the South West Africa People's Organization (SWAPO).

206. In pursuance of its policies of seeking to perpetuate racist domination in South Africa and to maintain illegal occupation of Namibia, as well as expand its imperialist influence beyond its borders, the Pretoria regime has resorted to constant acts of aggression, subversion, destabilization and terrorism against neighbouring independent African States, thereby aggravating existing international tensions.

207. It has built up a massive military machine and repressive apparatus and has embarked on acquisition of nuclear weapons capability in an attempt to suppress resistance by the oppressed people and terrorize neighbouring States into effective subservience.

208. Acquisition of military equipment and nuclear weapons capability by the racist regime of South Africa, with its record of violence and aggression, poses a grave menace to humanity.

209. The situation in southern Africa is, therefore, characterized by repeated breaches of the peace and acts of aggression and an ever-growing threat of a wider conflict with grave repercussions in Africa and the world.

210. The continuing political, economic and military collaboration of certain Western States and their transnational corporations with the racist regime of South Africa encourages its persistent intransigence and defiance of the international community and constitutes a major obstacle to the elimination of the inhuman and criminal system of apartheid in South Africa and the attainment of self-determination, freedom and national independence by the people of Namibia.

### Action by the international community

211. The United Nations and the international community must take energetic and concerted action because the oppressed people of South Africa and Namibia deserve full support in their legitimate struggle for self-determination, freedom and national independence. The independent sovereign States of southern Africa have a right to protection from the repeated armed attacks, acts of aggression and depredations by a racist regime which acts as an international outlaw.

212. The United Nations and the international community must take action to stop the continuing breaches of the peace, and to avert a wider conflict. Such action is urgent and indispensable for the maintenance of international peace and security; for the elimination of apartheid and illegal occupation; for the discharge of the solemn obligations to the people of Namibia; for ensuring the emancipation of Africa after centuries of oppression, exploitation and humiliation; and for promoting genuine international co-operation.

213. The Conference strongly condemns the minority racist regime of South Africa for its criminal policies and actions.

214. The Conference declares that the racist regime of South Africa—by its repression of the great majority of the people of the country and their national liberation movements, by its illegal occupation of Namibia, and by its acts of aggression against neighbouring States—bears full responsibility for the present conflict and for its inevitable escalation.

215. The Conference further stresses that this responsibility of South Africa is shared by those States whose assistance and multifaceted support encourage the aggressive policy of the Pretoria racist regime.

216. It expresses its deep conviction that the situation in South Africa, and in southern Africa as a whole, is of deep concern to all Governments and organizations and to humanity as a whole.

217. It declares that the United Nations and its family of organizations, as well as other intergovernmental organizations, have a vital interest in the elimination of apartheid and the achievement of genuine independence by Namibia. It recognizes that Governments, intergovernmental and non-governmental organizations, as well as men and women of conscience can and must play a role in the international effort to support the oppressed people of South Africa and Namibia.

218. It emphasizes the importance of close co-operation between the United Nations and OAU, as well as of co-operation between Governments and public organi-

zations to contribute to the elimination of apartheid and the independence of Namibia.

## Consensus achieved

219. During the many years that the United Nations and the international community have considered the problem of apartheid in South Africa and its international repercussions, a consensus has emerged on the fact that apartheid is a crime against the conscience and dignity of mankind, incompatible with the provisions of the United Nations Charter and the Universal Declaration of Human Rights. There is also consensus that reliance on violence and repression by the South African racist regime and its continuing denial of human and political rights to the great majority of the South African people will certainly lead to escalation of a violent conflict and to a racial conflagration in South Africa with serious international repercussions. The international community recognizes that the struggle of the South African people for the elimination of apartheid and for the establishment of a democratic society, in which all the people of South Africa as a whole, irrespective of race, colour or creed, will participate freely in the determination of their destiny, is legitimate.

220. There is also an international consensus on the legitimacy of the struggle of the Namibian people for self-determination, freedom and national independence. Namibia, being a direct responsibility of the United Nations, the international community has repeatedly condemned the continued illegal occupation of the territory by South Africa in defiance of United Nations decisions and the advisory opinion of the International Court of Justice of 21 June 1971. South Africa's brutal repression of the Namibian people and its ruthless exploitation of the resources of their territory is a matter of profound concern to the international community.

221. It is on the basis of the foregoing consensus and in response to the aspirations of the oppressed people of South Africa and Namibia that the Conference has made its recommendations.

222. It recalls that the United Nations and the international community have adopted a number of measures, including a mandatory arms embargo, aimed at forcing South Africa to abrogate all its racist and oppressive laws, to terminate its illegal occupation of Namibia, and to put an end forthwith to its repeated and flagrant violation of the sovereignty and territorial integrity of neighbouring African States. It is a source of the deepest regret and concern that those measures have been circumvented or not fully implemented, particularly by some of the very Security Council members who are essential parties to them. The Conference, therefore, considers that action taken so far by the international community has proved inadequate.

## Need for further action

223. The Conference considers it imperative that the Security Council should recognize that the situation in southern Africa, arising from the policies and actions of the racist regime of South Africa, is characterized by constant breaches of the peace and therefore, measures under Chapter VII of the United Nations Charter must be taken.

224. The Conference expresses its concern that the Security Council of the United Nations has yet been unable to effectively perform its solemn responsibilities in this connection due to the opposition of the Western permanent members of the Council. It draws the particular attention of those permanent members of the Security Council to their responsibilities under the Charter. It urges all Governments and organizations to exert their influence to facilitate action by the Security Council.

225. The Conference expresses grave concern and dismay that the Security Council, convened in April 1981 at the insistence of the member States of the OAU and the Movement of Non-Aligned States to impose comprehensive mandatory sanctions against South Africa for its continued illegal occupation of Namibia, failed to adopt the necessary decisions. The Conference supports the report of the OAU and the Movement of Non-Aligned Countries for an early meeting of the Security Council to adopt comprehensive and mandatory sanctions against the racist regime of South Africa for its policies of apartheid.

## The need for sanctions

226. The Conference affirms that the sanctions provided under Chapter VII of the United Nations Charter, universally applied, are the most appropriate and effective means to ensure South Africa's compliance with the decisions of the United Nations. The choice is between an escalation of conflict and the imposition of international sanctions, if all other attempts to reach a peaceful settlement have failed.

227. The Conference notes that an overwhelming majority of States—as well as most governmental and non-governmental organizations, including trade unions and religious organizations—share this view. It notes with appreciation the sacrifices made by many States, especially the developing States, in accordance with the decisions of the United Nations, OAU, and the Movement of Non-Aligned Countries to promote freedom and peace in southern Africa. It urges those Powers which have so far opposed sanctions, to heed the views of the rest of the international community and harmonize their policies in order to facilitate concerted action.

228. The purpose of sanctions is:

(*a*) to force South Africa to abandon its racist policy of apartheid and to put an end to its illegal occupation of Namibia;

(*b*) to demonstrate, by action, the universal abhorrence of apartheid and solidarity with the legitimate aspirations and struggles of the people of South Africa and Namibia;

(*c*) to deny the benefits of international co-operation to the South African regime so as to oblige it and its supporters to heed world opinion, to abandon the policy of racist domination and to seek a solution by consultation with the genuine leaders of the oppressed people;

(*d*) to undermine the ability of the South African regime to repress its people, commit acts of aggression against independent States and pose a threat to international peace and security;

(*e*) to remove economic support from apartheid so as to mitigate suffering in the course of the struggle of the people of South Africa and Namibia for freedom, and thereby promote as peaceful a transition as possible.

### A programme of sanctions

229. In the light of the above, the Conference urgently calls for a programme of sanctions and related measures against South Africa. The mandatory arms embargo against South Africa, instituted by a unanimous decision of the Security Council under Chapter VII of the Charter of the United Nations, must be effectively implemented and reinforced, so as to serve its purposes fully and should be the first step in the programme of sanctions.

230. The Conference attaches great importance and urgency: (1) to the cessation of all collaboration with South Africa in the military and nuclear fields; (2) to an effective oil embargo against South Africa; (3) to the cessation of investments in and loans to South Africa; (4) to the cessation of purchase and marketing of South African gold and other minerals as well as co-operation with South African marketing organizations for such minerals; and (5) to the denial to South Africa of certain essential supplies such as electronic and communications equipment, machinery and chemicals, as well as technology.

231. The Conference expresses its conviction that South Africa is vulnerable to sanctions and that sanctions under Chapter VII of the United Nations Charter are feasible and will be effective. South Africa is more dependent on world trade than the rest of the world is on trade with South Africa.

232. The Conference recognizes that sanctions against South Africa will involve adjustments and sacrifices by other States, as well as hardships for the oppressed people of South Africa. It takes into account the possibility that the South African regime may, in its desperation, retaliate against the oppressed majority of the population of South Africa as well as against neighbouring States.

233. Nevertheless, the Conference affirms that the cost of sanctions is very small compared to the cost of the existing human suffering and degradation in South Africa and to the dangerous consequences of a widening conflict in southern Africa, both to the people of southern Africa and to the international community.

234. The Conference considers that the international community can and should devise ways and means to enable the independent states of southern Africa to withstand the effects on them of sanctions against South Africa, rather than use their presumed plight as a pretext to avoid applying swift and effective sanctions against South Africa.

235. The Conference recognizes that for sanctions to be decisive, they must be effectively applied so as to remove their "immunization potentials" which prolong unnecessary suffering to innocent persons. Above all, they must implemented by all members of the international community, particularly the major trading partners of South Africa. Financial and economic relations with the South African racist regime, based on cheap labour and exploitation of resources which should be used to improve the quality of life of the majority of the population of South Africa, buttress and sustain the nefarious system of apartheid.

236. It urges all States to take note of the fact that their trade with the independent States of Africa alone—not to count their trade with all countries committed to sanctions against South Africa—is already far greater than trade with South Africa.

237. While stressing the importance of action by the major trading partners of South Africa, the Conference recognizes the importance of action by the entire international community, and of measures by the public.

238. The Conference considers that concerted action by all States and organizations committed to sanctions has not merely a moral value but can have a significant political, economic and material impact. Such action can also exert a positive influence on the attitudes of Governments opposing sanctions and facilitate mandatory action by the United Nations Security Council.

239. The Conference expresses appreciation of the measures taken by many States—members of the OAU and Non-Aligned Movement, the Socialist countries, the Nordic and some other West European States and hopes that other countries will take similar measures.

240. The Conference urges all States, while vigorously campaigning for action by the Security Council, to

take immediate unilateral and collective action to impose comprehensive sanctions against the racist regime of South Africa.

### Arms embargo

241. The Conference attaches utmost importance to the effective implementation and reinforcement of the existing mandatory arms embargo against South Africa.

242. The Conference endorses the recommendations submitted in September 1980 by the Security Council Committee established in pursuance of resolution 421 (1977) on the Question of South Africa for the implementation and reinforcement of the embargo and urges that the Security Council adopt them without delay. It expresses the hope that the Committee will be provided with all necessary means to accomplish fully the task which has been entrusted to it.

243. The embargo, as so far implemented, has not succeeded in reducing the danger of aggression and repression by the South African regime. To this end it calls upon all States to enact effective legislation or issue appropriate policy directives on the arms embargo, covering all forms of military collaboration, direct or indirect, transfers through third parties and involvement in arms production in South Africa, and including end-user clauses designed to monitor and enforce the embargo scrupulously. Such legislation should also cover the existing loop-holes with regard to "dual purpose" items and related materials including computers, electronic equipments and related technology.

244. The Conference further emphasizes the need for strengthening the relevant provision of Security Council resolution 418 (1977) in order to ensure the immediate cessation of all nuclear collaboration with South Africa.

245. The Conference expresses concern at reports regarding the efforts by the South African regime to force military alliances and arrangements involving certain Western Powers and certain regimes in other regions, and to convene a conference to that end.

246. It considers that any military alliances or arrangements with the South African regime would be an act of hostility against the legitimate struggle of the people of South Africa and Namibia and would greatly aggravate the situation in southern Africa. It commends those States which have firmly opposed any links by existing military alliances with the South African regime and calls for vigilance by the international community to prevent any military arrangements with that regime.

### Oil embargo

247. The Conference considers that an effective oil embargo against South Africa is an indispensable complement to the embargo on arms and nuclear co-opera-

tion. The racist regime of South Africa, having no oil of its own, is vulnerable to an oil embargo and will remain so notwithstanding the expansion of its oil-from-coal plants (SASOL).

248. Supplies of oil and petroleum products facilitate the acts of aggression and repression by the racist regime of South Africa. The need for an oil embargo is therefore urgent and complements the embargo on arms and nuclear collaboration.

249. The Conference notes with satisfaction that major oil-exporting States have imposed an embargo on the supply of their oil to South Africa. It further welcomes with appreciation their intention to consider establishing a mechanism, including a monitoring agency, to ensure that their oil embargo is effectively and scrupulously respected. It calls on other countries which supply oil or refined oil products to South Africa to join in implementing the oil embargo against South Africa through legislative measures or appropriate policy directives.

250. The Conference calls upon the Security Council of the United Nations to take action to support the measures by the oil-exporting countries, and to institute a mandatory embargo on the supply of oil and oil products to South Africa and on the provision of any assistance to the oil industry in South Africa.

### Economic sanctions

251. Pending action by the Security Council to impose comprehensive mandatory sanctions, the Conference urges all States to unilaterally and collectively impose economic sanctions against the apartheid regime of South Africa.

252. It recommends, as a first step, that all Governments end any promotion of trade with South Africa, including the exchange of trade missions, Government guarantees and insurance for trade with South Africa or investment in South Africa.

253. The Conference calls for a freeze on all new investments in, and financial loans to, South Africa. It is a well-established fact that foreign capital, loans and other financial facilities sustain the apartheid economy, provide it with resources to expand its repressive apparatus, as well as to acquire and increase its military and nuclear capability, to the detriment of peace and security in the entire southern African region.

254. It notes with satisfaction that the United Nations General Assembly has, repeatedly and by overwhelming majorities, recognized that "a cessation of new foreign investments in and financial loans to South Africa would constitute an important step in international action for the elimination of apartheid, as such investments and loans abet and encourage the apartheid policies in that country".

255. It welcomes the actions of those Governments which have taken legislative and other measures towards that end.

### Transport

256. The Conference calls for the adoption of measures aimed at terminating airline and other connections with apartheid South Africa and Namibia while under South African occupation. It further urges all countries concerned to take action to ensure that airlines registered in their countries terminate "pool arrangements" with South African airlines.

### Other measures

257. The Conference urges all States to take appropriate steps to prohibit sporting, cultural and scientific contacts with South Africa. Formal agreements promoting activities in these fields, except in dire humanitarian cases, should be abrogated.

258. The Conference also urges all States to take appropriate steps to prohibit or discourage emigration of their nationals to South Africa, especially of skilled personnel.

### Public actions

259. The Conference emphasizes the importance of action by local authorities, mass media, trade unions, religious bodies, co-operatives and other non-governmental organizations, as well as men and women of conscience, to demonstrate their abhorrence of apartheid and their solidarity with the legitimate struggle of the oppressed people of South Africa and Namibia.

260. It draws particular attention to the constructive value of consumer boycott, sports boycott, cultural and academic boycott, divestment from transnational corporations and financial institutions operating in South Africa. It encourages assistance to the victims of apartheid and their national liberation movements, as appropriate actions by the public, in support of international sanctions against South Africa.

### Assistance to neighbouring States

261. The Conference draws attention to the problems encountered by the independent States in southern Africa as a result of the aggressive actions of the South African regime, and the sacrifices they have made in the cause of freedom and human rights.

262. It recognizes that these States will be adversely affected by a programme of sanctions against South Africa.

263. It considers, therefore, that the imposition of sanctions must be accompanied by a programme of assistance to those States in the southern African region which would be seriously affected, in accordance with Article 50 of the United Nations Charter. Such assistance should include the provision of supplies of food, oil and other essential commodities, and the establishment of facilities for their stockpiling, as well as necessary financial assistance.

264. It urges support by all States to the Southern African Development Co-ordination Conference (SADCC) aimed at reducing the dependency of the neighbouring States on the racist regime of South Africa.

265. States carrying out their international duty of assistance to the liberation movements of southern Africa are entitled to the protection of the international law when confronting the violence of the racist regime and have the right to seek and obtain assistance from other States in protecting their territorial integrity and political independence.

### Conclusion

266. The Conference declares its solidarity with the oppressed people of South Africa and Namibia in their legitimate struggle for freedom, to all persons imprisoned, restricted or exiled for their participation in the struggle, and to the independent States in southern Africa.

267. The Conference affirms its solidarity with Nelson Mandela, as well as all other leaders and patriots, imprisoned or restricted for their part in the struggle for freedom and demands their immediate and unconditional release.

268. It recognizes the right of the oppressed people and their national liberation movements to choose their means of struggle, including armed struggle, for liberation from the oppressive regime in South Africa.

269. It declares that the racist regime of South Africa, by its escalating repression and defiance of world opinion, bears full responsibility for precipitating violent conflict. It draws the attention of those States which oppose sanctions but express their fulsome abhorrence at the brutalities of apartheid, particularly during dramatic crises such as Sharpeville and Soweto, that their policies are in effect aiding and abetting the escalation of violence. Sanctions are a legitimate and appropriate instrument of coercion prescribed by the Charter of the United Nations for the resolution of conflicts.

270. The Conference considers that the oppressed people of South Africa and Namibia and their national liberation movements, deserve the support of the international community in their legitimate struggle. It considers that comprehensive sanctions against South Africa constitute appropriate and effective support to facilitate freedom for the people of South Africa and Namibia and to put an end to racist violence.

271. The Conference recognizes the urgent need

for the mobilization of all Governments and peoples for comprehensive sanctions against the South African regime, as well as for all other appropriate assistance to the oppressed people of South Africa and Namibia and their national liberation movements.

272. It calls on all Governments and organizations committed to freedom and human dignity, to counteract all moves to assist and encourage the apartheid regime. It appeals to them to concert their efforts in an international campaign for comprehensive sanctions against South Africa, in the light of the discussions and decisions of the present conference.

273. It commends the United Nations Special Committee against Apartheid, the anti-apartheid and solidarity movements and other organizations for their efforts in support of comprehensive sanctions against South Africa.

274. It urges the United Nations, in co-operation with the OAU, and in close co-operation with the national liberation movements and other organizations, to take all necessary measures to promote, secure and monitor the programme of comprehensive sanctions against South Africa.

275. The Conference recognizes and pays tribute to the historic and continuing struggle of the peoples of South Africa and Namibia to end apartheid and illegal occupation, as well as to promote justice, freedom and independence in their countries. It is their courageous and persistent struggle which have made the Conference possible and relevant. The Conference responds to the noble aspirations and efforts of the South African and Namibian patriots and issues a fervent appeal for individual and collective support to them.

. . .

# Document 104

*Statement by the President of the Security Council, on behalf of the Council, concerning the proclamation of the "independent" state of Ciskei*

S/14794, 15 December 1981

The Security Council notes that on 4 December 1981, the South African regime proclaimed the Ciskei an integral part of South African territory, a so-called "independent" State, in pursuance of its apartheid and bantustanization policy.

The Security Council recalls its resolution 417 (1977), in which it demanded that the racist regime of South Africa should abolish the policy of bantustanization. It also recalls its resolutions 402 (1976) and 407 (1977), in which it endorsed General Assembly resolution 31/6 A of 26 October 1976 on this matter. The Council further takes note of General Assembly resolution 32/105 N of 14 December 1977 on the question of bantustans.

The Security Council does not recognize the so-called "independent homelands" in South Africa: it condemns the purported proclamation of the "independence" of the Ciskei and declares it totally invalid. This action by the South African regime, following similar proclamations in the case of the Transkei, Bophuthatswana and Venda, denounced by the international community, is designed to divide and dispossess the African people and establish client States under its domination in order to perpetuate apartheid. It seeks to create a class of foreign people in their own country. It further aggravates the situation in the region and hinders international efforts for just and lasting solutions.

The Security Council calls upon all Governments to deny any form of recognition to the so-called "independent" bantustans, to refrain from any dealings with them, to reject travel documents issued by them, and urges Governments of Member States to take effective measures within their constitutional framework to discourage all individuals, corporations and other institutions under their jurisdiction from having any dealings with the so-called "independent" bantustans.

# Document 105

## Declaration of the International Conference on Women and Apartheid, held at Brussels, 17-19 May 1982

A/AC.115/L.571, 14 July 1982

The International Conference on Women and Apartheid was held in the building of the European Parliament in Brussels, Belgium, from 17 to 19 May 1982 to consider the plight of women in South Africa and Namibia and their struggle for national liberation, measures to promote all necessary international assistance to them and action to demonstrate solidarity with them in their legitimate struggle.

The Conference declares that apartheid, especially as it affects women and children, is an international crime and an intolerable affront to the conscience of mankind.

The Pretoria regime has subjected the women of South Africa to oppression and humiliation, including forced deportations and separation of families. It has killed, imprisoned, restricted and tortured numerous women and children for opposing apartheid. It has committed repeated acts of aggression in southern Africa and even attacked and bombed refugee camps in neighbouring independent African States, killing women and children.

The Conference pays tribute to the courage and heroism of women in the legitimate struggle for liberation. It also pays tribute to the front-line States for their support of that struggle.

The Conference calls for effective international action in accordance with the United Nations resolutions, for the elimination of apartheid, the independence of Namibia and the establishment of a democratic society in South Africa.

The Conference deplores the actions of those governments, multinationals and interests which continue to collaborate with the apartheid regime and, in endorsing the relevant resolutions of the United Nations General Assembly, it calls upon the countries in question to end such collaboration.

The Conference reiterates its support for the resolutions adopted by the World Conference of the United Nations Decade for Women in Copenhagen condemning the expansion of the South African military and nuclear capacity as a threat to stability and world peace and calls for the implementation of the decisions reached by the United Nations and other international bodies on the military, nuclear and oil embargo against South Africa.

The Conference condemns the acts of aggression and intimidation perpetrated by the South African Government against the front-line States and, in particular, Angola and calls for the immediate and unconditional withdrawal of South African troops from the territory of the People's Republic of Angola.

The Conference supports Security Council resolution 435 on Namibia and calls on the "contact group" countries to bring pressure to bear on the South African Government to implement it as quickly as possible.

The Conference emphasizes, in this context, the urgent need for widest publicity to the plight of women in South Africa and Namibia, and their resistance against apartheid, as well as greatly increased international assistance to alleviate their hardships and enable them to develop further their participation in the struggle for liberation.

It appeals, in particular, for generous assistance by governments, organizations and individuals for relevant projects of the national liberation movements and front-line States.

It encourages the United Nations Special Committee against Apartheid and the International Committee of Solidarity with the Struggle of Women of South Africa and Namibia to redouble their efforts to promote publicity and assistance in close co-operation with the national liberation movements and front-line States. It appeals to all governments and organizations (particularly women's organizations and organizations concerned with development) to lend their full co-operation to the Special Committee and the International Committee.

The Conference extends its greetings to the Women of South Africa, Namibia and the front-line States, especially to all those persecuted for their role in the struggle for the liberation of South Africa and Namibia, and pledges the continued efforts of all participants in solidarity with them.

# Document 106

*General Assembly resolution: Policies of apartheid of the Government of South Africa—Situation in South Africa*

A/RES/37/69 A, 9 December 1982

*The General Assembly,*

...

*Gravely concerned* at the pronouncements, policies and actions of the Government of the United States of America which have provided comfort and encouragement to the racist regime of South Africa,

*Concerned* that some Western States and Israel continue military and nuclear cooperation with South Africa, in gross violation of the provisions of Security Council resolution 418 (1977), of 4 November 1977, and have failed to prevent corporations, institutions and individuals within their jurisdiction from carrying out such cooperation,

*Gravely concerned* that the racist regime of South Africa has continued to obtain military equipment and ammunition, as well as technology and know-how, to develop its armaments industry and to acquire nuclear-weapon capability,

*Recognizing* that any nuclear-weapon capability of the racist regime of South Africa constitutes a threat to international peace and security and a grave menace to Africa and the world,

...

1. *Strongly condemns* the apartheid regime of South Africa for its brutal repression and indiscriminate torture and killings of workers, schoolchildren and other opponents of apartheid, and the imposition of death sentences on freedom fighters;

2. *Vehemently condemns* the apartheid regime for its repeated acts of aggression, subversion and terrorism against independent African States, designed to destabilize the whole of southern Africa;

3. *Reiterates its firm conviction* that the apartheid regime has been encouraged to undertake these criminal acts by the protection afforded by major Western Powers against international sanctions;

...

11. *Requests* all intergovernmental organizations to exclude the racist regime of South Africa and to terminate all co-operation with it;

12. *Expresses serious concern* over the continued granting of credits by the International Monetary Fund to the racist regime of South Africa and requests it to terminate such credits forthwith;

13. *Requests* the International Atomic Energy Agency to refrain from extending to South Africa any facilities which may assist it in its nuclear plans and, in particular, to exclude South Africa from all its technical working groups;

...

20. *Urges* the United Nations Development Programme and other agencies of the United Nations system to expand their assistance to the oppressed people of South Africa and to the South African liberation movements recognized by the Organization of African Unity, namely, the African National Congress and the Pan Africanist Congress of Azania, in consultation with the Special Committee against apartheid;

...

# Document 107

*Statement by Mr. Alhaji Yusuff Maitama-Sule (Nigeria), Chairman of the Special Committee against Apartheid, at the meeting of the Committee on 13 January 1983*

Published by the United Nations Centre against Apartheid

Since its inception in 1963, this Special Committee has constantly reiterated that we do not view the problem in South Africa as a conflict between Black and White. We have said again and again that we seek—as indeed the great leaders of the Black people in South Africa seek—the establishment of a democratic society in which *all* the people will enjoy human rights and fundamental freedoms.

We have constantly stressed the danger of growing conflict if apartheid and repression continue, and pressed for a peaceful solution through consultations among genuine representatives of all the people of the country.

In view of the intransigence of the Pretoria regime, prodded along by its supporters, we have campaigned for sanctions against South Africa as the most effective peaceful measure to persuade that regime to heed world opinion and to seek a peaceful solution.

The interests of *all* the people of South Africa, and the averting of a gruesome racial conflict, have been the two main concerns of this Special Committee and of the international community.

In the discharge of its mandate, the Special Committee has followed developments in South Africa and repeatedly drawn attention to the constant deterioration of the situation. We have pointed to the obstinate moves of the Pretoria regime to consolidate White domination, to the enormous suffering caused by its policies and actions, and to its resolve to escalate repression in the hope of suppressing the legitimate resistance of the majority of the people of the country.

With the attainment of independence by the nations of central and southern Africa, and the growing mobilization of the South African people against apartheid, the regime has become ever more desperate and has not hesitated to violate international morality and law.

I need only point out that there are few parallels in history to the heroism of Black schoolchildren in Soweto and other townships who have since 16 June 1976, protested peacefully against apartheid, or to the inhumanity of the South African police who routinely resort to indiscriminate killing and maiming of thousands of children.

There are hardly any parallels in history to the actions of the Pretoria regime in the deporting and displacing of millions of Black people in South Africa, or to the attempted denationalization of over eight million Africans under the bantustan policy.

There are few parallels to the Pretoria regime's assassinations of South African refugees in neighbouring territories, to its invasions of independent African States, and organizing and supporting subversive elements in those States. The illegal and terrorist activities of South African intelligence agencies have even spread to distant lands like Seychelles, the United Kingdom and the United States of America.

In the past year, we have followed with utmost concern, anguish and indignation the torture of numerous leaders in prison—resulting in the death of a White physician in Johannesburg, a Black student in Soweto and a Lutheran priest in the bantustan of Venda. We have mourned the assassination of Mrs. Ruth First in Maputo.

Above all, on 9 December we learned with shock of the bestiality of the South African armed forces in Maseru —which entered the independent State of Lesotho in the middle of the night and in cold blood killed South African refugees as well as Lesotho nationals.

The excuses given by the Pretoria regime have proved to be totally false and the world has come to know that the South African army deliberately killed innocent men, women and children in order to terrorize Lesotho and the African National Congress of South Africa.

*Pretoria regime has lost its senses*

The Maseru massacre is not just another incident in a series of acts of aggression by the Pretoria regime, but something much more serious.

In the fifth century before Christ, a Greek philosopher, Euripides, wrote:

"Those whom God wishes to destroy, He first deprives of their senses."

There is little doubt that the Pretoria regime has lost its senses.

Does that regime realize—and do not its supporters realize—that this cowardly massacre cannot but provoke anger among the Black people? If they follow the Law of Moses:

"Eye for eye, tooth for tooth, hand for hand, foot for foot" (Exodus, XXI, 24), who can blame them?

Does not the Pretoria regime realize—and do not its supporters realize—that if the Black people stooped to the regime's level of morality, they could also kill innocent South African White men, women and children, in South Africa and abroad?

Is this what they want? Have they developed a death wish?

We must ask these questions because there is an explosive situation in southern Africa and a grave threat to international peace.

The Black people of South Africa have been seething with anger for many decades because of the injustice and oppression to which they have been subjected. Even the leaders of the present regime admit that they have committed many injustices since the National Party came to power in 1948.

But the leaders of the Black people and other opponents of apartheid tried by non-violent and humane means to obtain an end to injustice. They did so because they seek to build a non-racial society and not to wage a war against the privileged White minority.

They have "borne the cross" and suffered in the legendary non-violent resistance campaigns of the 1950s.

It was only after the Sharpeville massacre of 1960 and the banning of their liberation movements that they gave up strict adherence to non-violence. Even when they felt obliged to resort to armed resistance, they have taken great care to avoid the loss of innocent lives while risking their own lives in the process.

The Whites of South Africa must realize that it is very easy to kill in a country where every town has a Black majority, where every home has Black servants.

And the struggle of the Black people of South Africa has moved millions of people abroad so that there can be serious repercussions even outside the borders of South Africa.

### Restraint of the Black leaders

If there has been no wave of terrorism and killing of innocent Whites, it is not because of the weapons that the Whites and their regime possess, but because of the restraint by the leaders of the Black people.

Nelson Mandela, in a speech from the dock in April 1964, told a South African court and White people that:

"We of the ANC had always stood for a non-racial democracy and we shrank from any action which might drive the races further apart than they already were. But the hard facts were that fifty years of non-violence had brought the African people nothing. . ."

He pointed out that the African people had been talking of violence to win back their country. There had in fact been violent resistance in various parts of South Africa from 1957 and there was a grave danger of a drift to violent resistance as a rule of the struggle.

It was in that situation that the leaders of the ANC had decided, because they were left by the regime with no other choice, to resort to properly controlled violence, particularly sabotage of key installations, to persuade the White community, even at that late stage, to avoid the drift to disaster.

### Right to armed struggle

The Special Committee recognized—and on its recommendation the General Assembly recognized—the *right*—I repeat, the *right*—of the oppressed people of South Africa and their national liberation movement to choose their means of struggle, including armed struggle.

We have been criticized by delegations of some Member States—who have not hesitated to use massive violence in the pursuit of their supposed "national interests"—on the grounds that we were encouraging violence.

We have no apologies to make. In fact, we felt it imperative to recognize the sacred right of the people, in the face of the constant violence and terrorism of the regime. It had to be recognized because the profiteers from apartheid denied that right to the Black victims of their exploitation in South Africa. There are times when only armed resistance of the victims will stop the brigands from their crimes.

In fact, I am convinced that it is the support of the international community to the oppressed people of South Africa and their national liberation movement which has limited violence and averted uncontrolled conflict.

But after the gruesome massacre of Maseru, I feel it necessary to ask whether the situation is going out of control.

### Terrorism of the regime

Eleven years ago, on 28 February 1972, during the trial of the Anglican Dean of Johannesburg, the State counsel argued:

"Every ANC male member is a potential guerrilla fighter".

The regime seems now to have taken up that conclusion seriously.

A few weeks ago, Barbara Hogan, a young researcher, was sentenced to ten years' imprisonment for "high treason" with no evidence other than membership in the ANC and the sending of a study on unemployment to an ANC member in Botswana.

What does that mean?

According to polls in South Africa, despite all the intimidation, some 40 per cent of the Black people expressed support for the ANC. That is at least *ten* million people.

If every member of the ANC can be killed in cold blood—as was done in Maseru recently—cannot the ANC argue that every White household is a military target since all Whites are conscripted into the armed forces which are trained to kill unarmed Black men, women and children?

The violence of the Pretoria regime is due not only to its desperation, but to the comfort it has enjoyed from those who profit from apartheid, and those who are allied with it for various other reasons. We cannot but point out that since the election of a new administration in the United States of America in 1980, with its policy of so-called "constructive engagement" with Pretoria, the Botha regime has escalated terrorism. I need only point to the brazen raid into Matola, Mozambique, in January 1981, to the repeated acts of aggression against Angola and to the massacre in Maseru.

I must warn those governments which continue to oppose sanctions, and which continue to protect the Pretoria regime:

"If you think you are helping the Whites of South Africa you are mistaken. You are driving them to suicide for your own immoral profit or your short-sighted calculations. History will not forgive you."

### Message to the people of South Africa

I would like to conclude this statement with an appeal, especially to the White people of South Africa, the Africans of European descent.

I would like them to realize before it is too late that their destiny is with the Black majority and with the African continent—not with the greedy external forces which have no concern for the future of South Africa.

Let them listen to the true voice of the Black leaders of South Africa—not to the infamous propaganda which brands all Blacks struggling for their rights as "terrorists" and credits all African resistance against injustice to the activities of the Soviet Union or some other power.

Let them listen to the late Chief Albert Luthuli, the winner of the Nobel Peace Prize, who wrote in 1962:

"I am not opposed to the present Government because is it White. I am only opposed to it because it is undemocratic and repressive. . .

"My idea is a non-racial government consisting of the best men—merit rather than colour counting."

Let them listen to Nelson Mandela who declared his hatred of White domination, as well as Black domination, and his willingness to die, if need be, in the struggle for a democratic and free society in which all persons lived together in harmony and with equal opportunities.

Let them listen to Oliver Tambo who told the General Assembly in October 1976:

". . .we love our country and its people—*all* its people."

I have quoted only the leaders of the African National Congress, as the Pretoria regime has tried to picture them as the main enemies, but the views they have expressed are shared by all other Black leaders.

It is an offence to publish the writings or speeches of any of these leaders in South Africa!

These are men of firm convictions who have been prepared to risk their lives for their belief. They represent the truth.

There is only one sure way for peace and security in South Africa—release Nelson Mandela and all other political prisoners, declare amnesty for all political exiles, and undertake genuine consultations with them on the destiny of the nation.

Africa is a continent of reconciliation and I have no doubt that if they follow this course, the White people, now consumed by fear and insecurity, will be surprised at the compassion and generosity of the leaders of the Black people.

The militarists of the present regime and the inhuman tortures of the Security Police are leading the country to certain disaster. It is a tragedy that the White community remains silent and has shown no vision.

If they feel that they can terrorize African States or the national liberation movement, they have learned nothing from history. In our time, numerous African countries have suffered attacks from colonial powers for their support of liberation movements in neighbouring countries. But none has succumbed. And I have no doubt that the people of the States neighbouring South Africa will not betray their continent, whatever the price.

In all earnestness, I appeal to the men of religion, the educators, the jurists, the poets and writers and all others among the privileged minority in South Africa to wake up before it is too late, to curb those who rely on the gun and the instruments of torture, and seek peace.

The monopoly of political power enjoyed by the Whites must surely end, but it will be replaced by a more secure and glorious future for their children. Indeed, the whole of Africa will welcome them as brothers and sisters.

I would like to tell my brothers and sisters in the national !iberation movement in South Africa that we grieve with them for those who lost their lives and that we will stand with them, however hard the struggle may be, until South Africa and the entire continent are emancipated from all manifestations of racism. We are not moved by anger or the spirit of revenge, but the vision of freedom and peace.

I am sure I can say this not only on behalf of my African colleagues but on behalf of my colleagues from the Socialist States, from Asia and from Latin America who are in this Committee—and on behalf of countless governments and people outside this hall.

---

# Document 108

*Declaration adopted by the International Conference of Trade Unions on Sanctions and Other Actions against the Apartheid Regime in South Africa, held at Geneva, 10-11 June 1983*

A/38/272-S/15832, 16 June 1983

*The International Conference of Trade Unions on Sanctions and other Actions against the Apartheid Regime in South Africa* meeting in Geneva on 10 and 11 June 1983 with the participation of 375 delegates representing hundreds of millions of organized workers throughout the world:

*Recalling* that apartheid has been declared a crime against humanity and that the Security Council of the United Nations, since its resolution 182 (1963) adopted unanimously on 4 December 1963, has affirmed the conviction that the situation in South Africa is seriously disturbing international peace and security;

*Considering* the updated declaration of the International Labour Conference concerning the policy of apartheid in South Africa and the conclusions submitted by the sixth sitting of the Conference Committee on Apartheid and adopted by the Conference in 1981;

*Recalling* the United Nations General Assembly resolution (December 1981) which proclaimed 1982 International Year of Mobilization for Sanctions Against South Africa;

*Recalling* resolution 418 (1977) of November 1977 adopted by the United Nations Security Council instituting a mandatory arms embargo against South Africa, as well as ECOSOC resolution on Activities of Transnational Corporations in southern Africa and their collaboration with the racist minority regime in that area;

*Condemns* the South African minority apartheid regime for totally ignoring world opinion as expressed by the above-mentioned resolutions and consistently refusing to abide by international standards as enshrined in the United Nations Charter and the Declaration of Philadelphia;

*Warns* that South Africa's systematic violation of human and trade union rights in South Africa and the rapid escalation in the tightening and application of apartheid policies, constitute an imminent threat to world peace and security;

*Denounces* the division of South Africa into bantustans or so-called homelands, which is now being accelerated so as to complete the task of exiling the majority people of South Africa from their own country and denying their citizenship rights;

*Rejects* and *condemns* so-called constitutional changes, which totally exclude the Black majority people from all political rights and are designed to further consolidate apartheid, which have been strongly condemned by the independent Black trade union movement in South Africa;

*Stresses* that other so-called reforms in South Africa will continue being a mockery as long as violation of human and trade union rights remain institutionalized through the apartheid system;

*Deplores* and *condemns* South Africa's raids and incursions on sovereign neighbouring countries and the apartheid regime's efforts to destabilize the front-line states, which constitutes a breach of the peace;

*Vigorously condemns* the South African White minority racist regime for the annexation and illegal occupation of the territory of Namibia and the imposition of the apartheid system in that country;

*Stresses* that the cornerstone of the apartheid regime is exploitation of the cheap Black labour for the profit of the White minority and foreign investors;

*Denounces* and *condemns* continuing arrests, bannings, psychological and physical torture leading to deaths in detention, harassment and victimization of Black trade unionists and those assisting Black workers to organize themselves;

*Also denounces and condemns* the oppression of Black working women in South Africa, who because they are Black and of their sex, suffer two-fold discrimination;

*Salutes the Black workers of South Africa* for the courage and determination they have shown in organizing themselves into independent Black trade unions, which have become the strongest expression of the aspirations of the majority peoples of South Africa;

*Condemns* employers and investors in South Africa who directly or indirectly help to maintain the apartheid system and are collaborating with the apartheid regime in the military and nuclear fields and with its security forces;

*Disillusioned* with the various codes of conduct for companies with subsidiaries in South Africa, which have failed due to the fact that trade union demands for sanctions and a tripartite monitoring machinery were ignored;

*Appalled* that White emigration to South Africa is on the increase while unemployment among Black workers is escalating rapidly, reaching over 25 per cent in the so-called bantustans;

*Deplores* the failure of some States to fully implement United Nations resolutions and decisions on South Africa;

*Deplores* the fact that South Africa received a substantial loan from the International Monetary Fund despite opposition by the majority of the United Nations member States;

*Requests* the United Nations to make sanctions against South Africa mandatory;

*Endorses* the recommendations submitted in September 1980 by the Security Council Committee established in pursuance of resolution 421 (1977) on the question of South Africa, for the implementation and reinforcement of the arms embargo and urges that the Security Council adopt them without delay, extending the embargo to comprise all products that can be used in the manufacture of arms and military equipment;

*Urges* that the arms embargo be extended to also cover purchase of arms and military equipment manufactured by South Africa;

*Urges* the Security Council to further extend the

embargo beyond arms to raw materials and technology that can be used in the production of nuclear energy and to oil and petroleum products;

*Calls on Governments throughout the world to:*

(1) Make every effort, within the framework of the United Nations, to promote the adoption of mandatory economic sanctions against South Africa and pending a decision by the Security Council to take unilateral and regional action;

(2) Take immediate measures for an effective international arms embargo in line with the above-mentioned recommendations;

(3) Take immediate measures for the adoption of an oil embargo against South Africa and for this purpose and as a first step, to organize under UN auspices an international conference of oil-exporting and transporting countries; the Conference requests the UN Special Committee against Apartheid to produce, on a regular basis, lists of tankers and companies supplying oil and oil products to the racist regime in South Africa and to distribute these lists especially to unions of dock-terminal and oil transport workers;

(4) Initiate and intensify anti-apartheid action in all United Nations specialized agencies and inter-governmental organizations to stop dealings with banks cooperating with racist South Africa and to increase aid to the oppressed peoples of South Africa in cooperation with the international trade union movement;

(5) Ensure the speedy and full implementation of UN resolution 435 ending South Africa's illegal occupation of Namibia and restoring human and trade union rights through internationally supervised elections, failing which the UN should take immediate strongest punitive measures against South Africa.

*Further calls on* Governments throughout the world to:

-Sever political, cultural, sports, commercial and diplomatic relations with the South African regime and ensure that all existing cultural agreements with South Africa be revoked forthwith;

-Pass legislation to end all investment in South Africa;

-Withdraw pension funds and other forms of public investment from banks and companies collaborating with South Africa;

-Halt the transfer of patent rights (licences), and new technology to South Africa;

-Withdraw home company staff from South African subsidiaries;

-Put a halt to all incentives for exports to South Africa;

-Apply pressure on national and international institutions such as the IMF, to end cooperation with the South African regime on their overseas borrowing;

-Halt all scientific and technological cooperation with South Africa;

-Increase economic assistance to independent African States neighbouring South Africa, so as to reduce their economic dependence on South Africa, especially in transport and communication;

-Intensify necessary support to the liberation movements;

-Repeal any legislation in the home countries which prevents trade union solidarity action to support independent Black trade unions;

-Close South African recruitment offices;

-Refuse to transfer pensions and other State-sponsored benefit schemes to those choosing to emigrate to South Africa;

-Refuse recognition to any bantustan or so-called homeland.

*Calls on employers' organizations and companies to:*

-Take measures to sanction their members who maintain relations of any nature with South Africa and that economic and financial groups do not extend loans to South Africa and collaborate with the apartheid regime in any way;

-Request foreign companies which have invested in South Africa to withdraw their investments and to refrain from any cooperation with the South African regime in the economic and military field;

-Hire, train and promote Black labour lodging strongest protests against the influx control system, which is contrary to ILO employment Conventions and instrumental in maintaining job reservation;

-Fully meet obligations undertaken in the framework of the ILO Declaration concerning the policy of apartheid in South Africa.

*Strongly urges* all workers and their trade union organisations throughout the world to:

(1) Press on governments which have not yet done so to stop all kinds of aid to and investment in South Africa;

(2) Press on governments to pass national legislation and regulations to make it illegal to supply or transport oil and oil products to racist South Africa;

(3) Take industrial actions against the transnational corporations which are investing in South Africa;

(4) Expose by all possible means the crimes that are committed daily in South Africa by the racist White minority;

(5) Refrain from loading or unloading of any ships or planes destined to or coming from South Africa;

(6) Support by all means the attempts by Black workers in South Africa to set up their unions and assume trade union rights;

(7) Give full backing to the efforts of the United

Nations and of its committee against apartheid to end apartheid, liberate Namibia and establish the rule of majority in South Africa;

(8) Increase pressure for closure of South African recruitment offices and to picket such offices;

(9) Bring pressure to bear for the introduction of a ban on advertisements for jobs in South Africa;

(10) Organize meetings with shop stewards, workers' rallies within companies, the distribution of leaflets and posters, study circles and seminars and publish special features in trade union journals in order to mobilize the rank-and-file in solidarity action with the workers in South Africa;

(11) Organize, in cooperation with consumers' organizations, a boycott of goods imported directly or indirectly from South Africa, ensuring that the workers are widely informed about the needs for such boycott action;

(12) Eliminate any investment of trade union members' pension contributions and other trade union funds, in companies or investment schemes with interests in South Africa;

(13) Coordinate trade union action against apartheid in accordance with the resolution adopted by the Second World Trade Union Conference against Apartheid in 1977, and the updated ILO Declaration concerning the policy of apartheid in South Africa, making full use of the monitoring machinery established in that framework.

The Conference recommends that the Workers' group continues to work in close cooperation with all competent bodies of the United Nations, particularly the UN Special Committee against Apartheid.

# Document 109

## Introduction to the First Register of Entertainers, Actors and Others Who Have Performed in Apartheid South Africa, published by the Special Committee against apartheid, October 1983

United Nations Centre against Apartheid, Notes and Documents, No. 20/83, October 1983

The movement for a cultural boycott against South Africa, as a demonstration of opposition to apartheid, began many years ago. Father Trevor Huddleston, in an article in *The Observer*, London, in October 1954, wrote:

"I am pleading for a cultural boycott of South Africa. I am asking those who believe racialism to be sinful or wrong should refuse to encourage it by accepting any engagement to act, to perform as a musical artist or as a ballet dancer—in short, engage in any contracts which would provide entertainment for any one section of the community."

Over the years, many musicians, entertainers, artists, writers and others joined the boycott of South Africa. Many of them joined anti-apartheid movements and campaigns and lent their services for the benefit of the oppressed people of South Africa and their national liberation movement, as well as anti-apartheid movements.

The movement for a cultural boycott against South Africa gathered renewed momentum in 1965 when the apartheid regime in South Africa enacted stringent regulations prohibiting multiracial performances or audiences. The Special Committee against Apartheid held consultations with a number of anti-apartheid movements and cultural personalities and decided that the United Nations should promote and encourage the cultural boycott of South Africa. On its recommendation, the General Assembly—in resolution 2396 (XXIII) of 2 December 1968—requested "all States and organizations to suspend cultural, educational, sports and other exchanges with the racist regime and with organizations and institutions in South Africa which practise apartheid".

The apartheid regime defied international demands for an end to racial discrimination and segregation in the cultural field. In recent years, however, it became concerned over increasing isolation and tried to restore international cultural and sporting contacts. It relaxed some regulations so as to allow *some* mixed performances and mixed audiences in some theatres, *under permit*. (Segregation in theatres is still the rule, and exceptions are allowed mainly to attract foreign performers. The cinema theatres are totally segregated.) The Pretoria regime and its supporters tried to persuade artists that since multiracial performances and audiences were now possible, they should no more boycott South Africa. They also used secret funds and improper activities to break the boycott.

Many entertainers rejected South African offers, some at considerable sacrifice, because of their opposition to racism. They appreciated the position of the Black people of South Africa and of anti-apartheid movements that the so-called "reforms" were only a cover to divert attention from the entrenchment of apartheid, particularly through the bantustan policy designed to deprive the

African majority even of its citizenship, from forced removals of millions of African people from their homes and from brutal repression of opponents of apartheid, including the indiscriminate killing of schoolchildren protesting against racial discrimination.

Some entertainers, however, were enticed by the propaganda and the tempting financial offers of apartheid to defy the boycott and perform in South Africa.

In view of this, and on the recommendation of the Special Committee, the General Assembly adopted a separate resolution of 16 December 1980, calling for "cultural, academic and other boycotts of South Africa" (resolution 35/206 E). The Assembly adopted another separate resolution on the matter on 17 December 1981, as resolution 36/172 I.

The Special Committee intensified its efforts for a cultural boycott by appeals to artists and cultural groups which were reported to be planning tours of South Africa, and by publicity to the General Assembly resolutions on the matter. It encouraged and assisted anti-apartheid groups active in promoting the cultural boycott.

On 18 March 1982, it co-sponsored a forum on the cultural boycott at the United Nations with the participation of several South African artists and writers in exile. In August 1982, it publicized the declaration of O'Jays, the American singing group, supporting the boycott of South Africa and urged all others to follow the example. On 24 October 1982, it supported the establishment of the "Unity of Action" network in New York for a cultural boycott of South Africa. In September 1983, it encouraged and assisted Transafrica and associated groups to establish the "Artists and Athletes against Apartheid", under the leadership of Harry Belafonte and Arthur Ashe, to promote the cultural and sports boycott of South Africa.

It also initiated active efforts to mobilize cultural personalities in the international campaign against apartheid. It held hearings with several cultural personalities, and assisted in the organization of an international art exhibit against apartheid and in other projects.

It appealed to Governments to take appropriate measures such as the denial of visa-free entry to South Africans.

The efforts of the Special Committee found an encouraging response among Governments, cultural organizations and personalities.

The Government of Japan announced in June 1974 that no visas would be issued to South African nationals for the purpose of interchanges in the field of sports, culture and education. The Government of the Netherlands suspended its cultural agreement with South Africa after the Soweto massacre in 1976 and abrogated it in 1981. Several countries which had formerly provided visa-free entry to South Africans instituted visas.

Many cultural organizations and artists boycotted South Africa in response to appeals by the Special Committee in co-operation with anti-apartheid groups. To give but two recent examples: Sir Richard Attenborough, director of the film "Gandhi", cancelled plans to attend the showing of the film in South Africa in April 1983, and the South African delegation was forced to leave the film festival in Capri in September 1983.

The Special Committee also encouraged support for the cultural activities of the South African liberation movements recognized by the Organization of African Unity—the African National Congress of South Africa and the Pan Africanist Congress of Azania—and welcomed events which expressed solidarity with the cultural workers in the struggle for liberation in South Africa.

One important event was the "Culture and Resistance" festival and symposium which took place in Gaborone, Botswana, from 5 to 9 July 1982, with the participation of many South African musicians, writers, artists and other cultural workers. The Conference supported a cultural boycott of South Africa.

The Special Committee against Apartheid also encouraged the conference on "The Cultural Voice of Resistance—South African and Dutch Artists against apartheid", organized by the Netherlands Anti-Apartheid Movement in Amsterdam from 13 to 18 December 1982.

### Action in South Africa

The cultural boycott, strongly advocated by the liberation movements of South Africa which are banned in the country, received an impetus in 1980 when several legal organizations inside South Africa courageously called for action to dissuade foreign artists from performing in the country.

. . .

In March 1981, AZAPO called for a world-wide boycott of artists who performed in South Africa. The call was supported by other South African organizations such as the Congress of South African Students, Music, Drama, Art and Literature Institute (MDALI, a Black cultural organization), the Port Elizabeth Black Community Organization, and by numerous black leaders.

### Cooperation of anti-apartheid groups and other organizations

The Special Committee against Apartheid wishes to commend the intensified activities of anti-apartheid groups in several countries—particularly the United States of America, the United Kingdom, Ireland and Canada—in promoting the cultural boycott of South Africa.

It must make special mention of the United States of America where, because of the special efforts of South

Africa to lure Black American entertainers, a number of groups greatly intensified their activities to inform and persuade artists to boycott South Africa and to demand that those who had performed in South Africa undertake not to visit South Africa again but instead to support the liberation struggle. Among the most active organizations in the United States are the National Black United Front, the Patrice Lumumba Coalition, the African Jazz Artists Society and Studios (AJASS), Transafrica, the Black Music Association, the National Association of Black Owned Broadcasters, Operation PUSH, the American Committee on Africa, and the Continuation Committee of the Conference in Solidarity with the Liberation Struggle in Southern Africa. Their activities were supported by many local groups in different States and cities.

In 1982, the National Black United Front established the Coalition to End Cultural Collaboration with South Africa. The Coalition has been active in organizing demonstrations against artists who have performed in South Africa. The Patrice Lumumba Coalition and the African Jazz Associations and Studios (AJASS), established the "Unity in Action" network for similar action.

The recent establishment of "Artists and Athletes against Apartheid" reflects the growing support in the United States for the boycott of South Africa.

Special mention should also be made of activities in Wales in support of the cultural boycott. Three male voice choirs have been persuaded not to visit South Africa and in September 1983, the Welsh Anti-Apartheid Movement succeeded in securing the cancellation of a visit to the Welsh Arts Council by two members of a South African Government Commission.

## Support of boycott by artists

The Special Committee against Apartheid pays tribute to the numerous artists in all countries who have supported the boycott of apartheid South Africa. They include many of the greatest artists of our time.

It notes with particular appreciation the actions of those who rejected lucrative offers from South Africa because of their opposition to racism and solidarity with the oppressed people of South Africa.

In the United States, Ms. Roberta Flack, rhythm and blues singer, was reported to have rejected an offer of $2.5 million for performances in South Africa. Ms. Phyllis Hyman rejected a tempting offer from South Africa, and declared:

"I have a moral commitment that supersedes money".

Others who have rejected similar offers include: Ben Vereem, Gladys Knight and the Pips, the Floaters, The Jacksons, Diana Ross, Barry White, The Commodores,

The Third World, Lena Horne, Tony Bennett, Millie Jackson, Odyssey, Bross Townsend and Betty Wright. The Boston Ballet cancelled plans to tour South Africa in 1981 after representations by organizations and individuals. The Newport Jazz Festival rejected an offer in 1982 for performances in South Africa.

The Special Committee against Apartheid also notes with satisfaction that the O'Jays, James Moody and Lou Donaldson have undertaken not to perform in South Africa again. Tom Jones is among the British artists who refused offers to perform in South Africa. Eddy Amoo, member of the British group "The Real Thing", who visited South Africa in 1982, said on his return that the group would henceforth completely support the cultural ban. He said:

"Sun City" is an Afrikaner's paradise in a Black man's nightmare".

In Ireland, artists who turned down offers from South Africa include the Dubliners, Niall Toibin and Dusty Springfield.

## The collaborators

Despite the efforts of the Special Committee against Apartheid and many organizations, some musicians and entertainers continue to visit and perform in South Africa.

Many of them have appeared in "Sun City" in Bophuthatswana, where the management has organized a facade of multiracial audiences by bringing a few Blacks to attend.

Concerts, appearances and tours by cultural personalities have been used by the racist regime and its collaborators for propaganda purposes, as a proof of international acceptance of the apartheid system and so-called "reforms" within that system.

While some of the collaborators had perhaps visited South Africa because of ignorance of the situation, or lure of exorbitant fees, others have shown deliberate insensitivity or hostility to the legitimate aspirations of the oppressed people of South Africa.

. . .

## The Register

. . .

The Special Committee against Apartheid announced in September 1981 that it had decided to initiate a register of cultural contacts with South Africa in order to promote an effective boycott.

It is publishing the present register after numerous appeals and long notice to artists who have performed in South Africa. It intends periodically to publish supplements to the register. The names of persons who undertake not to perform in South Africa again will be deleted from the register.

. . .

The Special Committee hopes that this register will enable Governments, organizations and individuals to take all appropriate action to dissuade the artists concerned from continued collaboration with apartheid. It should be made clear to them that if they seek to profit from the system of inhuman oppression of the Black people in South Africa, they will not be allowed to benefit from the patronage of countries and peoples committed to the struggle against apartheid.

...

# Document 110

## *General Assembly resolution: Proposed new racial constitution of South Africa*

A/RES/38/11, 15 November 1983

*The General Assembly,*

*Recalling* its many resolutions and those of the Security Council calling on the authorities in South Africa to abandon apartheid, end oppression and repression of the Black majority and seek a peaceful, just and lasting solution in accordance with the principles of the Charter of the United Nations and the Universal Declaration of Human Rights,

*Reaffirming* that apartheid is a crime against humanity and a threat to international peace and security,

*Gravely concerned* that the so-called "constitutional proposals" endorsed, on 2 November 1983, by the exclusively White electorate in South Africa further entrench apartheid,

*Convinced* that the aim of the so-called "constitutional proposals" is to deprive the indigenous African majority of all fundamental rights, including the right of citizenship, and to transform South Africa into a country for "Whites only", in keeping with the declared policies of apartheid,

*Aware* that the inclusion in the "constitutional proposals" of the so-called "coloured" people and people of Asian origin is aimed at dividing the unity of the oppressed people of South Africa and fomenting internal conflict,

*Noting with grave concern* that one of the objectives of the so-called "constitutional proposals" of the racist regime is to make the "coloured" people and people of Asian origin in South Africa eligible for conscription into the apartheid armed forces for further internal repression and aggression against independent African States,

*Welcoming* the united resistance of the oppressed people of South Africa against these "constitutional" manoeuvres,

*Reaffirming* the legitimacy of the struggle of the oppressed people of South Africa for the elimination of apartheid and for the establishment of a society in which all the people of South Africa as a whole, irrespective of race, colour or creed, will enjoy equal and full political and other rights and participate freely in the determination of their destiny,

*Firmly convinced* that the implementation of these "constitutional proposals" will further aggravate the already explosive situation prevailing inside apartheid South Africa,

1. *Declares* that the so-called "constitutional proposals" are contrary to the principles of the Charter of the United Nations, that the results of the referendum are of no validity whatsoever and that the enforcement of the proposed "constitution" will inevitably aggravate tension and conflict in South Africa and in southern Africa as a whole;

2. *Rejects* the so-called "constitutional proposals" and all insidious manoeuvres by the racist minority regime of South Africa further to entrench White minority rule and apartheid;

3. *Further rejects* any so-called "negotiated settlement" based on bantustan structures or on the "constitutional proposals";

4. *Solemnly declares* that only the total eradication of apartheid and the establishment of a non-racial democratic society based on majority rule, through the full and free exercise of adult suffrage by all the people in a united and non-fragmented South Africa, can lead to a just and lasting solution of the explosive situation in South Africa;

5. *Urges* all Governments and organizations to take appropriate action, in cooperation with the United Nations and the Organization of African Unity and in accordance with the present resolution, to assist the oppressed people of South Africa in their legitimate struggle for a non-racial democratic society;

6. *Requests* the Security Council, as a matter of urgency, to consider the serious implications of the so-called "constitutional proposals" and to take all necessary measures, in accordance with the Charter, to avert the further aggravation of tension and conflict in South Africa and in southern Africa as a whole.

# Document 111

*Programme of Action against Apartheid, adopted by the General Assembly on 5 December 1983 in A/RES/38/39 B*

A/38/539-S/16102, 8 November 1983

## I. Introduction

1. Apartheid in South Africa, which has been denounced by the United Nations for over three decades, has become a grave menace to international peace and security. Urgent, effective and concerted action by the international community is essential in order to abolish that inhuman system and enable the people of South Africa to establish a democratic society in which all the people of the country, irrespective of race, colour or creed, will enjoy human rights and fundamental freedoms.

2. Apartheid has caused immense suffering to the people of South Africa and has been condemned as a crime against humanity.

3. The racist regime of South Africa, in its efforts to consolidate and perpetuate racist domination and exploitation, has forcibly moved and deported over 3 million people from their homes. It has imprisoned many millions of Africans under the humiliating "pass laws". It has segregated schools, hospitals and other amenities and enforced gross discrimination against the Black majority in education, health and other services.

4. In an effort to suppress resistance against its inhuman policies, it has banned many organizations and imprisoned or restricted thousands of persons. Scores of persons have died of torture in detention. Many eminent leaders of the people are imprisoned for life, without even any remissions and under harsh conditions, for espousing the principles of the Universal Declaration of Human Rights.

5. The apartheid regime has not hesitated to resort to massacres, even of schoolchildren.

6. Through its policy of bantustanization, it has established four so-called "independent" States—Transkei, Bophuthatswana, Venda and Ciskei—which are denounced by the United Nations and not recognized by any independent State. It has thereby purported to deprive over 8 million persons of the right to citizenship in South Africa. It seeks to deprive, through this policy, all the African majority of its citizenship, and perpetuate White domination.

7. It has continued its occupation of the international Territory of Namibia and escalated its war against the Namibian people in defiance of the United Nations which has assumed special responsibility for the people of Namibia. This constitutes an act of aggression against the Namibian people in terms of the definition of aggression contained in General Assembly resolution 3341 (XXIX) of 17 December 1974.

8. It has, moreover, committed numerous acts of aggression, destabilization and terrorism against neighbouring independent African States.

9. It acts as an outlaw in constant and flagrant violation of international law.

10. Its policies and actions have not only resulted in a serious threat to international peace and security, but have led to constant breaches of the peace and acts of aggression.

11. It has amassed military equipment and acquired nuclear weapon capability, with the support of certain Western countries and Israel, thereby posing an enormous threat to Africa and the world.

12. Despite the universal condemnation of apartheid and repeated calls for action by the United Nations, the apartheid regime has been able to survive and pose an ever greater threat to humanity, because of the support of the United States of America and other major Western Powers, Israel and other main trading partners of South Africa, which have continued collaboration with it and protected it from effective international sanctions. Their attitudes have enabled numerous transnational corporations and financial institutions to help to sustain the apartheid regime and profit from the inhuman exploitation of the oppressed majority in South Africa. They bear a grave responsibility for the sufferings of the South African people and for the threat to international peace resulting from the situation.

13. The continued collaboration with South Africa is the main obstacle to the elimination of apartheid. The United Nations has declared the legitimacy of the struggle of the South African people for the elimination of apartheid and the establishment of a non-racial society guaranteeing the enjoyment of equal rights by all the people of South Africa, irrespective of race, colour or creed. It has recognized the right of the oppressed people of South Africa to use all means at their disposal, including armed struggle.

14. It has declared that the struggle of the South African people against racism has been a notable contribution to the struggle of humanity for the principles of the Charter of the United Nations and the Universal Declaration of Human Rights. It has proclaimed that the United Nations and the international community have a

special responsibility towards the oppressed people of South Africa and their liberation movements and towards those imprisoned, restricted or exiled for their struggle against apartheid.

15. It has also laid down the lines of international action for the elimination of apartheid in the Lagos Declaration for Action against Apartheid of 1977, the Paris Declaration for Sanctions against South Africa of 1981, the Paris Declaration on Namibia adopted by the International Conference in Support of the Struggle of the People of Namibia for Independence of April 1983, the Programme of Action on Namibia which emanated from that Conference, and numerous resolutions of the General Assembly and the Security Council, calling for the total isolation of the apartheid regime and full support to the national liberation movements of South Africa and Namibia.

16. Outraged world opinion must translate these declarations and resolutions into universal action by exerting its influence on those Western Governments and Israel which continue to collaborate with the apartheid regime.

17. The need for international mobilization against apartheid is urgent and imperative.

18. In the name of peace, justice, human rights and international cooperation, all Governments and peoples should demand:

No arms to South Africa!

No collaboration with apartheid in any field and no profit from apartheid!

No compromise with racism!

Full support to the national liberation movement of South Africa!

## II. Action by Governments

19. All Governments, irrespective of any other differences, should unite in action against the crime of apartheid and take vigorous and concerted measures in implementation of United Nations resolutions to isolate the apartheid regime and assist the oppressed people of South Africa and their liberation movements recognized by the Organization of African Unity (OAU) to eliminate apartheid and establish a non-racial democratic society in which all the people of the country, irrespective of race, colour or creed, will enjoy equal rights.

20. All Governments should, in particular, take the following measures:

### A. *Diplomatic, consular and other official relations*

(1) Terminate diplomatic, consular and all other official relations with the racist regime of South Africa, or refrain from establishing such relations.

### B. *Military and nuclear collaboration*

(2) Implement fully the arms embargo against South Africa instituted by the Security Council by its resolution 418 (1977) of 4 November 1977, in letter and spirit, without any exceptions or reservations and, in this connection:

(a) Cease forthwith any provision to South Africa of arms and related *matériel* of all types, including the sale or transfer of weapons and ammunition, military vehicles and equipment and spare parts for the aforementioned;

(b) Cease forthwith the provision of all types of equipment and supplies and grants of licensing arrangements for the manufacture and maintenance of weapons and ammunition, military vehicles and equipment, paramilitary police equipment and spare parts for the aforementioned;

(c) Abrogate all existing contractual arrangements with and licences or patents granted to the racist regime of South Africa and South African companies relating to the manufacture and maintenance of arms, ammunition of all types and military equipment and vehicles;

(d) Refrain from any cooperation with South Africa in the nuclear field;

(e) Refrain from any supplies for the use of the armed forces, police and paramilitary organizations in South Africa;

(f) Prohibit investment in, or technical assistance for, the manufacture of arms and ammunition, aircraft, naval craft and other military vehicles and equipment in South Africa;

(g) Prohibit the transfer of technology and know-how to South Africa for the development of its armaments industry or nuclear weapon capability;

(h) Terminate any existing military arrangements with the racist regime of South Africa and refrain from entering into any such arrangements;

(i) Refrain from providing training for members of the South African armed forces;

(j) Refrain from any joint military exercises with South Africa;

(k) Prohibit warships or military aircraft from visiting South African ports and airports and South African warships or military craft from visiting their territories;

(l) Prohibit visits of military personnel to South Africa and visits by South African military personnel to their countries;

(m) Refrain from exchanges of military, naval or air attachés with South Africa;

(n) Refrain from purchasing any military supplies manufactured by, or in collaboration with, South Africa;

(o) Refrain from any communications or contacts with South African military establishment or installations;

(*p*) Prohibit any other form of military cooperation with South Africa;

(*q*) Take firm steps to prevent any cooperation or contacts with the racist regime of South Africa by military alliances to which they are parties;

(*r*) Prohibit any violations of the arms embargo by corporations, institutions or individuals within their jurisdiction;

(*s*) Prohibit any institutions, agencies or companies, within their national jurisdiction, from delivering to South Africa or placing at its disposal any reactors or other equipment or fissionable material or technology that will enable the racist regime of South Africa to acquire nuclear weapon technology;

(*t*) Take appropriate action to ensure the termination of all cooperation, direct or indirect, by the International Atomic Energy Agency with South Africa, except for inspection of nuclear facilities in South Africa under safeguards agreements;

(*u*) Assist persons compelled to leave South Africa because of their objections, on the grounds of conscience, to serving in the military or police forces of the apartheid regime;

(*v*) Support and facilitate the strengthening and reinforcement of the United Nations mandatory arms embargo against South Africa;

(*w*) Cooperate with the Security Council Committee established by resolution 421 (1977) concerning the question of South Africa and with the Special Committee against Apartheid.

## C. *Oil embargo*

(3) Take effective legislative and other measures to ensure the implementation of an oil embargo against South Africa, including:

(*a*) Enacting and enforcing "end-users" agreements to stop the supply of oil to South Africa directly or through third parties;

(*b*) Prohibiting the transport to South Africa of all crude oil or oil products, wherever they originate;

(*c*) Taking action against companies or individuals who supply or transport crude oil or oil products to South Africa;

(*d*) Seizing tankers owned by their nationals or registered in their countries which are used to transport oil or oil products to South Africa;

(*e*) Prohibiting all assistance to South Africa—through finance, technology, equipment or personnel—in the construction of oil-from-coal plants;

(*f*) Prohibiting the importation of oil-from-coal technology from South Africa;

(*g*) Preventing the efforts of South African corporate interests to maintain or expand their holdings in oil companies or properties outside South Africa;

(*h*) Banning the participation of corporations and individuals within their jurisdiction in the oil industry in South Africa, including exploration, storage, refining, transport and distribution.

## D. *Economic collaboration*

(4) Terminate all economic collaboration with South Africa and, in particular:

(*a*) Cease all direct or indirect trade or commercial transactions with South Africa;

(*b*) Refrain from supplying strategic materials to South Africa;

(*c*) Refrain from extending loans, investments and technical assistance to the racist regime of South Africa and companies registered in South Africa;

(*d*) Prohibit loans by banks or other financial institutions in their countries to the racist regime of South Africa or South African companies;

(*e*) Prohibit the sale of Krugerrands;

(*f*) Prohibit economic and financial interests under their national jurisdiction form cooperating with the racist regime of South Africa and companies registered in South Africa;

(*g*) Deny tariff and other preferences to South African exports and any inducements or guarantees for exports to, or investments in, South Africa;

(*h*) Take appropriate action in international and regional agencies and organization concerned, such as the European Economic Community, the General Agreement on Tariffs and Trade, the International Monetary Fund and the International Bank for Reconstruction and Development, to secure their denial of all assistance and commercial or other facilities to the South African regime;

(*i*) Take appropriate action, separately or collectively, against transnational corporations and financial institutions collaborating with South Africa.

## E. *Airlines and shipping lines*

(5) In dealing with airlines and shipping lines:

(*a*) Refuse landing and passage facilities to all aircraft belonging to the racist regime of South Africa and companies registered under the laws of South Africa;

(*b*) Close ports to all vessels flying the South African flag;

(*c*) Prohibit airlines and shipping lines registered in their countries from providing services to and from South Africa;

(*d*) Deny facilities to aircraft or shipping lines proceeding to, or returning from South Africa.

## F. *Emigration*

(6) In matters of emigration:

(*a*) Prohibit or discourage the flow of emigrants,

particularly skilled and technical personnel, to South Africa;

(*b*) Close South African recruitment offices and prohibit advertisements for employment in or immigration to South Africa.

### G. *Cultural, educational, sporting and other collaboration with South Africa*

(7) With regard to educational, cultural, sporting and other collaboration:

(*a*) Suspend cultural, educational, sporting and other exchanges with the racist regime and with organization or institutions in South Africa which practise apartheid;

(*b*) Implement United Nations resolutions on apartheid in sports and, in particular:

(i) Refrain from all contact with sports bodies established on the basis of apartheid and with racially selected sports teams from South Africa;

(ii) Withhold any support from sporting events organized with the participation of teams from South Africa;

(iii) Encourage sports organizations to refrain from any exchanges with teams from South Africa;

(*c*) Abrogate and cancel all cultural agreements and similar arrangements with the racist regime of South Africa;

(*d*) Cease any cultural and academic collaboration with South Africa, including the exchange of scientists, students and academic personalities, as well as cooperation in research programmes;

(*e*) Prevent any promotion of tourism to South Africa;

(*f*) Terminate visa-free entry privileges to South African nationals;

(*g*) Take appropriate action with respect to persons whose names appear in lists published by the Special Committee against Apartheid of sportsmen, entertainers and others visiting South Africa.

### H. *Comprehensive and mandatory sanctions against South Africa*

(8) With regard to comprehensive and mandatory sanctions:

(*a*) Support and facilitate the imposition by the Security Council of comprehensive and mandatory sanctions against South Africa, under Chapter VII of the Charter of the United Nations;

(*b*) Implement all possible measures against the racist regime of South Africa, separately or collectively in order totally to isolate it politically, economically, militarily and culturally, pending mandatory sanctions by the Security Council against South Africa.

### I. *Assistance to the oppressed people of South Africa and their liberation movements recognized by the Organization of African Unity*

(9) In assistance to the oppressed people of South Africa:

(*a*) Provide financial and/or material assistance, directly or through the Organization of African Unity, to the South African liberation movements recognized by that organization;

(*b*) Provide broadcasting facilities to the South African liberation movements;

(*c*) Provide transit and travel facilities and other assistance to the members of the liberation movements;

(*d*) Encourage public collections in the country for assistance to the South African liberation movements;

(*e*) Contribute generously and regularly to the United Nations Trust Fund for South Africa, the United Nations Educational and Training Programme for Southern Africa, the United Nations Trust Fund for Publicity against Apartheid and other intergovernmental and nongovernmental funds for humanitarian, educational and other assistance to the oppressed people of South Africa and their liberation movements;

(*f*) Encourage judicial organizations, other appropriate bodies and the public in general to provide assistance to those persecuted by the racist regime of South Africa for their struggle against apartheid;

(*g*) Grant asylum and extend travel facilities and educational and employment opportunities to refugees from South Africa;

(*h*) Encourage the activities of anti-apartheid and solidarity movements and other organizations engaged in providing political and material assistance to the victims of apartheid and to the South African liberation movements;

(*i*) Make generous contributions to the projects of the liberation movements and front-line States for assistance to refugee women and children from South Africa.

### J. *Assistance to independent African States*

(10) In assistance to independent African States:

(*a*) Provide, at their request, all necessary assistance to independent African States subjected to acts of aggression by the racist regime of South Africa in order to enable them to defend their sovereignty and territorial integrity;

(*b*) Assist the programmes of the Southern African Development Coordination Conference (SADCC).

### K. *Release of political prisoners and an end to repression*

(11) To achieve the release of political prisoners and an end to repression:

(*a*) Denounce the repression against opponents of

apartheid, including torture and ill-treatment of political prisoners, and demand an end to all repression and an amnesty to all those imprisoned, restricted or exiled for their opposition to apartheid, or acts arising therefore;

(*b*) Condemn the execution of freedom fighters and political prisoners, and exert all influence to prevent such executions;

(*c*) Demand that the racist regime of South Africa grant prisoner-of-war status to captured freedom fighters in accordance with Additional Protocol I of the Geneva Conventions of 12 August 1949;

(*d*) Demand that the racist regime of South Africa abrogate bans imposed on organizations and the media for their opposition to apartheid;

(*e*) Honour the leaders of the struggle against apartheid imprisoned by the racist regime of South Africa, and publicize their lives;

(*f*) Promote the world campaign for the release of political prisoners in South Africa.

## L. *Denial of all recognition to so-called "independent" bantustans*

(12) With regard to the so-called "independent" bantustans:

(*a*) Deny any form of recognition to the so-called "independent" bantustans, refrain from any dealings with them and reject travel documents issued by them;

(*b*) Deny facilities for the establishment of any offices of the so-called "independent" bantustans;

(*c*) Refuse recognition to postage stamps issued by the so-called "independent" bantustans;

(*d*) Take effective measures to prohibit all individuals, corporations and other institutions under their jurisdiction from having any dealings with the so-called "independent" bantustans or investing in them.

## M. *Dissemination of information on apartheid*

(13) With regard to dissemination of information on apartheid:

(*a*) Ensure, in cooperation with the United Nations and the national liberation movements of South Africa recognized by OAU, the widest possible dissemination of information on apartheid and on the struggle for liberation in South Africa, its legitimate objectives and its wider significance;

(*b*) Encourage the establishment of national organizations for the purpose of enlightening public opinion on the evils of apartheid;

(*c*) Encourage information media to contribute effectively to the international campaign against apartheid;

(*d*) Take all necessary measures to prevent the operations of propaganda organizations of the racist regime

of South Africa and of private organizations which advocate apartheid.

## N. *Other*

(14) In other matters:

(*a*) Accede to the International Convention on the Suppression and Punishment of the Crime of Apartheid;

(*b*) Observe annually the International Day for the Elimination of Racial Discrimination, 21 March; the International Day of Solidarity with the Struggling People of South Africa, 16 June; the International Day of Solidarity with the Struggle of Women of South Africa and Namibia, 9 August; and the Day of Solidarity with South African Political Prisoners, 11 October;

(*c*) Promote action by intergovernmental organizations in support of the struggle for liberation in South Africa;

(*d*) Support the World Campaign against Military and Nuclear Collaboration with South Africa, the International Defence and Aid Fund for Southern Africa, the International Committee of Solidarity with the Struggle of Women of South Africa and Namibia, and other bodies engaged in assistance to the struggle for liberation in South Africa;

(*e*) Exert all their influence to persuade those Governments which continue to collaborate with the apartheid regime to desist from such collaboration and implement United Nations resolutions against apartheid.

## III. Action by the specialized agencies and other intergovernmental organizations

21. All specialized agencies and other intergovernmental organizations should contribute to the maximum, within their respective mandates, to the international campaign against apartheid. In particular they should:

(*a*) Exclude the racist regime of South Africa from any participation in their organizations;

(*b*) Deny any assistance to the racist regime of South Africa;

(*c*) Invite representatives of the South African liberation movements recognized by the Organization of African Unity to attend their conferences and seminars and make financial provision for their participation;

(*d*) Provide appropriate assistance to the oppressed people of South Africa and to their liberation movements recognized by OAU;

(*e*) Disseminate information against apartheid in cooperation with the United Nations;

(*f*) Provide employment within their secretariats as appropriate and assistance for education and training to the oppressed people of South Africa;

(*g*) Withhold any facilities from, or investment of any funds in, banks, financial institutions and corporations that continue to give loans to or invest in South Africa;

(*h*) Refrain from any purchase of South African products, directly or indirectly;

(*i*) Deny any contracts or facilities to transnational corporations and financial institutions collaborating with South Africa;

(*j*) Prohibit any official travel by their employees in South African Airways or South African shipping lines;

(*k*) Deny any assistance to non-governmental organizations which collaborate with the apartheid regime and to institutions based on racial discrimination in South Africa;

(*l*) Cooperate with the Special Committee against Apartheid in the international campaign against apartheid;

22. The International Monetary Fund, in particular, should refrain from granting any credits to South Africa.

23. The International Atomic Energy Agency, in particular, should end all collaboration with the South African regime except with regard to inspection of nuclear facilities.

**IV. Action by trade unions, churches, anti-apartheid and solidarity movements and other non-governmental organizations and individuals**

24. All public organization should contribute to the international campaign against apartheid by mobilizing and organizing activities to educate public opinion about the crimes of the apartheid regime; to oppose the acts of aggression, destabilization and terrorism by the apartheid regime; to isolate the apartheid regime; and to assist the oppressed people and their liberation movements recognized by OAU in their struggle against apartheid.

25. They should concert and redouble their efforts, in cooperation with the Special Committee against Apartheid and the Centre against Apartheid, by contributing to this Programme of Action.

### A. *Education against apartheid*

26. All public organizations should pursue education programmes aimed at increasing understanding about the realities of apartheid.

27. Such programmes should involve the widest possible dissemination of information material (including leaflets and posters, pamphlets, films and other audiovisual material) with the purpose of:

(*a*) Informing the public of the crimes of apartheid;

(*b*) Exposing the apartheid regime bantustan policies;

(*c*) Demonstrating the consequences of South Af-

rica's policies of racial superiority in education, housing, employment, health care, land distribution, etc.;

(*d*) Alerting the public to the threat the policies of apartheid pose to international peace and security;

(*e*) Developing understanding of the legitimate struggle of the oppressed people of South Africa under the leadership of their national liberation movement for the eradication of apartheid and the establishment of a democratic society through the exercise of genuine self-determination by the people of the country as a whole.

### B. *Stop the apartheid war*

28. Public organizations should mobilize opposition to South Africa's policies of aggression, destabilization and terrorism aimed at independent African States in the region. Such mobilization should involve:

(*a*) Publicizing South Africa's acts of aggression against independent African States; its acts of international terrorism, including assassinations and abductions; its use of mercenaries and support of subversive groups; and its efforts to create political and economic instability in the region as a whole;

(*b*) Campaigning for effective solidarity with the front-line States and Lesotho, including assistance for the projects of the Southern African Development Coordination Conference;

(*c*) Alerting the public to the threat posed by South Africa's military and nuclear build-up and campaigning for an end to all forms of military and nuclear collaboration with South Africa:

(*d*) Providing assistance to victims of South African aggression;

(*e*) Upholding the right of the front-line States and Lesotho to defend their territorial integrity and security, including the securing of external military assistance for their defence against South African aggression.

### C. *No arms for apartheid*

29. All public organization should do everything in their power to ensure the strict implementation of the mandatory arms embargo against South Africa instituted by the Security Council and an end to all military collaboration with apartheid South Africa. In particular, public organizations should persuade Governments concerned to:

(*a*) Implement legislation to prevent the export of all forms of military, nuclear, police and other security material to South Africa, including all items which could enhance South Africa's military capability;

(*b*) Introduce measures to prevent South African-based subsidiaries or associates of parent companies under their jurisdiction from supplying arms or related material to the South African military or police;

(c) Ban the recruitment of mercenaries to serve in South Africa;

(d) Take all other necessary measures to ensure that the arms embargo is strengthened and strictly implemented.

30. They should organize campaigns to:

(a) Expose all breaches of the arms embargo;

(b) Focus attention on transnational corporations and other foreign interests involved, directly or through subsidiaries or affiliates, in supplying arms and related material to the South African military and police;

(c) Protest at any governmental action which undermines the arms embargo;

(d) Publicize the dangers ot international peace and security arising from the non-implementation of the arms embargo.

### D. *Stop the apartheid bomb*

31. Public organizations should be actively involved in the international campaign for a mandatory ban on all forms of nuclear collaboration with South Africa and in securing the support for such a measure from all Governments, especially the Western permanent members of the Security Council. They should organize to:

(a) Alert public opinion to the enormous dangers posed by continuing nuclear collaboration with South Africa;

(b) Press Governments concerned to:

(i) Terminate all agreements with South Africa in the nuclear field;

(ii) Prohibit the recruitment of nuclear scientists and engineers in their countries for South Africa's nuclear programme;

(iii) End all training, exchanges of personnel, information and know-how and all other related forms of collaboration in the nuclear field;

(iv) Stop imports of uranium from South Africa;

(v) Cease the delivery of any enriched uranium to South Africa;

(vi) Ensure the withdrawal of companies within their jurisdiction from South Africa's uranium industry;

(vii) End all forms of collaboration with South Africa's nuclear power programme, including government action to ban companies from tendering for nuclear contracts with South Africa.

### E. *Isolate apartheid South Africa*

32. Public organizations should press all Governments which continue to collaborate with apartheid South Africa to desist from such collaboration and to support the imposition of mandatory economic sanctions against South Africa under Chapter VII of the United Nations Charter. Such campaigns should focus in particular on the Western permanent members of the Security Council which have so far blocked such sanctions by the use or threat of veto. At the same time, public campaigns should be intensified in order to expose the role of economic collaboration in sustaining the apartheid system. These include campaigns for:

(a) The boycott of all products of apartheid South Africa;

(b) Disinvestment from companies operating in South Africa;

(c) Ending of loans to South Africa;

(d) The boycott of the major banks collaborating with South Africa;

(e) An embargo on the supply of oil and oil products to South Africa, focusing on the role of the major oil companies which continue to fuel the apartheid regime;

(f) An end to promotion of trade with South African through trade missions, export credits, etc.;

(g) An end to International Monetary Fund loans to South Africa;

(h) The boycott of South African Airways;

(i) Stopping airlines and shipping companies from providing services to and from South Africa.

33. Campaigns should be directed at particular companies whose collaboration with South Africa is strategically important. These campaigns should be organized in conjunction with educational activities designed to counter South African propaganda, e.g. alleged dependency on South African minerals, unemployment arising from sanctions, the consequences of sanctions for South Africa's Black population.

### F. *Don't play with apartheid*

34. Public organizations have a major contribution to make in strengthening the international sporting and cultural boycott of South Africa.

35. In the field of sports, they should press those Governments which have not yet done so to take effective measures to enforce the sports boycott, including the cancellation of visa-free entry privileges to South Africans, and the refusal of visas to South African sportsmen and women. In addition, campaigns should be organized to:

(a) Secure the expulsion of South Africa from all international sporting federations in which it still has membership;

(b) Mobilize opposition to all major sporting tours of South Africa and from South Africa;

(c) Persuade all national and local sporting organizations to sever all relations with apartheid sport;

(*d*)  Stop publicity or support by the media to sporting events, including the participation of South Africa;

(*e*)  Encourage individual sportsmen and women to refrain from participating in "pirate" tours and other sporting events in South Africa;

(*f*)  Counter South African propaganda promoting so-called "multinational" sport;

(*g*)  Support effective measures against individuals and sporting organizations which defy the international boycott;

(*h*)  Cooperate with the Special Committee against Apartheid in compiling the register of sports contacts with South Africa and securing action against those violating the boycott.

36.  The campaign to end all forms of collaboration in the cultural field should be intensified, including:

(*a*)  Action to persuade artists, musicians and entertainers to boycott South Africa;

(*b*)  Action to encourage authors, painters and filmmakers to refuse to allow their works to be performed or exhibited in South Africa;

(*c*)  Boycotts of pro-apartheid cultural groups undertaking international tours;

(*d*)  Support to appropriate measures against individuals and institutions which defy the cultural boycott;

(*e*)  Cooperation with the Special Committee against Apartheid in compiling and publicizing registers of collaborators with South Africa in the cultural field and in securing action against those violating the boycott.

### G.  *Don't work for apartheid*

37.  Public organizations can play a major role in discouraging individuals from emigrating to South Africa. Such activities include:

(*a*)  The dissemination of information setting out the case against emigrating to South Africa;

(*b*)  Demonstrating against South African recruitment activities;

(*c*)  Campaigning to secure the closure of recruitment offices for South Africa;

(*d*)  Action to stop the advertising of jobs in South Africa, including legislative measures.

### H.  *No apartheid tourism*

38.  Renewed efforts are required to stop tourism to South Africa which plays a dual function of strengthening the apartheid economy and promoting a false image of apartheid. Action in this respect should include:

(*a*)  Campaigning against companies and organizations promoting tourism to South Africa;

(*b*)  Picketing tourist agencies promoting tourism to South Africa;

(*c*)  Protesting against advertising promoting tourism to South Africa;

(*d*)  Demonstrating against offices of South African Airways and South African tourist organizations;

(*e*)  Distributing material setting out the case against visiting South Africa.

### I.  *Solidarity with South African political prisoners*

39.  Public organizations should intensify the international campaign for the release of South African political prisoners and educate public opinion about the repression by the apartheid regime against all those who resist apartheid. Activities should include:

(*a*)  Urging all Governments to intervene to secure the release of Nelson Mandela and all other political prisoners;

(*b*)  Giving special attention to the six PAC prisoners sentenced in 1963 and to women and juvenile prisoners;

(*c*)  Action to stop the execution of captured freedom fighters and to ensure that all such combatants are granted prisoner-of-war status in accordance with Additional Protocol I of the Geneva Conventions of 12 August 1949;

(*d*)  Organizing of protests against the inhuman and cruel treatment of detainees, including the use of torture resulting in deaths of detainees;

(*e*)  Providing assistance to the victims of South Africa's unjust laws by contributing to the International Defence and Aid Fund for Southern Africa.

### J.  *Solidarity with the South African liberation struggle*

40.  Public organizations can play an important role in educating public opinion about the long and heroic struggle against apartheid which involves all sections of the oppressed people, including trade unionists, women, youth and students, and religious organizations. They should organize material aid and other forms of solidarity with the liberation struggle. Essential actions should include:

(*a*)  Dissemination of information about the liberation struggle;

(*b*)  Establishment of solidarity funds;

(*c*)  Funding of projects for South African refugees;

(*d*)  Mobilizing solidarity with the day-to-day struggles of the oppressed people of South Africa;

(*e*)  Observing annually the International Day for the Elimination of Racial Discrimination, 21 March; the International Day of Solidarity with the Struggling People of South Africa, 16 June; the International Day of Solidarity with the Struggle of Women of South Africa and Namibia, 9 August; and the Day of Solidarity with South African Political Prisoners, 11 October.

Many public organizations can make specific contributions to this Programme of Action.

## 1. Trade unions

41. Trade unions should:

(a) Mobilize solidarity with the struggles of the Black workers of South Africa;

(b) Take action in response to the repression of Black workers and their unions;

(c) Refrain from loading or unloading any ships or planes destined for or coming from South Africa;

(d) Expose any collaboration between their employees and South Africa and take industrial action to stop it;

(e) Refuse to work on any military or nuclear project for South Africa;

(f) Ensure that trade union funds, pension funds, etc., are not invested in companies with South African subsidiaries or associates;

(g) Organize educational programmes involving the distribution of leaflets, posters, pamphlets, etc., for shop stewards, trade union activists and officials and trade union membership as a whole in order to mobilize effective solidarity with workers' struggles in South Africa;

(h) Support by all means possible the struggles of Black workers to form genuine trade unions and win trade union rights;

(i) Take disciplinary measures against trade unionists who emigrate to South Africa, including the withdrawal of their union membership cards.

42. Trade unions in particular industries can take certain specific actions. For instance, trade unions of printers can refuse to allow the publication of advertisements for jobs in South Africa.

## 2. Political parties

43. Political parties should:

(a) Pledge to implement the Programme of Action for Governments if elected to Government;

(b) Challenge the policies of governing parties which collaborate with apartheid South Africa;

(c) Encourage their members and supporters to join in anti-apartheid campaigns.

## 3. Corporations and employers

44. Corporations and employers should:

(a) Withdraw from any commercial operations with South Africa;

(b) Persuade employers' organizations to work for a policy of sanctions against South Africa;

(c) Implement the Declaration of the International Labour Organisation concerning the policy of apartheid in South Africa.

## 4. City and local authorities

45. City and local authorities should:

(a) Refrain from purchasing South African goods;

(b) Withdraw investments held by them in companies with interests in South Africa;

(c) Encourage the positive teaching of the history, culture and struggles of the oppressed people of South Africa;

(d) Ban South African propaganda from schools and libraries;

(e) Withhold the use of recreational facilities or other support for any sporting or cultural event with South African participation;

(f) Sever all official relations with South Africa and discourage economic links with South Africa;

(g) Honour leaders of the South African people.

## 5. Churches and religious organizations

46. Churches and religious organizations should:

(a) Ensure that their institutions divest totally from corporations with interests in South Africa and withdraw accounts with banks collaborating with apartheid;

(b) Organize protests against the persecution of religious leaders and other opponents of apartheid in South Africa;

(c) Disseminate information about the inhumanity of the apartheid system;

(d) Provide material assistance to the oppressed people of South Africa, refugees from South Africa, and the national liberation movement of South Africa;

(e) Mobilize their members and adherents in the anti-apartheid cause.

## 6. Sportsmen and women

47. Sportspersons should:

(a) Undertake not to participate in sporting events in South Africa or international events in which South Africa is represented;

(b) Ensure that their sporting organizations, local and national, have severed all relations with apartheid sport;

(c) Protest at the persecution of non-racial sportsmen and women and sports administrators who are struggling for non-racial sport;

(d) Campaign for the expulsion of South Africa from all international sports federations and competitions;

(e) Cooperate with the Special Committee against Apartheid and the South African Non-Racial Olympic Committee (SAN-ROC) in ensuring the total isolation of South Africa from international sport.

## 7. Writers, artists and musicians

48. Writers, artists and musicians should:

(a) Undertake not to participate in cultural events in South Africa or permit their works to be performed or exhibited in South Africa;

(b) Ensure that their trade union or association fully supports the cultural boycott;

(c) Contribute to the international campaign against apartheid by giving performances for assistance to South African refugees or their national liberation movement.

### 8. *Educationalists*

49. Educationalists should:

(a) Ensure that all forms of collaboration with the apartheid educational system are severed, including exchange visits;

(b) Encourage the positive teaching of the struggle against apartheid;

(c) Press for the banning of all South African propaganda from schools and other educational institutions.

### 9. *Women's organizations*

50. Women's organizations should:

(a) Mobilize women in solidarity with the struggles of the Black women of South Africa against apartheid;

(b) Distribute material highlighting the oppression experienced by Black women in South Africa and the role of women in the national liberation struggle:

(c) Protest at the victimization of women engaged in the struggle against apartheid;

(d) Provide material assistance for South African women refugees and the women's section of the liberation movements recognized by OAU.

### 10. *Youth and students*

51. Youth and students should:

(a) Campaign to break all ties between their educational institutions and South Africa including disinvestment from companies with interests in South Africa;

(b) Work for the banning of all South African products from their educational institutions;

(c) Mobilize solidarity with the struggles of the youth and students of South Africa including protests against the repression of youth and student leaders;

(d) Distribute material about the nature of the apartheid education system;

(e) Participate actively in anti-apartheid campaigns.

### 11. *Health workers*

52. Doctors, nurses and other health workers should:

(a) Campaign to sever all ties between medical and other health organizations, including professional bodies, with racist health bodies in South Africa;

(b) Protest at the abuse of health care in South Africa, including the complicity of health personnel with the South African security forces;

(c) Organize medical aid campaigns for the national liberation movement.

### 12. *Peace organizations*

53. Peace organizations should:

(a) Highlight the threat South Africa poses to international peace and security;

(b) Campaign against South Africa's nuclear plans and capability;

(c) Participate in campaigns to stop all military and nuclear collaboration with South Africa;

(d) Support the world campaign against military and nuclear collaboration with South Africa.

## V. Action by the Secretary-General of the United Nations

54. The Secretary-General of the United Nations should take all appropriate steps to promote the implementation of this Programme of Action, and provide all necessary services to the Special Committee against Apartheid to enable it to discharge its mandate.

55. He should, in particular:

(a) Instruct all relevant units of the Secretariat to cooperate fully with the Special Committee and the Centre against Apartheid in promoting the international campaign against apartheid;

(b) Withhold any facilities from, or investment of any funds in, banks, financial institutions and other corporations that continue to give loans to or invest in South Africa;

(c) Refrain from any purchase of South African products, directly or indirectly;

(d) Take action to prevent any officially sponsored travel of United Nations officials, consultants and others on South African Airways or South African shipping lines.

## VI. Action by the Special Committee against Apartheid and the Centre against Apartheid

56. The Special Committee against Apartheid, with the assistance of the Centre against Apartheid, should take all appropriate measures to promote concerted action against apartheid by Governments and intergovernmental and non-governmental organizations. It should promote coordinated international campaigns:

(a) For assistance to the oppressed people of South Africa and their national liberation movement, as well as independent African States subjected to acts of aggression, destabilization and terrorism by the apartheid regime;

(b) For an effective arms embargo against South Africa;

(c) Against all forms of nuclear cooperation with South Africa;

(d) Against all collaboration by Governments, banks and transnational corporations with South Africa;

*(e)* For comprehensive and mandatory sanctions against South Africa under Chapter VII of the Charter of the United Nations;

*(f)* Against propaganda by the racist regime of South Africa and its collaborators;

*(g)* For the unconditional release of South African political prisoners;

*(h)* For the boycott of racially selected South African sports teams;

*(i)* For an academic and cultural boycott of South Africa.

57. The Special Committee should mobilize the public—including writers, artists, entertainers, sportsmen, religious leaders, students, etc.—all over the world in support of the struggle for liberation in South Africa and for the total isolation of the apartheid regime.

58. It should continue and increase cooperation with parliaments, local authorities, anti-apartheid and solidarity movements, peace movements, trade unions, religious bodies, and other non-governmental organizations of students, women and others, as well as educational and other institutions, in promoting the international campaign against apartheid.

59. It should constantly review and publicize the implementation of United Nations resolutions against apartheid.

60. It should organize conferences and seminars, and arrange for studies, publications, films, exhibits, etc., on all aspects of the international campaign against apartheid, including collaboration with South Africa by Governments, transnational corporations, financial institutions and other interests.

# Document 112

*Appeal by the Special Committee against Apartheid to the cities of the world, issued on 21 March 1984*

A/AC.115/L.606, 4 April 1984

The Special Committee against Apartheid has followed with great interest and satisfaction the actions taken by cities in many countries to demonstrate their abhorrence of apartheid and their support for the just struggle of the oppressed peoples of South Africa and Namibia for freedom.

Many cities in African, non-aligned, Socialist and other nations have taken firm action for total isolation of South Africa. They were also joined by some cities in the West when the movement for the boycott of South Africa in 1959 took place.

More recently, the Special Committee was greatly encouraged by the support of over 200 mayors to the appeal launched by the Mayor of Glasgow in 1982 for the release of Nelson Mandela and all other political prisoners in South Africa. It was equally gratified by the action taken by a number of cities, especially in the United Kingdom, beginning with Sheffield, in adopting concrete declarations against apartheid and proclaiming themselves apartheid-free zones. It has warmly welcomed the actions of cities in the United States of America which have decided to disinvest their accounts and pension funds from corporations involved in South Africa.

These moves by cities were actively encouraged and commended by the Special Committee, as it attaches great importance to actions by cities against apartheid. The city authorities can take significant action, even within the limits of their legal powers, to stop collaboration with apartheid South Africa. They can help educate millions of citizens on the evils of apartheid and encourage their active participation in the campaign against apartheid. They can thereby encourage national Governments which have not yet done so to take energetic action in accordance with the United Nations resolutions on apartheid.

Actions by them are a source of great encouragement to the oppressed people of South Africa and give significant support to the efforts of the United Nations.

Many cities of the world are multiracial. Action against apartheid can be an integral part of their efforts against racism.

On this International Day for the Elimination of Racial Discrimination, the Special Committee makes an earnest appeal to all cities of the world to take appropriate action against apartheid, in the light of the present critical situation in southern Africa and in observance of the Second Decade of Action to Combat Racism and Racial Discrimination. It urges all citizens to promote and support such action.

In the light of the initiatives of the many cities which have already taken action, the Special Committee suggests the following for consideration, as appropriate:

1. Declare abhorrence of apartheid in South Africa and illegal occupation of Namibia;

2. Cease purchase of any goods originating from South Africa and Namibia;

3. Withdraw all investments in companies owned

or partly owned by South African interests, or operating in South Africa;

4. Take appropriate initiatives to discourage transnational corporations and financial institutions from investing in, or making loans to, South Africa;

5. Withhold city facilities from any sporting or cultural event involving South Africans and Namibians in contravention of United Nations resolutions, or sportsmen or entertainers who have toured South Africa and are included in the registers of the United Nations Special Committee against Apartheid;

6. Encourage teaching about evils of apartheid and the struggle of the oppressed peoples of South Africa and Namibia; arrange anti-apartheid exhibits and other such events;

7. Prohibit display or official South African propaganda in schools, libraries or other facilities;

8. Prohibit advertisement of South African products at sites and facilities controlled by the city;

9. Honour opponents of apartheid through award of freedom of city or naming of streets, buildings and parks;

10. Support the anti-apartheid movements in the region; and

11. Organize appropriate events to publicize its commitment against apartheid and encourage all citizens to take appropriate action.

The Special Committee appreciates that some of these measures are redundant in countries where national Governments have instituted comprehensive sanctions against South Africa. It recognizes that action by cities is particularly important in Western countries where the national Governments have failed to implement United Nations resolutions against apartheid. But in all countries, cities can and should take action appropriate and relevant to them.

Apartheid, an affront to the conscience and dignity of mankind, and indeed a crime against humanity, must be eradicated. The cities of the world can make an important contribution in meeting the supreme moral challenge of apartheid. The Special Committee trusts that they will act.

The Special Committee would appreciate information from all cities on action they have taken, or plan to take, in this respect.

# Document 113

*Security Council resolution: The question of South Africa*

S/RES/554 (1984), 17 August 1984

*The Security Council,*

  . . .

*Convinced* that the so-called "new constitution" endorsed on 2 November 1983 by the exclusively White electorate in South Africa would continue the process of denationalization of the indigenous African majority, depriving it of all fundamental rights, and further entrench apartheid, transforming South Africa into a country for "Whites only",

*Aware* that the inclusion in the "new constitution" of the so-called "coloured" people and people of Asian origin is aimed at dividing the unity of the oppressed people of South Africa and fomenting internal conflict,

*Noting with grave concern* that one of the objectives of the so-called "constitution" of the racist regime is to make the "coloured" people and people of Asian origin in South Africa eligible for conscription into the armed forces of the apartheid regime for further internal repression and aggressive acts against independent African States,

*Welcoming* the massive united resistance of the oppressed people of South Africa against these "constitutional" manoeuvres,

  . . .

*Firmly convinced* that the so-called "elections" to be organized by the Pretoria regime in the current month of August for the "coloured" people and people of Asian origin and the implementation of this "new constitution" will inevitably aggravate tension in South Africa and in southern Africa as a whole,

1. *Declares* that the so-called "new constitution" is contrary to the principles of the Charter of the United Nations, that the results of the referendum of 2 November 1983 are of no validity whatsoever and that the enforcement of the "new constitution" will further aggravate the already explosive situation prevailing inside apartheid South Africa;

2. *Strongly rejects and declares as null and void* the so-called "new constitution" and the "elections" to be organized in the current month of August for the "coloured" people and people of Asian origin as well as all insidious manoeuvres by the racist minority regime of South Africa further to entrench White minority rule and apartheid;

3. *Further rejects* any so-called "negotiated settlement" based on bantustan structures or on the so-called "new constitution";

4. *Solemnly declares* that only the total eradication

of apartheid and the establishment of a non-racial democratic society based on majority rule, through the full and free exercise of universal adult suffrage by all the people in a united and unfragmented South Africa, can lead to a just and lasting solution of the explosive situation in South Africa;

5. *Urges* all Governments and organizations not to accord recognition to the results of the so-called "elections" and to take appropriate action, in cooperation with the United Nations and the Organization of African Unity and in accordance with the present resolution, to assist the oppressed people of South Africa in their legitimate struggle for a non-racial, democratic society;

. . .

# Document 114

*Telegram dated 27 November 1984 from the Chairman of the Special Committee against Apartheid, Major-General J. N. Garba (Nigeria), to Mr. Walter Fauntroy, Mrs. Mary Frances Berry and Mr. Randall Robinson, Washington, D.C., commending non-violent direct action in support of the oppressed people of South Africa*

United Nations Centre against Apartheid Information Note No. 61/84

On behalf of United Nations Special Committee against Apartheid, I commend you for initiating non-violent direct action in support of the oppressed people of South Africa.

The apartheid regime has resorted to the deployment of armed forces against citizens of African townships, indiscriminate killings, detentions of public leaders, mass arrests and dismissals of thousands of workers in response to peaceful protests by the people against increases in rents and bus fares, gross discrimination in education, and an obnoxious new constitution denying any rights to the African majority. It hopes by brute force to suppress legitimate resistance against its diabolic plans to entrench White domination by dispossessing the African majority and even to enforce hegemony over southern Africa.

The regime has however become desperate because of courageous resistance by great majority of people of the country. Unfortunately, it continues to be encouraged in its disastrous course by policy of constructive engagement pursued by the United States.

The brutality of apartheid regime is an outrage against conscience of humanity, and international community must stay the hands of that criminal regime which does not hesitate to kill even little children in order to perpetuate itself in power.

We count in particular on action by people in the United States. The United States bears great responsibility and it has the power to stop the racist violence.

I hope that your commendable initiative, in the best traditions of the struggle for human rights in the United States, will receive widest support. We salute you.

[Editor's note: The three African-American leaders staged a sit-in at the South African Embassy in Washington on 21 November and were arrested. The Special Committee granted a hearing to Mr. Fauntroy and consulted with him on extending the direct action. Subsequently such actions took place in many cities and thousands of Americans courted arrest in the "Free South Africa Movement".]

# Document 115

*Statement by the President of the Security Council, on behalf of the Council, expressing grave concern over the killing and wounding of innocent people by the South African police in the town of Uitenhage, 21 March 1985*

S/17050, 22 March 1985

The members of the Security Council have entrusted me to express on their behalf their grave concern over the rapid deterioration of the situation in South Africa resulting from the spate of violence against defenceless opponents of apartheid throughout the country and most recently in the town of Uitenhage on 21 March 1985 where the South African police opened fire on innocent people proceeding to a funeral, killing and wounding scores of them.

The members of the Council strongly deplore such acts of violence, which can only further aggravate the situation in South Africa and make more difficult the search for a peaceful solution of the South African conflict.

The members of the Council recall the provisions of resolution 560 (1985), adopted unanimously on 12 March 1985, in which the Council noted with deep concern the intensification of repression in South Africa against apartheid, and reaffirmed the legitimacy of their struggle for a united, non-racial and democratic South Africa.

The members of the Council urge the Government of South Africa to end violence and repression against the Black people and other opponents of apartheid and to take urgent measures to eliminate apartheid.

# Document 116

*Security Council resolution: The question of South Africa*

S/RES/569 (1985), 26 July 1985

*The Security Council,*

*Deeply concerned* at the worsening of the situation in South Africa and at the continuance of the human suffering that the apartheid system, which the Council strongly condemns, is causing in that country,

*Outraged* at the repression, and condemning the arbitrary arrests of hundreds of persons,

*Considering* that the imposition of the state of emergency in thirty-six districts of the Republic of South Africa constitutes a grave deterioration in the situation in that country,

*Considering* as totally unacceptable the practice by the South African Government of detention without trial and of forcible removal, as well as the discriminatory legislation in force,

*Acknowledging* the legitimacy of the aspirations of the South African population as a whole to benefit from all civil and political rights and to establish a united non-racial and democratic society,

*Acknowledging* further that the very cause of the situation in South Africa lies in the policy of apartheid and the practices of the South African Government,

1. *Strongly condemns* the apartheid system and all the policies and practices deriving therefrom;

2. *Strongly condemns* the mass arrests and detentions recently carried out by the Pretoria Government and the murders which have been committed;

3. *Strongly condemns* the establishment of the state of emergency in the thirty-six districts in which it has been imposed and demands that it be lifted immediately;

4. *Calls upon* the South African Government to set free immediately and unconditionally all political prisoners and detainees, first of all Mr. Nelson Mandela;

5. *Reaffirms* that only the total elimination of apartheid and the establishment in South Africa of a free, united and democratic society on the basis of universal suffrage can lead to a solution;

6. *Urges* States Members of the United Nations to adopt measures against South Africa, such as the following:

(*a*) Suspension of all new investment in South Africa;

(*b*) Prohibition of the sale of krugerrands and all other coins minted in South Africa;

(*c*) Restrictions on sports and cultural relations;

(*d*) Suspension of guaranteed export loans;

(*e*) Prohibition of all new contracts in the nuclear field;

(*f*) Prohibition of all sales of computer equipment that may be used by the South African army and police;

7. *Commends* those States which have already adopted voluntary measures against the Pretoria Government and urges them to adopt new provisions, and invites those which have not yet done so to follow their example;

. . .

# Document 117

*Statement by the President of the Security Council, on behalf of the Council, on the situation in South Africa*

S/17413, 21 August 1985

The members of the Security Council, deeply alarmed by the worsening and deteriorating situation of the oppressed Black majority population in South Africa since the imposition of the state of emergency on 21 July 1985, express once again their profound concern at this deplorable situation.

The members of the Council condemn the Pretoria regime for its continued failure to heed the repeated appeals made by the international community including Security Council resolution 569 of 26 July 1985 and in particular the demand made in that resolution for the immediate lifting of the state of emergency.

The members of the Council strongly condemn the continuation of killings and the arbitrary mass arrests and detentions carried out by the Pretoria government. They call, once again, upon the South African government to set free immediately and unconditionally all political prisoners and detainees, first of all Mr. Nelson Mandela, whose home has lately been subjected to an act of arson.

The members of the Council believe that a just and lasting solution in South Africa must be based on the total eradication of the system of apartheid and the establishment of a free, united and democratic society in South Africa. Without concrete action towards such a just and lasting solution in South Africa any pronouncements of the Pretoria regime can represent nothing more than a reaffirmation of its attachment to apartheid and underline its continuing intransigence in the face of mounting domestic and international opposition to the continuation of this thoroughly unjustified political and social system. In this context, they express their grave concern at the latest pronouncement of the President of the Pretoria regime.

# Document 118

*General Assembly resolution: Policies of apartheid of the Government of South Africa—International Convention against Apartheid in Sports*

A/RES/40/64 G, 10 December 1985

[Editor's note: The International Convention against Apartheid in Sports came into force on 3 April 1988. As at 15 July 1994, 76 States had signed the Convention and 56 had ratified it or acceded to it.]

*The States Parties to the present Convention,*

*Recalling* the provisions of the Charter of the United Nations, in which all Members pledged themselves to take joint and separate action, in cooperation with the Organization, for the achievement of universal respect for, and observance of, human rights and fundamental freedoms for all without distinction as to race, sex, language or religion,

*Considering* that the Universal Declaration of Human Rights proclaims that all human beings are born free and equal in dignity and rights and that everyone is entitled to all the rights and freedoms set forth in the Declaration without distinction of any kind, particularly in regard to race, colour or national origin,

*Observing* that, in accordance with the International Convention on the Elimination of All Forms of Racial Discrimination, States Parties to that Convention particularly condemn racial segregation and apartheid and undertake to prevent, prohibit and eradicate all practices of this nature in all fields,

*Observing* that the General Assembly of the United Nations has adopted a number of resolutions condemning the practice of apartheid in sports and has affirmed its unqualified support for the Olympic principle that no discrimination be allowed on the grounds of race, religion or political affiliation and that merit should be the sole criterion for participation in sports activities,

*Considering* that the International Declaration against Apartheid in Sports, which was adopted by the General Assembly on 4 December 1977, solemnly affirms the necessity for the speedy elimination of apartheid in sports,

*Recalling* the provisions of the International Convention on the Suppression and Punishment of the Crime of Apartheid and recognizing, in particular, that participation in sports exchanges with teams selected on the basis of apartheid directly abets and encourages the commission of the crime of apartheid, as defined in that Convention,

*Resolved* to adopt all necessary measures to eradicate the practice of apartheid in sports and to promote international sports contacts based on the Olympic principle,

*Recognizing* that sports contact with any country practising apartheid in sports condones and strengthens apartheid in violation of the Olympic principle and thereby becomes the legitimate concern of all Governments,

*Desiring* to implement the principles embodied in the International Declaration against Apartheid in Sports and to secure the earliest adoption of practical measures to that end,

*Convinced* that the adoption of an International Convention against Apartheid in Sports would result in more effective measures at the international and national levels, with a view to eliminating apartheid in sports,

*Have agreed* as follows:

### Article 1

For the purposes of the present Convention:

(*a*) The expression "apartheid" shall mean a system of institutionalized racial segregation and discrimination for the purpose of establishing and maintaining domination by one racial group of persons over another racial group of persons and systematically oppressing them, such as that pursued by South Africa, and "apartheid in sports" shall mean the application of the policies and practices of such a system in sports activities, whether organized on a professional or an amateur basis;

(*b*) The expression "national sports facilities" shall mean any sports facility operated within the framework of a sports programme conducted under the auspices of a national government;

(*c*) The expression "Olympic principle" shall mean the principle that no discrimination be allowed on the grounds of race, religion or political affiliation;

(*d*) The expression "sports contracts" shall mean any contract concluded for the organization, promotion, performance or derivative rights, including servicing, of any sports activity;

(*e*) The expression "sports bodies" shall mean any organization constituted to organize sports activities at the national level, including national Olympic committees, national sports federations or national governing sports committees;

(*f*) The expression "team" shall mean a group of sportsmen organized for the purpose of participating in sports activities in competition with other such organized groups;

(*g*) The expression "sportsmen" shall mean men and women who participate in sports activities on an individual or team basis, as well as managers, coaches, trainers and other officials whose functions are essential for the operation of a team.

### Article 2

States Parties strongly condemn apartheid and undertake to pursue immediately by all appropriate means the policy of eliminating the practice of apartheid in all its forms from sports.

### Article 3

States Parties shall not permit sports contact with a country practising apartheid and shall take appropriate action to ensure that their sports bodies, teams, and individual sportsmen do not have such contact.

### Article 4

States Parties shall take all possible measures to prevent sports contact with a country practising apartheid and shall ensure that effective means exist for bringing about compliance with such measures.

### Article 5

States Parties shall refuse to provide financial or other assistance to enable their sports bodies, teams and individual sportsmen to participate in sports activities in a country practising apartheid or with teams or individual sportsmen selected on the basis of apartheid.

### Article 6

Each State Party shall take appropriate action against its sports bodies, teams and individual sportsmen that participate in sports activities in a country practising apartheid or with teams representing a country practising apartheid, which in particular shall include:

(*a*) Refusal to provide financial or other assistance for any purpose to such sports bodies, teams and individual sportsmen;

(*b*) Restriction of access to national sports facilities by such sports bodies, teams and individual sportsmen;

(*c*) Non-enforceability of all sports contracts which involve sports activities in a country practising apartheid or with teams or individual sportsmen selected on the basis of apartheid;

(*d*) Denial and withdrawal of national honours or awards in sports to such teams and individual sportsmen;

(*e*) Denial of official receptions in honour of such teams or sportsmen.

## Article 7

States Parties shall deny visas and/or entry to representatives of sports bodies, teams and individual sportsmen representing a country practising apartheid.

## Article 8

States Parties shall take all appropriate action to secure the expulsion of a country practising apartheid from international and regional sports bodies.

## Article 9

States Parties shall take all appropriate measures to prevent international sports bodies from imposing financial or other penalties on affiliated bodies which, in accordance with United Nations resolutions, the provisions of the present Convention and the spirit of the Olympic principle, refuse to participate in sports with a country practising apartheid.

## Article 10

1. States Parties shall use their best endeavours to ensure universal compliance with the Olympic principle of non-discrimination and the provisions of the present Convention.

2. Towards this end, States Parties shall prohibit entry into their countries of members of teams and individual sportsmen participating or who have participated in sports competitions in South Africa and shall prohibit entry into their countries of representatives of sports bodies, members of teams and individual sportsmen who invite on their own initiative sports bodies, teams and sportsmen officially representing a country practising apartheid and participating under its flag. States Parties may also prohibit entry of representatives of sports bodies, members of teams or individual sportsmen who maintain sports contacts with sports bodies, teams or sportsmen representing a country practising apartheid and participating under its flag. Prohibition of entry should not violate the regulations of the relevant sports federations which support the elimination of apartheid in sports and shall apply only to participation in sports activities.

3. States Parties shall advise their national representatives to international sports federations to take all possible and practical steps to prevent the participation of the sports bodies, teams and sportsmen referred to in paragraph 2 above in international sports competitions and shall, through their representatives in international sports organizations, take every possible measure:

(a) To ensure the expulsion of South Africa from all federations in which it still holds membership as well as to deny South Africa reinstatement to membership in any federation from which it has been expelled;

(b) In case of national federations condoning sports exchanges with a country practising apartheid, to impose sanctions against such national federations including, if necessary, expulsion from the relevant international sports organization and exclusion of their representatives from participation in international sports competitions.

4. In cases of flagrant violations of the provisions of the present Convention, States Parties shall take appropriate action as they deem fit, including, where necessary, steps aimed at the exclusion of the responsible national sports governing bodies, national sports federations or sportsmen of the countries concerned from international sports competition.

5. The provisions of the present article relating specifically to South Africa shall cease to apply when the system of apartheid is abolished in that country.

## Article 11

1. There shall be established a Commission against apartheid in Sports (hereinafter referred to as "the Commission") consisting of fifteen members of high moral character and committed to the struggle against apartheid, particular attention being paid to participation of persons having experience in sports administration, elected by the States Parties from among their nationals, having regard to the most equitable geographical distribution and the representation of the principal legal systems.

2. The members of the Commission shall be elected by secret ballot from a list of persons nominated by the States Parties. Each State Party may nominate one person from among its own nationals.

3. The initial election shall be held six months after the date of the entry into force of the present Convention. At least three months before the date of each election, the Secretary-General of the United Nations shall address a letter to the States Parties inviting them to submit their nominations within two months. The Secretary-General shall prepare a list in alphabetical order of all persons thus nominated, indicating the States Parties which have nominated them, and shall submit it to the States Parties.

4. Elections of the members of the Commission shall be held at a meeting of States Parties convened by the Secretary-General at United Nations Headquarters. At that meeting, for which two thirds of the States Parties shall constitute a quorum, the persons elected to the Commission shall be those nominees who obtain the largest number of votes and an absolute majority of the votes of the representatives of States Parties present and voting.

5. The members of the Commission shall be elected for a term of four years. However, the terms of nine of the members elected at the first election shall expire at the

end of two years; immediately after the first election, the names of these nine members shall be chosen by lot by the Chairman of the Commission.

6. For the filling of casual vacancies, the State Party whose national has ceased to function as a member of the Commission shall appoint another person from among its nationals, subject to the approval of the Commission.

7. States Parties shall be responsible for the expenses of the members of the Commission while they are in performance of Commission duties.

### Article 12

1. States Parties undertake to submit to the Secretary-General of the United Nations, for consideration by the Commission, a report on the legislative, judicial, administrative or other measures which they have adopted to give effect to the provisions of the present Convention within one year of its entry into force and thereafter every two years. The Commission may request further information from the States Parties.

2. The Commission shall report annually through the Secretary-General to the General Assembly of the United Nations on its activities and may make suggestions and general recommendations based on the examination of the reports and information received from the States Parties. Such suggestions and recommendations shall be reported to the General Assembly together with comments, if any, from States Parties concerned.

3. The Commission shall examine, in particular, the implementation of the provisions of article 10 of the present Convention and make recommendations on action to be undertaken.

4. A meeting of States Parties shall be convened by the Secretary-General at the request of a majority of the States Parties to consider further action with respect to the implementation of the provisions of article 10 of the present Convention. In cases of flagrant violation of the provisions of the present Convention, a meeting of States Parties shall be convened by the Secretary-General at the request of the Commission.

### Article 13

1. Any State Party may at any time declare that it recognizes the competence of the Commission to receive and examine complaints concerning breaches of the provisions of the present Convention submitted by States Parties which have also made such a declaration. The Commission may decide on the appropriate measures to be taken in respect of breaches.

2. States Parties against which a complaint has been made, in accordance with paragraph 1 of the present article, shall be entitled to be represented and take part in the proceedings of the Commission.

### Article 14

1. The Commission shall meet at least once a year.

2. The Commission shall adopt its own rules of procedure.

3. The secretariat of the Commission shall be provided by the Secretary-General of the United Nations.

4. The meetings of the Commission shall normally be held at United Nations Headquarters.

5. The Secretary-General shall convene the initial meeting of the Commission.

### Article 15

The Secretary-General of the United Nations shall be the depositary of the present Convention.

### Article 16

1. The present Convention shall be open for signature at United Nations Headquarters by all States until its entry into force.

2. The present Convention shall be subject to ratification, acceptance or approval by the signatory States.

### Article 17

The present Convention shall be open for accession by all States.

### Article 18

1. The present Convention shall enter into force on the thirtieth day after the date of deposit with the Secretary-General of the United Nations of the twenty-seventh instrument of ratification, acceptance, approval or accession.

2. For each State ratifying, accepting, approving or acceding to the present Convention after its entry into force, the Convention shall enter into force on the thirtieth day after the date of deposit of the relevant instrument.

### Article 19

Any dispute between States Parties arising out of the interpretation, application or implementation of the present Convention which is not settled by negotiation shall be brought before the International Court of Justice at the request and with the mutual consent of the States parties to the dispute, save where the Parties to the dispute have agreed on some other form of settlement.

### Article 20

1. Any State Party may propose an amendment or revision to the present Convention and file it with the depositary. The Secretary-General of the United Nations shall thereupon communicate the proposed amendment or revision to the States Parties with a request that they

notify him whether they favour a conference of States Parties for the purpose of considering and voting upon the proposal. In the event that at least one third of the States Parties favour such a conference, the Secretary-General shall convene the conference under the auspices of the United Nations. Any amendment or revision adopted by the majority of the States Parties present and voting at the conference shall be submitted to the General Assembly of the United Nations for approval.

2. Amendments or revisions shall come into force when they have been approved by the General Assembly and accepted by a two-thirds majority of the States Parties, in accordance with their respective constitutional processes.

3. When amendments or revisions come into force,

they shall be binding on those States Parties which have accepted them, other States Parties still being bound by the provisions of the present Convention and any earlier amendment or revision which they have accepted.

*Article 21*

A State Party may withdraw from the present Convention by written notification to the depositary. Such withdrawal shall take effect one year after the date of receipt of the notification by the depositary.

*Article 22*

The present Convention has been concluded in Arabic, Chinese, English, French, Russian and Spanish, all texts being equally authentic.

# Document 119

*Declaration adopted by the World Conference on Sanctions against Racist South Africa, Paris, 20 June 1986*

A/CONF.137/5, 1986

## I. Introduction

1. The World Conference on Sanctions against Racist South Africa met at a most critical time in South Africa and in southern Africa, emphasizing the need for urgent and effective international action.

2. The opening of the Conference coincided with the tenth anniversary of the brutal massacre of hundreds of innocent schoolchildren in Soweto. It served as a sombre reminder of the nature of the monstrous regime in Pretoria.

3. The day on which the Conference was convened coincided also with a resoundingly successful general strike, possibly the biggest in the history of South Africa, called by the Congress of South African Trade Unions and other democratic forces, clearly demonstrating that the draconian measures imposed by the regime have not cowed the people into submission.

4. The racist regime has stepped up its massive repression of, and violence against, the oppressed majority of the population of South Africa in a desperate attempt to suppress the intensified resistance of the people and to perpetuate racist domination. Rejecting a just, peaceful and negotiated settlement of the conflict with the genuine representatives of the vast majority of the people, it has declared a State of Emergency in the country and relied on force and violence to detain thousands of persons involved in the struggle against apartheid. It has increasingly resorted to aggression against, and destabilization of, the neighbouring independent African States

on the pretext that they have provided facilities to the liberation movements recognized by the Organization of African Unity, the Movement of Non-Aligned Countries and the United Nations. The entire region is engulfed in tension and conflict and, as a result of the policies and actions of the racist regime, there is a clear and present danger that arises from a manifest breach of international peace and security, with incalculable consequences in terms of bloodshed and loss of life and property.

5. However, the great advance of the struggle for freedom in South Africa and the international support that the peoples of Southern Africa have secured for their legitimate aspirations have brought closer the speedy and total elimination of apartheid and the attainment by those peoples of freedom and peace.

6. The present threat to international peace and security posed by the racist regime of South Africa arises, inter alia, from three principal causes: (a) its ever increasing internal repression and brutality in the perpetuation of apartheid; (b) its continuing illegal occupation of Namibia; and (c) its acts of aggression, subversion, destabilization and terrorism against the independent African States.

7. In spite of the actions of the regime to entrench apartheid and dispossess the Black majority of its rights through ruthless repression and violence, there is an unprecedented mass upsurge against apartheid.

8. The racist regime has failed to suppress the resistance despite the proclamation of a State of Emer-

gency, the greatly increased repression and violence, including the dispatch of armed forces into African townships and education institutions, the shooting of peaceful demonstrators and even mourners at funeral processions, and the use of vigilantes for terrorist acts against opponents of apartheid. Thousands of people, including many children, have been killed and wounded by the security forces who have been granted immunity for their acts. Many more have been imprisoned, tortured and restricted. Severe restrictions have been imposed on the media.

9. The South African regime has continued its illegal occupation of Namibia, a Territory for which the United Nations assumed direct responsibility in 1966, and has continued to use the Territory for aggression against independent African States. The struggle of the Namibian people for independence has greatly advanced under the leadership of the South West Africa People's Organization (SWAPO), which has gained ever wider and stronger support from the Namibian people as well as the recognition by the Organization of African Unity, the Movement of Non-Aligned Countries and the United Nations General Assembly as the sole and authentic representative of the Namibian people.

10. The South African regime, however, is preventing the implementation of the United Nations plan for the independence of Namibia, endorsed by the Security Council in resolution 435 (1978); it embarks on repeated attempts to impose its puppets on the people of Namibia, thereby prolonging the conflict and suffering.

11. The South African regime continues, moreover, to commit numerous acts of aggression, subversion, destabilization and terrorism against independent African States, including deliberate massacre of refugees, causing enormous human and material damage, as well as against the ships, aircraft and nationals of other countries. It has instigated and supported subversive groups engaged in terrorism in those States. It has defied United Nations resolutions calling for an immediate cessation of such actions and for the payment of compensation to the States concerned. The South African actions have been held to be a clear illustration of the policies of state terrorism.

12. The attacks by South African forces on the capitals of Botswana, Zimbabwe and Zambia on 19 May 1986, as well as new acts of aggression against Angola, reflect a more serious threat than ever before and underline the imperative need for international action with determination and a sense of urgency.

13. The racist regime persists, however, in attempting to perpetuate White domination instead of complying with the demands of the great majority of the people, and of the international community, for the release of all political prisoners, and for a cessation of repression and

for negotiations to eliminate apartheid and to establish a non-racial democratic State based on universal franchise and majority rule.

14. The World Conference stresses that the racist regime of South Africa, the only regime that practises racism as its official policy and has enshrined it in its so-called "constitution", has its roots in the same racist and bellicose ideology that provoked the Second World War and caused untold deaths and destruction. Appeasement of the racist regime therefore can only have the same disastrous consequences. The Conference notes that the policy and practices of the apartheid regime have already brought South Africa to the brink of a racial conflagration.

15. The World Conference holds the racist regime solely responsible for the conflict and violence in South Africa and Namibia, for the constant acts of aggression and breaches of the peace in the whole of southern Africa and for the growing threat to international peace and security. It acts as an outlaw, persistently violating the provisions of the Charter of the United Nations and defying the resolutions of the General Assembly and the Security Council. Its continued occupation of Namibia is, moreover, a direct challenge to the authority of the United Nations and of the International Court of Justice.

16. The elimination of apartheid, the root cause of the crisis in southern Africa, is indispensable for the attainment of peace and stability in the sub-region.

17. Apartheid is not only a crime against the people of South Africa and Namibia, but one of universal concern. The General Assembly has condemned the policy of apartheid as a crime against humanity.

18. Apartheid cannot be reformed and no encouragement should be given to any so-called reform. It must be totally uprooted and destroyed. The destiny of South Africa must be decided by all the people of the country exercising their right to self-determination—irrespective of race, colour, sex or creed—on the basis of complete equality.

19. The United Nations has a direct responsibility to ensure the independence of Namibia through free elections and the exercise of the right of self-determination by its people in accordance with all relevant General Assembly and Security Council resolutions, in particular, Security Council resolution 435 (1978). It has an inescapable responsibility to end South Africa's constant breaches of peace and acts of aggression in the region.

20. The World Conference considered the means by which the United Nations and the international community could discharge their responsibility in accordance with the Charter of the United Nations, including especially the application of comprehensive mandatory sanctions under Chapter VII of the Charter as the most

effective means to deal with threats to the peace, breaches of peace and acts of aggression.

## II. Growing support for concerted international action against apartheid

21. The World Conference recalls the International Conference on Sanctions against South Africa, held in 1981, made a series of recommendations for international action to avert the growing menace to peace in southern Africa.

22. Regrettably, in the period since that Conference, the Security Council has been unable to take the requisite mandatory action recommended due to the negative votes of the United Kingdom and Great Britain and Northern Ireland and the United States of America. Emboldened by the opposition reflected in those negative votes and the avowed policy of utilizing their extensive links with it to secure changes in its policies by persuasion, the racist regime embarked on increased aggression and destabilization against neighbouring African States in the hope of undermining the liberation struggles in South Africa and Namibia and even imposing hegemony over the entire region. It prevented the implementation of the United Nations plan for the independence of Namibia by introducing extraneous and unacceptable conditions.

23. In an attempt to further entrench apartheid the regime devised a new racist so-called "constitution" to try to divide the Black majority and embarked on a further intensification of its repressive reign of terror in order to impose that so-called "constitution" and to oppose the determined and ever-escalating resistance of the people.

24. However, the mobilization of the South African people in resistance to the regime's "total strategy" for the perpetuation of White domination, as well as the advance of the struggle of the Namibian people, frustrated the plans of the racist regime. The oppressed people of South Africa and Namibia, through their struggle and sacrifice, gained increasing support from world public opinion which was outraged by the atrocities of the racist regime and inspired by the just aspirations of the oppressed people.

25. The World Conference notes with satisfaction that the General Assembly, as well as the Organization of African Unity, the Movement of Non-Aligned Countries and many other international organizations, have called for greater pressure against the racist regime and greater assistance to the oppressed people. However, the Security Council has been unable, because of the opposition of certain Western Permanent Members, to institute any mandatory sanctions against South Africa except for the mandatory arms embargo of 1977.

26. The World Conference expresses deep concern and disappointment that the Security Council, during its meetings in November 1985 and in May 1986, convened at the request of the States members of OAU and of the Movement of Non-Aligned Countries to impose mandatory selective economic and other sanctions against South Africa as an effective means of combating the apartheid system and bringing peace and stability to southern Africa, failed to adopt the necessary decisions.

27. Countries including the members of the Non-Aligned Movement, the Socialist States, the members of the Organization of Petroleum Exporting Countries, the Nordic States and some other countries have taken far-reaching measures towards the total isolation and boycott of the apartheid regime. Besides the policy of isolation and boycott of the racist regime by those countries, many Western countries have taken a variety of measures. State and local authorities, trade unions, religious bodies, co-operatives and other organizations and institutions have also stepped up their actions against apartheid. The developments in southern Africa and the pressure of some Governments and public opinion abroad has persuaded some transnational corporations and financial institutions to suspend loans to South Africa and some corporations to reduce or terminate their operations in South Africa.

28. While these international, national and local actions are not adequate to deal with the grave situation in southern Africa, they have brought about a wider consensus that can help secure more effective action.

29. The World Conference notes with satisfaction that the overwhelming majority of States and world public opinion are now in favour of comprehensive mandatory sanctions against the apartheid regime and support to the people of South Africa and Namibia in their legitimate struggle for freedom.

30. There is thus an unprecedented opportunity for decisive international action to eliminate apartheid, ensure the speedy independence of Namibia and secure peace in southern Africa.

## III. Objectives of international action

31. The primary objectives of international action are: (a) to assist the South African people in eliminating apartheid and racial discrimination and building throughout the territory of South Africa a non-racial, equalitarian and democratic State; (b) to secure the independence of Namibia without further delay, in accordance with all relevant General Assembly and Security Council resolutions, in particular, with Security Council resolution 435 (1978); and (c) to restore peace in the region and thus ensure the maintenance of international peace and security.

32. The World Conference condemns the policy

and all repressive measure of the Pretoria regime that only serve to perpetuate the apartheid system, in particular the recent imposition of a nation-wide State of Emergency, the continued killings and the arrest and detention of thousands of persons involved in the struggle against apartheid. Furthermore, the Conference demands the immediate and unconditional release of all political prisoners as well as immediate lifting of the State of Emergency. There must be no recognition of the fragmentation of the country by the racist regime through the creation of so-called "independent" bantustans to dispossess the African majority.

33. The World Conference notes with serious concern that the actions of the racist regime undermine the possibility of an early negotiated solution of the conflict in South Africa. Indeed, it has sought to divert attention by professing to favour so-called "changes" and "reforms". These are not intended to eliminate the system of apartheid and racial discrimination but to perpetuate it. They are designed to deceive world opinion, divide the oppressed people and entrench apartheid. They are accompanied by greater repression of the Black people and all opponents of apartheid and have been firmly resisted by the majority of the population.

34. The World Conference stresses that the indispensable prerequisites for a negotiated, just and lasting solution in South Africa are:

(a) Acceptance of the objective of the speedy and total elimination of apartheid and the establishment of a non-racial democratic society in accordance with the principles of the Charter of the United Nations, the Declaration on the Granting of Independence to Colonial Countries and Peoples (General Assembly resolution 1514 (XV) and the Universal Declaration of Human Rights (Assembly resolution 217 A (III));

(b) Immediate and unconditional release of all political prisoners, abrogation of bans on political organizations and measures that prohibit full and free political organization and expression, and an end to censorship;

(c) Negotiations with genuine leaders of the oppressed people of South Africa.

35. As regards Namibia, the World Conference considers it intolerable that the racist regime continues its illegal occupation of Namibia almost two decades after the United Nations terminated its mandate and assumed direct responsibility for the Territory and its people. This illegal occupation—and the repression and military operations against the Namibian people and their national liberation movement—are not only an affront to but an attack against the United Nations and the international community.

36. The Namibian people must be freed of the illegal occupation immediately and unconditionally. Any attempt to introduce "linkage" between the termination of the illegal occupation of Namibia and the withdrawal of Cuban troops from Angola or any other extraneous issues must be totally rejected.

37. The World Conference considers it imperative that: (a) the international community demand that the South African regime proceed to implement forthwith the United Nations plan for the independence of Namibia without any conditions or delaying manoeuvres; and (b) that the Security Council decide immediately on effective sanctions against the racist regime under Chapter VII of the Charter of the United Nations. It trusts that all States will implement such measures and thereby enable the United Nations to discharge its solemn responsibility. It expresses confidence that public opinion will exert all its influence to ensure the universal implementation of the measures.

38. The World Conference notes with indignation the policies and the repeated acts of aggression, destabilization, subversion and terrorism perpetuated by the racist regime against the sovereign territories of the frontline and other neighbouring countries in an attempt to overthrow their legitimate Governments. In this regard, it is imperative that the international community exert pressure upon the Pretoria regime so that it desist from such policies and acts against those States.

## IV. Need for a comprehensive programme of action

39. In view of the extreme gravity of the situation in southern Africa, it is imperative that the international community should take all necessary action, with a sense of urgency, for the speedy abolition of apartheid and an end to its violence in South Africa, the illegal occupation of Namibia and aggression against independent African States. Any delays or weaknesses in action will prolong the suffering of the people and further aggravate the threat to the peace.

40. The World Conference considers that the international community should decide on a comprehensive programme of action. Mandatory sanctions against South Africa, under Chapter VII of the Charter, must be the central element of such a programme, which should also include additional actions by Governments and the public to isolate the racist regime and to render all appropriate assistance to those striving for freedom and peace in southern Africa.

41. Regrettably, certain Western Powers and other Governments and some transnational corporations, by their active collaboration with the racist regime in contravention of appeals by the United Nations, have enabled that regime to build up its military and repressive apparatus through breaches of United Nations embargoes. This has served to encourage that regime to pursue its

disastrous course of attempting to perpetuate racist domination in South Africa and Namibia. It has been a major obstacle to the efforts of the oppressed people and the international community for the elimination of apartheid, the independence of Namibia and the maintenance of peace and security in southern Africa.

42. The policy of "constructive engagement" has not contributed to the abolition of the system of "apartheid". On the contrary, this situation has continued and the Pretoria regime is maintaining its illegal occupation of Namibia and its policy of aggression, subversion and destabilization of different sorts against the front-line and other neighbouring States.

43. The World Conference takes note of the Declaration adopted by the Co-ordinating Bureau of the Movement of Non-Aligned Countries, held at New Delhi from 16 to 19 April 1986 which expressed its concern at the grave consequences for international peace and security of Israel's collaboration with South Africa, especially in the nuclear field.

44. The World Conference urges the Governments concerned to abandon policies based on collaboration with the racist regime, as such policies have led to disastrous consequences. It calls on the Governments, transnational corporations and others concerned to cease forthwith collaboration with and support of the racist regime of South Africa.

45. The World Conference notes with concern that the racist regime has taken advantage of international tension to secure protection against effective international action even while it has escalated violence and repression. It stresses the vital importance of concerted international action for the elimination of apartheid and the imperative need to oppose any attempts to interpret the situation in southern Africa as part of "East-West" or other conflicts.

46. The World Conference strongly condemns any attempts by South Africa and its supporters to destabilize independent States in southern Africa and, in particular, to assist subversive groups instigated and supported by the racist regime of South Africa. In that connection, it appeals to all States not to render any assistance to the UNITA criminal bandits.

## V. Comprehensive mandatory sanctions against South Africa under Chapter VII of the Charter of the United Nations

47. The World Conference notes that it is now recognized more widely than ever by Governments and peoples of the world that such sanctions against South Africa are the most appropriate and effective peaceful means available to the international community for the elimination of apartheid, the liberation of Namibia and the maintenance of peace in southern Africa.

48. It urges the few Western Powers that continue to oppose sanctions against South Africa—especially the United States and the United Kingdom of Great Britain and Northern Ireland, which have prevented the imposition of mandatory sanctions by the Security Council through the exercise of vetoes—to reassess their positions and co-operate in, rather than hinder, international action. By so doing, they can make a great contribution to peace and freedom in southern Africa and they have a responsibility to do so, as do the other main trading partners of South Africa.

49. The World Conference attaches particular importance and urgency to the adoption of comprehensive mandatory sanctions by the Security Council, to be implemented by all States, and to the adoption of effective measures especially by the major Western Powers that are also the main trading partners of South Africa. It urges all Governments to exert their influence to secure the co-operation of those Powers for such action with a view to facilitating mandatory action by the Security Council.

50. In view of the aggravation of the situation in South Africa and Namibia, the growing threat to the security of African States and the unwillingness of the racist regime to seek a peaceful and just solution, the World Conference urges the Security Council to consider, without delay, all appropriate action under the Charter, taking into account the appeals by the oppressed people of South Africa and Namibia, supported by the overwhelming majority of States and by world public opinion, for sanctions against the racist regime of South Africa. It suggests, as a first step, that the Security Council determine that the policies and actions of the racist regime of South Africa have caused and constitute a grave threat to the maintenance of international peace and security and that action under Chapter VII of the Charter is imperative. It urges further that the Security Council adopt comprehensive and mandatory sanctions against South Africa with special reference to the following most urgent measures.

### A. *Military and nuclear collaboration*

51. The World Conference notes with deep concern the massive military machine and repressive apparatus accumulated by the racist regime as well as its acquisition of nuclear weapons capability. Considering the record of violence and aggression of the regime, which poses an enormous menace to peace and security in southern Africa, the World Conference attaches the utmost importance to the immediate and complete cessation of all military and nuclear collaboration with the racist regime of South Africa as a first step to undermine the ability of that regime to resort to massive violence

against the people of South Africa and Namibia and to commit aggression against independent African States.

52. The World Conference expresses great concern that the mandatory arms embargo instituted in 1977 has not been effectively implemented. To this end it calls upon States that have not yet done so to enact and reinforce legislation or to issue appropriate policy directives on the arms embargo, covering all forms of military collaboration.

53. The World Conference expresses grave concern over the nuclear plans of the South African regime and urges effective measures for the termination of all collaboration with it in the nuclear field.

54. The World Conference therefore recommends that the mandatory arms embargo instituted by the Security Council in resolution 418 (1977) of 4 November 1977 be reinforced by calling upon all States:

(*a*) To end all military and nuclear collaboration with South Africa;

(*b*) To cease the sale or supply of "dual purpose" items and related matériel such as computers, radar and other electronic equipment and related technology to South Africa;

(*c*) To terminate all investments in corporations manufacturing military equipment or supplies in South Africa;

(*d*) To take measures to discourage or prevent enlistment of their nationals in the South African military forces and to give appropriate assistance to those who resist conscription or recruitment.

55. The World Conference further urges the Security Council to make mandatory its request to all States, in paragraph 2 of its resolution 558 (1984) of 13 December 1984, "to refrain from importing arms, ammunition of all types and military vehicles produced in South Africa" and to extend the embargo to cover all components and related *matériel* originating from South Africa.

56. It calls for more effective monitoring of the arms embargo against South Africa and in that connection urges action, without further delay, on the recommendations submitted in September 1980 by the Security Council Committee established by resolution 421 (1977) concerning the question of South Africa.

57. The World Conference welcomes the declaration of the International Seminar on Arms Embargo against South Africa (A/41/388-S/18121, annex), held in London from 28 to 30 May 1986, and believes that it is imperative that the measures recommended therein be taken to reinforce and strengthen the mandatory arms embargo by the Security Council in resolution 418 (1977).

58. It calls for the extension of the arms embargo to include the police sector.

## B. *Oil and petroleum products*

59. The World Conference considers oil a commodity of utmost strategic importance to the apartheid regime, being a crucial factor in its terror and repression meted out to the peoples of South Africa and Namibia, its illegal occupation of Namibia, and its acts of aggression against the front-line and neighbouring States.

60. Given, as well, the inability of the apartheid regime to meet its oil needs from domestic sources, the World Conference considers an oil embargo an essential component of international action against the racist regime.

61. The Conference notes that while oil-exporting States have committed themselves to the oil embargo against South Africa, very few major shipping States have done so.

62. The Conference welcomes the declaration adopted by the Seminar on Oil Embargo against South Africa (A/41/404-S/18141, annex), held at Oslo from 4 to 6 June 1986, and urges all States that have not yet done so to adopt and implement legislative and other specific measures for an effective oil embargo against the racist regime.

63. These measures should include, *inter alia*, the following: (a) the prevention of the sale, supply and transport of crude oil and petroleum products to South Africa; (b) the prohibition of all assistance to apartheid South Africa through the provision of finance, technology, equipment or personnel for the prospecting, development or production of hydrocarbon resources; (c) the prohibition of assistance in the construction or operation of oil-from-coal plants or the development and operation of plants producing fuel substitutes and additives such as ethanol and methanol; (d) the prohibition of the participation of corporations and individuals within their jurisdiction in the oil industry in South Africa, including exploration, storage, refining, transport and distribution; (e) the prohibition of the importation of oil-from-coal technology from South Africa; (f) the prohibition of the importation of oil or petroleum products and petrochemicals from South Africa; and (g) the prevention of the efforts of South African corporate interests to maintain or expand their holdings in oil companies or properties outside South Africa.

64. The World Conference urges all States that have not yet done so to take all possible legal actions against companies and individuals that have been involved in violating the oil embargo.

65. In order to monitor the compliance with the oil embargo, the World Conference urges the establishment of an intergovernmental monitoring agency. Such an intergovernmental monitoring agency would, among other functions, develop efficient techniques to monitor

the enforcement of the oil embargo.

66. The World Conference affirms the urgent need for the Security Council to adopt a mandatory oil embargo under Chapter VII of the Charter. It recommends that members of the Security Council, in consultation with oil-producing and oil-shipping States, co-ordinate action in ensuring that effective action at the level of the Security Council is taken as soon as possible.

67. The World Conference draws attention to the illegal prospecting for oil off the coast of Namibia carried out by the racist regime because it is contrary to decree No. 1 for the Protection of the Natural Resources of Namibia enacted by the United Nations Council for Namibia in 1974. All States are therefore requested to withhold co-operation from the racist regime in this exploitation.

### C. *Investments and loans*

68. The General Assembly has repeatedly and by overwhelming majorities recognized that a cessation of all new foreign investments in and financial loans to South Africa would constitute an important step in international action for the elimination of apartheid. Several Governments have taken legislative and other measures towards that end. In addition, some transnational corporations, as a result of government legislation, pressures of their shareholders and public action, have begun to reduce their operations in South Africa. Regrettably, other transnational corporations from some Western countries and Japan have most unscrupulously stepped in to fill the vacuum by new or increased investments, thus becoming very active collaborators in the perpetuation of apartheid. The World Conference condemns these corporations and calls for a list of such corporations to be published periodically by the Special Committee against Apartheid and other appropriate bodies of the United Nations. The Conference also calls for intensified vigilance to identify those corporations that may take advantage of withdrawal of others, with a view to subjecting them and those remaining in South Africa to a world-wide boycott campaign.

69. The World Conference recommends that the Security Council urgently consider a mandatory embargo on investments in and financial loans to South Africa.

70. It urges that Governments be requested to make every possible effort to exert their influence to persuade banks and financial institutions concerned to refrain from further rescheduling the debts of South Africa.

### D. *Other sanctions*

71. The World Conference urges the Security Council to consider other mandatory sanctions against South Africa, especially with respect to trade, e.g.:

(*a*) Prohibition of transfer of technology to South Africa;

(*b*) Cessation of export, sale or transport of oil and oil products to South Africa and of any co-operation with South Africa's oil industry;

(*c*) Cessation of further investment in and financial loans to South Africa or Namibia and of any governmental insurance or guarantee of credits to these regimes;

(*d*) An end to all promotion of or support for trade with South Africa, including assistance to trade missions;

(*e*) Prohibition of the sale of krugerrands and any other coins minted in South Africa;

(*f*) Prohibition of imports from South Africa of agricultural products, coal, uranium, etc.;

(*g*) Enactment of legislation or adoption of other measures to comply with Decree No. 1 for the Protection of the Natural Resources of Namibia enacted by the United Nations Council for Namibia in 1974;

(*h*) Termination of any visa-free entry privileges to South Africa;

(*i*) Termination of air and shipping links with South Africa;

(*j*) Cessation of all academic, cultural, scientific and sports relations with South Africa and of relations with individuals, institutions and other bodies endorsing or based on apartheid;

(*k*) Suspension or abrogation of agreements with South Africa, such as agreements on cultural and scientific co-operation.

72. It stresses, in particular, the need for an immediate embargo on the import of uranium and other products from Namibia in accordance with Decree No. 1 for the Protection of the Natural Resources of Namibia enacted by the United Nations Council for Namibia in 1974.

73. Pending a decision by the Security Council, the World Conference recommends the above-mentioned measures for urgent consideration of all Governments that have not yet taken such action and encourages anti-apartheid action by State and local authorities and by the public.

## VI. Actions by individual States

74. Such actions have resulted from the outrage of public opinion at the massive repression and violence of the racist regime. They were encouraged and promoted by General Assembly resolutions 39/72 G of 13 December 1984 and 40/64 I of 10 December 1985 on concerted international action for the elimination of apartheid and by the Security Council in its resolutions 566 (1985) of 19 June 1985 on Namibia and 569 (1985) of 26 July 1985 on South Africa.

75. The Nordic States adopted a new and expanded programme against apartheid in October 1985 that covered proposals for action by the United Nations as well as commitment for a series of national measures. The European Community and the Commonwealth have agreed on a number of specific measures.

76. The World Conference, while commending all States that have imposed sanctions against South Africa, expresses appreciation to those Governments and intergovernmental organizations that have now taken significant measures against apartheid and urges them to take further action.

77. It considers that national measures should be actively promoted and monitored, not only for their direct effect on the situation in South Africa, but as one of the means to promote mandatory action by the Security Council for universal implementation.

78. The World Conference takes note of the signing, by a significant number of States, of the International Convention against Apartheid in Sports (General Assembly resolution 40/64 G, annex) and urges other States to consider acceding to it.

## VII. Assistance

79. The World Conference affirms the legitimacy of the struggle of the people of South Africa for the elimination of apartheid and the establishment of a nonracial and democratic State and the struggle of the Namibian people for self-determination and independence. It recognizes and respects the right of the people of South Africa and Namibia and their national liberation movements to choose their means of struggle to attain those objectives.

80. The World Conference commends all Governments, organizations and individuals who have assisted the oppressed peoples of South Africa and Namibia and their national liberation movements and thereby demonstrated solidarity with their legitimate struggle for freedom. It stresses the need for much greater assistance at this critical time. It draws attention to the need for humanitarian and educational assistance, as well as all appropriate assistance for the struggle for the elimination of apartheid and the building of new societies. It draws special attention to the need for assistance to trade unions and other organizations in South Africa and Namibia that are playing an important role in this struggle.

81. The World Conference draws attention to the great importance of assistance to independent African States in southern Africa that have suffered greatly from aggression and destabilization by the racist regime of South Africa because of their support for freedom in South Africa and Namibia, and to the efforts of the States

members of the Southern African Development Coordination Conference to reduce their economic dependence on South Africa.

82. It recognizes that a programme of sanctions against South Africa must be complemented by a programme of assistance to these States, as well as to the oppressed people of South Africa and Namibia through their national liberation movements.

## VIII. Public action

83. The World Conference attaches great importance to public action in support of the struggle for freedom in South Africa and Namibia and commends all those organizations and individuals who have organized or promoted such action.

84. It notes with satisfaction the action taken by hundreds of State and local authorities in several countries and by trade unions, religious bodies, co-operatives, universities, anti-apartheid and solidarity movements and other organizations and institutions all over the world.

85. It encourages consumer, sports, cultural and other boycotts against racist South Africa and the campaign for disinvestment from South Africa. It recognizes the great importance of such campaigns that have not only encouraged millions of individuals to participate in action against the inhuman system of apartheid, but have sustained the faith of the oppressed peoples of South Africa and Namibia in international solidarity, especially in countries which continue to maintain economic and other relations with South Africa.

86. It commends musicians, artists, writers, sportsmen and others who have contributed to the campaigns against apartheid.

87. It expresses its great appreciation to anti-apartheid and solidarity movements and other organizations that have constantly tried to promote action for the isolation of the racist regime of South Africa and to promote support for the struggle for liberation in South Africa and Namibia.

88. It encourages further development of anti-apartheid campaigns in cooperation with the national liberation movements of South Africa and Namibia. It stresses, in particular, the need for international support for campaigns by the oppressed people of South Africa and Namibia, such as consumer boycotts, trade union actions and resistance against "Bantu" education.

89. The World Conference invites the United Nations, the Movement of Non-Aligned Countries and the Organization of African Unity to consult and consider more active efforts to promote public action against apartheid and in support of the struggle of the oppressed peoples of South Africa and Namibia.

## IX. Follow-up action

90. The World Conference invites the relevant United Nations bodies to examine the ways and means of implementing the present Declaration. It also invites the Secretary-General to report to the General Assembly on the follow-up action thereon.

## X. Conclusion

91. The World Conference pays tribute to all those who have laid down their lives or made sacrifices in the struggle against apartheid in South Africa, thereby espousing a non-racial democratic society in conformity with the principles of the Universal Declaration of Human Rights and in the true interests of all the people of South Africa. It notes with satisfaction the non-racial character of the movement for freedom in South Africa that represents diverse religious, ideological and other persuasions.

92. It condemns the racist regime for its brutal repression against that movement—which has inspired the world by its great non-violent campaigns, by its heroic resistance under most difficult conditions and its consistent rejection of all forms of racial discrimination and apartheid—and holds that regime responsible for precipitating all conflicts and violence.

93. The World Conference stresses that the international community has a sacred obligation to ensure the independence of the people of Namibia, who have grievously suffered under, and heroically fought against, ruthless oppression and virtual genocide. On the eve of the twentieth anniversary of the decision of the United Nations to assume direct responsibility for the Territory and people of Namibia, it makes a solemn appeal for all necessary international action to discharge the "sacred trust of civilization".

94. The independent African States in southern Africa have been unable to benefit fully from their hard-won independence and to ensure economic and social development for their peoples because of the constant acts of aggression and destabilization by the South African regime. They deserve the support of the international community.

95. Indeed, the legitimate aspirations of African States and peoples and of the Organization of African Unity for the total liberation of the continent of Africa from colonialism and racism merit the full support of the international community.

96. The World Conference highly commends the statesmanship of the Governments and liberation movements in southern Africa that have, despite the atrocities committed by the racist regime, consistently espoused a just solution in the interests of all the people in southern Africa.

97. It calls for an immediate end to collaboration with the racist regime of South Africa and to policies that endow legitimacy or lend respectability to a regime based on apartheid. The Conference condemns the imposition of the nation-wide State of Emergency over South Africa and demands its immediate lifting.

98. While reaffirming solidarity with Nelson Mandela, Zephania Mothopeng and all others imprisoned for their opposition to apartheid and their commitment to the struggle for freedom in South Africa and Namibia, the Conference demands that the Pretoria regime release them unconditionally and immediately. The participants in the Conference pledge their redoubled and concerted efforts to ensure that freedom and peace will prevail.

99. The World Conference notes with appreciation the efforts of the Commonwealth Group of Eminent Persons to provide a just and peaceful solution in South Africa.

100. It condemns any attempts to interpret the present conflict in southern Africa as an "East-West" conflict. The conflict in this area does not result from the "East-West" confrontation; it has its roots in the policies and practices of the apartheid regime. The World Conference calls for full and unconditional support of the legitimate aspirations of the peoples of southern Africa for peace, denuclearization, non-alignment and freedom. It invites the active and urgent support of all Governments, organizations, institutions, media and individuals for the present Declaration.

101. In conclusion, the World Conference reiterates its conviction that the most effective peaceful means available to the international community to end apartheid is to enforce comprehensive mandatory sanctions against the racist regime of South Africa. The alternative to sanctions is escalating violence and bloodshed. The situation brooks no delay. The time for concrete, immediate action has come. This is the call of this Conference.

## Message of solidarity with the struggling people of South Africa

On this tenth anniversary of the massacre of Soweto, the entire world has joined in manifestations of solidarity with the struggling people of South Africa and in prayers for peace and justice in that tormented country. In South Africa itself, the Government, spurning all opportunities for peace and reconciliation, turns to ever more desperate measures to keep in being the dark and cruel system of apartheid.

On this day we remember and commemorate the hundreds of young people who were killed in cold blood 10 years ago for no other crime than asking that they receive their education in English. Since then, thousands more have paid with their blood and lives the price of seeking justice and full rights as citizens of the land of their birth. In the last 20 months scarcely a day has passed without taking its toll of dead and wounded. The total killed so far has already exceeded the figure of 1,700.

The apartheid regime's aggressions have continued and multiplied in the face of repeated condemnations and warnings by the Security Council and notwithstanding South Africa's non-aggression agreements and understandings with neighbouring States. South Africa's depredations have imposed heavy costs on these countries and blighted their prospects of social and economic development.

But the oppressed and dispossessed people of South Africa have not flinched from sacrifice and suffering. The growing scope and intensity of the struggle in South Africa have shown that for the struggling people of South Africa there is no turning back and that they will continue the fight, enduring suffering and facing death until victory is won and the evil of apartheid vanquished.

In its arrogance and folly, the South African regime turned its back—as it has in the past—on the efforts, undertaken this time by the Commonwealth, to bring about a settlement through negotiation and peaceful change. It has shown thereby that it wants no settlement except on its own terms, and that these are calculated to maintain White supremacy and domination in one form or another at any cost.

The regime has again imposed a state of emergency over the entire country and given to every policeman and member of the security forces the right, at will, to imprison without warrant, without charge and without recourse, anyone he chooses to, indefinitely. Few Governments in the history of the world have assumed such untrammelled power of life and death over its citizens. It is clear that a new and more tragic chapter is opening in the bloodstained history of apartheid.

The World Conference on Sanctions against Racist South Africa convenes as storm clouds are gathering over South Africa. It wishes to send a message of solidarity to the people of South Africa in their struggle for liberation and equal rights. Let them be assured that they do not stand alone before the might of the apartheid State. The people of the world have, on this Soweto day, reaffirmed their support for the just struggle of the people of South Africa. The Governments gathered in this Conference represent all regions and races of the world, and have come together for the purpose of agreeing upon measures to support the South African people's valiant struggle for liberation and to lift the curse of apartheid from South Africa.

The racist regime has had too much leeway for too long. It has been led to believe that it would be allowed to continue in its ways indefinitely. Let it now understand that the days of apartheid are numbered and that the representatives of Governments and people who have gathered here are determined to do everything they can to see that apartheid shall be extirpated in the shortest possible time and replaced by a democratic, non-racial system in a united liberated South Africa.

# Document 120

*Statement by the President of the Security Council, on behalf of the Council, calling upon the South African authorities to revoke the decree of 10 April 1987, under which protests against detentions without trial or support for those detained are prohibited*

S/18808, 16 April 1987

The members of the Security Council express their deep concern about the decree issued by the South African authorities on 10 April 1987, under which nearly all forms of protest against detentions without trial or support for those detained are prohibited. The members of the Council express their strong indignation at this latest measure, which is based on the June 1986 decree imposing the nation-wide state of emergency, the lifting of which was called for by the members of the Council in the statement made by the President on their behalf at the 2690th meeting of the Council on 13 June 1986.

The members of the Council call upon the South African authorities to revoke the decree of 10 April 1987, which is contrary to fundamental human rights as envisaged in the Charter of the United Nations and to the relevant resolutions of the Security Council and can only aggravate the situation further, lead to an escalation of acts of violence and further intensify human suffering in South Africa.

The members of the Council, recognizing that the root cause of the situation in South Africa is apartheid, once again strongly condemn the apartheid system and all the policies and practices, including this latest decree, deriving therefrom. They again call upon the Government of South Africa to end the oppression and repression of the Black majority by bringing apartheid to an end and to seek a peaceful, just and lasting solution in accordance with the principles of the Charter of the United Nations and the Universal Declaration of Human Rights. They also call upon the Government of South Africa to set free immediately and unconditionally all political prisoners and detainees, in order to avoid further aggravating the situation.

They urge the Government of South Africa to enter into negotiations with the genuine representatives of the South African people with a view to the establishment in South Africa of a free, united and democratic society on the basis of universal suffrage.

# Document 121

*General Assembly resolution: Policies of apartheid of the Government of South Africa—International solidarity with the liberation struggle in South Africa*

A/RES/42/23 A, 20 November 1987

*The General Assembly,*

...

1. *Reaffirms* its full support to the people of South Africa in their struggle, under the leadership of their national liberation movements, to eradicate apartheid totally, so that they can exercise their right to self-determination in a free, democratic, unfragmented and nonracial South Africa;

...

3. *Condemns* the policy and practice of apartheid and, in particular, the execution of patriots and captured freedom fighters in South Africa and demands that the racist regime:

(a) Stay the execution of those now on death row;

(b) Abide by the Geneva Conventions of 12 August 1949 and Additional Protocol I of 1977 thereto;

4. *Demands again* that the racist regime end repression against the oppressed people of South Africa; lift the state of emergency; release unconditionally Nelson Mandela, Zephania Mothopeng, all other political prisoners, trade union leaders, detainees and restrictees and, in particular, detained children; lift the ban on the African National Congress of South Africa, the Pan Africanist Congress of Azania and other political parties and organizations; allow free political association and activity of the South African people and the return of all political exiles; put an end to the policy of bantustanization and forced population removals; eliminate apartheid laws and end military and paramilitary activities aimed at the neighbouring States;

5. *Considers* that the implementation of the above demands would create the appropriate conditions for free consultations among all the people of South Africa with a view to negotiating a just and lasting solution to the conflict in that country;

...

8. *Urges* all States to contribute generously to the Action for Resisting Invasion, Colonialism and Apartheid Fund set up by the Eighth Conference of Heads of State or Government of Non-Aligned Countries with the aim of increasing support to the liberation movements fighting the apartheid regime and to the front-line States;

...

# Document 122

*General Assembly resolution: Policies of apartheid of the Government of South Africa—Imposition, coordination and strict monitoring of measures against racist South Africa*

A/RES/43/50 D, 5 December 1988

*The General Assembly,*

*Recalling* its resolutions on sanctions against South Africa,

*Taking note* of the report of the Special Committee against Apartheid—in particular paragraphs 191 to 194, and of the Secretary-General's report on implementation of national measures adopted against South Africa,

*Considering* that measures taken by States individually and some collectively, while commendable, vary in coverage and degree of enforcement, which allows for the exploitation of existing gaps and loopholes,

*Concerned* at the increasing number of States that exploit the trade gaps created by the imposition of these measures,

*Commending* the action taken by labour unions, women's organizations, student groups and other antiapartheid organizations for the isolation of the apartheid regime,

1. *Urges* all States that have not yet done so, pending the imposition of comprehensive and mandatory sanctions, to adopt legislative and/or comparable measures to impose effective sanctions against South Africa and, in particular:

(*a*) To impose embargoes on the supply of all products, technologies, skills and services that can be used for the military and nuclear industry of South Africa, including military intelligence;

(*b*) To impose embargoes on the supply of oil and petroleum products;

(*c*) To prohibit the import of coal, gold, other minerals and agricultural products from South Africa and Namibia;

(*d*) To induce transnational corporations, banks and financial institutions to withdraw effectively from South Africa by ceasing equity and non-equity investment, transfer of technology and know-how, and provision of credit and loans;

(*e*) To sever all air, sea and other transport links with South Africa;

(*f*) To prevent, through appropriate measures, their citizens from serving in South Africa's armed forces and other sensitive sectors;

(*g*) To take appropriate measures to ensure the effectiveness of the sports and cultural boycott of the racist regime of South Africa;

2. *Also urges* all States to monitor strictly the implementation of the above measures and adopt when necessary legislation providing for penalties on individuals and enterprises violating those measures;

3. *Requests* the Secretary-General to report to the General Assembly at its forty-fourth session on new legislative and/or comparable measures adopted and implemented by States against South Africa, especially in areas in which the South African economy depends on the outside world.

---

# Document 123

*General Assembly resolution: Policies of apartheid of the Government of South Africa—Special session of the General Assembly on apartheid and its destructive consequences in southern Africa*

A/RES/43/50 G, 5 December 1988

*The General Assembly,*

*Gravely concerned* at the escalating repression mounted against the opponents of apartheid in South Africa,

*Further concerned* about the racist regime's continued aggression against the front-line States and its destructive consequences,

*Taking note* of the Declaration of the Conference of Foreign Ministers of Non-Aligned Countries held at Nicosia from 7 to 10 September 1988,

*Indignant* at the continued non-implementation of the General Assembly and Security Council resolutions by South Africa,

1. *Decides* to hold a special session of the General Assembly on apartheid and its destructive consequences in southern Africa before its forty-fourth session, on a date to be determined by the Secretary-General in consultation with the Special Committee against Apartheid;

2. *Requests* the Secretary-General to make the necessary administrative arrangements towards the convening of the special session.

# Document 124

*General Assembly resolution: Policies of apartheid of the Government of South Africa—International solidarity with the liberation struggle in South Africa*

A/RES/44/27 A, 22 November 1989

*The General Assembly,*

*Having considered* the report of the Special Committee against Apartheid,

*Gravely concerned* at the continuing repression of the majority population in South Africa and the continuation of the state of emergency,

*Expressing particular concern* at the continuing practice of arbitrary detentions and trials, including those of women and children, executions of political prisoners, the ongoing use of vigilante groups and the stifling of the press,

*Noting with serious concern* the regime's acts of aggression and destabilization against neighbouring independent African States,

1. *Reaffirms* the legitimacy of the struggle of the South African people for the total eradication of apartheid and for the establishment of a united, non-racial and democratic society in which all the people of South Africa, irrespective of race, colour or creed, enjoy the same fundamental freedoms and human rights;

2. *Reaffirms also* its full support to the national liberation movements, the African National Congress of South Africa and the Pan Africanist Congress of Azania, which pursue their noble objective to eliminate apartheid through political, armed and other forms of struggle and have reiterated their preference for reaching their legitimate objectives through peaceful means;

3. *Condemns* the regime's continuing practice of sentencing to death and executing its opponents and demands that it annul the capital punishment imposed on opponents of apartheid, including the "Upington Fourteen", and confer prisoner-of-war status on captured freedom fighters in accordance with the Geneva Conventions of 12 August 1949 and Additional Protocol I of 1977 thereto;

4. *Demands* that all political prisoners and detainees, particularly children, be released unconditionally and without subsequent restrictions and that the abhorrent practice of applying repressive measures to children and minors cease immediately;

5. *Calls* upon Governments, intergovernmental and non-governmental organizations and individuals to extend all possible assistance to the struggling people of South Africa, their national liberation movements and South African refugees, particularly women and children;

6. *Also calls upon* all Governments, intergovernmental and non-governmental organizations to step up material, financial and other forms of support to the front-line and other neighbouring independent States that are subject to acts of destabilization by South Africa;

7. *Appeals* to all Governments, intergovernmental and non-governmental organizations to contribute generously to the Action for Resisting Invasion, Colonialism and Apartheid Fund set up by the Eighth Conference of Heads of State or Government of Non-Aligned Countries, held at Harare from 1 to 6 September 1986;

8. *Decides* to continue the authorization of adequate financial provision in the regular budget of the United Nations to enable the South African liberation movements recognized by the Organization of African Unity - namely, the African National Congress of South Africa and the Pan Africanist Congress of Azania - to maintain offices in New York in order to participate effectively in the deliberations of the Special Committee against Apartheid and other appropriate bodies.

# Document 125

*General Assembly resolution: Policies of apartheid of the Government of South Africa—International support for the eradication of apartheid in South Africa through genuine negotiations*

A/RES/44/27 B, 22 November 1989

*The General Assembly,*

*Condemning once again* the policy and practice of apartheid,

*Convinced* that the continuation of the policy and practice of apartheid will lead to further violence and is detrimental to the vital interests of all the people of South Africa,

*Convinced* that the system of apartheid cannot be reformed but must be eliminated,

*Taking note* of the Declaration of the Ad Hoc Committee of the Organization of African Unity on Southern Africa on the question of South Africa, adopted at Harare on 21 August 1989,

1. *Reaffirms* its support for the establishment of a united, non-racial and democratic society in which all the people of South Africa, irrespective of race, colour or creed, will enjoy the same fundamental freedoms and human rights;

2. *Fully supports* the efforts of the South African people to arrive at a peaceful settlement of the conflict in their country through genuine negotiations;

3. *Strongly demands:*

(a) The lifting of the state of emergency;

(b) The immediate and unconditional release of Nelson Mandela and all other political prisoners and detainees;

(c) The lifting of the ban on all individuals and political organizations opposing apartheid and the repeal of restrictions on the press;

(d) The withdrawal of the troops from Black townships;

(e) The cessation of all political trials and political executions;

4. *Considers* that the implementation of the above demands would help create the necessary climate for genuine negotiations and calls upon all parties to take full advantage of opportunities arising therefrom, and further considers that this could also promote an agreement to end apartheid and bring about the cessation of violence;

5. *Calls upon* all Member States to use concerted and effective measures to ensure the prompt implementation of the present resolution;

6. *Requests* the Secretary-General to continue to promote efforts leading to the eradication of apartheid through genuine negotiations.

# Document 126

*General Assembly resolution: Policies of apartheid of the Government of South Africa—Comprehensive and mandatory sanctions against the racist regime of South Africa*

A/RES/44/27 C, 22 November 1989

*The General Assembly,*

*Recalling* its earlier resolutions and those of the Security Council calling for concerted international action to force the racist regime of South Africa to eradicate apartheid,

*Having considered* the report of the Special Committee against Apartheid, in particular paragraphs 255 to 275, and the report of the Commission against Apartheid in Sports,

*Gravely concerned* that, in spite of recent developments in South Africa, the system of apartheid remains intact and the regime maintains its repressive domestic practices, its policies of destabilization against neighbouring independent States and its intransigence towards the will of the international community for the prompt elimination of apartheid,

*Noting with grave concern* that sanctions and other measures recommended by the General Assembly, as well as measures introduced unilaterally by a number of States, lack comprehensiveness, co-ordination and adequate monitoring mechanisms,

*Gravely concerned* that some Member States and

transnational corporations have continued economic relations with South Africa, while others continue to exploit opportunities created by sanctions imposed by other States, thus substantially increasing their trade with that country, as indicated in paragraphs 109, 110, 112 and 265 of the report of the Special Committee against Apartheid,

*Convinced* that the imposition of comprehensive and mandatory sanctions by the Security Council under Chapter VII of the Charter of the United Nations remains the most appropriate and effective means to bring about a peaceful end to apartheid,

1. *Reaffirms* that apartheid is a crime against humanity and a threat to international peace and security, and that it is a primary responsibility of the United Nations to assist in efforts to eliminate apartheid peacefully without further delay;

2. *Calls upon* those States which have increased their trade with South Africa and, particularly, the Federal Republic of Germany, which recently emerged as the leading trading partner of South Africa, to sever trade relations with South Africa;

3. *Calls upon* those Governments which are still opposed to the application of comprehensive and mandatory sanctions to reassess their policies and cease their opposition to the application of such sanctions by the Security Council;

4. *Urges* the Security Council to consider immediate action under Chapter VII of the Charter of the United Nations with a view to applying comprehensive and mandatory sanctions against the racist regime of South Africa as long as it continues to disregard the demands of the majority of the people of South Africa and of the international community to eradicate apartheid.

# Document 127

*General Assembly resolution: Policies of apartheid of the Government of South Africa—Imposition, coordination and strict monitoring of measures against racist South Africa*

A/RES/44/27 D, 22 November 1989

*The General Assembly,*

*Recalling* its resolutions on sanctions against South Africa, in particular resolution 43/50 D of 5 December 1988,

*Taking note* of the report of the Special Committee against Apartheid and of the report of the Secretary-General on restrictive measures affecting externally dependent areas of the South African economy,

*Taking note with appreciation* of the recommendations made in the report of the Panel of Eminent Persons that held public hearings, at Geneva from 4 to 6 September 1989, on the activities of transnational corporations in South Africa and Namibia,

*Convinced* that sanctions and other restrictive measures have had a significant impact on recent developments in South Africa and remain a most effective and necessary instrument of pressure in contributing to a political solution to the crisis in that country,

*Considering* that measures taken by States individually or collectively, while commendable, vary in coverage and degree of enforcement and monitoring and are not always addressed to those areas of the South African economy which are vulnerable to international pressure,

*Concerned* at the increasing number of States that exploit the trade gaps created by the uneven and uncoordinated imposition of restrictive measures,

*Noting with concern* that a number of transnational corporations, including banks, continue to provide support to the apartheid economy by maintaining financial and technological and other ties with South Africa,

*Commending* those States which have already adopted strict measures against the apartheid regime in accordance with United Nations resolutions, as well as non-governmental organizations and individuals, for their contribution to the isolation of the apartheid regime,

1. *Urges* all States that have not yet done so, pending the imposition of comprehensive and mandatory sanctions, to adopt legislative and/or comparable measures to impose effective sanctions against South Africa and, in particular:

(*a*) To impose embargoes on the supply of all products, in particular computer and communications equipment, technologies, skills and services, including military intelligence, that can be used for the military and nuclear industry of South Africa;

(*b*) To impose embargoes on the supply of oil and petroleum products and oil technology;

(*c*) To prohibit the import of coal, gold, other minerals and agricultural products from South Africa;

(*d*) To induce transnational corporations, banks and financial institutions to withdraw effectively from South Africa by ceasing equity investment and cutting off non-equity links, particularly those involving transfer of high technology and know-how;

(e) To induce banks to cease the provision of new credits and loans;

(f) To consider ending promptly double taxation agreements with South Africa and any form of tax relief in respect of income from investments in that country;

(g) To restrict landing and port rights to South African air and sea carriers and to sever direct air, sea and other transport links with South Africa;

(h) To ensure, through appropriate measures, that their citizens refrain from serving in South Africa's armed forces and other sensitive sectors;

(i) To take appropriate measures to ensure the effectiveness of the sports and cultural boycott of apartheid South Africa;

2. *Also urges* all States to monitor strictly the implementation of the above measures and adopt, when necessary, legislation providing for penalties on individuals and enterprises violating those measures;

3. *Calls upon* Governments, intergovernmental organizations, the specialized agencies of the United Nations, non-governmental organizations and the public at large to take full account of the recommendations of the Panel of Eminent Persons that held public hearings on the activities of transnational corporations in South Africa and Namibia;

4. *Requests* the Secretary-General to report to the General Assembly at its forty-fifth session on measures to monitor sanctions undertaken by the United Nations system, governments and non-governmental agencies, taking fully into account reports of existing intergovernmental monitoring mechanisms.

# Document 128

*General Assembly resolution: Policies of apartheid of the Government of South Africa—International financial pressure on the apartheid economy of South Africa*

A/RES/44/27 E, 22 November 1989

*The General Assembly,*

*Noting* that the maintenance of the apartheid economy and the expansion of military and police expenditures substantially depend on the supply of further credits and loans by the international financial community,

*Deeply regretting* that the participating banks in the Third Interim Agreement with the apartheid regime, in spite of demands by the international community, have recently announced the rescheduling of South Africa's external debt, which was due for repayment in 1990,

*Considering* that the rescheduling of South Africa's external debt at this particular time represents an attempt to undermine the efforts of the international community to promote a peaceful resolution of the conflict in that country,

*Taking note* of the Kuala Lumpur Statement on Southern Africa adopted by the Commonwealth Heads of Government Meeting on 21 October 1989,

1. *Deplores* the Third Interim Agreement, particularly its terms and timing, which, by providing for the rescheduling over a period of three and a half years of a significant part of South Africa's debt, lessens the financial pressure on the apartheid regime;

2. *Strongly urges* Governments and private financial institutions to deny new bank loans to South Africa, whether to the public or private sectors;

3. *Calls upon* those States which continue to maintain trade and financial links with South Africa to restrict the provision of trade credits and cease loan insurance, in particular:

(a) By calling upon all the relevant banks and financial institutions to impose stricter conditions on day-to-day trade financing, specifically through reducing the maximum credit terms to 90 days;

(b) By taking South Africa "off cover" with official government agencies for official trade credit and insurance purposes, thus making its acquisition of trade credits more difficult;

4. *Calls upon* all Governments, intergovernmental and non-governmental organizations to use all appropriate means to induce banks and other financial institutions to give effect to the measures outlined above;

5. *Requests* the Secretary-General to report to the General Assembly at its forty-fifth session on the implementation of the present resolution.

# Document 129

*General Assembly resolution: Policies of apartheid of the Government of South Africa—Programme of work of the Special Committee against Apartheid*

A/RES/44/27 G, 22 November 1989

*The General Assembly,*

*Having considered* the report of the Special Committee against Apartheid,

1. *Commends* the Special Committee against Apartheid for its work in the discharge of its responsibilities in promoting international action against apartheid;

2. *Takes note* of the report of the Special Committee and endorses the recommendations contained in paragraph 275 of the report relating to its programme of work;

3. *Authorizes* the Special Committee, in accordance with its mandate and acting as a focal point for the international campaign against apartheid and with the support services of the Centre against Apartheid of the Secretariat, to continue:

(*a*) To monitor closely the situation in South Africa and the actions of the international community regarding the imposition and implementation of sanctions and other restrictive measures and their impact on apartheid South Africa;

(*b*) To mobilize international action against apartheid, *inter alia*, through collection, analysis and dissemination of information, through liaison with non-governmental organizations and relevant individuals and groups able to influence public opinion and decision-making, and through hearings, conferences, consultations, missions, publicity and other relevant activities;

4. *Appeals* to all Governments, intergovernmental and non-governmental organizations to increase their cooperation with the Special Committee in the discharge of its mandate;

5. *Requests* all United Nations bodies, organs and agencies to cooperate with the Special Committee and the Centre against Apartheid in their activities in order to ensure consistency and improve co ordination and the greatest use of available resources in the implementation of the relevant resolutions of the General Assembly and the Security Council;

6. *Requests* Governments and organizations to provide financial and other assistance for the special projects of the Special Committee and to make generous contributions to the Trust Fund for Publicity against Apartheid;

7. *Appeals* to all Governments, intergovernmental organizations, information media, non-governmental organizations and individuals to co operate with the Centre against Apartheid and the Department of Public Information of the Secretariat in their activities relating to apartheid and, in particular, in disseminating information on the situation in South Africa in order to mitigate the effects of the restraints on the press in South Africa and to counteract South African propaganda effectively;

8. *Decides* to make a special allocation of 430,000 United States dollars to the Special Committee for 1990 from the regular budget of the United Nations to cover the cost of special projects to be decided upon by the Committee.

# Document 130

*General Assembly resolution: Policies of apartheid of the Government of South Africa—Oil embargo against South Africa*

A/RES/44/27 H, 22 November 1989

*The General Assembly,*

*Having considered* the report of the Intergovernmental Group to Monitor the Supply and Shipping of Oil and Petroleum Products to South Africa,

*Recalling* its resolutions on an oil embargo against South Africa, in particular resolution 43/50 J of 5 December 1988,

*Noting* that, while oil-exporting States have committed themselves to an oil embargo against South Africa, very few major shipping States have done so,

*Concerned* that the racist regime of South Africa has been able to circumvent the oil embargoes and comparable measures adopted by States,

*Commending* action taken by labour unions, student groups and anti-apartheid organizations against companies involved in the violation of the oil embargo against South Africa, and for the enforcement of the embargo,

*Convinced* that an effective oil embargo against South Africa would complement the arms embargo against the apartheid regime, and serve to curtail both its acts of aggression against the front-line States and its repression of the people of South Africa,

1. *Takes* note of the report of the Intergovernmental Group to Monitor the Supply and Shipping of Oil and Petroleum Products to South Africa;

2. *Notes* the intention of the Intergovernmental Group to submit an interim report to the General Assembly at its forty-fourth session, in keeping with paragraph 44 of the Group's report;

3. *Takes note also* of the report of the Panel on the Hearings on the Oil Embargo against South Africa held in New York on 12 and 13 April 1989;

4. *Urges* the Security Council to take action without further delay to impose a mandatory embargo on the supply and shipping of oil and petroleum products to South Africa as well as on the supply of equipment and technology to, financing of and investment in its oil industry and coal liquefaction projects;

5. *Requests* all States concerned, pending a decision by the Security Council, to adopt effective measures and/or legislation to broaden the scope of the oil embargo in order to ensure the complete cessation of the supply and shipping of oil and petroleum products to South Africa, whether directly or indirectly, and in particular:

(*a*) To apply strictly the "end users" clause and other conditions concerning restriction on destination to ensure compliance with the embargo;

(*b*) To compel the companies originally selling or purchasing oil or petroleum products, as appropriate to each nation, to desist from selling, reselling or otherwise transferring oil and petroleum products to South Africa, whether directly or indirectly;

(*c*) To establish strict control over the supply of oil and petroleum products to South Africa by intermediaries, oil companies and traders by placing responsibility for the fulfilment of the contract on the first buyer or seller of oil and petroleum products who would, therefore, be liable for the actions of these parties;

(*d*) To prevent access by South Africa to other sources of energy, including the supply of raw materials, technical know-how, financial assistance and transport;

(*e*) To prohibit all assistance to apartheid South Africa, including the provision of finance, technology, equipment or personnel for the prospecting, development or production of hydrocarbon resources, the construction or operation of oil-from-coal or oil-from-gas plants or the development and operation of plants producing fuel substitutes and additives such as ethanol and methanol;

(*f*) To prevent South African corporations from maintaining or expanding their holdings in oil companies or properties outside South Africa;

(*g*) To terminate the transport of oil and petroleum products to South Africa by ships flying their flags, or by ships that are ultimately owned, managed or chartered by their nationals or by companies within their jurisdiction;

(*h*) To develop a system for registration of ships, registered or owned by their nationals, that have unloaded oil or petroleum products in South Africa in contravention of embargoes imposed, and to discourage such ships from calling at South African ports;

(*i*) To impose penal action against companies and individuals that have been involved in violating the oil embargo, and to publicize cases of successful prosecutions in conformity with their national laws;

(*j*) To gather, exchange and disseminate information regarding violations of the oil embargo, including ways and means to prevent such violations, and to take concerted measures against violators;

6. *Authorizes* the Intergovernmental Group to take action to promote public awareness of the oil embargo against South Africa, including, when necessary, sending missions and participating in relevant conferences and meetings;

7. *Requests* the Intergovernmental Group to submit to the General Assembly at its forty-fifth session a report on the implementation of the present resolution, including proposals for strengthening the mechanism to monitor the supply and shipment of oil and petroleum products to South Africa;

8. *Requests* all States to extend their cooperation to the Intergovernmental Group in the implementation of the present resolution, including submission of proposals for strengthening the mechanism to monitor the supply and shipment of oil and petroleum products to South Africa;

9. *Requests* the Secretary-General to provide the Intergovernmental Group with all necessary assistance for the implementation of the present resolution.

# Document 131

*General Assembly resolution: Policies of apartheid of the Government of South Africa—Military collaboration with South Africa*

A/RES/44/27 I, 22 November 1989

*The General Assembly,*

*Recalling* its resolutions and those of the Security Council on the arms embargo, as well as other resolutions on collaboration with South Africa,

*Taking note* of the report of the Special Committee against Apartheid,

*Reiterating* that the full implementation of an arms embargo against South Africa is an essential element of international action against apartheid,

*Taking note* of the statement adopted on 18 December 1987 by the Security Council Committee established by Council resolution 421 (1977) of 9 December 1977 concerning the question of South Africa, which "noted with alarm and great concern that large quantities of arms and military equipment, including highly sophisticated *matériel*, were still reaching South Africa directly or via clandestine routes",

*Expressing* serious concern at the increasing number of violations of the mandatory arms embargo against South Africa,

*Regretting* that some countries surreptitiously continue to deal in arms with South Africa and allow South Africa to participate in international arms exhibitions,

1. *Strongly deplores* the actions of those States and organizations which directly or indirectly continue to violate the arms embargo and collaborate with South Africa in the military, nuclear, intelligence and technology fields and, in particular, Israel, for providing nuclear technology and two corporations based in the Federal Republic of Germany, for supplying blueprints for the manufacture of submarines and other related military *matériel*; and calls upon Israel to terminate forthwith such hostile acts and upon the Government of the Federal Republic of Germany to honour its obligations under Security Council resolution 421 (1977) by prosecuting the said corporations;

2. *Deplores* the actions of Chile, which has become an important outlet for the sale of South Africa's military hardware and strongly urges it to refrain forthwith from such acts;

3. *Urges* the Security Council to consider immediate steps to ensure the scrupulous and full implementation of the arms embargo imposed by the Council in resolutions 418 (1977) of 4 November 1977 and 558 (1984) of 13 December 1984 and its effective monitoring;

4. *Requests* the Special Committee against Apartheid to keep the matter under constant review and to report thereon to the General Assembly and the Security Council as appropriate.

# Document 132

*General Assembly resolution: Policies of apartheid of the Government of South Africa—United Nations Trust Fund for South Africa*

A/RES/44/27 J, 22 November 1989

*The General Assembly,*

*Recalling* its earlier resolutions on the United Nations Trust Fund for South Africa, in particular resolution 43/50 I of 5 December 1988,

*Having considered* the report of the Secretary-General on the United Nations Trust Fund for South Africa, to which is annexed the report of the Committee of Trustees of the Trust Fund,

*Gravely concerned* at the continued nation-wide state of emergency and security regulations which crimi-nalize political dissent and protest,

*Alarmed* by the continued detentions without trials, forced removals, bannings, restriction orders, political trials, death sentences imposed on opponents of apartheid and harassment of trade unions, church and other organizations and individuals involved in peaceful protest and dissent,

*Reaffirming* that increased humanitarian and legal assistance by the international community to those persecuted under repressive and discriminatory legislation in

South Africa is more than ever necessary to alleviate their plight and sustain their efforts,

*Strongly convinced* that increased contributions to the Trust Fund and to the voluntary agencies concerned are necessary to enable them to meet the extensive needs for humanitarian and legal assistance,

1. *Endorses* the report of the Secretary-General on the United Nations Trust Fund for South Africa;

2. *Expresses its appreciation* to the Governments, organizations and individuals that have contributed to the Trust Fund and to the voluntary agencies engaged in rendering humanitarian and legal assistance to the victims of apartheid and racial discrimination;

3. *Appeals* for generous and increased contributions to the Trust Fund;

4. *Also appeals* for direct contributions to the voluntary agencies engaged in rendering assistance to the victims of apartheid and racial discrimination in South Africa;

5. *Commends* the Secretary-General and the Committee of Trustees of the Trust Fund for their persistent efforts to promote humanitarian and legal assistance to persons persecuted under repressive and discriminatory legislation in South Africa and Namibia, as well as assistance to their families and to refugees from South Africa.

# Document 133

*General Assembly resolution: Policies of apartheid of the Government of South Africa—Concerted international action for the elimination of apartheid*

A/RES/44/27 K, 22 November 1989

*The General Assembly,*

*Alarmed* by the critical situation in South Africa caused by the policy of apartheid and in particular by the extension of the nation-wide state of emergency,

*Convinced* that the root-cause of the crisis in southern Africa is the policy of apartheid,

*Noting with grave concern* that in order to perpetuate apartheid in South Africa the authorities there have committed acts of aggression and breaches of the peace,

*Recognizing* that the policy of bantustanization deprives the majority of the people of their citizenship and makes them foreigners in their own country,

*Noting* that the so-called reforms in South Africa have had the effect of further entrenching the apartheid system and further dividing the people of South Africa,

*Convinced* that only the total eradication of apartheid and the establishment of majority rule on the basis of the free and fair exercise of universal adult suffrage can lead to a peaceful and lasting solution in South Africa,

*Also convinced* that broad-based negotiations involving the genuine representatives of South Africa's majority population should be initiated immediately by the South African authorities with a view to establishing a free, democratic, united and non-racial South Africa,

*Recognizing* the responsibility of the United Nations and the international community to take all necessary action for the eradication of apartheid, and, in particular, the need for effective pressure on the South African authorities as a peaceful means of achieving the abolition of apartheid,

*Encouraged*, in this context, by the growing international consensus, as demonstrated by the adoption of Security Council resolution 569 (1985) of 26 July 1985, and the increase in and expansion of national, regional and intergovernmental measures to this end,

*Considering* sanctions to be the most effective peaceful means available to the international community to increase pressure on the South African authorities,

*Convinced* of the vital importance of the strict observance of Security Council resolution 418 (1977) of 4 November 1977, by which the Council instituted a mandatory arms embargo against South Africa, and Council resolution 558 (1984) of 13 December 1984 concerning the import of arms, ammunition and military vehicles produced in South Africa, and of the need to make these embargoes fully effective in conformity with Council resolution 591 (1986) of 28 November 1986,

*Commending* the national policies not to sell and export oil to South Africa,

*Considering* that measures to ensure effective and scrupulous implementation of such embargoes through international cooperation are essential and urgent,

*Noting*, in this respect, the efforts undertaken by the Intergovernmental Group to Monitor the Supply and Shipping of Oil and Petroleum Products to South Africa,

*Noting with deep concern* that, through a combination of military and economic pressures, in violation of international law, the authorities of South Africa have resorted to economic reprisals and aggression against and destabilization of neighbouring States,

*Alarmed* by the deteriorating situation of millions of refugees, returnees and displaced persons in southern Africa caused by these policies and actions,

*Considering* that contacts between apartheid South Africa and the front-line and other neighbouring States, necessitated by geography, colonial legacy and other reasons, should not be used by other States as a pretext for legitimizing the apartheid system or justifying attempts to break the international isolation of that system,

*Convinced* that the existence of apartheid will continue to lead to ever-increasing resistance by the oppressed people, by all possible means, and increased tension and conflict that will have far-reaching consequences for southern Africa and the world,

*Also convinced* that policies of collaboration with the apartheid regime, instead of respect for the legitimate aspirations of the genuine representatives of the great majority of the people, will encourage its repression and aggression against neighbouring States and its defiance of the United Nations,

*Expressing its full support* for the legitimate aspiration of African States and peoples and of the Organization of African Unity for the total liberation of the continent of Africa from colonialism and racism,

1. *Strongly condemns* the policy of apartheid that deprives the majority of the South African population of their dignity, fundamental freedoms and human rights;

2. *Also strongly condemns* the South African authorities for the killings, arbitrary mass arrests and the detention of members of mass organizations as well as other individuals who are opposing the apartheid system and the state of emergency, and for the detention of and even the use of violence against children;

3. *Condemns* the overt and the covert aggressive actions, which South Africa has carried out for the destabilization of neighbouring States, as well as those aimed against refugees from South Africa;

4. *Demands* that the authorities of South Africa:

(*a*) Release immediately, unconditionally and effectively Nelson Mandela and all other political prisoners, detainees and restrictees;

(*b*) Immediately lift the state of emergency;

(*c*) Abrogate discriminatory laws and lift bans on all organizations and individuals, as well as end restrictions on and censorship of news media;

(*d*) Cease all political trials and political executions;

(*e*) Grant freedom of association and full trade union rights to all workers of South Africa;

(*f*) Initiate a political dialogue with genuine leaders of the majority population with a view to eradicating apartheid without delay and establishing a representative government;

(*g*) Eradicate the bantustan structures;

(*h*) Immediately end the destabilization of front-line and neighbouring States;

5. *Urges* the Security Council to consider without delay the adoption of effective mandatory sanctions against South Africa;

6. *Also urges* the Security Council to take steps for the strict implementation of the mandatory arms embargo instituted by it in resolution 418 (1977) and of the arms embargo requested in its resolution 558 (1984) and, within the context of the relevant resolutions, to secure an end to military and nuclear cooperation with South Africa and the import of military equipment or supplies from South Africa;

7. *Appeals* to all States that have not yet done so, pending mandatory sanctions by the Security Council, to consider national legislative or other appropriate measures to exert pressure on the apartheid regime of South Africa, such as:

(*a*) Cessation of further investment in and financial loans to South Africa;

(*b*) An end to all promotion of and support for trade with South Africa;

(*c*) Prohibition of the sale of Krugerrands and all other coins minted in South Africa;

(*d*) Cessation of all forms of military, police or intelligence cooperation with the authorities of South Africa, in particular the sale of computer equipment;

(*e*) An end to nuclear collaboration with South Africa;

(*f*) Cessation of export and sale of oil and petroleum products to South Africa;

(*g*) Other measures within the economic and commercial fields;

8. *Recognizes* the pressing need, existing and potential, of South Africa's neighbouring States for economic assistance, as a complement and not as an alternative to sanctions against South Africa, and appeals to all States, organizations and institutions:

(*a*) To increase assistance to the front-line States and the Southern African Development Coordination Conference in order to increase their economic strength and independence from South Africa;

(b) To increase humanitarian, legal, educational and other such assistance and support to the victims of apartheid, to the liberation movements recognized by the Organization of African Unity and to all those struggling against apartheid and for a non-racial, democratic society in South Africa;

9. *Appeals* to all Governments and organizations to take appropriate action for the cessation of all academic, cultural, scientific and sports relations that would support the apartheid regime of South Africa, as well as relations with individuals, institutions and other bodies endorsing or based on apartheid;

10. *Commends* the States that have already adopted voluntary measures against the apartheid regime of South Africa in accordance with General Assembly resolution 43/50 K of 5 December 1988 and invites those which have not yet done so to follow their example;

11. *Reaffirms* the legitimacy of the struggle of the oppressed people of South Africa for the total eradication of apartheid and for the establishment of a non-racial, democratic society in which all the people, irrespective of race, colour or creed, enjoy fundamental freedoms and human rights;

12. *Pays tribute to and expresses solidarity with* organizations and individuals struggling against apartheid and for a non-racial, democratic society in accordance with the principles of the Universal Declaration of Human Rights;

13. *Requests* the Secretary-General to report to the General Assembly at its forty-fifth session on the implementation of the present resolution.

# Document 134

*General Assembly resolution: Policies of apartheid of the Government of South Africa—Support for the work of the Commission against Apartheid in Sports*

A/RES/44/27 L, 22 November 1989

*The General Assembly,*

*Recalling* its resolutions on the boycott of apartheid in sports and in particular resolution 32/105 M of 14 December 1977 by which it adopted the International Declaration against Apartheid in Sports and resolution 40/64 G of 10 December 1985, the annex to which contains the International Convention against Apartheid in Sports,

*Having considered* the report of the Commission against Apartheid in Sports and the relevant sections of the report of the Special Committee against Apartheid,

1. *Takes note* of the report of the Commission against Apartheid in Sports;

2. *Calls upon* those States which have signed the International Convention against Apartheid in Sports to ratify it and also calls upon other States to accede to it as soon as possible;

3. *Commends* those Governments, organizations and individual sportsmen and sportswomen that have taken action in accordance with the Register of Sports Contacts with South Africa with a view to achieving a total isolation of apartheid in sports;

4. *Requests* the Special Committee against Apartheid to continue issuing the Register of Sports Contacts with South Africa;

5. *Calls upon* those international sports organizations and federations that have not yet expelled South Africa or suspended its membership to do so without further delay;

6. *Requests* the Secretary-General to provide the Commission against Apartheid in Sports with all needed assistance.

# Document 135

*General Assembly resolution: Declaration on Apartheid and its Destructive Consequences in Southern Africa*

A/RES/S-16/1, 14 December 1989

*We, the States Members of the United Nations,*

*Assembled* at the sixteenth special session of the General Assembly, a special session on apartheid and its destructive consequences in southern Africa, guided by the fundamental and universal principles enshrined in the Charter of the United Nations and the Universal Declaration of Human Rights, in the context of our efforts to establish peace throughout the world by ending all conflicts through negotiations, and desirous of making serious efforts to bring an end to the unacceptable situation prevailing in southern Africa, which is a result of the policies and practices of apartheid, through negotiations based on the principle of justice and peace for all,

*Reaffirming* our conviction, which history confirms, that where colonial and racial domination or apartheid exists, there can be neither peace nor justice,

*Reiterating*, accordingly, that while the apartheid system in South Africa persists, the peoples of Africa as a whole cannot achieve the fundamental objectives of justice, human dignity and peace, which are both crucial in themselves and fundamental to the stability and development of the continent,

*Recognizing* that, with regard to southern Africa, the entire world is vitally interested that the processes in which that region is involved, leading to the genuine national independence of Namibia and peace in Angola and Mozambique, should succeed in the shortest possible time, and equally recognizing that the world is deeply concerned that destabilization by South Africa of the countries of the region, whether through direct aggression, sponsorship of surrogates, economic subversion or other means, is unacceptable in all its forms and must not occur,

*Also recognizing* the reality that permanent peace and stability in southern Africa can only be achieved when the system of apartheid in South Africa has been eradicated and South Africa has been transformed into a united, democratic and non-racial country, and therefore reiterating that all the necessary measures should be adopted now to bring a speedy end to the apartheid system in the interest of all the people of southern Africa, the continent and the world at large,

*Believing* that, as a result of the legitimate struggle of the South African people for the elimination of apartheid, and of international pressure against that system, as well as global efforts to resolve regional conflicts, possibilities exist for further movement towards the resolution of the problems facing the people of South Africa,

*Reaffirming* the right of all peoples, including the people of South Africa, to determine their own destiny and to work out for themselves the institutions and the system of government under which they will, by general consent, live and work together to build a harmonious society, and remaining committed to doing everything possible and necessary to assist the people of South Africa, in such ways as they may, through their genuine representatives, determine to achieve this objective,

*Making these commitments* because we believe that all people are equal and have equal rights to human dignity and respect, regardless of colour, race, sex or creed, that all men and women have the right and duty to participate in their own government, as equal members of society, and that no individual or group of individuals has any right to govern others without their democratic consent, and reiterating that the apartheid system violates all these fundamental and universal principles,

*Affirming* that apartheid, characterized as a crime against the conscience and dignity of mankind, is responsible for the death of countless numbers of people in South Africa, has sought to dehumanize entire peoples and has imposed a brutal war on the region of southern Africa, which has resulted in untold loss of life, destruction of property and massive displacement of innocent men, women and children and which is a scourge and affront to humanity that must be fought and eradicated in its totality,

*Therefore we support* and continue to support all those in South Africa who pursue this noble objective. We believe this to be our duty, carried out in the interest of all humanity,

While *extending this support* to those who strive for a non-racial and democratic society in South Africa, a point on which no compromise is possible, we have repeatedly expressed our objective of a solution arrived at by peaceful means; we note that the people of South Africa, and their liberation movements who felt compelled to take up arms, have also upheld their preference for this position for many decades and continue to do so,

*Welcoming* the Declaration of the Ad Hoc Committee of the Organization of African Unity on Southern Africa on the question of South Africa, adopted at Harare on 21 August 1989, and subsequently endorsed by the Heads of State or Government of Non-Aligned Countries at their Ninth Conference, held at Belgrade from

4 to 7 September 1989, as a reaffirmation of readiness to resolve the problems of South Africa through negotiations. The Declaration is consistent with the positions contained in the Lusaka Manifesto of two decades ago, in particular regarding the preference of the African people for peaceful change, and takes into account the changes that have taken place in southern Africa since then. The Declaration constitutes a new challenge to the Pretoria regime to join in the noble efforts to end the apartheid system, an objective to which the United Nations has always been committed,

*Noting with appreciation* that the Commonwealth Heads of Government, at their meeting held at Kuala Lumpur from 18 to 24 October 1989, noted with satisfaction the strong preference for the path of negotiated and peaceful settlement inherent in the Declaration adopted at Harare on 21 August 1989, and considered what further steps they might take to advance the prospects for negotiations,

*Also noting with appreciation* that the Third Francophone Conference of Heads of State and Government, held at Dakar from 24 to 26 May 1989, likewise called for negotiations between Pretoria and representatives of the majority of the people with a view to the establishment of a democratic and egalitarian system in South Africa,

Consequently, *we shall continue* to do everything in our power to increase support for the legitimate struggle of the South African people, including maintaining international pressure against the system of apartheid until that system is ended and South Africa is transformed into a united, democratic and non-racial country, with justice and security for all its citizens,

In keeping with this solemn resolve, and responding directly to the wishes of the majority of the people of South Africa, *we publicly pledge ourselves* to the positions contained hereunder, convinced that their implementation will lead to a speedy end of the apartheid system and herald the dawn of a new era of peace for all the peoples of Africa, in a continent finally free from racism, White minority rule and colonial domination,

*Declare as follows:*

1. A conjuncture of circumstances exists which, if there is a demonstrable readiness on the part of the South African regime to engage in negotiations genuinely and seriously, given the repeated expression of the majority of the people of South Africa of their long-standing preference to arrive at a political settlement, could create the possibility to end apartheid through negotiations.

2. We would therefore encourage the people of South Africa, as part of their legitimate struggle, to join together to negotiate an end to the apartheid system and agree on all the measures that are necessary to transform their country into a non-racial democracy. We support the position held by the majority of the people of South Africa that these objectives, and not the amendment or reform of the apartheid system, should be the goals of the negotiations.

3. We are at one with the people of South Africa that the outcome of such a process should be a new constitutional order determined by them and based on the Charter of the United Nations and the Universal Declaration of Human Rights. We therefore hold the following fundamental principles to be of importance:

(*a*) South Africa shall become a united, non-racial and democratic State;

(*b*) All its people shall enjoy common and equal citizenship and nationality, regardless of race, colour, sex or creed;

(*c*) All its people shall have the right to participate in the government and administration of the country on the basis of universal, equal suffrage, under a non-racial voters' roll, and by secret ballot, in a united and non-fragmented South Africa;

(*d*) All shall have the right to form and join any political party of their choice, provided that this is not in furtherance of racism;

(*e*) All shall enjoy universally recognized human rights, freedoms and civil liberties, protected under an entrenched bill of rights;

(*f*) South Africa shall have a legal system that will guarantee equality of all before the law;

(*g*) South Africa shall have an independent and non-racial judiciary;

(*h*) There shall be created an economic order that will promote and advance the well-being of all South Africans;

(*i*) A democratic South Africa shall respect the rights, sovereignty and territorial integrity of all countries and pursue a policy of peace, friendship and mutually beneficial cooperation with all peoples.

4. We believe that acceptance of these fundamental principles could constitute the basis for an internationally acceptable solution that will enable South Africa to take its rightful place as an equal partner among the world community of nations.

A. *Climate for negotiations*

5. We believe that it is essential that the necessary climate be created for negotiations. There is an urgent need to respond positively to this universally acclaimed demand and thus create this climate.

6. Accordingly, the present South African regime should, at the least:

(*a*) Release all political prisoners and detainees unconditionally and refrain from imposing any restrictions on them;

(b) Lift all bans and restrictions on all proscribed and restricted organizations and persons;

(c) Remove all troops from the townships;

(d) End the state of emergency and repeal all legislation, such as the Internal Security Act, designed to circumscribe political activity;

(e) Cease all political trials and political executions.

7. These measures would help create the necessary climate in which free political discussion can take place—an essential condition to ensure that the people themselves participate in the process of remaking their country.

### B. *Guidelines to the process of negotiations*

8. We are of the view that the parties concerned should, in the context of the necessary climate, negotiate the future of their country and its people in good faith and in an atmosphere which, by mutual agreement between the liberation movements and the South African regime, would be free of violence. The process could commence along the following guidelines:

(a) Agreement on the mechanism for the drawing up of a new constitution, based on, among others, the principles enunciated above, and the basis for its adoption;

(b) Agreement on the role to be played by the international community in ensuring a successful transition to a democratic order;

(c) Agreed transitional arrangements and modalities for the process of the drawing up and adoption of a new constitution, and for the transition to a democratic order, including the holding of elections.

### C. *Programme of action*

9. In pursuance of the objectives stated in this Declaration, we hereby decide:

(a) To remain seized of the issue of a political resolution of the South African question;

(b) To step up all-round support for the opponents of apartheid and to campaign internationally in pursuance of this objective;

(c) To use concerted and effective measures, including the full observance by all countries of the mandatory arms embargo, aimed at applying pressure to ensure a speedy end to apartheid;

(d) To ensure that the international community does not relax existing measures aimed at encouraging the South African regime to eradicate apartheid until there is clear evidence of profound and irreversible changes, bearing in mind the objectives of this Declaration;

(e) To render all possible assistance to the front-line and neighbouring States to enable them: to rebuild their economies, which have been adversely affected by South Africa's acts of aggression and destabilization; to withstand any further such acts; and to continue to support the peoples of Namibia and South Africa;

(f) To extend such assistance to the Governments of Angola and Mozambique as they may request in order to secure peace for their peoples, and to encourage and support peace initiatives undertaken by the Governments of Angola and Mozambique aimed at bringing about peace and normalization of life in their countries;

(g) The new South Africa shall, upon adoption of the new constitution, participate fully in relevant organs and specialized agencies of the United Nations.

10. We request the Secretary-General to transmit copies of the present Declaration to the South African Government and the representatives of the oppressed people of South Africa and also request the Secretary-General to prepare a report and submit it to the General Assembly by 1 July 1990 on the progress made in the implementation of the present Declaration.

---

# Document 136

*Report by the Secretary-General on progress made in the implementation of the Declaration on Apartheid and its Destructive Consequences in Southern Africa; includes statement by Nelson Mandela, Deputy President of the African National Congress, in the Special Committee against Apartheid on 22 June 1990*

A/44/1990, 1 July 1990

## I. Introduction

1. At its sixteenth special session, on 14 December 1989, the General Assembly adopted the Declaration on Apartheid and its Destructive Consequences in Southern Africa (resolution S-16/1) (annex VII). The Declaration, inter alia, encouraged the people of South Africa to join together to negotiate an end to the apartheid system and agree on all the measures that are necessary to transform

their country into a non-racial democracy. The Declaration dealt with fundamental principles for a new constitutional order (para. 3), with the creation of a climate for negotiations (paras. 5-7), with guidelines to the process of negotiations (para. 8) and with a programme of action in pursuance of the objectives of the Declaration (para. 9).

2. In paragraph 10 of the Declaration, the General Assembly requested the Secretary-General to transmit copies of the Declaration to the South African Government and the representatives of the people of South Africa, and to prepare a report on the progress made in the implementation of the Declaration and submit it to the Assembly by 1 July 1990.

3. Prior to the adoption of the Declaration, on 7 December 1989, the Minister for Foreign Affairs of the Republic of South Africa addressed a letter to the Secretary-General in which he outlined the position of the Government of South Africa relating to the draft declaration then under consideration (annex III).

4. Pursuant to paragraph 10 of the Declaration, on 12 January 1990, the Secretary-General personally transmitted to the Permanent Representative of South Africa to the United Nations a copy of the Declaration. He also transmitted copies of the Declaration to the Permanent Observers of the African National Congress and the Pan Africanist Congress of Azania on 7 February 1990. In addition, the text of the Declaration was transmitted to the Permanent Representatives of Member States by a note verbale dated 7 March 1990, requesting them to bring the Declaration to the attention of their Governments and to provide the Secretary-General with information on the action which their Governments had taken in respect to provisions of the Declaration that concerned them. The replies received to date from Member States are reproduced in annex II. In addition, the Secretary-General of the Organization of African Unity provided a copy of the report of the Monitoring Group of the OAU *Ad Hoc* Committee on Southern Africa, which is being issued separately as a document of the General Assembly.

5. Since it was important that the report be as factual as possible, the Secretary-General, while in Windhoek on 20 March 1990, sought the agreement of the State President of South Africa for a team of senior United Nations officials to visit the Republic at an appropriate date. While agreeing to this suggestion, the State President made it clear that this was without prejudice to the position of his Government on the question of non-interference in the internal affairs of South Africa.

. . .

## II. Observations

10. The Secretary-General has been greatly encouraged by the positive developments that have taken place within South Africa since the beginning of this year. The bold and courageous policy to which President de Klerk has committed his Government opens up distinct possibilities for the dismantling of the *apartheid* system. Equally encouraging and statesmanlike has been the vision and forebearance displayed by the Black leadership which, despite long years of injustice and oppression, has renewed its commitment to a peaceful process for ending apartheid and building a non-racial and democratic society.

11. The fact that the United Nations Team was able to meet with whom it wished, travel where it desired, and receive freely the views of all on political issues arising from the policy of apartheid, demonstrates, by itself, a significant change in the political climate.

12. Of the measures required by the Declaration on Apartheid and its Destructive Consequences in Southern Africa to create a climate for free political activity, the measure relating to the lifting of the ban on political parties and movements has been implemented in full. Other measures have been implemented in part. While it is evident that an important process has been set in motion, many believe that the Government should implement all measures in their totality to create the appropriate atmosphere.

13. Parallel with the need to establish an appropriate climate for the negotiations is the urgent requirement to end the violence. The issue of violence, not least in Natal, urgently needs to be addressed at the highest level since, if it is allowed to continue unrestrained, the consequences could well present serious difficulties for the political process. The Secretary-General therefore appeals to all parties to do whatever is necessary to end the violence and to work together to build a peaceful South Africa.

14. It is quite clear from the report of the Team that a substantial body of public opinion is anxious to see that the process for the dismantlement of the apartheid system be accelerated.

15. Some of the data in the report illustrate vividly the grave social injustices that have been inflicted by apartheid on the Black population. The Secretary-General would strongly endorse any measures aimed at redressing the social and economic imbalances, particularly in the area of housing, education, employment and health. Such measures would go a long way towards addressing effectively glaring inequities and instilling public confidence in the democratic process and in national institutions.

16. The Secretary-General was requested by the General Assembly to submit a report on the progress made in the implementation of the Declaration on Apartheid within six months of its adoption. As the report of the United Nations Team shows, the political process

towards the dismantlement of the apartheid system is still at an early stage. Political parties and movements are in the first phases of developing their responses to the negotiating process. For this reason the report does not comment in detail on some of the major issues covered by the Declaration, such as those envisaged in paragraph 8 of that document concerning the mechanisms for drafting a constitution, as well as the principles of the constitution itself.

...

## Annex VI

*Statement by Nelson Mandela, Deputy President of the African National Congress, to the 641st meeting of the Special Committee against Apartheid on 22 June 1990*

Your Excellency Ambassador Ibrahim Gambari, Permanent Representative of the Federal Republic of Nigeria and Chairman of the Special Committee against Apartheid; Your Excellency Mr. Joseph Garba, President of the General Assembly; Your Excellency Mr. Javier Pérez de Cuéllar, Secretary-General of the United Nations; Your Excellencies Permanent Representatives; Heads of Observer Missions; ladies and gentlemen, friends and comrades.

We feel especially honoured and privileged to have the possibility today to stand at this particular place, to speak to all of you, who represent the peoples of the world. We are most grateful to you, Mr. Chairman, the Special Committee against Apartheid, the Secretary-General and all Member States of the Organization for making it possible for us to be here.

The tragedy is that what has created the need for this gathering and made it seem natural that we must gather in this historic meeting place is the fact of the continuing commission of a crime against humanity. How much better it would have been if we were meeting to celebrate a victory in hand, a dream fulfilled, the triumph of justice over a tyrannical past, the realization of the vision enshrined in the United Nations Charter and the Universal Declaration of Human Rights.

It will for ever remain an indelible blight on human history that the apartheid crime ever occurred. Future generations will surely ask: what error was made that this system established itself in the wake of the adoption of a Universal Declaration of Human Rights?

It will for ever remain an accusation and a challenge to all men and women of conscience that it took as long as it has before all of us stood up to say enough is enough. Future generations will surely inquire: what error was made that this system established itself in the aftermath of the trials at Nuremberg?

These questions will arise because when this august body, the United Nations, first discussed the South African question, in 1946, it was discussing the issue of racism. They will be posed because the spur to the establishment of this Organization was the determination of all humanity never again to permit racist theory and practice to dragoon the world into the deathly clutches of war and genocide.

And yet, for all that, a racist tyranny established itself in our country. As they knew would happen, who refused to treat this matter as a quaint historical aberration, this tyranny has claimed its own conclave of victims. It has established its own brutal worth by the number of children it has killed and the orphans, the widows and widowers it can claim as its unique creation.

And still it lives on, provoking strange and monstrous debates about the means that its victims are obliged to use to rid themselves of this intolerable scourge, eliciting arguments from those who choose not to act, that to do nothing must be accepted as the very essence of civilized opposition to tyranny.

We hold it as an inviolable principle that racism must be opposed by all the means that humanity has at its disposal. Wherever it occurs it has the potential to result in a systematic and comprehensive denial of human rights to those who are discriminated against. This is because all racism is inherently a challenge to human rights, because it denies the view that every human being is a person of equal worth with any other, because it treats entire peoples as sub-human.

This is why it was correct to characterize the apartheid system as a crime against humanity and appropriate that the international community should decide that it should be suppressed and punishment meted out against its perpetrators. We pay tribute to this Organization and its Member States for this and other decisions and actions it took to expunge this crime.

We also take this opportunity to salute the Special Committee against Apartheid, which has been and is a very important instrument in our struggle against the iniquitous and oppressive policies of the South African Government. We salute also the States that make up its membership, which have been unrelenting in their resolve to contribute everything they could to ensure that the world was mobilized to act against the *apartheid* system.

In this connection also, Sir, allow us to express a well-deserved tribute to your country, Nigeria, which you so ably represent, as did your predecessor in this important office, His Excellency Major-General Joseph Garba, current President of the General Assembly, under whose leadership the United Nations Declaration on South Africa was adopted by consensus at the sixteenth special session of the General Assembly last December.

That Declaration will go down in history as one of the most important documents in the struggle of the international community against apartheid. The fact that it was adopted by consensus was itself a telling blow against the apartheid system and a vital statement underlining the unity of the world community on the South African question and its resolution.

We look forward to the report that the Secretary-General of the United Nations will submit dealing with the question of the implementation of the Declaration in South Africa. This report will also be important to the extent that it will provide a basis for further decisions by the United Nations regarding future action on the question of apartheid.

What must, however, be clear is that the apartheid system remains in place. None of the principles laid down in the Declaration has been implemented to provide what the Declaration characterized as an internationally acceptable solution of the South African question. Similarly, the profound and irreversible changes which the Declaration visualized have not yet occurred.

The conclusion from these observations would seem clear to us. It is that nothing which has happened in South Africa calls for a revision of the positions that this Organization has taken in its struggle against apartheid. We therefore strongly urge that there should be no relaxation of existing measures. The sanctions that have been imposed by the United Nations and by individual Governments should remain in place.

We also urge that the United Nations should do everything in its power to maintain the unity it achieved when it adopted the Declaration on South Africa last December. We therefore hope that all Member States will continue to act in concert so as not to create any situation in which those who are opposed to change in our country find encouragement to resist change, because some countries would have destroyed the consensus that has been achieved. In this regard, we take this opportunity once more to call on the countries of the European community, which are holding a summit meeting in a few days' time, themselves to remain faithful to the purposes of the Declaration to whose elaboration they were party and for which they voted.

At the initiative of ANC, the process has begun which could lead to a just political settlement in our country. At our well-known meeting in Cape Town, at the beginning of last month, we agreed with the South African Government on the removal of the obstacles to negotiations which are identified in the Declaration. The process of implementing that agreement has started, but as this distinguished gathering knows, a lot still remains to be done before we can say that a climate conducive to negotiations has been created.

We therefore still have some distance to travel before we undertake the further steps outlined in the Declaration, leading to negotiations for the adoption of a new, democratic constitution. The fact that a good beginning was made in Cape Town should not lead us to conclude that further progress is assured or that we will not have to confront major obstacles in future.

In this regard, we would like to reiterate what we have said before, that we believe that President de Klerk and his colleagues in the leadership of the ruling party are people of integrity. We are of the view that they will abide by decisions that are arrived at in the course of our discussions and negotiations. This, in itself, is an important victory of our common struggle because it is that struggle which has made the cost of maintaining the apartheid system too high and helped to convince the ruling group in our country that changes can no longer be resisted.

It is, however, also true that there are many among our White compatriots who are still committed to the maintenance of the evil system of White minority domination. Some are opposed because of their ideological adherence to racism. Others are resisting because they fear democratic majority rule. Some of these are armed and are to be found within the army and the police.

Outside of these State agencies, other Whites are working at a feverish pace to establish paramilitary groups whose stated aim is the physical liquidation of ANC, its leadership and membership, as well as other persons or formations which these right-wing terrorists see as a threat to the continued existence of the system of White minority domination. We cannot afford to underestimate the threat that these defenders of a brutal and continuing reality pose to the whole process of working towards a just political settlement.

The ANC is determined to do everything in its power to ensure speedy movement forward towards the peaceful abolition of the apartheid system. To this end we are engaged in many initiatives within South Africa aimed at bringing into the process of negotiations all the people and the representative political formations of our country. We have to overcome the mistrust that exists on both sides and reinforce the understanding that the only victory we should all seek is the victory of the people as a whole and not the victory of one party over another.

It is obvious that none of these processes can be easy. We are, however, inspired by the experience of the people of Namibia and our comrades-in-arms of the South West Africa People's Organization (SWAPO), who also overcame the divisions and the mistrust generated by the apartheid system, carried out a peaceful political process within a relatively short period of time and are today a proud nation of independent people. We take this opportunity to salute the representatives of the Namibian people who are present in this Hall and acknowledge the debt we owe them for the contribution they have made to our own liberation.

We also salute the front-line States of southern Africa and the rest of our continent for their own enormous contribution to the struggle against apartheid, which has brought us to the point today when we can say that the victory of the struggle for a united, democratic and non-racial South Africa is within our grasp.

Tribute is also due to the non-aligned countries and Movement and the peoples of the rest of the world for their own sterling efforts in pursuit of the common cause. What we must once more urge is that all these forces should maintain their unity around the perspectives contained in the United Nations and Harare Declarations on South Africa. How fast we progress towards liberation will depend on how successful we are in our efforts to sustain that united resolve.

This is for us a moving moment because we know that as we stand here we are among friends and people of conscience. We know this because we know what you did over the decades to secure my release and the release of other South African political prisoners from Pretoria's dungeons. We thank you most sincerely for this, especially because you have thus given us the opportunity to join hands with you in the search for a speedy solution to the enormous problems facing our country, our region and continent and humanity as a whole.

We know also that you harbour the hope that we will not relent or falter in the pursuit of that common vision which should result in the transformation of South Africa into a country of democracy, justice and peace. Standing before the nations of the world, we make that commitment, strengthened by the knowledge that you will fight on side by side with us until victory is achieved. We also take this opportunity to extend warm greetings to all others who fight for their liberation and their human rights, including the peoples of Palestine and Western Sahara. We commend their struggles to you, convinced that we are all moved by the fact that freedom is indivisible, convinced that the denial of the rights of one diminishes the freedom of others.

We thank you for your kind invitation to us to address this gathering and for the opportunity it has given us to pay homage to you all: to the Secretary-General, to the President of the General Assembly, to the Special Committee against Apartheid and to the United Nations itself for the work that has been done to end the apartheid crime against humanity.

The distance we still have to travel is not long. Let us travel it together. Let us, by our joint actions, vindicate the purposes for which this Organization was established and create a situation wherein its Charter and the Universal Declaration of Human Rights will become part of the body of law on which will be based the political and social order of a new South Africa. Our common victory is assured.

# Document 137

*General Assembly resolution: Policies of apartheid of the Government of South Africa*

A/RES/44/244, 17 September 1990

*The General Assembly,*

*Recalling* the Declaration on Apartheid and its Destructive Consequences in Southern Africa, adopted by consensus on 14 December 1989 at the sixteenth special session of the General Assembly,

*Bearing in mind* that the Declaration called upon the South African regime, *inter alia*, to undertake certain measures in order to create a climate suitable for negotiations in South Africa,

*Recalling* that the Declaration called upon the international community not to relax existing measures aimed at encouraging the South African regime to eradicate apartheid until there is clear evidence of profound and irreversible changes, bearing in mind the objectives of the Declaration,

*Noting* that the States Members of the United Na-

tions and the members of the international community have generally adhered to the programme of action contained in the Declaration and expressing its concern over any departures that have occurred from the international consensus reflected in the Declaration,

*Taking careful note* of the report of the Secretary-General on the progress made in the implementation of the Declaration and welcoming his contributions,

*Taking note* of the report of the Monitoring Group of the *Ad Hoc* Committee on Southern Africa of the Organization of African Unity,

*Taking note also* of other statements and reports from Member States and regional groups on this issue,

*Noting* that while some significant measures in the right direction have been undertaken by the South African regime, such as the unbanning of the African National Congress of South Africa, the Pan Africanist Congress of Azania and other political organizations and the release of some political prisoners, including Nelson Mandela, and the regime's declared commitment to abolish the apartheid system, continued efforts are needed to establish a climate fully conducive to negotiations and free political activity,

*Welcoming* the ongoing talks between the African National Congress of South Africa and the South African regime aimed at eliminating obstacles to the commencement of negotiations towards a peaceful settlement in South Africa, and the results achieved thus far as set out in the Groote Schuur Minute of 4 May 1990 and the Pretoria Minute of 6 August 1990,

*Gravely concerned* with the escalating violence in South Africa resulting largely from continued existence of the apartheid policies, practices and structures, and actions of those opposed to the democratic transformation of South Africa,

1. *Reaffirms* the provisions of the Declaration on Apartheid and its Destructive Consequences in Southern Africa and the need for their full and immediate implementation;

2. *Determines* that further steps need to be undertaken by the South African regime to implement the profound and irreversible changes called for in the Declaration;

3. *Calls upon* all Governments and intergovernmental organizations to adhere strictly to the programme of action contained in the Declaration by maintaining existing measures aimed at encouraging the South African regime to eradicate apartheid until there is clear evidence of profound and irreversible changes, bearing in mind the objectives of the Declaration;

4. *Calls upon* the South African regime to proceed without delay to establish a climate fully conducive to negotiations by taking all the steps stipulated in the Declaration, in particular, to implement its commitment to repeal all legislation, such as the Internal Security Act, designed to circumscribe political activity;

5. *Calls for* an immediate end to violence and urges the South African authorities to take urgent action to end it, specifically by dismantling the apartheid structures as well as ensuring effective and impartial action by the security forces and calls upon all parties concerned to contribute to the establishment of a climate free of violence;

6. *Welcomes* the fact that the African National Congress of South Africa and the South African regime have engaged in talks which have thus far resulted in the Groote Schuur and the Pretoria minutes aimed at facilitating the commencement of substantive negotiations;

7. *Commends* the African National Congress of South Africa for having taken the initiative in calling for talks with the South African regime and for its landmark decision to suspend the armed struggle;

8. *Urges* the international community and the Secretary-General, through the relevant United Nations agencies, to provide all possible assistance to facilitate the re-establishment of previously banned political organizations in South Africa as well as the reintegration of released political prisoners;

9. *Requests* the Secretary-General, through the relevant United Nations agencies, to provide all necessary assistance for the voluntary repatriation of the South African refugees and political exiles in safety and dignity, and requests the South African regime, the liberation movements and other organizations in South Africa and the international community to extend their full support to this endeavour;

10. *Also requests* the Secretary-General to remain actively seized of developments in South Africa and to submit by 30 June 1991 to the forty-fifth session of the General Assembly a report on further progress in the implementation of the Declaration.

---

# Document 138

*Statement by Secretary-General Javier Pérez de Cuéllar on the occasion of the International Day of Solidarity with South African Political Prisoners*

UN Press Release SG/SM/4504 - GA/AP/2001, 11 October 1990

Today's observance of the International Day of Solidarity with South African Political Prisoners is taking place at a historic juncture in South Africa. Political developments over the past year hold promise that more tangible progress will be made in dismantling the system of apartheid, thus removing a major cause for the unjust imprisonment of those who seek an equitable system of government under which the rights of all will be assured.

I know that I express the strong hope of all present here that the time will soon come when South Africa will be transformed into a united, democratic and non-racial society. It remains my conviction that such a transformation is within the grasp of the South African people and, given the political will, statesmanship and a scrupulous regard for the rights of all, I have no doubt that it will materialize.

These sentiments were expressed by the General Assembly in its Declaration on Apartheid last December. The Assembly affirmed its belief that certain measures were needed in order to create the necessary climate for negotiations. Among these was the requirement that the South African Government should release all political prisoners and detainees unconditionally and refrain from imposing any restrictions on them.

In this connection, we have all welcomed the developments that have led to the release from imprisonment of leaders such as Nelson Mandela, Zephania Mothopeng, Walter Sisulu and others. Their release was a vindication of all that we in this Organization cherish and hold dear.

The concern of the General Assembly towards political prisoners and exiles was again reflected in the resolution it adopted last month under which it requested me to provide all possible assistance, through relevant United Nations agencies, to facilitate the return of exiles and refugees, and the reintegration of released political prisoners into South African society. United Nations stands ready to do so. Consultations have in fact already begun between the United Nations High Commissioner for Refugees (UNHCR) and the concerned parties.

The agreements reached between the Government of South Africa and the African National Congress (ANC), at their meeting in Pretoria last August, provide for a plan for the release of ANC-related prisoners and the granting of indemnity to groups of persons in a phased manner. I was glad to learn yesterday that a further group of political prisoners has been released.

There is no doubt that the agreements reached in August will promote the confidence that will further contribute to the creation of a climate conducive to negotiations. Undoing the wrongs inflicted by apartheid and establishing fully the conditions in which free political activity can take place are necessary ingredients for national reconciliation. These are indispensable steps in strengthening the process for political change that has now been initiated in South Africa.

Let me again stress how critical it is that an atmosphere free from violence and intimidation be restored throughout South Africa. All parties concerned must contribute to the establishment of a peaceful climate which will assure security for all, and enable the energies of the people to be devoted towards nation-building.

Our thoughts today go to all political prisoners who still languish in jail and are sacrificing their freedom in the cause of democracy, decency and dignity. They too must be released.

# Document 139

*General Assembly resolution: Policies of apartheid of the Government of South Africa—International efforts to eradicate apartheid*

A/RES/45/176 A, 19 December 1990

*The General Assembly,*

*Reaffirming* the Declaration on Apartheid and its Destructive Consequences in Southern Africa, contained in the annex to its resolution S-16/1 of 14 December 1989, and its resolution 44/244 of 17 September 1990,

*Having considered* the report of the Special Committee against Apartheid, and the report of the Secretary-General on progress made in the implementation of the Declaration,

*Convinced* that the total eradication of apartheid and the establishment, through broad-based negotiations, of a non-racial democracy based on a new constitutional order providing for universal, equal suffrage under a non-racial voters' roll can lead to a peaceful and lasting solution to the problems facing the people of South Africa,

*Also convinced* that the policy and practice of apartheid breeds violence and its continuation would be detrimental to the vital interests of all the people of South Africa,

*Gravely concerned* at the continuing repression of the majority population in South Africa through the apartheid system, manifested, *inter alia*, by detentions without trial, continued possibility of executions of political prisoners, absence of full implementation of agreements regarding the return of political exiles without restrictions and repressive provisions in the Internal Security Act,

*Noting* that, while some significant measures in the right direction have been undertaken by the South African authorities, including the recent repeal of the Separate Amenities Act and the lifting of the state of emergency throughout the country, continuing effort is needed to facilitate free political activity and to foster a climate fully conducive to negotiations,

*Welcoming* the ongoing talks between the African National Congress of South Africa and the South African authorities aimed at facilitating the commencement of substantive broad-based negotiations,

*Noting* that the African National Congress, in an effort to contribute to an atmosphere free of violence, which is in accordance with the guidelines of the Declaration, and further to the agreements set out in the Pretoria Minute of 6 August 1990, has suspended its armed activities,

*Gravely concerned* that the recurring violence resulting largely from the persistence of apartheid and other factors, including actions of those opposed to the democratic transformation of South Africa, poses a threat to the negotiating process,

*Noting with serious concern* the continuing effects of the acts of aggression and destabilization that have been committed by South Africa against neighbouring independent African States, in particular against Angola and Mozambique,

*Noting* that the international community has generally adhered to the programme of action contained in the Declaration, and expressing its concern over any departures that have occurred from the international consensus reflected in the Declaration,

*Recognizing* the responsibility of the United Nations and the international community to take all necessary measures aimed at the eradication of apartheid through peaceful means, in particular by adhering to the programme of action contained in the Declaration by maintaining the measures aimed at encouraging the South African authorities to eradicate apartheid and to promote profound and irreversible change,

1. *Reaffirms* its support for the legitimate struggle of the South African people for the total eradication of apartheid and the establishment of a united, non-racial and democratic society in South Africa in which all its people, irrespective of race, colour, sex or creed, will enjoy the same fundamental freedoms and human rights;

2. *Takes note* of Pretoria's declared commitment to abolish the apartheid system;

3. *Reaffirms* the provisions of the Declaration on Apartheid and its Destructive Consequences in Southern Africa and the need for their full and immediate implementation;

4. *Fully supports* the efforts of the South African people to arrive at a peaceful settlement of the problems in their country through genuine negotiations, and welcomes the fact that the African National Congress of South Africa and the South African regime have engaged in talks that have thus far resulted in the agreements set out in the Groote Schuur Minute of 4 May 1990 and in the Pretoria Minute, aimed at facilitating the commencement of substantive negotiations;

5. *Calls upon* the South African authorities to continue their efforts to foster a climate fully conducive to negotiations and free political activity, in particular by repealing all repressive legislation, such as provisions in the Internal Security Act, by ending detentions without trial, by allowing the return of all political exiles without restrictions and by fully implementing all agreements reached so far with the African National Congress, including the release of all remaining political prisoners;

6. *Calls* for a speedy and full implementation of the agreements reached so far between the South African regime and the African National Congress;

7. *Welcomes* the progress made thus far aimed at facilitating the commencement of substantive broad-based negotiations and encourages all parties concerned, taking into account the guidelines to the process of negotiations contained in the Declaration, to participate fully in future negotiations, in order to secure the adoption of a new constitution and the establishment of a united, non-racial and democratic South Africa;

8. *Calls* for an immediate end to violence, which has resulted largely from the continued existence of the apartheid policies, practices and structures;

9. *Calls upon* the South African authorities to redouble their efforts to end recurring violence by ensuring effective and impartial actions by all branches of government and all competent authorities against all those responsible for violence, including vigilante groups, and calls upon all parties concerned to contribute to the establishment of an atmosphere free of violence;

10. *Considers* that while the South African authorities have declared their intention to eradicate apartheid and embark on negotiations for a new constitution, the process of change in South Africa remains at an early stage and further substantive progress needs to be made to promote the profound and irreversible changes called for in the Declaration;

11. *Calls upon* all Governments and intergovernmental organizations to adhere strictly to the programme of action contained in the Declaration by maintaining the measures aimed at applying pressure on the South African regime to eradicate apartheid and to promote profound and irreversible changes, bearing in mind the objectives of the Declaration, namely, the speedy eradication of apartheid and the establishment of a united, democratic, non-racial South Africa;

12. *Calls upon* all Governments, intergovernmental organizations and financial institutions to use concerted and effective measures, particularly in the areas of

economic and financial relations with apartheid South Africa, aimed at applying pressure to ensure a speedy end to apartheid;

13. *Calls upon* all Governments to observe fully the mandatory arms embargo and requests the Security Council to monitor effectively the strict implementation of the arms embargo;

14. *Appeals* to all Governments and organizations to render all possible assistance to the front-line States, particularly Angola and Mozambique, to enable them to reconstruct their economies, which have been devastated from years of destabilization;

15. *Appeals* to all States, organizations and institutions to increase economic, humanitarian, legal, educational and other assistance and support to the victims of apartheid and to all those, including previously banned organizations, who oppose apartheid and promote a united, non-racial, democratic society in South Africa;

16. *Urges* the international community and the Secretary-General, through the relevant United Nations agencies, to provide all possible assistance to facilitate the re-establishment of previously banned political organizations in South Africa as well as the reintegration of released political prisoners and returning South African refugees and exiles;

17. *Requests* the Secretary-General to ensure the coordination of activities of the United Nations system in the implementation of the Declaration and report thereon to the General Assembly at its forty-sixth session, and to continue monitoring the implementation of the Declaration as well as pursuing appropriate initiatives to facilitate all efforts leading to the peaceful eradication of apartheid.

# Document 140

*General Assembly resolution: Policies of apartheid of the Government of South Africa—Concerted and effective measures aimed at eradicating apartheid*

A/RES/45/176 B, 19 December 1990

*The General Assembly,*

*Recalling* the Declaration on Apartheid and its Destructive Consequences in Southern Africa, adopted by consensus on 14 December 1989 at its sixteenth special session, and its resolution 44/244 of 17 September 1990,

*Recalling also* its resolution 44/27 K of 22 November 1989 and other relevant resolutions,

*Taking note* of the report of the Special Committee against Apartheid and of the reports of the Secretary-General on international financial pressure on the apartheid economy of South Africa and measures to monitor sanctions undertaken by the United Nations system, Governments and non-governmental agencies,

*Gravely concerned* that, in spite of recent positive developments in South Africa, the system of apartheid and most of its main pillars, namely, the Land Acts, the Group Areas Act, the Population Registration Act, the Bantu Education Act and the acts establishing the tricameral Parliament and the bantustan system, still remain intact,

*Convinced* that sanctions and other restrictive measures have had a significant impact on recent developments in South Africa and remain a most effective and necessary instrument of pressure towards the peaceful resolution of the conflict in that country,

*Strongly convinced* that the imposition of comprehensive and mandatory sanctions by the Security Council under Chapter VII of the Charter of the United Nations remains the most appropriate and effective means to bring about a peaceful end to apartheid,

*Noting* that the States Members of the United Nations and the members of the international community have generally adhered to the programme of action contained in the Declaration and expressing its concern over any departures that have occurred from the international consensus reflected in the Declaration,

*Gravely concerned* that some Member States and transnational corporations have continued economic relations with South Africa, while others continue to undermine the sanctions imposed by other States, by establishing and/or increasing their trade with that country, as borne out in the report of the Special Committee,

*Noting with concern* that sanctions and other measures adopted by the General Assembly, as well as measures introduced unilaterally by a number of States, lack coordination, monitoring and enforcement mechanisms,

*Considering* that measures taken by States individually or collectively, while commendable, vary in coverage and degree of monitoring and enforcement, and are not always addressed to those areas of the South African economy which are responsive to international pressures,

*Noting with concern* the recent talks between the International Monetary Fund and representatives of the South African regime and any consideration by the Fund of loans to South Africa,

*Commending* those States which have not relaxed their existing measures and maintained their commitment to the international consensus expressed in the programme of action contained in the Declaration, whereby Member States of the United Nations decided that the international community should not relax existing measures,

1. *Reaffirms* that apartheid is a crime against the conscience and dignity of humankind and a threat to international peace and security, and that it is a primary responsibility of the United Nations to assist in efforts to eliminate it without further delay;

2. *Calls upon* all States, especially those States which have increased or initiated trade, financial and other links with South Africa, in particular the leading trading partners of South Africa, as indicated in the annual report of the Special Committee against Apartheid, to adhere fully to the programme of action contained in the Declaration on Apartheid and its Destructive Consequences in Southern Africa;

3. *Calls upon* all States to maintain existing measures aimed at applying pressure on apartheid South Africa, particularly in the following areas:

(*a*) Supply of all products, in particular computer and communications equipment, technologies, skills and services, including military intelligence, that can be used for the military and nuclear industry of South Africa;

(*b*) Import of coal, gold and other minerals and agricultural products from South Africa;

(*c*) Effective withdrawal of transnational corporations, banks and financial institutions from South Africa by ceasing equity investment and by cutting off non-equity links, particularly those involving transfer of high technology and know-how;

(*d*) Provision of new credits and loans;

(*e*) Double taxation agreements with South Africa and any form of tax relief in respect of income from investments in that country;

(*f*) Landing and port rights to South African air and sea carriers and direct air, sea and other transport links with South Africa;

4. *Appeals* to all Governments, organizations and individuals to refrain from any sports relations with South Africa and not entertain any cultural or academic links unless any particular activity in the cultural and academic fields has the intent and effect of opposing apartheid in line with United Nations policy on this matter, and to give appropriate assistance in these fields to the anti-apartheid forces and to the disadvantaged sections of South African society;

5. *Urges* Governments and private financial institutions, as well as the International Monetary Fund and the World Bank, not to extend loans and credits to South Africa, whether to the public or private sector, until there is clear evidence of profound and irreversible changes in South Africa, bearing in mind the objectives of the Declaration;

6. *Urges* all States to close existing loopholes in their existing measures, monitor strictly their implementation and adopt and apply, when necessary, legislation providing for penalties on individuals and enterprises violating those measures;

7. *Requests* the Special Committee to continue to monitor the implementation of existing measures aimed at the eradication of apartheid, and to report thereon to the General Assembly and the Security Council as appropriate;

8. *Requests* the Secretary-General to report to the General Assembly at its forty-sixth session on the implementation of the present resolution.

---

# Document 141

*General Assembly resolution: Policies of apartheid of the Government of South Africa—Military collaboration with South Africa*

A/RES/45/176 C, 19 December 1990

*The General Assembly,*

*Recalling* the Declaration on Apartheid and its Destructive Consequences in Southern Africa, adopted by consensus on 14 December 1989 at its sixteenth special session, and its resolution 44/244 of 17 September 1990,

*Recalling* its resolutions and those of the Security Council on the arms embargo, as well as other resolutions on collaboration with South Africa,

*Taking note* of the report of the Special Committee against Apartheid and the report of the Security Council Committee established by Council resolution 421 (1977) of 9 December 1977 concerning the question of South Africa on its activities during the period 1980-1989,

*Noting with grave concern* that the mandatory sanctions imposed by the Security Council in its resolution 418 (1977) of 4 November 1977 lack an effective monitoring and enforcement mechanism,

*Noting with appreciation* the resolve and coerciveness of the Security Council in its handling of questions relating to the preservation of international peace and security,

*Reiterating* that the full implementation of the arms embargo against South Africa is an essential element of international action against apartheid,

*Expressing serious concern* at the increasing number of violations of the mandatory arms embargo, particularly by those countries which surreptitiously continue to trade in arms with South Africa and allow South Africa to participate in international arms exhibitions,

*Gravely concerned* at the practice carried out by certain oil-producing States whereby oil is exchanged for South African arms,

*Noting with concern* that South Africa's external military relations, especially in the area of military technology and, in particular, in the production and testing of nuclear missiles, continue unabated,

1. *Strongly deplores* the actions of those States which, directly or indirectly, continue to violate the arms embargo and collaborate with South Africa in the military, nuclear, intelligence and technology fields, and calls upon those States to terminate forthwith such hostile acts and honour their obligations under Security Council resolution 421 (1977);

2. *Urges* all States to adopt strict legislation relating to the implementation of the arms embargo and prohibit the supply to South Africa of all products, in particular computer and communications equipment, technologies, skills and services, including military intelligence, that can be used for the military and nuclear industry of that country;

3. *Urges* the Security Council to consider immediate steps to ensure the scrupulous and full implementation and the effective monitoring of the arms embargo imposed by Council resolutions 418 (1977) and 558 (1984) of 13 December 1984, to consider strengthening the monitoring and the reporting of violations of the arms embargo and to provide information on a regular basis to the Secretary-General for general distribution to Member States;

4. *Also urges* the Security Council to implement the recommendations of the report of the Committee established under Council resolution 421 (1977) concerning appropriate measures against those States violating the mandatory arms embargo against South Africa;

5. *Requests* the Special Committee against Apartheid to keep the matter under constant review and to report thereon to the General Assembly and the Security Council as appropriate.

---

# Document 142

*General Assembly resolution: Policies of apartheid of the Government of South Africa—Programme of work of the Special Committee against Apartheid*

A/RES/45/176 E, 19 December 1990

*The General Assembly,*

*Having considered* the report of the Special Committee against Apartheid,

1. *Commends* the Special Committee against Apartheid for the diligent manner in which it has discharged its responsibilities in monitoring the situation in South Africa and promoting international action against apartheid;

2. *Takes note* of the report of the Special Committee and endorses its recommendations relating to its programme of work;

3. *Authorizes* the Special Committee, in accordance with its mandate and acting, with the support services of the United Nations Centre against Apartheid, as the focal point for the international campaign against apartheid and the promotion of the implementation of the Declaration on Apartheid and its Destructive Consequences in Southern Africa:

(*a*) To continue monitoring closely developments in South Africa and the actions of the international community, particularly regarding the need for maintaining pressure on South Africa as called for in the Declaration;

(*b*) To continue mobilizing international action against apartheid, *inter alia*, through collection, analysis and dissemination of information, through liaison and consultations with Governments, intergovernmental and non-governmental organizations and relevant individuals and groups, both inside and outside South Africa, able to influence public opinion and decision-making, and through missions, hearings, conferences, publicity and other relevant activities;

(*c*) To publish an interim annual report during the first half of 1991 on developments in South Africa and on the international response thereto and, in this context, undertake, as appropriate, consultations with the parties concerned;

4. *Appeals* to all Governments, intergovernmental and non-governmental organizations to increase their cooperation with the Special Committee and the Centre in the discharge of their mandates;

5. *Requests* all United Nations bodies, organs and agencies to cooperate with the Special Committee and the Centre in their activities in order to ensure consistency, improve coordination and efficient use of available resources and avoid duplication of efforts in the implementation of the relevant resolutions of the General Assembly and the Security Council;

6. *Requests* Governments and organizations to provide financial and other assistance for the special projects of the Special Committee and to make generous contributions to the Trust Fund for Publicity against Apartheid;

7. *Appeals* to all Governments, intergovernmental and non-governmental organizations, information media and individuals to cooperate with the Centre and the Department of Public Information of the Secretariat in their activities relating to apartheid and, in particular, in disseminating information on the evolving situation in South Africa;

8. *Decides* to continue the authorization of adequate financial provision in the regular budget of the United Nations to enable the African National Congress of South Africa and the Pan Africanist Congress of Azania to maintain offices in New York in order to participate effectively in the deliberations of the Special Committee and other appropriate bodies;

9. *Decides* to make a special allocation of 480,000 United States dollars to the Special Committee for 1991 from the regular budget of the United Nations to cover the cost of special projects to be decided upon by the Committee.

# Document 143

## General Assembly resolution: Policies of apartheid of the Government of South Africa—Oil embargo against South Africa

A/RES/45/176 F, 19 December 1990

*The General Assembly,*

*Having considered* the report of the Intergovernmental Group to Monitor the Supply and Shipping of Oil and Petroleum Products to South Africa, as well as its interim report, which was adopted unanimously on 12 June 1990,

*Recalling* its resolution 44/244 of 17 September 1990, in which it reaffirmed the Declaration on Apartheid and its Destructive Consequences in Southern Africa, which was adopted by consensus on 14 December 1989 by the General Assembly at its sixteenth special session,

*Recalling also* its resolutions on the oil embargo against South Africa, in particular resolution 44/27 H of 22 November 1989,

*Recognizing* the importance of the oil embargo and other existing measures imposed by the international community on the apartheid regime towards the elimination of apartheid through negotiations, as well as the importance of maintaining these measures until there is clear evidence of profound and irreversible changes, bearing in mind the objectives of the Declaration,

*Noting* that, while oil-exporting States have committed themselves to an oil embargo against South Africa, very few major shipping States have done so,

*Concerned* that the oil embargo against South Africa is still being violated and that South Africa, because of loopholes in the embargo, such as lack of effective legislation, has been able to acquire oil and petroleum products,

*Convinced* that an effective oil embargo against South Africa would contribute to the efforts of the international community to bring about a negotiated settlement and the establishment of a united, non-racial and democratic South Africa,

1. *Takes note* of the report of the Intergovernmental Group to Monitor the Supply and Shipping of Oil and Petroleum Products to South Africa and endorses its recommendations;

2. *Commends* the proposed model law for the effective enforcement of the oil embargo against South Africa annexed to the annual report of the Intergovernmental Group to States for their attention, including consideration of the adoption of the general principles of the draft within the context and framework of their own legal practices;

3. *Urges* the Security Council to take action under appropriate provisions of the Charter of the United Nations to ensure an effective embargo on the supply and shipping of oil and petroleum products to South Africa in order to effect a speedy and peaceful eradication of apartheid;

4. *Requests* all States, pending such decisions, to adopt effective measures and/or legislation to broaden the scope of the oil embargo in order to ensure the complete cessation of the supply and shipping of oil and petroleum

products to South Africa, whether directly or indirectly, and in particular:

(a) To apply strictly the "end users" clause and other conditions concerning restriction on destination to ensure compliance with the embargo;

(b) To compel the companies originally selling or purchasing oil or petroleum products, as appropriate to each nation, to desist from selling, reselling or otherwise transferring oil and petroleum products to South Africa, whether directly or indirectly;

(c) To establish strict control over the supply of oil and petroleum products to South Africa by intermediaries, oil companies and traders by placing responsibility for the fulfilment of the contract on the first buyer or seller of oil and petroleum products who would, therefore, be liable for the actions of these parties;

(d) To prevent access by South Africa to other sources of energy, including the supply of raw materials, technical know-how, financial assistance and transport;

(e) To prohibit all assistance to apartheid South Africa, including the provision of finance, technology, equipment or personnel for the prospecting, development or production of hydrocarbon resources, the construction or operation of oil-from-coal or oil-from-gas plants or the development and operation of plants producing fuel substitutes and additives such as ethanol and methanol;

(f) To prevent South African corporations from maintaining or expanding their holdings in oil companies or properties outside South Africa;

(g) To terminate the transport of oil and petroleum products to South Africa by ships flying their flags, or by ships that are ultimately owned, managed or chartered by their nationals or by companies within their jurisdiction;

(h) To develop a system for registration of ships, registered or owned by their nationals, that have un-loaded oil or petroleum products in South Africa in contravention of embargoes imposed, and to discourage such ships from calling at South African ports;

(i) To impose penal action against companies and individuals that have been involved in violating the oil embargo, and to publicize cases of successful prosecutions in conformity with their national laws;

(j) To gather, exchange and disseminate information regarding violations of the oil embargo, including ways and means to prevent such violations, and to take concerted measures against violators;

(k) To discourage ships capable of carrying oil or petroleum products in their national registries or owned or managed by companies or individuals within their jurisdiction from engaging in activities that give rise to violation of the oil embargo against South Africa, taking into account legislative and other measures already adopted;

5. *Authorizes* the Intergovernmental Group to take action to promote public awareness of the oil embargo against South Africa, including, when necessary, sending missions and participating in relevant conferences and meetings;

6. *Requests* the Intergovernmental Group to submit to the General Assembly at its forty-sixth session a report on the implementation of the present resolution;

7. *Requests* all States to extend their cooperation to the Intergovernmental Group in the implementation of the present resolution, including submission of proposals for strengthening the mechanism to monitor the supply and shipment of oil and petroleum products to South Africa;

8. *Requests* the Secretary-General to provide the Intergovernmental Group with all necessary assistance for the implementation of the present resolution.

# Document 144

*General Assembly resolution: Policies of apartheid of the Government of South Africa—Support for the work of the Commission against Apartheid in Sports*

A/RES/45/176 G, 19 December 1990

*The General Assembly,*

*Recalling* its resolutions on the boycott of apartheid in sports and in particular resolution 32/105 M of 14 December 1977 by which it adopted the International Declaration against Apartheid in Sports, resolution 40/64 G of 10 December 1985, the annex to which contains the International Convention against Apartheid in Sports, and resolution 44/27 L of 22 November 1989,

*Having considered* the report of the Commission against Apartheid in Sports and the relevant sections of the report of the Special Committee against Apartheid,

*Reiterating* that the sports boycott of South Africa should be maintained until profound and irreversible changes aimed at the total eradication of apartheid take place in that country,

1. *Takes note* of the report of the Commission against Apartheid in Sports;

2. *Calls upon* the States that have signed the International Convention against Apartheid in Sports to ratify it and also calls upon other States to accede to it as soon as possible;

3. *Commends* those Governments, organizations and individual sportsmen and sportswomen who have taken action in accordance with the Register of Sports Contacts with South Africa with a view to achieving the total isolation of apartheid in sports;

4. *Requests* the Special Committee against Apartheid to continue issuing the Register of Sports Contacts with South Africa;

5. *Calls upon* those international sports organiza-

tions and federations which have not yet expelled South Africa or suspended its membership to do so without further delay;

6. *Calls upon* all Governments and sports organizations to maintain the sports boycott of South Africa until profound and irreversible changes take place in that country;

7. *Urges* Governments and the international sporting community to assist the non-racial sports movement in South Africa to redress the structural inequalities created and sustained by the apartheid State;

8. *Requests* the Secretary-General to provide the Commission against Apartheid in Sports with all needed assistance.

---

# Document 145

*General Assembly resolution: Policies of apartheid of the Government of South Africa—United Nations Trust Fund for South Africa*

A/RES/45/176 H, 19 December 1990

*The General Assembly,*

*Recalling* its resolutions on the United Nations Trust Fund for South Africa, in particular resolution 44/27 J of 22 November 1989,

*Having considered* the report of the Secretary-General on the United Nations Trust Fund for South Africa, to which is annexed the report of the Committee of Trustees of the Trust Fund,

*Taking note* of resolution 44/244 adopted by consensus by the General Assembly on 17 September 1990, and in particular of its paragraph 8 relating to the reintegration of released political prisoners into the South African society,

*Welcoming* the release of Nelson Mandela and some other political prisoners, the suspension of executions and the unbanning of a number of political organizations, including the African National Congress of South Africa and the Pan Africanist Congress of Azania, and the lifting of the nation-wide state of emergency and the repeal of certain emergency regulations,

*Remaining seriously concerned* by the continued existence of basic laws sustaining the apartheid system and other discriminatory and repressive laws, rules and regulations in South Africa,

*Concerned* by the large number of political trials in 1990 and the continued application of criminal proceedings to cases that are clearly of a political nature,

*Reaffirming* that continued humanitarian and legal assistance by the international community is necessary to

alleviate the plight of those persecuted under repressive and discriminatory legislation in South Africa and to facilitate the reintegration of released political prisoners,

*Strongly convinced* that continued contributions to the Trust Fund and to the voluntary agencies concerned are necessary to enable them to meet the extensive needs for humanitarian, legal and relief assistance in this crucial period,

1. *Endorses* the report of the Secretary-General on the United Nations Trust Fund for South Africa;

2. *Decides*, in view of the independence of Namibia, to delete paragraph (*e*) of the terms of reference of the Trust Fund;

3. *Expresses* its appreciation to the Governments, organizations and individuals that have contributed to the Trust Fund and to the voluntary agencies engaged in rendering humanitarian and legal assistance to the victims of apartheid and racial discrimination in South Africa;

4. *Appeals* for generous contributions to the Trust Fund;

5. *Also appeals* for direct contributions to the voluntary agencies engaged in rendering assistance to the victims of apartheid and racial discrimination in South Africa;

6. *Commends* the Secretary-General and the Committee of Trustees of the Trust Fund for their persistent efforts to promote humanitarian and legal assistance to persons persecuted under repressive and discriminatory legislation in South Africa, as well as assistance to their families and to refugees from South Africa.

# Document 146

*Second report of the Secretary-General on progress made on the implementation of the Declaration on Apartheid and its Destructive Consequences in Southern Africa*

A/45/1052, 4 September 1991

. . .

## II.  Observations by the Secretary-General

6.  Over the last 12 months the process towards the end of apartheid in South Africa, although halting, remained on course. A most notable development was the repeal of major apartheid legal structures. Regrettably, the wave of violence that engulfed the country during the period became a severe test of confidence and a serious obstacle to the evolving political dialogue. As several measures necessary for a climate for negotiations as well as peace initiatives have been undertaken recently, South Africa appears to be moving ahead again towards the beginning of substantive negotiations.

7.  The complex process of change in which South Africa is presently engaged inevitably gives rise to reaction and political antagonisms. Such reaction has been manifest in a variety of ways, from violent acts by those opposing the democratic transformation of the country or wishing to obtain political advantage prior to negotiations to less overt activities by elements connected with the system. In this respect, the impartiality of the security forces has been called into question and the potential for destabilization by extremist groups remains a cause for concern.

8.  While the most basic laws of apartheid, as promised, were removed by last June, many of the concomitant attitudes and practices, as indeed the consequences of those laws, do persist. Delays in the implementation of the necessary measures envisaged by the Declaration to create a climate for negotiations, particularly with regard to political prisoners and exiles, the perceived ineffectual response to violence and disclosures of secret funding of organizations led to tensions and a crisis of confidence in the government structures.

9.  Yet a number of initiatives taken in the recent period, specifically to deal with violence, hold the promise that the momentum that started more than a year ago could regain strength. It is hoped that in the next few months, following the outcome of the peace initiative sponsored by religious and business leaders, steps will be taken towards an agreement regarding the drafting of a new constitution and the establishment of transitional arrangements.

10.  At the same time, this process may be relatively lengthy, and even vulnerable, and it may be affected by the magnitude of the socio-economic inequalities that persist in South Africa and the inadequacy of the measures taken so far to address them effectively. While the Government has introduced a number of positive measures, the problems facing the majority of South Africans are so vast that they require a comprehensive national programme of redress. The private sector would be required to play a more important role than it has until now. The serious socio-economic cleavages and the persistent negative attitudes towards change will have to be overcome so that the conditions of life of the disadvantaged sectors can be perceptibly improved. Access to the media and a sustained effort aimed at informing the public about the effects of apartheid on the majority population might contribute to building a consensus on the need to address these problems as early as possible.

11.  On the positive side, the broad consensus that human rights must be protected in a democratic South Africa is encouraging. In this connection, the ratification of the International Covenants on Human Rights would be a significant step.

12.  There appears also to be a growing convergence of the views of the parties concerned on a number of basic principles of a new constitution. However, the mechanism to draft a new constitution and the necessary arrangements for the transition to a democratic order are still to be agreed upon. It is encouraging that proposals on these matters are being elaborated and that a widening range of South African leaders are realizing that there is no other realistic option than to gather together and negotiate on a democratic, non-racial future for their country.

13.  A meeting of all parties concerned to discuss and agree on these matters, as foreseen in the Declaration, now appears to be at the top of the political agenda. Such a meeting could go a long way towards resolving outstanding issues regarding the atmosphere for negotiations and free political activity, and, by itself, could serve as a confidence-building measure. Certainly, there are eminent persons in the country who inspire general trust, for instance, from the religious, academic, labour and business sectors, who can play an important role in the transitional period.

14.  The response of the international community needs to be finely tuned to this complex and delicate

process. As the Declaration envisages, encouragement, pressure and assistance would need to be suitably applied as the process unfolds, bearing in mind that the ultimate objective is the establishment of a non-racial democracy in South Africa.

15. The United Nations system, in addition to its contribution in connection with the return of exiles, is preparing a concerted response to requests for assistance, particularly from disadvantaged sectors of the society. Furthermore, the Secretary-General stands ready, when requested by the South Africans themselves and the international community, to help in the promotion of the process and in the provision of assistance during the transitional period and beyond.

---

# Document 147

## General Assembly resolution: Policies of apartheid of the Government of South Africa—International efforts towards the total eradication of apartheid and support for the establishment of a united, non-racial and democratic South Africa

A/RES/46/79 A, 13 December 1991

*The General Assembly,*

*Recalling* the Declaration on Apartheid and its Destructive Consequences in Southern Africa, contained in the annex to its resolution S-16/1 of 14 December 1989, its resolution 45/176 A of 19 December 1990 and its decision 45/457 B of 13 September 1991,

*Taking note* of the report of the Special Committee against Apartheid and the second progress report of the Secretary-General on the implementation of the Declaration, as well as the reports of the Secretary-General on the coordinated approach by the United Nations system on questions relating to South Africa and on the concerted and effective measures aimed at eradicating apartheid,

*Convinced* that broad-based negotiations leading to a new constitutional order providing for universal, equal suffrage under a non-racial voters' roll will lead to the total eradication of apartheid through peaceful means and the establishment of a non-racial democracy in South Africa,

*Welcoming* the signing on 14 September 1991 of the National Peace Accord and expressing the hope that this will finally end the tragic bloodshed in South Africa,

*Welcoming* the efforts of all parties, including ongoing talks among them, such as the recently held Patriotic United Front conference, aimed at facilitating the commencement of substantive broad-based negotiations towards a new constitution and arrangements on the transition to a democratic order,

*Welcoming* the accession of South Africa on 10 July 1991 to the Treaty on the Non-Proliferation of Nuclear Weapons and subsequent conclusion and ratification of a related safeguards agreement,

*Noting with satisfaction* that fundamental principles for a new constitutional order, as set out in the Declaration, are receiving broad acceptance in South Africa,

*Welcoming* the convening of the preparatory meeting for the Convention for a Democratic South Africa,

*Noting* that while positive measures have been undertaken by the South African authorities, including the repeal and revision of the major apartheid and security laws, further efforts are needed to enhance the climate for free political activity and to address the inequities resulting from the legacy of these laws,

*Gravely concerned* that the persistence of violence, resulting largely from apartheid, including actions by those opposed to the democratic transformation of the country, poses a threat to the negotiating process and to the vital interests of all people of South Africa,

*Concerned* about any remaining obstacles to free political activity, as identified in the Declaration, including the delay in the full implementation of agreements regarding the release of any remaining political prisoners and the return of refugees and exiles, the use of repressive legislation still in place as well as other attempts aimed at undermining the democratic forces,

*Noting with serious concern* the remaining effects of the acts of aggression and destabilization that were committed by South Africa against neighbouring independent African States,

*Convinced* that international pressure, both that exerted by Governments and by individual citizens and organizations, has had and continues to have a significant impact on developments in South Africa,

*Recognizing* the responsibility of the United Nations and the international community, as envisaged in the Declaration, to continue to take all necessary measures aimed at the eradication of apartheid through peaceful means, in particular by adhering to the programme of action contained in the Declaration,

1. *Reaffirms* its support for the legitimate struggle of the South African people for the total eradication of apartheid through peaceful means and the establishment of a united, non-racial and democratic South Africa in which all its people, irrespective of race, colour, sex or creed, will enjoy the same fundamental freedoms and human rights;

2. *Reaffirms* the Declaration on Apartheid and its Destructive Consequences in Southern Africa and the need for the full and immediate implementation of the provisions not yet fulfilled;

3. *Calls for* an immediate end to violence and the removal of any remaining obstacles to free political activity;

4. *Urges* the South African authorities to take immediate further action to end the recurring violence and acts of terrorism, including actions by those opposed to the democratic transformation of the country, by ensuring that all competent authorities act effectively and impartially;

5. *Calls upon* all signatories of the National Peace Accord to manifest their commitment to peace by fully implementing its provisions, and calls upon all other parties to contribute to the attainment of its objectives;

6. *Calls upon* the South African authorities to enhance the climate conducive to negotiations by ensuring the immediate release of any remaining political prisoners, the unhindered return of refugees and exiles and the repeal of repressive and discriminatory legislation still in place, and to address the glaring inequalities created by apartheid;

7. *Calls upon* the representatives of the people of South Africa to commence in good faith, urgently, broad-based substantive negotiations towards an agreement on the basic principles of a new constitution, taking into account the fundamental principles in the Declaration and its suggested guidelines on the modalities for the elaboration of a new constitution, on transitional arrangements inspiring general confidence in the administration of the country until the new constitution takes effect, and on the role to be played by the international community in ensuring the successful transition to a democratic order;

8. *Appeals* to the international community to give its full and concerted support to the vulnerable and critical process now under way in South Africa through a phased application of appropriate pressure on the South African authorities, as warranted by developments, and to provide assistance to the opponents of apartheid and the disadvantaged sectors of society in order to ensure the rapid and peaceful attainment of the objectives of the Declaration;

9. *Calls upon* the international community, in view of progress made in overcoming obstacles to negotiations, to resume academic, scientific and cultural links with democratic anti-apartheid organizations and the individuals in these fields, to resume sports links with unified non-racial sporting organizations of South Africa which have received endorsement by appropriate non-racial sporting organizations within South Africa and to assist disadvantaged athletes in that country;

10. *Also calls upon* the international community, within the context of the need to respond appropriately to ongoing developments in South Africa, to review existing restrictive measures as warranted by positive developments, such as agreement by the parties on transitional arrangements, and agreement on a new, non-racial democratic constitution;

11. *Calls upon* all Governments to observe fully the mandatory arms embargo, requests the Security Council to continue to monitor effectively its strict implementation and urges States to adhere to the provisions of other Security Council resolutions on the import of arms from South Africa and the export of equipment and technology destined for military or police purposes in that country;

12. *Appeals* to the international community to increase humanitarian and legal assistance to the victims of apartheid, returning refugees and exiles and released political prisoners;

13. *Also appeals* to the international community to increase its material, financial and other contributions to the victims and opponents of apartheid to help them address the glaring socio-economic inequalities, particularly in the areas of education, health, housing and social welfare;

14. *Further appeals* to the international community to render all possible assistance to the front-line and neighbouring States to enable their economies to recover from the effects of years of destabilization and to support the current efforts to achieve a durable peace in Angola and Mozambique, which would contribute to the stability and prosperity of the region;

15. *Welcomes* the agreement reached on 4 September 1991 by the United Nations High Commissioner for Refugees with the South African authorities concerning the voluntary repatriation of South African refugees and exiles, and appeals to the international community to provide and urges the Secretary-General to facilitate, through the relevant United Nations agencies and offices in cooperation with the High Commissioner, all necessary humanitarian assistance to ensure the successful implementation of the repatriation programme;

16. *Urges* the Secretary-General to facilitate, through the relevant United Nations agencies and offices and in a concerted manner, humanitarian and educa-

tional assistance inside South Africa for the reintegration of political exiles and released political prisoners and to the disadvantaged sectors of South African society;

17. *Also urges* the Secretary-General, at the appropriate time, in the light of positive developments such as agreement on transitional arrangements, to expand, in a concerted manner, through the relevant United Nations offices and in collaboration with the specialized agencies, the scope of assistance provided inside South Africa aimed at addressing socio-economic issues, particularly in the areas of education, health, housing and social welfare, which may entail the physical presence of the United Nations system in that country;

18. *Requests* the Secretary-General to continue to ensure the coordination of activities of the United Nations system in the implementation of the Declaration and of the present resolution and to report thereon to the General Assembly at its forty-seventh session, and to continue monitoring the implementation of the Declaration as well as pursuing appropriate initiatives to facilitate all efforts leading to the peaceful eradication of apartheid.

---

# Document 148

*General Assembly resolution: Policies of apartheid of the Government of South Africa—Programme of work of the Special Committee against Apartheid*

A/RES/46/79 B, 13 December 1991

*The General Assembly,*

*Having considered* the report of the Special Committee against Apartheid,

1. *Commends* the Special Committee against Apartheid for the diligent manner in which it has discharged its responsibilities in monitoring the situation in South Africa and in promoting concerted international support for the process towards the early establishment of a democratic, non-racial society;

2. *Takes note* of the report of the Special Committee and endorses its recommendations relating to its programme of work;

3. *Authorizes* the Special Committee, in accordance with its mandate as the focal point for the international campaign against apartheid and for the promotion of the implementation of the Declaration on Apartheid and its Destructive Consequences in Southern Africa and acting with the support services of the Centre against Apartheid:

(*a*) To continue monitoring closely developments in South Africa and the actions of the international community, particularly regarding appropriate pressure on South Africa and timely assistance to the victims and opponents of apartheid;

(*b*) To continue mobilizing international action in support of the early establishment of a democratic, non-racial South Africa, *inter alia*, through collection, analysis and dissemination of information, through liaison and consultations with Governments, intergovernmental and non-governmental organizations and relevant individuals and groups, both inside and outside South Africa, able to influence public opinion and decision-making, and through missions, hearings, conferences, publicity and other pertinent activities, and to continue undertaking activities aimed at supporting the political process towards the establishment of a non-racial, democratic South Africa;

4. *Appeals* to all Governments, intergovernmental and non-governmental organizations to increase their cooperation with the Special Committee and the Centre in the discharge of their mandates;

5. *Requests* all components of the United Nations system to cooperate further with the Special Committee and the Centre in their activities in order to ensure consistency, improve coordination and efficient use of available resources and avoid duplication of efforts in the implementation of the relevant resolutions of the General Assembly and the Security Council;

6. *Appeals* to all Governments, intergovernmental and non-governmental organizations, information media and individuals to cooperate with the Centre and the Department of Public Information of the Secretariat in their activities relating to South Africa and, in particular, in disseminating information on the evolving situation in South Africa and on the considerable assistance needs of the opponents of apartheid and the disadvantaged sectors of South African society in rectifying the glaring socio-economic inequalities in their country, and further appeals to them to make generous contributions to the Trust Fund for Publicity against Apartheid;

7. *Decides* to continue the authorization of adequate financial provision in the regular budget of the United Nations to enable the African National Congress

of South Africa and the Pan Africanist Congress of Azania to maintain offices in New York in order to participate effectively in the deliberations of the Special Committee and other appropriate bodies;

8. *Also decides* that the special allocation of 480,000 United States dollars to the Special Committee for 1992 from the regular budget of the United Nations should be used towards the cost of special projects aimed at promoting the process towards the elimination of apartheid and the democratization of South Africa, with particular emphasis on the issues of constitution building, human rights, domestic peace, education and training and ways to help address the serious socio-economic inequalities in the country.

---

# Document 149

*General Assembly resolution: Policies of apartheid of the Government of South Africa—Military and other collaboration with South Africa*

A/RES/46/79 C, 13 December 1991

*The General Assembly,*

*Recalling* the Declaration on Apartheid and its Destructive Consequences in Southern Africa, its resolutions 45/176 B and C of 19 December 1990, as well as the resolutions of the Security Council on the arms embargo and military collaboration with South Africa,

*Taking note* of the report of the Special Committee against Apartheid and the report of the Security Council Committee established by Council resolution 421 (1977) of 9 December 1977 concerning the question of South Africa on its activities during the period 1980-1989,

*Noting* with appreciation the resolve and effectiveness of the Security Council in its handling of questions relating to the preservation of international peace and security,

*Noting* that the monitoring and enforcement mechanism of the mandatory sanctions imposed by the Security Council on South Africa in its resolution 418 (1977) of 4 November 1977 would benefit from further strengthening,

*Reiterating* that the full implementation of the mandatory arms embargo against South Africa is an essential element of international action towards the eradication of apartheid,

*Convinced* that sanctions and other restrictive measures have had a significant impact on recent developments in South Africa and that the phased application of appropriate pressure remains an effective and necessary instrument in the process towards the peaceful end to apartheid,

*Taking note* of the accession of South Africa on 10 July 1991 to the Treaty on the Non-Proliferation of Nuclear Weapons and subsequent conclusion and ratification of a related safeguards agreement,

*Expressing serious concern* about the continued violations of the mandatory arms embargo, particularly by those countries which surreptitiously trade in arms with South Africa,

*Expressing concern* that South Africa's external military relations, especially in the area of military technology and, in particular, in the production and testing of missiles, continue unabated, as mentioned in paragraphs 100 to 102 of the report of the Special Committee,

*Gravely concerned* about the practice carried out by certain oil-producing States whereby oil is exchanged for South African arms,

1. *Deplores* the actions of those States which, directly or indirectly, continue to violate the mandatory arms embargo and collaborate with South Africa in the military, nuclear, intelligence and technology fields, and calls upon those States to terminate forthwith any illegal acts and honour their obligations under Security Council resolution 418 (1977);

2. *Urges* all States to adopt strict legislation relating to the implementation of the arms embargo and prohibit the supply to South Africa of nuclear and military products, as well as computer and communications equipment, technological skills and services, including military intelligence, destined for use by the military, police and security agencies of that country, until free and fair elections have been held and a democratic government has been established;

3. *Calls* for the early and full disclosure by South Africa of its nuclear installations and materials in conformity with its treaty obligations as an essential element to the peace and security of the southern African region;

4. *Urges* the Security Council to consider immediate steps to ensure the full implementation and the effective monitoring of the arms embargo imposed by the Council in its resolutions 418 (1977) and 558 (1984) of 13 December 1984, to implement the recommendations of the Committee established under Council resolution 421 (1977) concerning appropriate measures in response to violations of the mandatory arms embargo and to provide information on a regular basis to the Secretary-

General for general distribution to Member States;

5. *Calls* upon all States to maintain existing financial measures, and, in particular, urges Governments and private financial institutions, as well as the International Monetary Fund and the World Bank, not to extend new loans and credits to South Africa, whether to the public or private sector, until agreement has been reached on a non-racial democratic constitution or until specific rec-

ommendations are made on this matter by the transitional authorities to be established by the Convention for a Democratic South Africa;

6. *Requests* the Special Committee against Apartheid to keep the issue of military and nuclear collaboration with South Africa under constant review and to report thereon to the General Assembly and the Security Council as appropriate.

---

# Document 150

*General Assembly resolution: Policies of apartheid of the Government of South Africa—Oil embargo against South Africa*

A/RES/46/79 E, 13 December 1991

*The General Assembly,*

*Having considered* the report of the Intergovernmental Group to Monitor the Supply and Shipping of Oil and Petroleum Products to South Africa,

*Recalling* its resolutions on the oil embargo against South Africa, in particular resolution 45/176 F of 19 December 1990,

*Recognizing* the importance of the oil embargo as a major contribution to the pressure exerted on South Africa towards the eradication of apartheid through negotiations, as well as the importance of maintaining pressure until there is clear evidence of profound and irreversible changes, bearing in mind the objectives of the Declaration on Apartheid and its Destructive Consequences in Southern Africa, such as the adoption of a non-racial and democratic constitution for a free South Africa,

*Noting* that the most effective way to enforce the oil embargo against South Africa remains the adoption by the Security Council of a mandatory embargo under Chapter VII of the Charter of the United Nations,

*Concerned* that the oil embargo against South Africa is still being violated and that South Africa, because of loopholes in the embargo, such as lack of effective legislation, has been able to acquire oil and petroleum products,

*Convinced* that an effective oil embargo against South Africa would contribute to the efforts of the international community to bring about a negotiated settlement and the establishment of a united, non-racial and democratic South Africa,

1. *Takes note* of the report of the Intergovernmental Group to Monitor the Supply and Shipping of Oil and Petroleum Products to South Africa and endorses its recommendations;

2. *Requests* all States to adopt, if they have not already done so, and otherwise to maintain and enforce

effective measures prohibiting the supply and shipping of oil and petroleum products to South Africa, whether directly or indirectly, and in particular:

(a) To apply strictly the "end users" clause and other conditions concerning restriction on destination to ensure compliance with the embargo;

(b) To compel the companies originally selling or purchasing oil or petroleum products, as appropriate to each nation, to desist from selling, reselling or otherwise transferring oil and petroleum products to South Africa, whether directly or indirectly;

(c) To establish strict control over the supply of oil and petroleum products to South Africa by intermediaries, oil companies and traders by placing responsibilities for the fulfilment of the contract on the first buyer or seller of oil and petroleum products who would, therefore, be liable for the actions of these parties;

(d) To prevent South African companies from acquiring holdings in oil companies outside South Africa;

(e) To prohibit all assistance to South Africa in the oil sector, including finance, technology, equipment or personnel;

(f) To prohibit the transport of oil and petroleum products to South Africa by ships flying their flags, or by ships that are ultimately owned, managed or chartered by their nationals or by companies within their jurisdiction;

(g) To develop a system for registration of ships, registered in their territory or owned by their nationals, that have violated the oil embargo, and to discourage such ships from calling at South African ports;

(h) To impose penal action against companies and individuals that have been involved in violating the oil embargo, and to publicize cases of successful prosecutions in conformity with their national laws;

(i) To gather, exchange and disseminate information regarding violations of the oil embargo, including ways and means to prevent such violations, and to take concerted measures against violators;

(*j*) To discourage ships within their jurisdiction from engaging in activities that give rise to violation of the oil embargo against South Africa, taking into account legislative and other measures already adopted;

3. *Commends* to Member States for their consideration the draft model law annexed to the report of the Intergovernmental Group and recommends that they strive for an effective oil embargo by adopting the general principles of the model law within the framework of their own legal practices;

4. *Authorizes* the Intergovernmental Group to take action to promote public awareness of the oil embargo against South Africa, including, when necessary, sending missions and participating in relevant conferences and meetings;

5. *Requests* the Intergovernmental Group to submit to the General Assembly at its forty-seventh session a report on the implementation of the present resolution;

6. *Requests* all States to extend their cooperation to the Intergovernmental Group with all necessary assistance for the implementation of the present resolution.

---

# Document 151

*General Assembly resolution: Policies of apartheid of the Government of South Africa—United Nations Trust Fund for South Africa*

A/RES/46/79 F, 13 December 1991

*The General Assembly,*

*Recalling* its resolutions on the United Nations Trust Fund for South Africa, in particular resolution 45/176 H of 19 December 1990,

*Having considered* the report of the Secretary-General on the United Nations Trust Fund for South Africa, to which is annexed the report of the Committee of Trustees of the Trust Fund,

*Taking note* of its resolution 45/176 A adopted without a vote on 19 December 1990, and in particular of paragraph 16, relating to the reintegration of released political prisoners into South African society,

*Welcoming* the repeal and revision of the major apartheid and security laws and a number of discriminatory and repressive laws, rules and regulations,

*Welcoming also* the release of a large number of political prisoners and the agreement reached between the South African authorities and the United Nations High Commissioner for Refugees allowing for the voluntary repatriation of political exiles and refugees,

*Further welcoming* the National Peace Accord signed on 14 September 1991 as a significant initiative towards addressing the critical issue of violence in the country and providing a framework within which substantive and broad-based discussions can take place,

*Remaining concerned* about the continued existence of a number of discriminatory and repressive laws, rules and regulations in South Africa,

*Concerned* about the delay in the full implementation of agreements regarding the release of any remaining political prisoners and the return of refugees and exiles and about reports that trials of politically motivated cases were carried out in 1991,

*Recognizing* the work carried out by the International Defence and Aid Fund for Southern Africa over the years in providing legal and humanitarian assistance to the victims of apartheid and their families and noting with satisfaction the transfer of programmes of the Fund to broad-based, impartial organizations inside South Africa,

*Strongly convinced* that continued, direct and substantial contributions to the Trust Fund and to the voluntary agencies concerned are necessary to enable them to meet the extensive needs for humanitarian, legal and relief assistance during the critical transition to a nonracial and democratic South Africa,

1. *Endorses* the report of the Secretary-General on the United Nations Trust Fund for South Africa;

2. *Supports* continued and substantial humanitarian, legal and educational assistance by the international community in order to alleviate the plight of those persecuted under discriminatory legislation in South Africa and their families, and to facilitate the reintegration of released political prisoners and returning exiles into South African society;

3. *Supports* assistance by the Trust Fund for work in the legal field aimed at ensuring effective implementation of legislation repealing major apartheid laws, redressing continuing adverse effects of these laws and encouraging increased confidence in the rule of law;

4. *Expresses its appreciation* to the Governments, organizations and individuals that have contributed to the Trust Fund and to the voluntary agencies engaged in rendering humanitarian and legal assistance to the victims of apartheid in South Africa;

5. *Appeals* for generous contributions to the Trust Fund;

6. *Also appeals* for direct contributions to the voluntary agencies engaged in rendering assistance to the victims of apartheid and racial discrimination in South Africa;

7. *Commends* the Secretary-General and the Committee of Trustees of the Trust Fund for their persistent efforts to promote humanitarian and legal assistance to persons persecuted under repressive and discriminatory legislation in South Africa, as well as assistance to their families and to refugees from South Africa.

# Document 152

*Statement by Secretary-General Boutros Boutros-Ghali at the first meeting in 1992 of the Special Committee against Apartheid*

UN Press Release SG/SM/4700 - GA/AP 2064, 18 February 1992

Throughout the years, I have followed with deep interest the situation in South Africa. The commitment of the United Nations, ably advocated by the Special Committee, to seek an end to apartheid and witness the birth of a democratic country, have undoubtedly contributed to the auspicious developments we are witnessing today.

The Special Committee against Apartheid has, over the years, played an important role in stirring the conscience of the international community. The consensus which the Special Committee helped forge recently in the General Assembly gave further impetus and weight to this role.

Mr. Chairman, it is a pleasure to join you at your first meeting of this year. I should like to congratulate you, Ambassador Gambari, as well as your colleagues on the bureau on your re-election to a new term of office.

The system of apartheid in South Africa, which has rightly been on the agenda of the United Nations for many years, is crumbling under the combined pressure of internal and external forces. It is possible now to envisage a new society in South Africa—a society which respects human rights, a society which does not discriminate on grounds of colour, sex, political affiliation or creed; an undivided society in which economic wealth and opportunity are shared by all.

It is these principles underpinning the United Nations Declaration on Apartheid—approved by consensus in 1989—which constitute the international community's blueprint for a future South Africa. It should be a source of satisfaction for all of us that negotiations towards a new constitution in South Africa are finally under way, in line with the proposals and guidelines of the Declaration.

Courageous political steps have been taken in South Africa in the past two years. The repeal of major apartheid laws and the beginning of the repatriation of exiles facilitated the start of the current negotiations. The launching of the Convention for a Democratic South Africa marked a new stage in the political life of the country, as concerned parties began the gradual process towards national reconciliation and agreement on a democratic constitution.

The presence of the United Nations at the Convention last December made it clear that we fully support this process. The inclusion of all parties concerned in the negotiations will, of course, enhance the prospects of achieving early and durable solutions. We hope, therefore, that others who have not yet done so will soon join these negotiations. It will be important to address as early as possible critical outstanding differences regarding transitional arrangements that will inspire general confidence in the administration of the country, and the necessary mechanism for drafting a new constitution. Delays in reaching agreement on these matters would only increase the threat emanating from those opposed to the democratic transformation of the country.

Persisting political violence and major socio-economic problems continue to endanger the process and require an effective response. Such a response would build confidence in the current negotiations and would be crucial to the success of national reconstruction. In this context, a number of specific suggestions were made by my distinguished predecessor in his last report to the General Assembly.

All who are and have been involved in this historic process are arriving, we must hope, at the end of a long night, and should be braced for arduous days ahead. If the people of South Africa are to make a peaceful transition to a true democracy in their country, they must all proceed together, with wisdom, imagination and generosity of spirit. The international community must continue to be vigilant and respond appropriately to developments as they occur. The Special Committee and I, in our respective—and allow me to say—mutually supportive roles, have the important and challenging duty of providing advice and assistance during this difficult transition and beyond. The General Assembly has defined the scope of our responsibilities and I am certain that the United Nations will continue to effectively support this critical process.

In closing, I wish to take this opportunity to pay tribute to Sotirios Mousouris who has made such a distinguished contribution as head of the Centre against Apartheid and who will now be assuming new functions. I am confident that James Jonah, Under-Secretary-General for Political Affairs, who will be taking over this important function, will provide exemplary support for the work of the Committee.

# Document 153

*Statement by the Spokesman for Secretary-General Boutros Boutros-Ghali concerning the results of the referendum in South Africa*

UN Press Release SG/SM/4717 - SAF/131, 18 March 1992

The Secretary-General welcomes the positive results of the referendum on democratic reform in South Africa.

These results constitute a major step forward towards the eradication of apartheid and the creation of a new, non-racial society in South Africa, based on the respect of human rights.

These prospects will constitute a new factor for peace and development throughout Africa.

# Document 154

*Statement by Secretary-General Boutros Boutros-Ghali at a meeting on the occasion of the observance of the International Day for the Elimination of Racial Discrimination*

UN Press Release SG/SM/4720/Rev.1 - GA/AP/2070/Rev.1 - RD/662/Rev.1, 20 March 1992

This observance of the International Day for the Elimination of Racial Discrimination is taking place at a time filled with hope. The process of negotiated change currently under way in South Africa should lead, in the near future, to the emergence of a new society—a society in which all South Africans, irrespective of their race, can live together in harmony as equal citizens of a non-racial democracy.

The results of the recent referendum in South Africa have clearly demonstrated that the overwhelming majority of White South Africans support the negotiation process for a non-racial democracy. The result underlines the commitment of the South African people as a whole to reform and change through peaceful means. It provides a fresh and compelling impetus to the negotiations now taking place within the framework of the Convention for a Democratic South Africa (CODESA).

The United Nations, which participated as an observer in the first meeting of CODESA in December, is fully committed to the negotiating process. It is hoped that all concerned parties which have not yet joined the negotiations will do so soon. A preliminary agreement was reached earlier this month regarding arrangements to oversee the initial phase of the transition process. Further progress in the negotiations should lead to transitional arrangements that will inspire general confidence in the administration of the country and facilitate the establishment of the necessary mechanism for drafting a new constitution.

It is important that the negotiations remain on course, so that a common vision for the management of South Africa's transition towards a non-racial democracy can emerge. Persistent violence and socio-economic inequalities, however, continue to complicate the transition process. Improvements in such crucial areas as housing, education, employment and health will help to ensure a peaceful transition to a post-apartheid South Africa.

We now have a new opportunity for accelerating the process towards a negotiated settlement.

A challenging period lies ahead for South Africa and the region as a whole. Member States, which have committed themselves, individually and collectively, within the framework of the United Nations Declaration on Apartheid, to monitoring and promoting a non-racial and constitutional democracy in South Africa, must remain vigilant. They should be ready to provide the support needed to facilitate the total eradication of apartheid and the establishment of a society in South Africa in which the aspirations of all its citizens for justice and equality are at long last fulfilled.

As we observe the International Day for the Elimination of Racial Discrimination, we must reaffirm our faith in fundamental human rights, in equality and the worth of the human person, in the equal rights of men and women.

There can be no development without respect for human rights, and there can be no respect for human rights without development.

Harmonious relations between nations and all efforts to consolidate world peace ultimately depend on our attitude towards human rights.

# Document 155

*Letter dated 10 July 1992 from Mr. L. M. Mangope, Chief Minister of Bophuthatswana, to the President of the Security Council*

Not issued as a United Nations document

I am informed that the Security Council is to have a formal meeting on Wednesday 15 July 1992 on the situation in the Republic of South Africa, more particularly on the question of violence.

My Government is a participant in the Conference for a Democratic South Africa (CODESA). As you are aware, Sir, it is the body involved in negotiating a peaceful transition to a new South Africa.

It is in that capacity that I request to be allowed to address the Security Council. I believe that information at my disposal can be of value to the Council and can make a contribution towards an informed debate.

As I need to make extensive travelling and accommodation arrangements, I would be most grateful if you could inform me as soon as possible of your and the Council's reactions and response to my request.

. . .

Your Excellency, please accept the assurance of my highest consideration and regard.

(*signed*)
L. M. MANGOPE

# Document 156

*Security Council resolution: The question of South Africa*

S/RES/765 (1992), 16 July 1992

*The Security Council,*

*Recalling* its resolutions 392 (1976) of 19 June 1976, 473 (1980) of 13 June 1980, 554 (1984) of 17 August 1984 and 556 (1984) of 23 October 1984,

*Gravely concerned* by the escalating violence in South Africa, which is causing a heavy loss of human life and by its consequences for the peaceful negotiations aimed at creating a democratic, non-racial and united South Africa,

*Concerned* that the continuation of this situation would seriously jeopardize peace and security in the region,

*Recalling* the Declaration on Apartheid and its Destructive Consequences in Southern Africa adopted by consensus by the General Assembly at its sixteenth special session, on 14 December 1989, which called for negotiations in South Africa to take place in a climate free of violence,

*Emphasizing* the responsibility of the South African authorities to take all necessary measures to stop the violence immediately and protect the life and property of all South Africans,

*Emphasizing also* the need for all parties to cooperate in combating violence and to exercise restraint,

*Concerned* at the break in the negotiating process and determined to help the people of South Africa in their legitimate struggle for a non-racial, democratic society,

1. *Condemns* the escalating violence in South Africa and in particular the massacre at Boipatong township on 17 June 1992, as well as subsequent incidents of violence including the shooting of unarmed protesters;

2. *Strongly urges* the South African authorities to take immediate measures to bring an effective end to the ongoing violence and to bring those responsible to justice;

3. *Calls upon* all the parties to cooperate in com-

bating violence and to ensure the effective implementation of the National Peace Accord;

4. *Invites* the Secretary-General to appoint, as a matter of urgency, a Special Representative for South Africa in order to recommend, after, *inter alia*, discussion with the parties, measures which would assist in bringing an effective end to the violence and in creating conditions for negotiations leading towards a peaceful transition to a democratic, non-racial and united South Africa, and to submit a report to the Security Council as early as possible;

5. *Urges* all parties to cooperate with the Special Representative of the Secretary-General in carrying out his mandate, and to remove the obstacles to the resumption of negotiations;

6. *Underlines*, in this regard, the importance of all parties cooperating in the resumption of the negotiating process as speedily as possible;

7. *Urges* the international community to maintain the existing measures imposed by the Council for the purpose of bringing an early end to apartheid in South Africa;

8. *Decides* to remain seized of the matter until a democratic, non-racial and united South Africa is established.

---

# Document 157

*Letter dated 27 July 1992 from the Secretary-General to Mr. Nelson Mandela, President of the African National Congress*

Not issued as a United Nations document

My Special Representative, Mr. Cyrus Vance, has been keeping me informed of the range and depth of his discussions in South Africa pursuant to the adoption of Security Council resolution 765 (1992).

I look forward to receiving his detailed views and recommendations on his return to New York and I wish, in the meantime, to thank you for the cooperation extended to him.

There is, however, one matter on which I want to address you immediately. I am deeply disturbed, on the basis of reports I have received from Mr. Vance, that there is a very real chance of the mass demonstrations planned for 3 August 1992 taking a turn towards violence. This I realize would be contrary to the wishes of all of the parties in South Africa. With a situation as delicately poised as that which now exists in your country, I fear violence can readily be sparked by provocateurs and that this must, by all means, be avoided. Indeed, it would be tragic and ironical in the extreme if the Vance mission were to be followed by an eruption of violence—a development that would be wholly inconsistent with the purposes of the Security Council's resolution.

May I, in light of these circumstances, urge you to do all in your power, in association with the leaders of the principal political parties, to stave off such an eventuality. The peaceful transition to a democratic, non-racial and united South Africa requires no less at this critical moment.

(*signed*)
Boutros BOUTROS-GHALI

---

# Document 158

*Report of the Secretary-General to the Security Council in pursuance of Security Council resolution 765 (1992)*

S/24389, 7 August 1992

. . .

## III. Observations

63. From my discussions with Mr. Vance and Mr. Dayal since their return from South Africa, I have been struck by the range and depth of the talks that the United Nations delegation held while in that country. I have also been profoundly impressed by the open and responsive manner in which they were received by all sectors of society. I view this as further evidence of a transformation taking place in that country as its leaders and peoples strive to create a democratic, non-racial and united South Africa.

64. The path to the attainment of this objective will not be easy. Violence in whatever form must be brought under control and conditions established to ensure the success of the negotiating process. Decades of apartheid have left a painful legacy of distrust and anguish, and these persist despite the resilience and courage of those who wish to see their country on an irreversible new course.

65. The unanimous adoption of resolution 765 (1992) by the Security Council strengthened the hands of those so motivated. It also heightened expectations that the continuous involvement of the Security Council in this new phase of South Africa's evolution will be marked by understanding and a readiness to contribute constructively to the process of peaceful change.

66. It is with this in mind, and in this spirit, that I recommend the measures that follow to bring an effective end to the violence and to create the conditions for the resumption of negotiations envisaged in resolution 765 (1992).

67. It is neither necessary nor possible here to recount the far-reaching work being undertaken by Justice Richard Goldstone, Chairman of the Commission of Enquiry into Public Violence and Intimidation. Suffice it to say that it commands widespread respect in South Africa and abroad. I believe that the efforts of the Goldstone Commission should be supported by the international community and the recommendations of the Commission should be fully and speedily implemented by the Government and, when so required, by the parties in South Africa.

68. Without wishing to select arbitrarily from among the many recommendations of the Goldstone Commission, I believe that those relating to a total ban on the public display of dangerous weapons and the security of hostels need to be acted upon with utmost urgency, as recent events have sadly proven necessary. Further, I believe that the Commission's code of conduct for mass demonstrations can do much to control violence. It is also necessary, in my view, that the leaders of the major political parties should, as the Goldstone Commission recommends, take firm steps to stop their supporters from participating in acts of violence.

69. The long-standing capacity for violence by the various political groups in South Africa is so central to the lack of trust in the political life of the country that I feel it must be remedied. Accordingly, I recommend that the Goldstone Commission undertake a series of investigations into the functioning and operations of certain agencies, *inter alia*, the army and police, the *Umkontho we Sizwe* (MK), the Azanian People's Liberation Army (APLA), the KwaZulu police and, more generally, certain private "security firms". My Special Representative has discussed this proposal with Justice Goldstone and certain of the parties who are of the view that such investigations could indeed serve to curb violence and be of benefit to the country as a whole. While such investigations would widen the scope of the work of the Goldstone Commission, they could be undertaken within its present terms of reference. Should the Commission need further financing for its expanded work, I would urge the Government to be forthcoming.

70. The Commission has welcomed suitable international assistance. Certainly the Waddington report and the assessorship of Justice Bhagwati have been very positive developments. It may well be useful in the future to have senior personnel seconded to the Commission, in addition to a pool of jurists to sit on the committees of inquiry. The choice of properly qualified, suitable and compatible persons will need to be adequately and sufficiently addressed. Should Justice Goldstone feel the need, at any stage, for assistance from the international community and the United Nations in this regard, I recommend that the Organization respond positively and appropriately.

71. The reports of the Goldstone Commission when written are, at present, submitted first to the State President and only after being reviewed by the Government are they made public more widely. I believe political and public opinion in South Africa would welcome the reports being made available to all signatories of the National Peace Accord within 24 hours of submission to the State President. I recommend this course of action, which would enhance the impact and credibility of the reports.

72. Finally, as far as the Goldstone Commission is concerned, I believe it is essential that any further investigations and prosecutions that are required pursuant to its reports should be undertaken promptly by the competent departments of the Government. Such action would enhance the credibility of the law enforcement machinery of the country.

73. The National Peace Accord of 14 September 1991 establishes a comprehensive framework, agreed upon by all the major parties, organizations and groups of South Africa, to end violence and to facilitate socio-economic development and reconstruction. The mechanisms foreseen under the Accord, however, lack teeth and need to be greatly strengthened. This was the unanimous view of all those who discussed this matter with the United Nations delegation, including those who are associated with the existing structures of the National Peace Secretariat.

74. Both the National Peace Committee and the National Peace Secretariat need to be more consistently and substantially supported from the highest political

levels, as do the 11 regional dispute resolution committees covering all parts of the country. Most importantly, they require financing and full-time staff of the requisite calibre. Further, there is desperate need for efficient, functioning offices or operations centres at the major "flashpoints"; these should be staffed on a 24-hour basis and fully funded and equipped. For each of such offices there should be a standing group composed of representatives of the Government, ANC, Inkatha and other concerned parties. Such offices should be capable at all times of acting immediately to defuse incipient problems; they should have prompt and direct access to law enforcement agencies. I recommend the earliest establishment of such offices.

75. I have reflected deeply on the many serious requests made to the United Nations to dispatch monitors to South Africa for the various purposes referred to above. I understand the concerns expressed and the anxieties they reflect. I am most appreciative of the many bold and constructive ideas conveyed to my Special Representative in the course of his discussions and I have weighed these most carefully.

76. Given the mechanisms already established by the National Peace Accord, to which all parties have agreed, I have concluded that, at this stage, the wisest course of action would be to strengthen and reinforce those mechanisms. Such action would, in my view, contribute tangibly to enhancing the capacity of indigenous structures that can play a major role in the building of peace, both in the present and in the future. I recommend, accordingly, that the United Nations make available some 30 observers to serve in South Africa, in close association with the National Peace Secretariat, in order to further the purposes of the Accord. The observers would be stationed in agreed upon locations, in various parts of South Africa. As necessary, their number could be supplemented by other appropriate international organizations, such as the Commonwealth, the EC and the Organization of African Unity (OAU). I am of the view that the practical arrangements stemming from this recommendation should be the subject of early and detailed discussions between the United Nations, the Government and the parties concerned. I believe, in this connection, that the experience gained by the dispatch of 10 United Nations observers to cover the present mass demonstrations could serve a valuable purpose in defining the tasks and methods of functioning of the larger group that I am recommending.

77. I would also urge that the Government act expeditiously to ensure the early appointment of the Justices of Peace and the establishment of the special criminal courts envisaged in the National Peace Accord.

78. The reasons for the violence in South Africa are, of course, complex and deep. But the special desperation that apartheid brought to the country can, in the long run, only be remedied by rapid progress towards the creation of the democratic, non-racial and united South Africa that is the goal of the negotiations and the objective not only of the CODESA process but of the international community as a whole.

79. The task of conducting these negotiations is uniquely the responsibility of South Africans themselves, and I was heartened by statements made to my Special Representative of the determination of the major parties to return, as early as possible, to the negotiating table. I urge such a course of action, for the time otherwise lost is precious and even more so are the lives. I am strongly of the view that actions such as the immediate release of all remaining political prisoners could contribute greatly to improving the political climate, creating trust and burying the unhappy past. In this connection, it is also important that reporting on State-owned radio and television be, and be seen to be, fair and objective.

80. For all of its shortcomings, the CODESA process must be pursued and improved. I believe it needs to encourage others, who have not yet joined, to do so, in the interests of the country and of peace. I am convinced that its processes must be better coordinated and made much more transparent. Considerable progress has been accomplished in the working groups, but too few know of this, or of the precise issues that need to be resolved. There is a manifest need to establish a deadlock-resolving machinery at the highest political level. In addition, there may well be need for CODESA to consider the appointment of an eminent and impartial person, who need not be a foreigner, to draw the strings together and to provide the impetus and cohesion that CODESA needs to accomplish its tasks. I recommend that these ideas be considered further by all concerned in South Africa.

81. In a time such as this, crucial to South Africa and the world alike, it is most important that the Security Council should have decided, in its resolution 765 (1992), to "remain seized of the matter until a democratic, non-racial and united South Africa is established".

82. To discharge its function, I believe that the Security Council should have before it information that is regular, impartial and objective. To this end, I would propose that missions such as that just completed should be undertaken on a quarterly basis or more frequently, if the situation so warrants, and that reports be provided to the Council.

83. The role of the international community and of the United Nations in particular can, at this moment, be profound and beneficial. It can facilitate a great and peaceful transition of historic proportion in a part of the world that has suffered too long.

# Document 159

*Letter dated 13 August 1992 from the Secretary-General to Mr. Abdou Diouf, President of Senegal and Chairman of the Organization of African Unity*

Not issued as a United Nations document

[Editor's note: Original in French]
As you know, the Security Council met recently at the request of the Organization of African Unity to consider the situation in South Africa. Your Minister for Foreign Affairs, H.E. Mr. Djibo Laïty Ka, who headed a high-level OAU delegation, explained the position of OAU to the Council in a particularly effective way.

The Security Council concluded the debate by adopting resolution 765 (1992) of 16 July 1992, which invites the Secretary-General to appoint, as a matter of urgency, a Special Representative for South Africa in order to recommend measures which would assist in bringing an effective end to the violence and in creating conditions for negotiations leading towards a peaceful transition to a democratic, non-racial and united South Africa.

I immediately appointed as Special Representative Mr. Cyrus Vance, who visited South Africa from 21 to 31 July and met with as many of the interested parties as possible. On his return, and pursuant to the Security Council's request, I submitted a report to the latter on 7 August. The Council will meet in the next few days to consider and take action on the recommendations contained therein.

I have the honour, Sir, to attach herewith a copy of this report and should like to keep in close contact with you concerning it.

Accept, Sir, the assurances of my highest consideration.

*(signed)* Boutros BOUTROS-GHALI

# Document 160

*Security Council resolution: The question of South Africa*

S/RES/772 (1992), 17 August 1992

*The Security Council,*

*Reaffirming* its resolution 765 (1992) of 16 July 1992,

*Having considered* the report of the Secretary-General of 7 August 1992 on the question of South Africa,

*Determined* to help the people of South Africa in their legitimate struggle for a non-racial, democratic society,

*Cognizant* of the expectations of the people of South Africa that the United Nations will assist with regard to the removal of all obstacles to the resumption of the process of negotiations,

*Bearing in mind* the areas of concern relevant to the question of violence in South Africa, including the issues of the hostels, dangerous weapons, the role of the security forces and other armed formations, the investigation and prosecution of criminal conduct, mass demonstrations and the conduct of political parties,

*Also bearing in mind* the need to strengthen and reinforce the indigenous mechanisms set up under the

National Peace Accord, so as to enhance their capacity in the building of peace, both in the present and in the future,

*Determined* to assist the people of South Africa to end violence, the continuation of which would seriously jeopardize peace and security in the region,

*Underlining*, in this regard, the importance of all parties cooperating in the resumption of the negotiating process as speedily as possible,

1. *Welcomes with appreciation* the report of the Secretary-General of 7 August 1992 on the question of South Africa;

2. *Expresses its appreciation* to all relevant parties in South Africa for the cooperation they extended to the Special Representative of the Secretary-General for South Africa;

3. *Calls upon* the South African Government and all parties in South Africa to implement urgently the relevant recommendations contained in the report of the Secretary-General;

4. *Authorizes* the Secretary-General to deploy, as a matter of urgency, United Nations observers in South Africa, in such a manner and in such numbers as he determines necessary to address effectively the areas of concern noted in his report, in coordination with the structures set up under the National Peace Accord;

5. *Invites* the Secretary-General to assist in the strengthening of the structures set up under the National Peace Accord in consultation with the relevant parties;

. . .

7. *Calls on* the Government of South Africa, parties and organizations, and the structures set up under the National Peace Accord, to extend their full cooperation to the United Nations observers to enable them to carry out their tasks effectively;

8. *Invites* international organizations such as the Organization of African Unity, the Commonwealth and the European Community to consider deploying their own observers in South Africa in coordination with United Nations and the structures set up under the National Peace Accord;

9. *Decides* to remain seized of the matter until a democratic, non-racial and united South Africa is established.

---

# Document 161

*Statement by the Spokesman for Secretary-General Boutros Boutros-Ghali concerning loss of life in Ciskei, and details on the United Nations Observer Mission in South Africa (UNOMSA)*

UN Press Release SG/SM/4807 - SAF/141, 9 September 1992

The Secretary-General deeply deplores the loss of life which occurred in Ciskei on 7 September during a demonstration organized by the African National Congress of South Africa (ANC).

The Secretary-General wishes to recall in that connection that by its resolution 772 (1992) of 17 August, the Security Council authorized the Secretary-General to deploy, as a matter of urgency, United Nations observers in South Africa, in such manner and in such numbers as he determines necessary to address effectively the areas of concern noted in his report (document S/24389), in coordination with the structures set up under the National Peace Accord, which was signed on 14 September 1991 to provide a framework and basis for putting an end to violence in the country.

The Council also invited the Secretary-General to assist in the strengthening of the structures set up under the National Peace Accord in consultation with the relevant parties. The Security Council further invited international organizations, such as the Organization of African Unity, the Commonwealth and the European Community, to consider deploying their own observers in South Africa in coordination with the United Nations and the structures set up under the National Peace Accord.

Following consultations with the Security Council, the Secretary-General has decided to deploy 50 United Nations observers in South Africa for the purposes indicated in Security Council resolution 772. Angela King of Jamaica has been appointed the Chief of Mission of the United Nations Observer Mission to South Africa. Ismat Steiner of the United Republic of Tanzania is the Deputy Chief of Mission.

Mr. Steiner will lead an advance party of 13 observers to South Africa on 11 September to establish the Mission. The 13 observers will be assigned to the Natal/KwaZulu area (Durban) and the Wits/Vaal area (Johannesburg). The total of 50 United Nations observers will be stationed in the following 11 areas to cover the entire country:

| | |
|---|---|
| Natal/KwaZulu | Northern Cape |
| Border/Ciskei | Far Northern Transvaal |
| Wits/Vaal | Northern Transvaal |
| Western Cape | Eastern Transvaal |
| Orange Free State | Eastern Cape |
| Western Transvaal | |

The headquarters of the Mission will be in Johannesburg.

# Document 162

*Statement by the President of the Security Council, on behalf of the Council, on the shooting of demonstrators in Ciskei*

S/24541, 10 September 1992

The members of the Security Council deplore the killing of 28 demonstrators and the wounding of nearly 200 others by security elements in South Africa on 7 September 1992. They reiterate their grave concern at the continued escalation of the violence in South Africa. They emphasize once again the responsibility of the South African authorities for the maintenance of law and order and call on them to take all measures to end the violence and to protect the right of all South Africans to engage in peaceful political activity without fear of intimidation or violence. They urge all parties in South Africa to cooperate in combating violence and to exercise maximum restraint in order to help break the spiralling cycle of violence.

The members of the Security Council emphasize the need to put an end to the violence and create conditions for negotiations leading to the establishment of a democratic, non-racial and united South Africa. They note in this regard that the Security Council, in its resolution 772 (1992) of 17 August 1992, authorized the Secretary-Gen-

eral to deploy United Nations observers in South Africa, in coordination with the structures set up under the National Peace Accord, to provide a framework and basis for putting an end to violence in the country. They welcome the Secretary-General's decision to deploy an advance party of 13 United Nations observers in South Africa on 11 September 1992 as part of the complement of 50 observers to be deployed within one month.

The members of the Council call upon the Government of South Africa, parties and organizations, and the structures set up under the National Peace Accord, to extend their full cooperation to the United Nations observers to enable them to carry out their tasks effectively. They reiterate their call to other relevant regional and intergovernmental organizations to consider deploying their own observers in South Africa in coordination with the United Nations and the structures set up under the National Peace Accord in order to facilitate the peace process.

---

# Document 163

*Letter dated 16 September 1992 from the Secretary-General to Justice R. J. Goldstone, Chairman of the Commission of Inquiry regarding the Prevention of Public Violence and Intimidation*

Not issued as a United Nations document

My Special Envoy, Mr. Cyrus Vance, has informed me of the useful discussions he had with you during his recent visit to South Africa. As you are aware, in my report to the Security Council, I stated that the international community should support the work of the Goldstone Commission and that its recommendations should be fully and speedily implemented by the Government and, when so required, by the parties in South Africa. In view of the fact that the Commission has welcomed suitable international assistance, I recommended that the international community and the United Nations respond positively and appropriately, as and when requested.

The Security Council has authorized me to deploy the United Nations observers in coordination with the structures set up under the National Peace Accord. This mandate requires the United Nations mission to deal with

all the relevant structures under the Accord, including your Commission. When fully deployed, the 50 United Nations observers would be in a position to undertake these important tasks.

As you know, the advance team of United Nations observers authorized by Security Council resolution 772 (1992) of 17 August 1992, arrived in South Africa on 13 September. The Head of the Mission, Ms. Angela King, is scheduled to arrive in Johannesburg on 23 September 1992. I am confident that you would wish to meet with Ms. King for a full discussion of the work of your Commission and the modalities for cooperation between it and the United Nations observer mission.

I deeply deplored the tragic loss of life which occurred in Ciskei on 7 September 1992. It is my fervent hope that the United Nations will contribute to a reduction of tensions and will serve as a catalyst for future positive developments.

I would like to commend you on the far-reaching work being undertaken by your Commission and to assure you of my readiness to consider in a positive light any request for assistance from the United Nations in support of the work of your Commission.

(*signed*)
Boutros BOUTROS-GHALI

# Document 164

*Letter dated 21 September 1992 from the Secretary-General to Mr. Roelof F. Botha, Minister for Foreign Affairs of the Republic of South Africa*

Not issued as a United Nations document

I have the honour to refer to resolution 772 (1992) of 17 August 1992 by which the United Nations Security Council has, *inter alia*, welcomed with appreciation the report of the Secretary-General on the question of South Africa contained in document S/24389 and authorized the Secretary-General to deploy, as a matter of urgency, United Nations observers in South Africa in such a manner and in such numbers as he determines necessary to address effectively the areas of concern noted in the above-mentioned report, in coordination with the structures set up under the National Peace Accord of 14 September 1991 which established a comprehensive framework, agreed upon by all the major parties, organizations and groups of South Africa, to end violence and to facilitate socio-economic development and reconstruction.

In order to facilitate the fulfilment of the purposes of the mission of the United Nations observers in South Africa, I propose that your Government, in implementation of its obligations under Article 105 of the Charter of the United Nations, extend to this mission, its property, funds and assets and to its personnel the provisions of the Convention on the Privileges and Immunities of the United Nations (the Convention).

In view of the importance of the functions which the mission of the United Nations observers will perform, I propose in particular that your Government extend to:

(i) the United Nations observers, including the Chief of mission, who are high-ranking officials of the Organization and whose names shall be communicated to your Government for this purpose, the privileges and immunities, exemptions and facilities which are enjoyed by diplomatic envoys in accordance with international law;

(ii) other officials of the United Nations assigned to serve with this mission, the privileges and immunities to which they are entitled under Articles V and VII of the Convention.

The privileges and immunities necessary for the fulfilment of the functions of the mission of the United Nations observers also include: freedom of entry and exit, without delay or hindrance of personnel, property, supplies, equipment and spare parts; complete freedom of movement on land, sea and in the air of personnel, equipment and means of transport; the acceptance of the United Nations registration of means of transport (on land, sea and in the air) and United Nations licensing of the operators thereof; the right to fly the United Nations flag on premises, observation posts, vehicles, aircraft and vessels; and the right of unrestricted communication by radio or by satellite, as well as by telephone, telegraph or other means.

It is understood that the Government of South Africa shall provide at no cost to the United Nations, all such premises as may be necessary for the accommodation and fulfilment of the functions of the United Nations observers, including office space. All such premises shall be inviolable and subject to the exclusive control and authority of the United Nations. Without prejudice to the use by the United Nations of its own means of transport and communication, it is understood that your Government shall, upon request of the Chief of mission provide at its own expense, any necessary means of transport and communication. The Government of South Africa shall further ensure the security and safety of the United Nations observers.

If these proposals meet with your approval, I would suggest that this letter and your reply should constitute an agreement between the United Nations and the Republic of South Africa to take effect immediately.

# Document 165

*Letter dated 23 September 1992 from the Secretary-General to Mr. Frederik Willem de Klerk, President of South Africa*

Not issued as a United Nations document

My Special Envoy, Mr. Virendra Dayal, has informed me of the critical stage that the talks have reached seeking to arrange a meeting between you and Mr. Mandela.

I am fully aware of the complexity of the issues involved. May I, however, urge you to ensure that the present obstacles are overcome and that the momentum created for the meeting is not allowed to dissipate. The announcement of an early date for a meeting would, I am sure, be received with the greatest satisfaction here in New York, where leaders from all over the world have gathered for the General Assembly. It would no less be a source of immense relief to all the peoples of South Africa whose destiny lies in the hands of their leaders.

(*signed*)
Boutros BOUTROS-GHALI

---

# Document 166

*Statement by the Spokesman for Secretary-General Boutros Boutros-Ghali concerning the arrival of Ms. Angela King, the Chief of UNOMSA, in Johannesburg*

UN Press Release SG/SM/4821 - SAF/145, 23 September 1992

Following the Secretary-General's announcement of 9 September, of his decision to deploy a mission of 50 United Nations observers in South Africa, Angela King, who is heading the Mission, has arrived in Johannesburg today, 23 September, to assume her duties as head of the United Nations Observer Mission in South Africa (UNOMSA).

A second group of six observers travelled with the Chief of the Mission, bringing the total number of observers in South Africa to 20. It will be recalled that an advance team of 14 United Nations observers, headed by Ismat Steiner, has been in South Africa since 13 September to make the necessary arrangements for the deployment of UNOMSA. The full contingent of observers is expected to be deployed in October.

By its resolution 772 (1992) of 17 August, the Security Council authorized the Secretary-General to deploy, as a matter of urgency, United Nations observers in South Africa, in such a manner and in such numbers as he determined necessary to address effectively the areas of concern noted in his report (S/24389), in coordination with the structures set up under the National Peace Accord.

The Observer Mission will cooperate, and coordinate its work, as appropriate, with the structures set up under the Accord, particularly the National Peace Committee, the National Peace Secretariat and the Commission of Inquiry regarding the Prevention of Public Violence and Intimidation. Arrangements are being made to ensure coordination between the United Nations observer team and those of the Commonwealth Secretariat, the European Community and the Organization of African Unity.

# Document 167

*Statement by the Spokesman for Secretary-General Boutros Boutros-Ghali concerning the forthcoming meeting between President de Klerk and Mr. Nelson Mandela, President of the African National Congress*

UN Press Release SG/SM/4822 - SAF/146, 24 September 1992

The Secretary-General has just been informed by Nelson Mandela that the obstacles preventing a meeting between President de Klerk and Mr. Mandela have been overcome and that a meeting between them is being arranged imminently.

The Secretary-General warmly welcomes this development and wishes to express his sincere appreciation to Messrs. de Klerk and Mandela for the perseverance and leadership they have shown in resolving the difficulties that had arisen. He trusts that their meeting will help to transform the political atmosphere in South Africa in a positive way and lead rapidly to the resumption of multilateral negotiations involving all parties concerned.

The early attainment of a democratic, non-racial and united South Africa is a goal of the utmost importance to the United Nations. The Organization will continue to make every effort to further this objective in a constructive and understanding manner.

# Document 168

*Letter dated 29 September 1992 from the Secretary-General to Chief Mangosuthu Buthelezi, President of the Inkatha Freedom Party of South Africa*

Not issued as a United Nations document

I should like to recall our meeting at the end of July in New York, when we had the opportunity to exchange views on the situation in South Africa during the period of the Security Council debate. I found those discussions most useful. The participation of all interested parties in the debate in the Security Council, as well as the depth and scope of resolutions 765 (1992) and 772 (1992), underscore the central role of the United Nations on the issue and its readiness to work with all parties to facilitate the peace process.

As part of the effort to advance the peace process, we have been urging President de Klerk and Mr. Mandela to reach early agreement for a resumption of multilateral negotiations. My Special Envoy, Mr. Virendra Dayal, who visited South Africa from 16 to 26 September, met with a delegation of the Inkatha Freedom Party led by Inkosi S. H. Gumede, Deputy Secretary-General, on 19 September 1992, to discuss this and other related developments. However, despite several attempts, it was not possible for Mr. Dayal to establish contact with you personally by telephone before his departure.

Following the meeting of 26 September 1992 between President de Klerk and Mr. Mandela which resulted in the Record of Understanding, it is now essential that all South African leaders make every effort, as a matter of urgency, to put an end to the violence and to facilitate the resumption of multilateral negotiations, which must necessarily include the Inkatha Freedom Party. Further efforts will be required to accelerate the momentum for constructive change which should lead to progress on the constitutional questions and also reduce the volatility of the political atmosphere.

In order to move the peace process forward and to achieve a lasting settlement, I should like to appeal to you, as President of the Inkatha Freedom Party, to make a renewed effort to meet urgently with Mr. Nelson Mandela, President of the African National Congress, in order to consider ways and means of putting an end to the violence and to spur the negotiation process. As you are no doubt aware, the situation in South Africa today is followed very closely here in New York, where leaders from all over the world have gathered for the General Assembly. I believe that they and the people of South Africa as a whole would welcome any initiative emanating from a meeting between yourself and Mr. Mandela, which should set the tone for national reconciliation and cooperation.

Your urgent attention to this matter will be highly appreciated.

(*signed*) Boutros BOUTROS -GHALI

# Document 169

*Letter dated 29 September 1992 from the Secretary-General to Mr. Nelson Mandela, President of the African National Congress*

Not issued as a United Nations document

I should like to refer to our most useful conversation of this morning in regard to action to follow up your meeting of 26 September with President de Klerk. I have taken particular note of your suggestion that there should be a meeting of the 21 South African parties.

I wish to inform you in this connection that I have appealed to Chief Buthelezi to make a renewed effort to meet urgently with you in order to consider ways and means of putting an end to the violence and to move the peace process forward. I believe that the people of South Africa as a whole would welcome any initiative emanating from such a meeting, which should set the tone for national reconciliation and cooperation. Such a meeting between the two of you should also prepare the ground for a meeting of the 21 South African parties.

I very much hope that you will find it possible to respond promptly to an invitation to meet Chief Buthelezi.

*(signed)*
Boutros BOUTROS-GHALI

---

# Document 170

*Statement by Secretary-General Boutros Boutros-Ghali at a meeting of the Special Committee against Apartheid for the observance of the International Day of Solidarity with South African Political Prisoners*

UN Press Release SG/SM/4832 - GA/AP/2095, 12 October 1992

Today we remember South Africans who have suffered, or who are suffering, imprisonment for their political beliefs. Their struggle has not been in vain. The ideology of apartheid has been defeated, its evils recognized.

The South African Government now accepts that apartheid is discredited and unsustainable. South African authorities have decided to set free those who remain in prison on political grounds.

This is a welcome decision.

But the struggle is not yet over. The structures of apartheid have not yet been wholly dismantled.

The cruelties of apartheid have left a bitter legacy of violence, economic repression, distrust and anguish.

We remember with gratitude the sufferings of those who fought against apartheid. We are inspired by them in our determination to press ahead in helping to build a democratic, non-racial and united South Africa, which is the aim of the international community and of the Convention for a Democratic South Africa (CODESA) process.

To bring apartheid to a peaceful end through negotiations is the obligation placed on us by the United Nations Declaration on Apartheid, adopted by consensus in 1989. The United Nations is working hard to that end.

My Special Envoy, Virendra Dayal, visited South Africa from 16 to 26 September to hold follow-up discussions on Security Council resolution 772 (1992). He met State President de Klerk, senior officials of the Government of South Africa, and the various political parties, including the African National Congress of South Africa (ANC), the Inkatha Freedom Party (IFP) and the Pan Africanist Congress of Azania (PAC).

The discussions focused on my last report to the Security Council as well as on recent political developments in the country. Following bilateral discussions between officials of the Government and ANC, President de Klerk met Mr. Mandela on 26 September.

It was agreed that all prisoners whose imprisonment is related to past political conflicts, and whose release can make a contribution to reconciliation, should be released by 15 November. The release of political prisoners is, I understand, proceeding according to schedule. This is a hopeful sign.

The United Nations is doing all it can to assist the peace process. For example, following resolution 772, I sent a group of observers to South Africa. Twenty-eight United Nations observers are now in South Africa, deployed, in particular, in those areas where political violence is most severe. They will be working alongside observers from other intergovernmental bodies.

I am happy that the United Nations has not only condemned apartheid, but is taking concrete, constructive steps to assist the process of peaceful transition in South Africa.

Our efforts can of course only be complementary to those of the various political groups in South Africa. Their participation, goodwill and political courage are essential for success. Responsibility for achieving a just and long-lasting agreement through negotiation must rest with the South Africans themselves.

Sadly, outbreaks of violence continue in South Af-

rica. Apartheid and violence are blood brothers. Eliminating apartheid and eliminating violence are part of the same process. Apartheid creates a special desperation. Replacing its legacy of violence with a new spirit of trust and cooperation must be our main challenge now.

I know I speak for all the membership of the United Nations: I urge those in positions of leadership in South Africa to redouble their efforts to end the agony which apartheid has produced; and to join in creating a new future for South Africa.

# Document 171

*Third report of the Secretary-General on the implementation of the Declaration of Apartheid and its Destructive Consequences in Southern Africa*

A/47/574, 6 November 1992

## I. Introduction

1. By its decision 45/457 B of 13 September 1991, and its resolution 46/79/A of 13 December 1991, the General Assembly, *inter alia*, requested the Secretary-General to promote all efforts leading to the eradication of apartheid through genuine negotiations, to remain actively seized of developments in South Africa and to submit a report on further progress in the implementation of the Declaration on Apartheid and its Destructive Consequences in Southern Africa. The present report is submitted in compliance with that request.

2. To prepare the report, the Secretariat sought the views of the Government, all political parties, movements and organizations, as well as several other interlocutors whom United Nations delegations met in South Africa during 1992. They were requested to transmit by 5 October 1992 their observations on the overall situation in South Africa and on any development regarding the implementation of the Declaration. An analysis based primarily on those views is contained in annex I to the present report.

3. The Secretary-General had the opportunity, on a number of occasions during the year, to discuss, with the Minister for Foreign Affairs of South Africa and the Permanent Representative of South Africa to the United Nations, developments relating to the situation in South Africa, in particular, the negotiation process under way in that country. The Secretary-General also met with the President of the African National Congress (ANC), Mr. Nelson Mandela, the President of the Pan Africanist Congress of Azania (PAC), Mr. Clarence Makwetu, and Chief Mangosuthu Buthelezi, President of the Inkatha Freedom Party (IFP), who provided him with an assess-

ment of the situation and the position of their movements on the developments in South Africa. In addition, the Secretary-General was represented in an observer capacity at the Convention for a Democratic South Africa (CODESA I and II), held, respectively, in December 1991 and May 1992. Further, the Special Representative of the Secretary-General, Mr. Cyrus Vance, also visited South Africa in July 1992 pursuant to Security Council resolution 765 (1992). Mr. Virendra Dayal, Special Envoy of the Secretary-General, visited South Africa in September 1992 to hold follow-up discussions with the relevant parties in connection with the implementation of Security Council resolution 772 (1992).

4. In addition, the Secretary-General drew certain provisions of resolution 46/79/A of 13 December 1992 to the attention of the United Nations organs and specialized agencies concerned. Details on the steps taken by the United Nations system to implement such provisions will be reported in a separate report to the General Assembly.

## II. Observations by the Secretary-General

5. Despite progress made in the negotiations initiated at CODESA I in December 1991, CODESA II ended in a stalemate as no agreement could be reached on transitional arrangements including the establishment of an interim government. Following the break in the multilateral negotiations, the escalation in political violence further aggravated the situation. The massacre in Boipatong township on 17 June 1992, as well as subsequent incidents of violence, including the tragedy at Bisho, Ciskei, on 7 September 1992, focused attention on the imperative need to put an end to the violence, and to

facilitate a peaceful transition to a democratic, non-racial and united South Africa.

6. After the visit to South Africa of my Special Representative, Mr. Cyrus Vance, at the end of July 1992, pursuant to Security Council resolution 765 (1992), I made specific recommendations, in the context of the resolution, to assist in bringing an effective end to the violence and to create conditions for the resumption of the multilateral negotiations. Subsequently, in its resolution 772 (1992), the Security Council, *inter alia*, called upon the Government of South Africa and all parties in South Africa to implement urgently the relevant recommendations contained in my report, and authorized me to deploy United Nations observers in South Africa. My Special Envoy, Mr. Virendra Dayal, visited South Africa from 16 to 26 September 1992 to hold follow-up discussions with the parties concerned on the above resolution as well as on recent political developments in the country.

7. At the request of the parties, 10 United Nations observers were deployed in South Africa in the first week of August 1992 to observe mass action organized by ANC. It is generally agreed that the presence of the 10 United Nations observers had an overall salutary effect on the political situation during that period. By the end of October 1992, 44 United Nations observers had been deployed in South Africa in accordance with relevant decisions of the Security Council. They have been well received by the structures established under the National Peace Accord with which they are working in coordination to address effectively the areas of concern noted in my report to the Security Council. The Government of South Africa, as well as the parties concerned, has welcomed the presence and contribution of the observers to the peace process. The United Nations Observer Mission is proceeding expeditiously to fulfil the mandate entrusted to it, in close cooperation with observers from the Commonwealth and the European Community, as well as the Organization of African Unity (OAU).

8. The meeting between President de Klerk and Mr. Nelson Mandela, President of ANC, on 26 September 1992, constitutes an important step forward towards breaking the CODESA II deadlock. Agreement was reached at the meeting on the key issues relating to the securing of hostels, the release of all remaining political prisoners and the prohibition of the carrying and display of dangerous weapons. Agreement was also reached on the need for a democratic constituent assembly/constitution-making body and constitutional continuity during the interim transitional period. These agreements are a most welcome development and should provide a basis for moving the negotiation process forward. However, I

remain particularly concerned by the rejection of these agreements by Chief Mangosuthu Buthelezi, President of the Inkatha Freedom Party (IFP). Taking these factors into account, I have emphasized to all concerned the need for a renewed and determined effort to put an end to the violence and to remove any remaining obstacles that might impede the resumption of negotiations.

9. The agreement reached between President de Klerk and Mr. Mandela should accelerate the momentum for constructive change and lead to progress on the constitutional front. However, great perils persist, not least in the volatility of the political atmosphere and the tendency to resort to intimidation and violence. It is imperative that political parties honour the commitments they have made as signatories to the National Peace Accord, as well as to the interim agreement reached between the parties on the conduct of public demonstrations based on proposals made by the Goldstone Commission. Here, I should also like to stress once again the responsibility of the South African authorities for the maintenance of law and order, and the need for them to take all measures to end the violence and to protect the rights of all South Africans to engage in peaceful political activity without fear of intimidation or violence. All parties in South Africa should cooperate in combating violence and exercise maximum restraint in order to help break the cycle of violence.

10. The United Nations has been active, through the United Nations High Commissioner for Refugees, through its Trust Funds for Southern Africa and the network of specialized agencies, in facilitating, respectively, the return of South African exiles, the reintegration of former political prisoners into South African society, and in providing educational and training assistance to disadvantaged South Africans. In addition, the United Nations stands ready to provide a concerted system-wide response to address the economic and social disparities resulting from the long practice of institutionalized racism.

11. The role of the international community in the establishment of a democratic, non-racial South Africa, can, of course, only be complementary to those of the various political groups in the country. Their participation, goodwill and political courage are essential for success. Responsibility for achieving a just and long-lasting agreement through negotiation must rest with the South Africans themselves. For its part, the United Nations will continue to seek creative ways to assist the people of South Africa as a whole to attain the goals that they have set for themselves and to which the General Assembly committed itself in its 1989 Declaration on Apartheid and its Destructive Consequences in Southern Africa.

# Document 172

*Report of the Special Committee against Apartheid*

A/47/22-S/24663, 6 November 1992

. . .

## VII. Conclusions and recommendations

175. With the creation of a negotiating framework in December 1991, the political process in South Africa reached a new stage. Despite wide political differences, these first broad-based negotiations, moving ahead for several months, brought hopes for an early political settlement in South Africa. But developments since May 1992 have demonstrated that the political process in that country is fragile and vulnerable, and that a sustained process to reach a peaceful, negotiated solution needs not only political will and tolerance among the leadership involved in the negotiations, but also a climate of domestic peace in the society as a whole.

176. Violence which has continued to bring fear and horror to the South African society and has constantly aggravated a lack of trust between the main political actors, culminated on the night of 17 June. The Boipatong massacre shocked the international community and highlighted the necessity of its urgent involvement in assisting to contain and bring the violence to an end. The decision of the Security Council, OAU, the Commonwealth and the European Community to send observers to monitor the political violence has been welcomed by all major political parties and organizations in South Africa and outside. There is a strong expectation that neutral observers would also help to defuse the political tension and promote an environment in which serious and constructive negotiations could bring about a long-lasting solution in South Africa.

177. Socio-economic inequalities, deeply rooted in decades of apartheid, continue to plague the majority of the South African population and could threaten to undermine a peaceful and stable development through a transition period and beyond. A United Nations seminar organized by the Special Committee and the Centre Against Apartheid at Windhoek in May 1992 (see paras. 160-163) demonstrated the will of the international community to help address the socio-economic problems facing South Africa. Now, as the socio-economic dimensions of South Africa's transition are moving into focus, the Special Committee and the Centre are ready to concentrate their attention on the requirements of the disadvantaged sectors of the South African society and to promote appropriate and coordinated responses from the international community. The Special Committee fully supports the establishment in South Africa of an eco-nomic negotiating forum which would seek an accord between government, business and labour. It is hoped that the forum will address, *inter alia*, the problem of resetting economic priorities towards the correction of socio-economic imbalances engendered by decades of apartheid and an economic growth process capable of sustaining a considerable widening of services, human resources development and economic participation.

178. The referendum of the White electorate on 17 March 1992, which clearly demonstrated that the overwhelming majority of White South Africans support the process of change, had an important impact on the political situation in South Africa. However, the Special Committee expressed its concern about the referendum's lack of universality, since it had involved only about 15 per cent of the total population of South Africa. The Special Committee hoped that this referendum would be the last in the history of the country to be conducted by only a segment of the South African population.

179. Unfulfilled expectations of the Black majority, violence, deprivation and decay in the townships and huge unemployment may threaten to bring the country to the edge of a civil war. Under these circumstances, any delay in bringing about a political settlement could be disastrous. The economic price of delaying a settlement is also growing rapidly. These are powerful factors which should move all parties in South Africa to reach an agreement as soon as possible. Time is on no one's side. South Africa urgently needs an interim government of national unity to prepare elections for a constitution-making body and to administer the country until a new government has been elected on the basis of an agreed democratic and non-racial constitution. This cannot come about unless negotiations are resumed in some form or other. The Special Committee has confidence that common sense will prevail and that the parties will be able to reach the consensus necessary for a new South Africa to emerge.

180. Apartheid will have been eradicated only when a new constitution has been adopted, and a new government has been installed as a result of a free and fair election based on this constitution. The Special Committee cannot, therefore, support the view that apartheid is a closed page in the history of South Africa. Old legislative and executive structures of an apartheid nature are still in place and the majority of the population has not yet been able to exercise the right to vote. While many

apartheid laws have been dismantled in the past two years, the legacy of apartheid continues to pose a threat to the process of democratization. Apartheid has not only bitterly divided a nation but has also resulted in glaring disparities in the socio-economic situation. Even after the adoption of a new constitution, the dismantling of a system which has been so deeply embedded in the structure and everyday life of the country will not be without difficulties and pain. The legacy left behind by apartheid will be complex and will take long years to overcome.

181. The Special Committee, therefore, recommends that the General Assembly should:

(*a*) Reaffirm its determination to support the South African people in their legitimate struggle for the total elimination of apartheid through peaceful means and in their efforts to build together a non-racial and democratic society;

(*b*) Reaffirm the principles and goals envisaged in the consensus Declaration on Apartheid and its Destructive Consequences in Southern Africa, contained in the annex to its resolution S-16/1 of 14 December 1989, which *inter alia* called for negotiations in a climate free of violence;

(*c*) Reiterate its conviction that broad-based negotiations resulting in a new non-racial and democratic constitution and its early entry into force will lead to the total elimination of apartheid through peaceful means;

(*d*) Reiterate its strong support for the peaceful negotiations process in South Africa;

(*e*) Note that while positive measures have been taken by the South African authorities towards the creation of a better climate for negotiations, including the repeal of key apartheid laws, the revision of major security legislation and the release of remaining political prisoners, serious obstacles to achieving a climate conducive to free political activity still remain;

(*f*) Welcome the decisions taken by the Security Council on 16 July and 17 August 1992, its statement on the spiralling cycle of violence on 10 September 1992, the Secretary-General's report on the mission to South Africa of his Special Representative, the recommendations contained in his report of 7 August 1992, and the measures taken by the Secretary-General to assist the process in South Africa in strengthening the structures set up under the National Peace Accord, including the deployment there of United Nations observers;

(*g*) Urge the South African authorities to fully and impartially exercise the primary responsiblity of government to bring to an end the ongoing violence, to protect the lives, security and property of all South Africans in all of South Africa, and to bring to justice those responsible for acts of violence;

(*h*) Urge the South African authorities to assume fully the responsibility to respect and protect the right of South Africans to demonstrate peacefully in public in order to convey their views effectively;

(*i*) Call upon the signatories to the National Peace Accord to recommit themselves to the process of peaceful change by fully and effectively implementing its provisions, by cooperating with each other to that end, and upon all parties in South Africa to refrain from acts of violence;

(*j*) Note with satisfaction the release of prisoners held for their political beliefs or activities, and the agreements reflected in the Record of Understanding of 26 September 1992, which paved the way for the negotiations;

(*k*) Urge the representatives of the people of South Africa to resume, without further delay, broad-based negotiations on transitional arrangements and basic principles for a process of reaching agreement on a new constitution and for its speedy entering into force;

(*l*) Call upon the international community to support the process in South Africa through a phased application of appropriate measures with regard to the South African authorities, as warranted by ongoing developments, and, within the context of the need to respond appropriately to them, to review existing restrictive measures as warranted by positive developments, such as agreement by the parties on transitional arrangements, including the election of a constitution-meeting structure, and agreement on a new, non-racial and democratic constitution;

(*m*) Urge the international community to respect the existing measures imposed by the Security Council for the purpose of bringing an early end to apartheid in South Africa, and request the Security Council to continue to monitor its effective implementation;

(*n*) Appeal to the international community to increase humanitarian and legal assistance to the victims of apartheid, in particular, to the returning refugees and exiles, and to released political prisoners;

(*o*) Appeal also to the international community to help create stable conditions for the rapid and peaceful attainment of a new South Africa based on a negotiated, democratic and non-racial constitution by providing appropriate material, financial and other assistance to South Africans in their efforts to address the serious socio-economic problems, particularly in the areas of human resources development and employment, health and housing;

(*p*) Request the Secretary-General to continue to ensure the coordination of activities of the United Nations and its agencies with regard to, and, as appropriate, inside South Africa, and to report to the General Assembly at its forty-eighth session on measures taken to facilitate the peaceful elimination of apartheid and the transition of South Africa to a non-racial and democratic society as envisaged in the Declaration on Apartheid;

(q) Authorize the Special Committee against Apartheid, in accordance with its mandate, to mobilize international support for the elimination of apartheid through the early establishment in South Africa of a society based on a peacefully negotiated democratic and non-racial constitution, and to this end (i) to continue to monitor the complex developments in South Africa, and to collect, analyse and disseminate factual information in this regard; (ii) to facilitate a peaceful and stable transition in South Africa by promoting international assistance in helping South Africans to overcome the negative social and economic consequences of the policies of apartheid, *inter alia*, by organizing seminars on well-defined and specific topics with the participation of experts in the relevant fields and in cooperation with relevant offices and agencies in the United Nations system and other intergovernmental organizations, institutions and non-governmental organizations; (iii) to conduct liaison and consult with Governments, intergovernmental and non-governmental organizations, foundations and institutions, as well as other relevant groups, both inside and outside South Africa; and (iv) to undertake other relevant activities aimed at supporting the political process of peaceful change in South Africa;

(r) Appeal to Governments, intergovernmental and non-governmental organizations to continue their cooperation with the Special Committee against Apartheid, and also request all relevant components of the United Nations system to continue to cooperate with the Special Committee and the United Nations Centre Against Apartheid in their activities in support of the ongoing process of peaceful elimination of apartheid in South Africa.

# Document 173

*Letter dated 20 November 1992 from the Secretary-General to Mr. Nelson Mandela, President of the African National Congress*

Not issued as a United Nations document

I wish to thank you for your very informative reply of 13 October 1992 to my letter of 29 September 1992 in regard to my appeal to Chief Buthelezi to make a renewed effort to meet with you urgently.

As you have so clearly stated, the violence that continues unabated in the country has exacted a heavy and unacceptable toll. It has also threatened to scuttle the peace process to which you have made a significant contribution and has cast a dark cloud on the hopes and aspirations of the people of South Africa for a democratic, non-racial and united country.

I strongly believe that the momentum for reconciliation and peace that has driven politics and society in South Africa during the recent past must not be allowed to lapse. I therefore consider it extremely important to reiterate that in order to move the peace process forward without further delay, it would be necessary for you and Chief Buthelezi to meet urgently. As you yourself have noted, various matters of the utmost importance to the people of South Africa, including in particular agreement on transitional arrangements leading to the establishment of an interim government, await to be concluded in order to pave the way for a lasting, democratic solution to the problems of the country.

(*signed*) Boutros BOUTRO S-GHALI

# Document 174

*Letter dated 20 November 1992 from the Secretary-General to Chief Mangosuthu Buthelezi, President of the Inkatha Freedom Party of South Africa*

Not issued as a United Nations document

I should like to refer to my letter of 29 September 1992 in which I appealed to you to make a renewed effort jointly with Mr. Nelson Mandela in order to consider ways and means of putting an end to the violence and to facilitate the resumption of multilateral negotiations.

The violence that continues unabated in the country has exacted a heavy and unacceptable toll and has threatened to scuttle the peace process to which you have made a significant contribution. It has also cast a dark cloud on the hopes and aspirations of the people of South Africa for a democratic, non-racial and united country.

I strongly believe that the momentum for reconciliation and peace that has driven politics and society in South Africa during the recent past must not be allowed to lapse. I therefore consider it extremely important to reiterate that in order to move the peace process forward without further delay, it would be necessary for you and Mr. Mandela, as two of the most important leaders in the country, to meet urgently to address the issues in question.

As you are well aware, various matters of the utmost importance to the people of South Africa, including in particular agreement on transitional arrangements leading to the establishment of an interim government, await to be concluded in order to pave the way for a lasting, democratic solution to the problems of the country.

I should like to avail myself of this opportunity to thank you for meeting with Ms. Angela King, Chief of the United Nations Observer Mission in South Africa (UNOMSA), on more than one occasion, to exchange views on the role of UNOMSA on how best it could facilitate an end to the violence in the country. As you know, UNOMSA established a regional office in Durban soon after the advance team arrived in the country two months ago. About a third of the observers are deployed in Natal/KwaZulu and have been working in close cooperation with the dispute resolution committees in the region.

Your urgent attention to this matter would be highly appreciated.

(*signed*)
Boutros BOUTROS-GHALI

---

# Document 175

*General Assembly resolution: Policies of apartheid of the Government of South Africa—International efforts towards the total eradication of apartheid and support for the establishment of a united, non-racial and democratic South Africa*

A/RES/47/116 A, 18 December 1992

*The General Assembly,*

. . .

*Welcoming* the initiative of the Organization of African Unity to place before the Security Council the question of violence in South Africa, and welcoming Security Council resolutions 765 (1992) of 16 July 1992 and 772 (1992) of 17 August 1992 and especially the decision to deploy United Nations observers to further the purposes of the National Peace Accord signed on 14 September 1991,

*Welcoming also* the deployment of observers from the Organization of African Unity, the Commonwealth and the European Community in South Africa in response to Security Council resolution 772 (1992),

*Taking note* of the report of the Secretary-General of 7 August 1992 on the mission of his Special Representative to South Africa,

*Also taking note* of the report of the Special Committee against Apartheid, and the third progress report of the Secretary-General on the implementation of the Declaration, as well as the report of the Secretary-General on the coordinated approach by the United Nations system on questions relating to South Africa,

*Welcoming* the safeguards agreement of 16 September 1991 between the International Atomic Energy Agency and the Government of South Africa and the report of the Director General of the International Atomic Energy Agency of 4 September 1992, on the completeness of the inventory of South Africa's nuclear installations and materials, under the terms of the safeguards agreement,

*Reiterating its conviction* that broad-based negotiations, initially undertaken by the Convention for a Democratic South Africa, resulting in a new non-racial and democratic constitution and its early entry into force will lead to the total elimination of apartheid through peaceful means,

*Noting* that while positive measures have been taken by the South African authorities, including the repeal of key apartheid laws and the revision of major security legislation, important obstacles to achieving a climate conducive to free political activity remain,

*Recognizing* the responsibility of the United Nations and the international community, as envisaged in the Declaration, to help the South African people in their legitimate struggle for the total elimination of apartheid through peaceful means,

*Gravely concerned* that continued and escalating

violence threatens to undermine the process of peaceful change, through negotiations, to a united, non-racial and democratic South Africa,

*Deeply concerned* at revelations of illegal covert activities carried out by military intelligence with a view to undermining a major party to the political process of peaceful change in South Africa,

*Noting with concern* that, despite the signing of the National Peace Accord, the tragic bloodshed in South Africa has not ended,

*Bearing in mind* the need to strengthen and reinforce the mechanisms set up in South Africa under the National Peace Accord and emphasizing the need for all parties to cooperate in combating violence and to exercise restraint,

*Encouraging* the efforts of all parties, including ongoing talks among them, aimed at facilitating the resumption of substantive broad-based negotiations towards a new constitution and arrangements on the transition to a democratic order,

*Taking note with satisfaction* of recent agreements between parties aimed at removing many obstacles to resuming broad-based negotiations and also noting with satisfaction the release of prisoners held for their political beliefs or activities,

*Noting with concern* the remaining effects of the acts of destabilization that were committed by South Africa against the neighbouring African States,

1. *Strongly urges* the South African authorities to exercise fully and impartially the primary responsibility of government to bring to an end the ongoing violence, to protect the lives, security and property of all South Africans in all of South Africa, and to bring to justice those responsible for acts of violence;

2. *Calls upon* all parties to refrain from acts of violence and to cooperate in combating violence;

3. *Strongly urges* the South African authorities to assume the full responsibility to respect and protect the right of South Africans to demonstrate peacefully in public in order to convey their views effectively;

4. *Urgently calls upon* all signatories to the National Peace Accord to recommit themselves to the process of peaceful change by fully and effectively implementing its provisions and by cooperating with each other to that end;

5. *Calls upon* all other parties to contribute to the achievement of the aims of the National Peace Accord;

6. *Takes note with approval* of the recommendations contained in the report of the Secretary-General and calls upon the Government of South Africa and all parties in South Africa to implement urgently those recommendations;

7. *Commends* the Secretary-General for those measures taken to address areas of concern noted in his report and particularly to assist in strengthening the structures set up under the National Peace Accord, including the deployment of United Nations observers in South Africa, and urges the Secretary-General to continue to address all the areas of concern noted in his report which fall within the purview of the United Nations;

8. *Welcomes* the deployment in South Africa of the observers of the Organization of African Unity, the Commonwealth and the European Community;

9. *Strongly urges* the Government of South Africa, as well as the other parties and movements, to lend their full cooperation to the Commission of Inquiry regarding the Prevention of Public Violence and Intimidation (Goldstone Commission) and to permit the Commission urgently and fully to carry out investigations into the functioning and operations of security forces and armed formations, as recommended by the Secretary-General in his report;

10. *Requests* the Secretary-General to respond positively and appropriately, as envisaged in his report, to requests for assistance from the Goldstone Commission in the context of the National Peace Accord;

11. *Urges* the representatives of the people of South Africa to resume, without further delay, broad-based negotiations on transitional arrangements and basic principles for a process of reaching agreement on a new democratic and non-racial constitution and for its speedy entry into force;

12. *Calls upon* the international community to support the vulnerable and critical process still under way in South Africa through a phased application of appropriate measures with regard to the South African authorities, as warranted by ongoing developments, and, within the context of the need to respond appropriately to them, to review existing restrictive measures as warranted by positive developments, such as agreement by the parties on transitional arrangements and agreement on a new, non-racial and democratic constitution;

13. *Calls upon* all Governments to observe fully the mandatory arms embargo, requests the Security Council to continue to monitor effectively its strict implementation and urges States to adhere to the provisions of other Council resolutions on the import of arms from South Africa and the export of equipment and technology destined for military or police purposes in that country;

14. *Appeals* to the international community to increase humanitarian and legal assistance to the victims of apartheid, returning refugees and exiles and released political prisoners;

15. *Calls upon* the international community to assist disadvantaged South African democratic anti-apartheid organizations and individuals in the academic, scientific and cultural fields;

16. *Also calls upon* the international community to assist the non-racial sports bodies which have been endorsed by representative anti-apartheid sports organizations in South Africa in redressing the continuing structural inequalities in sports;

17. *Appeals* to the international community to help create stable conditions for the rapid and peaceful attainment of a new South Africa, based on an agreed, democratic and non-racial constitution, by providing and increasing its material, financial and other assistance to South Africans in their efforts to address the serious socio-economic problems of the disadvantaged people of South Africa, particularly in the areas of education, employment, health and housing;

18. *Also appeals* to the international community to render all possible assistance to States neighbouring South Africa to enable them to recover from the effects of destabilization and thereby to contribute to the stability and prosperity of the subregion;

19. *Requests* the Secretary-General, in consultation with the parties concerned, to undertake preliminary examination of the assistance which the United Nations might provide in the electoral process leading to a united, non-racial and democratic South Africa;

20. *Also requests* the Secretary-General to continue to ensure the coordination of activities of the United Nations and its agencies with regard to South Africa and, as appropriate, inside that country, and to report to the General Assembly at its forty-eighth session on measures taken to facilitate the peaceful elimination of apartheid and the transition of South Africa to a non-racial and democratic society as envisaged in the Declaration on Apartheid and its Destructive Consequences in Southern Africa.

# Document 176

*Report of the Secretary-General on the question of South Africa*

S/25004, 22 December 1992

### Introduction

1. The Security Council considered the question of South Africa at its 3107th meeting on 17 August 1992, having before it the report of the Secretary-General (S/24389). At the same meeting, the Security Council adopted resolution 772 (1992).

2. The resolution, *inter alia*, authorized the Secretary-General to deploy United Nations observers in South Africa, called upon the Government of South Africa, parties and organizations to extend their full cooperation to the observers and invited international organizations to also consider deploying observers in South Africa. In resolution 772 (1992), the Council also decided to remain seized of the matter until a democratic, non-racial and united South Africa is established.

3. The present report is submitted pursuant to paragraph 6 of Security Council resolution 772 (1992).

4. Following the adoption of the resolution, the President of the Security Council made the following statement (S/24456) on behalf of the Council:

"It is the understanding of the members of the Council that the Secretary-General will consult the Council on the number of observers he has the intention to deploy from time to time".

5. On 10 September 1992, I informed members of the Security Council of my decision to dispatch an advance party of 13 United Nations observers to South Africa on 11 September 1992 as part of the complement of 50 observers to be deployed in the country within a month.

6. On the same day, following consultations held by the Security Council, the President of the Council read a statement to the press (S/24541), in which he stated, *inter alia*, that the members of the Security Council deplored the killing of 28 demonstrators and the wounding of nearly 200 others by security elements at Bisho, Ciskei, in South Africa on 7 September 1992. The members reiterated their grave concern at the continued escalation of the violence in South Africa. They emphasized once again the responsibility of the South African authorities for the maintenance of law and order and called on them to take all measures to end the violence and to protect the right of all South Africans to engage in peaceful political activity without fear of intimidation or violence. The members of the Council urged all parties in South Africa to cooperate in combating violence and to exercise maximum restraint in order to help break the spiralling cycle of violence.

7. The President of the Security Council also stated that the members of the Council emphasized the need to put an end to the violence and create conditions for negotiations leading to the establishment of a democratic, non-racial and united South Africa. They welcomed the Secretary-General's decision to deploy an advance party of 13 United Nations observers in South Africa.

8. The President further stated that the members of the Security Council called upon the Government of South Africa, parties and organizations, and the structures set up under the National Peace Accord, to extend their full cooperation to the United Nations observers to enable them to carry out their tasks effectively. They reiterated their call to other relevant regional and intergovernmental organizations to consider deploying their own observers in South Africa in coordination with the United Nations and the structures set up under the National Peace Accord in order to facilitate the peace process.

9. In a communication addressed to me, dated 4 September 1992 (S/24526), the Permanent Representative of the United Kingdom of Great Britain and Northern Ireland to the United Nations informed me that the European Community Troika of Foreign Ministers, composed of the Foreign and Commonwealth Secretary of the United Kingdom of Great Britain and Northern Ireland and the Foreign Ministers of Portugal and Denmark, visited South Africa on 2 and 3 September 1992. Mr. Hurd had announced at a press conference in Pretoria on 3 September that the parties had accepted the European Community's offer to send observers to South Africa to be associated with the structures of the National Peace Accord, as part of efforts to end the violence. He indicated that initially, approximately 15 European Community observers were expected to be sent and that they would work in close coordination with the United Nations and with other international organizations.

10. In a communication addressed to me, dated 9 September 1992 (S/24544), the Permanent Representative of South Africa to the United Nations transmitted a memorandum submitted by the South African Government on the events which took place at Bisho, Ciskei, on 7 September 1992.

11. Taking into account ongoing developments in South Africa, and following consultations with the Government of South Africa and the parties after the adoption of resolution 772 (1992), I designated two Special Envoys who carried out separate missions to South Africa. Mr. Virendra Dayal, former United Nations Under-Secretary-General, visited South Africa from 16 to 27 September 1992. Ambassador Tom Vraalsen, Assistant Secretary-General of the Ministry of Foreign Affairs of Norway and former Permanent Representative of Norway to the United Nations, carried out a mission to South Africa from 22 November to 9 December 1992.

12. During the course of their respective visits, the Special Envoys held discussions with State President F. W. de Klerk and senior officials of the Government. They also had meetings with Mr. Nelson Mandela, President of the African National Congress (ANC) and Chief Mangosuthu Buthelezi, President of the Inkatha Freedom Party (IFP), as well as with leaders of other relevant parties in regard to the latest developments. Similar meetings were held with the senior officials of the National Peace Committee and National Peace Secretariat, and the Commission of Enquiry regarding the Prevention of Public Violence and Intimidation (Goldstone Commission). In addition, discussions were held with representatives of non-governmental organizations, as well as with the business, religious, human rights and development communities, along with civic associations. Discussions were also held with the leaders of the international observer teams that have been deployed in South Africa by the Commonwealth, the European Community and the Organization of African Unity.

## I. Findings of the Special Envoys of the Secretary-General

13. Following these wide-ranging consultations, each of the Special Envoys reported his findings to me. Their findings are reflected below.

### Status of negotiations

14. In contrast with the relatively minimal contact between the parties immediately following the stalemate in CODESA II, the current period is marked by a series of high-level contacts between nearly all parties in South Africa, including some of the parties not involved in the earlier CODESA process.

15. All parties appear to agree, in principle, that multi-party negotiations offer the only way forward to resolving South Africa's political problems. However, agreement has yet to be reached on the form a multi-party forum should take and its desired outcome. These issues, along with questions regarding participation, the agenda and timing of such a meeting, are among the topics being addressed in bilateral meetings.

16. In bilateral talks in the first week of December 1992, the Government and ANC appear to have made considerable progress in narrowing differences. The talks took place against the background of the Government's proposed timetable for the transition, and the November 1992 meeting of the ANC's National Executive Committee which considered the establishment of interim governmental structures.

17. Although there are fundamental differences yet to be bridged between these two parties, there appears to be a convergence of positions and a willingness on both sides to negotiate with one another and with others. A continuation of bilateral talks between the Government and ANC is expected shortly. Both parties have strongly emphasized that their positions are to be considered as proposals, and that they are determined not to exclude other parties from the process. They have, nonetheless,

also expressed the strong feeling that no party should be permitted to block progress towards a negotiated transition.

18. Attempts are being made to arrange a meeting between the State President, Mr. F. W. de Klerk, and Chief Mangosuthu Buthelezi in order to address the question of the resumption of multi-party talks. A meeting between President de Klerk, Chief Buthelezi and the leaders of Bophuthatswana and Ciskei was held on 10 December 1992 to discuss the resumption of multi-party talks.

19. Following the agreement reached between ANC and IFP at the 24 November 1992 meeting of the National Peace Committee, preparations have begun for a meeting between Chief Buthelezi and Mr. Nelson Mandela. Both organizations have appointed subcommittees of their senior leadership to prepare for the meeting. It is hoped that the preparations would expedite arrangements for an early meeting of the two leaders.

20. The Government and the Pan Africanist Congress of Azania (PAC) held bilateral discussions in Gaborone in early November 1992, and agreed to meet again in South Africa on 9 December 1992 to discuss the convening of a multi-party forum. Subsequently, the Government has reacted strongly to the position taken by the PAC political leadership with regard to reports that its armed wing, the Azanian Peoples' Liberation Army (APLA), claimed responsibility for recent armed attacks at King William's Town and Queens Town and that APLA planned a campaign of attacks on "soft targets". Following this, arrangements for further meetings with PAC were cancelled.

21. Further political developments include the emergence in October of a loose coalition composed of the Conservative Party and other groups on the right, and the leaders of Bophuthatswana, Ciskei and KwaZulu. This "Concerned South Africans Group" (COSAG) is aimed at galvanizing opposition to what its members perceive as an alliance between ANC and the Government. Other organizations and entities across the entire political spectrum are also pursuing contacts with one another.

22. Bilateral talks between the parties have focused on serious constitutional discussions about regional structures and the devolution of powers, power-sharing provisions, and the constitutional provisions related thereto. The regional structure of a new South Africa, and the relationship of the regions to the central government, remains a major preoccupation with all the parties. Agreement on effective multi-party machinery based on the principle of inclusiveness remains an essential first step for a resumption of multi-party negotiations.

23. At CODESA II there was wide agreement in principle on the reincorporation of the homelands into South Africa, their participation in the transitional arrangements, provisions for testing the will of their people regarding their reincorporation, and the "restoration" of South African citizenship to those who chose reincorporation.

24. The leader of Ciskei has subsequently indicated his outright opposition to reincorporation, and Bophuthatswana continues to reject suggestions of reincorporation. On 1 December, Chief Buthelezi presented a new draft constitution for a "federal state of Natal/KwaZulu" which was ratified that same day by the KwaZulu Legislative Assembly.

### National Peace Accord

25. Since the stalemate at CODESA II, the National Peace Committee has been the focal point for efforts to bring the major parties together to facilitate the peace process. A meeting of signatories of the Peace Accord, called for by the National Peace Committee on 24 November 1992, will provide an opportunity for the parties to review developments and to consider ways of strengthening the peace structures.

26. The National Peace Accord and the structures established under it are among South Africa's most valuable tools for assisting in reducing violence and bringing about a peaceful transition to democracy. A series of contacts between the parties have been made at all levels through the National Peace Committee and the network of Regional and Local Dispute Resolution Committees. These bodies offer open channels of communication essential to building a culture of political tolerance in the country. In this regard, virtually all parties have expressed the view that the presence in South Africa of United Nations Observers has significantly enhanced and reinforced the structures under the National Peace Accord.

27. A matter of particular concern is that some of the homelands are not signatories to the Accord, and some of those which are parties to it have withdrawn from the peace structures. The homelands continue to be major flashpoints of violence, largely due to conflicts arising over the lack of free political expression. They retain on their statute books repressive legislation such as the Internal Security Act, whose provisions have the practical effect of prohibiting public gatherings and other forms of political activity. There is also evidence that the security forces of the homelands are involved in violence. The result of these repressive practices and violence are increased tension and rising numbers of dead, injured and displaced, both inside the homelands themselves and in border areas. The responsibility of the Government of South Africa to redress this situation cannot be overemphasized.

28.   Some 13,000 returnees are receiving protection and assistance from the Office of the United Nations High Commissioner for Refugees (UNHCR) in South Africa and another 5,000 refugees have applied to return. UNHCR's mandate in the country has been extended for another year in order to address problems of reintegration and to facilitate the return of exiles. UNHCR has reached agreement with the South African Government for the involvement of the United Nations Children's Fund (UNICEF) in reintegration, focusing on the needs of women and children. A recent United Nations Development Programme (UNDP) mission to South Africa recommended that since rehabilitation programmes are not normally within the mandate of UNHCR, consideration should be given to establishing a modest UNDP presence in South Africa, within UNHCR, to assist with the rehabilitation aspects of resettling returnees.

*Areas of concern identified in the previous report of the Secretary-General (S/24389) and Security Council resolution 772 (1992)*

*Violence*

29.   Fear of violence and violence itself continue to be features of daily life in South Africa, particularly in the Witwatersrand/Vaal and Natal/KwaZulu regions. These regions account for most of the politically motivated violence in the country, which has been attributed to conflict between supporters of ANC and IFP. This conflict often manifests itself at the local or regional level where parties engage in violence and intimidation to establish and secure claims to a specific geographical area as their political base.

30.   Hostility between ANC and IFP supporters in many areas is openly acknowledged, but there is a growing sentiment that it fails to explain a significant proportion of the violence. There is strong evidence of conspiracy in some quarters and the use of agents provocateurs to incite and direct violence calculated to discredit and disrupt the peace process. Here it should be emphasized that grave concern continues to be expressed regarding the existence of covert operations, apparently sanctioned at high levels of Military Intelligence, as recently as December 1992.

31.   Socio-economic factors and crime often trigger political violence. "Commercial" violence often becomes politicized, destabilizing entire communities. High unemployment, inadequate housing and the lack of basic services such as water and sanitation pit groups against one another. To this volatile mix must be added the existence in the townships of certain "self-defence units" of dubious legitimacy, and right-wing "commandos" in some mostly rural areas of the country. Another critical element is the apparently growing cross-border traffic in weaponry, particularly from Mozambique. Indications are that the senior political leadership lacks political control over groups that engage in violence.

32.   Despite continued violence, there is wide agreement that without the deployment of international observers in the country the level of violence would be higher. The presence of the observers is viewed as having a salutary effect on the situation.

*Measures to reduce violence*

33.   While the primary responsibility of the South African Government for maintaining law and order is not questioned, there is a growing recognition that political leaders across the spectrum also have a responsibility to actively discourage violence on the part of their supporters.

*Investigations and prosecutions of criminal activity*

34.   In South Africa's current political context, there is troubling evidence of serious deficiencies in the law enforcement establishment's ability to promptly investigate violent crimes and prosecute offenders. At worst, these deficiencies translate into public perceptions of security force conspiracy or complicity in such crimes, which has frequently contributed to further violence, often directed at individual policemen. At best, such deficiencies are viewed as proof that the number of competent police personnel is inadequate.

*Efforts at police reform*

35.   There is a pervasive public sense of disbelief at the failure of the South African police (SAP) to maintain law and order and a widely held perception that the Government has failed to make full use of its law enforcement powers to stop violence. However, there appears to be an ongoing effort on its part to improve the image and methods of work of SAP. Organizational change in SAP is to be welcomed and encouraged. International exchange of expertise and training is being sought. Particular emphasis is being placed on community policing with the stated intention of moving away from the concept of a police "force" to that of a police "service". Reform of this kind demands political guidance and support from the highest levels of government, as well as consistency, perseverance and mobilization of resources. This level of commitment is indispensable.

*Investigations into the security forces and other armed formations*

36.   Evidence of conspiracy by at least some elements in the security establishment, recent armed attacks, the continued recruitment and training of individuals for service in non-governmental armed formations, the presence of arms caches and the cross-border flow of weapons all contribute to the level of violence and risk jeopardizing the

transition to democracy. In his statement to the press on 16 November 1992, Justice Goldstone referred to the Secretary-General's recommendation that the Goldstone Commission undertake a series of investigations into the security forces and other armed formations. Justice Goldstone called on "all political parties and groups in South Africa, and particularly the Government, to authorize and empower the Commission, or any other independent body, to carry out urgently and fully the recommendations of the Secretary-General". He also called on the international community to assist in this regard.

37. Justice Goldstone assured the Special Envoys that the Commission has all the legal powers needed to carry out its mandate. He stressed that he was entirely satisfied with the response that he had received from the State President regarding the resources which would be put at the Commission's disposal to conduct the necessary investigations. He also expressed satisfaction with the Government officials designated to work with him, and the principles agreed with the Government concerning access to information. The Government's commitments to Justice Goldstone were subsequently confirmed at the highest level.

38. The highest levels of the ANC have also pledged to cooperate with the Goldstone Commission and facilitate its work. Such cooperation is not forthcoming from PAC with regard to APLA, or the Chief Minister of KwaZulu, who has refused to cooperate in investigations of the KwaZulu police. Justice Goldstone indicated that in his investigation, he would welcome assistance from the international community and the United Nations in particular, in order to secure the cooperation of Governments which served as hosts to training camps and bases for armed formations operating in South Africa.

*Status of Battalions 31, 32 and Koevoet*

39. The status of Battalions 31 and 32 continue to be a source of concern. The South African Minister of Defence and Public Works confirmed to my Special Envoy, Ambassador Vraalsen, the Government's intention to disband Battalion 32 and transfer its members to existing units around the country by 30 November 1993. With regard to Battalion 31, the Minister stated that "it is regarded as essential" that "the whole San community . . . with its unique characteristics should be accommodated in one place. . . . The military members within the community will be deployed in existing military units in the vicinity of Schmidtsdrift." He added that "It is, however possible that some members presently at Schmidtsdrift may in due course prefer to return to their countries of origin. Should this be the case liaison will be established with the international community."

40. To date Battalions 31, 32 and Koevoet have not been disbanded as indicated by the Government of South Africa. There is a strong feeling in South Africa that merely dispersing their personnel among other military units is unsatisfactory. In this connection, it is believed that their continued existence, in whatever formation or form, does not have a place in a new South African dispensation.

*Question of hostels*

41. Violence between hostel dwellers and the surrounding communities is the result of a complex mix of factors including overcrowding, unemployment, competition over scarce resources and ethnic differences. Key among these factors is the rivalry between supporters of IFP and ANC. Violence between hostel dwellers and surrounding communities is widely perceived as an extension of the "turf battles" between these two groups elsewhere in the country, particularly in Natal/KwaZulu.

42. The urgency of improving security at the hostels in line with the recommendations of the Goldstone Commission, which called for the fencing of hostels, has been noted (see S/24389). The securing of hostels was one of three main issues discussed at the meeting between the State President, F. W. de Klerk and Mr. Nelson Mandela, President of ANC, on 26 September 1992, at which time it was agreed that further measures would be taken, including fencing and policing to prevent criminality by hostel dwellers and to protect hostel dwellers against external aggression. It was agreed that progress will be reported to the Goldstone Commission and the National Peace Secretariat. United Nations observers could witness the progress in cooperation with the Goldstone Commission and the National Peace Secretariat (S/24606).

43. The Government should take immediate steps to improve the security situation at those hostels known to be flashpoints for violence. Continuing efforts to address the problem of improving the security and living conditions at the hostels and in the surrounding communities, in consultation with their residents, should be facilitated by all parties.

*Dangerous weapons*

44. A similar situation obtains with regard to dangerous weapons. At the 26 September 1992 meeting between the Government and ANC, referred to above, the Government informed ANC that it would issue a proclamation within weeks to prohibit countrywide the carrying and display of dangerous weapons at all public occasions subject to exemptions based on guidelines being prepared by the Goldstone Commission. It should be noted that a proclamation to give effect to Justice Goldstone's recommendation to restrict the carrying of dangerous weapons in public has yet to be issued, although the measure has been drafted for some time.

45. The debate over restrictions on "cultural weapons" often diverts attention away from the critical issue of the supply of automatic weapons and other firearms

to which all factions have ready access. The Government and all other parties should make a concerted effort to reduce the supply and control the use of firearms and other sophisticated weapons.

46. Effective steps to address the carrying and public display of dangerous weapons can contribute significantly to creating an atmosphere of political tolerance. It is imperative that political leaders call on their supporters to disavow violence and to cease equating political rivalry with warfare. It is equally important that the South African Government take the necessary legal security measures to act promptly and impartially to prevent and quell violence, whatever its source.

## II. Activities of the United Nations Observer Mission in South Africa

47. The terms of reference of the United Nations Observer Mission in South Africa (UNOMSA) are reflected in Security Council resolution 772 (1992) as well as in the last report of the Secretary-General on the question of South Africa to the Security Council (S/24389). Following consultations with the Security Council, I announced on 9 September 1992 the decision to deploy a mission of up to 50 United Nations observers in South Africa in implementation of the relevant provision of the above resolution. Ms. Angela King, Director, Staff Administration and Training Division, Office of Human Resources Management, was appointed Chief of the United Nations Observer Mission in South Africa and took up her post on 23 September. An advance team of United Nations observers headed by the Deputy Chief preceded her by a week. By the end of October, UNOMSA observers were deployed in all 11 regions of South Africa. The full complement of 50 observers was attained at end-November 1992.

48. The headquarters of UNOMSA is in Johannesburg and it has a regional office in Durban, headed by the Deputy Chief of Mission. UNOMSA's current deployment is weighted towards the Witswatersrand/Vaal and Natal/KwaZulu regions, where 70 per cent of the political violence occurs.

49. UNOMSA personnel observe demonstrations, marches and other forms of mass action, noting the conduct of all parties, and endeavour to obtain information indicating the degree to which the parties' actions are consistent with the principles of the National Peace Accord and the Goldstone Commission guidelines for marches and political gatherings. Observers supplement their field observations by establishing and maintaining informal contacts at all levels with established governmental structures, political parties and organizations, as well as community-based "alternative structures" such as civic associations and other groups.

50. The functions of the structures established under the National Peace Accord with which UNOMSA was requested to cooperate are varied but also interrelated. The National Peace Committee is charged with the resolution of disputes concerning interpretation and alleged transgression of the code of conduct for political parties and organizations and with the promotion of social and economic reconstruction and development. The National Peace Secretariat has the responsibility to establish and coordinate the work of regional and local dispute resolution committees.

### The Goldstone Commission

51. In my earlier report to the Council, I commended the work of the Goldstone Commission and stated that should Judge Goldstone need assistance, he could request it from the international community. In this regard, following consultation with the European Community, six legal experts were seconded to the Commission. The United Nations has at Judge Goldstone's request provided an expert with a background in crime-prevention, security and criminal law to assist the Commission and several members of the UNOMSA team with the requisite legal background are also specifically assigned to the Commission in addition to their other duties.

52. The observer teams in various parts of the country also attend the hearings of the Commission held in their respective locations.

### Strengthening of the peace structures

53. In its role of strengthening the peace structures, UNOMSA initiated through the National Peace Secretariat courtesy calls and visits to homelands other than Ciskei, Bophuthatswana and KwaZulu, which were visited separately. The meetings were designed to enable the United Nations, European Community, Commonwealth and OAU observers to familiarize themselves with measures being taken within these territories to promote the peace process and support the National Peace Accord, and to explain the role of UNOMSA and other observer missions.

54. Fact-finding trips were made to QwaQwa, Lebowa and KaNgwane. The UNOMSA observer team based in Pretoria (Northern Transvaal region) made frequent trips to KwaNdebele. In each case, the observer groups were received by the Chief Minister, cabinet members, local political party representation and senior administration officials.

### Cooperation with other international observers

55. Security Council resolution 772 (1992) invited the Organization of African Unity (OAU), the Commonwealth and the European Community to deploy their observers in coordination with UNOMSA.

56. The UNOMSA observers were joined in South Africa on 18 October 1992 by the first Commonwealth observers, currently 17-strong. The European Community observers began arriving on 29 October and now total 14 members, while 11 OAU observers arrived between 15 and 23 November.

57. A weekly coordination and briefing session is held at UNOMSA headquarters in Johannesburg for the leaders of the observer groups. In addition, regularly scheduled morning briefings are open to all team members. Similar arrangements are in place at the UNOMSA office in Durban.

58. Because many of the Commonwealth and European Community observers come from a police background, a small task force has been set up under UNOMSA coordination to examine different aspects of SAP ranging from its structures and training to its performance at the community level.

59. The international observer teams have established close working relationships at the field and headquarters levels. They exchange information regularly and frequently observe events and meetings as mixed teams.

60. Throughout the country, the teams frequently pool their resources to ensure attendance and coverage of key events which may be scheduled simultaneously at different and often widely dispersed venues.

### Contacts with political parties

61. Since her arrival in South Africa, the Chief of Mission has held discussions with a wide range of government officials and leaders of political parties and organizations in the country. At these meetings, the Chief of Mission briefed her interlocutors on the role of UNOMSA, its deployment and activities.

## III. Consultations and communications of the Secretary-General

62. Following the massacre on 7 September 1992 at Bisho, Ciskei, President de Klerk called for an urgent meeting between the Government and ANC at the leadership level to discuss the question of violence.

63. In response to the proposal by the Government, Mr. Mandela agreed to meet with President de Klerk, on the understanding that the Government would make prior commitments to address three key issues, namely, the display of dangerous weapons, the securing of hostels, and the release of political prisoners.

64. Bilateral discussions were immediately resumed between ANC and the Government to address these three issues, in order to prepare the ground for the meeting between President de Klerk and Mr. Mandela. I instructed my Special Envoy, Mr. Dayal, to immediately upon his arrival in South Africa establish contacts with both parties, in order to assist, as necessary, and to make his services available to expedite the process of negotiation.

65. Given the critical importance of such a meeting, I addressed identical messages to President de Klerk and Mr. Mandela, urging them to ensure that the prevailing obstacles were overcome. I added that such a meeting would, no less, be a source of immense relief to all of the peoples of South Africa whose destiny lies in the hands of their leaders.

66. On 24 September 1992, I made a statement indicating that the obstacles preventing a meeting between President de Klerk and Mr. Mandela had been overcome, and that a meeting between them was being arranged imminently. This meeting took place on 26 September 1992. A detailed self-explanatory Record of Understanding agreed to at the meeting has been issued as a Security Council document (S/24606). Agreement was reached at the meeting on the key issues relating to the securing of hostels, release of all remaining political prisoners and the prohibition of the carrying and display of dangerous weapons. Agreement was also reached on the need for a democratic constituent assembly/constitution-making body and constitutional continuity during the interim transitional period. These developments constitute an important step forward towards breaking the CODESA II deadlock. It will be recalled that these three issues were the subject of specific observations in my report of 7 August 1992 (S/24389).

67. Regrettably, following the agreement reached between President de Klerk and Mr. Mandela, Chief Buthelezi announced his withdrawal from any constitutional negotiations on South Africa's future, and challenged the agreement reached in the Record of Understanding, particularly concerning the ban on carrying and display of dangerous weapons, including "cultural weapons".

68. On 29 September 1992, I telephoned President de Klerk and Mr. Mandela to congratulate them on their agreement of 26 September 1992. In regard to the position taken by Chief Buthelezi, I decided to contact him to urge him to support the resumption of multi-party negotiations based on the agreement reached between the State President and Mr. Mandela.

69. On 29 September 1992, I addressed a letter to Chief Buthelezi, in which I appealed to him to make a renewed effort to meet urgently with Mr. Mandela, in order to move the peace process forward and to achieve a lasting settlement. I also wrote to Mr. Mandela informing him that I believed that the people of South Africa as a whole would welcome any initiative emanating from such a meeting, which should set the tone for national reconciliation and cooperation. I pursued this matter in subsequent communications with both Mr. Mandela and Chief Buthelezi.

70. I also addressed letters to the leaders in the homelands, urging that all concerned redouble their efforts to expedite the resumption of multilateral negotiations, and emphasizing the need for a renewed and determined effort to put an end to the violence and to remove any remaining obstacles that might impede the resumption of negotiations.

71. I also addressed Mr. Clarence Makwetu, President of PAC, on the same subject.

72. On a regular basis I have had the opportunity to discuss the situation in South Africa with the Permanent Representative of that country to the United Nations as well as with other interlocutors. Through him, I urged the Government of South Africa to resume, as rapidly as possible, multi-party negotiations aimed at ending the present stalemate. I also expressed my concern at the escalating violence.

73. During the course of the forty-seventh session of the General Assembly, I met with Mr. Thabo Mbeki, Director, International Affairs Department of ANC and Mr. Clarence Makwetu, President of PAC. Mr. Mbeki briefed me on the latest developments concerning bilateral discussions between the Government and ANC. Mr. Makwetu informed me of the outcome of discussions held between PAC and the Government in Gaborone in November 1992. I impressed upon both the importance of resuming multi-party negotiations and containing violence so prevalent in South Africa.

74. The situation in South Africa was also reviewed with the Chairman of OAU, President Diouf of Senegal, and the Secretary-General of OAU, Mr. Salim Ahmed Salim, during their visits to the United Nations.

75. All my interlocutors expressed support for the efforts being made by the United Nations to facilitate a peaceful transition to a democratic society in South Africa and assured me of their continued cooperation.

76. On 27 November 1992, I received a letter from the Permanent Representative of South Africa (S/24866) containing a statement and accompanying background paper issued by State President F. W. de Klerk setting out a proposed timetable for the transitional process in South Africa. The timetable envisages that a fully representative government of national unity will be in place no later than the first half of 1994.

77. On 4 December 1992, a joint media statement was issued by the Government of South Africa and ANC which indicated that they had held bilateral discussions from 2 to 4 December 1992. The discussions recognized the importance of resuming multilateral negotiations as soon as possible to ensure speedy movement to a democratic dispensation. To this end, bilateral discussions will continue.

78. On 17 December 1992, I met with Mr. Roelf Meyer, Minister for Constitutional Development of South Africa, who reported to me on the progress being made regarding bilateral discussions between the Government and the parties and prospects for the resumption of multilateral negotiations which would involve all parties. Various other issues relating to the situation in South Africa were also discussed.

## IV. Observations

79. Based on my consultations and the reports of my two Special Envoys, I would make the following observations and recommendations concerning the situation in South Africa for consideration by the Security Council.

80. All parties must recognize that continued uncertainty over the country's future can only lead to further violence, instability and economic decline. Recent developments therefore give cause for guarded optimism about the prospect for progress towards a negotiated settlement in South Africa. I am pleased to note that there is substantial agreement to expedite arrangements for multi-party negotiations. These are positive trends which should be encouraged and supported by the international community. With respect to the CODESA process, the principle of inclusiveness must be recognized as essential for achieving the transition to democratic rule through free elections and new constitutional arrangements. It is imperative that all parties refrain from unilateral actions or public statements which alienate others or render the process more difficult.

81. While it is recognized that the Government has primary responsibility for the maintenance of law and order, all political leaders must take immediate action to curb political violence. To this end I would urge all parties to attend the planned meeting of signatories to the National Peace Accord in order to examine ways and means of putting an end to the violence and to strengthen the structures. Lack of political freedom in the homelands continues to be a source of tension and violence. Those in a position to influence the authorities in the homelands should strongly urge the repeal of repressive legislation and restraint of their security forces. Scrupulous adherence by all parties to the Goldstone Commission guidelines for the conduct of public demonstrations would also foster and sustain the peace process.

82. At the 26 September 1992 meeting between State President de Klerk and Mr. Mandela, an agreement was reached in respect of the release of all political prisoners, the securing of hostels, as well as the banning of the display of dangerous weapons. Regarding political prisoners, a Joint Committee consisting of government and ANC representatives has made considerable progress. By 15 November 1992, the agreed date for the release of political prisoners, 536 cases had been disposed

of by the Joint Committee. At the same time some of the cases submitted by ANC have yet to be resolved. The Government stated it would issue a proclamation to prohibit, countrywide, the carrying and display of dangerous weapons at all public occasions subject to exemptions based on guidelines being prepared by the Goldstone Commission. The granting of exemptions was to be entrusted to one or more retired judges. On this basis, the terms of the proclamation and mechanism for exemption shall be prepared with the assistance of the Goldstone Commission. I would urge the South African Government to take steps to expedite the full implementation of the agreements on these issues. All parties have expressed their deep concern over the illegal flow of weapons into the country. Consideration might be given to ways of cutting off the illegal supply of weapons from whatever source they may derive.

83. I welcome the decision of the Government of South Africa to extend the necessary assistance to the Goldstone Commission in order to facilitate its work and urge all parties in South Africa to cooperate fully with the Goldstone Commission's forthcoming investigation into the security forces and other armed formations. I also welcome the assurance given by the highest level of leadership of ANC to cooperate with the Goldstone Commission and facilitate its work. Justice Goldstone's standing in the international community and the United Nations active support for him and his Commission have reinforced the Commission's capacity to address difficult and sensitive issues. The United Nations and the international community will continue to assist the Commission, as requested by Mr. Justice Goldstone, in conducting its investigations. For my part, I will continue to extend all necessary support to the work of the Goldstone Commission.

84. As a means of building community confidence in and developing the human resources of the South African police, I would urge expansion of the present programmes for the exchange of information and expertise between South Africa and other countries on community-policing techniques, as well as on the recruitment, training and management of police personnel. Such programmes can only improve the morale and stature of the police, and enhance their credibility as an impartial service dedicated to public safety and security of all South Africans.

85. In order to help the South African police improve its investigative policies and procedures, and the skills of its personnel, police officers of various countries with the requisite skills and experience should be invited to South Africa to observe and, as appropriate, advise South African police personnel on the conduct of investigations. These international police officers would be deployed as technical advisers, and would be separate from the police officers already participating in the international observer missions presently in the country.

86. Women's organizations emphasize their concern over violence and intimidation directed at women from a variety of sources, including the police. I would strongly urge that special attention be given to this question, especially in view of the crucial role women can play in maintaining cohesion and stability in their communities. One aspect of democratization which should not be overlooked is the need to bring the country's women into the political process as full partners. Political violence, intimidation, poverty and dislocation of families and communities are among the factors currently preventing their full participation. Future democracy, reconciliation and development in South Africa cannot take place without the contribution of all its people.

87. The contribution of the international observer teams has been welcomed by all concerned. Some nevertheless have contended that UNOMSA needs to be strengthened and others are of the view that its mandate should be expanded. Effective means have been established for coordinating the work of UNOMSA with that of the other international observer teams from the Commonwealth, the European Community and OAU operating under Security Council resolution 772 (1992). By all accounts, the international observers have performed well in adapting their operations to meet the needs on the ground and have had a salutary effect on the political situation in general. Given the delicate situation now prevailing in South Africa, characterized by unacceptable and in some locales rising levels of violence, I intend to modestly reinforce UNOMSA with an increment of 10 additional observers.

88. While progress has been made in enhancing and reinforcing the structures established under the National Peace Accord, much more remains to be done particularly with regard to the National Peace Committee and the National Peace Secretariat. The Government of South Africa should ensure that adequate resources are made available to facilitate the operations of the National Peace Committee and the National Peace Secretariat at all levels.

89. There has been distinct progress in implementing the observations and recommendations made in my report of 7 August 1992 (S/24389). It remains essential that the Security Council stay actively seized of the situation, as it has undertaken to do. The goal of a democratic, non-racial and united South Africa must remain one of the highest priority to the Organization and I shall keep the Council informed of further developments, so that it can react, as needed, with understanding of the process under way.

# Document 177

*Letter dated 18 January 1993 from Mr. Thabo Mbeki, Secretary for International Affairs of the African National Congress, to the Secretary-General*

Not issued as a United Nations document

I take this opportunity to extend seasonal greetings to you.

The people of South Africa will enter 1993 eagerly looking forward to a future of democracy and social progress, without apartheid and violence. After many difficulties, the negotiations process is once again under way in our country. That requires the ANC to use all its resources to ensure that elections for a Constitutional Assembly take place before the end of 1993 and an Interim Government of National Unity established.

We therefore believe 1993 will be a decisive year for the people of South Africa. We take this opportunity to extend our warm appreciation to you for your consistent opposition to apartheid and your support for democracy in our country. Knowing you and working with you over the years has proved to be a great source of inspiration.

It is vital that as we enter this most critical stage of our struggle, we meet together to analyse the situation and together work out appropriate strategies for successfully marching the last mile to freedom.

The ANC has therefore decided to convene an International Conference under the theme—*From Apartheid to Peace, Democracy and Development*—to be held here in Johannesburg from 19 to 21 February 1993.

We believe that this major International Conference on South African soil will be one of the most significant conferences ever held on the issue of South Africa. It will give us the opportunity not only jointly to work out initiatives that will ensure that democratic foundations are firmly established in 1993, but will also enable us to take measures that will help us consolidate and defend the new democracy. . . .

President Nelson Mandela and other senior leaders of the ANC will also actively participate in the Conference.

I extend an invitation to you to participate in this historic Conference.

. . .

(*signed*)
Thabo MBEKI

---

# Document 178

*Letter dated 9 March 1993 from the Secretary-General to President de Klerk of South Africa*

Not issued as a United Nations document

I was pleased to learn from Ms. Angela King, Chief of the United Nations Observer Mission in South Africa, about the successful conclusion of the Multi-party Planning Conference in Johannesburg. It was encouraging that so many of the parties and political groups in South Africa participated in this initial stage. Ms. King has informed me that the next stage of the Multi-party negotiations will take place no later than 5 April.

I am confident that the next round of meetings will be equally successful and will lead to an agreement on the transitional arrangements.

I wish to assure you that the United Nations is following the situation in South Africa very closely and it will continue to remain a matter of high priority for the United Nations.

Ms. King and her team of Observers will stay on in South Africa, not only to contribute to the efforts to reduce the violence but also as a symbol of United Nations' commitment to help South Africa's transition to a united, democratic, non-racial country.

Please accept, Excellency, the assurances of my highest consideration.

(*signed*)
Boutros BOUTROS-GHALI

# Document 179

*Remarks by Secretary-General Boutros Boutros-Ghali at the
annual ceremony to receive contributions and pledges to
United Nations assistance programmes and funds
for southern Africa*

UN Press Release SG/SM/4947 - SAF/155, 22 March 1993

I am delighted to welcome you here today. This is an occasion at which we formally receive, and acknowledge, contributions and pledges made to United Nations assistance funds for Southern Africa.

For more than 25 years, the United Nations Trust Fund for South Africa and the United Nations Educational and Training Programme for Southern Africa have been providing humanitarian, legal and educational assistance to the victims of apartheid.

This assistance has been of crucial importance. Individuals were enabled to realize their potential. Communities saw they were not alone. As a result, the oppressed regained their self-confidence. Fatal cracks appeared in the unjust system of apartheid.

We are now entering what is almost certainly the final phase of the struggle against institutional racism in southern Africa. It has been a long and, at times, bitter struggle. It has been a struggle waged mainly by the people of southern Africa themselves.

But we should not overlook the key role of international humanitarian assistance in supporting the people of the region. Solidarity has been an important factor.

That solidarity, that generosity, is needed now more than ever. South Africa is beginning a process of transition. To assist that process, generous international support will be vital. The country, and the region, face massive tasks of political and social transformation. Expectations are, understandably, running high.

So, as I pay tribute to the support given in 1992 and before, I have to say that the task is not over. We will have to call forth even more generosity in future.

I hope I can rely on the continued support of Member States for these programmes. They constitute the humanitarian component of United Nations efforts for the peaceful settlement of the conflict in South Africa.

But it is a real pleasure to acknowledge the generous contributions made in 1992. This support by Member States has been generous. It is a clear indication of the long-standing commitment of Governments to promote progress towards a peaceful negotiated political settlement in South Africa. It is a clear indication of international solidarity and generosity in the humanitarian field.

The United Nations Trust Fund for South Africa has for over 27 years supported South African victims of apartheid, both inside and outside the country. It has provided legal assistance and humanitarian relief. Following a change in its mandate agreed by the General Assembly two years ago, the Trust Fund is now working through broad-based, impartial organizations in South Africa itself. It is assisting the reintegration of released political prisoners and former exiles. It is providing legal assistance and support to individuals, and working for the effective implementation of legislation repealing apartheid laws.

The United Nations Educational and Training Programme for Southern Africa provides scholarship assistance to South Africans. At present about 2,100 students are being supported in priority fields. Like the Fund, the Programme has adjusted rapidly to changing conditions. Now many of its projects involve training South Africans within South Africa itself. It is well placed to support the education and training of disadvantaged South Africans in the critical area of human resources development.

So, in acknowledging the help given in the past, I call on you to redouble your efforts to support the important work of the Fund and the Programme.

In conclusion, I must express my appreciation for the unstinting support I have received from the Chairman of the Committee of Trustees of the Trust Fund, Ambassador Osvald of Sweden; the Chairman of the Advisory Committee on the United Nations Educational and Training Programme for Southern Africa, Ambassador Huslid of Norway; and the Chairman of the Special Committee against Apartheid, Ambassador Gambari of Nigeria.

Finally, I ask that you convey to your Governments my deep appreciation of the contributions and pledges that they have made today.

# Document 180

*Statement by Secretary-General Boutros Boutros-Ghali at the solemn meeting by the Special Committee against Apartheid in observance of the International Day for the Elimination of Racial Discrimination*

UN Press Release SG/SM/4948 - GA/AP/2118, 22 March 1993

This day, observed annually as the International Day for the Elimination of Racial Discrimination, was inaugurated by a resolution of the General Assembly in 1966. It honours the memory of the 69 peaceful demonstrators—mainly women and children—who were massacred at Sharpeville in 1960. And it calls on the international community to redouble its efforts to eliminate all forms of racial discrimination.

Each year the world community has honoured those who died at Sharpeville. It has reflected on their sacrifice. It has mobilized its thoughts, and its efforts, on behalf of the suffering victims of apartheid. And it has, increasingly, focused on the gigantic task of building the new South Africa.

This year, for example, the international observer missions in South Africa have called on all South Africans to dedicate themselves, on this day, to peace and reconciliation.

This year, the observance of the International Day for the Elimination of Racial Discrimination coincides with an important moment in the process of negotiations in South Africa. They have entered a new phase.

Two weeks ago, on 5 and 6 March, a Multi-party Planning Conference was held at Kempton Park, South Africa, to plan for the resumption of full-scale, multi-party constitutional negotiations. It was attended by 26 delegations representing the broadest spectrum of political parties and organizations ever assembled on South African soil. In a far-reaching decision, participants committed themselves, individually and collectively, to multi-party constitutional negotiations to take place within the multi-party forum, as a matter of national urgency, not later than 5 April 1993.

This historic meeting is, in a sense, a tribute to the resilience, wisdom and determination of the South African leadership, both Black and White, to forge ahead and rise above their differences to build a common future.

The United Nations—which is committed to facilitating the negotiating process, has spared no effort in bringing about peace and reconciliation. In July 1992, while the country was engulfed in endless recriminations, turmoil and politically motivated violence, the Security Council offered a forum to South African political leaders to state their positions. At the same time, it urged them to renounce violence and remove the remaining obstacles

to resume negotiations. At the request of the Council, I deployed United Nations observers to assist in the strengthening of the mechanism of the National Peace Accord. Other international and regional organizations were invited likewise to send their own observers.

Today, it is generally recognized that these timely decisions and actions by the United Nations and other international organizations have helped in reducing political tension in South Africa. They have also had a positive impact on the political situation in the country.

At this point, I urge the leaders of all the parties and organizations to persevere in their efforts to reach an agreement on the principles and modalities for the difficult transition ahead. It is important that this agreement be based on the principles of inclusiveness, mutual tolerance and respect which are so essential to bring about democratic rule through free elections and a new constitutional dispensation.

In these endeavours, they can rest assured of the support of the United Nations and the international community at large.

But time is of the essence in South Africa as elsewhere. A speedy settlement in South Africa is essential to allow the nation to address the serious socio-economic imbalances resulting from decades of apartheid, and to return to the path of sustained economic growth.

At a symposium last year, in Windhoek, organs and agencies of the United Nations system looked into ways and means of addressing these imbalances. They are preparing now for the time when they can bring their full contributions to bear, particularly in the critical areas of health, education and housing, with special regard to the needs of children and women, the most vulnerable groups in South Africa.

It should be recalled in this connection that the United Nations has long been providing humanitarian, legal, educational and relief assistance to victims of apartheid—largely through the Trust Fund for South Africa and the United Nations Educational and Training Programme for Southern Africa.

Last year, at the pledging conference for assistance programmes for southern Africa, 27 Governments contributed a total of $7 million.

At the pledging conference this morning, I also received important contributions from a number of Governments. I wish to thank all the donor countries for their generous contributions and hope that other countries will also join in this genuine international humanitarian effort.

The massacre at Sharpeville—and the contempt which it showed for the rights of Black South Africans—illustrated the horrors of apartheid at its worst.

But there are other forms of racism besides the hideous institutional racism of apartheid. In too many countries, minorities feel threatened by intolerance and racial bigotry.

Democracy—rule of the majority—can easily become the tyranny of the majority unless there are safeguards.

Opposition to racism and racial discrimination is inherent to the United Nations and its Charter. The Charter not only recognizes the importance of fundamental human rights, equality and the intrinsic value of each and every human being; it sees them as the essential foundation of true progress and lasting development.

The United Nations, in upholding the Charter, proclaims the universal values of human rights and the dignity of all human beings. Later this year, in Vienna in June, we will be holding the World Conference on Human Rights. This will provide an excellent opportunity to consider practical measures to protect and enhance human rights in the world.

The struggle against racism is not confined to southern Africa; and it must not be limited to words only. Human rights, including protection against racial discrimination, need to be put into law, and monitored and upheld in practice.

We are at the dawn of a new era in South Africa. An era marked by a desire for reconciliation and renewed determination to overcome difficulties of all kinds through negotiation and dialogue, which have already resumed.

Chance mishaps, admittedly, have occurred in the past. No one can predict the future. One fact is certain: for the first time, one can see the light at the end of the tunnel in South Africa. Yesterday's enemies have gathered together at Kempton Park in order to conduct a dialogue and begin to define the elements of a process that will lead, soon, it is our hope, to a new, non-racial and democratic South Africa.

The day will come when South Africa, a land that is so rich and so tormented, will have overcome the upheaval of the transition. In its restored dignity, the abundance of its means and the commitment of a people reconciled with itself, South Africa will be able then to look to the future with confidence. Its victory, of course, will, first of all, be the victory of all South Africans, and all Africans. But it will also be the victory of mankind as a whole.

# Document 181

*Letter dated 24 April 1993 from the Secretary-General to Mr. Nelson Mandela, President of the African National Congress*

Not issued as a United Nations document

It was with a profound sense of loss and sorrow that I learned this morning of the death of Oliver Tambo, National Chairman of the African National Congress. I had known and worked with Oliver during his tenure as President of ANC. He was a remarkable man with a deep sense of conviction and compassion, a man of extraordinary intellect and knowledge, a man of courage and vision.

I know that Oliver's death is a very great loss to you personally in view of the long friendship you enjoyed and the deep commitment and sacrifices you shared in the service of your people. Like you, Oliver was as committed to the struggle to eradicate the apartheid system as he was to the imperative to build in its wake a South Africa in which all races and creeds could live in peace and harmony. He will be remembered for his many achievements in the service of oppressed people in Africa and around the world.

At this critical phase of the multi-party negotiations on the country's future, a stern trial of character and will may now face the country, its leaders and people. South Africans as a whole can continue to count on the goodwill of the entire international community in facing this challenge. I have no doubt that in your endeavours, the legacy of Oliver will help sustain the way forward.

I would like to extend to you and through you to the entire leadership and supporters of ANC, my most sincere condolences on the loss of a great comrade and friend. I have also extended deep condolences to Oliver's widow and family.

With my profound sympathy and my warmest regards.

(*signed*)
Boutros BOUTROS-GHALI

# Document 182

*Statement by a Spokesman for Secretary-General Boutros Boutros-Ghali expressing "outrage" at right-wing Afrikaners' "brazen display" of force and intimidation against multi-party negotiations*

UN Press Release SG/SM/5028, 27 June 1993

The Secretary-General was outraged at the brazen display of force and intimidation by members of the right-wing Afrikaner National Front (ANF) against delegates engaged in multi-party negotiations in Johannesburg to facilitate South Africa's transition to a non-racial, democratic and united country. It has become apparent that progress in the multi-party negotiations threatens extremist elements that continue to espouse racist policies and practices.

The Secretary-General stresses that the overwhelming majority of South Africans have committed themselves to peace, equality and democracy. In this quest, they enjoy the strong encouragement and support of the international community.

The Secretary-General reiterates his call on all South Africans to renounce violence and intimidation. He urges them to commit themselves to the negotiation process which provides the only alternative to the establishment of lasting peace and democracy in South Africa.

# Document 183

*Letter dated 6 August 1993 from the Secretary-General to Chief Mangosuthu Buthelezi, President of the Inkatha Freedom Party of South Africa*

Not issued as a United Nations document

I wish to recall the very fruitful talks we had in Rome on 18 April 1993 regarding the situation in and relating to South Africa. I have continued to follow closely developments in South Africa with renewed hope but also with equal concern.

Among the issues of major concern is the recent spate of violence which has claimed scores of lives in the Wits/Vaal area. Most of the violence continues to be directed at supporters of both the Inkatha Freedom Party and the African National Congress.

You will recall that both during our meeting in Rome and in my communications to you prior to and subsequent to that meeting, I had expressed the hope that all efforts would be deployed to settle the problems of the future of South Africa through a broad-based dialogue amongst South Africans. I was therefore very concerned when IFP decided recently to suspend its participation in the multi-party negotiation process.

As one of the major political parties in the country, the participation of IFP in the ongoing negotiations is extremely important for the success of the peace process.

It is widely held that the issues of priority concern to IFP regarding the transitional arrangements would best be addressed in the context of the multi-party negotiations, not outside them. There is also the danger that IFP's withdrawal could be misconstrued by some of its supporters who could then consider violence as the only option open to pursue their political goals.

I wish to reiterate to you the readiness of the United Nations to continue to contribute to the efforts to resolve the remaining problems through negotiations. As you are aware, consideration is being given to the possibilities of expanding the United Nations role in the efforts to reach agreement on the transitional arrangements and process in South Africa.

In order to move the peace process forward and to make a positive contribution to the efforts to reduce the violence that is exacting a heavy toll particularly in the townships, it would be imperative for IFP to return to the negotiations as soon as possible.

(*signed*)
Boutros BOUTROS-GHALI

# Document 184

*Statement by the President of the Security Council, on behalf of the Council, on the upsurge of violence in South Africa*

S/26347, 24 August 1993

The Security Council deplores the recent upsurge in violence and discord in South Africa, especially in the East Rand. This violence—terrible in its human toll—is even more tragic as the country proceeds on the path to a democratic, non-racial and united South Africa and a new, more promising future for all its citizens.

The Council recalls its statement in resolution 765 (1992) that it is the responsibility of the South African authorities to take all necessary measures to stop the violence immediately and protect the life and property of all South Africans. The Council affirms that all parties in South Africa must assist the Government in preventing opponents of democracy from using violence to threaten the country's democratic transition. In this regard, the Council notes the proposal for a national peace force to restore and maintain order in volatile areas. Any such force should be genuinely representative of South African society and its major political bodies. Just as importantly, it must have the confidence, support and cooperation of the people of South Africa. The Council also welcomes efforts by the leaders of the African National Congress and the Inkatha Freedom Party to convince their followers to avoid further violence. The Council urges all of South Africa's leaders to work jointly to prevent violence in the election period ahead.

The Security Council commends the international community, including the Organization of African Unity, the European Community and the Commonwealth, for playing a constructive role in helping to curb the violence in South Africa. The United Nations Peace Monitors, under the able supervision of the chief of the United Nations Observer Mission in South Africa, have made a difference. People are alive today because of the tireless and courageous efforts of these and other international peace monitors. Yet far too many are dying. The world community must continue to signal firmly that it will not allow the violence to derail South Africa's political transition.

The Council emphasizes the key role of the multi-party negotiating process in securing the transition to a democratic, non-racial and united South Africa. It urges the parties to reaffirm their commitment to the multi-party negotiating process, to redouble their efforts to reach consensus on the transitional arrangements and constitutional issues still outstanding and to proceed to elections as planned in the coming year.

The Council reaffirms its determination to remain supportive of efforts to facilitate the peaceful transition to a non-racial democracy for the benefit of all South Africans. The Council is following developments in South Africa closely and will remain seized of the matter.

# Document 185

*Statement by the Spokesman for Secretary-General Boutros Boutros-Ghali concerning a meeting of the Secretary-General with President de Klerk of South Africa*

UN Press Release SG/SM/5104 - SAF/160, 23 September 1993

The Secretary-General met President F.W. de Klerk of South Africa this afternoon. The Secretary-General congratulated President de Klerk on the historic decision adopted this morning by the South African parliament on the establishment of the Transitional Executive Council.

The Secretary-General informed President de Klerk of his intention to increase the strength of the United Nations Observer Mission in South Africa (UNOMSA).

They also discussed regional issues in Africa, particularly the situations in Angola and Mozambique. The Secretary-General expressed his support of the agreement reached between South Africa and Namibia on the status of Walvis Bay.

President de Klerk expressed his appreciation for the presence of the United Nations in South Africa and for the constructive role played by the Organization in encouraging the multi-party negotiating process in the country.

The Secretary-General assured President de Klerk that the United Nations stands ready to assist the people of South Africa in the ongoing efforts aimed at the establishment of a democratic, non-racist South Africa.

# Document 186

*Statement by Mr. Nelson Mandela, President of the African National Congress, to the Special Committee against Apartheid*

A/AC.115/SR.669, 24 September 1993, and United Nations Centre against Apartheid Notes and Documents, No. 8/93, September 1993

We are most grateful to the Special Committee against Apartheid and its distinguished Chairman, His Excellency Professor Ibrahim Gambari, as well as the United Nations as a whole, for enabling us to address this gathering today.

We have, together, walked a very long road. We have travelled together to reach a common destination.

The common destination towards which we have been advancing defines the very reason for the existence of this world Organization.

The goal we have sought to reach is the consummation of the yearning of all humankind for human dignity and human fulfilment. For that reason, we have been outraged and enraged that there could be imposed on any people the criminal system of apartheid.

Each and every one of us have felt our humanity denied by the mere existence of this system. Each and every one of us have felt brandished as subhuman by the fact that some could treat others as though they were no more than disposable garbage.

In the end, there was nobody of conscience who could stand by and do nothing in the search for an end to the apartheid crime against humanity.

We are here today to convey to you, who are the representatives of the peoples of the world, the profound gratitude of the people of South Africa for your engagement, over the decades, in the common struggle to end the system of apartheid.

We are deeply moved by the fact that, almost from its birth, this Organization has kept on its agenda the vital question of the liquidation of the system of apartheid and White minority rule in our country.

Throughout the many years of struggle, we, as South Africans, have been greatly inspired and strengthened as you took action both severally and collectively, to escalate your offensive against apartheid rule, as the White minority regime itself took new steps in its own offensive further to entrench its illegitimate rule and draw tribute from those it had enslaved.

In particular, we are most grateful for the measures that the United Nations, the Organization of African Unity, the Commonwealth, the Non-Aligned Movement, the European Community and other intergovernmental organizations have taken to isolate apartheid South Africa.

We are deeply appreciative of similar initiatives that individual countries, non-governmental organizations, local communities and even single individuals have taken, as part of their contribution to the common effort to deny the apartheid system all international sustenance.

This global struggle, perhaps without precedent in the inestimable number of people it united around one common issue, has helped decisively to bring us to where we are today.

Finally, the apartheid regime was forced to concede that the system of White minority rule could no longer be sustained. It was forced to accept that it had to enter into negotiations with the genuine representatives of our people to arrive at a solution which, as agreed at the first sitting of the Convention for a Democratic South Africa (CODESA), would transform South Africa into a united, non-racial and non-sexist country.

This and other agreements have now been translated into a specific programme that will enable our country to take a leap forward from its dark, painful and turbulent past to a glorious future, which our people will strive with all their strength to make a future of democracy, peace, stability and prosperity.

The countdown to democracy in South Africa has begun. The date for the demise of the White minority regime has been determined, agreed and set.

Seven months from now, on 27 April 1994, all the people of South Africa, without discrimination on grounds of gender, race, colour or belief, will join in the historic act of electing a government of their choice.

The legislation has also been passed to create the institutions of State, the statutory organs that will ensure that these elections are held and that they are free and fair.

As a consequence of the creation of these statutory

instruments, we have arrived at the point where our country will no longer be governed exclusively by a White minority regime.

The Transitional Executive Council, provided for in this legislation, will mark the first participation ever by the majority of our people at governmental level in the process of determining the destiny of our country.

It will be the historic precursor to the Interim Government of National Unity which will be formed after the democratic elections of 27 April.

The other structures now provided for in law, the Independent Election Commission and the Independent Broadcasting Authority, will themselves play their specified roles in ensuring a process of transition and a result which our people as a whole will accept as having been legitimate and therefore acceptable.

We must, however, warn that we are not yet out of the woods.

Negotiations are continuing to agree on the interim constitution, according to which the country will be governed as the elected national assembly works on the final constitution.

There will, therefore, be a continuing need for this Organization, and the world movement for a democratic South Africa as a whole, to sustain their focus on the transitional process, so that everybody concerned in our country is left in no doubt about the continuing determination of the international community to help see us through to democracy.

The reality is that there are various forces within South Africa which do not accept the inevitability of the common outcome which all humanity seeks.

Within our country, these forces, which seek to deny us liberty by resort to brute force, and which have already murdered and maimed people in the tens of thousands, represent a minority of the people.

They derive their strength not from the people, but from the fear, insecurity and destabilization which they seek to impose through a campaign of terrorism conducted by unknown killers whose hallmark is brutality and total disregard for the value of human life.

There are other forces which, because of narrow, sectarian interest, are also opposed to genuine change. These are engaged in other actions which seek to create obstacles on the way to a smooth transition to democracy.

We believe that it is critically important that these forces too should understand that the international community has the will and determination to act in concert with the majority of the people of our country, to ensure that the democratic change which is long overdue is not delayed.

The apartheid system has left a swathe of disaster in its trail. We have an economy that is tottering on the brink of an even deeper depression than the one we are experiencing now.

What this means in practical terms is millions of people who have no food, no jobs and no homes.

The very fabric of society is threatened by a process of disintegration, characterized by high and increasing rates of violent crime, growth in the numbers of people so brutalized that they will kill for a pittance, and the collapse of all social norms.

In addition, the absence of a legitimate State authority, enjoying the support of the majority of the people, immensely exacerbates this general crisis, emphasizing the critical importance of speedy movement forward to democratic change.

In sum, acting together, we must, at all costs, resist and rebuff any tendency of a slide towards another Somalia or a Bosnia, a development that would have disastrous repercussions extending far beyond the borders of South Africa.

What we have just said is not intended to alarm this august gathering. Rather, it is meant to say: now is the time to take new steps to move us forward to the common victory we have all fought for!

We believe the moment has come when the United Nations and the international community as a whole should take stock of the decisive advances that have been made to create the setting for the victory of the cause of democracy in our country.

We further believe that the moment has come when this same community should lay the basis for halting the slide to a socio-economic disaster in South Africa, as one of the imperatives in ensuring the very success of the democratic transformation itself.

In response to the historic advances towards democracy that have been achieved, further to give added impetus to this process, to strengthen the forces of democratic change and to help create the necessary conditions for stability and social progress, we believe the time has come when the international community should lift all economic sanctions against South Africa.

We therefore extend an earnest appeal to you, the Governments and peoples you represent, to take all necessary measures to end the economic sanctions you imposed, which have brought us to the point where the transition to democracy has now been enshrined in the law of our country.

We further urge that this historic step, marking a turning-point in the history of the relations between South Africa and the rest of the world, should not be viewed as an act of abstention but one of engagement.

Let us all treat this new reality as an opportunity and a challenge to engage with the South African situation in a way that will advance the democratic cause and create the best possible social and economic conditions for the victory of that cause.

The Special Committee against Apartheid has itself led the process of preparing the United Nations and its specialized agencies for the new reality that is the fruit of our common struggle. We trust that the United Nations family will, therefore, not delay in engaging the people of South Africa in a new way.

We trust also that the Governments across the globe, that have been so central in the effort to defeat the system of apartheid, will do what they can to help us ensure the upliftment of our people.

A similar appeal extends to the millions of people organized in the broad non-governmental anti-apartheid movement themselves to remain involved in the continuing struggle for a democratic South Africa, and to add to their programmes the extension of all-round development assistance from people to people.

We hope that both the South African and the international investor communities will also take this opportunity themselves to help regenerate the South African economy, to their mutual benefit.

As you know, our people have not yet elected a democratic government. It is therefore important that the White minority government, which remains in place in our country, should not be granted recognition and treated as though it were representative of all the people of South Africa.

The Transitional Executive Council provides the appropriate mechanism for such interaction as should take place between ourselves and the international community in the period between now and the formation of the new government.

We should mention here that, within the ambit of the diplomatic sanctions which many countries imposed, we also believe that such countries may now establish a diplomatic presence in South Africa to enhance their capacity to assist the people of our country in realizing the common objectives.

This Organization also imposed special sanctions relating to arms, nuclear matters and oil. In this regard, we would like to urge that the mandatory sanctions be maintained until the new government has been formed. We would leave the issue of the oil embargo to the discretion of the Committee of the General Assembly responsible for the enforcement of this particular sanction.

We would further like to request the Security Council to begin consideration of the very important issue of what this Organization should do to assist in the process of organizing for the forthcoming elections and ensuring that they are indeed free and fair.

This, naturally, should be accompanied by a review of the important contribution that has been made by the United Nations Observer Mission in South Africa, which is helping us to address the issue of political violence, to ensure that this contribution addresses this continuing problem adequately.

. . .

Our common victory against the only system to be declared a crime against humanity since the defeat of Nazism is in sight.

The historic need to end this crime as speedily and peacefully as possible requires that we, the peoples of the world, should remain as united as we have been and as committed as we have been to the cause of democracy, peace, human dignity and prosperity for all the people of South Africa.

Standing among you today, we continue to be moved by the selfless solidarity you have extended to our people. We are aware that by our common actions we have sought not only the liberation of the people of South Africa but also the extension of the frontiers of democracy, non-racism, non-sexism and human solidarity throughout the world.

Understanding that, we undertake before you all that we will not rest until the noble cause which unites us all emerges triumphant and a new South Africa fully rejoins the rest of the international community as a country of which we can all be proud.

# Document 187

*General Assembly resolution: Lifting of sanctions against South Africa*

A/RES/48/1, 8 October 1993

*The General Assembly,*

*Bearing in mind* the objectives of the Declaration on Apartheid and its Destructive Consequences in Southern Africa, adopted by consensus on 14 December 1989,

*Noting* that the transition to democracy has now been enshrined in the law of South Africa,

1. *Decides* that all provisions adopted by the General Assembly relating to prohibitions or restrictions on economic relations with South Africa and its nationals, whether corporate or natural, including the areas of trade, investment, finance, travel and transportation, shall cease to have effect as of the date of the adoption of the present resolution, and requests all States to take appropriate meas-

ures within their jurisdiction to lift the restrictions and prohibitions they had imposed to implement the previous resolutions and decisions of the General Assembly;

2. *Also decides* that all provisions adopted by the General Assembly relating to the imposition of an embargo on the supply of petroleum and petroleum products to South Africa, and on investment in the petroleum industry there, shall cease to have effect as of the date that the Transitional Executive Council becomes operational, and requests all States to take appropriate measures within their jurisdiction to lift any restrictions or prohibitions they had imposed to implement previous resolutions and decisions of the General Assembly in this respect.

# Document 188

*Statement by the Spokesman for Secretary-General Boutros Boutros-Ghali congratulating President de Klerk of South Africa and ANC President Mandela on their being awarded the Nobel Peace Prize*

UN Press Release SG/SM/5129, 15 October 1993

The Secretary-General has received with great satisfaction the announcement of the awarding of the Nobel Peace Prize to President Frederik W. de Klerk of South Africa and Nelson Mandela, President of the African National Congress of South Africa (ANC).

He applauds those two courageous leaders who are

working together along with the people of South Africa to eradicate the evil of apartheid. He extends to them his warm congratulations. He pledges his full support to work with them in the coming months for the establishment of South Africa as a non-racist, democratic society.

# Document 189

*Statement by the Spokesman for Secretary-General Boutros Boutros-Ghali applauding the "historic agreement" on an interim constitution for South Africa*

UN Press Release SG/SM/5157 - SAF/163, 18 November 1993

The Secretary-General applauds the historic agreement reached yesterday on an interim constitution for South Africa's transition to democracy by participants at the Multi-party Negotiations in Johannesburg. The agreement crowns three years of very difficult negotiations that would lay the framework for South Africa's transition to a united, democratic and non-racial country.

The Secretary-General congratulates all South Africans

who have continued to support and to contribute to the peace process despite the many impediments that faced the process amid mounting violence and intimidation. He reiterates the continued support of the United Nations to the peace process and its readiness to assist the people of South Africa in the formidable challenges that lie ahead, including in efforts to facilitate the country's first multiparty democratic elections scheduled for 27 April 1994.

# Document 190

*Statement by the President of the Security Council, on behalf of the Council, welcoming the successful completion of the Multi-party Negotiating Process, looking forward to the elections in South Africa in April 1994 and urging the early establishment of the Transitional Executive Council and Independent Electoral Commission.*

S/26785, 23 November 1993

The Security Council welcomes the successful completion of the Multi-party Negotiating Process in South Africa, and the conclusion of agreements reached therein on an interim constitution and electoral bill. These agreements constitute a historic step forward in establishing a democratic, non-racial and united South Africa.

The Council looks forward to the elections to be held in South Africa in April 1994. It urges all parties in South Africa, including those which did not participate fully in the multi-party talks, to respect agreements reached during the negotiations, to re-commit themselves to democratic principles, to take part in the elections and to resolve outstanding issues by peaceful means only.

The Council reiterates its determination to continue to support the process of peaceful democratic change in South Africa for the benefit of all South Africans. It commends once again the work being done by the Secretary-General and the United Nations Observer Mission in South Africa in assisting that process. It invites the Secretary-General to accelerate contingency planning for a possible United Nations role in the election process, including coordination with the observer missions of the Organization of African Unity, the European Community and the Commonwealth, to enable expeditious consideration of a request to the United Nations for such assistance. In this connection, the Council urges early establishment of the Transitional Executive Council and the Independent Electoral Commission.

The Council considers that South Africa's transition to democracy must be underpinned by economic and social reconstruction and development, and calls on the international community to assist in this regard.

# Document 191

*Letter dated 3 December 1993 from the Secretary-General to Mr. Roelof F. Botha, Minister for Foreign Affairs of South Africa*

Not issued as a United Nations document

I wish to acknowledge receipt of your letter of 2 December 1993 concerning the forthcoming elections in South Africa, in which you suggested that immediate consideration be given to advance planning, in order to ensure that the United Nations is in a position to mount an effective operation when the Independent Electoral Commission (IEC) and the Transitional Executive Council (TEC) become operational.

Following consultations, I have undertaken steps to accelerate contingency planning for a possible United Nations role in the election process, including coordination with the observer missions of the Organization of African Unity (OAU), the European Economic Community (EEC) and the Commonwealth Secretariat.

Taking into account your suggestion, I have decided to send a survey mission to South Africa which will depart from New York on 9 December for a period of ten days for consultations, to facilitate preparatory arrangements in respect of the role envisaged for the United Nations in the electoral process. Particulars of the members of the mission, as well as their itinerary, will be communicated to your Government as soon as they are finalized.

I should be most grateful if your Government would extend all necessary assistance to the mission during the period of its stay in South Africa.

Please accept, Excellency, the assurances of my highest consideration.

(*signed*) Boutros BOUTROS-GHALI

# Document 192

*Fourth progress report of the Secretary-General on the implementation of the Declaration on Apartheid and its Destructive Consequences in Southern Africa*

A/48/691, 6 December 1993

## I. Introduction

1. In paragraph 20 of its resolution 47/116 A of 18 December 1992, the General Assembly, *inter alia*, requested the Secretary-General to report to it at its forty-eighth session on measures taken to facilitate the peaceful elimination of apartheid and the transition of South Africa to a non-racial and democratic society as envisaged in the Declaration on Apartheid and its Destructive Consequences in southern Africa. The present report is submitted in compliance with that request.

2. To prepare the report, the Secretariat sought the observations of the Government, political parties, movements and organizations represented at the Multi-party Negotiating Process, as well as those of South African non-governmental organizations, on the overall situation in South Africa, including developments regarding the implementation of the Declaration since September 1992. The annex to the present report contains an analysis based primarily on the views of the respondents.

3. In its resolution 47/116 A, the General Assembly also requested the Secretary-General to continue to ensure the coordination of activities of the United Nations and its agencies with regard to, and, as appropriate, inside South Africa. Details on the steps taken by the United Nations system to implement those provisions are contained in a separate report that I have submitted to the General Assembly (A/48/467 and Add.1).

## II. Observations

4. In my last progress report, I had stated that the role of the international community in the establishment of a democratic, non-racial South Africa could only be complementary to those of the various parties in the country, and that the primary responsibility for achieving a just and long-lasting agreement through negotiations must rest with the people of South Africa as a whole. During the period under review, I designated Ambassador Tom Erik Vraalsen, Assistant Secretary-General of the Ministry of Foreign Affairs of Norway and former Permanent Representative of Norway to the United Nations, as my Special Envoy to South Africa for consultation with the parties concerned on political developments in the country. Mr. Vraalsen visited South Africa from 22 November to 9 December 1992. Subsequently, I submitted a detailed report to the Security Council on his mission

and that of his predecessor, former Under-Secretary-General Virendra Dayal (S/25004).

5. The resumption of multi-party negotiations in April 1993 with broader representation than the Conference for a Democratic South Africa (CODESA), after a 10-month suspension, was a most welcome development, which resulted in significant breakthroughs, including agreement on a date for South Africa's first non-racial, democratic elections. This was followed by the enactment into law of most of the principal provisions of the transitional arrangements to the negotiations, including a Transitional Executive Council, an Independent Electoral Commission, an Independent Media Commission and an Independent Broadcasting Authority, and an interim constitution. The broad-based representation of the South African parties in the negotiating process and the determination and commitment of most of them to a peaceful political settlement have been decisive factors leading to these positive developments.

6. The United Nations Observer Mission in South Africa was established in October 1992 to assist the parties in South Africa in their efforts to put an end to the violence. Initially 50 United Nations observers were deployed. Subsequently, the Security Council approved my recommendation to increase the number of observers to 100. The United Nations observers have been deployed, along with those from the Organization of African Unity, the Commonwealth and the European Union, in various parts of South Africa, particularly in areas where violence is taking its worst toll. In accordance with the mandate entrusted to the Mission by the Security Council, the observers have been cooperating with the National Peace Secretariat and its local and regional dispute resolution committees and with the Commission of Inquiry regarding the Prevention of Public Violence and Intimidation (Goldstone Commission). It is generally agreed in South Africa that the presence of United Nations observers has had a salutary effect on the peace process.

7. However, violence continues to pose a major threat to the peace process. To break the escalating cycle of violence requires the cooperation of the Government and all parties in South Africa. Such cooperation is also essential to the efforts to resolve any remaining difficulties peacefully and to facilitate the establishment of the arrangements for South Africa's transition to a democratic,

non-racial and united country. Since my last report, I have on various occasions expressed my concern at the increasing violence, which has reached new heights, and urged the parties to resolve their differences through the negotiating process.

8. During the period under review, I had occasion to meet with all the major political leaders in the country and to discuss the situation in and relating to South Africa. I met in New York with President de Klerk and Mr. Mandela on 23 and 29 September 1993, respectively. While on a visit to Maputo, I arranged to meet Mr. Clarence Makwetu, Chief Mangosuthu G. Buthelezi and Foreign Minister Roelof Botha.

9. With all my South African interlocutors, I underlined the importance the United Nations attached to the peace process in the country and reiterated the support of the international community to the efforts to establish a democratic, non-racial and united South Africa. I also stressed the imperative need to end the violence in the country in order to facilitate a peaceful transition and the holding of free and fair elections.

10. During my meeting with Chief Buthelezi, I stressed the importance accorded to the multi-party negotiations by the international community and to the formation of the Transitional Executive Council, and that it was only by participating in the negotiations, no matter how difficult, that all parties could ensure that their views were heard, discussed and reflected in the interim constitution. I also urged the Freedom Alliance through Chief Buthelezi to participate in the peace process and underlined that its participation was essential to the establishment of a democratic, non-racial and united South Africa.

11. While in Maputo, I also met with the chairmen of the National Peace Committee and its secretariat, Mr. John Hall and Mr. Antonie Gildenhuys, respectively. My discussions with the chairmen of the National Peace Committee and its secretariat centred on how the peace structures could be strengthened to defuse increasing violence and broadened to be more representative of the population as a whole.

12. Taking into account the progress reached in the peace process, the General Assembly on 29 September 1993 adopted resolution 48/1, by which it decided to lift all provisions relating to prohibitions or restrictions imposed by it on economic relations with South Africa. The United Nations will remain active, through its offices and agencies and relevant Trust Funds as well as in cooperation with intergovernmental organizations, in providing assistance, as appropriate, to disadvantaged South Africans. It will also consider the preparation of a concerted system-wide response to address the economic and social disparities resulting from the long practice of institutionalized racism.

13. Among the initiatives being undertaken is the organization of a donors' conference for human resource development in a post-apartheid South Africa. The United Nations and the Commonwealth Secretariat have been holding consultations with a view to organizing such a conference, which would provide concrete assistance to South Africa in the transition period. Those consultations have involved a group of interested organizations, including the United Nations, the Commonwealth Secretariat, the United Nations Development Programme, the World Bank, the African Development Bank, the Organization of African Unity, the European Union and the Agence de coopération culturelle et technique. Several meetings of these organizations have been held to make preliminary plans for the donors' conference. The main objective of the conference, which is tentatively scheduled to take place in June 1994, will be to mobilize international support for addressing the human resource development needs of a post-apartheid South Africa, particularly those of the disadvantaged sectors of society. It has been agreed that the conference would be convened only after a democratically elected, non-racial Government has been established and be held under its sponsorship. Accordingly, the United Nations and the Commonwealth have made it clear that the conference would be organized in close cooperation with the new Transitional Executive Council.

14. I applauded the historic agreement reached by the participants at the Multi-party Negotiating Process on 17 November 1993 on an interim constitution and noted that the agreement crowned three years of difficult negotiations to lay the framework for South Africa's transition to a democratic, non-racial and united country. I also reiterated the continued support of the United Nations to the peace process and its readiness to assist the people of South Africa in the formidable challenges that lie ahead, including in efforts to facilitate the country's first multi-party democratic elections scheduled for 27 April 1994. With regard to these developments, I am accelerating contingency planning for a possible United Nations role in the election process, including coordination with the observer missions of the Organization of African Unity, the European Union and the Commonwealth, to enable expeditious consideration of the request to the United Nations for such assistance.

15. In concluding, I wish to urge all parties in South Africa to cooperate in the full and timely implementation of the transitional arrangement in order to ensure the early establishment of a non-racial, democratic society in South Africa. For my part, I shall continue to provide all necessary assistance to facilitate the success of the transitional process.

# Document 193

*Statement by the President of the General Assembly, Mr. S. R. Insanally (Guyana), on the lifting of the oil embargo against South Africa*

A/48/PV.72, 9 December 1993

. . .

I have received letters dated 7 December 1993 from the Chairmen of the Special Committee against Apartheid and the Intergovernmental Group to Monitor the Supply and Shipping of Oil and Petroleum Products to South Africa informing me that the Transitional Executive Council [TEC] in South Africa is now operational. I also received a letter from the Permanent Representative of South Africa to the United Nations informing me that the Transitional Executive Council met on 7 December.

In view of this information and with respect to [operative] paragraph 2 of the General Assembly resolution which I have just read out [resolution 48/1 of 8 October 1993], I am pleased to inform the Assembly that the embargo related to the supply of petroleum and petroleum products to South Africa and investment in the petroleum industry there is now lifted.

. . .

---

# Document 194

*General Assembly resolution: Elimination of apartheid and establishment of a united, democratic and non-racial South Africa—International efforts towards the total eradication of apartheid and support for the establishment of a united, non-racial and democratic South Africa*

A/RES/48/159 A, 20 December 1993

*The General Assembly,*

*Recalling* the Declaration on Apartheid and its Destructive Consequences in Southern Africa, set forth in the annex to its resolution S-16/1, adopted by consensus on 14 December 1989,

*Also recalling* its resolution 48/1 of 8 October 1993 on the lifting of sanctions against South Africa,

*Further recalling* the initiative of the Organization of African Unity to place before the Security Council the question of violence in South Africa,

*Recalling with satisfaction* Security Council resolutions 765 (1992) of 16 July 1992 and 772 (1992) of 17 August 1992, in which the Council authorized the deployment of the United Nations Observer Mission in South Africa and invited the deployment there of observers from the Organization of African Unity, the Commonwealth and the European Community,

*Welcoming* the statement of the extraordinary session with Ministers for Foreign Affairs of the Ad Hoc Committee on Southern Africa of the Organization of African Unity, held in New York on 29 September 1993,

*Taking note* of the report of the Special Committee against Apartheid and of the report of the Chairman of the Special Committee against Apartheid on his mission to South Africa, as well as of the report of the Secretary-General on the coordinated approach by the United Nations system on questions relating to South Africa and the fourth progress report of the Secretary-General on the implementation of the Declaration on Apartheid,

*Recognizing* the responsibility of the United Nations and the international community, as envisaged in the Declaration on Apartheid, to help the South African people in their legitimate struggle for the total elimination of apartheid through peaceful means,

*Noting* the agreements reached within the framework of the resumed multi-party negotiations on holding elections on 27 April 1994, and on the establishment of the Transitional Executive Council, the Independent Electoral Commission, the Independent Media Commission and the Independent Broadcasting Authority,

*Also noting* the endorsement by the parties in the multi-party negotiations of the Constitution for the Transitional Period and the Electoral Bill,

*Gravely concerned* that continued and escalating violence threatens to undermine the process of peaceful change, through negotiated agreements, to a united, non-racial and democratic South Africa,

*Bearing in mind* the need to strengthen and reinforce

all mechanisms set up to prevent violence in South Africa, and emphasizing the need for all parties to cooperate in combating violence and to exercise restraint,

*Encouraging* the efforts of all parties, including ongoing talks among them, aimed at establishing arrangements for the transition to a democratic order,

*Noting with concern* the remaining effects of the acts of destabilization that were committed by South Africa against the neighbouring African States,

1. *Welcomes* the agreements reached within the framework of the multi-party negotiations on holding elections on 27 April 1994, on the establishment of the Transitional Executive Council, the Independent Electoral Commission, the Independent Media Commission and the Independent Broadcasting Authority, and on the Constitution for the Transitional Period, as well as the Electoral Bill;

2. *Strongly urges* the South African authorities to exercise fully and impartially the primary responsibility of government to bring to an end the ongoing violence, to protect the lives, security and property of all South Africans in all of South Africa and to promote and protect their right to participate in the democratic process, including the right to demonstrate peacefully in public, to organize and participate in political rallies in all parts of South Africa and to run for election and participate in the elections without intimidation;

3. *Calls upon* the South African authorities in this context to bring to justice those responsible for acts of violence, to take the necessary measures for the peaceful reincorporation of the "homelands" into South Africa and to ensure that the populations in those territories can freely participate in the elections and that all political parties will be able to run election campaigns there free of intimidation;

4. *Calls upon* all parties to refrain from acts of violence and to do their utmost to combat violence;

5. *Urgently calls upon* all signatories to the National Peace Accord to recommit themselves to the process of peaceful change by fully and effectively implementing its provisions, and by cooperating with each other to that end;

6. *Calls upon* all other parties to contribute to the achievement of the aims of the National Peace Accord;

7. *Commends* the Secretary-General for those measures taken to address areas of concern noted in his reports and particularly to assist in strengthening the structures set up under the National Peace Accord, including the deployment of United Nations observers in South Africa, and expresses its appreciation for the activities carried out by the United Nations Observer Mission in South Africa;

8. *Supports* the recommendation of the Secretary-General for the additional deployment of observers in South Africa to further the purposes of the National Peace Accord, and urges him to continue to address all the areas of concern noted in his report that fall within the purview of the United Nations;

9. *Welcomes* the continuing role of the observers of the Organization of African Unity, the Commonwealth and the European Union deployed in South Africa;

10. *Urges* all parties in South Africa, including those which did not participate fully in the multi-party talks, to respect agreements reached during the negotiations, to recommit themselves to democratic principles, to take part in the elections and to resolve outstanding issues by peaceful means only;

11. *Calls upon* all Governments to observe fully the mandatory arms embargo imposed by the Security Council, requests the Council to continue to monitor effectively the strict implementation of that embargo, and urges States to adhere to the provisions of other Council resolutions on the import of arms from South Africa and the export of equipment and technology destined for military purposes in that country;

12. *Demands* the immediate release of remaining political prisoners;

13. *Appeals* to the international community to increase humanitarian and legal assistance to the victims of apartheid, to the returning refugees and exiles and to released political prisoners;

14. *Calls upon* the international community to continue to assist disadvantaged South African democratic anti-apartheid organizations and individuals in the academic, scientific and cultural fields;

15. *Also calls upon* the international community to assist the non-racial sports bodies in South Africa in redressing the continuing structural inequalities in sports in that country;

16. *Strongly urges* the international community, following the adoption of resolution 48/1 on 8 October 1993, to respond to the appeal by the people of South Africa for assistance in the economic reconstruction of their country and to ensure that the new South Africa begins its existence on a firm economic base;

17. *Appeals* to the international community to render all possible assistance to States neighbouring South Africa to enable them to recover from the effects of past acts of destabilization and to contribute to the stability and prosperity of the subregion;

18. *Calls upon* the Secretary-General to respond promptly and positively to a request for electoral assistance from the transitional authorities in South Africa, bearing in mind that the elections are set for 27 April 1994;

19. *Requests* the Secretary-General to accelerate planning for a United Nations role in the election process, in

consultation with the Security Council and in coordination with the observer missions of the Organization of African Unity, the Commonwealth and the European Union;

20. *Also requests* the Secretary-General to take the necessary measures for the initiation and coordination among the United Nations and its agencies of detailed planning for programmes of socio-economic assistance, particularly in the areas of human resource development, employment, health and housing, and to ensure also that those programmes are coordinated with other international agencies and with legitimate non-racial structures in South Africa;

21. *Commends* the Secretary-General of the United Nations and the Secretary-General of the Commonwealth for their initiative to start planning for an international donors' conference on human resource development for post-apartheid South Africa, to take place following the election of a non-racial and democratic Government;

22. *Calls upon* the international community to continue to exercise vigilance with respect to developments in South Africa to ensure that the common objective of the people of South Africa and the international community is achieved, without deviation or obstruction, by the establishment of a united, non-racial and democratic South Africa.

---

# Document 195

*General Assembly resolution: Elimination of apartheid and establishment of a united, democratic and non-racial South Africa—Programme of work of the Special Committee against Apartheid*

A/RES/48/159 B, 20 December 1993

*The General Assembly,*

*Having considered* the report of the Special Committee against Apartheid,

*Recognizing* the important role that the Special Committee has held in mobilizing international support for the elimination of apartheid and in promoting an international consensus on this critical issue, as reflected in the adoption by consensus on 14 December 1989 of the Declaration on Apartheid and its Destructive Consequences in Southern Africa, in General Assembly decision 45/457 B of 13 September 1991 and in Assembly resolutions 45/176 A of 19 December 1990, 46/79 A of 13 December 1991 and 47/116 A and B of 18 December 1992,

1. *Takes note with appreciation* of the report of the Special Committee against Apartheid on its work, under its mandate, in support of the peaceful elimination of apartheid through the process of a negotiated transition of South Africa to a democratic, non-racial society;

2. *Also takes note with appreciation* of the report of the Chairman of the Special Committee on his mission, together with a delegation of the Committee, to South Africa from 1 to 11 March 1993;

3. *Commends* the Special Committee for organizing, together with the Institute for a Democratic Alternative for South Africa and the Institute for Multi-Party Democracy, the Symposium on Political Tolerance in South Africa: Role of Opinion-Makers and Media, which was held at Cape Town from 30 July to 1 August 1993;

4. *Authorizes* the Special Committee, until the completion of its mandate following the establishment of a democratically elected non-racial Government in South Africa:

(*a*) To follow closely developments in South Africa;

(*b*) To continue to facilitate a peaceful and stable transition in South Africa by promoting international assistance in helping South Africans to overcome the negative social and economic consequences of the policies of apartheid;

(*c*) To maintain contacts with academic institutions and the labour, business and civic communities, including community-based and other non-governmental organizations in South Africa;

(*d*) To consult with the parties participating in the political process, with legitimate non-racial structures and with a democratically elected non-racial Government with a view to facilitating the resumption of the participation of South Africa in the work of the General Assembly;

(*e*) To submit, as soon as possible following the establishment of a democratically elected non-racial Government, a final report to the General Assembly;

(*f*) To undertake other relevant activities aimed at supporting the political process of peaceful change until a democratically elected non-racial Government has been established in South Africa;

5. *Expresses its appreciation* for the cooperation extended to the Special Committee by Governments, intergovernmental and non-governmental organizations and relevant components of the United Nations system, and invites them to continue their cooperation;

6. *Decides* that the special allocation of 240,000 United States dollars to the Special Committee for 1994 from the regular budget of the United Nations should be used towards the cost of special projects aimed at promoting the process towards the elimination of apartheid through the establishment of a democratically elected and non-racial Government in South Africa;

7. *Also decides* to continue to authorize adequate financial provision in the regular budget of the United Nations to enable the African National Congress of South Africa and the Pan Africanist Congress of Azania to maintain offices in New York so that they may participate effectively in the deliberations of the Special Committee and in deliberations relating to the situation in South Africa in other relevant United Nations bodies, on the understanding that such grants will continue until the situation of the two organizations as political parties has been regularized.

# Document 196

*General Assembly resolution: Elimination of apartheid and establishment of a united, democratic and non-racial South Africa—Work of the Intergovernmental Group to Monitor the Supply and Shipping of Oil and Petroleum Products to South Africa*

A/RES/48/159 C, 20 December 1993

*The General Assembly,*

*Having considered* the report of the Intergovernmental Group to Monitor the Supply and Shipping of Oil and Petroleum Products to South Africa,

*Recalling* its resolutions 47/116 D of 18 December 1992 and 48/1 of 8 October 1993,

*Welcoming* the establishment of the Transitional Executive Council in South Africa,

1. *Takes note with appreciation* of the report of the Intergovernmental Group to Monitor the Supply and Shipping of Oil and Petroleum Products and endorses its recommendations;

2. *Decides* to terminate the mandate of the Intergovernmental Group as of the date of the adoption of the present resolution;

3. *Requests* the Secretary-General to issue by 30 January 1994, as addenda to the report of the Intergovernmental Group, the responses of States to requests addressed to them regarding the cases contained in the annexes to that report.

# Document 197

*General Assembly resolution: Elimination of apartheid and establishment of a united, democratic and non-racial South Africa—United Nations Trust Fund for South Africa*

A/RES/48/159 D, 20 December 1993

*The General Assembly,*

*Recalling* its resolutions on the United Nations Trust Fund for South Africa, in particular resolution 47/116 C of 18 December 1992,

*Having considered* the report of the Secretary-General on the United Nations Trust Fund for South Africa, to which is annexed the report of the Committee of Trustees of the Trust Fund,

*Taking note* of its resolution 46/79 F, adopted without a vote on 13 December 1991, in particular paragraph 3, relating to assistance by the Trust Fund for work in the legal field,

*Welcoming* the agreements reached within the framework of the resumed multi-party negotiations and approved by Parliament to hold elections in 1994 on the basis of universal suffrage and to establish a Transitional Executive Council, as well as legislative and other measures adopted to promote free political activity in the run-up to free and fair elections,

*Recognizing* the work being carried out by broad-based, impartial voluntary organizations inside South Africa in providing legal and humanitarian assistance to victims of apartheid and racial discrimination, and noting with satisfaction the working relationship that the Trust Fund has established with those South African organizations,

*Concerned* about continued political violence and the dangers it represents for the democratic process and for the country at large,

*Convinced* that the time is nearing when South African authorities, within new, non-racial and democratic structures, will take responsibility for matters which have been within the mandate of the Trust Fund,

1. *Endorses* the report of the Secretary-General on the United Nations Trust Fund for South Africa;

2. *Supports* continued humanitarian, legal and educational assistance by the international community towards alleviating the plight of victims of apartheid in South Africa and towards facilitating the reintegration of released political prisoners and returning exiles into South African society;

3. *Endorses* the decision of the Trust Fund to channel its assistance through appropriate non-governmental organizations inside South Africa;

4. *Expresses its appreciation* to the Governments, organizations and individuals that have contributed to the Trust Fund and to the voluntary agencies engaged in rendering humanitarian and legal assistance to the victims of apartheid in South Africa;

5. *Expresses its conviction* that the Trust Fund has an important role to play during the final stage of the elimination of apartheid by assisting efforts in the legal field aimed at ensuring effective implementation of legislation repealing major apartheid laws, redressing the continuing adverse effects of those laws and encouraging increased public confidence in the role of law, and, therefore, appeals for generous contributions to the Fund;

6. *Commends* the Secretary-General and the Committee of Trustees of the Trust Fund for their persistent and worthy efforts throughout the years to promote humanitarian and legal assistance to the victims of apartheid and racial discrimination.

# Document 198

*General Assembly resolution: United Nations Educational and Training Programme for Southern Africa*

A/RES/48/160, 20 December 1993

*The General Assembly,*

*Recalling* its resolutions on the United Nations Educational and Training Programme for Southern Africa, in particular resolution 47/117 of 18 December 1992,

*Having considered* the report of the Secretary-General containing an account of the work of the Advisory Committee on the United Nations Educational and Training Programme for Southern Africa and the administration of the Programme for the period from 1 September 1992 to 31 August 1993,

Noting with satisfaction that the recommendations of the evaluation of the Programme undertaken in 1989 as endorsed by the Advisory Committee continued to be implemented,

*Recognizing* the valuable assistance rendered by the Programme to the peoples of South Africa and Namibia,

*Emphasizing* the need for assistance to the people of South Africa particularly in the field of education during the transitional period,

*Fully recognizing* the need to provide continuing educational opportunities and counselling to students from South Africa in a wide variety of professional, cultural and linguistic disciplines, as well as opportunities for vocational and technical training and for advanced studies at graduate and postgraduate levels in priority fields of study, as often as possible at educational and training institutions within South Africa,

*Noting* that, in order to address the priority needs of disadvantaged South Africans, the programme is continuing to allocate a higher proportion of resources for the purpose of institution-building in South Africa, in particular by strengthening the historically Black and other institutions of higher learning, especially the *technikons*, through specialized training courses with built-in employability of graduates,

1. *Endorses* the report of the Secretary-General on the United Nations Educational and Training Programme for Southern Africa;

2. *Commends* the Secretary-General and the Advisory Committee on the United Nations Educational and Training Programme for Southern Africa for their efforts to adjust the Programme so that it can best help meet the needs evolving from changing circumstances in South Africa, to promote generous contributions to the Pro-

gramme and to enhance cooperation with governmental, intergovernmental and non-governmental agencies involved in educational and technical assistance to South Africa;

3. *Also endorses* the Programme activities aimed at contributing to South Africa's human resources needs, especially during the transition period, by:

(*a*) Supporting co-sponsored projects with *technikons* and the historically Black and other universities;

(*b*) Strengthening the institutional, technical and financial capacity as well a the decision-making of non-governmental organizations, community-based organizations and educational institutions that serve the needs and interests of disadvantaged South Africans;

(*c*) Engaging educational institutions, non-governmental organizations and the private sector in South Africa in co-sponsorship arrangements and job placement of graduates;

4. *Welcomes* the fact that educational and training activities of the Programme inside South Africa have expanded, and the Programme's close cooperation with South African non-governmental organizations, universities and *technikons*;

5. *Calls upon* non-governmental educational institutions, private organizations and individuals concerned to assist the Programme by entering into cost-sharing and other arrangements with it and by facilitating the re-turnability and job placement of its graduates;

6. *Appeals* to Governments, intergovernmental and non-governmental organizations, international professional associations and individual to assist, within their areas of activity and influence inside South Africa, graduates of the Programme in obtaining access to job opportunities so that they can effectively contribute their professional competence and expertise towards the political, economic and social development of South Africa during the period of transition and beyond;

7. *Considers* that the activities of the Programme, under changing circumstances, should be planned in such a manner as to ensure that commitments made with regard to educational and training assistance to disadvantaged South Africans can be fully met;

8. *Requests* the Secretary-General to include the United Nations Educational and Training Programme for Southern Africa in the annual United Nations Pledging Conference for Development Activities;

9. *Expresses its appreciation* to all those who have supported the Programme by providing contributions, scholarships or places in their educational institutions;

10. *Appeals* to all States, institutions, organizations and individuals to offer such financial and other assistance to the Programme so as to enable it to carry out its programmed activities.

---

# Document 199

*Report of the Secretary-General concerning arrangements for United Nations monitoring of the electoral process in South Africa and coordination of activities of internal observers*

A/48/845 - S/1994/16, 10 January 1994

## I. Introduction

1. It will be recalled that following the Boipatong massacre on 17 June 1992, the Security Council unanimously adopted resolution 765 (1992) on 16 July by which it, *inter alia*, invited me to appoint a Special Representative for South Africa in order to recommend, after discussion with the parties in the country, measures which would assist in bringing an effective end to the violence and in creating conditions for negotiations leading towards a peaceful transition to a democratic, non-racial and united South Africa. Immediately after the adoption of the resolution, I appointed Mr. Cyrus R. Vance as my Special Representative for South Africa and he visited the country from 21 to 31 July 1992. On 7 August 1992, I submitted a report to the Security Council on the basis of Mr. Vance's discussions with a wide range of prominent figures and parties in South Africa (S/24389).

2. After considering my report, the Security Council adopted resolution 772 (1992) on 17 August by which it, *inter alia*, authorized me to deploy, as a matter of urgency, United Nations observers in South Africa, and invited me to assist in the strengthening of the structures set up under the National Peace Accord. It also invited international organizations such as the Organization of African Unity (OAU), the Commonwealth and the European Community to consider deploying their own observers in South Africa in coordination with the United Nations and the structures set up under the National Peace Accord.

3. Soon thereafter, the United Nations Observer Mission in South Africa (UNOMSA) was established and

the first group of observers arrived in the country in September 1992. By the end of the year, the full complement of the authorized strength of 50 observers was deployed in all the regions of the country. Taking into account the progress in the multi-party negotiations, the Security Council authorized two increases in the number of observers—10 in February and 40 in September 1993, for a total complement of 100 observers—to serve as a nucleus for the anticipated United Nations role in the electoral process in South Africa.

4. Following consultations with the Government and relevant parties, I designated two Special Envoys, Messrs. Virendra Dayal and Tom Vraalsen, who carried out separate missions to South Africa in September and November/December 1992, respectively, to assist me in the implementation of the two above-mentioned resolutions of the Security Council. On 22 December 1992, I submitted a report to the Council on the findings of my two Special Envoys and on the activities of UNOMSA (S/25004).

5. On 23 November 1993, the President of the Security Council issued a statement on behalf of the Council in which it welcomed the successful completion of the multi-party negotiating process and the conclusion of agreements reached therein on an interim constitution and electoral bill, and invited me to accelerate contingency planning for a possible United Nations role in the election process in South Africa (S/26785). At its first meeting on 7 December 1993, the Transitional Executive Council (TEC) endorsed a resolution that was adopted the previous day by the Multi-Party Negotiating Council (MPNC) requesting, *inter alia*, the United Nations to provide a sufficient number of international observers to monitor the electoral process and to coordinate the activities of the international observers provided by OAU, the European Union (EU) and the Commonwealth as well as those provided by Governments. Accordingly, I dispatched a survey team to South Africa on 9 December 1993 to assess the needs of the United Nations in carrying out the requests made to it for electoral assistance.

6. Furthermore, pursuant to Security Council resolutions 765 (1992) and 772 (1992) and taking into account the progress achieved in the peace process including the establishment of TEC on 7 December 1993, I advised the President of the Security Council on 13 December 1993 of my intention to appoint Mr. Lakhdar Brahimi, former Minister for Foreign Affairs of Algeria, as my Special Representative for South Africa to assist me in the implementation of the relevant Security Council resolutions and decisions concerning South Africa and to coordinate the activities of other international observers as requested by TEC (S/26883). The President of the Council informed me on 16 December 1993 that the members of

the Council agreed with my proposal (S/26884). In earlier discussions with me, both Mr. Mandela and Foreign Minister R. F. Botha had welcomed my suggestion to appoint a Special Representative as soon as possible in order to facilitate the peace process.

7. Immediately after his appointment, I requested Mr. Brahimi to visit South Africa for consultations with the parties and the officials of the relevant transitional institutions they have established on the scope and modalities of United Nations involvement in the electoral process in the country. Assisted by a small team from the Secretariat led by Mr. Hisham Omayad, Director in the Department of Political Affairs, Mr. Brahimi visited South Africa from 16 to 23 December 1993. During his stay in Johannesburg, Mr. Brahimi was briefed by the survey team on its findings.

## II. Consultations of the special representative

### A. *Background*

8. In 1989, various parties in South Africa, including the Government and the African National Congress of South Africa (ANC), decided to commit themselves to a negotiated political settlement of the conflict in the country. The international community lent its support and encouragement to the commitment made by the parties with the adoption of the Harare Declaration of August 1989 which was endorsed by the General Assembly on 14 December of the same year in its Declaration on Apartheid and its Destructive Consequences in Southern Africa (resolution S-16/1).

9. Early in February of 1990, Mr. Nelson Mandela and other prominent political prisoners were released from prison. The Government also announced the unbanning of a number of political organizations including ANC, the Pan Africanist Congress of Azania (PAC) and the South African Community Party (SACP), and its intention to repeal apartheid and emergency restrictions. During 1990 and 1991, discriminatory legislation, particularly that constituting the "pillars of apartheid"—the Land Acts, Population Registration Act and the Group Areas Act—was repealed.

10. Soon after the release of Mr. Mandela, bilateral talks between the Government and ANC led to two preliminary agreements: the Groote Schuur Minute of 4 May 1990 (A/45/268, annex), by which the two parties agreed on a common commitment towards the resolution of the existing climate of violence as well as to stability, and to a peaceful process of negotiations; and the Pretoria Minute of 6 August 1990 by which ANC announced the suspension of all armed action with immediate effect.

11. Formal negotiations on constitutional reform began in December 1991 with the establishment of the

Convention for a Democratic South Africa (CODESA I). Despite the positive atmosphere of the talks and the progress made in some areas, agreement on the crucial issue of a new constitutional dispensation eluded the parties. The following May, the parties made another attempt at CODESA II. However, the Boipatong massacre prompted ANC to suspend its participation in the talks until the Government took more decisive action to put a halt to the violence in the townships.

12. Despite the breakdown of the CODESA process, the Government and ANC continued informal contacts which led to the signing on 26 September 1992 of a Record of Understanding, by which the Government agreed to a number of the conditions put forward by ANC for returning to the negotiations. Further bilateral talks resulted, on 5 March 1993, in a number of informal understandings which made possible the convening of a new conference with broader representation than at CODESA—the Multi-Party Negotiating Council (MPNC).

13. After protracted and difficult negotiations, MPNC adopted on 18 November 1993 a number of constitutional principles and institutions which would guide South Africa during a transitional period lasting until 27 April 1999. They included the Transitional Executive Council (TEC), the Interim Constitution, the Independent Electoral Commission (IEC), the Independent Media Commission (IMC) and the Independent Broadcasting Authority (IBA). TEC will remain in existence until the entry into force of the interim constitution on 27 April 1994.

14. The main objective of TEC is to facilitate, in conjunction with all existing legislative and executive governmental structures at national, regional and local levels, the transition to, and preparation for, the implementation of a democratic system of Government in South Africa by the holding of free and fair elections for a Parliament which will consist of a 400-member National Assembly and a 90-member Senate. The joint sitting of the Assembly and the Senate will form the Constitutional Assembly whose main task would be to draft during the first two years of the transition period, by acting as a Constituent Assembly, a final constitution for the country. The interim constitution stipulates that the future South Africa will be divided into nine provinces, each of which will have a provincial legislature, government and executive council.

15. The Head of State will be an Executive President who will be chosen by the governing party. The Cabinet will be composed of, on the basis of the principle of proportional representation, those political parties that will obtain 5 per cent or more of the vote in the elections. Decisions in the Cabinet will be taken by consensus, in a manner which will give consideration to the spirit underlying the concept of a government of national unity as well as the need for the effective administration of the country.

16. The future Constitutional Court of South Africa will have the final jurisdiction regarding matters pertaining to the interpretation, protection and enforcement of the interim constitution at all levels of government. A decision by the Constitutional Court will be final and binding.

## B. *Discussions with the Government*

17. My Special Representative met with President F. W. de Klerk in Cape Town and with Foreign Minister R. F. Botha in Johannesburg on 17 December and 23 December 1993, respectively. The President noted that South Africa was capable of and had extensive experience in organizing and conducting elections. He said that the electoral process would be complicated for most of the electorate, and national and international assistance in voter education would be welcomed.

18. Both the President and the Foreign Minister stressed that the most difficult problem facing the transition process was political violence and intimidation. They also noted that the United Nations has contributed appreciably through UNOMSA to the efforts to curb such violence and to encourage dialogue and tolerance. In the process, the United Nations has succeeded in establishing its credibility and objectivity among the South African population at large. They stressed the historical importance of the elections and the critical need for the electoral process and its outcome to be, and seen to be, both free and fair as well as legitimate.

19. The President stated that the transitional arrangements were resilient institutions and enjoyed substantial influence and authority to facilitate a successful outcome of the peace process. The State President and the Foreign Minister shared the view that international support for and assistance to the transitional structures would enhance their prestige and ability to contribute positively to the peace process. In this regard, the Minister expressed the hope that the United Nations would allocate resources to provide the largest possible number of observers needed to do the job.

## C. *Discussions with the political parties*

20. My Special Representative met with Mr. Nelson Mandela, President of ANC, in Johannesburg on 18 December 1993. Mr. Mandela said that he and President de Klerk were coordinating their efforts to bring the members of the Freedom Alliance—the Inkatha Freedom Party (IFP), the Conservative Party (CP), the Afrikaner Volksfront (AVF) and the homelands of Ciskei and Bo-

phuthatswana—to the peace process, and expressed cautious optimism that most—if not all—of them would eventually cooperate and agree to participate in the elections. He noted that the groups which had the potential to disrupt the electoral process were those that enjoyed support within the military police and security forces as well as within the bureaucracy. Mr. Mandela stressed that it was important for the United Nations to maintain lines of communication open with the Freedom Alliance and urged my Special Representative to meet with them during his visit to the country.

21. My Special Representative had actually asked to see all political leaders but appointments could not be arranged with some of them because of the holiday season. Chief Buthelezi suggested a meeting on Tuesday, 21 December. However my Special Representative was in Harare, Zimbabwe, on that day and he asked to meet the leader of IFP as early as possible in the New Year.

22. Mr. Mandela recognized the positive contributions made by UNOMSA to the peace process and called for a strong United Nations presence during the electoral process. In his view, if the resources were available, the United Nations should consider deploying a large number of observers—no less than 5,000—in support of the efforts deployed by the people of South Africa to ensure that the elections were free and fair.

23. My Special Representative also met with the leader of the Democratic Party, Mr. Zach de Beer, in Johannesburg on 23 December 1993. The discussion centred on the arrangements for the elections and on the role that the United Nations could play in support of the electoral process. Mr. de Beer observed that the interim constitution and the other transitional arrangements enjoyed the support of the overwhelming majority of South Africans. He noted that the more observers the United Nations could deploy, the better.

24. It should be noted that, before leaving New York, my Special Representative had met with Mr. Thabo Mbeki, Chairman of ANC, as well as with Mr. Benny Alexander, Secretary-General of PAC. While in Harare, he met with Mr. Johnson P. Mlambo and Mr. Gora Ibrahim, respectively First Deputy President and Foreign Secretary of PAC, who explained that their party will participate in the elections but was not, for the moment, willing to be represented on TEC.

### D. Discussions with represe ntatives of the transitional institutions

25. While he was in Cape Town on 17 December 1993, my Special Representative met with Mr. Zam Titus, Co-Chairperson of TEC. On 23 December 1993, he met in Johannesburg with a delegation of the newly appointed Independent Electoral Commission (IEC) led by its Chairman, Judge J. C. Kriegler, and including the Rev. Frank Chikane and Mr. C. Nupen, members of IEC and Dr. R. Mokate, Chief Executive Officer of IEC.

26. With both Messrs. Titus and Kriegler, my Special Representative exchanged views on the responsibilities entrusted to TEC and IEC with respect to the electoral process and as to how best the United Nations could assist them in that regard. It was recognized that the relationship between the United Nations and the two structures would need to be further discussed and clarified.

27. Judge Kriegler emphasized that IEC was determined to meet the deadline of 27 April 1994 for holding the elections. IEC would like to know as soon as possible the programmes of assistance to the electoral process planned by the United Nations and other intergovernmental organizations, particularly regarding voter education and election monitoring. Early coordination and liaison between IEC and the United Nations will help achieve the common objective of facilitating a successful electoral process. He said that United Nations assistance would be needed to conduct polling in foreign countries where South Africa did not have political representation and noted that IEC would welcome United Nations expertise and assistance on the technical aspects of monitoring.

### E. Discussions with other intergovernmental observer missions

28. During his stay in Johannesburg, my Special Representative also met on 18 December 1993 with the Head of the OAU Observer Mission in South Africa, Ambassador Legwaila J. Legwaila, and with a team of the Commonwealth Observer Mission in South Africa (COMSA) led by Mr. John Syson, Senior Adviser for southern Africa. The discussions with both missions centred around the existing cooperation between them and UNOMSA and how this could be further strengthened and broadened in connection with the electoral process. They exchanged preliminary ideas about the planned expansion in the size of each mission and how best they can coordinate their activities with a view to their future coordination in the deployment and training of observers.

### F. Discussions with leaders of the national peace structures, and leading individuals

29. On 17 December 1993, my Special Representative met in Cape Town with Archbishop Desmond Tutu and with Justice Richard Goldstone, Chairman of the Commission of Inquiry into Public Violence and Intimidation. Archbishop Tutu, who had recently met with Chief Buthelezi and talked to Mr. Mandela and other leaders, apprised my Special Representative about the efforts being made to convince all parties to partici-

pate in the electoral process. Despite the decision of the Freedom Alliance not to participate in the electoral process and the violence in the East Rand and Natal/KwaZulu, Archbishop Tutu was optimistic that the transitional arrangements would succeed.

30. Justice Goldstone stressed that intimidation and violence remained the most difficult challenge to the peace process. He said he might seek United Nations expert assistance for the investigative unit of his Commission. My Special Representative observed that personnel with police background could be included in the United Nations Mission to respond to such needs.

31. On 22 December 1993, my Special Representative met in Johannesburg with Mr. John Hall and Dr. Antonie Gildenhuys, Chairpersons of the National Peace Committee and its Secretariat, respectively. The role that the two bodies would play in the electoral process and the cooperation between them and UNOMSA was discussed. Dr. Gildenhuys informed my Special Representative that the various regional and local peace committees will continue to be involved in promoting peace but will not observe the electoral process. Since all relevant parties in South Africa, including some which are not participating in the multi-party talks, are members of the committees, the Secretariat cannot pass judgement on the electoral process or its outcome. The most useful contribution it can make is to continue to promote peace and dialogue among all the parties.

### G. *Visit to Harare, Zimbabwe*

32. In response to an invitation by the Government of Zimbabwe, my Special Representative visited Harare to attend the Summit Meeting of the Front-line States which took place on 20 December 1993. President Mugabe, who holds the chairmanship of this group, expressed his satisfaction at the positive developments which had taken place on the South African scene. He appealed to all parties to cease acts of violence so that the elections of 27 April 1994 could take place in favourable conditions. In this connection, the Conference welcomed the appointment of a Special Representative of the Secretary-General and stressed the positive role which the United Nations should play to ensure the success of the electoral process in South Africa. The participants in the Conference emphasized, in particular, the importance for the United Nations to mobilize a large number of observers (President Mugabe mentioned a figure of 7,000) to cover the elections in South Africa.

### H. *Discussions with the diplomatic community in South Africa*

33. During his visit to South Africa, my Special Representative had occasion to meet with Mr. Peter Bruckner, Ambassador of Denmark and Dean of the Diplomatic Corps; Mr. Princeton Lyman, Sir Anthony Reeve and Mr. Marc Brault, Ambassadors of the United States, the United Kingdom of Great Britain and Northern Ireland and Canada, respectively; and with a group of African heads of mission in South Africa led by Ambassador William Khoza of Malawi. All his interlocutors welcomed the involvement of the United Nations in the electoral process in South Africa and noted that it would have a salutary effect both on the process and its outcome. They also recognized the positive contributions of UNOMSA to the transitional process in South Africa and to the efforts to curb violence.

34. There was a meeting of minds among the diplomatic community on the need for as close cooperation and coordination as possible between the United Nations on the one hand and EU, OAU and the Commonwealth on the other. All ambassadors stressed that the United Nations must have adequate observers to cover fully the electoral process and to ensure the success of the transition period. Some ambassadors cited the figure of 2,000 as a rough estimate of United Nations observers that would be needed. Others asked whether 2,000 or even 3,000 observers would be enough, considering the violence, and the tensions which existed between security forces and large sections of the population, and given that up to 9,000 voting stations would be opened on election day. Many diplomats underlined the importance of providing common training to all international observers in order to avoid—or at least limit—confusion and disagreement. All ambassadors spoke of the importance of the success of the peace process in South Africa for Africa and the world. They also stressed the importance of voter education and saw a role for the United Nations in that regard.

### III. Activities of the United Nations Observer Mission in South Africa

#### A. *Main activities*

35. UNOMSA continued to carry out its tasks in all regions and at both regional and local levels. In this context, the Chief of Mission held a series of meetings with a cross-section of political, church and community leaders including President de Klerk, Mr. Mandela and Chief Buthelezi, Mr. Clarence Makwetu, President of the PAC, General Constand Viljoen, leader of AVF and Professor Mosala, President of the Azanian People's Organization (AZAPO), to discuss a range of issues related to the peace process, and in particular the question of political violence and developments in the multi-party negotiations. Pursuant to the recommendations of the Secretary-General in December 1992 (S/25004) and Sep-

tember 1993 (S/26558) and their approval by the Security Council in February and October 1993, (S/25315 and S/26559) additional observers are to be deployed, bringing the total to 100 early in 1994. This expanded group will serve also as the nucleus for the activities of UNOMSA in the South African electoral process.

36. Among the main events covered and activities undertaken by UNOMSA observers in this period were:

(*a*) Demonstrations, marches, rallies, funerals and other forms of mass action. UNOMSA observers worked closely with organizers and the security forces to ensure that events were adequately planned and that the Goldstone Commission guidelines for marches and political gatherings were complied with. Observers also held 832 informal bilateral meetings and often acted as channels of communication between groups across the political and social spectrum, including officials of the Government and security forces, political parties and non-governmental organizations which are actively involved in the peace process;

(*b*) Meetings of local and regional peace committee and other structures established under the National Peace Accord to whose activities full support was given. In the past six months alone, UNOMSA has been represented at about 1,320 meetings of the peace structures. In total, UNOMSA observers have attended well over 9,000 meetings and events throughout the country in the 15 months during which the Mission has been in South Africa;

(*c*) The Goldstone Commission hearings at which a UNOMSA jurist continued to play a role as an objective commentator on the Commission's *modus operandi* and balance;

(*d*) Serving as a channel of communication and coordination among international observer missions. This role has contributed to enhancing the effectiveness and harmonizing the activities of the OAU, Commonwealth and European Union observer missions and has been reinforced by the recent call of the Transitional Executive Council on the United Nations to coordinate the activities of all international observers in South Africa.

### B. *Peace structures*

37. The structures established under the National Peace Accord have all been functioning at national, regional and local levels, with the number of peace committees going from 50 to about 200 in the past six months. The performance of the structures has been far from uniform. In most cases, the lack of agreement between political parties on the measures to be taken or their failure to implement decisions agreed upon have been the major causes for the ineffectiveness of many of the peace structures. Furthermore, most peace committees continue

to suffer from budgetary constraints, lack of competent and committed staff as well as absence of political commitment on the part of major role players, including the police and security forces.

38. The Goldstone Commission, one of the most credible institutions in South Africa in terms of its contribution for peaceful transition towards democracy and non-racialism, has recently issued some important findings.

39. With regard to the vital area of socio-economic reconstruction and development (SERD), concerted efforts have been exerted in various regions to establish regional and local SERD committees and appoint regional coordinators, notably in the Wits/Vaal, Northern Transvaal and the Natal/KwaZulu regions. However, these evolving SERD structures are still ill equipped to mobilize resources, especially in terms of generating local interests and political support for project formulation, planning and implementation and in identifying appropriate sources of funding. The lack of technical expertise, the lengthy bureaucratic procedures for appointing SERD coordinators, the absence of clear criteria for funding mechanisms, the seemingly low priority of socio-economic development on the current political agenda of different groups and, most importantly, the scarcity of funds for development, have all contributed to the quasi-stagnation of development activities at the regional and local levels.

40. UNOMSA has been called upon to play a more pro-active role in the SERD process, regionally and locally, in view of the diversified pool of expertise available to it. The international observers will thus share in their research, documentation and knowledge, bringing in relevant experience in development from other areas. This is a crucial step forward for the international observers, as it paves the way for technical assistance and the whole array of development activities already pledged to the new South Africa.

### C. *Violence*

41. The major area of concern still remains that of public violence attributed mostly to conflict between political parties, taxi associations and between township and hostel residents. Criminal elements, often victims of social deprivation and unemployment, especially among the youth, contribute to a significant extent to the perpetuation of violence. In many instances, they receive protection from political groups or disappear in the anonymity or complicity of the township population.

42. Political violence continues to be mainly concentrated in Natal and the East Rand, mostly in the townships of Katlehong and Thokoza. According to the Human Rights Commission, 2,768 people have died in

political violence between the beginning of June and the end of November 1993, an increase of 46 per cent over the same period last year. The East Rand and Natal together have accounted for approximately 90 per cent of the death toll. In the East Rand alone, 1,299 people have died as a result of political violence during the period. This represents 54 per cent of the total number of victims in the country and 87 per cent of the Pretoria-Witwatersrand-Veereeniging (PWV) region. According to the reports from the Human Rights Commission, the month of July, during which the date for the election was announced, was the highest for the past three years with 581 deaths, followed by the month of August with 554. Since then the number of deaths has decreased slightly but violence in the affected areas has not been brought under control, despite the efforts of the peace structures and the international observers.

43. Right-wing violence is also on the increase. On 25 June, right-wingers armed with guns, many of them members of the Afrikaner Resistance Movement, Afrikaanse Weerstandsbeweging (AWB), forcibly broke into and occupied the World Trade Centre, where multi-party negotiations were taking place. Many have appeared in the Magistrate's Court and have been charged with trespassing. On 13 December, in a gruesome racist attack in Randfontein, on the West Rand of the PWV, white men in camouflage uniform forced two cars off the road and shot their black occupants, killing three people and injuring four others.

44. The increased violence in the East Rand and Natal has coincided with the collapse or at least the paralysis of the peace structures in the areas. While numerous initiatives have been undertaken to curb violence, the overall result is far from reassuring. However, in circumstances where joint action was taken by political parties and the police, tangible results were often achieved. Initiatives to prevent violence around hostels in the Wits/Vaal area have also been undertaken by church leaders as well as hostel and township residents. The newly created National Youth Development Forum and the Peace Corps project of the Wits/Vaal Peace Secretariat are efforts being undertaken to engage young people in meaningful and productive activities and thereby reduce their criminal activities. With regard to taxi violence, mediation by peace structures has helped to mitigate the worst excesses of taxi wars, but long-term changes are required to end taxi violence. UNOMSA teams have played a major role in the resolution of similar problems in Border/Ciskei and Western Cape.

D. *Security forces and National Peace-keeping Force*

45. In the absence of hard evidence as to causes, the paralysis in law enforcement tends to be explained in terms of collusion or indifference on the part of the security forces, or the involvement of a "third force" or an unknown number of covert forces in the more systematic acts of violence. The Goldstone Commission has investigated several specific allegations of this type and, except for some members of the KwaZulu police, has found no conclusive evidence in support. Nevertheless, the average citizen tends to believe otherwise. Consequently a cloud of suspicion and hostility continues to hang over the security services, particularly in the townships, as a result of a general dissatisfaction with their performance and their previous role as enforcers of apartheid.

46. A national peace-keeping force for the maintenance of peace and public order in the electioneering period has been proposed. Though the task of establishing the National Peace-keeping Force has been entrusted to the Transitional Executive Council (TEC) through its Subcouncil on Defence and some ideas on the modalities have been put forward, the prospect of such a Force coming into being effectively before the elections is remote. As a result, the task of maintaining law and order would remain the responsibility of the current security forces. The Internal Stability Unit, whose reform in line with community policing and incorporation into the police force is being considered by TEC, remains a controversial body and its removal from some townships is still being demanded. Though much remains to be done, the security forces and the Minister of Law and Order have started to respond to the demands of the community and dictates of changing situations. Of signal importance is the recent call for technical assistance from the international community and the willingness not to declare "unrest areas" without consultations with the communities and peace structures concerned.

47. The establishment of the National Peace-keeping Force should be distinguished from the long-term issue of the integration of armed formations. One of the tasks entrusted to the Subcouncil on Defence is to oversee the planning, preparation and training of a future National Defence Force. The Multi-party Forum agreed on an integrated force to be known as the National Defence Force, consisting of the current South African Defence Force (SADF), the defence forces of the Transkei, Bophuthatswana, Venda and Ciskei (TBVC) states, and other armed formations. This is an area of concern cited under resolution 772 (1992) where major progress has been made in the fourth quarter instanced by regular meetings between SADF and the Umkhonto we Sizwe (MK Spear of the Nation) leadership, joined more recently by officials of Ciskei, Venda, Transkei and the Azanian Peoples' Liberation Army (APLA).

## IV. The electoral process

### A. *The legal framework of the electoral process*

48. The legal framework of the electoral process is defined by the Independent Electoral Commission (IEC) and the Electoral Acts, the Independent Media Commission Act and the Independent Broadcasting Authority Act. These four Acts are the product of lengthy discussions and were approved by consensus. They provide a legitimate framework for the conduct of free and fair elections, and many of their provisions are quite innovative. The recent appointments to the Independent Electoral Commission are a further reassurance of good faith and cooperation on all sides.

49. As formal preparations for the elections now get under way, several concerns should be noted. Owing to the delay in the establishment of the electoral structures, the elections will be organized under significant time pressures. The limited lead time is particularly critical with regard to the issuance of voter documentation (whether identity cards or the voter identification cards envisioned in the Electoral Act). Approximately 4 million eligible voters are currently without enabling documentation, 2 million of them residents of the TBVC states. There is no doubt that IEC will do all it can to ensure that all eligible voters willing to obtain the necessary documentation will be able to do so in time and without unnecessarily cumbersome procedures.

50. A second concern is voter education. At present, only a few non-governmental organizations are providing quality non-partisan voter education. Experience has shown that the most important element in a free and fair election is an informed voting public. The Independent Electoral Commission should reinforce the voter education campaign and emphasize three crucial components: the secrecy of the vote, the need for political tolerance and the mechanics of voting, including the procedure for obtaining enabling documentation.

51. The third main concern is the spread of violence and the need for impartiality in election-related police actions. There is a great need for measures that will increase the public accountability of the police and promote meaningful community involvement—factors essential to the effectiveness of the police in serving the public. This is all the more important as it is unlikely that the National Peacekeeping Force will come into being before the elections.

52. Finally, the transparency and fairness of the appointment procedures for electoral officials at all levels will have a clear impact on the perceived legitimacy of the elections. Adequate appointment procedures will supplement the detailed provisions of the Electoral Law in ensuring the full confidence of the public in their electoral institutions.

### B. *The framework for observation of the elections*

53. The Independent Electoral Commission Act defines two categories of observers: international observers and domestic monitors. International observers are defined as the accredited representatives of intergovernmental organizations or foreign Governments. Monitors are appointed electoral officers who will observe different aspects of the electoral process and report to the Chief Director of the IEC Monitoring Directorate on any irregularities. The Monitoring Directorate will operate under the direct supervision of IEC. Additional definitions are provided by the Electoral Act, which specifies the powers, duties and functions of party election and voting agents.

54. At present, there are no detailed regulations or guidelines for international observers. As soon as the Monitoring Directorate is established, it will be expected to register observers and regulate their activities, publish guidelines and, eventually, prepare a Code of Conduct for international observers which will be binding. Once the guidelines have been prepared, the Directorate will probably consider similar arrangements with regard to observers from national and international non-governmental organizations.

55. One of the closing acts of the Multi-Party Negotiating Council, ratified by the Management Committee of the Transitional Executive Council (TEC) at its first session, was to request the United Nations, the Commonwealth, the European Community and the Organization of African Unity as well as individual foreign Governments to provide a sufficient number of international observers to oversee the electoral process. On 1 December 1993, the Minister for Foreign Affairs of South Africa wrote me a letter suggesting that immediate consideration be given to advance planning in order to ensure that the United Nations would be in a position to mount an effective operation when IEC or TEC became operational.

### C. *An expanded mandate for the United Nations Observer Mission in South Africa*

56. In response to the above request, I would propose that the mandate of the United Nations Observer Mission in South Africa (UNOMSA) be expanded to include the observation of the elections scheduled for 27 April 1994. In this new context, UNOMSA would have a significant role not only in assessing the ultimate freedom and fairness of the elections, but in monitoring the electoral process at each stage. Based on its long-term activities, UNOMSA would be uniquely capable of evaluating the extent to which the April elections truly reflect the will of the South African people.

57. Under the proposed expanded mandate, UNOMSA would be required to:

(*a*) Observe the actions of the Independent Electoral Commission and its organs in all aspects and stages of the electoral process, verifying their compatibility with the conduct of a free and fair election under the Independent Electoral Commission and Electoral Acts;

(*b*) Observe the extent of freedom of organization, movement, assembly and expression during the electoral campaign and ascertain the adequacy of the measures taken to ensure that political parties and alliances enjoy those freedoms without hindrance or intimidation;

(*c*) Monitor the compliance of the security forces with the requirements of the relevant laws and the decisions of the Transitional Executive Council (TEC);

(*d*) Verify the satisfactory implementation of the dispositions of the Independent Media Commission and the Independent Broadcasting Authority Acts;

(*e*) Verify that the voter education efforts of the electoral authorities and other interested parties are sufficient and will result in voters being adequately informed on both the meaning of the vote and its procedural aspects;

(*f*) Verify that qualified voters are not denied the identification documents or temporary voter's cards that will enable them to exercise their right to vote;

(*g*) Verify that voting occurs on election days in an environment free of intimidation and in conditions which ensure free access to voting stations and the secrecy of the vote; and verify that adequate measures have been taken to ensure proper transport and custody of ballots, security of the vote count and timely announcement of results;

(*h*) Coordinate the activities of observers from international governmental organizations and foreign Governments so as to ensure that they are deployed in an effective and coordinated manner; establish effective cooperation with South African and foreign non-governmental organizations, which will also monitor the electoral process.

58. Based on the above activities, UNOMSA will report to the electoral authorities on complaints, irregularities and interferences reported or observed, and, as appropriate, will request the electoral authorities to take remedial action. UNOMSA will be expected to prepare all of its reports on the basis of factual information about the conduct of the elections. UNOMSA will establish a direct relationship with the Independent Electoral Commission and make constructive suggestions and comments as appropriate in order to contribute to the success of each stage of the electoral process.

59. UNOMSA will also prepare periodic reports on the evolution of the electoral process which will be submitted to the Secretary-General through his Special Representative.

## D. *The operational approach*

60. In order to define the operational approach for the observation, it is important to note the difference between the observation of the electoral campaign and the observation of a specific polling day. The difference is particularly important in the case of UNOMSA, since many of the electoral campaign observation activities will be similar to those already undertaken within the current mandate. UNOMSA has been observing "demonstrations, marches and other forms of mass action, noting the conduct of all parties, and endeavouring to obtain information indicating the degree to which the parties' actions are consistent with the principles of the National Peace Accord and the Goldstone Commission guidelines for marches and political gatherings". (S/25004, para. 47)

61. During the two/three months preceding the elections, the focus of this original UNOMSA activity will change and become more closely related to the electoral process. The network of contacts established by UNOMSA will expand to include new electoral actors. The framework for evaluating the incidents observed will be the guidelines and regulations issued by the Independent Electoral Commission (IEC) rather than the National Peace Accord and Goldstone Commission guidelines. UNOMSA will continue to cooperate with the structures established under the National Peace Accord, whose activities will also increasingly concentrate on the electoral process. In this context, the violence-monitoring activities of UNOMSA are almost indistinguishable from the campaign observation activities contained in the electoral mandate suggested above.

62. The current UNOMSA mandate does not, however, cover a variety of activities that are essential for adequate electoral campaign coverage. These must therefore be added. These activities include: observation of IEC activities and of dispositions relating to the media; verification of the adequacy of voter education efforts; verification that qualified voters are not denied the identification documents or temporary voter's cards that will enable them to vote; and new responsibilities related to coordination. Furthermore, since a very large increase in the volume and intensity of events can be anticipated, arrangements must be made now to ensure sufficient resources for the mission.

63. In contrast to campaign observation, polling day observation is qualitatively and quantitatively different. While the electoral campaign as a whole may include thousands of demonstrations and marches, it is unlikely that more than a few hundred will take place on any given day. This will be the general pattern for most of the electoral events observed during the campaign period. In contrast, events to be observed on polling day will take place simultaneously at 10,000 different polling stations.

While the events of an electoral campaign are usually heterogeneous and have a high emotional content, polling day events tend to be the opposite. They are highly mechanical, repetitive and predictable, since the electoral authorities will clearly establish each step in the voting procedure. Furthermore, the incidence of violence and intimidation is unlikely to decrease.

64. As a result, polling day observation requires a much larger number of observers, who will perform a simpler task. Previous United Nations electoral missions have followed two different approaches regarding voting day observers. In cases where the number of polling stations was small (as in Namibia) or where a large number of polling stations is concentrated in a few polling centres (as in El Salvador), it has been possible to deploy at least one observer to each polling centre, thus maintaining a continuous presence at all times. However, this approach has not been feasible in cases where there has been a large number of dispersed polling stations (as in Nicaragua, Haiti, Angola or Eritrea). In those cases, mobile teams were used to visit several polling stations each. The homogenous character of the activities to be observed allows the systematic use of statistical samples and random visits with very effective results.

65. The presence of national monitors is not essential to the first approach, since international observers are present everywhere. With the second approach, however, the presence of national monitors at every polling station is a necessary precondition for an effective operation. In such cases, national monitors constitute a first line of observation, providing information on irregularities to the international observers when they visit the polling stations. The mutual controls implicit in the presence of monitors representing competing parties and/or independent non-governmental organizations will facilitate cross-verification of the information received. As the international observers will be expected to visit each polling station more than once, the direct and indirect information thus collected will be sufficient for a very detailed evaluation of the events on polling days.

66. The case of South Africa presents special considerations. There will be a very large number of polling stations (about 10,000), and distances to be travelled in the rural areas are considerable. Violence is concentrated in a few limited areas, with the Natal/KwaZulu and Wits/Vaal regions accounting for a very large percentage. The participation of national monitors is expected to be significant. Several parties will be able to place one monitor in each of the polling stations, and non-governmental organizations interested in the electoral process are forming their own observer network.

67. Therefore, the operational approach for election day observation suggested for South Africa is a combination of the two approaches used in previous missions. Observation will be conducted by mobile teams in those areas of the country where expectations of violence are low. The number of polling stations monitored by an observer team will vary. In rural districts, an observation team will be able to visit 4 to 10 polling stations per polling day depending on local conditions. In urban areas, each observation team will observe 14 to 20 polling stations per polling day. However, in districts with a history of violence, one observer will be assigned to each polling station.

## E. Coordination with other intergovernmental organizations

68. The resolution adopted by the Negotiating Council on 6 December 1993 and ratified by the Transitional Executive Council calls upon the United Nations to coordinate all international observers as defined in the Independent Electoral Commission Act and, as a matter of urgency, to put in place the necessary arrangements to that effect, in particular ensuring that the international observers are deployed in an effective and coordinated manner in close cooperation with IEC. The Independent Electoral Commission Act defines an international observer as "any person appointed as a representative of the United Nations, the Organization of African Unity, the European Community, the Commonwealth or any other intergovernmental organization or foreign Government accredited for that purpose by the Subcouncil on Foreign Affairs of the Transitional Council in consultation with the Department of Foreign Affairs, in order to observe and to report on the electoral process".

69. All of the intergovernmental organizations specifically mentioned in the Independent Electoral Commission Act have already deployed observers in South Africa and plan to expand their number in the near future. The Organization of African Unity currently has 13 observers working with the National Peace Accord structures and plans a gradual increase to 50 observers in early April. The European Union now has 17 observers monitoring public violence. It plans a separate group of up to 322 observers by the election date. The Commonwealth Observer Mission to South Africa (COMSA) presently comprises 20 observers. For the elections the Commonwealth will organize a Commonwealth Observer Group (COGSA) comprising a total of 70 senior observers beginning in early April. All three organizations have expressed their support for a United Nations role as the coordinator of international electoral observation efforts.

70. Several Governments have expressed interest in sending observers in addition to those to be provided by the missions organized by the United Nations, the Organization of African Unity, the European Union or the

Commonwealth and in having them included under the United Nations coordination umbrella. Although a sizeable number of such observers is expected to join the international effort, precise numbers are not yet available.

71. Effective coordination must go beyond the simple exchange of information. I would suggest the creation of a Coordinating Committee, comprising the chiefs of the four major missions present for the observation. Given the special responsibility assigned to the United Nations, my Special Representative or the Chief of Mission will act as its Chairperson. The Committee should provide overall political leadership for the common efforts and assume responsibility for the joint statement after the elections. Under the Committee there should be a Technical Task Force comprising the four Chief Electoral Officers of the four missions, chaired by the Head of the Electoral Division of UNOMSA, with the function of overseeing the activities of a Joint Operations Unit that will also be responsible for establishing cooperation links with the non-governmental organizations that send observer delegations. The Secretary of the Technical Task Force, an officer appointed by the United Nations, will head the Joint Operations Unit.

72. The Joint Operations Unit will concentrate on preparing the deployment of the large number of additional observers who will arrive for election day. This will require a substantial amount of preparatory work, including problem-solving related to transportation, communications and accommodation of the additional observers; the compilation of information for each of the small areas in which each of the observer teams will be working; organization of their deployment, which will include a sojourn of two to three days in their respective areas so that they can get acquainted with local conditions as well as with the electoral authorities and political representatives; the preparation of a manual, guidelines and training programmes; and the organization of observer arrival and departure. However, the initial attention of the Joint Operations Unit will be devoted to building on the informal coordination arrangements already established by UNOMSA in collaboration with the other three missions, developing common forms for the observation of events such as mass demonstrations, and organizing the databanks where information collected by the observers will be systematically recorded and maintained for the use of all four missions.

73. The proposed coordination will include the preparation of a joint statement after the election which will reflect the consensual opinion of the four missions in relation to the electoral process. Following standard practice, it is expected that each mission will prepare an independent, detailed report to its respective mandating organ. However, it must be noted that the primary responsibility for the verification of the elections as free and fair rests with the Independent Electoral Commission (IEC).

### F.  *Cooperation with national and foreign non-governmental organizations*

74. The resolution of the Transitional Executive Council regarding the participation of international observers also expressed "the hope that all international observers and other observers from South African and foreign non-governmental organizations would cooperate closely in the performance of their task to oversee the electoral process at all stages". Given the interest shown to date in the situation in South Africa, one can anticipate a very large involvement of foreign non-governmental organizations in the forthcoming elections. In many cases, such involvement will consist of support to South African organizations for voter education and training and organization of monitor networks and other election-related activities.

75. Although foreign non-governmental organization observers will be present during the campaign period, their presence will increase significantly in the two weeks prior to the elections. However, their numbers, together with the variety of their sponsoring organizations, will prevent them from coordinating their observation in the systematic manner being planned for international governmental organizations and foreign government delegations. Nevertheless, efforts will be made to establish a cooperative relationship with the foreign non-governmental organizations, as they will contribute to the overall impact of the international observer presence. Cooperation might include the sharing of background materials, briefings and coordinated deployments.

76. Efforts will also be made to establish working relationships with national non-governmental entities involved in various aspects of the elections such as civic education and the organization of domestic monitoring networks. Several national non-governmental organizations are currently organizing a network of independent monitors in order to integrate their efforts. Since the presence of domestic monitors at every polling station is critical to the overall success of the observation, the international observer teams will seek to establish direct contact with the national monitors in polling stations throughout their assigned areas.

### G.  *Trust Fund for Observers from Developing Countries*

77. Most of the Member States that are sending observers are industrialized societies. Similarly, an overwhelming majority of the foreign non-governmental organizations that will participate in the process are

headquartered in those countries. On the other hand, many developing countries, although deeply interested in the situation in South Africa, do not have the resources to send their own observers. Even if the geographical distribution of the observers funded from the United Nations budget is more balanced, an overrepresentation of observers from Western, industrialized societies can be expected. I will set up a special Trust Fund to finance the participation of additional observers from African and developing countries, and I hope that some Member States will be willing to make voluntary contributions to this Fund.

## V. Resource requirements

### A. *Organizational constraints*

78. The election has been scheduled for 27 April 1994. The time remaining to establish an efficient support system is therefore extremely short and significantly limits the range of otherwise viable options. As a result, the operational plan for the expanded mission must be formulated on the basis of what can realistically be accomplished in the time-frame available. This applies to the calculation of the number of observers that can be selected and dispatched to UNOMSA in time to follow the electoral campaign; the overall number of observers that can be fielded to monitor the actual elections (considering relevant logistical support limitations on site); the type of communications network that can be established; and the manner in which additional resources such as vehicles and other relevant equipment can be made available to the observers in due time. Furthermore, only a limited amount of preparatory work can actually commence immediately, and many of the necessary financial commitments can only be undertaken once the revised mission budget is approved.

### B. *Organizational structure and personnel requirements*

79. Under the expanded mandate of UNOMSA, the Mission will be headed by my Special Representative, supported by a Deputy Special Representative and assisted by a Senior Advisory Committee comprised of distinguished personalities, which will meet as required, and supported by a small unit comprised of two Senior Advisers, four Professional staff and support staff. The current and future work of UNOMSA will be fully integrated.

80. UNOMSA will have two operating arms: a Peace Promotion Division and an Electoral Division. The Peace Promotion Division will be headed by a D-2 reporting to the Deputy Special Representative. The work of the nine Regional Offices will be coordinated by that Division, and its teams will continue to follow rallies and

other public events, investigate instances of intimidation and related complaints, continue to coordinate with the peace structures, and will expand its network of contacts to include the monitoring branch of the IEC.

81. The Director in charge of the Peace Promotion Division will be supported by three Area Coordinators at the D-1 level. There will also be nine Regional Coordinators for the Northern Cape, Western Cape, Eastern Cape, KwaZulu/Natal, Orange Free State, Northwest, Pretoria-Witwatersrand-Vaal (PWV), Northern Transvaal and Eastern Transvaal regions. To cope with the expected large increase in the volume of activities to be monitored by the Division, it is proposed that the present 50 observers now being increased to 100 by the end of January should be further increased to 500 by March 1994. This will allow the monitoring teams to increase their coverage in terms of number of events, geographical spread and political complexity and intimidation.

82. The Electoral Division will also be headed by a Director at the D-2 level who will report to the Deputy Special Representative. The Director will be supported by a Deputy Director responsible for logistic matters at the D-1 level. There will be three other areas: electoral, voter education and media - as well as a small complement of statistical and research officers. Two electoral officers, both with electoral/voter education backgrounds, will be posted in each region. Although all personnel in each region will be under the coordination and guidance of the regional coordinators, the electoral specialists will maintain a functional liaison with the Electoral Division at headquarters at Johannesburg.

83. Considering the substantial expansion of the mandate of the Mission, with the resulting enlargement of its substantive staff, the administrative component of UNOMSA must be augmented significantly. In order to ensure that adequate logistical support for the observers is provided in a timely manner, a Chief Administrative Officer must be appointed to head the Administrative Service, including Personnel, Finance, Procurement, Transport, Communications and General Services. The strength of international staff of the service will gradually expand from the currently authorized level of 14, which includes clerical staff, to an election period total of 50 people of various ranks, plus one Senior Administrative Officer assigned to each regional office. Approximately 300 local staff, including drivers and interpreters, would be required on at least a part-time basis by February and an additional 700 for the last phase.

84. The organizational structure outlined in the previous paragraphs should be fully in place by the end of February. It is expected that OAU, EU and the Commonwealth will have 15, 150 and 20 observers respectively by that date. During March, UNOMSA will have

incrementally increased by 200 observers each month, so as to cover the increased number of public mass activities that will take place in the last phase of the electoral campaign and to help to prepare the ground for election-day observers. OAU and EU will increase their numbers by 15 and 50 respectively, and the Commonwealth will maintain its previous strength.

85. The Joint Operations Unit (see paras. 71 and 72 above) will be comprised of one liaison officer from OAU, EU and the Commonwealth, with a small complement of three computer programmer assistants, one demographer and one cartographer. A liaison officer will be responsible for non-governmental organization contacts as well as keeping track of contacts with Member States related to the identification and deployment of observers. In order to support the activities of the Joint Operations Unit at the regional level, there will be one logistics officer attached to each of the regional offices. As in the case of the electoral officers, they will be under the coordination and guidance of the Regional Coordinator and related functionally to the Joint Operations Unit.

### C. Observers on election day

86. South Africans have high expectations regarding the number of international electoral observers anticipated for the elections. This was brought to the attention of my Special Representative in almost all of his interviews. The range in the number of requested observers is very wide. Some groups, based on the number of observers that were present in Namibia (1,758 electoral and 1,035 police observers supervised 358 polling stations), have requested the presence of 25,000 to 30,000 observers. Some sectors have requested the presence of at least one observer for each polling station, which would entail a minimum of 10,000 observers, while others have asked for numbers ranging between 5,000 and 7,000 observers.

87. Most of the requests referred to observers who would arrive shortly before election day, as the proximity of election day places a clear limitation on the number of long-term observers that can be usefully incorporated into UNOMSA in a limited time. However, the experience of the United Nations since Namibia clearly indicates that long-term observers who follow the electoral campaign and establish relevant networks of contacts are far more useful and influential than those who arrive just a few days before the elections and concentrate their attention on the closing episodes of the campaign and on the events of the voting days. Furthermore, as I have pointed out in previous reports, additional observers—or resources—cannot compensate for a possible lack of political will of the competing parties or for attempted sabotage of the process by non-participating groups.

88. It will not be difficult to identify a very large number of observers for the election, as a large number of Member States have closely followed the negotiation process in South Africa. However, other than the limited usefulness of observers concentrating on election day events, there are several practical considerations in calculating the necessary number of observers. The larger the number of observers, the greater the time and resources required for planning their arrival and deployment. And as the limited resources of the Joint Operational Unit can be easily overwhelmed, a large part of the preparatory work could fall on the long-term observers who will be following the campaign and monitoring violence. Given the special importance attached to their work, such changed emphasis would constitute a misuse of resources.

89. For these reasons I have proposed the use of a combination of earlier approaches, using mobile teams to cover a certain number of polling stations in those areas with low expectations of violence and one observer in each polling station in those areas with a history of violence.

90. The number of required observers, as estimated by the survey mission team, is based on several assumptions:

(a) That the number of polling stations, presently estimated at 7,880 on the basis of demographic information, will increase by 20 per cent after adjustments based on more detailed physical evaluation of sites and consultations with the political parties;

(b) That approximately 40 per cent of the polling stations will be located in non-violent rural milieus. Based on the experience of mobile teams in previous missions, a mobile team of two observers should be able to effectively cover 4 to 10 polling stations on each polling day;

(c) That approximately 50 per cent of the polling stations will be located in non-violent urban and semi-urban areas, and that mobile teams of two observers should be able to adequately cover 14 to 20 polling stations per polling day;

(d) That 10 per cent of the polling stations will be located in areas with a history of violence, and that one observer will be placed in each of them;

(e) That counting will be conducted at counting stations and will start the morning after the elections so that observers who have followed the voting will also be able to monitor counting (without requiring any additional observers to monitor the count);

(f) That a 10 per cent reserve will be sufficient to cover unforeseen requirements and other complementary activities related to the observation.

91. The total number of observers required on the basis of previous assumptions is 2,840. This number refers to the subset of international observers that will function under a joint operational approach. The total number of international observers, including those representing foreign non-governmental organizations and

other groups, will be much larger and will probably exceed 5,000. Although there will be close liaison with the non-governmental organizations, their large number and heterogeneity will make it impossible to establish the same kind of coordination.

92. The core observer group of 2,840 will comprise 50 observers from OAU, 322 from EU, and 70 from the Commonwealth. Observers from three other sources will be integrated into the joint group: observers provided by some Member States, over and above those covered by the United Nations budget; observers from developing countries financed through the Trust Fund proposed above; and members of the diplomatic community, particularly the surrounding African countries, who participate in the observation process. If a conservative estimate of 600 observers from these sources is introduced, then the total number of observers to be provided by the United Nations is 1,778. As there will already be 500 United Nations observers, the additional number to be fielded for the last phase is 1,278.

93. Although these estimates are as realistic as possible based on the information available, there may be subsequent changes in the electoral organization procedures (for example, the number of polling stations, the counting immediately after the close of polls and the number of election days) or in the spread of violence, which could affect the numbers required. If so, I intend to resort to the three other intergovernmental organizations and to Member States to provide additional observers or to make additional contributions to the Trust Fund described above. Only if that proves impossible will I request the competent organs to authorize an additional number of observers.

### D. *Other resource requirements*

94. All vehicles used by the mission are rented locally, and the experience with this arrangement has been very favourable. Considering that the rental agencies have confirmed their ability to meet the mission's entire vehicle requirements during the election, it is foreseen that all sedan-type vehicles will be rented locally. Difficulties may arise in obtaining suitable dirt-road vehicles, as they are in short supply at the car rental agencies and the time remaining to effect international purchases is too short. While it would be desirable to provide at least 10 per cent of the mobile election teams with this type of vehicle, at this stage this may prove impossible. Air transport will be provided on a rental basis as required.

95. A functional communications network is of vital importance for the effective execution of the observation and poll-monitoring duties. Therefore, particular attention must be given to the timely establishment of a reliable and responsive communications system throughout South Africa. The survey team found that communications systems in South Africa are, as expected, of a very high technical standard and are available in most parts of the country, although their coverage in rural areas and in the vast squatter camp areas on the outskirts of the big cities is unsatisfactory.

96. Owing to the size of the country and the very short time remaining, it is not deemed feasible to establish the usual independent, country-wide, high-technology United Nations communications network. Even if very substantial financial commitments were entered into, the resulting network would, in all likelihood, be of marginal quality. Future efforts will be geared towards the determination of appropriate local solutions to establish suitable means of communication. In traditionally non-violent areas, local telephone and pager networks will be utilized as far as possible. In areas with a history of violence, efforts will be made to establish independent, direct, two-way communication systems. They will be coordinated by a Senior Communications Officer who will supervise a team of technicians to be deployed as soon as possible.

---

# Document 200

*Security Council resolution: The question of South Africa*

S/RES/894 (1994), 14 January 1994

*The Security Council,*

   ...

*Welcoming* the further progress made in establishing a democratic, non-racial and united South Africa, and in particular the establishment of the Transitional Executive Council and the Independent Electoral Commission, and the agreement on the Interim Constitution,

*Noting* that the legal framework of the electoral process in South Africa leading to the elections to be held on 27 April 1994 is defined by the Independent Electoral Commission (IEC) and the Electoral Acts, the Independent Media Commission Act and the Independent Broadcasting Authority Act,

*Commending* the positive contribution already made by the United Nations Observer Mission in South Africa (UNOMSA) to the transitional process in South Africa and to efforts to curb violence,

*Commending also* the positive contribution of the

Organization of African Unity, the Commonwealth and the European Union in this regard,

*Reiterating* its determination to continue to support the process of peaceful democratic change in South Africa for the benefit of all South Africans,

...

*Having considered* the request of the Transitional Executive Council that the United Nations provide a sufficient number of international observers to monitor the electoral process and to coordinate the activities of the international observers provided by the Organization of African Unity, the Commonwealth and the European Union as well as those provided by Governments, and *accepting* the need to respond urgently to this request,

1. *Welcomes with appreciation* the report of the Secretary-General of 10 January 1994 and *agrees* with the proposals contained therein concerning the mandate and size of the United Nations Observer Mission in South Africa, including the proposals for the coordination of the activities of the international observers provided by the Organization of African Unity, the Commonwealth

and the European Union as well as those provided by any other intergovernmental organizations or Governments;

2. *Urges* all parties in South Africa, including those which did not participate fully in the multi-party talks, to respect agreements reached during the negotiations, to adhere to democratic principles, and to take part in the elections;

3. *Calls upon* all parties in South Africa to take measures to end the violence and intimidation and thus contribute to the conduct of free and fair elections, and *expects* that anyone who seeks to disrupt the elections will be held accountable for such actions;

4. *Calls also upon* all parties in South Africa to respect the safety and security of the international observers and to facilitate the carrying out of their mandate;

5. *Welcomes* the intention of the Secretary-General to set up a special Trust Fund to finance the participation of additional observers from Africa and other developing countries and *urges* States to contribute generously to this Fund;

6. *Decides* to remain seized of the matter until a democratic, non-racial and united South Africa is established.

---

# Document 201

*General Assembly resolution: Elimination of apartheid and establishment of a united, democratic and non-racial South Africa—Democratic and non-racial elections in South Africa*

A/RES/48/233, 21 January 1994

The General Assembly,

*Recalling* its resolution 48/159 A, adopted by consensus on 20 December 1993, as well as its resolution 48/230 of 23 December 1993,

*Recalling also* Security Council resolutions 765 (1992) of 16 July 1992 and 772 (1992) of 17 August 1992,

*Welcoming* the agreement reached within the framework of multi-party negotiations to hold the first democratic elections in South Africa on 27 April 1994,

*Welcoming also* the adoption by Parliament, of 22 December 1993, of the Constitution for the Transitional Period as well as the Electoral Bill, and encouraging the efforts of all parties, including ongoing talks among them, aimed at the widest possible agreement on the arrangements for the transition to a democratic order,

*Noting* the request by the Transitional Executive Council to the United Nations for the provision of a sufficient number of international observers to monitor the electoral process, which also called upon the United Nations to coordinate, in close cooperation with the Independent Electoral Commission, the activities of the international observers provided by the Organization of

African Unity, the Commonwealth and the European Union, as well as those provided by Governments,

*Noting with appreciation* the report of the Secretary-General on the question of South Africa,

1. *Commends* the Secretary-General for his prompt response to the request contained in paragraphs 18 and 19 of its resolution 48/159 A, and *welcomes* the proposals contained in the report of the Secretary-General;

2. *Takes note with satisfaction* of Security Council resolution 894 (1994), adopted on 14 January 1994, by which the Council accepted the need to respond urgently to the request by the Transitional Executive Council and agreed with the proposal contained in the report of the Secretary-General concerning the mandate and size of the United Nations Observer Mission in South Africa, including the proposals for the coordination of the activities of the international observers provided by the Organization of African Unity, the Commonwealth and the European Union as well as those provided by other intergovernmental organization or Governments;

3. *Encourages* Member States to respond positively to the request of the Secretary-General for election observers;

4. *Urges* all parties in South Africa, including those which did not participate fully in the multi-party talks, to respect agreements reached during the negotiations, to adhere to democratic principles and to take part in the elections;

5. *Expresses its grave concern* at the threat of the ongoing violence to the process of peaceful change, and calls upon all parties to promote the full participation of all South Africans in the democratic process in all parts of South Africa by exercising restraint and by refraining from acts of violence and intimidation;

6. *Calls upon* the South African authorities, including the Independent Electoral Commission, under the supervision and guidance of the Transitional Executive Council, to take the necessary measures to protect the rights of all South Africans to organize and participate in peaceful public manifestations and political rallies, to run for election and to participate in the polls in all parts of South Africa, including the "homelands", free of intimidation;

7. *Calls upon* all parties in South Africa to respect the safety and security of the international observers and to facilitate the carrying out of their mandate;

8. *Welcomes* the intention of the Secretary-General to set up a special trust fund to finance the participation of additional observers from African and other developing countries, and urges States to contribute generously to this fund.

# Document 202

*Statement by the Spokesman for Secretary-General Boutros Boutros-Ghali concerning the declaration by Mr. Nelson Mandela offering new concessions to the Freedom Alliance in order to secure participation by all parties in the forthcoming elections*

UN Press Release SG/SM/5228 - SAF/170, 17 February 1994

The Secretary-General did receive from his Special Representative in South Africa the full text of the declaration made by Nelson Mandela on Wednesday, 16 February, and offering new concessions to the Freedom Alliance in an effort to secure participation by all parties in the forthcoming elections in South Africa.

We understand from the first press reports that this initiative was rather well received in South Africa, and it is certain that everyone hopes that all political parties will take part in the elections. It is difficult not to share Mr. Mandela's view that history and future generations would judge the current South African leadership harshly if [they] failed to take all the necessary measures to resolve South Africa's problems peacefully and through dialogue.

As you all know, there is great interest and support for South Africa the world over. You also know that through the Special Representative of the Secretary-General and the United Nations Observer Mission in South Africa (UNOMSA), the United Nations has a presence in South Africa and is strongly supportive of the peaceful process towards the new, non-racial and democratic South Africa.

For all these reasons, the Secretary-General is following very closely indeed all the news that comes out of South Africa.

# Document 203

*Joint statement dated 1 March 1994 by Mr. Nelson Mandela, President of the African National Congress, and Mr. Mangosuthu Buthelezi, President of the Inkatha Freedom Party*

Not issued as a United Nations document

Both parties approached this meeting with a determination to promote conditions in which the people of South Africa as a whole can exercise their democratic right to make political choices in accordance with their beliefs and conscience.

Notwithstanding differences on constitutional matters, the parties recognised the right of people to participate or not to participate in the forthcoming general elections.

After a constructive exchange of views, the parties agreed to work together to ensure that canvassing for respective views should be able to take place without let or hindrance.

In an effort to resolve outstanding constitutional

deadlocks, the parties agreed to explore with their principals the possibility of international mediation and in this regard the IFP would consider provisional registration in terms of the Electoral Act.

Both parties agreed that the present levels of violence in our society were totally unacceptable and were jeopardising conditions for socio-economic reconstruction and development.

They therefore resolved to redouble their efforts to encourage their respective constituencies to participate in and support National Peace Accord structures and all peace initiatives.

While recognising the fact that members of the ANC and IFP are involved in political violence, the parties are of the view that the primary responsibility for the maintenance of law and order remains with the Government of the day.

The parties also explored the possibility of making greater use of international expertise in areas such as conflict resolution and the investigation of political violence.

It was agreed that a Task Group would be established in order to facilitate the strengthening of peace committees and to attend to communication between the parties.

---

# Document 204

*Letter dated 2 March 1994 from the Secretary-General to Mr. Nelson Mandela, President of the African National Congress*

Not issued as a United Nations document

I was delighted to learn yesterday of the outcome of your meeting with Chief Buthelezi. This positive development should provide a framework for all political parties to participate in the transitional arrangements, including the electoral process.

I congratulate you and Chief Buthelezi on the bold initiatives you have taken to promote national reconciliation and peace in South Africa. Mr. Brahimi is keeping me informed of developments. Please be sure that the United Nations will continue to support your efforts to resolve all outstanding issues which are impeding the peace process and to put an end to the violence.

*(signed)*
Boutros BOUTROS-GHALI

---

# Document 205

*Letter dated 11 March 1994 from the Secretary-General to Mr. André Ouellet, Minister for Foreign Affairs and International Trade of Canada*

Not issued as a United Nations document

[Editor's note: Original in French]
Thank you for your letter of 24 February and for the good news it contains. Since my talk with you and Mr. Chrétien on 9 January, when I asked for your help in the elections to take place on 26 April in South Africa, I knew that I could count on the usual generosity of Canada, which always responds positively to the appeals of the United Nations.

By sending, at no cost to the Organization, a group of experts on control of violence and specialists on elections, Canada is remaining true to its commendable tradition in the area of humanitarian assistance, cooperation for development, support for democratization and peace-keeping.

I note with gratitude, in particular, that since the creation of our Electoral Assistance Unit in April 1992, Canada has provided us with specialists and observers for electoral assistance projects in Burundi, the Congo, Kenya, Lesotho, Uganda and the Central African Republic.

Through its latest contribution, Canada will be helping to bring about a free, democratic and non-racial South Africa, finally delivered from the terrible scourge of apartheid. For this it deserves our thanks.

Accept, Sir, the assurances of my highest consideration.

*(signed)*
Boutros BOUTROS-GHALI

# Document 206

## Letter dated 19 April 1994 from the Secretary-General to Mr. Nelson Mandela, President of the African National Congress

Not issued as a United Nations document

I am pleased to learn of the positive outcome of the meeting between yourself, President F. W. de Klerk and Chief Mangosuthu Buthelezi which will facilitate the participation of the Inkatha Freedom Party in the elections to be held from 26 to 28 April 1994. I congratulate you warmly on this important achievement.

The agreement constitutes a decisive step towards an overall settlement which will make it possible, even at this late hour, for all parties who wish to do so to participate in the historic elections. It is my fervent hope that all groups, whatever their political orientation, who remain outside the electoral process will respect the right of those who wish to vote. I call upon all parties to give the Independent Electoral Commission their fullest cooperation and to contribute to the success of the elections.

I take this opportunity to assure you once again that the United Nations will continue to support your efforts for South Africa's peaceful transition to a non-racial, democratic and united country.

(*signed*)
Boutros BOUTROS-GHALI

# Document 207

## Statement by the Spokesman for Secretary-General Boutros Boutros-Ghali welcoming the breakthrough agreement in South Africa

UN Press Release SG/SM/5268 - SAF/172, 19 April 1994

The Secretary-General welcomes the breakthrough agreement reached today between Frederik Willem de Klerk, State President of South Africa, Nelson Mandela, President of the African National Congress of South Africa, and Chief Mangosuthu Buthelezi, Chief Minister of KwaZulu and President of the Inkatha Freedom Party.

The Secretary-General congratulates the parties and hopes that this historic decision will ensure that the elections, in which all South Africans will be able to participate, will take place later this month under calm and peaceful conditions.

# Document 208

## Statement by the President of the Security Council on behalf of the Council welcoming the agreement reached on 19 April between the Inkatha Freedom Party, the African National Congress and the Government of South Africa, following which the Inkatha Freedom Party decided to participate in the forthcoming elections

S/PRST/1994/20, 19 April 1994

The Security Council has noted with appreciation the Secretary-General's report of 14 April 1994 (S/1994/435) on the question of South Africa, as well as the oral information received from the Secretariat on the latest developments in the electoral process.

The Council welcomes the agreement reached on 19 April 1994 between the Inkatha Freedom Party (IFP), the African National Congress (ANC) and the Government of South Africa, following which the IFP has decided to participate in the forthcoming elections in South Africa. It commends all the parties involved for the statesmanship and goodwill which they have displayed in reaching this result.

The Council expresses the hope that this agreement will bring an end to the violence which has scarred South Africa and that it will promote lasting reconciliation among the people of South Africa. It calls upon all parties to contribute to the conduct of free and fair elections in which all South Africans will be able to participate peacefully.

The Council commends the positive contribution by the United Nations Observer Mission in South Africa (UNOMSA) and the international community to the transitional process in South Africa and reiterates its determination to support the process of peaceful democratic change for the benefit of all South Africans. It calls upon all parties to respect the safety and security of the international election observers and to assist them to carry out their mandate.

The Council looks forward to the successful completion of the electoral process in South Africa and to the establishment of a democratic, non-racial and united South Africa that will take its place in the international community.

# Document 209

*Statement by the Spokesman for Secretary-General Boutros Boutros-Ghali applauding the election process in South Africa*

UN Press Release SG/SM/5282 - SAF/176, 6 May 1994

Judge Johann Kriegler, Chairman of the Independent Electoral Commission in South Africa, has proclaimed the results of the elections and has declared them to have been "sufficiently free and fair". The Secretary-General welcomes this declaration and once again expresses his warm congratulations to the people of South Africa and all their leaders.

The Secretary-General also congratulates very warmly the Chairman and members of the Electoral Commission for the remarkable work they have done. Thanks to their dedication and courage, they have made it possible for the South African people to express peacefully and freely their collective aspiration for a better future and their determination to ensure a life of dignity, equality and freedom for every man and woman in their country.

The United Nations has been involved with the situation in South Africa for more than four decades. It has spearheaded the international campaign against apartheid and initiated and supported programmes aimed at alleviating the suffering of its victims. It has also provided a forum for the representatives of South African organizations such as the African National Congress of South Africa (ANC) to advance the anti-apartheid campaign.

Since September 1992, in particular, the United Nations has been represented in South Africa by an Observer Mission with the express mandate of contributing to a peaceful transition from apartheid to a new, democratic, non-racial and united South Africa.

This was the largest electoral observer mission mounted by the United Nations. No fewer than 2,120 men and women took part, including staff members of the United Nations and specialized agencies and recruits from some 120 Member States.

To all of them, the Secretary-General wishes to express his appreciation for the work they have accomplished. They served the United Nations well. They also served the people of South Africa at a critical moment of their history; and they served the cause of democracy.

The United Nations will remain committed to South Africa. The Secretary-General looks forward to the contribution the Government and people of South Africa will make to the activities of the United Nations.

# Document 210

*Statement by Secretary-General Boutros Boutros-Ghali in Pretoria at the luncheon following the inauguration of Mr. Nelson Mandela as President of South Africa*

UN Press Release SG/SM/5286, 10 May 1994

On behalf of the United Nations, I congratulate you, Mr. President, on your inauguration today as State President of the Republic of South Africa. I congratulate Deputy President Mbeki and Deputy President de Klerk. Today, we have been privileged to witness a turning-point in the history of a nation. Today, South Africa regains its rightful place in Africa, in the United Nations and in the family of nations.

The United Nations raised its flag against the evil of apartheid. The world joined against it. Repeatedly, the nations and the peoples of the international community expressed their solidarity and support for the people of South Africa. We demonstrate that solidarity again, by our presence, by your presence today. Today's celebrations truly belong to all South Africans, whatever their party or affiliation. I pay tribute to all who had the vision to lead. I pay tribute to all who had the courage to join in this undertaking. I pay tribute to the international organizations and the Member States who contributed and who stood together with you.

Guided by wise and able leaders, South Africa has earned the respect and the admiration of all. Tireless in the search for understanding and vigorous in the pursuit of peace, you have refused to let the difference defeat you. You, Mr. President, have worked long and suffered greatly to see this day. The firmness of your resolve to build a new,

non-racial society in South Africa is not in doubt. Your resolve will be needed, your political will will be tested. But I am confident that through your courage and determination, you and South Africa will prevail.

Deputy President de Klerk, your vision and courage have contributed to this great day. You have won the lasting respect of all who yearn for justice.

I call on all nations and on the institutions and the programmes and the agencies of the international community to support the new democracy in South Africa. I appeal to all South Africans to support the principle of tolerance and reconciliation, principles that provide the only sure foundation for peace, security and progress. The people of South Africa have spoken. You assume office, Mr. President, with a historic mandate and supported by great goodwill.

We welcome you with happiness, we embrace you with pride. On behalf of the United Nations and the agencies and programmes of the United Nations, I pledge our continued support for the achievement of dignity, equal rights and social progress for all the people of this great country.

# Document 211

*Letter dated 18 May 1994 from President Nelson Mandela of South Africa to the President of the Security Council*

S/1994/606, 23 May 1994

Thank you very much for your letter dated 10 May 1994 in which you conveyed the Security Council's congratulations on the conclusion of the first democratic and multiparty elections in South Africa, as well as on my election to the office of President of the Republic of South Africa.

On behalf of all the people of South Africa and myself, I wish to assure the Security Council, and you in particular, of our appreciation and gratitude for your unstinting support and encouragement.

The successful conclusion of the electoral process

and political change in South Africa have certainly brought an end to the need for international sanctions to be imposed on the country. In order to allow South Africa to resume its rightful place in the international community, I therefore wish to call upon the United Nations Security Council to consider revoking all the remaining sanctions still enforced against the country at the earliest possible occasion.

*(signed)* N. R. MANDELA

# Document 212

*Statement by Mr. Thabo Mbeki, First Deputy President of South Africa, in the Security Council*

S/PV.3379, 25 May 1994

. . .

This eminent body is meeting today to close a particular chapter in the history of the relations between our

country, South Africa, and the nations of the world, as represented by the United Nations.

We trust that, at the conclusion of its meeting today,

the Security Council will terminate the mandatory sanctions imposed against South Africa under the terms of resolutions 418 (1977), 558 (1984) and 591 (1986).

We are most grateful to the Council for the opportunity it has kindly granted to our delegation to participate in its proceedings, and would like to take this opportunity to convey to you, Mr. President, and to the other members of the Council, the greetings of our President, Nelson Mandela, and the rest of the Government of democratic South Africa.

We are indeed moved by the fact that the Council is meeting on Africa Day to consider the specific matter on its agenda of lifting the arms embargo against South Africa.

When this embargo was imposed pursuant to the provisions of Chapter VII of the Charter of the United Nations, it was because the prevailing system of government in our country and the actions carried out by that Government constituted, demonstrably, a threat to international peace and security.

We therefore view the decisions that the Council will take today as an acceptance by the world body that we have become a democratic country, and a country that can be counted on to subscribe and adhere to the pursuit of the important goals of international peace and security. Like millions of other people across the globe, we count on this body to continue to act as the principal protagonist in the global struggle for peace, security and stability.

We firmly commit our country, as a Member of the United Nations and as a responsible citizen of the world, to live up to its obligations in this regard and, consequently, to contribute what it can to the making of the peaceful world which is the right of the peoples. Our Government and people are determined to ensure that within our borders we banish from our national life all those things that make for war and violent conflict.

The successful transition to a democratic order constitutes the firm foundation for peace which our people have yearned for, for generations. It constitutes also the basis from which we will move in the search for a negotiated, just and stable regional security system for all the peoples of southern Africa, which would guarantee the sovereignty of all the countries of our region and ensure that never again should any country fall victim to aggression and destabilization.

Our Government has also begun discussions to see what further contribution we can make to the search for peace in Angola and Mozambique, in support of the efforts of the United Nations and the Governments and peoples of those two countries. We are also committed to participating to the full extent of our abilities in the efforts spearheaded by the Organization of African Unity (OAU)

to address the related issues of peace, security, stability, cooperation and development on our continent.

We are accordingly ready to begin discussions with the OAU, the United Nations and all concerned with regard to what can and should be done concerning the tragic situation in Rwanda.

And as we have said, we are otherwise determined to discharge our responsibilities as a Member of the Organization in the collective effort to secure peace for ourselves and for the peoples of the world. We must, in this context, mention the fact that serious steps have already been taken to address the matter of proliferation of weapons of mass destruction and the regulation of the sale of conventional weapons. Among other things, this has been marked by accession to the Nuclear Non-Proliferation Treaty, the Chemical Weapons Convention and the Biological Weapons Convention, as well as the passage of domestic legislation relating to these matters.

Our Government is determined to ensure that we do indeed honour all the obligations which derive from these international agreements, including such agreements as may regulate the movement of equipment and technology which can be used in the production of missiles capable of delivering weapons of mass destruction. South Africa is also in the process of converting its military technology to civilian application. We would greatly appreciate the assistance of the international community with regard to this matter. Our Government is also keen that a treaty for an African nuclear-weapons-free zone be concluded as soon as possible.

We would also like to take this opportunity to extend our sincere thanks to the Security Council, to the Secretary-General of the United Nations, His Excellency Mr. Boutros Boutros-Ghali and the United Nations as a whole for the outstanding contribution this Organization has made in bringing South Africa to the happy situation in which it is today. This, of course, has included the dispatch of observers to help us deal with the matter of political violence and the observers, who played such an important role in ensuring a successful first democratic and non-racial election.

The victory that has been won in South Africa belongs as much to the people of our country as to this Organization and the peoples of the world. As we proceed to confront the enormous challenge of consolidating this victory, we shall continue to count on your support. Precisely because we are conscious of what the world has done for us, we too are determined to contribute what we can to the making of a better world for all.

We are especially pleased that today we meet under your [Mr. Kingibe of Nigeria] presidency—Sir, end apartheid's crime against humanity and to give birth to a society that is determined to live up to the ideals contained in the United Nations Charter and the Universal Declaration of Human Rights. Please count on us to behave as an exemplary Member of this Organization, in which the hopes of millions reside.

. . .

# Document 213

*Security Council resolution: The question of South Africa*

S/RES/919 (1994), 25 May 1994

*The Security Council,*

*Recalling* its resolutions on the question of South Africa, in particular resolutions 282 (1970) of 23 July 1970, 418 (1977) of 4 November 1977, 421 (1977) of 9 December 1977, 558 (1984) of 13 December 1984 and 591 (1986) of 28 November 1986,

*Welcoming* the first all-race multi-party election and the establishment of a united, democratic, non-racial Government of South Africa, which was inaugurated on 10 May 1994,

*Taking note* of the letter of 18 May 1994 from President Nelson R. Mandela of the Republic of South Africa (S/1994/606; annex),

*Stressing* the urgent need to facilitate the process of reintegration of South Africa in the international community, including the United Nations system,

1. *Decides,* acting under Chapter VII of the Charter of the United Nations, to terminate forthwith the mandatory arms embargo and other restrictions related to South Africa imposed by resolution 418 (1977) of 4 November 1977;

2. *Decides also* to end forthwith all other measures against South Africa contained in resolutions of the Security Council, in particular those referred to in resolutions 282 (1970) of 23 July 1970, 558 (1984) of 13 December 1984 and 591 (1986) of 28 November 1986;

3. *Decides further* to dissolve the Committee of the Security Council established by resolution 421 (1977) concerning the question of South Africa, in accordance with rule 28 of the provisional rules of procedure of the Security Council, effective from the date of the adoption of the present resolution;

4. *Invites* all States to consider reflecting the provisions of this resolution, as appropriate, in their legislation.

# Document 214

*Report of the Committee of Trustees of the United Nations Trust Fund for South Africa*

A/48/523/Add.1, Annex, 13 June 1994

1. The United Nations Trust Fund for South Africa was established in 1965 as a programme of legal, educational and relief assistance to political prisoners and their families and to refugees and other victims of apartheid. It was conceived as a humanitarian component of the United Nations commitment to the peaceful elimination of apartheid.

2. Its original mandate was expanded by the General Assembly in its resolution 46/79 F of 13 December 1991 to include, *inter alia*, assistance to facilitate the reintegration of political prisoners and returning exiles into South African society, as well as legal assistance aimed at redressing continuing adverse effects of apartheid laws.

3. In December 1993, the General Assembly, by its resolution 48/159 D of 20 December 1993, expressed its conviction that the Trust Fund had an important role to play during the final stage of the elimination of apartheid by assisting efforts in the legal field aimed at ensuring effective implementation of legislation repealing major apartheid laws and encouraging increased public confidence in the rule of law.

4. Since it was established in 1965, the Trust Fund has spent US$ 50 million on programmes of humanitarian, legal and educational assistance within the purview of its mandate. Thousands of victims of apartheid owe their very survival and hopes for the future to the activities of the Trust Fund.

5. In the execution of its mandate, the Committee made grants to the Office of the United Nations High

Commissioner for Refugees, and to voluntary agencies, principally located outside South Africa, whose dedication and commitment has remained exemplary throughout the years: the International Defence and Aid Fund for Southern Africa, Amnesty International, the World Council of Churches, the Freedom from Fear International Charitable Foundation, Christian Action (Southern Africa Education Fund), the Lawyers Committee for Civil Rights under Law, the Executive Council of the Episcopal Church, the International Confederation of Free Trade Unions, the International University Exchange Fund, the National Council of Churches of Christ, the South African Council of Churches, the National Council of Churches and the Catholic Institute of International Relations.

6. Over the past three years, in the light of positive developments in South Africa and the expanded mandate from the General Assembly, the Committee has provided assistance directly to South African voluntary agencies involved particularly in constitutional and human rights litigation, land and housing issues and legal representation for disadvantaged communities, children's rights, gender discrimination, needs of marginalized youths and environmental issues. These agencies, which are all based in South Africa and whose professionalism, impartiality and dedication have been widely recognized, are the South African Legal Defence Fund, the Association of Ex-Political Prisoners, the Legal Resources Centre, the National Association of Democratic Lawyers and the Black Lawyers Association.

7. Through these agencies, the Trust Fund also contributed to the training and deployment of paralegals to assist disadvantaged communities and promote a culture of human rights in South Africa.

. . .

11. The first universal-suffrage elections in South Africa were held from 26 to 29 April 1994 and were declared free and fair by the Independent Electoral Commission and international observers.

12. On 9 May, the new Parliament unanimously elected Mr. Nelson Mandela as the State President of the Republic of South Africa. His inauguration took place at Pretoria the following day.

13. Under these extraordinary circumstances, which ushered in a new, non-racial constitutional order in South Africa, the Committee of Trustees decided at a meeting on 31 May 1994 to recommend to a resumed meeting of the General Assembly at its forty-eighth session that the Committee had fulfilled its mandate. It further decided to recommend that the balance in the Trust Fund be transferred to the United Nations Educational and Training Programme for Southern Africa for use in its educational and training projects in South Africa. The Committee also noted with satisfaction that arrangements were being made with the Comptroller's office to ensure accountability for the last grants made by the Committee of Trustees at its meeting on 13 April 1994.

14. Taking into account the need to address the legacies of apartheid, the Committee decided further to call on members of the international community to provide financial and material support to the reconstruction and development efforts of the new South African Government and to continue to assist civic society in South Africa.

15. The Committee of Trustees would like to express its gratitude to the donor countries without whose steadfast and generous contributions its work could not have been accomplished, to the voluntary agencies for their professionalism and dedication beyond the call of duty, to the host countries of refugees, and to the countless men and women throughout the world and in South Africa who, sometimes at great risk to themselves, ensured that legal, educational and relief assistance to thousands of opponents and victims of apartheid could be effectively rendered.

16. The Committee wishes finally to record its deep thanks to the Secretary-General for his encouragement and untiring support to the Committee's work for nearly three decades.

# Document 215

*Report of the Special Committee against Apartheid*

A/48/22/Add.1 - S/26714/Add.1, 14 June 1994

. . .

**Goldstone Commission report on involvement of security forces in political violence**

. . .

78. At a joint press conference held on 18 March with President de Klerk, Justice Richard Goldstone re-

leased a 100-page report entitled "The Interim Report on Criminal Political Violence by Elements within the South African Police (SAP), the KwaZulu police and the Inkatha Freedom Party (IFP)". The report disclosed the involvement of senior South African Police officers, senior IFP officials and senior officials of the KwaZulu police in a conspiracy aimed at destabilizing South Africa's first democratic elections. The 20 officials named included Lt. Gen. Basie Smit, Deputy Commissioner of Police; Major Gen. Krappies Engelbrecht, head of Counter-Intelligence; the Chief of the Division of Crime Prevention and Investigation, Lt. Gen. Johan Le Roux and Mr. Themba Khoza, IFP leader of the Transvaal.

79. The report substantiated allegations of the involvement of members of the South African Police in the activities of a so-called "Third Force", which have included perpetrating and financing assassinations of political opponents (in particular, members of ANC) and organizing and training IFP "hit squads" to attack commuters and township residents. According to evidence given to the Commission, senior officials who had access to a large secret slush fund supplied IFP from 1989 until "the very recent past" with large quantities of arms both domestically manufactured and brought in from Namibia and Mozambique that were channelled to IFP for use against ANC. Furthermore, the report disclosed evidence of widespread financial corruption and attempted blackmail by senior police officers in an attempt to stop the inquiry by the Goldstone Commission.

80. President de Klerk suspended the officers named from active duty, denied that the Government of South Africa had prior knowledge of the activities and stated that an international task force would be invited to investigate the charges further. ANC also called for an international investigation. IFP termed the report "a dirty trick" to discredit its leadership.

81. In a statement dated 16 March, the Human Rights Commission of South Africa stated that by mid-April 1994, 4,500 IFP members would have received military training at the Mlaba Camp in Natal and that the KwaZulu Legislative Assembly had provided funding for the camp. On 26 April, Security Forces raided the camp and seized weapons and arrested persons at the camp suspected to be members of "hit squads".

. . .

4. Missions of the Special Committee against Apartheid to South Africa, 28 February - 5 March 1994 and 6 - 10 June 1994

. . .

174. The second mission [of the Special Committee], also led by the Committee's Chairman, Professor Ibrahim A. Gambari (Nigeria), took place between 6 and 10 June 1994. The other members of the mission to South Africa were: Dr. Jayaraj Acharya (Nepal), Vice-Chairman of the Special Committee; Mr. Simbarashe Mumbengegwi (Zimbabwe); Dr. Fernando Guillen (Peru); Mr. Suresh Goel (India), Rapporteur; Mr. Abdullahi Gwary (Nigeria) and Mr. Amer Araim, Secretary of the Special Committee.

175. The Chairman of the Special Committee set the objectives of the mission by emphasizing at various meetings that this was a fact-finding mission in order to enable the Special Committee to incorporate its assessment of the situation in South Africa in its final report to the General Assembly. The Chairman congratulated the people of South Africa on the success of the elections, which were recognized as free and fair. The elections demonstrated the courage and determination of the people of South Africa to bring about the end of apartheid by establishing a democratic and non-racial society. The Chairman stated that the United Nations had responded to the changes that had taken place in South Africa by lifting all restrictions against South Africa. Furthermore, the Special Committee was looking forward to South Africa resuming its seat in the General Assembly and its active participation in all the activities of the United Nations system. The Chairman also highlighted the importance of a coordinated manner in which the United Nations should continue to remain engaged in South Africa and the reconstruction and development of the country in the post-apartheid era. He emphasized the continuing role of the international community in enabling South Africa to overcome the legacy of apartheid.

176. In the course of the mission to South Africa, members of the delegation held discussions with the leaders of four political parties in the country (ANC, NP, IFP and PAC); the President of the Senate, the Speaker of the National Assembly and several members of the new Parliament; church leaders; the Chairman of IEC; Officials of the National Olympic Committee of South Africa (NOCSA); the editor of a leading South African newspaper, *The Sowetan*, as well as some other senior media representatives; the ambassadors and diplomats of the United States and several other Western countries resident in South Africa; the Ministers of Public Enterprises, Safety and Security, Constitutional and Provincial Affairs, and Home Affairs and also a number of Deputy Ministers including, in particular, the Deputy Minister of Foreign Affairs and Deputy Presidents T. Mbeki and F. W. de Klerk. The highlight of the mission, however, was the audience with President Mandela.

177. The Chairman and other members of the mission were received in audience by President Mandela on Tuesday, 7 June 1994. President Mandela praised the work of the Special Committee, which had made a tremendous contribution to the elimination of apartheid. He also stated that the mission by the Special Committee symbolized the changes that had already happened in South Africa. President Mandela stressed that there now existed a great deal of good will amongst the political parties of South Africa and its people. The elections, as well as the subsequent actions, including the estab-

lishment of the Government of National Unity, had brought about a new spirit of cooperation. He also stated that South Africa needed the support of the international community, especially for the Government's socio-economic programmes contained in the Reconstruction and Development Programme (RDP).

178. The Chairman of the Special Committee assured President Mandela that the final report of the Special Committee would include recommendations on the future role of the United Nations in South Africa, and he wished to know the views of the Government and people of the country on what such a role should be. The members of the mission would also continue to work on assistance for South Africa as representatives of their respective countries in the United Nations, both at the bilateral level and through different United Nations programmes. He also emphasized that the members of the Special Committee had had a deep-rooted commitment to the end of apartheid and its consequences in South Africa and that their interest in South Africa would continue even after the termination of the Special Committee's mandate.

179. At various meetings of the mission, there was a unanimous expression of appreciation and praise for the role played by the United Nations, the Secretary-General and the United Nations Observer Mission in South Africa, as well as the Special Committee. There was a general recognition that the changes that had taken place in South Africa were achieved through the determination of the people of South Africa to eliminate apartheid. The United Nations efforts, through both pressure and persuasion and assistance to the opponents of apartheid, had contributed to the process in a significant manner. It was also recognized that the changes in South Africa would benefit all the sectors of the society and that the contributions of all ethnic and cultural groups would strengthen the unity of the people.

180. The leaders of South Africa expressed the hope that their country would soon resume its place in the General Assembly and begin to participate actively in the work of the United Nations. They also hoped that the question of arrears would be considered in a favourable manner, keeping in mind related circumstances. South Africa is also looking forward to playing an active role in OAU, the Non-Aligned Movement, the Commonwealth and other organizations.

181. The question of development assistance was emphasized throughout the visit, particularly in respect of education and training for South African youth who are unemployed. The phenomenon of unemployment among the Black majority is a matter of great concern to the political leadership of South Africa. With the establishment of the new Government in South Africa, there is a considerable keenness in the country to attract foreign investment. The Government is planning various policy initiatives and strategies to encourage foreign enterprises to participate in the South African economy. Such participation and investment would contribute substantially to the growth and development of the country. It was stated that the long-term goal of the Government would be to make the enterprises internationally competitive.

182. South Africa is also looking forward to the establishment of regional mechanisms in southern Africa which would not only promote the regional trade and economic development but also contribute to peace and security in the region. South Africa, with its existing infrastructure and resources, could play an important role in such a regional mechanism.

183. The mission had extensive discussions on the election process in South Africa. It was explained that notwithstanding the administrative difficulties faced in the conduct of the elections, including the late decision by IFP to participate in the elections, the results were generally representative of public opinion. IEC made every effort to deal with the problems. The cooperation extended by SADF to IEC in the redistribution of voting materials, contributed significantly to re-establishing the former's credibility. As an indicator of the success of voter education, it was said that only 1 per cent of the total vote was invalid. Subsequent analysis by IEC concluded that in a 68 per cent sample of the vote, there was only a 2 per cent margin of error.

184. The presence of international observers had a salutary effect in promoting a peaceful atmosphere during the elections. IEC recognizes the importance of the international support of the election process, particularly that of UNOMSA and other observer groups. This support not only enhanced the credibility of the elections, but also helped in the very conduct of the elections.

185. The mission is satisfied that the democratization process in South Africa, the Constitutional Principles, the Interim Constitution and the political will of the South African leadership will enable the people and the Government of South Africa to achieve their objective of building a new, democratic and non-racial society.

186. After the elections, the new Parliament and the Government of National Unity face an intensive agenda. The immediate task for the Government of National Unity is to establish priorities for economic development which would most likely draw heavily upon the Reconstruction and Development Programme of ANC. The budget to be shortly presented by the Government would clearly indicate these priorities. It was, however, emphasized by many prominent personalities, including those from the media, church and business groups, that the Government would need to give a definite indication

of some progress in the areas of socio-economic development in the immediate time-frame. It was suggested by a business group and others that active support of business in South Africa towards those goals would generate substantial confidence of the people in the Government. The leaders also stressed that notwithstanding the availability of resources for such programmes, financial assistance from the international community would not only be desirable but also essential. It was also felt that "the end-of-apartheid dividend" might to a considerable extent be offset by the cost of dismantling several structures and administrative anomalies created by apartheid, in particular those relating to the homelands.

187. The Parliament, composed of the National Assembly and the Senate, has the task ahead of legislative action to give shape to the programmes of various ministries of the Government, including, in particular, the need for affirmative action to redress the socio-economic inequities in South Africa. In its capacity as the Constituent Assembly, the Interim Parliament will have the task of addressing the pending issues of federalism, provincial powers, minority rights in the field of education and culture, and the *volkstaat*. The process of constitutional review in the Constituent Assembly will be based on the Constitutional Principles as annexed to the Interim Constitution. It is expected that the final Constitution will be adopted within the two-year period as envisaged earlier, but the present Government will continue to function for a period of five years to promote national stability.

188. The mission believes that the role of the international community, in general, and the United Nations, in particular, in helping the people and the Government of South Africa to overcome the legacies of apartheid cannot be underestimated or overlooked. And to this end, an informal group of friends of South Africa in the General Assembly may be established to provide necessary support.

189. There are a number of issues of concern that require the continuing support of the international community. The mission believes that South Africa should be allowed to resume its seat in the General Assembly without further delay. South Africa has already been readmitted to a number of specialized agencies and other international organizations. The democratization process should be encouraged. Development assistance at the bilateral and multilateral levels to South Africa should be a priority item on the agenda of the States which are able to do so as well as international organizations. The United Nations should continue to be the catalyst for support and development assistance to South Africa. The mission would therefore recommend that, in consultation with the Government of South Africa, a high-level coordinator be appointed for all United Nations development activities in South Africa for

the next five years, that is, to coincide with the tenure of the Government of National Unity.

190. The mission was impressed with the determination of the South African leadership to cooperate at the bilateral, regional and multilateral levels to achieve those goals.

191. The mission is thankful for the cooperation it received from the Government of South Africa, the political parties, religious, business and other segments of the South African society, as well as for the recognition of the role of the United Nations and the Special Committee in the successful achievement by the people of South Africa in establishing a democratic, non-racial and United South Africa.

. . .

## VI. Conclusions and recommendations

197. With the entry into force, on 27 April 1994, of South Africa's first non-racial and democratic Constitution, and the holding of the first non-racial elections from 26 to 29 April 1994, apartheid came to an end.

198. This is, first of all, a victory for all South Africans of all races, and the success of their political leaders who have manifested an extraordinary degree of courage, wisdom and resilience in negotiating broad-based agreements for bringing apartheid to a peaceful end and for laying the foundations for a new, non-racial and democratic South Africa with equal and guaranteed rights for each and all.

199. The United Nations, the Special Committee and the international community at large can take just pride in the contribution they have made, over several decades, to the efforts leading to the elimination of apartheid, and the support they have given to all those South Africans who have courageously struggled against apartheid and suffered from it.

200. Also in this respect, the international community can take pride in the positive contributions made to the political process of negotiations and the electoral process itself by the presence and activities of the observer missions in South Africa of the United Nations, the Commonwealth, the European Union and OAU. The efforts of the Secretary-General of the United Nations, including his active support of the process through, *inter alia*, frequent contacts with the parties and his rapid actions to put into effect the mandates given to him by the Security Council and the General Assembly, deserves the appreciation of the international community.

201. The South African elections were held under markedly difficult circumstances, largely owing to the very short time available to IEC to make the necessary arrangements. While not flawless, however, South Africa's first non-racial and democratic elections were sufficiently free and fair. It was the observation of the heads

of the international observer missions in South Africa, including that of the United Nations, that the people of South Africa had expressed their determination to create a peaceful, non-racial and democratic South Africa.

202. The parties to the political multi-party process leading to the end of apartheid and a new non-racial South Africa have, in their dedication to pursue a peaceful settlement, developed habits and skills, and devised unique mechanisms for finding broadly agreed solutions, which hold out a promise for continued reconciliation and inclusiveness in the process of economic and social recovery and reconstruction that will now begin in South Africa.

203. As South Africa returns to the family of nations, we look forward to its contribution to the purposes of the United Nations.

204. The socio-economic disparities caused by apartheid need to be urgently addressed to ensure the stable and peaceful development of post-apartheid South Africa and, in this respect, assistance from the international community will be vital.

205. The system of apartheid having been brought to an end, the Special Committee against Apartheid established by the General Assembly on 6 November 1962 (resolution 1761 (XVII)) has fulfilled its mandate in accordance with the provisions of relevant General Assembly resolutions, in particular resolution 2671 (XXV) of 8 December 1970 and resolution S-16/1 of 14 December 1989, containing the Declaration on Apartheid and its Destructive Consequences in Southern Africa, and has successfully concluded its work.

---

# Document 216

*Final report of the Secretary-General on the question of South Africa*

S/1994/717, 16 June 1994

## I. Introduction

1. On 14 April 1994, I submitted a report to the Security Council on the situation in South Africa and the work of the United Nations Observer Mission (UNOMSA) in that country (S/1994/435). The present report, also submitted pursuant to Security Council resolutions 772 (1992) and 894 (1994) of 17 August 1992 and 14 January 1994, respectively, will be, happily, my last on the question of South Africa as regards the work of UNOMSA and the transitional process in that country.

## II. The transitional process in South Africa

2. For obvious reasons, my report will focus this time on the electoral mandate of UNOMSA and on the breathtaking developments that took place in South Africa during the month of April 1994, culminating in the holding of elections from 26 to 29 April 1994, the proclamation of the official results on 5 May 1994 and the memorable inauguration of the new President of the Republic of South Africa, Mr. Nelson Rolihlala Mandela, on 10 May 1994.

3. In my previous report I spoke of the mixed feelings of hope and fear shared by South Africans of all backgrounds and foreign observers alike as the date of the election neared: hopes arising from the determination of the main political players to see the process through to its logical conclusion, a substantially free and fair election, and fears because violence continued at an ever-increasing level and some significant political forces still refused to join the peace and reconciliation process and participate in the election.

4. The fears peaked on Monday, 28 March, when a public march organized in Johannesburg by Inkatha Freedom Party (IFP) followers in support of the demands of Zulu King Goodwill Zwelithini for a constitutional provision concerning the role of the King in the Interim Constitution ended in bloodshed, with over 50 people dead and 250 wounded.

5. The Security Council, concerned by the deplorable events in Johannesburg, held informal consultations on the subject. Consequently, the President of the Council for that month, His Excellency Mr. Jean-Bernard Mérimée, Ambassador of France, made the following statement on behalf of the Council members on 29 March 1994:

> "We deplore in the strongest possible terms yesterday's violence in Johannesburg, which is clearly aimed at derailing the South African transition process.

> "Intimidation, violence and provocation cannot be permitted to deny the South African people their opportunity to join the community of democratic States.

> "We call upon all the people of South Africa to eschew violence and hope that all parties will participate peacefully in the elections.

> "The Council reiterates the importance it attaches to the holding of the first general, free and democratic elections in South Africa on 27 April 1994, as previously agreed upon.

"The Council considers that this question is of the utmost importance and is determined to follow the election process closely."

6. In Johannesburg, my Special Representative and his colleagues the heads of the missions of the Organization of African Unity (OAU), the Commonwealth and the European Union (EU) called a press conference and made the following joint statement on 29 March:

"The international observer missions of the United Nations, the Organization of African Unity, the Commonwealth and the European Union deplore, in the strongest possible terms, the needless violence and loss of life in Johannesburg yesterday. The pain of these deaths is felt all the more strongly because they could have been prevented. The failure to plan adequately for yesterday's march, to define routes and to take steps for effective crowd control contributed to the violence. The tragic violence in Johannesburg, and events throughout the country in recent weeks, and even today, compel us to speak out.

"First, we must call for reason and responsibility on the part of political leaders. This means they must carry the message—and *actions*—of peace and democracy to all corners of the communities they claim to serve and represent. Failure by political leaders and security forces to act together to prevent a senseless slaughter is inexcusable. In this, the political parties, the Government and the security forces—at the community level and at the national level—share responsibility.

"Second, we must express our deepening concern over the impact of 'war talk', threats and challenges that are calculated to unleash emotions in the population. Such language, in the current critical stage, threatens the very future of this country.

"Third, we have repeatedly deplored the carrying of weapons in public demonstrations. The consequences of this practice were demonstrated only too clearly again yesterday. The time for words on this issue is past. Consequently, we strongly urge political leaders not to permit any marches that are not properly planned and in which their supporters are carrying weapons.

"Violence obviously frustrates the work of the Independent Electoral Commission. The IEC is already straining under the burden placed upon it, and the pressure increases daily. It is labouring, despite repeated political reverses and practical obstacles, to establish in time the infrastructure needed to put the vote within reach of all South Africans who wish to exercise that right. The IEC is also seeking to foster the climate necessary to guarantee that the election can be considered free and fair.

"In the current context, we call on President de Klerk, Mr. Mandela and Chief Buthelezi to find at their meeting tomorrow, 30 March, a way out of the present crisis and to create conditions for a peaceful transition.

"International observers are present throughout South Africa, providing us with detailed reports of what is happening in areas not always reached or covered by the media. We are, in a very real sense, side by side with South Africans. Observers were also present in the streets of Johannesburg yesterday, providing first-hand reports as the situation deteriorated. We are willing to discuss our observations with all parties which, in the interest of peace, are seeking to understand how yesterday's events unfolded.

"The international observer missions are in this country as sympathetic witnesses. But we are not passive witnesses. We are working closely with South Africans from the ground level up, in the hope of reinforcing their efforts to bring about democracy in their country. We continue to work closely with the national peace structures and all others engaged in initiatives that favour peace and dialogue. As our mandate sets forth, we are providing whatever support and assistance we can to South Africans who are committed to peace and democracy.

"We do this in cooperation with the Independent Electoral Commission, with leaders and members of all political parties and groups, with the Government and the Transitional Executive Council. Our common goal is to provide moral support and reassurance to South Africans who are committed to peaceful change through democratic means. Free political activity and a willingness to respect the right of others to hold opinions different from one's own are prerequisites for peace.

"The task of national reconciliation becomes more difficult with every death related to political violence. Reconciliation does not begin with elections, nor does it depend solely on initiatives at the national level. We appeal also to local and provincial leaders—be they traditional leaders or political representatives—to consider the lives of their people and their children before they embark on any action which could lead to further violence."

7. The events in Johannesburg contributed to increasing the tension—already very high—in KwaZulu as well as in the East Rand area of the Pretoria-Witwatersrand-Vereeniging (PWV) province. The political leaders,

nevertheless, remained undeterred in their determination that dialogue and constitutional negotiations must be kept going at all costs and that, somehow, solutions must be arrived at to allow the holding of a legitimate, credible and all-inclusive election. Thus, again and again, State President de Klerk met with King Goodwill Zwelithini or Chief Mangosuthu Buthelezi or both. Continuously, Mr. Mandela offered new suggestions and put forward new ideas. Similarly, the African National Congress (ANC) and the Government unceasingly engaged the IFP, the right wing and the homeland leaders in various talks to sort out differences, to address concerns and to come to new compromises.

8. However, the constitutional negotiations were further complicated by King Zwelithini's call on 18 March for the restoration of the Zulu kingdom. A meeting planned for that day between Mr. Mandela and the King to address the latter's concerns was cancelled, amid fears for the safety of Mr. Mandela. Faced with continued defiance on the part of KwaZulu authorities, on 23 March the Transitional Executive Council (TEC) authorized its management committee to take all steps necessary to ensure free and fair elections in KwaZulu. However, the KwaZulu Legislative Assembly rebuffed an attempt by Judge Johann Kriegler, Chairman of the IEC, on 24 March to secure the homeland administration's cooperation with the Commission in its efforts to prepare for and conduct the election. These developments, coupled with the upsurge in violence in KwaZulu/Natal following the events in Johannesburg, were probably decisive factors in the decision taken on 31 March by State President F. W. de Klerk to proclaim, with TEC support, a state of emergency in the province.

9. Another noteworthy political development was that the situation with respect to the so-called independent homelands dramatically changed as elections neared. The Bophuthatswana administration led by Lucas Mangope had repeatedly rejected participation in the elections. The result of the Mangope administration's intransigence was a popular uprising, accompanied by many deaths and extensive destruction of property, which culminated in the regime's overthrow. The TEC and the Government moved quickly to take over administration of the territory in order to prevent further bloodshed, restore order and prepare for the elections. The Bophuthatswana crisis reverberated in other homelands where demands and concerns were similar. Brigadier-General Oupa Gqozo, the leader of Ciskei, resigned under pressure on 22 March and was replaced by administrators appointed by the Government and the TEC.

10. A further meeting between President de Klerk, Mr. Mandela, Chief Buthelezi and King Zwelithini took place on 8 April in an attempt to reach an all-inclusive

political settlement and to secure IFP participation in the elections. No breakthrough was achieved, however, and violence continued at an alarming level in KwaZulu/Natal.

11. The agreement reached in March between Mr. Mandela and Chief Buthelezi to seek foreign help through international mediation to resolve the political impasse was revived and a team of mediators including Dr. Henry Kissinger and Lord Carrington was hastily called in. They arrived in the country on 12 April and were scheduled to start work the next day, but it was discovered that there was no agreement between the parties on the terms of reference for the talks. The election date emerged as the central issue, with the IFP demanding that the mediators address the question of whether the election should be held on the appointed date or postponed, while the Government and the ANC firmly held that the date could not be changed and that it should, therefore, remain outside the field of competence of the mediators.

12. Not having made any progress, the mediators left, but again the South African leaders refused to give up. A further, intense round of consultations took place in which Professor Washington Okumu, from Kenya, participated. Patience and determination at last paid off and, at a meeting on 19 April, the Government, the ANC and the IFP, led by President de Klerk, Mr. Mandela and Chief Buthelezi, reached agreement providing for:

(a) IFP participation in national and provincial elections to be held on the scheduled dates of 26, 27 and 28 April;

(b) Entrenchment of safeguards for the Zulu monarchy in the provincial constitution of KwaZulu/Natal;

(c) International mediation to address outstanding issues relating to the Zulu monarchy and regional powers, after the elections.

13. In a statement issued on 19 April, I welcomed the breakthrough agreement reached between State President F. W. de Klerk, ANC President Nelson Mandela and Chief Mangosuthu Buthelezi. I also addressed letters to the three leaders, congratulating them and expressing the hope that this historic decision would ensure that the elections, in which all South Africans would be able to participate, would take place later in the month under calm and peaceful conditions.

14. On 23 April, after protracted negotiations, the Government, the ANC and General Constand Viljoen, acting on behalf of the Freedom Front, signed an accord that provided for the establishment of a *Volkstaat* Council and further negotiations after the elections to discuss the feasibility of a *volkstaat*. This move was aimed at encouraging the right wing to participate in the elections and to pursue their objectives through peaceful negotiations.

15. The Multi-party Negotiating Council ap-

proved the agreement on 24 April. It also passed a resolution committing all parties to accept the election results. Parliament reconvened on 25 April and adopted amendments to the Interim Constitution and the Electoral Act, 1993, thus giving legislative effect to the agreement.

16. The IFP decision to participate in the elections resulted in an immediate and dramatic reduction in violence, and, for a while, the country experienced reduced tension and relative calm.

17. In all, a total of 19 parties participated in the elections at the national level. The Azanian People's Organization, the Black Consciousness Movement, the Conservative Party, and the Afrikaner Volksfront did not participate.

## III. Deployment and activities of observers of the United Nations Observer Mission prior to the elections

18. The operational plan contained in my report of 10 January 1994 to the Council (A/48/845-S/1994/16 and Add.1) called for the deployment of almost 2,000 United Nations observers during the election period. Following the approval by the General Assembly, in its resolution 48/230 B of 14 February 1994, of the financing for the expansion of UNOMSA, the staged deployment of observers proceeded rapidly. By the end of March 1994, 500 observers were deployed in a total of some 60 IEC operational locations. Also, it should be noted that bilateral agreements were concluded between the United Nations and Finland, the Netherlands, Sweden and Switzerland for the provision by their Governments of electoral observers for UNOMSA.

19. The final phase of deployment came during the period from 17 to 20 April 1994, when a total of 1,485 additional international electoral observers joined UNOMSA. The Joint Operations Unit developed the electoral deployment plan in consultation with the other intergovernmental observer missions, taking into account their additional 542 international electoral observers (OAU 102; Commonwealth 118; and EU 322). During the elections, observers fielded by the intergovernmental observer missions working in coordination with UNOMSA totalled 2,527 (including the Mission's own 1,985 observers).

20. Under its expanded mandate in accordance with Security Council resolution 894 (1994), UNOMSA continued its activities relating to peace promotion and the reduction of violence. Under the direction of the Mission's Peace Promotion Division, observers continued to assist and cooperate with the National Peace Accord structures. As the electoral period progressed, the Division expanded its network of contacts to include the Monitoring Directorate of the IEC.

21. In the run-up to the elections, observers' activi-

ties expanded to include observing and reporting on voter education, issuance of temporary voter's cards, and IEC attempts to select sites for and establish voting and counting stations. The UNOMSA peace promotion activities facilitated the Mission's electoral phase by providing access to grass-roots contacts and non-governmental organization networks built up during the Mission's first 16 months in the country. Information provided by UNOMSA observers to IEC monitors, both before and during the elections, allowed the latter constantly to address and resolve many problems.

22. UNOMSA officials continued to interact with political parties, attend rallies and other public events, investigate instances of intimidation and related complaints and work closely with the IEC and national, regional and local peace structures. Weekly meetings continued, at the level of heads or deputy heads of mission, between the intergovernmental observer missions and the National Peace Secretariat, but increasing emphasis was necessarily placed on interaction with the structures of the IEC. This took place both formally, through weekly meetings between the Coordinating Committee and the Chairman of the IEC and with directorate-level IEC officials and Commissioners at meetings of the Technical Task Force, and informally, through constant contacts conducted by my Special Representative, his Deputy and senior staff of the Electoral Division.

23. The frequency and level of violence, particularly in the townships of KwaZulu/Natal and PWV, reflected the continued uncertainty during the final stages of the negotiations among the political parties. The Human Rights Commission of South Africa recorded 450 politically related killings during the month of April—at least 311 in KwaZulu/Natal alone, the highest monthly toll recorded in more than four years. Although ANC-IFP rivalry was generally acknowledged as the prime cause of the killings, it failed to explain all incidents of violence. Many suspected that much township violence was orchestrated by an unknown "third force" linked to extremists seeking to derail the election process.

24. A Commission of Inquiry regarding the Prevention of Public Violence and Intimidation (Goldstone Commission) report of 18 March and a TEC report released on 29 March both implicated top South African police officers and members of the IFP in gun-running and political violence. Both reports appeared to confirm suspicions concerning the existence of a "third force" and its involvement in instigating political violence.

25. A series of initiatives by the Government, the ANC and mediators aimed at including the IFP in the process, as noted earlier, resulted in a breakthrough a week before the elections when, on 19 April, the IFP

announced that it would participate in the elections. With this announcement, there was an immediate and dramatic reduction in violence. Months of tension throughout the country, particularly in the warring townships of KwaZulu/Natal and PWV, eased perceptibly and levels of violence dramatically dropped.

26. Within days, however, concerns about a potential resurgence of violence were heightened when a car bomb exploded in Johannesburg near ANC headquarters on 24 April, marking the start of a cross-country spate of bombings. Some 21 people died in these attacks and some 200 were injured.

27. Tension was high and anonymous phone calls to various radio stations threatening that more was to come and that what would happen next would make the bombs of the last few days look like a picnic did not help matters. On 26 April, the day of special voting, a bomb went off at Johannesburg Airport, injuring a few people. Luckily no one was killed, although extensive damage was caused to property.

28. There was general concern about security and intimidation. Several questions were on everyone's mind: Would people be intimidated, stay home and refuse to vote? What would the reaction be if, as a result of the problems the IEC might not have solved by election day, some polling stations did not open on time or, for one reason or another, voting could not proceed as it should?

29. Highly conscious of these difficulties, the heads of the international observer missions called a press conference to appeal to people to remain calm and not to fall into the trap of provocation. Their statement made on 25 April read as follows:

"In less than 24 hours, South Africans of all races will at last be able to exercise the fundamental right to vote—for which they have waited so long.

"For over 18 months we have closely followed the transitional process. We welcome the recent agreements which have made the process more inclusive, allowing people of all political persuasions to participate in the elections. We hope that they will be able to do so peacefully and without any hindrance.

"We deplore in the strongest possible terms the violent incidents in Ulundi on Saturday, in Johannesburg on Sunday and continuing incidents calculated to instil fear in voters.

"We wish to emphasize the paramount importance of peaceful conduct during the voting, both at voting stations and in the surrounding communities. Political leaders and voters themselves should strictly observe the Electoral Code of Conduct. They should refrain from any activity which may disrupt the voting. Communities and security forces should ex-

tend the hand of cooperation to one another in the interest of maintaining peace and good order.

"We unanimously believe that in a very short period, the IEC has achieved an extraordinary feat in the work they have done to prepare for these elections. We have shared with the IEC our observations on the electoral process, in order to enhance the Commission's ability to detect and resolve difficulties. The IEC has been receptive to our comments, which we have always offered in a constructive and supportive spirit.

"In view of all the constraints that have complicated the IEC's work, and considering the enormous logistical tasks they face, we appeal to all South Africans to be patient and cooperative if they encounter problems, such as the late opening of voting stations, which might make voting a long and tiring exercise in certain areas.

"Voters should rest assured that their vote is secret. We welcome the pledge affirming the secrecy of the vote by leaders of political parties last week. We wholeheartedly welcome the resolution adopted unanimously on 20 April by the Multi-party Negotiating Council under which the parties pledge that they 'will accept the results of the election and will abide by the decision of the Independent Electoral Commission in respect of the fairness and freeness of the elections'. We urge all parties which have not explicitly endorsed this resolution to do so.

"By adhering to this principle, and acting in the interest of peace, democracy and national reconciliation, the people and political parties of South Africa will send a powerful message of national reconciliation to peoples around the world."

30. The security forces moved quickly and, almost immediately after the blast at the airport, arrested a number of extreme right-wing militants accused of having been amongst those who planted the bombs. No other bombs went off and in spite of continuing fears of violence during the voting period, South Africans came out in their millions, refusing to be intimidated and determined to make their voices heard; they queued for hours in calm, discipline and dignity, and voted.

## IV. Electoral process and organization

### A. *Legal framework*

31. The legal framework for the election was set out in the Constitution of the Republic of South Africa Act, 1993; the Independent Electoral Commission Act, 1993; the Electoral Act, 1993; the Independent Media Commission Act, 1993; and the Independent Broadcast-

ing Authority Act (1993). The Constitution of the Republic of South Africa Act and the Electoral Act were both amended significantly in the period immediately preceding the election. Changes to the Electoral Act were facilitated by an amendment adopted by Parliament that empowered the State President to amend the Act by proclamation in consultation with the IEC and the TEC.

32. Under the Independent Electoral Commission Act, 1993, the IEC was to consist of not less than seven and no more than 11 members, appointed by the State President upon the advice of the TEC. In accordance with the Act, the appointment as members of not more than five persons from the international community was made. The Electoral Act empowered the IEC to introduce regulations having the force of law on a wide range of topics. Several sets of regulations were, in fact, established by the IEC. The mandated objectives of the IEC were:

"(a)  To administer, organize, supervise and conduct, whether directly or indirectly, free and fair elections for the National Assembly and all other legislatures in terms of the Constitution and the Electoral Act;

"(b)  To promote conditions conducive to free and fair elections;

"(c)  To determine and certify the results of elections, and to certify to what extent such elections have been free and fair;

"(d)  To conduct voter education;

"(e)  To make and enforce regulations for the achievement of such objectives".

33. The Independent Electoral Commission Act provided for an Election Administration Directorate of the IEC, headed by a Chief Director, Administration. The position of Chief Director, Administration, carried a number of statutory functions under the Electoral Act. More generally, the Election Administration Directorate was that part of the bureaucratic structure of the IEC which was responsible for the actual preparation for and conduct of the polling.

34. Provision was also made for an Election Monitoring Directorate of the IEC, headed by a Chief Director, Monitoring. The Chief Director, Monitoring, was required under the Electoral Act to undertake the following tasks, among other things:

(a)  To appoint monitors to observe and report on the electoral process, including political meetings, canvassing, advertising and other campaigns. Such monitors were to work directly for the Election Monitoring Directorate;

(b)  To register observers (other than official observers from foreign Governments and intergovernmental organizations), and publish guidelines and if necessary a code of conduct binding on all such observers;

(c)  To facilitate the role of official observers from Governments and intergovernmental organizations, and provide them with information and assistance to enable them to perform their duties.

35. The Chief Director, Monitoring, was also given extensive powers to investigate electoral offenses, to issue and execute search warrants and to undertake mediation between parties to a dispute. Chapters VI, VII and VIII of the Independent Electoral Commission Act established a special hierarchical judicial structure for the purposes of the election, consisting of Electoral Tribunals, Electoral Appeal Tribunals and a Special Electoral Court. An Election Adjudication Secretariat was also created, the role of which was:

(a)  To coordinate the functions of the Electoral Tribunals, the Electoral Appeal Tribunals and the Special Electoral Court;

(b)  To perform the administrative work connected with the performance of the functions of those Tribunals and that Court.

36. For the purposes of the election, the Constitution divided South Africa into nine provinces. A Provincial Electoral Officer was to be appointed for each province, together with one or more deputies. According to the Electoral Act, the Provincial Electoral Officer would, subject to the control of the Chief Director, Administration, assume responsibility for the administration, organization, supervision and conduct of the election for both the National Assembly and the provincial legislature in the province in respect of which he or she had been appointed.

37. Each province was further divided into electoral districts, corresponding to the existing magisterial districts, and totalling 374 nationwide. For each district, a District Electoral Officer was appointed, together with one or more deputies. The District Electoral Officer was required, subject to the control of the Provincial Electoral Officer, to exercise delegated powers in relation to the administration, organization, supervision and conduct of the election in the electoral district. Within the 374 electoral districts there were to be established voting stations, some of them static and others mobile, each with a Presiding Officer. Presiding Officers were to be in charge of the overall management of their respective voting stations.

38. Each voting station was to have a staff of voting officers working under the direction of the Presiding Officer. The IEC initially estimated that there would be an average of about 18 voting officers per voting station. This figure was subsequently altered in view of the decision to issue separate ballot papers for elections to the

National Assembly and provincial legislatures.

39. The counting of the ordinary ballots in districts was to be conducted at counting stations rather than at voting stations. The IEC anticipated that ordinary votes from an average of about nine voting stations would be dealt with at each counting station. Each counting station was to be managed by a Counting Officer, assisted by enumerators.

### B. *Outline of prescribed election procedures*

40. Voting was to be by secret ballot. For each registered political party participating in the election, the ballot paper showed the party's name, its distinguishing mark or symbol (in colour), the abbreviated name of the party and a photograph of the leader(s) of the party or, in lieu thereof, a photograph of such other candidate as the party determined. Each voter was entitled to vote for a single registered political party—not individual candidates. The order of the parties on the ballot paper was to be alphabetical, except that the commencing letter of the alphabet was to be determined by lot.

41. No specific registration of voters took place prior to the election. Voters were therefore not required to produce any special voter registration card, but rather had to produce a voter's eligibility document, which, according to section 1 (LXVII) of the Electoral Act, meant:

"(*a*)  An identity document or a temporary identity certificate issued in terms of the Identification Act, 1986 (Act No. 72 of 1986), or any other applicable law of the Republic, as the case may be;

"(*b*)  A temporary voter's card;

"(*c*)  A reference book issued in terms of the repealed Blacks (Abolition of Passes and Coordination of Documents) Act, 1952 (Act No. 67 of 1952); or

"(*d*)  An identity document referred to in section 13 of the Population Registration Act, 1950 (Act No. 30 of 1950); and

"(*e*)  For the purpose of voting at any foreign voting station, also a valid South African passport".

42. Section 17 of the Electoral Act provided for the issuance of temporary voter's cards. The IEC and the Director-General of the Department of Home Affairs, under the supervision of the IEC, were empowered to issue such cards to persons eligible to vote.

43. The voting period was to consist of one day for "special votes", Tuesday, 26 April 1994, followed by two days for general voting, Wednesday, 27 April and Thursday, 28 April. Wednesday, 27 April 1994, was to be a public holiday. The hours of polling on each voting day were to be from 7 a.m. to 7 p.m. During the election, votes were to be cast at static voting stations (which were to remain open for voting at one place on both general voting days) and at mobile voting stations (which were to move from place to place during the course of the polling period). The District Electoral Officer for the district in which a mobile voting station was to operate was required to make known the locations and estimated times at which the mobile voting station would function during voting day. The Electoral Act also provided that the Presiding Officer of a mobile voting station, any other Electoral Officer and any prescribed number of party voting agents might enter upon any land or building with such mobile voting station for the purposes of voting.

44. A voter was entitled to vote at the voting station of his or her choice, and a vote so cast was counted in respect of the province in which the voting station was located. Voters were not subject to any requirement to vote in the province or district in which they were ordinarily resident. There were to be two different ways of recording a vote. It was envisaged that most voters would cast an "ordinary ballot". They were simply to be issued with a ballot paper, which they would then mark and place directly in the ballot box. However, a voter was to be entitled to record a "special vote" (a) if he or she, because of his or her illness or physical infirmity or physical disability or, in the case of a woman voter, her pregnancy, would not be able to attend a voting station at any time during the voting hours on the days specified for general voting; or (b) if he or she was a convicted prisoner or a person awaiting trial being detained, who was not legally excluded from voting.

45. In practice, the distinction between ordinary and special voting became blurred. The Electoral Act had originally provided that the ballot paper marked by a person recording a special vote would not be placed directly in a ballot box, but would instead be placed in a ballot paper envelope, which would then be placed in an outer envelope. The outer envelope would then be handed to the Presiding Officer of the voting station and placed by him or her in a sealed ballot box. The Act had also provided that a person wishing to record a special vote would be required, by means of a declaration under oath or affirmation in a prescribed form, to satisfy the Presiding Officer that he or she was entitled to record a special vote, and would not be able to attend a voting station at any time during voting hours on any day for general voting. Prior to the election, the Electoral Act was amended to delete both the requirement to place special votes in envelopes and the requirement for the making of oaths or affirmations in support of applications for special votes.

46. The IEC was also obliged by the Electoral Act to establish such number of foreign voting stations out-

side the Republic at such locations, including South African diplomatic missions, as it might consider appropriate in order to facilitate the casting of votes by voters who were outside the Republic during the voting period. A voter at a foreign voting station was to be required to specify at the time of voting the province in respect of which his or her vote was to be counted at the election. Each registered political party was to be entitled to appoint voting agents to monitor the conduct of the election at the voting stations and the counting process.

47. A qualified voter who had not voted previously at the election was to be entitled to vote. The question of whether or not a person was a qualified voter was to be determined by his or her producing a voter's eligibility document. If everything appeared to be in order, the person was to be regarded as entitled to vote and was, after showing that he or she had not voted previously at the election, to be allowed to cast an ordinary ballot. The question of whether or not a person had voted before was to be dealt with in a much more basic way. When a person was actually issued with a ballot paper, his or her fingers were to be marked with an indelible dye visible only under ultraviolet light. When a person applied to vote, his or her fingers were to be examined to determine whether they had already been marked with the dye. A voter whose fingers had been marked was not to be allowed to vote.

48. A duly appointed party election or voting agent was to be entitled to object formally to a person's right to vote. The Electoral Act provided that an objection could only be made on the ground (a) that the voter was not the person described in the voter's eligibility document which he or she had submitted; (b) that the voter had already voted in the election; or (c) that the voter was not entitled to vote.

49. Once it had been determined that a person was entitled to vote, he or she was to be issued with a ballot paper. He or she was then to (a) proceed alone to the screened voting compartment within the voting station; (b) mark the ballot paper by placing a cross or other clear mark against the party for which he or she wished to vote; (c) display the ballot paper to a voting officer at the ballot box in such a way that the official mark stamped on the back of the ballot paper could be clearly recognized; and (d) place the ballot paper in the ballot box.

50. A blind or otherwise disabled voter could be assisted in marking his or her vote by (a) a person of his or her choice, who had to be at least 18 years old; or (b) by the Presiding Officer, in the presence of at least two monitors, South African or international observers or, in their absence, any two other IEC officials. An illiterate voter was to be entitled to be assisted only by the Presiding Officer, in the presence of at least two monitors, observers or international observers or, in their absence, any two other IEC officials.

51. The counting of ordinary votes cast at static and mobile voting stations was to take place at predetermined counting centres. After the close of the poll on the last day of polling, the ballot boxes containing ordinary ballots were to be sealed and dispatched under guard to the District Electoral Officer or a designated Deputy District Electoral Officer. Votes were then to be counted as follows:

(a) The seals applied to the ballot boxes were to be inspected to confirm that they had not been tampered with. The ballot boxes were then to be opened and the ballot papers they contained were to be check-counted. Any inconsistencies between this ballot paper count and the records provided by the Presiding Officer were then to be examined, a record of them was to be made and the Chief Director, Administration, was to be informed;

(b) The ballot papers were then to be checked for correct marking. Any invalidly marked ballots were to be rejected and the remaining ballots were then to be sorted according to the party for which the voter voted. The numbers of votes recorded for each party were then to be counted;

(c) After all ordinary and special votes had been counted, the IEC was to determine the total number of votes each registered party had received overall and in respect of each province, and was to determine the number of seats won by each party in the National Assembly and the various provincial legislatures.

### C. *Problems faced by the Independent Electoral Commission*

52. In implementing the procedures described above, the IEC faced a number of severe constraints. Firstly, in contrast to the situation prevailing in many other countries, the IEC had no independent opportunity to advise the Government as to the feasibility of the chosen election dates, since the dates were determined well before the creation of the IEC. The time-frame within which the Commission was expected not only to conduct the elections, but also to establish a large and complex electoral administrative structure, was extraordinarily short and problematical.

53. In addition, a number of significant changes to voting procedures, agreed at the political level after the IEC had commenced its work, created massive practical problems. The most significant of these changes were (a) the decision to use different ballot papers for the National Assembly and provincial legislature elections; and (b) the decision taken, only one week before the election, to include the IFP on the ballot papers. The IEC was also

faced with great difficulties in mounting its operation in the former homelands. In Bophuthatswana, the IEC was prevented from undertaking preparatory work in the field until the Mangope regime fell and was replaced by administrators. In Transkei, major problems arose from the fact that Transkei identity documents had not been issued for several years. Finally, in KwaZulu, severe obstacles were placed in the way of the IEC until the IFP decided, only a week before the commencement of the polling, to join the electoral process.

### D. *The electoral mandate of the United Nations Observer Mission*

54. The mandate of UNOMSA in relation to the observation of the elections was spelt out in paragraphs 56 to 59 of my report of 10 January 1994 (A/48/845-S/1994/16 and Add.1) and agreed to by the Security Council in its resolution 894 (1994) of 14 January. Specifically, in paragraph 57 it was proposed that under its expanded mandate UNOMSA would be required, among other things, to:

"(*a*) Observe the actions of the Independent Electoral Commission and its organs in all aspects and stages of the electoral process, verifying their compatibility with the conduct of a free and fair election under the Independent Electoral Commission and Electoral Acts;

"(*b*) Observe the extent of freedom of organization, movement, assembly and expression during the electoral campaign and ascertain the adequacy of the measures taken to ensure that political parties and alliances enjoy those freedoms without hindrance or intimidation;

"(*c*) Monitor the compliance of the security forces with the requirements of the relevant laws and the decisions of the Transitional Executive Council;

"(*d*) Verify the satisfactory implementation of the dispositions of the Independent Media Commission and the Independent Broadcasting Authority Acts;

"(*e*) Verify that the voter education efforts of the electoral authorities and other interested parties are sufficient and will result in voters being adequately informed on both the meaning of the vote and its procedural aspects;

"(*f*) Verify that qualified voters are not denied the identification documents or temporary voter's cards that will allow them to exercise their right to vote;

"(*g*) Verify that voting occurs on election days in an environment free of intimidation and in conditions which ensure free access to voting stations and the secrecy of the vote; and verify that adequate

measures have been taken to ensure proper transport and custody of ballots, security of the vote count and timely announcement of results;

"(*h*) Coordinate the activities of observers from international governmental organizations and foreign Governments so as to ensure that they are deployed in an effective and coordinated manner; establish effective cooperation with South African and foreign non-governmental organizations, which will also monitor the electoral process."

### E. *Observation and verification methodology adopted by the United Nations Observer Mission*

55. Shortly after the expansion of its mandate, the Observer Mission developed plans for the observation and verification methodology. In relation to the observation called for in subparagraph 57 (*a*) of my report of the actions of the Independent Electoral Commission, a distinction was drawn between the central preparations by the IEC for the election, which would be monitored from the headquarters of the Mission, with extensive liaison with the IEC on issues of concern, and the IEC's field preparations, which would be monitored by field staff, in accordance with guidelines developed centrally. Monitoring of field preparations focused specifically on (a) establishment by the IEC of essential field structures; (b) choice of premises for voting stations; and (c) provision of staff and equipment for voting stations.

56. Observation of the extent of freedom of organization, movement, assembly and expression (subpara. 57 (*b*)) was undertaken by field staff of the Mission, in accordance with precise guidelines that drew heavily on the extensive experience with such observation developed by UNOMSA prior to the expansion of its mandate.

57. Verification of the sufficiency and effectiveness of the voter education process (subpara. 57 (*e*)) was undertaken both centrally and by field staff of the Mission. Guidelines and documentation relating to the observation of voter education events were issued on 4 March 1994. Verification of the non-denial to voters of identity documents that would entitle them to vote (subpara. 57 (*f*)) was undertaken by field staff in accordance with guidelines developed centrally and issued on 2 March 1994. The verification called for in subparagraph 57 (*g*) of the report was undertaken as a coordinated operation involving all four international observer missions. For the purposes of the operation a manual and associated reporting forms were jointly developed by all four missions.

58. At all stages of the process, UNOMSA faced significant difficulties in that many of its tasks were directly dependent on the performance of the IEC. For example, the legal framework for the election continued

to undergo changes until literally days before the commencement of polling: the critical amendments to the Electoral Act providing for the inclusion of the IFP on the ballot via the attachment of stickers to all ballots were made only five days before the polling commenced. There were also frequent procedural changes: the IEC issued 19 "Technical Updates" to its own staff between 13 and 25 April 1994. Finally, the Commission's tardiness in definitively identifying voting stations created major problems for UNOMSA in planning coordinated itineraries for observers.

### F. Actions of the Independent Electoral Commission and its organs

59. UNOMSA was able, with the cooperation of the IEC, to observe closely its preparations for the election. In the field, UNOMSA maintained close liaison with local IEC representatives and many problems were solved directly at that level. Other problems were referred to IEC headquarters in Johannesburg. While a great deal was achieved by the IEC in a short space of time, shortcomings in IEC performance and looming problem areas were identified by UNOMSA shortly after the mission's mandate was expanded. The following specific issues were discussed early in March 1994 by the Coordinating Committee, comprising the heads of the four international observer missions, and were canvassed in discussions between UNOMSA and the Chairman of the IEC. At the beginning of March 1994:

(a) Only a minute fraction of the IEC field staff necessary for the conduct of the election had been appointed. This represented a major slippage of deadlines earlier spelt out by the IEC to the four international observer missions. Neither the District Electoral Officers nor the Presiding Officers had been appointed and when such provincial staff were appointed they were working out of offices that were scarcely functional;

(b) Major delays in the accurate identification of polling station sites were apparent. It was clear that this problem, related to the late deployment of field staff, had the potential to disrupt in a significant way much of the other election planning, which depended on accurate knowledge of voting station locations;

(c) The IEC's ballot box requirement had increased threefold in the preceding three weeks, owing (i) to the requirement for a separate ballot box into which the provincial ballots were to be deposited; and (ii) to the requirement set out in regulation 34 (3) of the Electoral Regulations for a further ballot box in which disputed ballot papers were to be deposited. In early March, the IEC estimated its requirement for ballot boxes at 126,000, of which only 33,003 were on hand;

(d) It could be expected that the service provided to voters would be manifestly better in the low-density areas in which people had voted before than in the high-density townships where voters would be novices;

(e) The IEC had no plausible plan in place for securely consolidating, packing, warehousing and distributing critical electoral equipment and materials. Since the development of such a plan invariably requires detailed input from the field, elaborate marshalling of usually scarce resources (vehicles, drivers, aircraft, etc.) and significant lead times, the absence of a stable IEC field structure to undertake these tasks was seen at the time as a critical failing;

(f) UNOMSA noted that the sheer number of ballot boxes, ballot papers and other voting materials required meant that their secure movement and storage before, during and after the polling would be a massive logistical operation. As at early March 1994, no plausible plan for that operation was in place. On the one hand this reflected the late development of an overall security plan; but again the absence of field staff to fill in the details required for such a plan was critical;

(g) It was unclear what mechanism was proposed by the IEC for the compilation and announcement of the election results. Such a mechanism was one which had not been required in the same form at previous South African elections, which were constituency-based and had not required a timely tallying of national voting figures. The area is one which is notoriously fraught with complications; and it was, moreover, clear that the exercise would have to be undertaken at a time when the IEC would be under great pressure;

(h) Complex computer systems were being developed under a highly attenuated system development lifecycle, with few if any specifications being given to analyst programmers and with inadequate time for proper testing. Because of this, there was a relatively high probability that they would fail, under the public gaze, when put into operation.

60. The above major systemic issues continued to be a predominant concern to UNOMSA throughout preparations for the elections. Constructive representations made by UNOMSA on the issues were welcomed by the IEC. The Special Representative, in his meetings with the IEC Chairman, UNOMSA officers working at the technical level in daily contact with IEC officers, as well as field staff in meetings with their IEC counterparts expressed concerns of the Mission up to the time of the election. Many more specific and technical issues were also raised informally with the IEC.

61. It was not possible for the IEC to solve all problems identified by UNOMSA for several reasons. IEC field staff were appointed too late in the process. Many of them were still not functioning on a sound basis

at election time. Until just days before the election, voting station sites remained problematical in a number of areas, notably in KwaZulu/Natal, Eastern Cape, and parts of PWV. This contributed substantially to the many practical problems that arose during the polling. IEC plans for the timely and secure distribution of election materials remained manifestly inadequate in many areas of the country, with major consequences: proper accounting for and control of the movement of sensitive items such as ballot papers was lost in many areas. In addition, poor planning of the movement of ballot boxes to counting centres contributed substantially to delays in the conduct of the count. Finally, the IEC experienced difficulties with critical computer systems and was forced to replace the computerized tallying of voting figures with a more reliable manual system.

62. These systemic problems virtually guaranteed that a significant proportion of the electorate would experience some difficulty in voting. In view of this, the Special Representative and the heads of the other international observer missions convened a press conference on 25 April in which they urged South Africans to remain peaceful and patient if they encountered problems such as delays in the opening of voting stations (see para. 30 above).

## V. Electoral observation

### A. *Voter education*

63. Voter education was a key component in the organization of South Africa's first elections by universal suffrage. The elections presented a huge educational task. The vast majority of the electorate of nearly 20 million were first-time voters. The electoral procedures would also differ from those followed in previous elections and people would be voting for a new form of government. Voter education programmes aimed at reaching all potential voters but focused in particular on those previously disenfranchised. Programmes were needed to reach a target audience—of whom one half or more were illiterate or semi-literate—speaking a variety of languages. The majority were to be found in peri-urban and rural areas, many out of the reach of newspapers, television and, in some cases, radio. Special measures were therefore needed to reach beyond mainstream modes of communication.

64. UNOMSA was required to verify that the voter education efforts of the electoral authorities and other interested parties were sufficient and would result in voters being adequately informed about both the meaning of the vote and its procedural aspects. A Voter Education Section, established as part of the Electoral Division, was charged with making this assessment. UNOMSA observers re-

viewed the programmes of major implementing organizations and liaised with and reviewed the work of the national and provincial voter education staff of the IEC. They also assessed the state of voter education in each province and monitored media initiatives nationwide.

65. Motivation amongst the electorate to vote was generally high, but new voters needed detailed information about the voting process in order to instil confidence and minimize the number of spoilt ballots. Convincing people of the secrecy of the ballot was particularly important. Many potential voters lacked the requisite voter eligibility documents and needed explanations about how to obtain them. It was essential, however, that the voter education campaign go beyond the technical aspects of the electoral process to address the issue of the nature and process of democracy and the role of elections.

### 1. *Implementation of voter education campaigns*

66. Among the groups carrying out voter education were church groups, trade unions, civic organizations, business groups and other non-governmental organizations, as well as commercial companies and political organizations. A significant proportion of voter education was funded by the international community. Recognizing the need for a coordinated and consolidated approach to voter education, the Independent Forum for Electoral Education, a coalition of 32 organizations, was formed in October 1993. Through its Commission on Voter Education and Training, the Forum facilitated coordination of its members' activities and sharing of materials.

### 2. *Direct non-partisan voter education*

67. Many organizations initially emphasized training voter educators. Thousands of people attended nationwide workshops held between mid-1992 and throughout 1993. Several organizations developed reading materials. Thousands of workshops were organized nationwide and attended by hundreds of thousands of people. Mobile units showing videos and distributing written materials in various languages visited places where gaps in coverage had been detected. Pamphlets, booklets and sample ballot papers were widely distributed at events, through door-to-door programmes, from information kiosks, at taxi ranks and stations and by many other means.

68. UNOMSA observers reported that over 90 per cent of the events they attended included clear and effective presentations covering the secrecy of the ballot, democratic principles and values, and election procedures.

### 3. *The role of the Independent Electoral Commission*

69. The Voter Education Directorate of the IEC was charged with carrying out the voter education mandate. The Directorate was to identify and fill existing gaps

in coverage by using its own resources and those of the more than 100 organizations whose programmes it accredited.

70. The immensity of the task was such that, in addition to commissioning organizations, the IEC hired voter educators, many of whom had been previously trained by non-governmental organizations. They worked in all provinces, with several thousand deployed in critical areas such as Bophuthatswana in the North-West Province and, in the final week of the electoral campaign, throughout KwaZulu/Natal. During March and April, several million leaflets, booklets and sample ballot papers and 5,000 videos on the voting process were distributed as part of an intensive information campaign. The IEC media campaign, which commenced in February, broadcast and published information that, *inter alia*, clarified its role, assured the electorate of the secrecy of the ballot, described eligibility documents and provided updates on electoral procedures. Several political parties included voter education as an integral part of their political campaign activities.

### 4. *The media and voter education*

71. Voter education on radio and television began in earnest in late 1993 following the formation of the Democracy Education Broadcast Initiative, with groups such as the Independent Forum for Electoral Education, the Institute for a Democratic Alternative for South Africa, the Business Election Fund and the Initiative itself producing an array of voter education programming aired for up to 41 hours per week. Radio programmes were transmitted on the South African Broadcasting Corporation's 21 radio services in different languages. Television programming included informational productions using drama, documentary, animation and puppets. Several political debates were also broadcast on television and radio. Newspaper campaigns addressed issues such as the secrecy of the ballot and identification documents, and also motivated people to vote.

### 5. *Problems and constraints affecting voter education*

72. Voter education was hampered by resource constraints, including personnel and equipment. Problems with transportation had a negative effect on the ability of groups to work extensively in remote rural areas. Delays in establishing the IEC Voter Education Directorate and in deploying provincial staff exacerbated time constraints. The voter educators' job was complicated by the several late revisions in electoral procedures, such as the decision in February to change from a single- to a double-ballot system. These procedural changes were also often not reported by the IEC to the relevant organizations in an efficient manner.

73. Access also posed a problem in several areas. Voter education for farm workers was limited as many organizations were unable to gain access to farms. Until the change of administration in Bophuthatswana in March, restrictions on election-related activity made the implementation of programmes in that area very difficult. A number of "voter education no-go areas" existed in KwaZulu/Natal where, on several occasions, voter educators were harassed. Several were killed.

74. The massive voter education campaign carried out in preparation for South Africa's first fully democratic elections, although concentrated in urban and peri-urban areas and often limited to explanations of the voting procedure, reached the majority of the electorate. Relatively few voters needed assistance at the polls due to illiteracy. The high voter turnout, the low number of spoilt ballots (0.99 per cent) and the fact that in most areas most voters proceeded smoothly through the process indicated that most people had been adequately informed and motivated to vote.

### B. *Identity documents*

75. Although a range of documents could be presented at voting stations as voter's eligibility documents, in practice the time lags involved in issuing such documents gave rise to the need for temporary voter's cards, which could be issued to applicants at the time at which their applications were made. Although the voting population requiring temporary voter's cards was variously estimated as between 2 and 4 million, no reliable figures were available.

76. UNOMSA's observation of the process of issuing temporary voter's cards during the weeks preceding the election indicated that the quality of performance of the card-issuing authorities was very uneven: while in some areas units were issuing cards at a rate of about one every 10 minutes, elsewhere the process took up to two hours. Very often inadequate measures were taken to publicize the existence or opening hours of temporary voter's card units, with the result that output was unacceptably low. In some areas, people already possessing valid voter's eligibility documents applied for temporary voter's cards as well, thereby preventing the process from properly serving those in genuine need.

77. Numerous allegations were made regarding irregularities in the issuing of temporary voter's cards. These encompassed such alleged practices as the issuing of cards to underage persons; confiscation of cards by chiefs and farmers; misuse of baptismal certificates as supporting documents for applications; contrived shortages of mobile card centres where they were most needed; refusal to issue cards to persons who had applied for substantive identity documents; contrived shortages of forms; lack of cameras and other necessary issuing equip-

ment; bias in favour of one or another party (e.g. dispatch of mobile centres only to areas populated by party supporters, establishment of centres in political party offices); demands for payment by card-issuing officials; refusal to issue temporary voter's cards to South African citizens resident and working in neighbouring countries; and issuing of cards to immigrant workers from neighbouring countries. However, apart from the observed shortcomings in the publicizing of the operation in certain areas, the irregularities were as a rule not backed by official and duly substantiated complaints.

78. In a number of "no-go areas" card-issuing officials' lives were threatened or they were otherwise prevented by the local community from operating. This problem was tackled with some success by the IEC, through concentrated campaigns in the affected areas. Notwithstanding these problems, by the time of the election it was clear that in most parts of the country, major and substantially successful efforts had been made to ensure that voters were given a proper opportunity to obtain the documents they required. The political parties themselves were substantially satisfied with the progress made in this regard. In areas where problems remained until election time, last-minute difficulties were addressed by operating card-issuing centres near the voting stations during the polling.

## C. *Conduct of the polling*

79. On 26 April 1994, the day reserved for special voting, observers visited and reported upon a total of 2,960 special voting points. The most striking findings of their reports were that election materials were in short supply at 23.44 per cent of special voting stations, while voting procedures were correctly applied in 73.72 per cent of the stations visited. The pattern of inadequacy was uneven across the country: the province of Northern Transvaal was conspicuously the worst overall, with procedures observed to have been correctly applied at only 42.08 per cent of special voting points visited and sufficient electoral materials and supplies at only 56.71 per cent of the stations. There was also considerable variation within provinces: while, for example, performance overall was good in Western Cape and Eastern Cape, major problems were experienced with the delivery of election materials in the townships in the Cape Flats area of Western Cape, and throughout the former homelands of Transkei and Ciskei in Eastern Cape. The East Rand of PWV also proved to be a particular problem area, with severe shortages of materials at a large number of special voting points. In the course of the day, observers provided frequent oral reports regarding problems through the UNOMSA communications system, many of which were fed directly to the IEC's crisis centre for prompt remedial action.

80. Shortages were experienced in supplies of ballot boxes, ballot papers, ultraviolet lights and invisible ink. In response, the IEC attempted to redeploy materials, obtained additional ultraviolet lights from Lesotho, had additional invisible ink manufactured and printed additional ballot papers within the country. The printing and distribution of these additional ballot papers was poorly controlled by the IEC: in a number of areas of the country great uncertainty existed as to what materials had been supplied to specific voting stations, significantly complicating the process of accounting for electoral materials at the commencement of the count, as required by law.

81. Also on 26 April, United Nations observers monitored voting at 119 foreign voting stations in 57 countries. This was managed by the Electoral Assistance Unit in New York, with extensive assistance from the United Nations Development Programme (UNDP) offices and United Nations information centres. A similar methodology of observation was applied to that adopted within South Africa: an observation form was completed at each foreign voting station and sent to the Electoral Assistance Unit for compilation and analysis of statistics. Overall, no major problems were reported: 76 per cent of the observers viewed the electoral process at foreign voting stations as satisfactory, while the rest determined that the process had been satisfactory with minor problems.

82. On 27 and 28 April, observers in South Africa visited 7,430 of the 8,478 voting stations. Late fluctuations in the proposed numbers of voting stations in various parts of the country made it impossible to achieve 100 per cent coverage. The pattern of performance observed was broadly similar to that of 26 April. Some improvement in the correct implementation of procedures was noted, with 81.13 per cent of voting stations observed to be applying procedures correctly. Problems continued with the supply of materials, however: only 75.71 per cent of voting stations observed had a sufficient supply of materials. UNOMSA continued to convey to the IEC details of specific problems observed in the field.

83. As a result of the major problems encountered with the polling, on the evening of 27 April a decision was taken to declare 28 April a public holiday. On the evening of 28 April, polling was extended to 29 April in Transkei, Ciskei, Venda, Lebowa, Gazankulu and KwaZulu. A total of 47 observer teams were deployed to observe the extended polling in Transkei and Ciskei; 65 teams were deployed in KwaZulu/Natal; and 68 teams were deployed in Lebowa, Gazankulu and Venda.

84. The problems were manifestations of systemic problems that the international observer missions had raised with the IEC in the months preceding the election. The patience and forbearance shown by the voters them-

selves prevented these problems from carrying more serious consequences for the overall legitimacy of the electoral process.

85. After the end of the voting, on 30 April, my Special Representative in South Africa and the heads of the observer missions of the Commonwealth, EU and OAU issued a statement in which they stated that:

"With the end of voting in these historic national and provincial elections in South Africa, in which all South Africans could vote for the first time, we the heads of Mission of the United Nations, Organization of African Unity, Commonwealth, and European Union election observer groups have jointly agreed on an interim assessment of the process up until the end of voting and before counting is completed. Our assessment is based on the work of more than 2,500 election observers deployed throughout the country, under the coordination of the United Nations.

"We have benefited from the work of colleagues representing our organizations who have been in South Africa since late 1992, supporting the peace structures and observing the transitional process. They were concerned in particular with the central problems of violence and intimidation.

"While the time-frame for these elections was determined in the Multi-party Negotiation Process almost one year ago, the Independent Electoral Commission (IEC) was set up only in December 1993. From the outset it was faced with the extraordinarily difficult task of mounting elections in four months, a task which normally would have demanded much more time. The Commission was required to cater for the entire voting population, including the former homelands, and for South Africans overseas.

"The people of South Africa clearly demonstrated their commitment to the end of apartheid and the transformation to non-racial democracy by turning out in enormous numbers to vote—most for the first time in their lives. They did so with obvious patience and enthusiasm—and not a little stoicism.

"Queues formed from the early hours of the first day of voting and at many stations were several kilometres long even before voting began. People evidently felt confident about the arrangements for voting and in particular the secrecy of the ballot. We are satisfied that the people of South Africa were able to participate freely in the voting.

"The escalation of violence was widely predicted and feared and did not happen. In a remarkable departure from recent trends there was a dramatic reduction in the scope and intensity of violence during the polling. A spate of bombs which led to the brutal and senseless killing of 21 people and injuring of hundreds in the days leading up to and even during the poll failed to intimidate and deter the voters. The voting days themselves were virtually free of any significant evidence of intimidation.

"It is not surprising, given the short lead time to organize the elections and the constant changes typified by the last-minute political decision to place an additional party on the ballot papers, that major administrative and logistical problems were experienced. These included: difficulties in the provision of identity documents, including temporary voter's cards; the late recruitment of polling staff; the delayed and constantly changing decisions on the siting of polling stations; shortcomings in the supply, control and delivery of voting materials; and uncertainties, even during the voting days, concerning administrative regulations.

"The IEC remained firmly committed throughout to ensuring that every eligible South African who wished to vote could do so. In that endeavour, we maintained a fruitful and open dialogue with the Chairman of the IEC and his fellow Commissioners, who were always responsive to our suggestions.

"Constructive intervention of the IEC's own monitoring mechanisms in many cases not only identified the problems but found solutions to them. We were impressed too with the efficiency, dedication and perseverance shown by the many thousands of well trained IEC voting officials.

"We also commend members of the army and the police for their professional approach to the particular demands placed on them, including assistance at critical times with the transport of election materials. We also take this opportunity to express our gratitude to them for the constant cooperation they gave us. We commend the many thousands of peace monitors who contributed to the achievement of a peaceful election.

"What we have observed, over the four days of voting from 26 to 29 April 1994, has been a great achievement for South Africa: a people who have, in the past, been systematically separated came together in a historic national expression of their determination to create a peaceful, non-racial and democratic South Africa."

### D. *Conduct of the counting*

86. The systemic problems identified and conveyed to the IEC well before the election were again manifest in the counting. Staff had been recruited late and many had

not been properly trained. Inadequate planning for the arrival of ballot boxes and other materials at counting centres caused much confusion and delay. In many cases reconciliation of ballot papers found in ballot boxes to ballot papers provided to voting stations proved difficult or impossible, because records of materials issued were inadequate.

87. The extent to which UNOMSA was able to monitor the actual conduct of the count was limited by the need, for budgetary reasons, to withdraw most international electoral observers before the end of the count. This problem was compounded by the IEC's decision to postpone the start of the counting by one day, from 29 to 30 April, owing to the extension of voting in some areas; and by the fact that the count took much longer than the IEC had anticipated. It was not until Thursday, 5 May, that the IEC was able to announce the final election results. In addition, the IEC's decision to conduct round-the-clock counting at some 700 separate "counting streams" meant that it was impossible for UNOMSA to cover the counting process fully. My Special Representative therefore decided, on the recommendation of the Joint Operations Unit, that counting at a sample number of stations should be observed.

88. Reports were received on the conduct of the process at a total of 458 counting stations. In general, these reports again revealed problems that were a manifestation of broader systemic failings within the IEC. Observers' reports indicated that only 84.06 per cent of counting stations had sufficient staff and facilities to ensure uninterrupted counting. At only 78.82 per cent of counting stations were the prescribed procedures for the delivery of materials adhered to. At only 74.45 per cent of counting stations were the official ballot paper reconciliation procedures adhered to; in fact this reflected, at least in part, a decision, announced by the Chairman of the IEC after the start of the count, that the reconciliation procedures had proved too onerous and were to be modified. In only 81.66 per cent of counting stations were the official counting procedures observed to have been strictly adhered to.

89. In certain parts of the country allegations of fraudulent interference with ballot materials emerged during the counting. It was not possible for UNOMSA to make an independent judgement on these allegations.

### E. Observation of the media

90. Among the tasks of the Public Information and Media Analysis Section of UNOMSA was that of verifying the satisfactory implementation of and compliance with the Independent Media Commission and Independent Broadcasting Authority Acts. The Section observed the work of the Independent Media Commission (IMC) and Independent Broadcasting Authority (IBA) established under those acts.

### 1. Independent Media Commission

91. The IMC was established on 22 January 1994 to ensure equitable treatment of all political parties by broadcasting services, and to ensure that State-financed publications and State information services were not used to advance the interests of any political party. With respect to broadcasting, the IMC issued editorial guidelines for broadcasters that set standards for equitable treatment. The IMC also granted political parties free air time for party election broadcasts on public service radio stations, according to a formula calculated to ensure equitable treatment.

92. The South African Communications Services monitored the media on behalf of the Commission's Broadcasting Directorate, measuring the length of broadcasts allocated to political parties by various broadcast services. The Media Monitoring Project, an independent monitoring service, also provided qualitative daily monitoring reports to the Broadcasting Directorate. The Directorate used the data provided to evaluate the media's treatment of political parties and also attempted to resolve disputes between parties and broadcasters prior to the submission of formal complaints to the IMC. Most of the 27 formal and informal complaints received were resolved in this manner. However, four complaints, one from the ANC, one from the African Christian Democratic Party (ACDP) and two from the Inkatha Federal Party (IFP), were submitted to the Commission.

93. Under the terms of section 23 of the Independent Media Commission Act, the IMC received a written complaint from the ANC against the South African Broadcasting Corporation concerning its news coverage of an IFP march in Johannesburg on 28 March. According to the complaint, the Corporation's radio and television broadcasts continually referred to marchers as "Zulus". The use of this term to describe supporters of the IFP, according to the ANC, was not only inaccurate but also carried the potential to increase ethnic tension. One of the Federal Party's complaints concerned the inequitable television coverage of its leader during the voting period compared with those of other smaller parties. The two complaints brought by the Federal Party were heard and adjudicated, while the ANC and ACDP complaints were withdrawn. Based on the principle of equitable access and the monitoring of the content of news and current affairs coverage, the IMC found that from the start of the election period to the start of voting the treatment of contesting parties had been broadly equitable on radio stations and television.

94. With regard to the monitoring of State publications and State information services, the IMC convened

a meeting of heads of departments of all State information services. It was decided to review especially those publications which could be regarded as sensitive during the election period. The Directorate received a total of 534 publications, defined by the Act as newspapers, books, periodicals, pamphlets, posters or any other printed material, or any other object recorded for reproduction. In addition, 498 press releases published by ministries, State departments, provincial administrations, political parties, homelands and self-governing territories were received. In the case of the KwaNdebele magazine *In Progress*, the Commission found that section 22 (5) of the Act had been contravened in that the KwaNdebele authority had used the publication to promote support for the ANC. There were a few contraventions of the IMC Act but no single action could be deemed to have had a significant impact on the outcome of the elections.

95. It should be noted that, in the implementation of its mandate, the IMC encountered considerable obstacles. It functioned without a chairman for several weeks; it was required to act as both policeman and judge; it was required to put in place an administrative, legal and monitoring infrastructure in a very short time; and it faced many logistical problems, including a mid-stream move to new premises. Despite these problems, the Commission was successful, not only in largely achieving its objectives but also in establishing a model for future action.

### 2. Independent Broadcasting Authority

96. The IBA was established on 28 March 1994 to regulate broadcasting services in the public interest. According to its enabling legislation, it should function wholly independently of State, Government and party political influences and free from political or other bias or interference. Among the functions of the IBA's eight counsellors were control of the broadcasting frequency spectrum; the issuance of broadcasting signal distribution licences and broadcasting licences; development of a code of conduct for broadcasting services; as well as the monitoring and adjudication of complaints. Since its inception the IBA dealt with the question of interim broadcast licences.

### 3. Print media

97. Monitoring the commercial media did not fall under the mandate of the IMC. However, the Public Information and Media Analysis Section itself, with the assistance of UNOMSA observers in the provincial offices, monitored major national, regional and local daily press and selected periodicals in Afrikaans, English, Xhosa and Zulu. Political debate received broad coverage. Both large and small newspapers contributed towards voter education. It is safe to conclude that the print

media contributed positively to creating an atmosphere conducive to free and fair elections. It is worth noting a public opinion survey conducted by the Independent Forum for Electoral Education, which indicated that some 75 per cent of respondents depended on the print and broadcast media for voter education.

98. UNOMSA was of the view that media coverage of the electoral process was balanced and did not disadvantage any one political party.

### F. Observing electoral adjudication

### 1. Mandate and suitability of procedures

99. The Adjudication Section of UNOMSA was charged with observing how complaints relating to the violation of the Electoral Act were dealt with by the IEC. Investigation, legality, fairness and dispatch were the criteria for judging the process. IEC adjudication procedures were somewhat too rigid for election purposes. For example, the fact that serious cases contemplated in section 70, such as de-registration of political parties and candidates, could only be referred for a decision to the Commission upon a recommendation by an Appeal Tribunal, would have made it difficult to respond promptly had the need arisen to de-register a political party in terms of section 69 (2) (b) (i), or a candidate under section 69 (2) (c) (ii).

### 2. Number and nature of cases reported

100. Out of a total of 3,558 registered complaints, the IEC reported 1,013 as complaints of alleged intimidation; 177 as cases of violence against people; 147 as cases of violence against property; 322 as cases of obstruction or interference with canvassing; 267 as cases of destruction of posters; 106 as cases relating to chapter X matters (undue influence, bribery, impersonation, interference with election materials, interference with canvassing, failure to comply with the law, etc.); 540 as cases of various voting infringements; 143 as cases of illegal identity cards; 206 as cases of illegal temporary voter's cards; 298 as cases relating to the violation of the Electoral Code of Conduct; and 115 relating to voter education. The balance of 688 were other, undefined types of violations.

101. The largest number of complaints was registered in KwaZulu/Natal with 741, followed by Western Cape with 475 and PWV with 409. Northern Cape had the lowest number at 44. On the basis of the cases received by UNOMSA, intimidation constituted the single largest group of violations, accounting for 335 (32.6 per cent) out of 1,027 cases reported. A number of complaints were made against employers, including farmers, regarding access to premises and voters.

102. The objective of investigations, mediation and adjudication was to prevent or minimize the level of

conflict and violence during the election campaign. Of the 3,558 cases recorded by the IEC, 278 complaints were sent for mediation. No explanation was provided on how mediation was done (i.e. on what principles and under what circumstances it was accomplished). Fifty-two cases were sent for adjudication.

103. An election is an activity of intense, often highly emotional, competition and should be conducted on the basis of very strict rules. Every aspect should be legally defined and controlled to maximize freedom of competition. Although legal requirements in the South African election were not always strictly met, it is the view of UNOMSA observers that the adjudication process worked reasonably well.

### G. *Joint final statement by the heads of the international observer missions*

104. On 5 May, the IEC, after careful consideration of numerous issues raised by various parties relating to alleged or actual irregularities in the polling and counting and in pursuance of its statutory duty, pronounced the elections for the National Assembly and for each of the provincial legislatures to have been substantially free and fair. The following day, the Special Representative of the Secretary-General in South Africa and the Heads of the observer missions of the Commonwealth, EU and OAU issued the following statement:

"Judge Johann Kriegler, the Chairman of the Independent Electoral Commission, has just announced the results of South Africa's first democratic elections and has pronounced them substantially free and fair.

"On 30 April, the international observer missions noted in an interim statement that despite administrative and logistical problems in some areas, South Africans turned out in enormous numbers to vote. Their confidence in the secrecy of the ballot was manifest and they were able to participate freely in the elections.

"The counting process has also been characterized by logistical and administrative problems which have again revealed serious inadequacies in the control and accounting of sensitive election materials. For instance, it became evident that, given the size of some counting centres, it would prove extremely difficult— if not impossible—to carry out the prescribed reconciliation within the time allowed, and this led the IEC to modify the procedures. On the positive side, the great strength of this process—conducted in the presence of party agents, IEC monitors and electoral observers from South Africa and the international community—has been its transparency.

"As the count proceeded, evidence of irregularities also emerged which gave rise to formal complaints by various parties. In addition, the IEC's own investigations have produced *prima facie* evidence of malfeasance which exacerbated problems in the supply of voting materials experienced during the election. This evidence is now under investigation by the IEC and the South African Police. We urge the IEC to proceed diligently with the mediation and adjudication of outstanding disputes, and that any criminal investigations be pursued.

"The resolution of these cases is critical to the credibility of the IEC and will hold important lessons for future South African elections. Successful resolution of these outstanding matters will also further the cause of national reconciliation by allowing political parties and the South African people to turn their attention to the tasks ahead.

"The international observer missions welcome the spirit of reconciliation that animated the remarks made by President de Klerk and President-elect Mandela on 2 May. The tolerance and patience demonstrated by South Africans during the voting period, the dramatic drop in the level of political violence, and the expressed commitment of the political parties to national reconciliation augur well for the new South Africa.

"The international community has lent its support to the struggle for democracy in South Africa. But South Africans themselves have managed the entire transitional process - from the start of negotiations through the organization and conduct of the elections. In this, South Africa is unique. Despite the problems encountered, the strenuous efforts of the IEC, combined with the patience and determination of the South African people, have borne fruit. While taking into account the difficulties noted in this and our earlier statement, the international observer missions share the collective view that the outcome of the elections reflects the will of the people of South Africa."

105. On the same day at United Nations Headquarters I issued a statement that read as follows:

"Judge Johann Kriegler, Chairman of the Independent Electoral Commission in South Africa, has proclaimed the results of the elections and has declared them to have been substantially free and fair'.

"The Secretary-General welcomes this declaration and once again expresses his warm congratulations to the people of South Africa and all their leaders.

"The Secretary-General also congratulates very

warmly the Chairman and members of the IEC for the remarkable work they have done. Thanks to their dedication and courage, they have made it possible for the South African people to express peacefully and freely their collective aspiration for a better future and their determination to ensure a life of dignity, equality and freedom for every man and woman in their country.

"The United Nations has been involved with the situation in South Africa for more than four decades. It has spearheaded the international campaign against apartheid and initiated and supported programmes aimed at alleviating the suffering of its victims. It has also provided a forum for the representatives of South African organizations such as the ANC to advance the anti-apartheid campaign.

"Since September 1992, in particular, the United Nations has been represented in South Africa by an Observer Mission with the express mandate of contributing to a peaceful transition from apartheid to a new, democratic, non-racial and united South Africa.

"This was the largest electoral observation mission mounted by the United Nations. No fewer than 2,120 men and women took part, including staff members from the United Nations and specialized agencies and recruits from some 120 Member States. To all of them, the Secretary-General wishes to express his appreciation for the work they have accomplished. They served the United Nations well. They also served the people of South Africa at a critical moment of their history; and they served the cause of democracy.

"The United Nations will remain committed to South Africa. The Secretary-General looks forward to the contribution the Government and the people of South Africa will make to the activities of the United Nations."

## VI. Coordination with other international observer missions

### A. Coordinating Committee

106. In carrying out its initial mandate, UNOMSA worked closely with the observer missions of the Commonwealth, EU and OAU. At regular joint meetings, both at UNOMSA headquarters and in the field, members of the four missions exchanged information on current developments throughout the country, planned joint deployments for major events and coordinated their activities to ensure maximum coverage of developments throughout the country. Regular consultation among the missions also resulted in common positions and action-oriented decisions regarding particularly important developments or issues. Decisions were made regarding approaches to individuals or groups in order to express the international community's concerns or to outline possible options for dealing with problems. Representatives of the international observer missions met regularly, for example, with the Executive of the National Peace Secretariat, the Commissioner of Police and the Minister of Law and Order with a view to evaluating such matters as police-community relations, unnecessary use of force by security personnel, as well as improvement in police recruitment procedures and training. The international observer missions, working together, became an important conduit for information from the grass-roots level to reach decision makers in Government, political parties and the security forces regarding situations that might exacerbate tensions or lead to violence.

107. South Africa's Multi-party Negotiating Council on 6 December 1993 adopted a resolution, later ratified by the TEC, calling upon the United Nations to coordinate activities of international observers provided by the Commonwealth, EU and OAU, as well as those provided by any other intergovernmental organization or Government. It also requested that the United Nations put in place the necessary arrangements to that effect, in particular ensuring that the international observers were deployed in an effective and coordinated manner in close cooperation with the IEC. Against this background, and in accordance with my earlier report of 10 January 1994 (A/48/845-S/1994/16 and Add.1), a Coordinating Committee, consisting of the heads of the observer missions of the United Nations, Commonwealth, OAU and EU, was set up under the chairmanship of my Special Representative for South Africa, Mr. Lakhdar Brahimi.

108. The Coordinating Committee met at least once a week to consider reports from the Joint Operations Unit, consisting of representatives of the four observer missions, and the Technical Task Force, comprising representatives of the heads of the election units of the four observer missions, and also other issues raised by any committee member. The Technical Task Force also met regularly and interacted with IEC officials under the chairmanship of the Deputy Special Representative. The Joint Operations Unit, chaired by UNOMSA, prepared a training and deployment plan for the large number of international electoral observers to be deployed during the elections and developed data banks for systematically recording and maintaining information collected by observers.

109. The Coordinating Committee also met regularly with Judge Kriegler. At those meetings reports sub-

mitted by the missions' observer teams in all provinces were brought to the attention of the IEC. For his part, Judge Kriegler briefed the Committee on progress in the Commission's work in preparing for the elections. The missions brought to his attention field reports of slippages and shortcomings in the election preparations at the local level, on which the Commission acted. Overall, cooperation between the Coordinating Committee and the IEC was constructive and mutually beneficial. The international observer missions provided the IEC with support and encouragement not only at the policy level, but also at the level of the Technical Task Force and the Joint Operations Unit. Officials of the electoral units of the four observer missions also met with IEC election officials to address problems as they arose.

110. With regard to reporting and public statements, while each international observer mission reported to its parent organization, UNOMSA coordinated the drafting and release of joint statements on various aspects of the transition process. One such statement, on 29 March 1994, deplored the violence that had occurred in central Johannesburg during a Zulu march in support of King Zwelithini. A joint statement by the international observer missions issued on the eve of the voting (25 April) condemned acts of violence that threatened the election and emphasized the paramount importance of peaceful conduct during the election. A statement issued after the voting (30 April) expressed the missions' satisfaction that South Africa's people were able to participate freely in the voting. On 6 May, after the announcement of the election results by the IEC, the missions issued a statement expressing the collective view of international observers that, in spite of the difficulties encountered, the outcome of the elections reflected the will of the people of South Africa.

### B. *Technical Task Force*

111. In paragraph 71 of my report of 10 January 1994 it was proposed that there should be established, under the Coordinating Committee, a Technical Task Force comprising the four Chief Electoral Officers of the four international observer missions, chaired by the Head of the Electoral Division of UNOMSA, with the function of overseeing the activities of the Joint Operations Unit. In practice, however, Technical Task Force meetings were chaired by the Deputy Special Representative or the Director of the UNOMSA Electoral Division, while the Division's Deputy Director served as Secretary.

112. The Technical Task Force held its first meeting on 27 January 1994 and met 11 times thereafter. IEC officials attended eight of these meetings on a standing invitation from the Coordinating Committee. At its first meeting, the Technical Task Force agreed that the Joint Operations Unit would operate as a full-time project team, rather than as a committee or periodic working group. At its 3 February meeting, the Technical Task Force approved a list of tasks to be performed by the Joint Operations Unit as the basis for the latter's work.

113. Once the Joint Operations Unit was established, technical issues were dealt with mostly at that level. The Technical Task Force examined only major resource issues. The Joint Operations Unit worked largely autonomously and the degree of supervision required of the Technical Task Force was minimal. This pattern became more pronounced as the election approached. The Technical Task Force also served as a forum for coordination of the responses of the international observer missions to requests for technical assistance from the IEC. This function accounted for a significant proportion of the Technical Task Force's time.

### C. *The Joint Operations Unit*

114. The Joint Operations Unit's role was concentrated in two main areas: coordination with the three other international observer missions and preparation for the arrival of the large number of international electoral observers for the elections.

115. The Unit, to which each observer mission assigned representatives, initially devoted its attention to building on the informal coordination arrangements already established by UNOMSA. In collaboration with the other international observer missions, the Unit developed common forms for observation of voting and counting stations, and prepared computer programs and organized data banks for systematically recording and maintaining data for use by all four missions. Regular Joint Operations Unit meetings were held to discuss issues of concern and to seek agreement on proposed actions.

116. The Unit was deeply involved in preparation of the deployment plan for the large number of international electoral observers needed to observe the elections. This required a substantial amount of preparatory work, particularly in the area of training, which included development of appropriate briefing and training materials and strategies. The Unit also cooperated with the UNOMSA Division of Administration in solving problems relating to transportation, communications, conference facilities and accommodation for some 1,485 newly arrived international electoral observers, along with their deployment to the provinces. The Joint Operations Unit also liaised with the IEC in order to compile information on each group of voting stations to be visited by observer teams during voting days, and produced a manual comprising background information and operational guidelines used by international electoral observers of all four international observer missions.

## VII. Cooperation with non-governmental organizations

### A. *UNOMSA and non-governmental organizations*

117. Under the terms of Security Council resolution 772 (1992), UNOMSA cooperated with a wide range of non-governmental organizations, especially in the areas of violence monitoring, peace promotion, human rights and civic education. From the start of the mission one UNOMSA observer was assigned to work as a non-governmental organization liaison officer. With the expanded mandate under Security Council resolution 894 (1994), UNOMSA's cooperation with institutions of civil society expanded to include those involved in observing the electoral process and voter education.

118. In my report of 10 January, I noted the crucial role that domestic and foreign non-governmental organizations were bound to play in the overall success of the observation process. Responding to a wish expressed by the TEC that all international observers and other observers cooperate closely in the performance of their task to oversee the electoral process at all stages, I stated (paras. 75 and 76) that efforts would be made to establish a cooperative relationship with the foreign non-governmental organizations and working relationships with national non-governmental entities involved in various aspects of the elections such as civic education and the organization of domestic monitoring networks.

119. An NGO Liaison Office was established in the UNOMSA Electoral Division to implement this policy. UNOMSA observers were urged to expand upon existing contacts with non-governmental organizations, especially community-based organizations and those involved in peace-building and conflict resolution, as well as those observing the electoral process. The NGO Liaison Office maintained contacts with relevant non-governmental organizations, both domestic and foreign, briefing them on the UNOMSA mandate and replying to requests for information. The Liaison Office represented UNOMSA, for example, at meetings of the National Electoral Observer Network, an organization formed in December 1993 to coordinate the efforts of both domestic and foreign non-governmental organizations involved in observing the elections, as well as at the meetings of the Panel of Religious Leaders on Electoral Justice and the Ecumenical Monitoring Programme in South Africa. The IEC, in turn, also consulted the Liaison Office with regard to foreign non-governmental organizations.

120. The international observer missions were invited to cooperate with representatives of churches, the business sector, trade unions, peace monitoring organizations and various domestic and foreign non-governmental organizations by appointing a representative to the Management Committee of the National Electoral Observer Network. Similar cooperation developed at provincial, sub-provincial and district levels with the structures of the Network and with other non-governmental organizations. In several areas, joint forums were established to exchange information, to devise common strategies for monitoring events and to discuss deployment plans for the election. In many instances, peace structures and non-governmental organizations provided orientation and access to local communities for international electoral observers. The latter, in return, supplied assistance and advice when requested.

### B. *Non-governmental organization observers*

121. South African non-governmental organizations carried out the bulk of civic and voter education and shaped the concept of election monitoring by civil society. The IEC accredited a total of 30 domestic non-governmental organizations, of which the National Electoral Observer Network was the largest. These organizations deployed nearly 25,000 observers throughout the country for the election. In addition, 97 foreign non-governmental organizations provided more than 2,000 observers from all over the world. Among the most important institutions was the Association of Western European Parliamentarians, which deployed nearly 400 parliamentarians to observe the South African election. UNOMSA shared with them briefing and logistical information and maintained close contact with observers of the Association at central and provincial levels. In addition, many non-governmental organizations provided the IEC with qualified and trained personnel, particularly to its Monitoring Directorate. The Women's National Coalition ensured a wider participation of women in the democratization process in South Africa. Non-governmental organizations involved in election observation were asked to sign a code of conduct and were provided with IEC identification cards and apparel that gave them access to voting stations.

122. The contribution of institutions of civil society during the election days went far beyond observing the election. Administrative and logistical shortcomings of the IEC led non-governmental organization observers to perform tasks beyond their original mandate. In many voting stations, they formed part of the team of officials and monitors. They were called on by the IEC to assist election officials ad hoc. At the IEC's request, the religious community provided some 1,200 people to assist with the counting of ballots, when it became clear that this phase of the election process was seriously hindered by a lack of qualified personnel. Many observers recruited as volunteers felt after the election that they had been unfairly treated and demanded to be paid, as were IEC officials and monitors.

123. The contribution of non-governmental or-

ganization observers was vital to the election even if, for lack of time, not all observers were properly trained and certain areas were not covered. The participation of non-governmental organizations helped complete the electoral process despite administrative and logistical difficulties. Non-governmental organization action also allowed South Africans to participate more broadly in the election, making it, in the words of IEC Chairman Judge Johann Kriegler, a "people's election".

## VIII.  Administration

### A.  *Resources: personnel*

124.  As indicated earlier in the present report, the expanded mandate of UNOMSA called for a sharp increase in the number of observers within a short time-frame, necessitating the establishment of a support system with little lead time. The Mission's electoral phase was relatively short. As a result, the administrative and logistical support required to carry out its mandate effectively constituted a massive undertaking, particularly in the periods immediately before and after the elections. Between the end of January 1994, when the General Assembly approved the budget of the expanded UNOMSA, and the end of April 1994, UNOMSA planned and executed the deployment of 1,985 international electoral observers. This represented a vast increase over the 100 observers in-country beginning in February 1994.

125.  The deployment exercise reached its peak immediately before the elections with the arrival of most of the international electoral observers. UNOMSA's administrative components and the Joint Operations Unit processed incoming international electoral observers, transferred them to training centres and deployed them to their assigned locations. Immediately after the elections, the observers were repatriated. This entire exercise was accomplished within 12 days by a limited number of support staff. Factors outside UNOMSA's control required constant adjustment in the Mission's deployment plan, including problems encountered at United Nations Headquarters in finalizing numbers and lists of observers. Difficulties experienced by the IEC, which delayed finalization of the list of voting stations right up to the voting days, as well as the extension of the voting and counting days, necessitated numerous last-minute changes in UNOMSA's deployment and logistical plans.

### B.  *Communications*

126.  Installation of a UNOMSA radio communications system to cover the entire country was not possible, given the short time available and the size of the country. A VHF radio communications network was therefore established to cover those areas with a history of violence or where violence was expected. In order to work within the limits of an extremely cluttered VHF band, a commercial trunking radio system was used to cover the Durban and Johannesburg areas. To enhance radio communications in potentially violent areas, two light helicopters equipped with radio repeaters served as airborne repeaters in the event ground-based equipment failed. UNOMSA teams were equipped with telephones and fax facilities in most of the country, except in a few very remote areas. UNOMSA also provided communications facilities to the observer missions of the Commonwealth, EU and OAU, with these missions paying a proportionate share of installation and operating costs.

### C.  *Aviation support and vehicles*

127.  The UNOMSA budget provided for chartered aircraft to deploy international electoral observers and for communications purposes. With few exceptions, however, provincial capitals could be reached by bus or commercial airlines. For most air travel within the mission area, regular commercial airlines were used.

128.  During the elections, 11 light helicopters and one light fixed-wing aircraft were chartered. Two helicopters were used as airborne radio repeater stations, as described above; one in PWV and one in KwaZulu/Natal. In addition, one helicopter was stationed in each of the nine provinces to provide medical, casualty and emergency evacuation, and to permit provincial coordinators to travel quickly to problem areas if required. In Northern Cape, where the large distances to be covered exceeded the range of helicopters, a small fixed-wing aircraft was provided.

129.  Redeployment of the international electoral observers back to Johannesburg was initially envisaged to be the reverse of deployment. The extension of the voting days, however, required last-minute changes and incorporated the use of chartered aircraft to ensure the timely out-processing and repatriation of observers. In addition, an AN26 aircraft, on loan from the United Nations Operation in Mozambique, was used in the repatriation exercise.

130.  The UNOMSA surface transport fleet of 1,077 vehicles was hired from car rental agencies in the country. In the run-up to the elections, 300 vehicles were rented. This number was increased by an additional 777 vehicles for international electoral observers during the elections themselves. UNOMSA also hired 20 vehicles for use by OAU observers. In this instance, UNOMSA acted as centralized purchasing agent on behalf of the OAU observer mission.

### D.  *Security issues*

131.  The safety and security of international observers was a concern expressed in Security Council

resolution 894 (1994), which called upon all parties in South Africa to respect the safety and security of international observers and to facilitate the carrying out of their mandate. This request was brought to the attention of the relevant government departments and the political parties.

132. The security of UNOMSA staff was a key concern throughout the Mission. Staff were at risk of:

(a) Common criminal attack: there were a number of such incidents, the majority in Johannesburg;

(b) Accidental involvement in violence at demonstrations, rallies or in areas where rivalry between different factions sometimes developed into exchanges of gunfire and the like. The most serious incident of this kind was a grenade attack at a demonstration in Kimberley on 25 May 1993 in which a UNOMSA observer was among those injured;

(c) Deliberate attack: throughout the Mission there was a degree of threat from extremists objecting to the role of the United Nations in South Africa. Verbal abuse, carriage of weapons in a threatening manner and the alleged inclusion of international observer missions on a target list apparently sent by an extremist group to a newspaper were among the manifestations of this threat. However, there were no deliberate physical attacks on any members of the international observer missions.

133. Close and constructive liaison was established at all levels with the South African Police and the South African Defence Force. Senior UNOMSA staff discussed security matters with officials at all levels of government and with representatives of political parties. Under UNOMSA's peace promotion mandate, observers were often able to use these links to defuse confrontation between the security forces and demonstrators. During the election the South African security forces made special provisions for the safety of international observers. For example, the SADF agreed to the use of communications facilities and barracks by United Nations observers in the event of an emergency.

134. Primary responsibility for the protection of observers rested with the Government of South Africa. UNOMSA recognized, however, that the security forces were unable to protect observers at all times. Measures to improve mission security included security awareness training for all observers and planning in accordance with guidelines in the United Nations Field Security Handbook. Prior to the elections, coordinators were designated at UNOMSA provincial and headquarters offices to liaise with the security forces, prepare security plans and advise observers. Most but not all these coordinators had experience in security matters. Frequent liaison with other international observer missions regarding security issues meant that a common approach was developed. The exchange of information was encouraged at all levels to ensure that observers were not placed at risk.

## IX. Concluding observations

135. South Africa's first democratic elections were truly historic. There is no doubt that the elections provided a framework for the entire population to unite and endorse the ideal of the new, non-racial, democratic and united South Africa.

136. The United Nations, through UNOMSA, has reaped a wealth of experience. Its achievements, as well as its mistakes and shortcomings, will be recalled when similar missions are planned in the future. I have asked the various departments directly concerned to cooperate with senior UNOMSA staff in order to draw lessons from this experience.

137. In the course of the transitional process, a high level of cooperation was achieved between UNOMSA, the IEC and other South African institutions. This was highly beneficial to all parties. It contributed, in particular, to the early solution of a large number of problems faced by the IEC. The experience gained and the relations established can be built on in the future. Indeed, this experience as well as South African expertise are already in the process of being used elsewhere.

138. The close cooperation between UNOMSA and the observer missions of the Commonwealth, the European Union and the Organization of African Unity also benefited all concerned, including South African structures. The level of understanding and like-mindedness achieved found its ultimate expression in the two key joint statements made by all four missions: first to assess the manner in which the voting took place and, a few days later, to make the final assessment of the electoral process.

139. As an exercise in preventive diplomacy, drawing on the strengths of several international organizations to support indigenous efforts towards peace and national reconciliation, the international community's efforts in South Africa since 1992 offer a unique and positive demonstration of the benefits of such cooperation. I wish to record here the expression of my warmest congratulations to the Organization of African Unity, the Commonwealth and the European Union for the excellent work they have done in South Africa and my gratitude for the cooperation their missions gave UNOMSA at all levels. This was probably the closest form of cooperation achieved by our organizations so far. We should not be complacent, however: there is still ample room for improvement and I intend to invite the three organizations and, indeed, other concerned regional organizations, to work out together guidelines for future cooperation based on the success, as well as the mistakes, of our common experience in South Africa and elsewhere.

140. Another lesson worth learning from the South African experience is the concept of the National Peace Accord and the structures to which it gave birth: the National Peace Committee, the National Peace Secretariat and the Goldstone Commission. Even if many peace committees lost momentum at some stage, the high value of their contribution to the whole process cannot be overlooked. An added tribute is owed to them for the training provided within the peace structures to thousands of people who were thus able to come to the assistance of the IEC during the elections, either directly as its employees or indirectly as volunteers. Of course, the South African experience cannot be automatically transposed elsewhere but there may be situations in the world today or in the future—particularly in Africa—to which South African experiences, initiatives and attitudes might be applicable.

141. The Independent Electoral Commission succeeded in delivering an election against colossal odds and deserves to be congratulated. The performance of South Africa's electoral machinery was not perfect, as the Commission itself was the first to admit. Fortunately, the perseverance and spirit of compromise that prevailed in the negotiations was sustained. The political parties demonstrated remarkable maturity and responsibility, thus helping to achieve an overall acceptable, credible result. This is one of the great lessons to be drawn from the whole South African process of change. Throughout the transitional process, South African political leaders have stayed the course, reaching deep into their own reserves of energy and imagination to overcome each stumbling block in their path. For this they deserve our admiration, congratulations and continued support.

142. In conclusion, I would like to pay a warm tribute to my Special Representative for South Africa, Mr. Lakhdar Brahimi, for his selfless dedication and outstanding leadership of UNOMSA. I wish also to thank the Deputy Special Representative, Ms. Angela King, for her contribution to the success of the mission. Finally, I wish to thank all those who served or collaborated with UNOMSA, whose collective contribution ensured that the mandate entrusted to me by the Security Council regarding South Africa was fulfilled in both its letter and spirit.

---

# Document 217

*Statement by Secretary-General Boutros Boutros-Ghali to the General Assembly plenary meeting on the resumption of South Africa's participation in the work of the Assembly*

A/48/PV.95, 23 June 1994

The people of South Africa have found their voice. A new South Africa now takes its place among the family of nations. Today, South Africa regains its place as a full partner in the work of the United Nations.

The fight against apartheid was the most important struggle of our century. The destruction of apartheid is a tribute to the people of South Africa. It is a testament to the commitment of the international community.

It was a struggle that extended far beyond South Africa's borders. It was a struggle that helped to shape the United Nations and to shape the international community as a whole.

South Africa's success, therefore, is also a success for the United Nations. Through the United Nations, the international community expressed its solidarity with the people of South Africa. Through the United Nations, the international community showed its support for their cause and for their struggle.

The contribution of the United Nations was substantial. Its role was significant. By forcefully condemning apartheid, the United Nations reinforced the moral dimension of the struggle. By isolating South Africa, and by assisting the opponents of apartheid, the United Nations expanded the political dimensions of the struggle. By urging and imposing sanctions, the international community added a vital economic dimension to the struggle.

In moral and in human terms, the voice of the international community was clearly heard. The General Assembly declared apartheid to be a violation of the Charter. It held apartheid to be a violation of the Universal Declaration of Human Rights. It labelled apartheid as a crime against the conscience and dignity of all humanity. It monitored and publicized brutality. It worked to mobilize public opinion against injustice.

Politically, the United Nations helped to build and cement an international consensus in support of change. A Special Committee against Apartheid was established in 1962 with the aim of promoting opposition to apartheid. In 1974, the General Assembly barred South Africa from participating in its work, and invited liberation movements to participate as observers. A Trust Fund was established to aid political prisoners and their families.

International Anti-Apartheid Year was proclaimed in 1978. Special international days were designated in solidarity with opponents of apartheid. The political message against apartheid was clear.

The United Nations was also instrumental in strengthening the economic dimension of the struggle against apartheid. The Security Council imposed a mandatory arms embargo on South Africa under Chapter VII of the Charter. The General Assembly declared 1982 International Year of Mobilization for Sanctions against South Africa. These actions gave new momentum to anti-apartheid efforts in many Member States.

I am especially proud that the United Nations was also central to international efforts to promote the establishment of a democratic and non-racial South Africa.

The adoption in 1989 of the Declaration on Apartheid and its Destructive Consequences in Southern Africa was a turning-point. Its adoption cemented a new consensus on South Africa. This consensus was a significant element in creating the conditions for a negotiated solution.

United Nations representatives were made available during the long negotiations. United Nations observers were sent in August 1992 to build confidence and help diminish the spread of political violence. At the request of the Transitional Executive Council, 1,600 United Nations election monitors were sent to observe South Africa's first free and democratic elections in April of this year. The successful installation of a Government of national unity is a fitting reward for South Africa, for the United Nations and for the international community as a whole.

At a time when the African continent too often offers the sad spectacle of ethnic clashes, civil war and border conflicts that compound the economic misery and underdevelopment affecting a large portion of its population, South Africa has offered us, this spring, unforgettable images of faith in the future.

At the recent OAU summit in Tunis, I had occasion to note how historically important were the first elections by universal suffrage in South Africa and the accession of Nelson Mandela to the presidency of a democratic and non-racial South Africa.

Those images of national reconciliation are of a memorable event that will find a lasting place in the annals of history. And for us, they offer a model.

Welcoming South Africa into the General Assembly and the various organs and agencies of the United Nations is a definite source of pride to us today. It is also a source of legitimate gratification to the United Nations, for it is true that the Organization has, for several decades, been unstinting in its efforts to help the South African people to combat apartheid and recover their dignity.

Now it is our turn to ask South Africa to give us its support in our struggle for peace and development on the African continent. Yes, democratic and non-racial South Africa can help the African continent along the road to stability, tolerance and democracy.

The remarkable way in which South Africans have been able to overcome their differences and lay the foundation for a multi-party and non-racial democracy offers a model. The courage, persistence and historic vision that were needed in overcoming extraordinary difficulties and ensuring a peaceful transition should give the whole African continent grounds for hope.

As a regional economic Power, South Africa can also contribute to the development of the African continent. Moreover, it can be a factor for stability in the region.

Within the General Assembly, South Africa has an immense role to play. Much is expected of it from the African continent, as well as from the international community as a whole.

In other words, it is with as much joy as hope, and not without deep emotion, that I today welcome South Africa into the General Assembly of the United Nations!

---

# Document 218

*General Assembly resolution: Elimination of apartheid and establishment of a united, democratic and non-racial South Africa—Work of the Special Committee against Apartheid*

A/RES/48/258 A, 23 June 1994

*The General Assembly,*

*Recalling* its resolutions S-16/1 of 14 December 1989, 46/79 A of 13 December 1991, 47/116 A of 18 December 1992, 48/1 of 8 October 1993, 48/159 A of 20 December 1993 and 48/233 of 21 January 1994, which were all adopted by consensus,

*Also recalling* its resolution 1761 (XVII) of 6 November 1962, by which it established the Special Committee against Apartheid, and its resolutions 47/116 B of 18 December 1992 and 48/159 B of 20 December 1993 on the programme of work of the Special Committee, which were adopted by consensus,

*Taking note with appreciation* of the final report of the Special Committee against Apartheid, submitted in accordance with paragraph 4 (e) of resolution 48/159 B,

*Also taking note with appreciation* of the report of the Chairman of the Special Committee against Apartheid on his missions to South Africa, together with a delegation of the Special Committee, from 28 February to 5 March and from 6 to 10 June 1994, as reflected in the final report of the Special Committee,

*Recalling* the contributions over the decades of the United Nations, its Special Committee against Apartheid, Member States of the United Nations, regional and non-governmental organizations and the international community as a whole to the efforts leading to the end of apartheid,

*Also recalling* Security Council resolution 919 (1994) of 25 May 1994,

*Noting with great satisfaction* that South Africa, having resumed its rightful place in the international community, intends to participate in the work of the United Nations in accordance with the principles and purposes of the Charter of the Organization,

1. *Expresses its profound satisfaction* at the entry into force of South Africa's first non-racial and democratic constitution on 27 April 1994, the holding of one-person/one-vote elections from 26 to 29 April 1994, the convening of South Africa's new parliament on 5 May 1994 and the installation on 10 May 1994 of its State President and the Government of National Unity;

2. *Congratulates* all South Africans and their political leaders on their success in bringing apartheid to an end and in laying, through broad-based negotiations, the foundations for a new, non-racial and democratic South Africa with equal and guaranteed rights for each and all;

3. *Notes* the importance of actions taken by the General Assembly and the Security Council, which have contributed significantly to the end of apartheid and the establishment of a democratic and united, non-racial South Africa;

4. *Commends* the Secretary-General for the successful implementation and conclusion of the mandates entrusted to him by relevant Security Council and General Assembly resolutions, in particular Security Council resolutions 765 (1992) of 16 July 1992, 772 (1992) of 17 August 1992 and 894 (1994) of 14 January 1994, through the efforts of his Special Representative, and General Assembly resolution 48/159 A of 20 December

1993 relating to the United Nations Observer Mission in South Africa;

5. *Also commends* the Organization of African Unity, the Commonwealth and the European Union for their important contributions, *inter alia*, through their observer missions, as well as the Movement of Non-Aligned Countries, for their support to the process of peaceful change culminating in the elections;

6. *Expresses its appreciation* to the Special Committee against Apartheid for the important role it has played as a focal point for international action in support of the efforts to eliminate apartheid in South Africa and to establish a non-racial and democratic society in that country;

7. *Welcomes* South Africa back to the community of nations as represented in the General Assembly of the United Nations, and calls upon specialized agencies and related organizations of the United Nations system to take all necessary actions to re-establish full membership of South Africa;

8. *Decides* to consider, as an exceptional measure, that the arrears of South Africa that have accrued to date were due to conditions beyond its control and, accordingly, that the question of the applicability of Article 19 of the Charter of the United Nations related to the loss of voting rights in the General Assembly in this respect will not arise;

9. *Considers*, as stated in the final report of the Special Committee against Apartheid, that the mandate of the Special Committee has been successfully concluded, and decides to terminate it as at the date of adoption of the present resolution;

10. *Requests* the Secretary-General to facilitate the transfer of the Art against Apartheid Collection to and its installation at an institution agreed on with designated representatives of the Government of South Africa;

11. *Strongly appeals* to Member States and the international community to provide generous assistance to the Government and people of South Africa in the implementation of the reconstruction and development programmes of their country, and requests the Secretary-General to consider the appointment, in consultation with the Government of South Africa, of a high-level coordinator for United Nations development activities in that country;

12. *Decides* to remove from the provisional agenda of its forty-ninth session the item entitled "Elimination of apartheid and establishment of a united, democratic and non-racial South Africa".

# Document 219

*General Assembly resolution: Elimination of apartheid and establishment of a united, democratic and non-racial South Africa—United Nations Trust Fund for South Africa*

A/RES/48/258 B, 23 June 1994

*The General Assembly,*

*Recalling* its resolutions on the United Nations Trust Fund for South Africa, in particular resolution 48/159 D of 20 December 1993,

*Recalling also* its resolution 48/160 of 20 December 1993 on the United Nations Educational and Training Programme for Southern Africa,

*Having considered* the report of the Secretary-General on the United Nations Trust Fund for South Africa,

*Recognizing* the valuable work carried out over the years by the Secretary-General and the Committee of Trustees of the United Nations Trust Fund for South Africa in rendering legal, educational and relief assistance to persons persecuted under repressive and discriminatory legislation in South Africa and their dependents and to former political prisoners and returning exiles in order to facilitate their reintegration into South African society,

*Taking note* of the recommendations in the final report of the Special Committee against Apartheid,

*Recognizing* the valuable assistance rendered by the United Nations Educational and Training Programme for Southern Africa to disadvantaged students in South Africa, its support for institution-building in that country and the measures it has taken to ensure that commitments made with regard to educational and training assistance can be met in full,

*Recognizing also* that the legacies of apartheid will continue to affect disadvantaged South Africans for years to come,

1. *Expresses its satisfaction* at the successful holding, from 26 to 29 April 1994, of the first non-racial and democratic elections in South Africa, the establishment of the Government of National Unity and the coming into effect of a non-racial and democratic constitution for the transitional period;

2. *Agrees* with the view of the Committee of Trustees of the United Nations Trust Fund for South Africa, expressed in the annex to the report of the Secretary-General, that the Fund has now fulfilled its mandate;

3. *Endorses* the recommendations of the Committee of Trustees that remaining funds of the Trust Fund be transferred to the United Nations Educational and Training Programme for Southern Africa to be used for the purposes of that Programme and that residual administrative matters relating to the programme of the Trust Fund be handled by the Secretariat unit responsible for the administration of the Programme;

4. *Also endorses* the recommendation of the Committee of Trustees that its functions be discontinued;

5. *Expresses its appreciation* to the Governments, organizations and individuals that have made generous contributions to the Trust Fund and to the voluntary agencies that have been engaged in rendering legal, educational and relief assistance to the victims of apartheid in South Africa over the years;

6. *Expresses its gratitude* to the Secretary-General and to the Committee of Trustees for their persistent humanitarian efforts in South Africa;

7. *Appeals* to Member States to offer financial and material support to the reconstruction and development efforts of the new Government of National Unity of South Africa and to continue to assist civic society in that country.

---

# Document 220

*Security Council resolution: The question of South Africa*

S/RES/930 (1994), 27 June 1994

*The Security Council,*

*Recalling* its resolutions 772 (1992) of 17 August 1992 and 894 (1994) of 14 January 1994,

*Noting with great satisfaction* the establishment of a united, non-racial and democratic government of South Africa,

*Welcoming* General Assembly resolutions A/RES/48/13 C and A/RES/48/258 A of 23 June 1994,

1. *Welcomes* the final report of the Secretary-General on the United Nations Observer Mission in South Africa (UNOMSA) (S/1994/717);

2. *Commends* the vital role played by the Special Representative of the Secretary-General and the United Nations Observer Mission in South Africa, together with the Organization of African Unity, the Commonwealth and the European Union, in support of the establishment of a united, non-racial and democratic South Africa;

3. *Decides* that, with the successful completion of its mandate, the United Nations Observer Mission in South Africa is terminated forthwith;

4. *Also decides* that it has concluded its consideration of the item entitled "The question of South Africa" and hereby *removes* this item from the list of matters of which the Council is seized.

---

# Document 221

## *Address by President Nelson Mandela of South Africa to the forty-ninth session of the General Assembly*

A/49/PV.14, 3 October 1994

It surely must be one of the great ironies of our age that this Assembly is being addressed for the first time in its 49 years' history by a South African head of State drawn from among the African majority of what is an African country.

Future generations will find it strange in the extreme that it was only so late in the 20th century that it was possible for our delegation to take its seat in the Assembly, recognized both by our people and by the nations of the world as the legitimate representative of the people of our country.

It is indeed a most welcome thing that the Organization will mark its 50th anniversary next year with the apartheid system vanquished and consigned to the past. That historic change has come about not least because of the great efforts in which the United Nations engaged to ensure the suppression of the apartheid crime against humanity. Even as it was still in the process of establishing its institutions, the United Nations was confronted by the challenge of the accession to power of the party of apartheid domination in our country. Everything this system stood for represented the very opposite of all the noble purposes for which this Organization was established. Because apartheid reduced and undermined the credibility of the United Nations as an effective international instrument to end racism and secure the fundamental human rights of all people, its establishment and consolidation of apartheid constituted a brazen challenge to the very existence of the Organization.

The United Nations was born out of the titanic struggle against nazism and fascism with their pernicious doctrines and practices of racial superiority and genocide. It therefore could not stand by while, in South Africa, a similar system was being established by a government which also had the temerity to claim representation within the United Nations.

We believe that it was indeed of great importance to the universal efficacy of, and respect for, the Declaration on Human Rights and the United Nations Charter, that the United Nations should have spurned the pleas of the apartheid regime that the gross violation of human rights in South Africa was a domestic matter of no legal or legitimate concern to the world body.

We stand here today to salute the United Nations Organization and its Member States, both singly and collectively, for joining forces with the masses of our people in a common struggle that has brought about our emancipation and pushed back the frontiers of racism.

The millions of our people say "thank you" and "thank you again because the respect for your own dignity as human beings inspired you to act to ensure the restoration of our dignity as well".

We have together traversed a course which we are convinced has strengthened human solidarity in general and reinforced the bonds of friendship between our peoples and the nations of the world. This dates back to the early days when India put the question of racism in South Africa on the Assembly's agenda, to the moment when the world community, as represented here, could adopt consensus resolutions against apartheid with none dissenting.

It was therefore with great joy that at our inauguration as President of our Republic we received, among others, such high and distinguished officials of this Organization as the Secretary-General, the President of the General Assembly and the Chairman of the Special Committee against Apartheid. Their presence reaffirmed the incontrovertible truth that the victory over apartheid, the success of the cause of democracy, non-racialism and non-sexism in our country belongs as much to our people as it does to the United Nations.

And so we have embarked on the road to the remaking of our country, basing ourselves both on the democratic Constitution which came into force on 27 April this year and on the Reconstruction and Development Programme, which has become the property of all our people.

Clearly, these documents would have no life unless the people give them life. The words printed in them must inspire common ownership by all our people and their common allegiance to the process and the results which these documents intend. For this to happen, as we propagate the vision these documents contain, we must at the same time engage in a historic effort of redefinition of ourselves as a new nation.

Our watchwords must be justice, peace, reconciliation and nation-building in the pursuit of a democratic, non-racial and non-sexist country. In all that we do, we have to ensure the healing of the wounds inflicted on all our people across the great dividing line imposed on our society by centuries of colonialism and apartheid.

We must ensure that colour, race and gender become only a God-given gift to each one of us, and not an indelible mark or attribute that accords a special status to any.

We must work for the day when we as South Africans see one another and interact with one another as equal human beings and as part of one nation united, rather than torn asunder, by its diversity.

The road we shall have to travel to reach this destination will by no means be easy. All of us know how stubbornly racism can cling to the mind and how deeply it can infect the human soul. Where it is sustained by the racial ordering of the material world, as is the case in our country, that stubbornness can multiply a hundred-fold.

And yet, however hard the battle may be, we will not surrender. Whatever the time it may take, we will not tire. The very fact that racism degrades both the perpetrator and the victim commands that, if we are true to our commitment to protect human dignity, we fight on until victory is achieved.

We firmly believe that we who have particular experience of the destructive and anti-human force of racism, owe it to ourselves to centre our transformation on the creation of a truly non-racial society. Because we know racism so intimately, we must stand a good chance of developing and nurturing its opposite.

It will perhaps come to be that we, who have harboured in our country the worst example of racism since the defeat of nazism, will make a contribution to human civilisation by ordering our affairs in such a manner that we strike an effective and lasting blow against racism everywhere.

Some of the steps that we have taken already including the establishment of a Government of National Unity, the orderly transformation of the institutions of state and the cultivation of a national consensus on the major issues of the day, have started us off on a correct footing with regard to continuing the processes leading to the creation of the just society we have been speaking of.

Our political emancipation has also brought into sharp focus the urgent need to engage in the struggle to secure our people's freedom from want, from hunger and from ignorance. We have written on our banners: that the society we seek to create must be a people-centred society; all its institutions and its resources must be dedicated to the pursuit of a better life for all our citizens. That better life must mean an end to poverty, to joblessness, homelessness and the despair that comes of deprivation. This is an end in itself because the happiness of the human being must, in any society, be an end in itself.

At the same time, we are intensely conscious of the fact that the stability of the democratic settlement itself and the possibility actually to create a non-racial and non-sexist society depend on our ability to change the material conditions of life of our people so that they not only have the vote, but have bread and work as well.

We therefore return to the United Nations to make the commitment that, as we undertook never to rest until the system of apartheid was defeated, so do we now undertake that we cannot rest while millions of our people suffer the pain and indignity of poverty in all its forms.

At the same time, we turn once more to this world body to say, We are going to need your continued support to achieve the goal of the betterment of the conditions of life of our people. We are pleased and inspired that both the Secretary-General and the specialized agencies of the United Nations have taken up the development challenge in South Africa with the enthusiasm that they have.

We believe that it is in the common interest that we sustain the common victory that we have scored in South Africa, and take it further by achieving success not only in politics but also in the socio-economic sphere.

It is perhaps common cause among us that everywhere on our globe there is an unmistakable process leading to the entrenchment of democractic systems of government. The empowerment of the ordinary people of our world freely to determine their destiny, unhindered by tyrants and dictators, is at the very heart of the reason for the existence of this Organization.

But it is equally true that hundreds of millions of these politically empowered masses are caught in the deathly trap of poverty, unable to live life in its fullness.

Out of all this are born social conflicts which produce insecurity and instability, civil and other wars that claim many lives, millions of desperate refugees and the destruction of the little wealth that poor countries are able to accumulate. Out of this cauldron are also born tyrants, dictators and demagogues who not only take away or restrict the rights of the people but also make it impossible to do the things that must be done to bring lasting prosperity to the people.

At the same time, the reality can no longer be ignored that we live in an interdependent world which is bound together to a common destiny. The very response of the international community to the challenge of apartheid confirmed this very point that we all understood, that as long as apartheid existed in South Africa, so long would the whole of humanity feel demeaned and degraded.

The United Nations understood very well that racism in our country could not but feed racism in other parts of the world as well. The universal struggle against apartheid was therefore not an act of charity arising out of pity for our people, but an affirmation of our common humanity. We believe that that act of affirmation requires that this Organization should once more turn its focused and sustained attention to the basics of everything that makes for a better world for all humanity.

The elaboration of a new world order must, of necessity, centre on this world body. In it we should find the appropriate forum in which we can all participate to help determine the shape of the new world.

The four elements that will need to be knit together in fashioning that new universal reality are the issues of democracy, peace, prosperity and interdependence.

The great challenge of our age to the United Nations is to answer the question "Given the interdependence of the nations of the world, what is it that we can and must do to ensure that democracy, peace and prosperity prevail everywhere?"

We are aware of the fact that the United Nations is addressing these questions in many ways; yet there can be no gainsaying the fact that such progress as we have made has been more by stealth than in the bold and determined fashion that the world crisis demands.

Perhaps a new and forceful initiative is required. Such an initiative should inspire all of humanity because of the seriousness of its intent. It should also have a chance to succeed because it will have been underwritten by the commitment of the masses of the people in each member country to join hands with other nations, to address together the related issues of democracy, peace and prosperity in an interdependent world.

We are aware of the fact that the dictates of *realpolitik* militate against the speedy realization of such an initiative. But we do believe that the reality of life and the realism of policy will, at some point, bring to the fore the fact that the delay we impose on ourselves today will only serve to increase the pressure on all of us to incorporate within what we consider possible, a sustainable vision of a common world that will rise or fall together.

Undoubtedly, to inspire greater confidence in itself among all the Member States and to reflect better the impulse towards the democratization of international relations, the United Nations will have to continue looking at itself to determine what restructuring of itself it should effect.

This process must naturally assert among others, on the structure and functioning of the Security Council and the peacemaking and peace-keeping issues raised by the Secretary-General in "An Agenda for Peace".

Democratic South Africa rejoins the world community of nations determined to play its role in helping to strengthen the United Nations and to contribute what it can to the furtherance of its purposes. Among other things, we have this morning acceded to the covenants and conventions adopted by this Organization, which address various matters such as economic, social and cultural rights, civil and political rights, and the elimination of all forms of racial discrimination, to say nothing of our irrevocable commitment to the realization of the objectives contained in the Universal Declaration of Human Rights.

We are determined to play our full part in all processes that address the important question of the non-proliferation and destruction of weapons of mass elimination. Our Government has also decided to become a signatory to the Convention on Prohibition and Restrictions on the Use of Certain Conventional Weapons.

In a similar vein, we shall not be found wanting in the quest for sustainable development that is in keeping with the Rio de Janeiro Declaration on the Environment and Development as well as with Agenda 21.

Equally, our own national interest dictates that we join forces with the United Nations and all its Member States in the common struggle to contain and end the traffic in narcotics.

Even in constitutional terms, we are committed to the advancement of the objective of the emancipation of women, through the creation of a non-sexist society. Apart from anything else, we are therefore actively engaged in the preparations for what we are convinced will be a successful Beijing Conference.

We are part of the region of southern Africa and the continent of Africa. As members of the Southern African Development Community and the Organization of African Unity (OAU), and an equal partner with other Member States, we will play our role in the struggles of those organizations to build a continent and a region that will help to create for themselves and all humanity a common world of peace and prosperity.

Ours must surely become a continent free of such tragedies as those that have afflicted our own country, as well as Rwanda, Somalia, Angola, Mozambique, Sudan and Liberia. Happily, the OAU is actively addressing this issue of peace and stability on our continent.

We are greatly encouraged that the countries of our region, faced with a crisis in Lesotho, acted together speedily and, with the cooperation of the Government and people of that country, succeeded in demonstrating that together we have the will to defend democracy, peace and national reconciliation.

Furthermore, as members of the Non-Aligned Movement and the Group of 77, we are committed especially to the promotion of South-South cooperation and to the strengthening of the voice of the poor and disadvantaged in the ordering of world affairs.

We would like to take this opportunity to express our appreciation to the members of the General Assembly for the speed and readiness with which they accepted the credentials of democratic South Africa, enabling us to participate in the work of the last General Assembly. We are pleased to note that this same spirit characterized the approach of other international organizations towards our new democracy, including the Commonwealth and the European Union.

We would like to close by congratulating you, Mr. President, on your election to your high post, and we express our confidence that you will guide the work of the Assembly with the wisdom and sense of purpose for which we admire you.

The millions across our globe who stand expectant at the gates of hope look to this Organization to bring them peace, to bring them life, to bring them a life worth living.

We pray that the new South Africa which the General Assembly helped bring into being and so warmly welcomed among the community of nations, will, in its own and in the wider interest, make its own contribution, however small, to the realization of those hopes.

Our common humanity and the urgency of the knock on the door of this great edifice demand that we must attempt even the impossible.

# VI  Subject index to documents

*[This subject index to the documents reproduced in this book should be used in conjunction with the index on pages 133-145. A complete listing of the documents indexed below appears on pages 205-219.]*

## A

**Academic freedom.**
– Document 97
*See also*: Education. Right to communicate.

**Action for Resisting Invasion, Colonialism and Apartheid Fund.**
– Document 121

**Advisory Committee on the United Nations Educational and Training Programme for Southern Africa.**
– Document 198

**Africa Liberation Day (25 May).**
– Documents 99, 103

**African National Congress of South Africa.**
– Documents 6, 36, 39, 40, 55, 95, 98, 99, 106, 107, 121, 124, 136, 137, 142, 148, 161, 170, 177, 181, 183, 203, 208, 215

**African Summit Conference (1960: Addis Ababa).**
– Document 16

**African Summit Conference (1963: Addis Ababa).**
– Document 26

**Afrikaner National Front.**
– Document 182

**Agricultural products.**
– Documents 13, 122, 127
*See also*: Raw materials.

**Aid coordination.**
*See*: Aid programmes. Coordination within UN system. Development assistance. Technical cooperation.

**Aid programmes.**
– Document 95
*See also*: Development assistance. Economic assistance. Humanitarian assistance. Military assistance. Refugee assistance. Technical cooperation.

**Airlines.**
– Document 111

**Amnesty.**
– Documents 37, 41, 97
*See also*: Political prisoners.

**Anniversaries.**
– Documents 98, 99

**Anti-apartheid movements.**
– Documents 22, 38, 49, 56, 65, 68, 72, 76, 81, 83, 87, 92, 100, 112, 114, 119, 121, 124, 175
*See also*: National liberation movements.

**Apartheid.**
*See*: Anti-apartheid movements. Bantustans. Foreign interests. Front-line states. South African refugees.

**Arbitrary detention.**
– Document 56
*See also*: Detained persons. Human rights.

**Armaments.**
*See*: Armed forces. Strategic materials.

**Armed forces.**
– Documents 94, 122, 127, 176
*See also*: Mercenaries.

**Armed incidents.**
– Documents 14, 15, 24, 82, 103, 107, 115, 216
*See also*: Military activity.

**Armistices.**
*See*: Peace.

**Arms embargo.**
– Documents 27, 28, 34, 41, 44, 46, 49, 58, 64, 68, 69, 87, 89, 90, 93, 97, 103, 108, 111, 119, 131, 133, 139, 141, 147, 149, 175, 194, 213
*See also*: Oil embargo.

**Arms industry.**
*See*: Arms transfers. Military technology.

**Arms transfers.**
– Document 89
*See also*: Military assistance.

**Arrest.**
*See*: Detained persons.

Art works.
– Document 218

Assassination.
*See*: Extralegal executions. Political violence.

Associations.
*See*: Professional associations.

Asylum.
*See*: Territorial asylum.

Athletes.
*See*: Sports.

Australia—Anti-apartheid movements.
– Document 72

# B

Balance of payments.
*See*: External debt.

Bank loans.
– Document 103
*See also*: Credit.

Banks.
*See*: Transnational banks.

Bantustans.
– Documents 60, 62, 77, 85, 88, 96, 104, 110, 113, 121, 133, 194, 201, 215

Botha, Roelof.
– Documents 164, 191, 192

Boutros-Ghali, Boutros.
– Documents 152-155, 157-159, 161, 163-171, 173, 174, 176-183, 185, 188, 189, 191, 192, 199, 202, 204-207, 209, 210, 216, 217

Boycotts.
– Documents 24, 29, 60, 61, 65, 72, 100, 102, 109, 116, 118, 122, 127, 133, 134, 144
*See also*: Trade boycotts.

Brain drain.
*See*: Emigration. Skilled workers.

Budget contributions.
*See*: Pledging conferences.

Buthelezi, Mangosuthu G.
– Documents 168, 173, 174, 176, 183, 192, 203, 204, 206

# C

Capital movements.
*See*: Foreign investments.

Capital punishment.
– Documents 41, 106, 121, 124, 133
*See also*: Extralegal executions. Summary executions.

Censorship.
– Document 133
*See also*: Freedom of the press.

Charter of the United Nations (1945).
– Documents 28, 34, 41, 213

Child refugees.
– Documents 95, 101
*See also*: Women refugees.

Children.
– Documents 45, 82, 95, 101, 121, 124, 133
*See also*: Child refugees.

Chile—Military relations.
– Document 131

Ciskei—political status.
– Document 104

Ciskei—political violence.
– Document 161, 162

Cities.
– Document 112

Civil and political rights.
– Documents 12, 64, 97, 135, 201
*See also*: Academic freedom. Equality before the law. Freedom of association. Freedom of the press. Right to communicate. Self-determination of peoples.

Civil disobedience.
*See*: Conscientious objectors. Non-violence. Political crimes. Protest movements.

Coal.
– Documents 122, 127

Colonial countries.
*See*: Colonialism. Decolonization. Foreign interests. Independence.

Colonialism.
– Documents 42, 57, 68
*See also*: Self-determination of peoples.

Commissions of inquiry.
– Documents 7, 215
*See also*: Special missions.

Commodities.
*See*: Agricultural products. Minerals. Raw materials.

Commonwealth.
– Document 160

Commonwealth Observer Group.
– Document 175

Commonwealth of Independent States.
– Document 176

Commonwealth Secretariat.
– Documents 194, 200, 201, 220

Communication process.
*See*: Right to communicate.

Computers.
– Documents 116, 127, 133

Conferences.
*See*: Hearings. Pledging conferences.

Conscientious objectors.
– Document 94

Constitutional law.
*See*: Civil and political rights. Constitutions.

Constitutions.
– Documents 110, 113, 136, 146-148, 171, 172,
189, 192, 215, 218

Consultants.
*See*: Experts.

Consultations.
– Documents 41, 80, 101, 176
*See also*: Negotiation.

Contracts.
– Document 103

Conventions.
*See*: Treaties.

Cooperation between organizations.
– Documents 76, 103, 129, 147, 176, 195, 198,
200, 201, 216
*See also*: Inter-agency cooperation. International
organizations.

Coordination within UN system.
– Documents 139, 142, 147
*See also*: Inter-agency cooperation. Specialized
agencies.

Corporal punishment.
*See*: Torture and other cruel treatment.

Credit.
– Documents 106, 128

Crime.
*See*: Crime victims. Military offences. Political
crimes.

Crime victims.
– Document 175

Crimes against humanity.
– Documents 49, 56, 60, 70, 82, 140
*See also*: Human rights violations. Massacres.

Crimes against peace.
– Documents 14, 82

Criminal investigation.
– Documents 101, 175
*See also*: Police.

Criminal justice.
– Documents 156, 158, 175

Cultural exchanges.
– Document 100
*See also*: Cultural relations. Educational exchanges.
Scientific exchanges.

Cultural property.
*See*: Art works.

Cultural relations.
– Documents 100, 103, 109, 111, 116, 119, 122,
127, 133, 140
*See also*: Cultural exchanges.

# D

Dayal, Virendra.
– Documents 165, 168

De Klerk, Frederik Willem.
– Documents 165, 167-169, 176, 178, 185, 188,
192, 206, 210

Death penalty.
*See*: Capital punishment.

Debt.
*See*: Credit. External debt.

Debt renegotiation.
– Document 128
*See also*: External debt.

Declaration on Apartheid and its Destructive
Consequences in Southern Africa (1989).
– Documents 135-137, 139, 140, 142, 146-148, 152,
171, 172, 192

Declaration on South Africa (1979).
– Document 96

Declarations.
– Documents 34, 87, 96, 103, 119, 135-137, 139,
140, 142, 146-148, 152, 171, 172

**Decolonization.**
– Document 84
*See also*: Independence. Namibia. Self-determination
of peoples.

**Democracy.**
– Documents 37, 139, 147, 148, 187, 190, 194,
195, 199-201, 219-221
*See also*: Equality.

**Denial of justice.**
*See*: Equality before the law. Summary executions.

**Detained persons.**
– Documents 28, 32, 34, 41, 52, 64, 88, 103, 116,
120, 121, 124, 133, 139, 214
*See also*: Arbitrary detention. Extralegal executions.
Political prisoners. Prisoner treatment. Torture and
other cruel treatment.

**Detention.**
*See*: Arbitrary detention. Detained persons.

**Developing countries.**
– Documents 200, 201

**Development assistance.**
– Documents 103, 139, 147, 148, 175, 194, 214,
215, 218, 219
*See also*: Economic assistance. International
cooperation. Technical cooperation.

**Development strategies.**
– Document 177

**Diouf, Abdou.**
– Document 159

**Diplomacy.**
*See*: Diplomatic relations. Negotiation. State visits.

**Diplomatic relations.**
– Documents 23, 26, 111

**Discrimination.**
*See*: Equality. Human rights violations. Minorities.
Racial discrimination. Tolerance.

**Diseases.**
– Document 39

**Disinvestment.**
*See*: Divestment.

**Dispute settlement.**
*See*: Commissions of inquiry. Consultations.
Negotiation. Peace. Special missions.

**Dissemination of information.**
*See*: Information dissemination.

**Dissidents.**
*See*: Protest movements.

**Divestment.**
– Documents 49, 111, 116, 119, 133
*See also*: Sanctions.

**Domestic security.**
*See*: Internal security.

**Double taxation.**
– Documents 127, 140

**Due process of law.**
*See*: Civil and political rights.

**Economic assistance.**
– Documents 95, 133, 194
*See also*: Development assistance. Financial
assistance. Humanitarian assistance. Military
assistance. Reconstruction.

# E

**Economic conditions.**
– Documents 44, 172, 215
*See also*: Political conditions. Social conditions.

**Economic integration.**
– Document 11

**Economic relations.**
– Documents 26, 103, 111
*See also*: Foreign trade.

**Economic, social and cultural rights.**
– Document 12
*See also*: Right to education. Right to labour. Trade
union rights.

**Education.**
– Documents 39, 175
*See also*: Academic freedom. Educational institutions.
Higher education. Right to education.

**Educational assistance.**
– Documents 37, 41, 45, 64, 95, 131, 139, 148, 179,
197, 198, 214
*See also*: Educational exchanges. Scholarships.
Training programmes.

**Educational exchanges.**
– Documents 100, 111
*See also*: Cultural exchanges. Educational assistance.
Scientific exchanges.

**Educational financing.**
*See*: Educational assistance. Scholarships.

**Educational institutions.**
– Document 198
*See also*: Education. Universities and colleges.

**Election law.**
– Document 216
*See also*: Elections.

**Election verification.**
– Documents 175, 191, 194, 199-201, 205, 208, 209, 216
*See also*: Elections. Technical cooperation. Voter registration. Voting.

**Elections.**
– Documents 113, 149, 190, 191, 194, 199-206, 208-210, 215-218
*See also*: Election law. Election verification. Political representation. Voter registration. Voting.

**Electoral assistance.**
*See*: Election verification.

**Electronics industry.**
– Document 127

**Embargo.**
*See*: Sanctions. Sanctions compliance.

**Emergency powers.**
*See*: State of emergency.

**Emergency relief.**
*See*: Humanitarian assistance.

**Emigration.**
– Documents 65, 100, 111
*See also*: Repatriation.

**Employees' rights.**
*See*: Workers' rights.

**Employment policy.**
– Document 37
*See also*: Right to labour.

**Employment services.**
*See*: Employment policy.

**Entertainment.**
*See*: Sports.

**Equality.**
– Documents 12, 96
*See also*: Democracy.

**Espionage.**
*See*: Intelligence services.

**Ethnic and racial groups.**
– Document 70
*See also*: Minorities. Race relations.

**European Community.**
– Documents 10, 65 160, 176

**European Communities Observer Mission in South Africa.**
– Document 175

**European Union.**
– Documents 194, 200, 201, 220

**Exiles.**
– Documents 121, 139, 142, 147, 172, 194, 197

**Experts.**
– Document 52
*See also*: Groups of experts.

**External debt.**
– Documents 119, 128
*See also*: Debt renegotiation. Foreign loans.

**Extralegal executions.**
– Documents 32, 41, 56
*See also*: Capital punishment. Detained persons. Massacres. Political prisoners. Summary executions. Torture and other cruel treatment.

# F

**Fact-finding missions.**
*See*: Commissions of inquiry. Special missions.

**Family.**
*See*: Children.

**Feasibility studies.**
– Document 44

**Federal Republic of Germany.**
*See*: Germany, Federal Republic of.

**Fellowships.**
*See*: Educational assistance. Scholarships.

**Financial assistance.**
– Documents 52, 106, 124, 175, 179

**Financial institutions.**
– Documents 127, 128, 140

**Financial resources.**
*See*: Financial assistance. Funds.

**Financing.**
*See*: Funds. Trade financing.

**Fischer, Abram.**
– Document 52

**Focal points.**
– Document 129

**Food shortage.**
*See*: Malnutrition.

**Forced labour.**
– Document 69
*See also*: Labour exploitation. Workers' rights.

**Foreign interests.**
– Documents 56, 60, 63, 65
*See also*: Foreign investments. Transnational corporations.

**Foreign investments.**
– Document 86, 108
*See also*: Foreign interests.

**Foreign loans.**
– Documents 111, 116, 127, 128, 133, 140, 149
*See also*: External debt.

**Foreign policy.**
*See*: Aid programmes. Foreign relations. Intervention.

**Foreign relations.**
– Documents 1, 49
*See also*: Diplomatic relations. Economic relations. Military relations. Political cooperation.

**Foreign trade.**
– Documents 49, 103, 111, 126, 131, 133, 140
*See also*: Economic relations.

**Freedom Charter (1955).**
– Documents 12, 98, 99

**Freedom of association.**
– Documents 121, 125, 133
*See also*: Right to communicate. Trade union rights. Workers' rights.

**Freedom of expression.**
*See*: Academic freedom. Censorship. Freedom of the press. Right to communicate.

**Freedom of information.**
*See*: Censorship. Freedom of the press.

**Freedom of the press.**
– Documents 24, 97, 125, 133
*See also*: Censorship. Right to communicate.

**Freedom of thought.**
*See*: Academic freedom. Political prisoners.

**Front-line states.**
– Documents 94, 101, 103, 106, 121, 124, 133, 139, 147, 194

**Funds.**
– Document 64
*See also*: Trust funds.

# G

**General Agreement on Tariffs and Trade.**
– Document 65

**Geneva Convention relative to the treatment of prisoners of war (1949).**
– Document 56

**Geneva Conventions (1949).**
– Document 121

**Germany, Federal Republic of—Foreign trade.**
– Documents 126, 131

**Germany, Federal Republic of—Military relations.**
– Document 131

**Gold.**
– Documents 122, 127, 133

**Gold sales.**
– Documents 103, 111, 116

**Goldberg, Dennis.**
– Document 40

**Goldstone, Richard J.**
– Document 163

**Groups of experts.**
– Documents 34, 41, 44
*See also*: Experts. Task forces. Working groups.

**Guerrillas.**
*See*: Armed forces. National liberation movements.

# H

**Hammarskjöld, Dag.**
– Document 18

**Harbours.**
*See*: Ports.

**Health.**
– Document 175

**Higher education.**
– Document 46
*See also*: Students. Universities and colleges.

**Homelands (South Africa).**
*See*: Bantustans.

**Housing.**
– Document 175

**Human resources development.**
– Document 194

# I

International Conference on Women and Apartheid (1982: Brussels).
– Document 105

International Convention Against Apartheid in Sports (1985).
– Documents 118, 119, 134, 144

International Convention on the Suppression and Punishment of the Crime of Apartheid (1973).
– Documents 70, 111, 118

International Cooperation.
– Documents 49, 79, 92
*See also*: Cooperation between organizations. Development assistance. Intergovernmental organizations. International days. International decades. International relations. Non-governmental organizations. Reconstruction. Technical cooperation.

International Court of Justice.
– Document 70

International Day for the Elimination of Racial Discrimination (21 Mar.).
– Documents 47, 154, 180

International Day of Solidarity with Political Prisoners in South Africa (11 Oct.).
– Document 138

International Day of Solidarity with the Struggle of Women of South Africa and Namibia (9 Aug.).
– Document 101

International days.
– Documents 47, 99, 101, 103, 119, 138, 154, 180
*See also*: International cooperation. International decades.

International Decades.
– Document 101
*See also*: International cooperation. International days.

International Donors' Conference on Human Resource Development for a Post-Apartheid South Africa.
– Document 192

International investment.
*See*: Foreign investments.

International law.
– Document 56
*See also*: International relations.

International Monetary Fund.
– Documents 65, 106, 111, 140, 149

International obligations.
– Documents 1, 21
*See also*: Treaties.

International offences.
*See*: Crimes against humanity. Crimes against peace.

International organizations.
– Documents 103, 106
*See also*: Cooperation between organizations. Intergovernmental organizations. Non-governmental organizations.

International relations.
– Documents 11, 74
*See also*: Foreign relations. International cooperation. International law. International security. Political cooperation.

International relief.
*See*: Humanitarian assistance. Refugee assistance.

International security.
– Documents 49, 103
*See also*: Front-line states. International relations. Intervention. Peace.

International Seminar on Apartheid, Racial Discrimination and Colonialism in Southern Africa (1967: Kitwe, Zambia).
– Document 53

International Seminar on Women and Apartheid (1980: Helsinki).
– Document 101

International trade.
– Document 66
*See also*: Foreign trade.

Intervention.
– Documents 56, 96
*See also:* International security.

Investments.
*See*: Divestment. Foreign investments.

Israel—Foreign trade.
– Document 131

Israel—Military relations.
– Document 131

Israel—Nuclear technology.
– Document 131

# K

Kathrada, Ahmed.
– Document 40

King, Angela.
– Documents 161, 163, 166, 178

# L

**Labour exploitation.**
– Document 69
*See also*: Forced labour. Trade union rights. Workers' rights.

**Labour movements.**
*See*: Political movements. Trade unions.

**Labour unions.**
*See*: Trade unions.

**Lagos Declaration for Action against Apartheid (1977).**
– Document 87

**Land rights.**
– Document 12

**Law.**
*See*: International law. Laws and regulations.

**Law enforcement officials.**
*See*: Police.

**Laws and regulations.**
– Documents 103, 137, 139, 151, 176, 213
*See also*: Legislative process.

**Legal aid.**
– Documents 43, 45, 48, 111, 128, 132, 133, 139, 145, 151, 175, 194, 197, 214

**Legislative process.**
– Document 78
*See also*: Laws and regulations.

**Licences.**
– Document 89

**Living conditions.**
*See*: Economic conditions. Housing. Social conditions.

**Loans.**
*See*: Bank loans. Credit. Foreign loans.

**Location of offices.**
– Documents 95, 142, 148

**Luthuli, Albert J.**
– Document 107

# M

**Malnutrition.**
– Document 39

**Mandela, Nelson.**
– Documents 33, 39, 40, 52, 107, 116, 121, 125, 136, 157, 167-169, 173, 174, 176, 177, 181, 182, 186, 188, 192, 202-204, 206, 210, 211, 221

**Mangope, L. M.**
– Document 135

**Manpower development.**
– Document 198
*See also*: Training programmes.

**Martial law.**
*See*: State of emergency.

**Mass media.**
– Documents 88, 97, 142, 194, 195, 216
*See also*: Propaganda.

**Massacres.**
– Documents 24, 83, 156, 161, 180
*See also*: Crimes against humanity. Extralegal executions. Political violence.

**Materials.**
*See*: Nuclear materials. Raw materials. Strategic materials.

**Matthews, Z. K.**
– Document 6

**Mbeki, Govan.**
– Documents 38, 40

**Mbeki, Thabo.**
– Documents 38, 177, 212

**Mercenaries.**
– Documents 96, 119
*See also*: Armed forces.

**Mhlaba, Raymond.**
– Document 40

**Military activity.**
– Documents 37, 53, 56, 97, 107, 176
*See also*: Armed incidents.

**Military assistance.**
– Document 103
*See also*: Arms transfers. Economic assistance. Military relations.

**Military offences.**
– Document 17

**Military personnel.**
*See*: Armed forces.

**Military policy.**
– Document 103

**Military relations.**
– Documents 96, 111, 119, 122, 127, 131, 140, 141, 149
*See also*: Military assistance.

Military technology.
– Document 175

Mineral resources.
– Documents 122, 127, 140
*See also*: Raw materials.

Minorities.
– Documents 1, 3
*See also*: Ethnic and racial groups.

Minors.
*See*: Children. Youth.

Mlangeni, Andrew.
– Document 40

Mothopeng, Zephania.
– Document 119

Motsoaledi, Elias.
– Document 40

Multinational corporations.
*See*: Transnational corporations.

# N

Namibia.
– Documents 103, 108, 119
*See also*: Decolonization. Namibian refugees.

Namibia—Agricultural products.
– Document 122

Namibia—Coal.
– Document 122

Namibia—Gold.
– Document 122

Namibia—Independence.
– Document 145

Namibia—Mineral resources.
– Document 122

Namibia—National liberation movements.
– Document 105

Namibia—Natural resources.
– Document 103

Namibia—Women.
– Document 105
See also: Decolonization. Namibia. Namibian refugees.

Namibian refugees.
– Document 101
*See also*: Namibia.

National liberation movements.
– Documents 22, 36, 40, 55, 65, 68, 71, 72, 78, 79, 81, 87, 92, 95, 101, 103, 105-107, 111, 121, 124, 133, 136, 137
*See also*: Anti-apartheid movements. Observer missions.

National Peace Accord (South Africa) (1991).
– Documents 147, 156, 158, 160-162, 172, 175, 176, 192, 194

National security.
*See*: Intelligence services. Internal security. International security. Military policy. State of emergency.

Nationalism.
*See*: National liberation movements. Self-determination of peoples.

Natural resources.
– Document 103
*See also*: Mineral resources. Raw materials.

Negotiation.
– Documents 34, 37, 117, 125, 135-137, 139, 142, 146, 147, 152, 154, 156, 158, 160, 162, 167, 169-172, 175, 176, 182, 190, 192, 194, 199-201, 215, 216
*See also*: Consultations.

Neighbouring states.
*See*: Front-line states.

New Zealand—Anti-apartheid movements.
– Document 72

Newly industrialized countries.
*See*: Developing countries.

Nobel Peace Prize.
– Document 188

Non-governmental organizations.
– Documents 49, 52, 92, 103, 111, 124, 127-129, 142, 148, 195, 197-199, 215, 216
*See also:* Intergovernmental organizations. International cooperation.

Non-violence.
– Document 40, 114

Nuclear facilities.
– Documents 96, 106, 141, 149

Nuclear materials.
– Document 149

Nuclear non-proliferation.
*See*: Nuclear weapons.

**Nuclear technology.**
– Documents 103, 111, 116, 122, 127, 131, 133, 141
*See also*: Nuclear weapons.

**Nuclear weapons.**
– Documents 87, 89, 93
*See also*: Nuclear technology.

**Nutrition.**
*See*: Malnutrition.

# O

**Observers.**
– Documents 163, 164, 166, 171, 175, 176, 178, 185, 190, 192, 194, 200, 209, 215, 218, 220
*See also*: Intergovernmental organizations. National liberation movements.

**Oil embargo.**
– Documents 16, 44, 80, 103, 108, 111, 119, 122, 127, 130, 133, 143, 150, 187, 193, 196
*See also*: Arms embargo.

**Organization of African Unity.**
– Documents 57, 65, 66, 71, 76, 79, 92, 95, 101, 106, 159, 160, 175, 176, 194, 200, 201, 220

**Ouellet, André.**
– Document 205

# P

**Pan Africanist Congress of Azania (South Africa).**
– Documents 95, 106, 121, 124, 142, 148, 176

**Payments agreements.**
– Document 128

**Peace.**
– Document 31
*See also*: International security. Peace treaties. Peace-keeping operations. Peacemaking.

**Peace treaties.**
– Document 175
*See also*: Peace.

**Peace-keeping operations.**
– Document 216
*See also*: Peace. Peacemaking.

**Peacemaking.**
– Documents 18, 155, 159, 163-166, 168, 169, 173, 174, 177, 178, 183, 185, 186
*See also*: Peace. Peace-keeping operations.

**Pérez de Cuéllar, Javier.**
– Document 138

**Periodic reports.**
– Document 70

**Petitions.**
– Document 70

**Petroleum.**
*See*: Oil embargo.

**Plebiscites.**
– Document 153
*See also*: Elections. Self-determination of peoples.

**Pledging conferences.**
– Document 198

**Police.**
– Documents 94, 176
*See also*: Criminal investigation.

**Political conditions.**
– Documents 15, 17, 19, 37, 53, 55, 136, 142, 146-148, 152, 156, 158-160, 162, 168, 170, 171, 174, 176, 184-186, 190, 199, 215, 218, 219
*See also*: Economic conditions. Independence. Interim governments. Self-determination of peoples.

**Political cooperation.**
– Document 92
*See also*: Foreign relations. International relations.

**Political crimes.**
– Document 146
*See also*: Political prisoners. Political trials. Political violence.

**Political movements.**
– Document 182
*See also*: Political participation. Protest movements.

**Political participation.**
– Documents 194, 195, 201-203, 207
*See also*: Political movements. Political representation. Popular participation. Voting.

**Political parties.**
– Documents 97, 111, 121, 137, 139, 142, 162, 167, 169, 170, 175, 176, 178, 182-184, 194, 195, 199-204, 207, 208, 216

**Political prisoners.**
– Documents 24, 28, 29, 32-38, 40, 41, 43, 45, 50-52, 56, 64, 65, 78, 79, 87, 88, 97, 106, 107, 111, 116, 120, 121, 124, 125, 133, 136-139, 146, 147, 151, 170-172, 175, 176, 180, 194, 197, 214
*See also*: Amnesty. Detained persons. Extralegal executions. Political crimes. Political trials. Prisoner treatment. Torture and other cruel treatment.

**Political representation.**
– Document 199
*See also*: Elections. Political participation.

**Political trials.**
– Documents 33, 38, 97, 125, 133
*See also*: Political crimes. Political prisoners.

**Political violence.**
– Documents 14, 16, 24, 36, 37, 43, 82, 83, 88, 97, 107, 115, 136, 137, 139, 146, 147, 154, 156-158, 160-163, 170-176, 183, 184, 192, 194, 199-201, 215, 216
*See also*: Massacres. Political crimes. State of emergency.

**Popular participation.**
– Document 201
*See also*: Political participation.

**Ports.**
– Documents 23, 127, 140

**Poverty.**
– Document 39

**Press.**
*See*: Freedom of the press.

**Prisoner treatment.**
– Documents 50-52, 88, 97
*See also*: Detained persons. Political prisoners. Torture and other cruel treatment.

**Prisoners.**
*See*: Detained persons. Political prisoners. Prisoner treatment.

**Prisoners of conscience.**
*See*: Political prisoners.

**Privileges and immunities.**
– Document 164

**Professional associations.**
– Document 198
*See also*: Trade unions.

**Programme of Action against Apartheid (1983).**
– Document 111

**Programmes of action.**
*See*: Declarations. Guidelines.

**Propaganda.**
– Document 96
*See also*: Public information.

**Protest movements.**
– Documents 88, 124
*See also*: Student movements.

**Provisional governments.**
*See*: Interim governments.

**Public administration.**
*See*: Administration. Institution building.

**Public debt.**
*See*: Debt renegotiation. External debt.

**Public information.**
– Documents 48, 216
*See also*: Information dissemination. Propaganda.

**Public institutions.**
*See*: Institution-building.

**Public opinion.**
*See*: Propaganda.

**Punishment.**
*See*: Amnesty. Capital punishment. Torture and other cruel treatment.

# R

**Race.**
*See*: Ethnic and racial groups. Race relations. Racial discrimination.

**Race relations.**
– Documents 6-8
*See also*: Ethnic and racial groups. Racial discrimination.

**Racial discrimination.**
– Documents 2-5, 8, 9, 11, 21, 23, 25, 26, 29, 42, 47-49, 57, 60, 61, 67, 70, 81, 180
*See also*: Race relations.

**Racial groups.**
*See*: Ethnic and racial groups.

**Racism.**
*See*: Racial discrimination.

**Radio broadcasting.**
– Document 91

**Raw materials.**
– Documents 80, 130, 143
*See also*: Agricultural products. Natural resources. Strategic materials.

**Reconstruction.**
– Documents 139, 147, 194, 210, 217-219, 221
*See also*: Economic assistance. International cooperation.

**Refugee assistance.**
– Documents 101, 175, 194, 214
*See also*: Humanitarian assistance.

South Africa. President.
– Document 210

South African Airways.
– Document 118

Southern Africa.
*See*: Front-line states. Namibia.

Southern Africa—Colonialism.
– Document 57

Southern Africa—Educational assistance.
– Documents 179, 198

Southern Africa—Financial assistance.
– Document 179

Southern Africa—Humanitarian assistance.
– Document 179

Southern Africa—Manpower development.
– Document 198

Southern Africa—National liberation movements.
– Documents 55, 68, 103

Southern Africa—Political conditions.
– Document 55

Southern Africa—Racial discrimination.
– Document 57

Southern Africa—Technical cooperation.
– Document 198

Southern Africa—Training programmes.
– Documents 179, 198

Southern African Development Coordination
Conference.
– Document 124

Southern African refugees.
– Document 45
*See also*: Namibian refugees. Refugees.

Southern Rhodesia—Intervention.
– Document 56

Southern Rhodesia—Military activity.
– Document 56

Special missions.
– Documents 158, 160-162, 171, 176, 190, 199-201, 216
*See also*: Commissions of inquiry. Humanitarian
assistance.

Specialized agencies.
– Documents 41, 49, 111
*See also*: Coordination within UN system.

Sports.
– Documents 60, 61, 65, 100, 102, 103, 111, 116, 118, 119, 122, 127, 133, 134, 140, 144, 147, 194

State of emergency.
– Documents 116, 117, 125, 133, 136
*See also*: Internal security. Political violence.

State visits.
– Document 18

Steiner, Ismat.
– Document 161

Strategic materials.
– Document 80
*See also*: Raw materials.

Student exchanges.
*See*: Educational exchanges.

Student movements.
– Document 83
*See also*: Protest movements.

Students.
– Document 82
*See also*: Higher education.

Summary executions.
– Document 121
*See also*: Capital punishment. Extralegal executions.
Torture and other cruel treatment.

South West Africa People's Organization.
– Document 103

Symposium on Political Tolerance in South Africa:
Role of Opinion-makers and Media (1993: Cape
Town).
– Document 195

# T

Tambo, Oliver.
– Documents 55, 77, 99, 107, 181

Task forces.
– Document 216
*See also*: Groups of experts. Working groups.

Taxation.
*See*: Double taxation.

Technical cooperation.
– Documents 127, 198, 216
*See also*: Aid programmes. Development assistance.
Election verification.

Technical cooperation among developing countries.
*See*: Developing countries. Focal points.

**Technical training.**
– Document 46
*See also*: Vocational training.

**Technology.**
*See*: Nuclear technology.

**Technology transfer.**
– Documents 127, 130, 140, 141, 143

**Territorial asylum.**
– Document 49

**Thant, U.**
– Documents 25, 42

**Third World.**
*See*: Developing countries.

**Tolerance.**
– Document 195

**Torture and other cruel treatment.**
– Documents 36, 50-52, 106, 107
*See also*: Detained persons. Extralegal executions. Political prisoners. Prisoner treatment. Summary executions.

**Tourism.**
– Documents 100, 111
*See also*: Travel costs.

**Trade.**
*See*: Foreign trade. International trade.

**Trade boycotts.**
– Documents 13, 16, 23, 60, 111, 112, 116, 119, 122, 126, 127, 130, 140, 141, 143

**Trade embargo.**
– Documents 68, 69

**Trade financing.**
– Document 128

**Trade union rights.**
– Document 133
*See also*: Freedom of association. Labour exploitation. Trade unions. Workers' rights.

**Trade unions.**
– Documents 37, 63, 66, 69, 103, 108, 111
*See also*: Professional associations. Trade union rights.

**Training programmes.**
– Documents 37, 41, 179, 198
*See also*: Educational assistance. Manpower development.

**Transitional Executive Council.**
– Documents 190, 194, 200, 201, 215

**Transitional governments.**
*See*: Interim governments.

**Transkei.**
– Document 85

**Transkei—Decolonization.**
– Document 84

**Transnational banks.**
– Document 127

**Transnational corporations.**
– Documents 53, 103, 122, 127, 140
*See also*: Foreign interests. Transnational banks.

**Transport.**
– Documents 122, 127, 140, 143
*See also*: Maritime transport.

**Travel.**
*See*: Tourism. Transport. Travel costs. Visas.

**Travel costs.**
– Document 66
*See also*: Tourism.

**Travel documents.**
*See*: Visas.

**Travel reimbursement.**
*See*: Travel costs.

**Travel restrictions.**
*See*: Sanctions.

**Treaties.**
– Documents 56, 70, 111, 118, 119, 121, 134, 144
*See also*: International obligations. Peace treaties. Signatures, accessions, ratifications.

**Trials.**
*See*: Political trials.

**Tributes.**
– Documents 181, 188

**Trust funds.**
– Documents 45, 48, 199-201, 219

**Trust territories.**
*See*: Namibia.

# U

**Umkhonto We Sizwe.**
– Document 22

UN Observer Mission in South Africa.
– Documents 161, 176, 185, 190, 192, 194, 199-201, 208, 216

UN Observer Mission in South Africa—Dissolution.
– Document 220

UN Pledging Conference for Development Activities.
– Document 198

UN Trust Fund for South Africa.
– Documents 45, 48, 145, 179

UN Trust Fund for South Africa—Budget Contributions.
– Documents 132, 145, 214

UN Trust Fund for South Africa—Dissolution.
– Document 219

UN Trust Fund for South Africa—Terms of reference.
– Document 145

UN Trust Fund for South Africa. Committee of Trustees.
– Documents 45, 54, 214

UN Trust Fund for South Africa. Committee of Trustees—Dissolution.
– Document 219

Underground movements.
See: National liberation movements.

UNDP.
– Document 106

Union of South Africa.
See: South Africa.

United Kingdom—Trade boycotts.
– Document 13

Universal Declaration of Human Rights (1948).
– Document 34

Universities and colleges.
– Document 198
See also: Higher education.

Uranium.
– Document 111

## V

Vance, Cyrus R.
– Documents 157-159

Violence.
See: Political violence.

Violent deaths.
See: Massacres.

Visas.
– Documents 94, 100, 118

Visiting missions.
See: Special missions.

Visits of state.
See: State visits.

Vocational education.
See: Manpower development. Vocational training.

Vocational training.
– Document 37
See also: Technical training.

Voter registration.
– Document 216
See also: Election verification. Elections.

Voting.
– Document 218
See also: Election verification. Elections.

Vraalsen, Tom Erik.
– Document 192

## W

Waldheim, Kurt.
– Documents 67, 90

Women.
– Documents 95, 101, 105, 124
See also: Women refugees. Women's organizations.

Women refugees.
– Documents 95, 101
See also: Child refugees.

Women's organizations.
– Document 111
See also: Women.

Workers' rights.
– Document 12
See also: Forced labour. Freedom of association. Labour exploitation. Right to labour. Trade union rights.

Working conditions.
See: Workers' rights.

Working groups.
– Document 52
See also: Groups of experts. Task forces.

**World Bank.**

*See*: International Bank for Reconstruction and Development.

**World Conference for Action Against Apartheid (1977: Lagos).**
– Document 87

**World Conference of the United Nations Decade for Women (1980: Copenhagen).**
– Document 101

**World Conference on Sanctions Against Racist South Africa (1986: Paris).**
– Document 119

# Y

**Youth.**
– Document 94

**Youth exchanges.**
*See*: Educational exchanges. Youth.

**Youth movements.**
*See*: Political movements. Student movements. Youth.

# Z

**Zimbabwe.**
*See*: Southern Rhodesia.

**Zimbabwe African People's Union.**
– Document 55

# United Nations publications of related interest

The following UN publications may be obtained from the addresses indicated below, or at your local distributor:

*Building Peace and Development, 1994*
Annual Report of the Work of the Organization
By Boutros Boutros-Ghali,
Secretary-General of the United Nations
E.95.I.3   92-1-100541-8   299pp.

*An Agenda for Peace*
By Boutros Boutros-Ghali,
Secretary-General of the United Nations
E.DPI/1247   57pp.

*New Dimensions of Arms Regulation snd Disarmament in the Post–Cold War Era*
By Boutros Boutros-Ghali,
Secretary-General of the United Nations
E.93.IX.8   92-1-142192-6   53pp. $9.95

*Basic Facts About the United Nations*
E.93.I.2   92-1-100499-3   290pp. $5.00

*Demographic Yearbook, Vol.44*
B.94.XIII.1   92-1-051083-6   1992   823pp.
$125.00

*Disarmament—New Realities:
Disarmament, Peace-Building and Global Security*
E.93.IX.14   92-1-142199-3   397pp.   $35.00

*United Nations Disarmament Yearbook, Vol.18*
E.94.IX.1   92-1-142204-3 1993   419pp.
$50.00

*Statistical Yearbook, 39th Edition*
B.94.XVII.1 H   92-1-061159-4   1992/93
1,174pp. $110.00

*Women: Challenges to the Year 2000*
E.91.I.21   92-1-100458-6   96pp.   $12.95

*World Economic and Social Survey 1994*
E.94.II.C.1   92-1-109128-4   308pp.   $55.00

*World Investment Report 1994—
Transnational Corporations, Employment and the Work Place*
E.94.II.A.14   92-1-104435-9   446pp.
$45.00

*Yearbook of the United Nations, Vol. 46*
E.93.I.1   0-7923-2583-4   1992   1277pp.
$150.00

United Nations Publications
2 United Nations Plaza, Room DC2-853
New York, NY 10017
United States of America

United Nations Publications
Sales Office and Bookshop
CH-1211 Geneva 10
Switzerland

 Typeset by the Copy Preparation and Proofreading Section
Printed on recycled paper by the United Nations Reproduction Section

7677